IFIP Advances in Information and Communication Technology 405

IFIP – The International Federation for Information Processing

IFIP was founded in 1960 under the auspices of UNESCO, following the First World Computer Congress held in Paris the previous year. An umbrella organization for societies working in information processing, IFIP's aim is two-fold: to support information processing within its member countries and to encourage technology transfer to developing nations. As its mission statement clearly states,

> IFIP's mission is to be the leading, truly international, apolitical organization which encourages and assists in the development, exploitation and application of information technology for the benefit of all people.

IFIP is a non-profitmaking organization, run almost solely by 2500 volunteers. It operates through a number of technical committees, which organize events and publications. IFIP's events range from an international congress to local seminars, but the most important are:

- The IFIP World Computer Congress, held every second year;
- Open conferences;
- Working conferences.

The flagship event is the IFIP World Computer Congress, at which both invited and contributed papers are presented. Contributed papers are rigorously refereed and the rejection rate is high.

As with the Congress, participation in the open conferences is open to all and papers may be invited or submitted. Again, submitted papers are stringently refereed.

The working conferences are structured differently. They are usually run by a working group and attendance is small and by invitation only. Their purpose is to create an atmosphere conducive to innovation and development. Refereeing is also rigorous and papers are subjected to extensive group discussion.

Publications arising from IFIP events vary. The papers presented at the IFIP World Computer Congress and at open conferences are published as conference proceedings, while the results of the working conferences are often published as collections of selected and edited papers.

Any national society whose primary activity is about information processing may apply to become a full member of IFIP, although full membership is restricted to one society per country. Full members are entitled to vote at the annual General Assembly. National societies preferring a less committed involvement may apply for associate or corresponding membership. Associate members enjoy the same benefits as full members, but without voting rights. Corresponding members are not represented in IFIP bodies. Affiliated membership is open to non-national societies, and individual and honorary membership schemes are also offered.

Lech J. Janczewski   Henry B. Wolfe
Sujeet Shenoi (Eds.)

Security
and Privacy Protection
in Information
Processing Systems

28th IFIP TC 11 International Conference, SEC 2013
Auckland, New Zealand, July 8-10, 2013
Proceedings

 Springer

Volume Editors

Lech J. Janczewski
The University of Auckland
Private Bag 92019, Auckland 1142, New Zealand
E-mail: lech@auckland.ac.nz

Henry B. Wolfe
University of Otago
P.O. Box 56, Dunedin 9016, New Zealand
E-mail: hwolfe@infoscience.otago.ac.nz

Sujeet Shenoi
The University of Tulsa
800 South Tucker Drive, Tulsa, OK 74104-3189, USA
E-mail: sujeet@utulsa.edu

ISBN 978-3-642-43139-5   ISBN 978-3-642-39218-4 (eBook)
DOI 10.1007/978-3-642-39218-4
Springer Heidelberg Dordrecht London New York

CR Subject Classification (1998): C.2, K.6.5, D.4.6, E.3, H.4, J.1

Typesetting: Camera-ready by author, data conversion by Scientific Publishing Services, Chennai, India

Printed on acid-free paper

Springer is part of Springer Science+Business Media (www.springer.com)

Preface

IFIP TC-11 Sec 2013, the 28th annual IFIP TC-11 Conference, was sponsored by the International Federation for Information Processing (IFIP), in cooperation with the University of Auckland Business School, the Institute of IT Professionals NZ (former New Zealand Computer Society), the US Office of Naval Research, International Business Machine Corporation, the New Zealand Security Information Forum, Insomnia, and many other business organizations. The conference was held in the beautiful city of Auckland.

The Program Committee, consisting of 70 members, considered 83 papers. These proceedings include the revised versions of the 31 papers presented at the conference. These papers were selected on the basis of originality, quality, and relevance to security and privacy. As a result, they should give a proper picture of how the field is evolving. Revisions were not checked and the authors bear full responsibility for the contents of their papers.

The selection of papers was a difficult and challenging task. Each submission was refereed usually by three reviewers. We wish to thank the Program Committee members, who did an excellent job. In addition, we gratefully acknowledge the help of a large number of colleagues who reviewed submissions in their areas of expertise. They are listed in the section following this Preface. We apologize for any inadvertent omission.

Many thanks to the creators of *EasyChair* without which the management of submissions for this conference would have been a nightmare. It would be difficult to imagine organizing and administering a conference without this valuable tool.

Formatting of the proceedings was done with the help of Vladimir Petranovic. The website was hosted at the University of Auckland School of Business, and a lot of work was done by Andrew Colarik, Romena Lim, and Wayne Gray. Thank you guys!

It is important for those of us involved with the administration of this conference to acknowledge and thank the US Office of Naval Research for, in addition to sponsoring the conference, specifically underwriting the substantial cost of this proceedings publication. Their contribution is much appreciated.

Finally, we wish to thank all the authors who submitted papers, for making this conference possible by creating the scientific material, and especially the authors of accepted papers. I would also like to thank the publisher, Springer-Verlag, for working within a tight schedule in order to produce these proceedings in due time.

July 2013

Lech Janczewski
Henry B. Wolfe
Sujeet Shenoi

Organization

IFIP TC-11 SEC 2013

8–10 July 2013, Auckland, New Zealand

Sponsored by the
International Federation for Information Processing (IFIP)

in cooperation with the

University of Auckland Business School
Institute of IT Professionals NZ
US Office of Naval Research
New Zealand Security Information Forum
International Business Machine Corporation
Insomnia

General Chair

Lech J. Janczewski	University of Auckland, New Zealand
Brian Cusack	AUT University, New Zealand

Program Chair

Henry B. Wolfe	University of Otago, New Zealand
Sujeet Shenoi	University of Tulsa, USA

Program Committee

Andreas Albers	Goethe University Frankfurt, Germany
Alessandro Aldini	University of Urbino, Italy
Portmann Armand	Hochschule für Wirtschaft , Switzerland
Vijay Atluri, Rutgers	The State University of New Jersey, USA
Richard Baskerville	Georgia State University, USA
Reinhardt Botha	NMMU, South Africa
Dagmar Brechlerova	Academy of Sciences of CR, Czech Republic
Jonathan Butts	Air Force Institute of Technology, USA
William Caelli	Queensland University of Technology, Australia
Jan Camenisch	IBM Research, Switzerland
Nathan Clarke	University of Plymouth, UK
Richard Clayton	University of Cambridge, UK

Ryoichi Sasaki   Tokyo Denki University, Japan
Ingrid Schaumüller-Bichl   University of Applied Sciences Upper Austria,
                               Austria
Annikken Seip   Finanstilsynet, Norway
Eugene Spafford   Purdue University, USA
Clark Thomborson   The University of Auckland, New Zealand
Vijay Varadharajan   Macquarie University, Australia
Pedro Veiga   Universidade de Lisboa, Portugal
Teemupekka Virtanen   Ministry of Social Affairs and Health, Finland
Rossouw von Solms   NMMU, South Africa
Jozef Vyskoc   VaF, Slovakia
Christian Weber   Ostfalia University of Applied Sciences,
                               Germany
Tatjana Welzer   University of Maribor, Slovenia
Brian Whitworth   Massey University, New Zealand
Louise Yngstrom   University of Stockholm, Sweden

Additional Reviewers

Ahmad Sabouri   Hüsler René
Andrew Colarik   Italo Dacosta
Anna Krasnova   Jan Vossaert
Brian Cusack   Janus Dam Nielsen
Chris Roberts   Ji Qingguang
Cristina Alcaraz   Markus Tschersich
Fatbardh Veseli   Paolo Gasti
Frédéric Cuppens   Philipp Winter
Fredrik Bjorck   Sujeet Shenoi
Gabriele Costa   Weiping Wen
Gergely Alpár   Wouter Lueks
Goekhan Bal

Table of Contents

Software Security

Policy Compliance and Obligations

Privacy Protection

Risk Analysis and Security Metrics

Social Engineering

Security Management/Forensic

Exploring Timeline-Based Malware Classification

Rafiqul Islam[1], Irfan Altas[1], and Md. Saiful Islam[1,2]

[1] Charles Sturt University, Australia
{mislam,ialtas}@csu.edu.au
[2] Swinburne University of Technology, Australia
mdsaifulislam@swin.edu.au

Abstract. Over the decades or so, Anti-Malware (AM) communities have been faced with a substantial increase in malware activity, including the development of ever-more-sophisticated methods of evading detection. Researchers have argued that an AM strategy which is successful in a given time period cannot work at a much later date due to the changes in malware design. Despite this argument, in this paper, we convincingly demonstrate a malware detection approach, which retains high accuracy over an extended time period. To the best of our knowledge, this work is the first to examine malware executables collected over a span of 10 years. By combining both static and dynamic features of malware and cleanware, and accumulating these features over intervals in the 10-year period in our test, we construct a high accuracy malware detection method which retains almost steady accuracy over the period. While the trend is a slight down, our results strongly support the hypothesis that perhaps it is possible to develop a malware detection strategy that can work well enough into the future.

Keywords: Timeline, Malware Detection, Static and Dynamic Features.

1   Introduction

Malware is one of the biggest challenges all over the world nowadays among the Internet users. Malware writers use various obfuscation techniques to transform a malicious program into undetectable variants with the same core functionalities of the parent malware program [1], [4], [7], [13], [15], [21]. Anti-Malware (AM) communities are trying hard to combat malware obfuscation techniques adopted by the malware writers by discovering the behavioral patterns of their parent malwares. However, one of the biggest challenges is that an AM strategy that has been found to be successful in a given time period cannot work at a much later time. This philosophy is supported by the works found in [1], [2], [9], [15], [16], [20] and [21], which indicates that current techniques fail to find the distinctive patterns of malicious software which can be used to identify future malwares. The argument is that malware evolves with time and eventually becomes unrecognizable from the original form; in addition completely new malware is designed which is unlike any known malware and so would not be detected by anti-virus software constructed to detect known types of malware. In fact, the assumption that malwares which are completely unlike earlier

L.J. Janczewski, H.B. Wolfe, and S. Shenoi (Eds.): SEC 2013, IFIP AICT 405, pp. 1–13, 2013.

malwares designed on a major scale is known to be false as indicated by the statistics in [3] showing that barely 25% of malwares found in 2006 are not variants of known malwares.

Despite the strong support in the literature of the assumption that malware detection methods cannot easily detect future malware, in this paper, we convincingly demonstrate that perhaps, it is possible to develop a malware detection strategy which can retain high accuracy over an extended time period. To the best of our knowledge, this paper is the first to examine malware executables collected over a span of 10 years. The key contributions of this paper are two-folds:

(a) A novel approach to feature collection by accumulating malware features over time segments of the 10 years span.
(b) A novel malware detection method retaining steady accuracy over an extended period of time.

The rest of the paper is organized as follows: Section 2 provides a review of the literature and Section 3 describes the set-up for the testing. In Section 4, we provide a detailed discussion of the experiment and present the results and in Section 5, we discuss the analysis and its implications for future work.

2   Related Work

A substantial research has been done on malware classification and detection. In this section, we present only a few of the existing works that are either closely related to or motivate us to conduct our research in this paper. The study in [20] investigates malicious attacks on several websites by creating web honey pots and collecting website-based malware executables over a period of five months. In their study, they collect and analyze malware samples using 6 different antivirus programs, and conduct the same experiment four months later using the updated versions of the 6 programs to determine their efficacy. Additionally, the work of Rajab et al. [10] also focuses on mitigating web-based malware. They study a dataset collected over a period of four years and demonstrate that existing malware characteristic can aid in detecting future malware. Both aforementioned works demonstrate that, some anti-virus software can significantly improve detection rates with training on older malware.

The research conducted by Rosyid et al. [11] is focused on detecting malicious attack patterns in botnets attacking a honeypot during the year 2009. After extracting the log files of malware sequences, they then apply the *PrefixSpan* algorithm to discover subsequence patterns. The authors extend their work by identifying attack patterns based on IP address and timestamp. The authors argue that the signature of a single malware file is not enough to detect the complex variants of the attacks by botnets. In [1], the authors apply a dynamic method for classifying malware, considering the interactions between the operating system and malicious programs as behavioral features. In their study they use three different evaluation techniques: completeness, conciseness, and consistency. The authors mention that one limitation of their methodology is the failure to "detect fine-grained characteristics of the observed behaviors".

Another group of researchers, [6], build their malware detection and classification framework based on comparisons of extracted strings using static analysis.

They claim that the similarity between two files can be determined by comparing the character strings, which in turn is used to identify and determine whether the two instances are variants. The authors present a three-step methodology of extraction, refinement and comparison. The authors show that if a mutated instance of malware is detected, it is reflected as a huge peak under the respective malware family.

In [5], the authors use a combination of static and dynamic analysis to achieve a high level of accuracy over an 8 year time period. We are not the first to integrate dynamic with static features however (see for example [12]), though we are the first to use this method applied over a long time period. In order to understand the evolution of malware over a long period of time and its effects on future malware, in this paper, we consider two types of analysis: static and dynamic, as these features are predominant for malware analysis in the literature.

3 Experimental Setup

3.1 The Methodology

Static and dynamic analyses are two of the most popular forms of malware analysis techniques predominant in the literature [1], [5], [6], [9], [12], [17], [18], [19], [20]. However, each of these analysis techniques comes with its own merits and demerits. Static analysis can analyze a wide spectrum of possible execution paths of an executable, thus providing a good global view of the whole executable and of the entire program logic without running it. But, static analysis is susceptible to inaccuracies due to obfuscation and polymorphic techniques.

On the otherhand, dynamic analysis monitors the behavior of the binary executable file during its execution, which enables it to collect a profile of the operations performed by the binary thus offering potentially greater insight into the code itself. The main limitation of dynamic analysis is that analysis results are only based on malware behavior during a specific execution run. Since some of the malware's behaviour may be triggered only under specific conditions, such behaviour would be easy to miss with only a single execution.

In our experiments, we extract both static and dynamic features from the malware and cleanware files collected over the 10 years period and learn our classifier to detect future malwares. More specifically, we extract from each executable (a) static features: printable string information (PSI) and function length frequency (FLF), (b) dynamic features: API calls including their parameters and (c) integrated features: a combination of the two static and the dynamic features. The WEKA library of data mining algorithms [8] is used to learn the classifiers and derive the detection results based on the extracted feature vectors as input.

3.2 Data (Malware and Cleanware) Collection

The malware executables used in the experiment were collected from CA's VET Zoo[1] over a span of 8 years (2002-2010) and we collect (2011-2012) manually from open

---

[1] www.ca.com.au

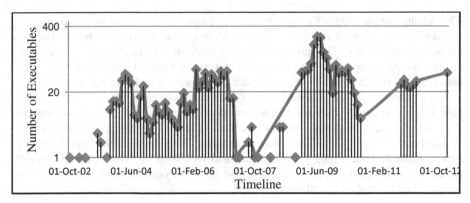

Fig. 1. Collection of malware executables from 2002 to 2012

sources (www.offensivecomputing.net, http://www.virussign.com); the cleanware executables were collected manually from various versions of Win32 based systems. Fig. 1 indicates the dates at which malware files were collected.

The total numbers of malware and cleanware executables, used in our experiments, are 2617 and 541 respectively. Table 1 shows the executables family by family.

3.3   Timeline Data Preparation

The date of a malware file was associated with the file when the file was collected. We exported all files, along with their dates, into our Ida2DBMS schema [18] and based on the dates broke the data into groups as described in Fig. 2.

To generate groups of malware for use in the testing, we begin with the earliest malware and add month by month across the timeline until all data are grouped. As the first data group, MG_1, we take the earliest-dated 10% of the files. There are 262 executables in this group which covers the period from October 2002 to December 2004. The second data group, MG_2, comprises the data collected during the period October 2002 to January 2005, and so on. When too few files appear in a subsequent month to justify including that month as a group, we jump to the following month. In all, this results in 65 malware data groups which are labeled as MG_1, MG_2,...,MG_{65}. Fig. 2 indicates the spread of malware across the sixty five groups with each bar corresponding to a group.

Throughout the test, the set of 541 WIN32 cleanware files is treated as a single group, cleanware group *(CG)*. However, when it is tested against a particular malware group, depending on the comparative size of the two groups, the cleanware group may be divided into subgroups.

3.4   Cumulative Feature Vector (CFV) Generation

To test malware against cleanware, we fix a malware group and use an equal portion of malware and of cleanware data. Fig. 3 shows the data preparation process. The selected malware group MG_i is compared with CG. If $|MG_i|$ is smaller than $|CG|$ then we compute the integer part of $|CG|/|MG_i|$ and the integer reminder $0 \le R < |MG_i|$ as in $|CG| = k |MG_i| + R$, for some positive integer k.

Table 1. Experimental set of 3158 files

Type		Family	Detection Date Starting ⇒ ending	Number of Executables	Number of Instances
Malware	Trojan	Bambo	2003-07 ⇒ 2006-01	44	5100
		Boxed	2004-06 ⇒ 2007-09	178	56662
		Alureon	2005-05 ⇒ 2007-11	41	7635
		Robknot	2005-10 ⇒ 2007-08	78	10411
		Clagger	2005-11 ⇒ 2007-01	44	4520
		Robzips	2006-03 ⇒ 2007-08	72	6549
		Tracur	2011-08⇒2011-11	42	7365
		Cridex	2011-10 ⇒2012-02	56	8692
	Worms	SillyDl	2009-01 ⇒ 2010-08	439	56933
		Vundo	2009-01 ⇒ 2010-08	80	1660
		Lefgroo	2012-12⇒2012-12	121	35421
		Frethog	2009-01 ⇒ 2010-08	174	28042
		SillyAutorun	2009-01 ⇒ 2010-05	87	9965
	Virus	Gamepass	2009-01 ⇒ 2010-07	179	23730
		Bancos	2009-01 ⇒ 2010-07	446	89554
		Adclicker	2009-01 ⇒ 2010-08	65	11637
		Banker	2009-01⇒ 2010-06	47	12112
		Agobot	2002-10 ⇒ 2006-04	283	216430
		Looked	2003-07 ⇒ 2006-09	66	36644
		Emerleox	2006-11 ⇒ 2008-11	75	61242
Total of malware files			*2002 ⇒ 2012*	**2617**	**690304**
Cleanware				**541**	81154
TOTAL				**3158**	**771458**

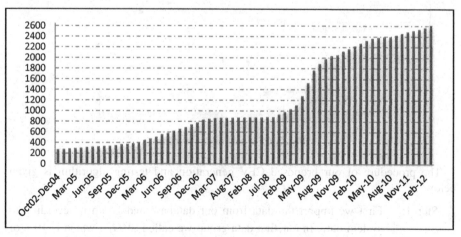

Fig. 2. Number of malware executables accumulated by date

We then divide *CG* into *k* disjoint groups of equal size. If $R > 0$, then the remaining elements must be padded out to a $(k+1)$'st group CG_{k+1}. However, if $R = 0$, this set is empty and is not used.

If $|MG_i|$ is bigger than $|CG|$ then we compute the integer part of $|MG_i|/|CG|$ and proceed in the same way. This procedure is repeated for every malware group.

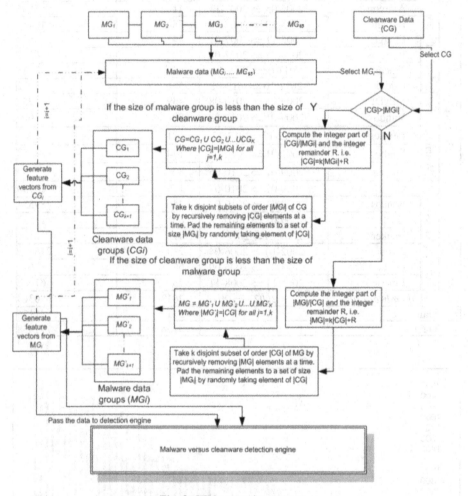

Fig. 3. CFV generation process

The procedure of our proposed CFV generation and testing algorithm is given below:

Step 1:   First we import the data from our database and group it according to system date. In our first data-group we called "*MG₁*", which is 10% of total malware from early malware executables. Then, we do remaining groups as month by month.

Step 2:   We add the data in increasing order as mentioned earlier, so that each data-group MG_i is the $MG_i = MG_i + MG_{i-1}$.

Step 3:   Since our test is based on malware versus cleanware test, we again divide each data-group MGi into subgroups, same size of cleanware, if the malware size is bigger; and vice versa for cleanware, if the cleanware size is bigger.

Step 4:   Select a data-group (both from malware and cleanware) and extract the feature information (explained in the following section).

Step 5:   Create CFV and construct the .arff file (WEKA) format.

Step 6:   Select the data group and split it into n (n = 10) folds.

Step 7:   Build training data using n-1 folds (90% of the total data) and the remaining fold as test data (10% of the total data). The detail can be found in Section 3.6.

Step 8:   Call WEKA libraries to train the classifier using training data.

Step 9:   Evaluate the test data set.

Step 10:   Repeat until finish for all n folds (each fold should be used as test data and the remaining folds as training data).

Step 11:   Repeat for other classifiers.

Step 12:   Repeat until finish all data groups.

3.5   Feature Vector Generation

In our experiment, we use both static and dynamic features as explained before. We also use a combined version of these two features for the purpose of detecting future malwares.

Static Features. From each of the executables, we extract two static features, function length frequency (FLF) and printable string information (PSI). These features are extracted from unpacked malware executables by means of a command line AV engine. The AV engine identifies and unpacks the packed executables in batch mode and identifies functions and printable strings.

To extract FLF features, we follow the methodology described in [17]. However, in order to determine an appropriate number of intervals, we follow Sturges' well-established statistical formula [14], which recommends the use of approximately $1+log_2(n)$ bins, where n represents the number of instances in the experiment. Based on our value of $n = 771458$ we use 20 bins.

As an example, consider an executable file with 22 functions which have the following lengths in bytes, presented in increasing order of size: 5, 6, 12, 12, 15, 18, 18, 50, 50, 130, 210, 360, 410, 448, 546, 544, 728, 848, 1344, 1538, 3138, 4632. For the purposes of illustration, we create 10 bins of function length ranges. The distribution of lengths across the bins is as shown in Table 2.

This produces a vector of length 10 using the entries in the second column of Table 2: (0.0, 2.0, 5.0, 2.0, 1.0, 4.0, 4.0, 3.0, 1.0, 0.0) which corresponds to the function length frequency for the file chosen.

In extracting PSI features, we use the methodology of [18] for generating vectors to use in the classification process. We illustrate this with an example. Consider a global ordered string list containing 10 distinct strings:

{"LoadMemory","GetNextFileA",   "FindLastFileA"   "GetProcAddress", "RegQueryValueExW", "CreateFileW", "OpenFile", "FindFirstFileA", "FindNextFileA", "CopyMemory"}

Suppose that a particular executable has the following set of printable strings:

{"GetProcAddress", "RegQueryValueExW","CreateFileW","GetProcAddress"}

The PSI vector for this executable file records, first of all, the total number of distinct strings in the file followed by a binary report on the presence of each string in the global list, where a 'true' represents the fact that the string is present and a 'false' that it is not. Table 3 presents the corresponding data for this executable file. The vector for this example becomes (4, false, false, false, true, true, true, false, false, false, false).

Table 2. Example of FLF bin distribution

FLF Bin distribution	
Length of functions	FLF Vectors
1-2	0.0
3-8	2.0
9-21	5.0
22-59	2.0
60-166	1.0
167-464	4.0
465-1291	4.0
1292-3593	3.0
3594-9999	1.0
>=10000	0.0

Table 3. Example of PSI vector generation

PSI Vector generation	
Printable string	PSI Vector
String number	4
LoadMemory	false
GetNextFileA	false
FindLastFileA	false
GetProcAddress	true
RegQueryValueExW	true
CreateFileW	true
OpenFile	false
FindFirstFileA	false
FindNextFielA	false
CopyMemory	false

Dynamic Features. To extract this feature, we follow the methodology to generate dynamic logs, described in [19]. For generating a normalized feature vector from dynamic log files we construct a global feature list from all extracted API calls and API parameters. We treat the functions and parameters as separate entities as they may separately affect the ability to detect and identify the executable. For illustration, consider the following global API feature list:

{"RegOpenKeyEx","RegQueryValueExW","Compositing","RegOpenKeyExW","0x54", "ControlPanel\Desktop","LameButtonText","LoadLibraryW",".\UxTheme.dll","LoadLibrary ExW", "MessageBoxW"}.

We now list the distinct features in the global list and generate a vector for the executable based on the frequency of these features. Table 4 shows the distinct global feature list with corresponding frequencies for this particular example and the corresponding feature vector is (0, 2, 1, 1, 1, 1, 1, 1, 2, 1, 0).

Table 4. Example of dynamic feature vector generation

Dynamic feature vector generation	
Global feature	Frequency
RegOpenKeyEx	0
RegQueryValueExW	2
Compositing	1
RegOpenKeyExW	1
0x54	1
ControlPanel\Desktop	1
LameButtonText	1
LoadLibraryW	1
.\UxTheme.dll	2
LoadLibraryExW	2
MessageBoxW	0

3.6   Detection Method

In our classification process, we input the generated feature vectors into the WEKA classification system [8] for which we have developed an interface. In all of our experiments, 10-fold cross validation is applied to ensure a thorough mixing of the sample data and thereby, reducing the biasness as much as possible. In this procedure, we first select one group of malware data from a particular data set and divide it into ten portions of equal size. Then we select cleanware data of the same size as the group of malware data and also divide it into ten portions. The portions are, then, tested against each other. The whole process is repeated for each group and we then calculate average classification results. In our test, we have multiple tests within each group. The following Fig. 4 shows the number of tests within a period range.

To establish the training set, our detection engine takes nine portions from each of the malware and cleanware. The remaining portions from both malware and cleanware are used for the testing set. As is customary, the training set is used to establish the model and the testing set is used to validate it. The whole process is repeated so that every portion of both malware and cleanware is chosen as testing data. The results are then averaged. In order to ensure that the input vectors are trained and tested over a

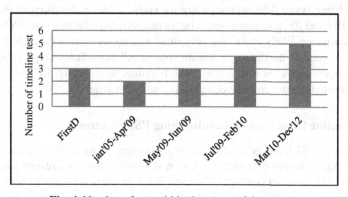

Fig. 4. Number of test within the group of data set

broad spectrum of classifiers, we chose the following four classifiers from WEKA [8] as they represent differing approaches to statistical analysis of data: Support Vector Machines (SVM), Random Forest (RF), Decision Table (DT) and IB1.

4   Experiments and Results

We have run the entire experiment using each of the four base classifiers SVM, IB1, DT and RF mentioned in Section 3.6. In addition, each test was run five times and the results averaged in order to ensure that any anomalies in the experimental set-up were discounted. The following sections present our empirical results.

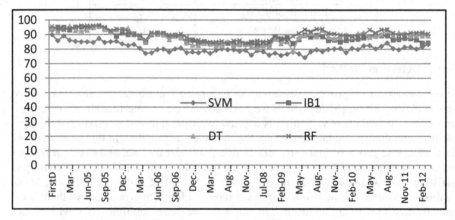

Fig. 5. Timeline results based on FLF features

4.1   Timeline Classification Results Using FLF Features

As mentioned in Section 3.5, the total number of FLF features used is fixed at 20 (bins) throughout the tests. Fig. 5 shows the result over the 10 year timeline. The x-axis shows the timeline data group and the y-axis shows the detection ratio of malware. It is clear that we achieve better detection accuracy for early malware compared to that for later malware. IB1 and RF give consistently better results across the timeline. SVM gives the worst performance, likely due to the very small feature set used in the experiment given that it is designed to handle large feature spaces. All classifiers except SVM maintain their accuracies above 80% throughout the timeline. Specifically, RF maintains better accuracy throughout the timeline compared to other classifiers.

4.2   Timeline Classification Results Using PSI Features

The number of PSI features used for each data group grows across the timeline, varying from approximately 800 to 2085. Fig. 6 shows the detection results using the PSI feature set. All classifiers except DT maintains their accuracies above 80% using PSI features. However, once again RF maintains better accuracy compared to the other classifiers throughout the timeline.

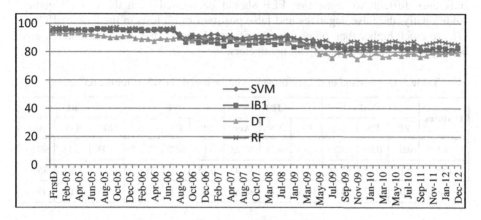

Fig. 6. Timeline results based on PSI features

4.3   Timeline Classification Results Using Dynamic Features

The number of features used in this test increases from approximately 2600 to 8800 over the timeline. Fig. 7 shows the detection accuracy of the dynamic feature set which is based on API calls and API parameters.

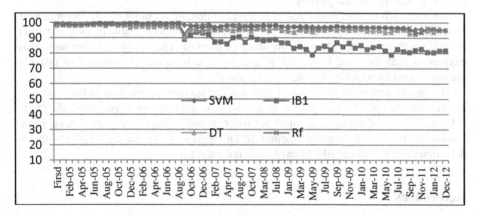

Fig. 7. Timeline results based on dynamic test

For all but the IB1 classifier, the dynamic feature results give almost consistent and better performance compared to either of the static features (i.e., FLF and PSI). With a large feature set, IB1 is inclined to make errors when building the training sets, which is likely to account for the poor performance here.

In Table 5, we have summarized the detection results for the last group, the 65th group of our data set, which includes all of the executables, showing the false positive (FP) and false negative (FN) rates and also the accuracies. Note the very poor accuracy of SVM with PSI while, with IB1, FLF has slightly better accuracy than the dynamic and PSI test, and with DT and RF, the results for dynamics features are better.

It is thus difficult to argue that FLF should be deleted from the test altogether. Additionally, the false negatives and false positives of all tests in the case of IB1 and DT are much higher than other two classifiers. However, the dynamic features give better performances comparing all parameters.

Table 5. Comparison of the performances of the tested classifiers for the 65th group

Features	SVM			IB1			DT			RF		
	FP	FN	Acc	FP	FN	Acc	FP	FN	Acc	FP	FN	Acc
FLF	0.07	0.66	83.26	0.14	0.25	84.23	0.17	0.28	89.17	0.03	0.11	90.51
PSI	0.12	0.25	81.98	0.1	0.23	82.92	0.15	0.24	78.87	0.12	0.21	85.33
Dynamic	0.01	0.12	94.81	0.17	0.16	81.65	0.02	0.08	95.35	0.03	0.04	95.29

5   Conclusion and Future Work

In this paper, we have presented a cumulative timeline approach for identifying malware from cleanware and demonstrated that perhaps it is possible to develop a malware detection strategy that can retains high accuracy over the long time period. The results presented in Section 4 indicate that our method retains fairly consistent accuracy over the 10 year period.

Our approach to feature collection is novel in that we accumulate the features over time segments of the 10 year span. In progressively adding malware over the time period, we thereby strengthen the accuracy of the test. The implication for anti-virus engines is that they are then able to use previously detected malware to provide features based on which to test new executables.

The results presented in section 4 indicate that no one feature type is the most significant for the specific classifier over the 10 year span. In our experiment, the static (FLF and PSI) and dynamic features act independently. Therefore, it is expected that combining static and dynamic features in an integrated manner could give a better detection rate. We would like to explore in our future work.

References

1. Bailey, M., Oberheide, J., Andersen, J., Mao, Z.M., Jahanian, F., Nazario, J.: Automated classification and analysis of internet malware. In: Kruegel, C., Lippmann, R., Clark, A. (eds.) RAID 2007. LNCS, vol. 4637, pp. 178–197. Springer, Heidelberg (2007)
2. Barford, P., Yegneswaran, V.: An inside look at botnets. In: Christodorescu, M., Jha, S., Maughan, D., Song, D., Wang, C. (eds.) Malware Detection, Advances in Information Security, vol. 27, pp. 171–191. Springer US (2007)
3. Braverman, M., Williams, J., Mador, Z.: Microsoft security intelligence report (January-June 2006), http://www.microsoft.com/en-us/download/details.aspx?id=5454 (accessed on May 19, 2011)

4. Fossi, M., Johnson, E., Mack, T., Turner, D., Blackbird, J., Low, M.K., Adams, T., Mckinney, D., Entwisle, S., Laucht, M.P., Wueest, C., Wood, P., Bleaken, D., Ahmad, G., Kemp, D.: Samnani: Symantec global internet security threat report trends for 2009. Technical report (2009)
5. Islam, R., Tian, R., Batten, L.M., Versteeg, S.: Classification of malware based on integrated static and dynamic features. J. Network and Computer Applications 36(2), 646–656 (2013)
6. Lee, J., Im, C., Jeong, H.: A study of malware detection and classification by comparing extracted strings. In: Proc. of the 5th International Conference on Ubiquitous Information Management and Communication, pp. 75:1–75:4. ACM, New York (2011)
7. Marcus, D., Greve, P., Masiello, S., Scharoun, D.: Mcafee threats report: Third quarter 2009. Technical report, Mcafee (2009)
8. Mark, H., Eibe, F., Geoffrey, H., Bernhard, P., Peter, R., Ian, H.W.: The WEKA Data Mining Software: An Update. SIGKDD Explorations 11(1), 10–18 (2009)
9. Nair, V.P., Jain, H., Golecha, Y.K., Gaur, M.S., Laxmi, V.: Medusa: Metamorphic malware dynamic analysis using signature from API. In: Proceedings of the 3rd International Conference on Security of Information and Networks, SIN 2010, pp. 263–269. ACM, New York (2010)
10. Rajab, M., Ballard, L., Jagpal, N., Mavrommatis, P., Nojiri, D., Provos, N., Schmidt, L.: Trends in circumventing web-malware detection. Google Tech. Rep. (2011)
11. Rosyid, N.R., Ohrui, M., Kikuchi, H., Sooraksa, P., Terada, M.: A discovery of sequential attack patterns of malware in botnets. In: SMC, pp. 2564–2570 (2010)
12. Roundy, K.A., Miller, B.P.: Hybrid analysis and control of malware. In: Jha, S., Sommer, R., Kreibich, C. (eds.) RAID 2010. LNCS, vol. 6307, pp. 317–338. Springer, Heidelberg (2010)
13. Soltani, S., Khayam, S.A., Radha, H.: Detecting malware outbreaks using a statistical model of blackhole traffic. In: ICC, pp. 1593–1597 (2008)
14. Sturges, H.A.: The choice of a class interval. Journal of the American Statistical Association 21(153), 65–66 (1926)
15. Sukwong, O., Kim, H., Hoe, J.: Commercial antivirus software effectiveness: An empirical study. Computer 44(3), 63–70 (2011)
16. Tang, H., Zhu, B., Ren, K.: A new approach to malware detection. In: Park, J.H., Chen, H.-H., Atiquzzaman, M., Lee, C., Kim, T.-H., Yeo, S.-S. (eds.) ISA 2009. LNCS, vol. 5576, pp. 229–238. Springer, Heidelberg (2009)
17. Tian, R., Batten, L.M., Versteeg, S.C.: Function length as a tool for malware classification. In: Proc. of the 3rd International Conference on Malicious and Unwanted Software: MALWARE 2008, pp. 69–76 (2008)
18. Tian, R., Batten, L., Islam, R., Versteeg, S.: An automated classification system based on the strings of Trojan and virus families. In: Proc. of the 4th International Conference on Malicious and Unwanted Software: MALWARE 2009, pp. 23–30 (2009)
19. Tian, R., Islam, R., Batten, L., Versteeg, S.: Differentiating malware from cleanware using behavioural analysis. In: Proceedings of the 5th International Conference on Malicious and Unwanted Software: MALWARE 2010 (2010)
20. Yagi, T., Tanimoto, N., Hariu, T., Itoh, M.: Investigation and analysis of malware on websites. In: Lucca, G.A.D., Kienle, H.M. (eds.) WSE, pp. 73–81. IEEE Computer Society (2010)
21. You, I., Yim, K.: Malware obfuscation techniques: A brief survey. In: BWCCA, pp. 297–300 (2010)

Screening Smartphone Applications Using Behavioral Signatures

Suyeon Lee, Jehyun Lee, and Heejo Lee*

Division of Computer and Communication Engineering,
Korea University,
Seoul, Korea
{suyeonl,arondit,heejo}@korea.ac.kr

Abstract. The sharp increase of smartphone malwares has become one of the most serious security problems. The most significant part of the growth is the variants of existing malwares. A legacy approach for malware, the signature matching, is efficient in temporal dimension, but it is not practical because of its lack of robustness against the variants. A counter approach, the behavior analysis to handle the variant issue, takes too much time and resources. We propose a variant detection mechanism using runtime semantic signature. Our key idea is to reduce the control and data flow analysis overhead by using binary patterns for the control and data flow of critical actions as a signature. The flow information is a significant part of behavior analysis but takes high analysis overhead. In contrast to the previous behavioral signatures, the runtime semantic signature has higher family classification accuracy without the flow analysis overhead, because the binary patterns of flow parts is hardly shared by the out of family members. Using the proposed signature, we detect the new variants of known malwares by static matching efficiently and accurately. We evaluated our mechanism with 1,759 randomly collected real-world Android applications including 79 variants of 4 malware families. As the experimental result, our mechanism showed 99.89% of accuracy on variant detection. We also showed that the mechanism has a linear time complexity as the number of target applications. It is fully practical and advanced performance than the previous works in both of accuracy and efficiency.

Keywords: Smartphone security, Android, Malware, Runtime semantic signature.

1 Introduction

Smart devices are now facing a serious threat posed by surging malwares. Smartphone has become the most popular target for malware writers since it contains a great deal of user information and has capability for mobile billing. The majority of smartphone malwares leak user information and perform user unwanted billing

---

* Corresponding author.

L.J. Janczewski, H.B. Wolfe, and S. Shenoi (Eds.): SEC 2013, IFIP AICT 405, pp. 14–27, 2013.
© IFIP International Federation for Information Processing 2013

by abusing smartphone's original functionality. Recently, smartphone malwares have adopted several obfuscation techniques such as metamorphism to avoid detection. According to F-Secure's report [1], about 82% of newly discovered mobile malware are revealed as a variant of known malware family. Such trend is especially remarkable on *Google Android*. Overall, smartphone malwares can cause more direct invasion of privacy and credential damage to the users compared with the desktop malwares. However, the flood of metamorphic malwares on the smartphones impedes an efficient dealing of malware attack. Accordingly, a mechanism which prevents malwares by filtering variant of known malwares, efficiently, is needed to retain smartphone security and user privacy.

Previous approaches for variant detection based on behavior analysis were not appropriate to identify the malware family where a detected malware variant belongs to. Those approaches detect the variants by estimating similarity of behavior such as API call frequency or API call sequence [2], with a known malware. Extracting and comparing the behaviors from numbers of target executables takes heavy computing overhead. Detection based on similarity of behavior is a helpful way for unknown detection, but it does not provide and use any evidence to show that certain variants are derived from same malware.

In opposite, a representative signature that usually has been used by AV vendors is effective to define and detect malware family. It is also efficient in contrast to the behavior based approaches in terms of time and space complexity. However, the signatures have not only narrow detection coverage on a malware family due to the lack of semantic but also easily defeated by the malwares which are adopted code obfuscation such as metamorphism. As a conclusion, re-investigation of overall code area for behavior analysis and to make an additional signature for slight modulation of a malware is an inefficient way against the little effort that consumed for making a variant.

In this paper, we propose a variant detection mechanism which filters new variants of known malware family. Since the most Android malwares are repackaged version of legitimate executable file, the malwares in same family retain semantics unchanged. Using this feature, we detect the variants efficiently and accurately by analyzing such semantics in static. The proposed mechanism uses a runtime semantic signature of known malwares. The runtime semantic signature is a malware family signature including the family representative binary patterns for control and data flow instructions and character strings, as well as API calls. The signatures including flow instructions and family representative signatures contribute to achieve accurate variant detection and family classification reducing analysis overhead.

In experimental evaluation, our mechanism show high detection performance and consumes practically low time in variant detection. We evaluated our mechanism with 1,759 real-world Android applications including 79 variants of 4 malware families, *DroidDream*, *Geinimi*, *KMIN*, and *PjApps*. The experimental set is randomly collected by automated crawler during the period of September 2011-December 2011. For performance evaluation, first, we created runtime semantic signatures for 4 malware families. Our mechanism showed over 99% of detection accuracy and near 97% of recall performance, on average, from 10-fold cross validation. Second, for unknown detection performance, we compared the four family signatures with unidentified 100 malwares. Our mechanism detected 56 malwares from the experiment set. This result shows that our mechanism detects code-level invariants with same semantics, while legacy signature-based approaches are generally not able to detect such variants. Finally, in the scalability evaluation, our mechanism screens a thousand of applications with also a thousand of signatures within 23 seconds. To consider efficiency and accuracy against variant detection of our mechanism, it is applicable for screening Android applications before they are uploaded on public app markets.

Our contributions are two folds:

- We proposed a runtime semantic signature that is used for detecting variants of known malware family accurately and efficiently. The runtime signature is a signature for a malware family sharing its API calls and representative part of codes having control and data flow semantics. It solves an existing malware detection issue, by combining malware semantic with sequence information. This contribution makes it possible to detect malware including their variants, even if the variant adopted evasion technique such as metamorphism.
- We reduced the number of signatures. The runtime signature representing a malware family on a single set of signature and covers numbers of family members including newly appeared variants. The runtime signature is based on the sequence of API calls which are shared among the malwares which have similar behaviors, but the adaptation of family representative binary patterns enable to detect and to classify malware families in practical accuracy. It enables to efficiently respond to the exponentially increasing number of malwares.

The rest of this paper organized as follows: we will start from describe details of mechanisms and assumptions of our proposition in section 2. Next, we will present experimental result of our system on Android in section 3. After distinguishing our work with previous works in section 4, we will discuss about limitations, future work and finally conclude our work in section 5.

2 Malicious Application Detection Using Behavioral Signature

2.1 Mechanism Overview

Our detection mechanism is an advanced type of signature-based approach. On a smartphone, the number of target of inspection (i.e. applications) are increasing sheerly and malware variants are taking the majority share of new malwares.

Legacy signature-based approach scans a lot of applications in a timely manner. However, since the performance of signature-based approach is highly dependent on its signature, it is not robust against a number of malware variants. Therefore, we added runtime semantic to complement the weakness of signature-based approach.

To detect malware variants belonging to a family by a single robust signature set, we basically use the malicious behaviors shared by family members represented by API calls and control and data flow between the calls. The API call sequence is one of the well-known behavior based approaches for detecting malware variants and reducing the volume of signatures. However, it has false detection problem in the smartphone environment because the legitimate smartphone applications have much more similar behavior to the malicious applications in contrast to the legacy PC environment's. Due to the problem, in the smartphone environment, the variant detection should be performed with more critical evidences representing the membership of a family. We overcome this challenge by adapting binary patterns of instructions between API calls for control and data processing to the behavioral signature. In the legacy PC environments, the binary patterns of control and data processing have too many variations and not so useful due to the numbers of various APIs. However, the executables working on a smartphone have relatively small variety of APIs and instructions enough to use as a behavioral signature. The binary patterns of the control and data flow, the runtime semantics, are general enough to detect the variants of a malware generated by code and class reusing or repackaging but rarely shared to the other family members and benign applications. The proposed detection mechanism using the behavioral signatures shows practical enough detection performance in both of efficiency and accuracy in our evaluation.

The key features of proposed behavioral signature structure are two-folds. First, the signature contains binary patterns of API call instructions on an executable file. In case of the Android environment, an application has its executable code as a *Dalvik Executable(DEX)* file. Second, the signature contains runtime semantic for reducing control and data flow analysis time and classifying malware families. Runtime semantic is also bytecode patterns that are used for the data and control flow between API calls. While analyzing known malwares, we monitor the taint flow of sensitive APIs and associate flow between APIs with three relationship, flow, call and condition. Figure 1 shows the overall architecture of our proposed mechanism. To efficiently and reliably winnow new malwares from target applications, our mechanism conducts two phases of analysis. Each analysis phases are quite straightforward. We first construct the behavioral signatures based on the known malware binaries and analysis report of them. Then we match the signatures with target DEX files. These analysis phases consequently produce a set of similarities between signatures and target applications as well as the security report of target applications. In the remainder of this section, we will detail each phases.

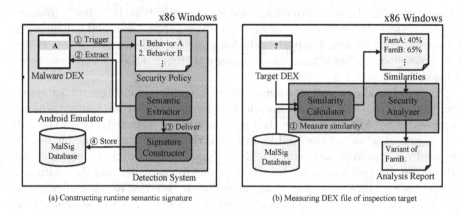

(a) Constructing runtime semantic signature   (b) Measuring DEX file of inspection target

Fig. 1. Overview of the proposed variant detection mechanism

2.2   Signature Construction

In this section, we explain the proposed behavior signature from the definition of malicious behavior. Signature construction is started from detecting the malicious behaviors by dynamic analysis. The signature construction process extracts the binary patterns and character strings from known malwares and estimates the weight of each pattern and string depending on the family where they belong to.

Malicious Behavior Definition. Before scanning applications, we need to clarify what behaviors will be considered as malicious behaviors. According to the 'Malicious payload' classification of Y. Zhou *et al.* [3], we selected four severe behaviors for malware detection. We detailed the definition of each behavior below.

- **Privilege Escalation** Since Android platform consists of more than 90 open-source libraries as well as linux kernel, flaws included in such libraries naturally incur vulnerabilities of whole Android system. As the time of research, seven exploits have been reported that are possible to gain the root privilege of an Android device. By adopting the exploits, application is being able to perform kernel-level control of the device without any user notification. The most risky and widespread malwares such as *DroidDream* and *DroidKungfu* initially contain exploits to perform high-risk malicious activities surreptitiously. Since the exploitation is the most serious threat for users, we detect known privilege escalation exploits that either contained in known malwares or be searched on internet forums.
- **Remote Control** Over 90% of currently reported Android malwares have remote control capability. Specifically, Android malwares that have remote control capability follow the commands from designated C&C server via

HTTP web request or SMS messages. More recently, malware authors obfuscate the C&C server IP address or the commands to make malware analysis be effortful. We identified three specific behaviors to detect remote control behavior, (1) establishing internet procedure and registering broadcast intent for SMS messages, (2) receiving internet packet or SMS messages, (3) and application or kernel-level runtime execution of received data.

- **Financial Charge** Financial charge is the most profitable way for malware authors. Since SMS messages can be sent surreptitiously i.e. without any user notification on Android, many malwares are designed to send premium-rate SMS or phone call. In early times, malwares have had hard-coded numbers to make charge for users. However, recent malwares with financial charging capability are being more complicated by changing their phone number gaining method such as runtime push-down from C&C server and to get from a encrypted file inside of the package. To detect financial charge capability, we monitor APIs that send messages (e.g. sendTextMessage) to hard-coded number.

- **Information Collection** Since a smartphone is one of the most trusted and user-friendly devices, it contains a great deal of information which are deeply related to the owner's social life and credentials. Therefore, malware authors are trying to get wide range of information from device-specific information (e.g. IMEI, IMSI and phone number) to the owner's information (e.g. contact book, SMS messages, call log and credentials). The exfilteration of such information will affect not only the user oneself but also the people around him/her both directly and indirectly. We identify the APIs that provide such information and network transfer API that will possibly send the information to remote server.

Malicious Behavior Detection. We identify each behavior as a set of APIs. However, defining APIs that form each behavior is difficult because the APIs vary depending on the sort of malware. For efficient and reliable analysis, we dynamically analyze known malware samples and extract APIs that are considered to malicious behaviors based on the corresponding malware reports. Additionally, to classify the family if target application has identified as a malware, we extract characteristics from malware that can represent the whole malware family. Variants of many Android malwares have common strings, constants or even classes or methods in practice. We extract the characteristics that only appear in each family. Common strings and constants between families are not considered as proper characteristics.

Signature Construction. Our signature is devised to provide knowledge-base for further investigations. To achieve reliable and efficient malware detection, we need to design our signature structure to meet four requirements in below. Basically, signatures should contain (1) behavioral semantics for basic detection capability. And, if a target application identified as a variant of known malware, then it could be (2) identifiable as a member of certain malware family. Also, to overcome the pitfalls of legacy signature-based approach, our signature should be (3) reliable against different evasion techniques while maintaining (4) the efficiency as a signature-based approach.

Figure 2 illustrates the structure of behavioral signature with an example. A signature represents a malware family. In other words, it is capable to know whether the target application is a new member of known malware family with a single matching. The signature consists of three main elements. The first one is malicious APIs and their runtime semantics for control and data flow. We extract APIs that make malicious behavior mentioned in *Malicious Behavior Detection*. When extracting APIs, runtime semantics such as repeated count of the API or the relationship between the former and latter APIs will also be extracted to infuse semantics into signatures. The second one is family characteristics. Since Android applications share broad range of behaviors even they are the member of each different malware families, identifiable information for malware family is necessary. Android malwares which included in same family tend to share same strings, constants, methods or even classes in most cases. Based on this tendency, we extract family common string, constants, methods and classes as family characteristics for family identification. The third one is weights of each behavior within family. Note that the signature contains sets of APIs and semantics according to that signature represents every behaviors appear in every variants of certain family. More frequently used API will take greater weight.

In conclusion, by using signature, our mechanism detects malicious behaviors semantically with APIs and their runtime semantics and also identifies the family of newly detected malware with API weights and family characteristics simultaneously.

In terms of signature matching, since a signature represents one malware family, it is possible to use only a small number of signatures to cover a large number of malwares. Our mechanism scans the signatures with target applications efficiently in conjunction with a static matching algorithm. We will describe the matching algorithm in detail in following section.

2.3   Malware Detection

Similarity Measurement. Similarity calculator compares and estimates the similarity between the DEX file of target application and behavioral signatures. Each signature has a weight of each behavior based on its discernment on malware family identification. Similarity calculator first scan all potentially malicious behaviors that contained in a DEX file, based on the APIs and semantics that stored in each signature. Specifically, the behavior is represented as the name and DEX bytecode patterns of API calls for faster scanning. However, DEXs are different by applications even if they contain same APIs. Thus direct matching bytecode patterns gathered from a known malware and from a target application is implausible. Instead, we separate constant area and variable area from DEX bytecodes. For example, *invoke-virtual (arg1, arg2, arg3, arg4, arg5) methodA* in Dalvik instruction is corresponds to *6e 35c (4bit, 4bit, 4bit, 4bit, 4bit,*

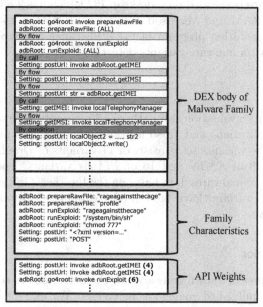

```
adbRoot: go4root: invoke prepareRawFile
adbRoot: prepareRawFile: (ALL)
By flow
adbRoot: go4root: invoke runExploid
adbRoot: runExploid: (ALL)
By call
Setting: postUrl: invoke adbRoot.getIMEI
By flow
Setting: postUrl: invoke adbRoot.getIMSI
By flow
Setting: postUrl: str = adbRoot.getIMEI
By call
Setting: getIMEI: invoke localTelephonyManager
By flow
Setting: getIMSI: invoke localTelephonyManager
By condition
Setting: postUrl: localObject2 = ...... str2
Setting: postUrl: localObject2.write()
                    ⋮

                    ⋮
```
— DEX body of Malware Family

```
adbRoot: prepareRawFile: "rageagainstthecage"
adbRoot: prepareRawFile: "profile"
adbRoot: runExploid: "rageagainstthecage"
adbRoot: runExploid: "/system/bin/sh"
adbRoot: runExploid: "chmod 777"
Setting: postUrl: "<?xml version=..."
Setting: postUrl: "POST"
                    ⋮
```
— Family Characteristics

```
Setting: postUrl: invoke adbRoot.getIMEI (4)
Setting: postUrl: invoke adbRoot.getIMSI (4)
adbRoot: go4root: invoke runExploit (6)
                    ⋮
```
— API Weights

Signature example of malware family DroidDream

Fig. 2. An example of malware family signature, *DroidDream*

4bit) 16bit in hexadecimal code. In this case, *6e 35c* is constant part that does not differ by application and *(4bit, 4bit, 4bit, 4bit, 4bit, 4bit) 16bit* is variable part that differs by application. And second, similarity calculator estimates the similarity $S(T, A)$ between target DEX 'T' and a signature 'A'. The similarity measuring is alike as follows:

$$S(T,A) = \frac{\sum_{j=1}^{n} W(b_j \mid b_j \in (T \cap A))}{\sum_{i=1}^{m} W(b_i \mid b_i \in A)}$$

Security Analysis. Security analyzer decides the maliciousness of a target application and discerns the most similar malware family with the target application. The decision method is quite straightforward. Among the resulted similarities for each family signature, the family which has the highest similarity is decided as the original family of target application. If the application has approximately equal similarities with multiple malware family, then the family characteristics are additionally used for more accurate identification.

3   Performance Evaluation

To evaluate the practicality of our malware detection mechanism, we performed time efficiency and detection performance evaluation experimentally.

The experiments are performed on a desktop PC which has 2.8 GHz Intel dual-cores CPU, 2GB RAM and Microsoft Windows XP SP3 as the OS. Our self-developed experimentation program in C++ measures time consumption and detection accuracy on malware variants detection.

3.1   Data Set

For the performance evaluation, we gathered 79 variants on four famous malicious Android applications and 1,680 legitimate applications published in real world. In detail, the variants set consists of 11 variants of *DroidDream*, 12 variants of *Geimini*, 40 of *KMIN* and 16 of *PjApps* variants. The malwares are gathered from public malwares data bases on the Internet. On average, the DEX files of the malware variants have 340 KB of size and the legitimate applications have 260 KB of size.

3.2   Signature Set

Behavioral signatures of known malwares for the detection are constructed from pre-analyzed and published malicious behaviors. We extracted class names, method instruction bodies and internal strings of methods which works for the malicious activities from the DEX files. In our experiments, the signatures which are extracted from randomly chosen training set have approximately 10 KB of size per a malware family. On the other hand, the white signatures which are trained from over a thousand of sample legitimate applications have 3 KB of size.

3.3   Experimental Result

Variant Detection Performance. The proposed system detects and identifies a new malware as a variant of known malware first. The major part of variant detection is similarity calculation. In contrast to the legacy signature matching method, our detection method investigates how much similar a new application is to the known malicious ones. The similarity to a malware family of an application is determined by the ratio of shared signatures. The detailed way for similarity calculation is explained at the *Signature Similarity Calculation* section. If it is determined as an unknown in this step, it means that the target application is the legitimate or a new malware family which is not corresponding to any known malware families. The application needs to be analyzed at the dynamic analysis phase.

For variant detection and identification performance evaluation, we performed 10-fold cross validation with the real-world malware samples. We made ten groups per a malware family. Then we took one group for signature extraction and rest nine groups as detection targets. We performed the testing ten times with randomly generated group configurations.

The variant detection system shows reliable detection performance. In the best threshold configuration, it shows 99.89% of accuracy and 98.73% of F-measure value on the 10-fold cross-validation results. Even though the volume of legitimate samples are much more than the malware samples, the performance showed on Table 2 is remarkable compared to other previous approaches.

The experimental result illustrated on left side of Figure 3 shows the recall rate more than 90% of even in the detection thresholds higher than 30% of similarity which have no false positive rate. Recall rate is the rate of detecting variants as a corresponding family. Though several variants of *Geimini* and *DroidDream* share some methods and strings and show over 30% of similarity, there are no family-mismatched detection cases. If they share many same malicious functionalities, their signature likely share the same API calls and methods. In these cases, the detection results of malwares belonging to of the similar families have the false negative decisions. At last, analysis for the false detection of legitimate application will be discussed with effect of the white signature.

The malware family which shows the lowest detection performance is *Droid-Dream*. According to our manual investigation results using decompiling, the major reasons of the lower similarity are the difference of included classes and methods. Several *DroidDream* variants only take rooter and self-alarm event methods within the known malicious functionalities of the *DroidDream*. One possible guessing is that the malwares share just a small part of code with the *DroidDream* such as the popular rooting exploit *rageagainstthecage*.

The detection system is also effectible to detect unknown malware not yet analyzed. Because several malicious actions and their code are commonly utilized on different kinds of malware, the trained signatures enable to detect the functionally similar unknown malwares. Table 1 shows the detection result on one hundred of non-labeled Android malwares using four signature sets and 25% similarity threshold. As the result, 56% of malwares are detected as the variants of four known malware families. It means that the 56% of malwares has the same name, strings, or same methods whose definition is identical to the one of the four malware families. In contrast, the rest 44% of malwares means that they have new methods and classes which are not included to any of the four signatures. In terms of the detection rate, the unknown malware detection rate could be increased to practical level if the knowledge-base had various and many enough signature sets.

Time Efficiency. Our malware detection system has an advantage on its time efficiency. A variant of a known malware whose behavioral signature is in a data base is detected as a variant of the known before a detailed and heavy inspection such as source level analysis or run-time testing on a sand-box. In our implementation for the experiments, the behavioral signature matching uses a matching algorithm using a hash-tree which takes a constant time [4]. As illustrated on Figure 4, the number of signatures has little effect to its time consumption. Consequently, the mechanism shows linearly increasing time consumption along with the amount of target applications. It means that this front line variant

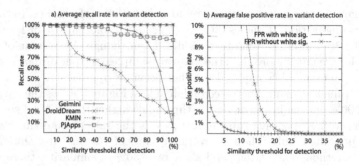

Fig. 3. Average recall(left) and false positive rate(right) on the variants detection experiment

Table 1. Investigation result for non-labeled malwares

DroidDream	Geimini	KMIN	PjApps	Total
4%	23%	29%	0%	56%

detection mechanism reduces the amount of target applications to be analyzed much smaller with a reasonable time overhead.

Effect of White Signature and Redundant Removal. The proposed system reduces the false detection by adopting white signatures. By giving negative points to the applications which have the anti-malicious methods and classes, the detection system avoids false detection of critical but safe applications.

The DEX bytecode patterns and strings which appear in both of malicious and legitimate applications are considered as the redundant. The redundant patterns are removed the signatures and ignored on the detection process. The bytecodes patterns and strings which are only in the legitimate applications and representative for the legitimate applications are considered as a white signature. In contrast to the redundant patterns, a white signature is rarely gathered because a white signature must be only on authenticated legitimate applications but not shared to any malware even though a repackaged malware also has legitimate codes on its DEX file.

For evaluating the effect of white signature and redundant removal, we performed the static variant detection to 1,680 of legitimate Android applications using the signature sets which are used at the variant detection experiment. The right side of Figure 3 shows the effect of adopting white signatures in false positive reduction. Among all the ranges of false positive occurrence, the rates are significantly decreased.

In the comparison with the static analysis study of Schmidt et al. [5] on classifying Android executables, our approach shows better performance on the correctly classified instances rate keeping non-false positive rate. In comparison with the study of Shabtai et al. [6] applying machine learning using hundreds

Table 2. Detection Performance Comparison Table

Method	Accuracy	Recall	Precision	F-measure
Androguard	93.04%	49.58%	99.16%	66.11%
DroidMat	97.87%	87.39%	96.74%	91.83%
Proposed	99.89%	97.73%	99.74%	98.73%

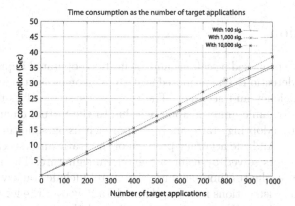

Fig. 4. Time consumption for detection as the number of target applications and signatures

of features extracted from DEX and XML, our classifying result shows better performance than the accuracy of their best configuration.

4 Related Work

The previous work for Android malware is mainly focused on the behavior and trainable features of source code and executable files. The studies which take the machine learning approach [6,7] attempt to classify the malware from the legitimate applications using characteristic features of malware. The classifying approaches using machine learning are robust to the small changes on malware variants. However, the malware has much different behavior and capability along with their family, and the result of these works are hard to give information and detection evidences. Furthermore, the base legitimate applications significantly affect their function and API call statistics. In contrast, our approach classify the malware into each malware family and it gives the detailed information about their behavior.

The behavior analysis approaches are classified into static approaches [2,5,8] and dynamic approaches [9,10]. The static approaches not limited on the behavior based approaches are light-weight and scalable. However, they have a limitation on the accuracy because it is hard to tracking the exact behavior even though the target application can be decompiled. In contrast, the dynamic analysis approaches using taint analysis and API monitoring have ability to tracking

the behavior accurately on run-time. But the dynamic analysis approaches have
the efficiency problem because of the requirement of time and resources including a virtual environment and test execution. In terms of efficiency, our work
takes a matching approach which is fast as the static analysis and even more
efficient against the numbers of variants using the behavioral signature. And the
behavioral signature we proposed proves pre-investigated behaviors with exact
evidences.

5   Conclusion

In this paper, we proposed a scalable and accurate co-operated approach for Android malware detection. The proposed system overcomes the trade-off problem
between the efficiency and accuracy. The proposed system solves the efficiency
problem of the dynamic analysis approach due to the virtual environment and
test execution by adopting static analysis approach using signatures which are
faster and lighter. And the accuracy problem of the static analysis caused by the
lack of robustness is solved by using a behavioral signature. The proposed behavioral signature, the runtime semantic signature, includes binary patterns for
entity names and instructions for control and data flow over the legacy API calls
for malicious acitvities. We experimentally showed that the runtime semantic
signature improves the accuracy compared with the previous static approaches.
In addition, the static analysis for the malware variants detection has practical
time consumption, only tens of second to investigate a thousand of targets. And
the time consumption has linear increasing manner to the increase of the number of targets. In conclusion, the proposed system has enough investigation performance for responding the rapidly growing numbers of Android applications.
Therefore, it is helpful to protect users from information leakage and economic
damages by malware on their smartphone.

Acknowledgment. This research was supported by the public welfare
& safety research program through the National Research Foundation of
Korea(NRF) funded by the Ministry of Education, Science and Technol-
ogy (2012M3A2A1051118 2012051118) and the KCC(Korea Communications
Commission), Korea, under the R&D program supervised by the KCA(Korea
Communications Agency)(KCA-2012-12-911-01-111).

References

1. F-Secure: Mobile threat report q2 2012. Report, F-Secure (2012)
2. Kwon, J., Lee, H.: Bingraph: Discovering mutant malware using hierarchical semantic signatures. In: Proc. of 7th International Conference on Malicious and Unwanted Software, MALWARE 2012 (2012)
3. Zhou, Y., Jiang, X.: Dissecting android malware: Characterization and evolution.
   In: Proc. of the 2012 IEEE Symposium on Security and Privacy, pp. 95–109 (2012)

4. Microsoft: Atl collection classes (2010), http://msdn.microsoft.com/en-us/library/vstudio/15e672bd(v=vs.100).aspx
5. Schmidt, A.D., Bye, R., Schmidt, H.G., Clausen, J., Kiraz, O., Yuksel, K., Camtepe, S., Albayrak, S.: Static analysis of executables for collaborative malware detection on android. In: Proc. of the IEEE International Conference on Communications (ICC 2009), pp. 1–5 (June 2009)
6. Shabtai, A., Fledel, Y., Elovici, Y.: Automated static code analysis for classifying android applications using machine learning. In: Proc. of International Conference on Computational Intelligence and Security (CIS 2010), pp. 329–333 (December 2010)
7. Burguera, I., Zurutuza, U., Nadjm-Tehrani, S.: Crowdroid: behavior-based malware detection system for android. In: Proc. of the 1st ACM Workshop on Security and Privacy in Smartphones and Mobile Devices (SPSM 2011), pp. 15–26. ACM (2011)
8. Lee, J., Jeong, K., Lee, H.: Detecting metamorphic malwares using code graphs. In: Proc. of the 2010 ACM Symposium on Applied Computing (SAC 2010), pp. 1970–1977. ACM (2010)
9. Enck, W., Gilbert, P., Chun, B.G., Cox, L.P., Jung, J., McDaniel, P., Sheth, A.N.: Taintdroid: an information-flow tracking system for realtime privacy monitoring on smartphones. In: Proc. of the 9th USENIX Conference on Operating Systems Design and Implementation (OSDI 2010), pp. 1–6. USENIX Association (2010)
10. Gilbert, P., Chun, B.G., Cox, L.P., Jung, J.: Vision: automated security validation of mobile apps at app markets. In: Proc. of the Second International Workshop on Mobile Cloud Computing and Services (MCS 2011), pp. 21–26. ACM (2011)
11. Blasing, T., Batyuk, L., Schmidt, A.D., Camtepe, S., Albayrak, S.: An android application sandbox system for suspicious software detection. In: Proc. of the 5th International Conference on Malicious and Unwanted Software (MALWARE 2010), pp. 55–62 (October 2010)
12. Barrera, D., Kayacik, H.G., van Oorschot, P.C., Somayaji, A.: A methodology for empirical analysis of permission-based security models and its application to android. In: Proc. of the 17th ACM Conference on Computer and Communications Security (CCS 2010), pp. 73–84. ACM (2010)
13. Shabtai, A., Fledel, Y., Kanonov, U., Elovici, Y., Dolev, S., Glezer, C.: Google android: A comprehensive security assessment. IEEE Security and Privacy 8(2), 35–44 (2010)
14. Enck, W.: Defending users against smartphone apps: Techniques and future directions. In: Jajodia, S., Mazumdar, C. (eds.) ICISS 2011. LNCS, vol. 7093, pp. 49–70. Springer, Heidelberg (2011)
15. Felt, A.P., Finifter, M., Chin, E., Hanna, S., Wagner, D.: A survey of mobile malware in the wild. In: Proc. of the 1st ACM Workshop on Security and Privacy in Smartphones and Mobile Devices (SPSM 2011), pp. 3–14. ACM (2011)
16. Whitney, L.: Android's popularity makes it open target for malware, says study. Technical report, CNET (December 2011)

Game Theoretic Approach for Cost-Benefit Analysis of Malware Proliferation Prevention*

Theodoros Spyridopoulos, George Oikonomou, Theo Tryfonas, and Mengmeng Ge

Cryptography Group, University of Bristol
Merchant Venturers Building, Woodland Road, Clifton BS8 1UB, UK
{th.spyridopoulos,g.oikonomou,theo.tryfonas}@bristol.ac.uk,
gemengmeng.2011@my.bristol.ac.uk

Abstract. Many existing research efforts in the field of malware proliferation aim at modelling and analysing its spread dynamics. Many malware dissemination models are based on the characteristics of biological disease spread in human populations. In this work, we utilise game theory in order to extend two very commonly used malware spread models (SIS and SIR) by incorporating defence strategies against malware proliferation. We consider three different security mechanisms, "patch", "removal" and "patch and removal" on which our model is based. We also propose a cost-benefit model that describes optimal strategies the defender could follow when cost is taken into account. Lastly, as a way of illustration, we apply our models on the well studied Code-Red worm.

1   Introduction

With the ever growing importance of networked computing, malicious software, known as malware, has been a considerable threat to the realm of interconnected computers. Often built by cyber criminals, malware aims to compromise target computers with the ultimate goal of stealing sensitive data or gaining access to private systems. Malware includes a variety of malicious software such as computer viruses, worms, trojan horses, key-loggers and many others.

Defence mechanisms such as firewalls and anti-viruses have been developed in order to defend against malicious software. Those mechanisms investigate the problem of malware at micro level by utilising experimental and heuristic findings, such as virus signatures, in order to prevent or detect and cure a computer's infection. Nevertheless, malware spread in a network of computers underlines the need for a network-level solution. The increasing number of malware which bases its function on new techniques that are difficult to detect and mitigate renders conventional defence mechanisms unsuitable. In light of these challenges epidemiological models which can describe the dynamics of malware proliferation over a computer network have been proposed.

Additionally, Game Theory has been introduced in a number of occasions across the fields of computer and network security (e.g. [1,2]) to describe the interactions between attacker and defender and the ways they may affect each other. As malware acts based

* This work has been kindly supported by the Faculty of Engineering's Systems Centre and its Industrial Partners.

L.J. Janczewski, H.B. Wolfe, and S. Shenoi (Eds.): SEC 2013, IFIP AICT 405, pp. 28–41, 2013.
© IFIP International Federation for Information Processing 2013

on inscribed behaviour coded by cyber criminals, approaching it as a threat agent on its own right under the premise of game theory becomes a reasonable assumption.

Our work aims at combining well-known epidemiology models with a game theoretic framework that can describe the state of the system when the defender uses various strategies against the proliferation of a random-scanning worm. We develop a game between defender and malware, taking into account the spread dynamics, so that defenders manage to compute their optimal strategy by minimising the cost of security, on a cost-benefit basis.

The rest of the paper is structured as follows. In Section 2 we give a basic background on epidemiology models and game theory as it is applied in malware analysis. Special emphasis is given to the "FLIPIT" game. In Section 3 we present the models and methods that we have developed. In Section 4 we present an application of our approach to the well studied case of the Code-Red worm computing an optimal strategy for the defender. Finally, Section 5 discusses the conclusions drawn form this work.

2   Background

2.1   General Description of Epidemiology Models

The way that viruses and worms spread in a computer network shares common characteristics with the dissemination of biological diseases in human populations, in a way that the analysis of malware can benefit from investigating the behaviour of biological diseases. There are two kinds of models for analysing malware proliferation in epidemiology: stochastic models and deterministic models. Stochastic models are used to analyse small-scale networks, while deterministic models are used to analyse large-scale networks [3]. In our work, in order to study the effect of mass action, we consider malware spread in a large computer network, thus we utilise deterministic models.

In general, individuals in the epidemic population have several states, including susceptible, infected, recovered. A large fraction of the models used, rely on the transitions between those states. Among these, two models have been widely used, the Susceptible-Infected-Recovered (SIR) created by Kermack and McKendrick in 1927 [4,5,6] and a modified version of it, known as the Susceptible-Infected-Susceptible (SIS) model. Both models assume that all individuals within a closed population (i.e. no births and deaths) are susceptible to the malware in the initial phase and an individual may go through each state sequentially.

In the SIS model, the state transitions of an individual form a circulation. The individual may recover from the infection, but there is still a chance to be reinfected. In other words, an individual becomes again susceptible to the malware after its recovery. In the SIR model, the final state is described as the recovered state. An infected individual can recover from the infection and become immune to the malware. An immunised individual cannot be reinfected by the same malware.

Typically, disease spread depends on common shared characteristics of the individuals in a population. In a network of computers, malware exploits certain vulnerabilities in the system in order to infect a host. Common practice of malware is to exploit vulnerabilities in software that the victim-host has installed. Thus, in order for a host to be considered as susceptible to a certain malware, it has to have installed the specific software version that bears the vulnerability that the malware can exploit. In case it doesn't then it cannot be infected and thus cannot be considered as susceptible. In the real world, not every host in a network carries the same vulnerabilities. However, in our work, in order to simplify our model, we have made the assumption that our network is homogeneous. In other words, in a single network architecture an individual can infect every other individual. Furthermore, the network is assumed to be symmetric so that no preferential direction of the malware proliferation exists.

2.2   Mathematical Specification of Standard Epidemiology Models

In this section we present the mathematical specification of two commonly used epidemiology models, SIR and SIS. In general, such models are formulated over a fixed-size network. Nodes represent individuals. Links or edges between nodes represent contacts between individuals. The infection spreads along direct links between nodes.

The SIR Model. In the SIR model [4,5,6], the total population is divided into three parts: i) susceptible nodes (denoted by S), ii) infected nodes (denoted by I) and iii) recovered nodes (denoted by R). The differential equations 1, 2 and 3 depict the rate of change of the susceptible nodes, infected nodes and recovered nodes respectively over time [7]. Here β denotes the probability of a susceptible node to be infected by another infected node when they come in contact in each time unit, also regarded as the infection rate; γ denotes the probability of an infected node to recover from an infection and become immune to the malware in each time unit, also regarded as the recovery rate. In our research a contact is considered as a network link between two nodes, and since all nodes are connected with each other, either directly or through a number of hops depending on the network's topology, they are always in contact with each other.

$$\frac{dS}{dt} = -\beta IS \tag{1}$$

$$\frac{dI}{dt} = \beta IS - \gamma I \tag{2}$$

$$\frac{dR}{dt} = \gamma I \tag{3}$$

The SIS Model. In the SIS model, the total population is divided into two parts, susceptible nodes (denoted by S) and infected nodes (denoted by I). Equations 4 and 5 model the rate of change of susceptible nodes and infected nodes respectively over time [8]. Again, β denotes the probability of a susceptible node to get infected by an infected node when they come in contact in each time unit, also regarded as the infection rate; γ denotes the probability of an infected node to recover from an infection and become susceptible again to the malware in each time unit, also regarded as the recovery rate. Even though the term "recovery rate" is used in both the SIR and the SIS model, it is used for different purposes.

$$\frac{dS}{dt} = -\beta IS + \gamma I \tag{4}$$

$$\frac{dI}{dt} = \beta IS - \gamma I \tag{5}$$

2.3 Brief Introduction to Game Theory

Game theory provides us with a set of analytical tools designed to describe and analyse the phenomena observed when two or more decision makers interact [9]. Decision makers are identified as unique players and the formal description of the interaction between them is denoted as a game [10]. The basic assumption of game theory is that every player acts rationally, aiming at the best possible outcome, and take into account other players' decisions. Solution to a game is the description of the strategies that each player has to follow in order to achieve the best possible outcome. *Nash equilibrium* is the solution of the game that describes a steady state, where each player gets the best possible payoff. A deviation from the Nash Equilibrium strategy always leads in lesser payoff. Games are divided in various categories based on the nature of their parts:

- *Cooperative - Non-cooperative Games.* In general, games are divided into cooperative and non-cooperative games based on the way that players interact with each other. In cooperative games, all players try to maximise the overall payoff, while in non-cooperative games, each player cares only about his own gain and cost. In the field of network security, the research falls under the category of non-cooperative games since there is no cooperation between the attacker and the defender [1].
- *Static - Dynamic Games.* Under the category of non-cooperation, games are divided into static and dynamic games. In static games, all players make their decisions simultaneously not knowing other player strategies. They are one-shot games where each player has a pre-computed move list, each move denoted as a strategy, from which he has to choose the best move in order to maximise his personal benefit. Benefit, also known as payoff, refers to a player's net gain when he choses to play a strategy, and is described by Equation 6. In dynamic games, a player can alter his move during the game. The game is played into stages in each of which each player has to choose his move. A strategy in such games is defined as the combination of sequential moves chosen by the player in order to maximise his total benefit. Each stage of a dynamic game can be considered as a static game leading to a structure of sequential static games.

$$Benefit = Gain - Cost \tag{6}$$

- *Perfect - Imperfect Games.* A game where the players choose their strategies simultaneously, without knowing the choices of the other players, is an imperfect information game. Contrary, in perfect information games every player knows exactly the strategies that other players have followed before his turn. Thus only games where players play sequentially can be considered as perfect information games.
- *Complete - Incomplete Information Games.* Complete information games indicate that players know the available strategies and payoffs of the other players but do not necessarily know the strategies that have been played by other players. On the contrary, in incomplete information games players may not have access to other players' available strategies and payoffs during the game.

- *Pure - Mixed Strategies.* Pure strategies refer to deterministic actions taken by a player in the game for every possible situation that s/he can face (for every other players' actions). In mixed strategies a player's move is not based on a deterministic action-decision, but involves a probabilistic combination of the available pure strategies [9].

2.4   Game Theory in Security and Malware Analysis

Traditional network security mechanisms such as Intrusion Detection and/or Prevention Systems (IDS/IPS) analyse malware at a level of specific technical detail. They focus on collecting, dissecting and recording its structure and behaviour. This allows them to respond to attacks that are based on well known techniques. For instance, IDS algorithms apply malware-signature identification or make use of heuristic algorithms to detect suspicious system behaviours that indicate possible infection. Nevertheless, since they mostly rely on such experimental findings, they are proved to be insufficient against sophisticated attacks which may utilise unknown techniques (e.g. zero-day attacks).

A shortcoming of the traditional network security solutions is that they lack a macro-level quantitative decision framework [1] and various researchers have focused their work on utilising game theory in order to provide a holistic solution [11,12,13,2]. The relationship between attacker and defender can be modelled as the interaction between two competing parts in a game theoretic scenario. The malware's goal is to spread widely, whereas the defender aims at protecting the network against the attack (minimising spread) whilst keeping costs as low as possible. Game theory can be used for studying decision making problems in multiplayer scenarios, to examine and evaluate all possible scenarios given the outcomes of each player's strategy and return the best one.

The "FLIPIT" Game: In order to develop our game we first devised a cost-benefit model to help us compute the gain of each strategy. The cost-benefit model was originally based on another game theoretic model known as "The FLIPIT Game" [2]. In FLIPIT, the authors have developed a model that describes the situation in which an attacker periodically takes over a system and is not immediately detected by the defender. There are two players, the attacker and the defender, and a shared resource. The two opponents compete to control the shared resource. The attacker tries to put the resource into a bad state, while the defender puts the resource into a good state. The objective of each player is to control the resource for the largest possible fraction of time and minimise at the same time their total cost. Players do not know the current situation of the game when other players make a move; they learn that only when they make a move. Making a move incurs cost and taking over control gains benefit. Each player loses some points per move and gains some points per second when he is in control.

The mathematical description of the game is provided below. Here we assume that the defender is player 0 and the attacker is player 1. Player i pays k_i points per move and gains one point per second when the source is under his control.

$$\gamma_i(t) = \frac{G_i(t)}{t} \tag{7}$$

The total period of time t is the time the resource is controlled by the defender plus the time controlled by the attacker as shown in Equation 8.

$$G_0(t) + G_1(t) = t \tag{8}$$

Thus, for each player, the gain rate $\gamma_i(t)$ is equal to the fraction of time that player i has the shared resource under control, as shown in Equation 9.

$$\gamma_0(t) + \gamma_1(t) = 1 \tag{9}$$

Equation 10 calculates the benefit of a strategy, which is denoted as the gain minus the total cost. The aim of each player in the game is to maximise the value of benefit.

$$B_i(t) = G_i(t) - k_i \cdot N_i(t) \tag{10}$$

The generic description of a shared resource taken under control by an attacker is suitable to describe the situation of a computer network under attack from a worm. In our work we view the network as the shared resource which both attacker and defender try to take under control. However, in this context the shared resource cannot be instantly fully taken over, since a worm spreads in a fraction of the total population in each time step rather the whole population. Hence, only a fraction of the shared resource can be taken over by the attacker.

3 Models and Methods

3.1 Game Theoretical Models of Malware Proliferation

Worms have the ability to self-replicate and spread without human intervention in a network [14], resembling human viruses. In the human virus spread example this could mean that all individuals are always in contact with each other. In a network it means that an infected node can infect every other node in the network since all nodes are linked with one anoother. Random-scan worms have the ability to spread without topology constrains since they rely on random IP scans. On the other hand, worms spreading via emails have specific routes according to the email list of each infected computer. In our work we model random-scan worms.

There are three security mitigation practices against worm dissemination: i) Remove, ii) Patch and iii) both Patch and Remove. Under the SIR and SIS models, a susceptible node can either be patched against the certain worm and become immune to it or stay in the susceptible state. If a susceptible node is infected then it can either stay infected and consequently spread the worm or it can use the removal tool (e.g. an antivirus) in order to remove the worm. However, the removal tool does not encompass immunisation functionality. Thus, when an infected node removes the worm it returns back to the susceptible state where it can subsequently be reinfected. However, if an infected node uses both the remove tool and the patch against the worm then it moves to recovery state where it is immune against the specific worm. For each of the three security strategies we set up differential mathematical expressions, as in SIR and SIS models, which describe the dynamics of the system.

Patch Strategy: When the Patch Strategy is used, susceptible nodes can become immune to the worm, but infected nodes cannot recover from the infection. In this case, the worm and the defender seem to take part in a race. If the worm spreads very fast, it will infect most computers in a short time before defenders notice it; if people in the network can patch their computers much faster than the worm proliferation, the wide-range infection can be avoided. The model is depicted in Figure 1.

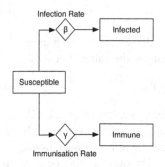

Recovery Rate

Infection Rate

Susceptible   Infected

Fig. 1. Patch Strategy Model   **Fig. 2.** Removal Strategy Model

The mathematical specification of the Patch Strategy is given in Equations 11,12 and 13, where S is the susceptible population, I is the infected population and R is the immune population. β is the probability that a susceptible node gets infected in each time unit, also regarded as infection fraction, and γ is the immunisation rate.

$$\frac{dS}{dt} = -\beta IS - \gamma S \tag{11}$$

$$\frac{dI}{dt} = \beta IS \tag{12}$$

$$\frac{dR}{dt} = \gamma S \tag{13}$$

Removal Strategy: When Removal Strategy is used, infected nodes can recover from the infection when the worm is detected and removed. However, nodes that have recovered from an infection are still susceptible to the specific worm since no immunisation against it is included. In this case the model is transformed into a SIS model where the system reaches an equilibrium where the number of infected nodes and the number of susceptible nodes stay almost constant. The model is depicted in Figure 2.

The mathematical specification of Removal Strategy is given in Equations 14 and 15. Again, S refers to the susceptible population and I refers to the infected population. β is the probability that a susceptible node gets infected and r is the removal or recovery rate. As seen, no recovered population is found in the system.

$$\frac{dS}{dt} = -\beta IS + \gamma I \tag{14}$$

$$\frac{dI}{dt} = \beta IS - \gamma I \tag{15}$$

Patch and Removal Strategy: The last strategy devised is the Patch and Removal. In this strategy both moves of patch and removal are available. A susceptible node can become immune to the worm when patch is used. Furthermore, an infected node can recover from the infection if the worm is removed and then become immune to the worm by using the patch. This is the most efficient, yet costly, way to eliminate malware spread. Eventually, all nodes in the network will be immune against the specific worm. The strategy model is shown in Figure 3.

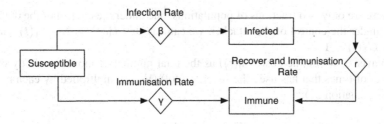

Fig. 3. Patch and Removal Strategy Model

The differential equations that describe the dynamics of the model are shown in Equations 16, 17, 18 and 19. S refers to the susceptible population, I refers to the infected population, R is used for the recovered and immunised population and Q for the population that becomes immune to the malware. As before, β is the probability that a susceptible node gets infected, γ refers to the immunisation rate when a susceptible node uses the specific patch and λ is the "removal and patch" rate.

$$\frac{dS}{dt} = -\beta IS - \gamma S \tag{16}$$

$$\frac{dI}{dt} = \beta IS - \lambda I \tag{17}$$

$$\frac{dR}{dt} = \lambda I \tag{18}$$

$$\frac{dQ}{dt} = \gamma S + \lambda I \tag{19}$$

3.2 Cost-Benefit Analysis

In "FLIPIT", two opponents compete in order to gain full control of a shared resource and gain is defined by the time the resource is under one's control. In our epidemiology model, the shared resource is the node population of the network. In each time unit the two opponents (attacker and defender) perform actions to take under their control a part of the population (a number of neighbouring nodes). For instance, the attacker takes under control I nodes in each time unit, and I changes according to the equations presented above. Hence, gain is defined by the average fraction of node population under one's control. Therefore, by considering player 0 as defender and player 1 as attacker we define $G_i(t)$ the gain of player i and calculate it as shown in Equation 20, where $P_i(t)$ is the fraction of population under control by player i over time and t_k is the total time for which our model is running.

$$G_i(t) = \frac{1}{t_k} \int_0^{t_k} P_i(t)dt \qquad (20)$$

Since there are only two fractions of populations, one under the control of the defender and one under the control of the attacker, we can say that $P_0(t) = 1 - P_1(t)$. Hence: $G_0(t) + G_1(t) = 1$.

For player 0, we define cost ($C_0(t)$) as the total number of moves made by player 0 (number of times that has used the security tool) ($n_0(t)$), multiplied by each move's cost (k_0) (Equation 21).

$$C_0(t) = n_0(t)k_0 \qquad (21)$$

We define as cost for player 1 the perceived complexity of the algorithm that their malware implements.

Each player's benefit is equal to the player's total gain minus the cost (Eq. 22).

$$B_i(t) = G_i(t) - C_i(t) \qquad (22)$$

In order to compute cost, we utilise quantitative tables of operational complexity. A strategy by either player (e.g. Patch Strategy for the defender or Code-Red worm for the attacker) may encompass several actions, with each action characterised by a complexity level. We set up empirically three levels of perceived complexity, low, medium and high, and assign a score to each of them, 1, 2 and 3 respectively. Therefore, the cost of a move for player 0 or the total cost of player 1 is equal to the sum of the costs of the actions it involves.

4   Application of the Model to Code-Red's Parameters

In this section we apply our game theoretic model to a real case of malware proliferation, the well known Code-Red worm. Albeit old, we chose Code-Red because it is a random-scanning worm with no topology constraints and so its characteristics fit well into the generic nature of our abstraction. It is self-activated by exploiting a vulnerability which exists in the host operating system. Other worms, such as Conficker, utilise various spread methods, e.g. through email, which would warrant specialisation of the differential equations describing the proliferation and mitigation strategies.

4.1   Code-Red

Code-Red was discovered in July 2001. It exploits a buffer-overflow vulnerability in Microsoft IIS Web Server [15]. It produces a list of random IP addresses and launches 99 threads to search each computer in the list in order to infect as many vulnerable computers as possible. It has two versions: Code-Red v1 and Code-Red v2. Code-Red v1 spreads slowly because it generates an identical list by using a static seed. Code-Red v2 is the variant of Code-Red v1. It can infect new nodes by using a random seed for its pseudo-random generator. Therefore, the latter version has a higher spread speed. The greatest damage caused by the worm is that it could launch a massive DoS attack. Finally, this worm is memory resident. Thus a reboot can clear the worm from a host node. However, in order to prevent the infection or reinfection, nodes have to use a specific patch [15].

We make the assumption of a network with a population of 10,000 susceptible nodes and 1,000 nodes immune to the worm due to not every node running susceptible software - a Microsoft ISS Web Server. We set the maximum time of worm spread period at one week or $t_k = 168$ hours. According to [16], an infected node infects other nodes with rate 1.62 nodes per hour. Thus the probability of a susceptible node in our network to get infected by an infected node in each second is equal to $1.62/N$ where N is the total population. Hence, $\beta = 1.47 \cdot 10^{-4}$. The costs for each player are shown in Tables 1 and 2. Since the attacker uses a specific malware that is not able of changing behaviour, there is no reason in computing an optimal strategy since this has already been chosen (the Code-Red worm's inscribed behaviour). We analytically compute the defender's gain according to Equation 20, however the calculations are not shown in this paper due to space restrictions.

Table 1. The cost for Code-Red worm

Actions	Complexity Low:1 Medium:2 High:3			Total
Exploit the buffer vulnerability		2		
Generate random IP addresses	1			4
Launch 99 threads with generated IP addresses	1			

Using Vensim as a simulation environment, we set up three simulations for the three security strategies (Patch, Remove, Patch and Remove) respectively, according to our models, in order to find the best strategy that the defender can follow. In our case study we assume that the defender has already chosen a patch rate or a removal rate so that he has only to chose the security strategy that he will follow. In an alternative scenario, the defender could also utilise our model in order to find both the security strategy and the rates that could give him the best possible benefit.

4.2   Patch Strategy

For the Patch Strategy the state of our system is shown in Figure 4. It can be seen that at the early hours of the worm spread the number of infected nodes increases

Table 2. The cost of each move for the defender

Actions		Complexity Low:1 Medium:2 High:3	Total
Patch	Detection	2	4
	Patch	2	
Removal	Detection	2	3
	Reboot	1	
Patch and Removal	Detection	2	5
	Reboot	1	
	Patch	2	

sharply while on the other hand the number of susceptible nodes decreases. Since infected nodes cannot recover and patched nodes cannot be infected, the system reaches soon its equilibrium where the Infected population is near 8,351 nodes and the immunised population around 1,649 nodes. If the defender used a much larger patch rate then they might be able to compete with the attacker in this race. However, this would not be easy since the number of infected nodes increases exponentially, whereas the number of immunised nodes linearly. Furthermore, an increase in the security rate would increase the total security cost. Based on the results of the simulation, the cost (using the Table 2) and the gain (the average number of non-infected nodes) of the Patch strategy are given by Equation 23. Thus the Benefit for the Patch strategy is equal to $B_0 = G_0 - C_0 = -4,652$.

$$C_0 = number\ of\ patches \times cost\ of\ patch = 1649 \cdot 4 = 6596$$
$$G_0 = 1944 \tag{23}$$

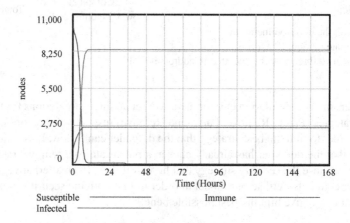

Fig. 4. Patch Strategy

4.3 Removal Strategy

For the Removal Strategy the state of our system is shown in Figure 5. It can be seen that after a period of time the system reaches an equilibrium where the populations of susceptible and infected nodes remain constant, 222 and 9,778 respectively. Again, the results would be better if the defender used a larger recovery rate. Based on simulation results, the cost and the gain (the average number of non-infected nodes) of the Removal strategy are given in Equation 24. Thus the Benefit for the Removal strategy is equal to $B_0 = G_0 - C_0 \simeq -156,152$.

$$C_0 = number\ of\ removals \times cost\ of\ removal = 52236 \cdot 3 = 156708$$
$$G_0 = 556 \tag{24}$$

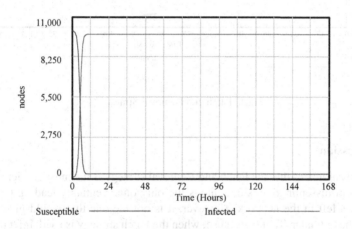

Fig. 5. Removal Strategy

4.4 Patch and Removal Strategy

The state of our system in time is shown in Figure 6. At the early hours of dissemination, the worm spreads exponentially into the network. However, as time passes more and more infected nodes recover form the infection and get immunised against the worm. Furthermore, the number of susceptible that are patched also increases. Thus, eventually every node in the network will be patched and thereby immunised against the worm. The dissemination slowly fades. Based on the results of the simulation, the cost and the gain of the Patch and Removal strategy are given in Equation 25. Hence, the Benefit for the defender's Patch and Removal strategy is equal to $B_0 = G_0 - C_0 \simeq -39,519$.

$$C_0 = number\ of\ patches \times cost\ of\ patch + number\ of\ removals \times cost\ of$$
$$patch\ and\ removal = 1771 \cdot 4 + 8188 \cdot 5 = 48024$$
$$G_0 = 8505 \tag{25}$$

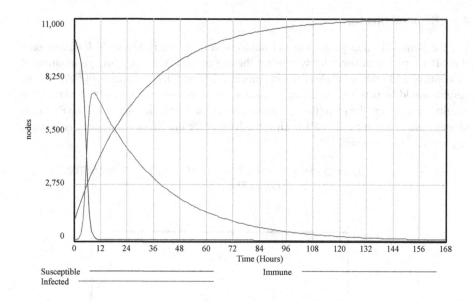

Fig. 6. Patch and Removal Strategy

4.5 Discussion

Our analysis indicates that the Patch and Removal strategy is the most efficient defence against worm dissemination, since this is the only one eventually leading to zero infected nodes left in the network. However, it is not the one that would give the best benefit to the defender. That is because, when the Patch strategy is used, infected nodes cannot be patched. Thus the total number of patches is significantly smaller and hence the total cost for the defender is lower. Therefore, although Patch and Removal is the most efficient strategy, when there are cost restrictions Patch strategy can also be used. An interesting approach could be the usage of a mixed strategy based on them.

5   Conclusions

In this paper we have integrated premises of game theory with malware proliferation models and developed a cost-benefit game-theoretic approach to evaluate defence strategies that mitigate malware proliferation. We applied our approach to a case study where defender could choose between three strategies i) "patch", ii) "removal" and iii) "patch and removal" and discuss our results for both the spread and the cost-benefit strategy selection. Our model can be extended by introducing more options for the defender, such as the ability to change the security (i.e. patch and removal) rate; as well as the attacker, e.g. change the manifested behaviour of the worm deployed.

As mentioned, we kept the rates of patch, removal and the infection rate constant in our simulations. However, defender can vary their security rates in order to achieve better results. Furthermore, an even more complicated approach would be to give the attacker the option to choose among strategies, in other words vary the malware's behaviour (e.g. metamorphic viruses). Thereby, we could establish a game where both players try to find their optimal strategies.

References

1. Roy, S., Ellis, C., Shiva, S., Dasgupta, D., Shandilya, V., Wu, Q.: A survey of game theory as applied to network security. In: 2010 43rd Hawaii International Conference on System Sciences (HICSS), pp. 1–10 (January 2010)
2. van Dijk, M., Juels, A., Oprea, A., Rivest, R.L.: FlipIt: the game of "Stealthy takeover". Technical Report 103 (2012)
3. Andersson, H., Britton, T.: Stochastic Epidemic Models and Their Statistical Analysis. Springer (July 2000)
4. Kermack, W.O., McKendrick, A.G.: A contribution to the mathematical theory of epidemics. Proceedings of the Royal Society of London. Series A 115(772), 700–721 (1927)
5. Kermack, W.O., McKendrick, A.G.: Contributions to the mathematical theory of epidemics. II. the problem of endemicity. Proceedings of the Royal Society of London. Series A 138(834), 55–83 (1932)
6. Kermack, W.O., McKendrick, A.G.: Contributions to the mathematical theory of epidemics. III. further studies of the problem of endemicity. Proceedings of the Royal Society of London. Series A 141(843), 94–122 (1933)
7. Capasso, V., Serio, G.: A generalization of the kermack-McKendrick deterministic epidemic model. Mathematical Biosciences 42(12), 43–61 (1978)
8. Van der Molen, H.: Math on malware. ISACA Journal 3, 40–47 (2011)
9. Osborne, M.J., Rubinstein, A.: A course in game theory. MIT Press, Cambridge (1996)
10. Turocy, T.: Texas a&m university. Bernhard von Stengel, London School of Economics "Game Theory" CDAM Research Report (October 2001)
11. Lin, J.C., Chen, J.M., Chen, C.C., Chien, Y.S.: A game theoretic approach to decision and analysis in strategies of attack and defense. In: Proceedings of the 2009 Third IEEE International Conference on Secure Software Integration and Reliability Improvement, SSIRI 2009, pp. 75–81. IEEE Computer Society, Washington, DC (2009)
12. Wu, Q., Shiva, S., Roy, S., Ellis, C., Datla, V.: On modeling and simulation of game theory-based defense mechanisms against DoS and DDoS attacks. In: Proceedings of the 2010 Spring Simulation Multiconference, SpringSim 2010, pp. 159:1–159:8. Society for Computer Simulation International, San Diego (2010)
13. Khouzani, M., Sarkar, S., Altman, E.: A dynamic game solution to malware attack. In: 2011 Proceedings IEEE INFOCOM, pp. 2138–2146. IEEE (2011)
14. Saudi, M., Tamil, E., Nor, S., Idris, M., Seman, K.: Edowa worm classification. In: Proceedings of the World Congress on Engineering, vol. 1 (2008)
15. Moore, D., Shannon, C., Brown, J.: Code-Red: a case study on the spread and victims of an Internet worm. In: ACM SIGCOMM/USENIX Internet Measurement Workshop (IMW), Marseille, France, pp. 273–284 (November 2002)
16. Vojnovic, M., Ganesh, A.: On the race of worms, alerts, and patches. IEEE/ACM Transactions on Networking (TON) 16(5), 1066–1079 (2008)

Evolving a Secure Internet

William J. Caelli[1], Lam-For Kwok[2], and Dennis Longley[3]

[1] Queensland University of Technology, Brisbane
[2] Department of Computer Science, City University of Hong Kong
[3] International Information Security Consultants Pty Ltd.
{w.caelli,d.longley}@iisec.com.au, cslfkwok@cityu.edu.hk

Abstract. Internet insecurity is inevitable if a high proportion of Internet users are insufficiently aware of the inherent risks involved, whilst those cognizant of those risks are denied the facilities to manage and control them. This paper highlights the first issue and discusses a potential approach to the second.

Keywords: Secure Internet, trust relationship model, Internet trust relationships.

1   Introduction

Forty years ago Scott Graham and Peter Denning [1] wrote:

On the basis of the foregoing argument, we conclude that the protection system is correct and will operate exactly as intended among trustworthy subjects. Untrustworthy subjects cannot be dealt with completely by mechanisms of the protection system. External regulation, together with a system for detecting and reporting violations, is required.

Forty years later this advice is relevant because it emphasises the key role of pre-existing trust relationships within information security. The focus of information security has evolved from government mainframes, to corporate information processing systems, small business and home computing and now the Internet and mobile devices. These developments involved major corresponding changes in the host environment trust relationships.

When information security developed as a topic in its own right, and as a profession, there was a natural tendency to concentrate on common themes of information security systems, perhaps at the expense of the fundamental role of pre-existing trust relationships in the host environment.

In the 1980's it was commonly assumed that the global communication offered by the Internet would facilitate social cohesion; but now it would appear that the Internet can produce some damaging impacts upon society. If the current impacts have been caused by petty criminals, one could well fear the potential future impacts from organised crime or a rogue government; hence the current widespread concerns for cyber insecurity, coupled with calls for greater regulation, sophisticated defence systems and even hints of assured mutual disruption.

L.J. Janczewski, H.B. Wolfe, and S. Shenoi (Eds.): SEC 2013, IFIP AICT 405, pp. 42–54, 2013.
© IFIP International Federation for Information Processing 2013

The host environment of the Internet comprises that of the 2 billion Internet users. Whilst the Internet itself, may be viewed from a network security viewpoint, Internet security must be directed at the trust network of the host global user society. When governments are faced with some of the social evils arising from the Internet, e.g. cyber bullying, network security techniques alone offer no solution.

Taking a broad brush approach to Internet security we could recognise that the pre-Internet society had, over millennia, evolved a remarkably successful social trust network, bonding a set of highly complex social systems. The Internet, as a computer network, certainly offers an opportunity of increasing social cohesion. Taking the lead from Graham and Denning it seems clear that the role of Internet security should be defined in terms of enhancing the effectiveness of that trust network.

This paper seeks to explore the approach based upon the concept of the Internet as communication system designed to enhance a highly evolved social trust relationship infrastructure. It suggests that a better understanding of the role and functions of existing social trust relationships could lead to the evolution of a secure sub-Internet, expanding and gradually replacing the current anarchic Internet

The paper first describes an informal personal trust relationship model, and then reviews the current state of Internet trust relationships from a user - supplier viewpoint. Finally there is a discussion on the evolution of a secure Internet service complementing the trust relationships in traditional personal activities: banking, information retrieval, social networking, entertainment etc.

2   Personal Trust

2.1   Overview

The role of trust in society has been widely discussed [2]. The term trust has such emotive affiliations that for the purposes of this paper a pragmatic definition will be adopted:

An entity trusts another entity if it is confident that it can predict the behaviour of that entity in a specified context.

Example: a householder predicts that the plumber will successfully repair a dripping tap.

Trust relationships are formed in the cot; trust relationship training and experiential learning continues throughout a lifetime. Society successfully evolved from small hunting parties, through tribal societies, agricultural communities, the industrial revolution, to the pre-Internet trust relationships, because increasingly complex societies were rendered viable by a vast trust relationship infrastructure.

One of the consequences of this infrastructure was that individuals exploited trust relationships instinctively and became less conscious of their existence. Hence a late nineteenth worker in a small village was probably more acutely aware of the importance of such personal trust relationships than a teenager in the Internet era.

This apparent current lack of awareness had significant consequences in the explosive growth of the Internet.

Example: compare the attitude of a nineteenth century village child to a stranger, as compared with that of a modern teenager in a bulletin board session.

A trust relationship model is defined below and is used in a discussion on the role of such relationships on the Internet.

2.2   Trust Relationship Model

Overview.   Fig 1 illustrates the Trust Relationship Model. The model parameters are:

- Context – the total set of potential actions requested from the Activator;
- Initiator – the party that establishes the trust relationship and subsequently sends transaction requests to the Activator;
- Activator – the party that performs the requested transactions;
- Security Attribute – details of the Activators ability and previous performance in performing the transactions;
- Trust Level – the Initiators' estimate of the probability that requested transactions will be successfully completed by the Activator.

In general the Activator predicts that the Initiator will provide some recompense for the completion of individual transactions. Hence most trust relationships are bilateral: party A predicts that party B will satisfactorily perform the transaction, whilst party B predicts that party A will pay the bill. Hence each party plays the Initiator role, in one of the constituent relationships, and the Activator role in the other.

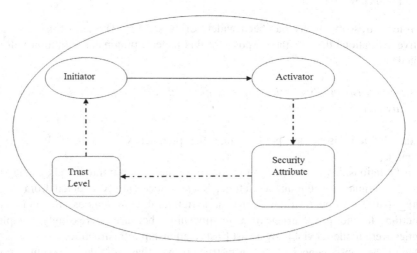

Fig. 1. Trust Relationship Model: The Initiator predicts that within the context of the trust relationship the Activator will behave as predicted with a probability equal to the Trust Level value; the Trust Level is a function of the Activators Security Attribute, which in turn is based upon the Activator's qualifications and reputation in the relationship context

Forming a Trust Relationship. The Initiator evaluates the Activator via the security attribute (see Fig. 1) and estimates the trust level associated that security attribute. The Activator will also set a risk profile and conduct a risk analysis; estimating the impact value of a failed transaction and estimating the risk from the impact value and trust level. If this risk is within the boundaries of the risk profile, the Initiator will propose the formation of the trust relationship with the Activator, who will usually undertake a similar process for the second half of a bilateral relationship, and accept or reject the offer.

Zero Trust Relationship. A multitude of transactions are conducted outside the trust relationship model described above, every day such one-off zero trust relationships are employed when the potential impact is low, or the risk of not requesting the transaction is high. One common example of the zero trust relationship arises when one requests directions from a stranger. Such one-off zero trust relationships are based upon the assumptions:

- The net benefit from a large number of such relationships justifies their usage;
- There would appear to be no benefit to a malicious activator;
- The initiator has some limited basis, e.g. activator's appearance, demeanour to assume a beneficial outcome.

Surfing the Web provides an example of the common usage of zero trust relationships.

Transitive Trust. The difficulties associated with the task of identifying and evaluating activators is commonly bypassed with transitive trust relationships, e.g. recommendations from a trusted friend.

In a unilateral transitive trust relationship A trusts C and C trusts B, which can lead to a transitive trust relationship: A trusts B (See Fig 2). Corresponding bilateral transitive trust relationship Transitive trust can take one of three forms:

- Introduction: C merely passes B's identifier to A.
- Recommendation: A's trust level in B is influenced by C.
- Delegation: B is merely a component in the performance of the tasks; the trust level assigned by A in the A trusts B relationship, is equal to that of A's trust level with C, e.g. B is an employee in Bank C.

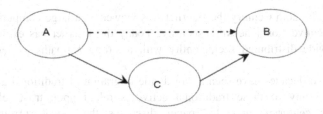

Fig. 2. Transitive Trust: A trusts C, C trusts B, A has a transitive trust relationship with B

A recommendation transitive trust is commonly employed when C is in a better position to evaluate B's security attribute than A, and in general A should have a high trust level in C; such transitive trust levels are highly conditional, e.g.

- The context of A's trust in B must be a subset of the context C's trust in B;
- If there are a large number of C's trusting a unique B then an average of these trust levels may be appropriate in the estimation of the transitive trust relationship;
- There should be no significant time gap between the last transaction of the C trusts B relationship and the first transaction of the A trusts B relationship.
- C's identifier for B must be unique in the union of population sets known to A and C.

The trust level between A and B can be no higher than the minimum of the A-C and C-B trust levels. If transitive chains are extended then trust levels between the initiators and activators and the ends of the chain could well fall below acceptable levels for even moderate impact transactions.

Transitive trust chains may become quite long and it is essential that they commence with a non-transitive trust relationship. This condition is significant for Internet users where transitive trust is commonly employed, because, as discussed below, there are extreme difficulties in forming non-transitive trust relationships on the Internet.

Appeal Systems.   In bilateral relationships both parties experience a degree of risk with each individual transaction. An appeal system, trusted by both parties, can reassure them that any disputes may be resolved impartially. In effect the existence of the appeal system may be a component of each party's security attributes, effectively increasing each party's trust level.

Appeal systems may play an important role in transitive chains, counteracting the inevitable decline of trust levels along long chains; provided, of course, that the transitive chain does not extend outside the realm of an appeal system common to both parties.

3   Internet Trust Relationships

3.1   Overview

At the end of the 20th Century the Internet was viewed as a large computer network amenable to conventional network security. Today the Internet has evolved into a novel worldwide distributed social entity with a strong antipathy to security and regulation.

The past two decades have seen a worldwide migration of traditional activities to the Internet. Many of these traditional activities relied upon trust relationships evolved over centuries, and this paper discusses the issues surrounding the establishment of corresponding trust relationships on the Internet.

The establishment of trust relationships in a small community was facilitated by propinquity and multichannel communication, i.e. a few people in close proximity who using one or more their five senses in their interactions. The Internet user population, on the other hand, represents of the order of 30% of the world population, and a major part of its traffic is restricted to the exchange of text and graphics. This environment seriously complicates the establishment of trust relationships as discussed below.

3.2   Establishing an Internet Trust Relationship

Activator Identification and Evaluation. Initially the initiator must locate and identify a potential activator; the initiator must then select a set of activator attributes rendering that individual unique amongst the population known to the initiator, so that the initiator will be able to identify the activator when requesting future transactions. If the initiator and activator live in a small community then the activator's physical appearance will suffice. However, as activators are selected from increasingly large populations the number of personal attributes required for unique identification grows rapidly.

The unique identification of the activator becomes even more problematic as information is collected to determine the activator's qualifications relevant to the context of the proposed trust relationship. Again such evaluation in respect of a local plumber in a small community is straightforward, but becomes increasingly problematic when such information must be collected from a variety remote sources and the initiator must verify that the activator identifying information, provided by each source, corresponds only the selected activator.

The initiator must aim at the collection of sufficient information, about the activator's potential performance in the relationship context, to estimate a trust level for the proposed relationship. Then a decision is made on whether or not that trust level is consistent with the initiator's risk profile.

Having collected the security attribute information, either directly from the activator or one or more other sources, a chicken-egg problem becomes apparent. How does the initiator verify the integrity of the information collected over the Internet? If the initiator has a trusted source of security attribute information, how was the trust relationship formed with that source? A similar problem arises if the initiator bypasses the identification and evaluation process with a transitive trust relationship. Hence it is apparent that trust relationships can only be formed on the Internet after some root trust relationship has been formed outside the Internet.

When the initiator has selected a specific activator then the initiator's problem of ensuring that future transactions are initiated with the correct activator must be addressed. Since the communication is via the Internet, the initiator and activator need to agree upon some effective authentication process for future communications. If the relationship is non-transitive root then this exchange of authentication details, e.g. public key certificates, should also be undertaken securely outside the Internet.

Authentication processes employed in communication channels assume that the communicating parties do not deliberately provide masquerading entities with the authentication parameters. Hence such authentication processes should be backed by some regulatory authority such that an individual would be held legally responsible for actions undertaken in any such masquerades.

Once the root trust relationship has been formed the Internet is, from an information security viewpoint, merely a computer network and the security facilities offered by public key cryptography may be deployed.

It would appear from the above discussion that the combination of trust relationships, formed in the traditional manner outside the Internet, may be used to provide secure roots for Internet transitive trust relationships and even trust relationship chains, thus combining the best of both worlds. This approach requires both a reconsideration of current approaches to Internet security, and a secure deployment of public key cryptography.

4   A Secure Internet Service

4.1   Overview

The period preceding the Internet experienced amazing technological advances in electronics and communications; these advances resulted in qualitative and quantitative changes; mass production of microelectronic devices provided mass access to computing and communication services. In the early years of computing developments Governments largely drove the agenda, but the Internet advances mainly resulted from market forces exploiting low cost consumer electronics. Such market forces tended to view security as a costly obstacle and the consumer was provided with a choice in many aspects of the Internet, except the level of personal security.

In conventional trust relationships the user weighs the advantages of undertaking transactions on the balance of potential gain and risk; the risk itself is measured in terms of impact probability and value. Over the past two decades it has become clear that a significant proportion of Internet users lack the detailed knowledge of Internet technology to evaluate their risks, e.g. they are unaware of potential unfavourable outcomes and associated impacts. For example: malicious code downloads, monitoring of users' Web usage, penalties of intellectual properties transgressions, lack of privacy etc.

Moreover a high proportion of Internet usage, i.e. surfing the Web, comprises apparently one off zero trust transactions (See Zero Trust Relationship in 2.2). Asking a stranger for directions is considered relatively safe because for any such single transaction the wrong information has limited impact, and the stranger is unlikely to benefit from deliberately malicious behaviour. Web surfing, however, may not fit this pattern, e.g.

- a malicious posted set of false information will impact upon multiple Internet users;
- monitoring of user Web actions may in some circumstances have significant long term impacts on specific users.

In recent years many users have been virtually compelled to employ Internet services because the off-line alternatives are not locally available or are too expensive. At the same time the average Internet user is provided with few opportunities to protect themselves apart from subscribing to anti-virus services and avoiding obvious pitfalls with passwords. It is proposed here that Internet users should be provided with the option of a security policy providing similar levels of security to that offered by traditional off line trust relationships, e.g. manual banking compared with current Internet banking.

The proposed secure Internet service is intended to complement, rather than replace, current Internet services, and could therefore commence with a few applications allowing user demand for security to determine its success.

Internet applications may be broadly listed in two categories: text/graphics and audio-visual. The text-graphics type Internet applications consist of financial services, commercial services, information retrieval, social networking and email, and interactive education; whereas audio-visual type Internet applications include music, movies and education presentation. The following sub-sections discuss the trust relationships of these Internet applications.

4.2   Text – Graphics Trust Relationships

Financial Services. These applications normally involve a pre-existing off-line trust relationship between the financial institution and the Internet user, and could be offered with a high level of user security. The client and financial institution are in a position to exchange mutual authentication data off-line and the Internet user security then depends upon the technology employed for the authentication process (See 4.4 PKI and Secure Interface Devices) , and the security of the institutional computers.

Commercial Services. Most on-line shoppers have no pre-existing trust relationship with the Internet supplier, and few Internet users would be in a position, or prepared, to establish such relationships with individual Internet suppliers. In this case transitive trust relationships are the only option for the secure Internet service, which implies some organisation, termed here root organization, is prepared to provide a root trust relationship for Internet users (See Transitive Trust in 2.2). Consumer Protection Authorities, for example, would be well placed for such a root organization role. Such agencies not only have some role with suppliers in specific geographic areas, they often have regulatory powers and access to some appeals system.

In the proposed scheme the suppliers would register with the root organization, and supply authentication data, off line. The Internet user would also register with this root organization offline and collect its authentication data. Having located a supplier on-line, and checked that it is registered with the root organisation, the user collects the supplier authentication data established with the root organization, and initiates the transaction with that supplier. The user supplier trust relationships could also be in a bilateral form, in which case the user would supply authentication data at time of registration with the root organization.

The obvious objection to this proposed scheme lies in the limited range of suppliers associated with a particular root organization; implying that Internet users would be restricted to a few suppliers, according to user's ability to register off line with various root organizations. If, however, diverse root organizations are prepared to offer reciprocal regulatory protection then they may merge off-line and provide their registered users with high trust level relationships over a much larger range of suppliers. One of the major advantages of the proposed scheme lies in the regulatory powers of the root organisation increasing the trust level of the user - supplier relationship.

The success of such a proposal is dependent upon market forces but it has the advantage that such a scheme could evolve from a small base.

Information Retrieval. Information retrieval probably represents the most important single application on the Internet. Search engines provide access to a host of relevant information. Web surfing is commonly regarded as a low risk activity, although the associated privacy risk to users is underplayed. However, users are on occasions concerned about the authenticity of accessed information; if one considers print based information retrieval it is apparent that the users on such occasions are strongly influenced by the provenance of written text ranging from newspapers, legal documents to respected text or reference books.

The risk associated with Internet information retrieval was apparent in Australia when an environmental activist, armed only a mobile phone and laptop, produced a fake Internet press report causing a sharp fall in the stock market value of a mining company. Medical and health warning information is now commonly accessed over the Internet by medical practitioners and the general public; one hesitates to list the potential dangers of this situation.

In traditional information retrieval the user can easily distinguish between a leaflet, a respected newspaper or reference book in the library, whereas URLs provide only limited guarantees of provenance and even these are commonly ignored. Even if users access a reputable site, they can be seriously misled by malicious hacker alterations in the text.

In the proposed scheme a reputable publisher acts as a root organisation (see Commercial Services in 4.2) for various Web publishers, although such a root organisation would normally have limited, if any, regulatory powers. The user obtains the Web publisher authentication data from the root organisation and checks a digital signature included in the Web page, thus providing assurance on the source and integrity of the displayed text.

Social Networking and Email. Social Networking did not feature in the early security vulnerable areas of the Internet, but the current level of cyber bullying is now a topic of government concern. Faced with the Pandora's Box opened by youthful entrepreneurs one can only compare the dangers faced by teenage parents in the pre-Internet days with their woe-begotten current counterparts.

Most parents traditionally adopted individual and group strategies in relationship to their off springs' companions. At an individual level the identity, security attribute and trust level of the candidate activator were routinely assessed, because this information was available. At the group level the culture surrounding clubs for various age groups and interests highlights the interesting trust relationships between club members and the organising committee. The members trusted the local committee to vet potential members and effectively used that trust in the formation of transitive trust relationships between current and new members. Is it conceivable that a similar approach could be used to form high trust transitive social trust networks on the Internet?

Email security is particularly interesting in the context of this paper because PGP (pretty good privacy) [3] addressed email security concerns and used both public key cryptography, and transitive trust for the development of a certificate chain. Email addresses can be masqueraded and from time to time one receives emails with a colleagues email address but with associated text clearly derived from another source. There are good arguments for more use of PKI in emails, particularly in large organisations, where sender certificates could include attributes informing the recipient of the role and authority of the sender within the company.

The fundamental risks associated with emails arise, however, from the curse of immediacy. In the pre-Internet era many people re-read their outgoing correspondence before sealing the envelope, reflecting on the contents and potential reactions of the recipients.

Interactive Education. If the Internet is to have an increasing role within education, in particular higher education, the risks associated with online tutorials and assessment deserve detailed consideration. The potential pitfalls, and associated litigation, arising from tutor – student interactions and assessment decisions suggest that a serious re-consideration of academic trust relationships, and their implementation in a global Internet based educational network, would be advisable.

4.3   Audi-Visual Trust Relationships

Overview. Originally Internet security was based upon conventional network security dealing with primarily with textual data. One of the perhaps more surprising outcomes of enhancing a single sense channel (sight) with a second channel (sound) is that two teenagers with Web cams can now securely mutually authenticate over the Internet without the aid of cryptography.

Audio visual applications have at least two significant security implications: intellectual property and privacy. Governments have been concerned both with protection with corporate profits and the impacts of cyber bullying, responding with strict legislation for the one, and serious hand wringing for the other.

Intellectual Property. The trust relationships associated with theatres and cinemas normally took the form that the client predicted the quality of entertainment provided would be compatible with the price of the entrance ticket, the supplier predicted that the audience would not express significant disapproval during or after the performance. Such trust relationships are significantly different when the client plays back some digitised music or video. The supplier now takes the risk of loss of income from piracy of the digitised information, whilst playing back such digitised information make involve the risk of penalties for intellectual property legislation transgressions.

In a previous generation the music industry employed technology that made illegal copying expensive; the publisher bore the cost of producing vinyl disks and the consumer purchased a hi-fi system capable of playing, but not reproducing, that disk. Digitisation revolutionised this industry, the supplier was no longer burdened with the cost and distribution of the disks, and the consumer purchased equipment capable of both play and reproduction. The downside from the supplier's viewpoint was the potential theft of their intellectual property. Their solution is to pass the responsibility of the protection of their intellectual property to the user, with major financial penalties for transgression; at least some governments have actively supported this initiative. An alternative solution to the intellectual property dilemma involves a reversion to the previous situation in which the supplier product was supplied in a form that could be played but not cheaply reproduced.

Cryptography combined with a special purpose secure playback devices could provide such a solution. In effect, the encrypted digitised data supplied could only be decrypted and played in the secure device holding a private key technologically protected against illegal access.

Privacy. There are no current technological solutions to the age old problem of the presumed friend who maliciously passes on intimate secrets. Social networking has unfortunately provided an international broadcast audio visual system for such indiscretions. As such it has exemplified the problems of the Internet world lacking effective social trust relationships. In previous generations teenagers were at least inculcated into the imperfect world of personal trust relationships (see Social Networking and Email in 4.2).

4.4   PKI and Secure Interface Devices

PKI. An Internet-wide PKI would provide a parent-child hierarchy of Certificate Authorities and presumably unique identification for each user. However such a system could pose a significantly enhanced threat of identity theft since it would rely upon the cryptographic strength of a particular public key algorithm, and the integrity of a vast host of employees charged with issuing certificates as well as the underlying computer systems used to create, store and distribute the base certificates themselves.

The proposed Internet trust relationship networks with root organizations uses a local PKI, and extends it with sibling certificates issued by the root organizations to their trusted individual Internet suppliers and, if appropriate, to their registered users. The user, and supplier, offline registration process with the root organization would thus involve face to face authentication and exchange of certificates.

Secure Interface Devices. The theme of this paper is that an Internet user should have the opportunity to benefit from trust relationships similar to that enjoyed in the pre-Internet era. Exploiting the proposed Internet transitive trust relationship network requires:

- secure end to end authentication;
- security of communication channels;
- some means of estimating trust levels over transitive chains, which may extend beyond the aegis of local appeal systems.

PKI Certificates exchanged between activators and initiators can facilitate unilateral or bilateral mutual authentication, and the exchange of cryptographically secured messages. The advantage of this proposed system is that it can mimic the conventional trust relationships practised outside the Internet where users make value judgements on transactions based upon impact and trust levels.

The user private key in this arrangement is the keystone to user security; its value and processing must be protected from the malicious code inevitably residing in the user's computer. Current technology has produced a plethora of handheld smart devices and hence a cost effective secure interface device capable of protecting cryptographic private keys and public key certificates can be reasonably postulated.

In keeping with the principle that the Internet trust relationships are either established outside the Internet or via transitive trust chains, certificates for non-transitive trust relationships, e.g. Internet banking, and root transitive trust servers would be loaded directly into the secure device.

The secure device has the task of extracting and checking certificates and supplier public keys derived from certificates, including sibling certificate chains, aided by attributes of the various certificates, and performing the corresponding cryptographic operations.

The sibling certificates may also be employed to facilitate end to end trust levels in long transitive chains. Attributes of these certificates may contain details of link trust levels and existence/ non-existence of end to end appeal facilities. Given some monetary impact value for the transaction the secure device could even provide warnings of risky transactions.

5   Conclusions

The user's security role is perhaps the most significant issue arising from this paper. In conventional information security environments, similar to those addressed by Scott Graham and Denning [1], the host organization information security system was designed to strengthen the pre-existing organisational trust framework. To this extent the user had a somewhat passive security role, e.g. protection of passwords etc. With Internet security, however, there is no host organization and the users have a major security role, including responsibility for their own risk analysis and management. Unfortunately the average user is neither equipped to fulfil this role, nor in a position to establish a requisite level of security. It is therefore of some concern when suggestions are made that users should be held liable for security breaches, e.g. penalties for harbouring botnets.

This paper emphasises the key role of users in Internet security and highlights two major factors of that role: user Internet security education, and facilities for the deployment of trust relationships with trust levels consistent with user risk. Such a user education requirement is not particularly novel; vehicle drivers are not legally permitted to use public highways with skills limited to manipulation of automobile controls, and total ignorance of road traffic interactions. The current Internet user security awareness situation may perhaps be traced to an ill-informed replacement of traditional IT education with minimalist mouse icon click training, and should be redressed as a matter of urgency.

The, hopefully increasing, proportion of Internet users with sufficient knowledge and skills to protect themselves will be the key drivers, and only hope, of a future adequately secure Internet. This paper discusses the harnessing of traditional trust relationship skills, and the facilities required to implement secure Internet trust relationships. The fundamental problem of establishing secure Internet trust relationships is addressed with a proposal for transitive trust relationships, supported with secure authentication, rooted on traditional trust relationships formed off line

References

1. Graham, G.S., Denning, P.J.: Protection Principles and Practice. In: Proc. AFIPS Spring Joint Computer Conference, pp. 417–429 (1972)
2. Fukuyama, F.: Trust: The Social Virtues and the Creation of Prosperity. Penguin Books (1996)
3. Zimmermann, P.: The Official PGP User's Manual. MIT Press (1995)

Enhancing Click-Draw Based Graphical Passwords Using Multi-Touch on Mobile Phones

Yuxin Meng[1], Wenjuan Li[2], and Lam-For Kwok[1]

[1] Department of Computer Science, City University of Hong Kong, Hong Kong, China
`yuxin.meng@my.cityu.edu.hk`, `cslfkwok@cityu.edu.hk`
[2] Computer Science Division, Zhaoqing Foreign Language College, Guangdong, China
`wenjuan.anastatia@gmail.com`

Abstract. Graphical password based authentication systems are now becoming one of the potential alternatives to alleviate current over-reliance on traditional text-based password authentication. With the rapid development of mobile devices (i.e., the increase of computing power), this kind of authentication systems has been implemented on mobile phones to authenticate legitimate users and detect impostors. But in real deployment, we notice that users can utilize more actions like multi-touch on a mobile phone than on a common computer. The action of multi-touch, which refers to the process of touching a touchscreen with multiple fingers at the same time, is a distinguished feature on a touchscreen mobile phone. In this paper, we therefore attempt to explore the effect of multi-touch on creating graphical passwords in the aspect of security and usability. In particular, we conduct a study of using click-draw based graphical passwords in the evaluation, which combines current input types in the area of graphical passwords, and we further develop a multi-touch enabled scheme on mobile phones. Three experiments were conducted with 60 participants and the experimental results indicate that, by integrating the action of multi-touch, graphical passwords can be generally enhanced in the aspect of both security and usability.

Keywords: Graphical Passwords, User Authentication, Multi-Touch, Human Factors, Mobile Phones, Mobile Security.

1   Introduction

User authentication on mobile phones has become more and more important with modern mobile devices being comparable to a PC (i.e., with the continuous increase of computing power). With the popularity of mobile phones, users are likely to store a lot of sensitive information (e.g., credit card numbers) on their mobile phones [11] and to use their phones for security sensitive tasks (e.g., authorizing commercial transactions) due to their fast data connection and wireless connectivity [8].

In these cases, it is crucial to develop and implement user authentication mechanisms for a mobile phone to authenticate legitimate users and detect imposters. To mitigate the limitations of traditional text-based password authentication (i.e., users have difficulty in remembering complex and random passwords which is known as long-term memory (LTM) limitations), authenticating users by means of images is one of the possible

L.J. Janczewski, H.B. Wolfe, and S. Shenoi (Eds.): SEC 2013, IFIP AICT 405, pp. 55–68, 2013.

alternatives in which several studies [17,19] have shown that human brain was better at remembering and recognizing images than text. Along with this observation, several graphical password applications have been proposed on mobile phones like *Android unlock pattern*[1], a graphical password based Android application in which users are required to input correct unlock patterns to unlock their Android screen [5].

Generally, graphical password based authentication can be categorized into three folders based on their input methods[2]: *click-based graphical passwords*, *choice-based graphical passwords* and *draw-based graphical passwords*. In particular, the click-based schemes require users to click on the provided image(s) (i.e., choosing an object or element of the image), the choice-based schemes require users to select a series of images (i.e., selecting images in an order), and the draw-based schemes require users to draw some secrets to be authenticated (i.e., drawing a user signature). Several security studies regarding graphical passwords can be referred to [3], [7] and [9].

Motivation. In real deployment, we find that users can utilize more actions like *multi-touch* in creating graphical passwords on a mobile phone than on a common computer. The *multi-touch* refers to the process of touching a touchscreen device with multiple fingers simultaneously, which is a distinguished feature for current touchscreen mobile phones. This observation indicates that the creation of graphical passwords may be different on distinct platforms due to different types of input actions. In addition, touchscreens are becoming the leading input method on the mobile platform where 74% of all phones in the market using a touch screen [16]. Our motivation is therefore to explore the impact of *multi-touch* on creating graphical passwords.

Contributions. In this paper, we attempt to investigate the impact of multi-touch on creating graphical passwords in the aspect of security and usability and use it to enhance the creation of graphical passwords. In particular, we employ click-draw graphical password scheme (*CD-GPS*) in the evaluation which combines current inputs of creating a graphical password. Our contributions can be summarized as below.

- We give a detailed analysis of the possible impact of using multi-touch on the creation of *CD-GPS* passwords. Based on the original *CD-GPS* scheme, we develop an example system of *multi-touch enabled CD-GPS scheme* on a mobile phone that enables users to create the *CD-GPS* passwords using the action of multi-touch.
- To verify our analysis, we conducted three experiments with a total number of 60 participants. By comparing the obtained results, we find that the action of multi-touch can positively enhance the construction of graphical passwords in the aspect of both security and usability.

The remaining parts of this paper are organized as follows: in Section 2, we briefly introduce the click-draw based graphical password scheme (*CD-GPS*); Section 3 analyzes the potential impact of multi-touch on creating *CD-GPS* passwords; Section 4 presents our developed *multi-touch enabled CD-GPS scheme* and our experimental

---

[1] http://code.google.com/p/androidunlockpatternswitch/

[2] Another graphical password classification (e.g., [3,20]): recognition based scheme (i.e., recognizing images), pure recall based scheme (i.e., reproducing a drawing without a hint) and cued recall based scheme (i.e., reproducing a drawing with hints).

methodology; Section 5 describes the experimental results and Section 6 reviews some related work; at last, Section 7 concludes our paper and points out future work.

2   Click-Draw Based Graphical Password Scheme

The click-draw based graphical password scheme (shortly *CD-GPS*) [14] was developed with the purpose of enhancing traditional graphical passwords by combining existing input types from click-based, choice-based and draw-based graphical passwords. A general *CD-GPS scheme* mainly consists of two operational steps: *image selection* and *secret drawing*.

The first step is *image selection* where users are required to select several images from an image pool (i.e., the pool may contain a number of images with different themes) in an ordered sequence, and remember this order of images like a story to assist memorization. Then, users are required to further select one or more images to draw their secrets. In the step of *secret drawing*, users can freely *click-draw* their secrets (e.g., a number, a letter) on their selected image(s). The action of *click-draw* requires users to draw a secret by using a series of clicks. To facilitate the use of *click-draw*, the *CD-GPS scheme* partitions the selected image, which is used for click-drawing secrets, into a $N \times N$ table.

In [14], an example system of CD-GPS was also implemented in which the image pool contains 10 different images (i.e., themes like fruits, landscape, people, etc). In the first step, users are required to select 4 images out of the image pool and organize these images in a story order. Then, in the second step of *secret drawing*, users have to further select 1 image for click-drawing their own secrets. The selected image in the example system will be divided into a 16×16 table with 256 clickable squares. The user study with 42 participants showed that the *CD-GPS scheme* could provide suitable properties in the aspect of both usability and security. Detailed analysis about the *CD-GPS* can be referred to [14].

3   Multi-Touch

In real deployment, we notice that the way of creating graphical passwords may be different on a computer and on a touchscreen mobile phone. For instance, users can use more actions (e.g., multi-touch) on a mobile phone than on a common computer (e.g., PC). Nowadays, *multi-touch* is becoming a distinguished feature on a touchscreen mobile phone (or other touchscreen based devices) that users can touch the screen with multiple fingers at the same time. Next, we analyze the potential impact of multi-touch on creating the *CD-GPS* passwords.

Common Computer. In a computer (e.g., a PC) with mouse as the input device, users can only create the *CD-GPS* passwords (i.e., drawing a secret by means of click-draw) with the action of single-click. In this scenario, the potential password space of *CD-GPS* passwords can be calculated as follows [14]:

$$\frac{N_1!}{(N_1 - n)!} \times \frac{n!}{k! \times (n-k)!} \times \prod_k \frac{N_c!}{(N_c - K_i)!} (i = 1, 2, 3, ...)$$

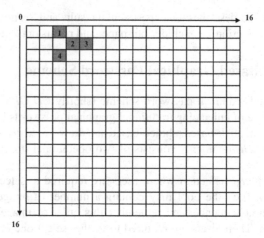

Fig. 1. An example of creating CD-GPS: drawing a symbol of arrow '>'

Where N_1 is the number of images in the image pool, n is the number of selected images in a story-sequence, k is the number of further selected images for click-drawing, N_c is the number of clickable squares and K_i means there are totally i clicks on a selected image. $\frac{N_1!}{(N_1-n)!}$ means that selecting n images out of N_1 images in a story sequence. $\frac{n!}{k! \times (n-k)!}$ means that choosing k images out of n images for secret drawing without considering the image sequence. Finally, $\prod_k \frac{N_c!}{(N_c-K_i)!}$ means the product of password space in selected k images.

Thus for the example system of the *CD-GPS* (where N_1=10, n=4, k=1 and N_c=256), the potential password space can be specified as below:

$$(10-4)! \times 4 \times \frac{256!}{(256-K_i)!} (i=1,2,3,...)$$

Touchscreen Mobile Phone. On a mobile phone with touchscreen as the main input device, users can perform more actions like *multi-touch* on the screen than on a common computer. The action of *multi-touch* greatly distinguishes the creation of graphical passwords on a mobile phone from that on a computer. For example, as shown in Fig. 1, our target is to draw a symbol of arrow '>'. To better illustrate the process of creation, we further assume the ordered sequence of drawing is 1, 2, 3 and 4. On a computer with mouse as the input device, because the *CD-GPS scheme* does not consider the sequence of clicks, there is only one choice to sequentially click these 4 squares.

However, with the action of *multi-touch* (i.e., only considering two fingers), there exist other 4 choices to complete the creation: {multi-touch{1, 2}, multi-touch{3, 4}}, {1, multi-touch{2, 3}, 4}, {1, 2, multi-touch{3, 4}}, {multi-touch{1, 2}, 3, 4}. In addition, if we do not limit the click sequence to 1, 2, 3 and 4, then the number of click choices can be increased to $4 \times 2 = 8$. This case indicates that the potential password space of *CD-GPS* can be further enlarged by integrating the action of *multi-touch* into the creation of graphical passwords.

If we only consider the multi-touch with 2 fingers (i.e., two squares can be selected at the same time), then the potential password space can be represented as below:

$$\frac{K_i!}{2!} \times \frac{N_1!}{(N_1 - n)!} \times \frac{n!}{k! \times (n - k)!} \times \prod_k \frac{N_c!}{(N_c - K_i)!} (i = 1, 2, 3, ...)$$

Correspondingly, for the example system of the *CD-GPS* in [14], its potential password space can be specified as below:

$$\frac{K_i!}{2!} \times (10 - 4)! \times 4 \times \frac{256!}{(256 - K_i)!} (i = 1, 2, 3, ...)$$

That is, by integrating the multi-touch with only 2 fingers, the password space can be further enlarged by $\frac{K_i!}{2!}$ times in theory. Note that the user study in [14] has showed that K_i is usually bigger than 5. Moreover, with the multi-touch, users may complete their drawings more quickly as two squares can be selected simultaneously.

4 User Study

With the above analysis of *multi-touch*, we therefore attempt to verify the impact of *multi-touch* on creating graphical passwords. In this section, we begin by describing our developed example system of *multi-touch enabled CD-GPS* on an Android phone and we then present our experimental methodology in the user study.

4.1 Multi-Touch Enabled CD-GPS

To enable the creation of *CD-GPS* passwords with the action of *multi-touch*, we design and develop an example system of *multi-touch enabled CD-GPS* that can collect multi-touch clicks. This system, as shown in Fig. 2, authenticates whether a user is legitimate by combining the click-coordinate information with multi-touch records.

Fig. 2 (a) illustrates the developed *multi-touch enabled CD-GPS scheme*. Similarly, the image pool contains 10 images (arranged in 5×2 grids) with different themes such as fruits, landscape, cartoon characters, food, sport, buildings, cars, animals, books and people. All used images have the same pixel size of 400×400. In the first step, users are required to select 4 images out of the image pool and organize these images in a story order. Then, users are required to select 1 image for drawing their secrets. Different from the *CD-GPS scheme* on a computer, users can utilize the multi-touch with two fingers to complete their drawings in the developed *multi-touch enabled CD-GPS scheme*. The *multi-touch enabled CD-GPS scheme* also divides an image into a 16×16 table with 256 clickable squares in which each square has a pixel size of 25×25.

Fig. 2 (b) shows the authentication process in our developed example system. When users finish their drawings, the authentication system collects all the inputs (e.g., clicked squares' coordinates) and multi-touch information (i.e., coordinates with multi-touch), and then constructs a signature in the phase of *signature construction*. Take the clicks in Fig. 1 as an example, if the squares with 2 and 3 are clicked with multi-touch, the relevant plaintext signature is recorded as: $\{(3, 1), \text{multi-touch}\{(4, 2), (5, 2)\}, (3, 3)\}$.

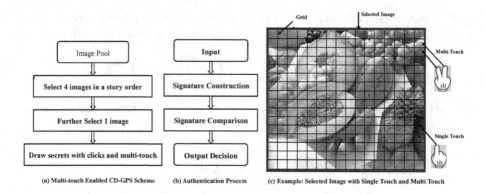

Fig. 2. An example system of *multi-touch enabled CD-GPS scheme*: (a) Multi-touch Enabled CD-GPS Scheme; (b) Authentication Process in the Example System; (c) An example of single touch and multi-touch on a selected image

In the phase of *signature comparison*, the authentication system can detect an imposter by comparing current collected signature with the pre-defined normal signature. The comparison process is described as follows:

- If signature matching is successful, then the user is regarded as a legitimate user.
- If signature matching is failed, then the user is regarded as an imposter.

Finally, the authentication system outputs the decision and can require users to perform extra validation (i.e., inputting a correct PIN) if they are identified as imposters. In addition, Fig. 2 (c) illustrates an example of *single touch* and *multi-touch* on a selected image (*fruit theme*) in the example system. Users can use either *single touch* or *multi-touch* to draw their own secrets.

In the evaluation, the above example system of *multi-touch enabled CD-GPS* was implemented on an Google/HTC Nexus One Android phone (with resolution 480×800 px and CPU 1GHz). In the current smartphone market, Android OS and iOS make up the largest share with a combined 80% of smartphones [16]. In addition, the merits of using this particular phone is that its stock Android system can be replaced by a modified customized OS version. Specifically, we updated the phone with a modified Android OS version 2.2 based on CyanogenMod[3]. The modification mainly consists of changes to the application framework layer to record the multi-touch input and relevant coordinate information from the touchscreen. The implementation details are similar to our previous work [15].

4.2 Experimental Methodology

To evaluate the performance of the *multi-touch enabled CD-GPS scheme*, we conducted an in-lab user study that consisted of three major experiments with totally 60 participants those who were interested in our work. All participants are volunteer with diverse

---

[3] http://www.cyanogenmod.com/

Table 1. Participants information in the user study

Age Range	Male	Female
15-25	10	10
25-35	10	8
35-45	6	6
45-55	6	4

backgrounds including both students and senior people. Particularly, 30 participants (13 females and 17 males) are from the computer science department (but not security related major). All participants are regular web, mobile phone users and ranged in age from 18 to 55 years. The detailed information of participants is shown in Table 1.

In the user study, we mainly attempt to identify the effect of multi-touch by collecting user's feedback. To avoid any bias, we employed a *double-blind manner* in the user study that we did not uncover the name of these two schemes but we introduced our objectives in the user study and gave a detailed description of using these two example systems. Specifically, the original *CD-GPS scheme* was implemented on a computer with mouse as the input device [14] while the *multi-touch enabled CD-GPS scheme* was deployed on an Android phone with a touchscreen as the input device. To further avoid the bias of platforms, we evaluate the *multi-touch enabled CD-GPS scheme* by enabling and disabling multi-touch on the Android phone respectively.

Every participants can complete 3 practice trials for each scheme to get familiar with the platforms before they start to complete real trails. Therefore, a total of three experiments were conducted with the same 60 participants and the detailed steps in each experiment are described as below:

- *Experiment1.* This experiment was conducted on a desktop computer and each participant had to create 5 *CD-GPS* passwords.
  - Step 1. *CD-GPS* Creation: Creating a *CD-GPS* password by following the two steps in the scheme: *image selection* and *secret drawing*.
  - Step 2. *CD-GPS* Confirmation: Confirming the password by re-selecting images in the correct order and re-drawing secrets in the correct place. If users incorrectly confirm their password, they can retry the confirmation or return to Step 1.
  - Step 3. Feedback: All participants are required to complete a *feedback form* about the password creation and confirmation.

In the second day, all participants were required to complete a login session and gave their feedback.

  - Step 4. *CD-GPS* Login: Logging in the example system with all created *CD-GPS* passwords. Users can cancel an attempted login if they noticed an error and try again.
  - Step 5. Feedback: All participants should complete a *feedback form* about the password login.
- *Experiment2.* This experiment was conducted on an Android phone by enabling the action of multi-touch, and the steps are similar to *Experiement1*.

- Step 1. *Multi-touch enabled CD-GPS scheme* Creation: Creating 5 *CD-GPS* passwords based on the two steps in the scheme. Multi-touch is available during the creation.
- Step 2. *Multi-touch enabled CD-GPS scheme* Confirmation: This step is similar to *Experiment1*, but multi-touch is enabled.
- Step 3. Feedback collection.

In the second day, all participants were required to complete a login session and gave their feedback.

- Step 4. *Multi-touch enabled CD-GPS scheme* Login: Logging in the example system with all created passwords. The action of multi-touch is enabled.
- Step 5. Feedback collection.

– *Experiment3*. This experiment was conducted on an Android phone by disabling the action of multi-touch with the purpose of avoiding the bias regarding the platforms. The steps are similar to *Experiment2*.

- Step 1. *Multi-touch disabled CD-GPS scheme* Creation: Creating 5 *CD-GPS* passwords based on the steps in the scheme. Multi-touch is disabled during the creation.
- Step 2. *Multi-touch disabled CD-GPS scheme* Confirmation: Confirming the password with multi-touch disabled.
- Step 3. Feedback collection.

In the second day, all participants were required to complete a login session and gave their feedback.

- Step 4. *Multi-touch disabled CD-GPS scheme* Login: Logging in the example system with all created passwords. Different from *Experiment2*, the action of multi-touch is disabled.
- Step 5. Feedback collection.

Ten-point Likert scales were used in each feedback question where 1-score indicates strong disagreement and 10-score indicates strong agreement. We denoted 5-score as the meaning of "It is hard to say" for a question. In the analysis, these collected questions and scores for each experiment can be used to investigate the impact of multi-touch on creating graphical passwords. During the evaluation, 300 real trails were recorded for *Experiment1*, *Experiment2* and *Experiment3* respectively.

5   Results and Analysis

In this section, we present the results obtained in the experiments and analyze the results by means of the collected users' feedback. The *success rate* and *average completion time* regarding the step of creation, confirmation and login in *Experiment1*, *Experiment2* and *Experiment3* are shown in Table 2.

Particularly, the *success rate* in the step of *Creation* means that participants created their passwords without restarting, the *success rate* in the step of *Confirmation* means that participants confirmed their passwords without restarting and failed attempts for the first time, while the *success rate* in the step of *Login* means that participants, for the first time, pressed the login button and entered into the example system successfully. The *average completion time* is an average value computed by all participants.

Table 2. Success rate and average completion time for the step of creation, confirmation and login in *Experiment1*, *Experiment2* and *Experiment3*

Experiment1	Creation	Confirmation	Login
Success Rate (the first time)	223/300 (74.3%)	271/300 (90.3%)	254/300 (84.7%)
Completion Time (Average in seconds)	20.2	15.7	14.3
Standard Deviation (SD in seconds)	7.6	7.5	5.3
Experiment2	Creation	Confirmation	Login
Success Rate (the first time)	270/300 (90.0%)	288/300 (96.0%)	276/300 (92.0%)
Completion Time (Average in seconds)	12.1	7.1	7.6
Standard Deviation (SD in seconds)	5.3	3.5	3.2
Experiment2	Creation	Confirmation	Login
Success Rate (the first time)	258/300 (86.0%)	276/300 (92.0%)	265/300 (88.3%)
Completion Time (Average in seconds)	16.8	11.2	9.6
Standard Deviation (SD in seconds)	5.9	6.5	4.2

Success Rate. In *Experiment1*, as shown in Table 2, the success rate is 74.3% in the *Creation step*, several participants restarted the *password creation* (i.e., click-drawing another secret) because they changed their minds in drawing the secrets. The success rate is 90.3% in the *Confirmation step*, some restarting and failed attempts were detected since these participants clicked a wrong square. In the *Login step*, most participants could enter their passwords successfully with a success rate of 84.7%, some failed attempts were identified since these participants forgot their selected images or clicked on a wrong square for the first time.

In *Experiment2*, the success rate is 90% in the *Creation step* which is higher than the corresponding results in both *Experiment1* and *Experiment3*. The success rate achieves 96% in the *Confirmation step* which is also higher than both *Experiment1* and *Experiment3*. Most participants indicated that they could create and confirm their passwords more easily by using the action of multi-touch. That is, it is easier for them to remember their passwords by reducing the number of touch gestures. In the *Login step*, the success rate again achieves a higher value of 92% compared to both *Experiment1* and *Experiment3*. Participants indicated that the action of multi-touch could facilitate their construction and memorization.

In *Experiment3*, by disabling the multi-touch, the success rate is decreased to 86%, 92% and 88.3% with regard to the *Creation step*, *Confirmation step* and *Login step* respectively. Participants indicated that they should use more touch gestures to construct a secret without multi-touch. But the results obtained in this experiment are still better than those obtained in *Experiment1*. Participants reflected that they could use a touch gesture more conveniently and accurately than a mouse-click.

Completion Time. In *Experiment1*, the average completion time is around 20 seconds in the *Creation step* since participants should spend more time in deciding the image-order and selecting the images. The average consuming time is gradually decreased to 15.7 seconds and 14.3 seconds in the *Confirmation step* and *Login step* respectively. The main reason is that participants only need to re-create their passwords without spending additional time in constructing a new one.

In *Experiment2*, the average completion time is 12.1 seconds regarding the *Creation step*, which reduces about 40.1% of the time consumption in creating the passwords compared to *Experiment1*. The same as *Experiment1*, the average time consumption in *Experiment2* continuously decreases to 7.1 seconds and 7.6 seconds for the *Confirmation step* and *Login step* respectively. Most participants indicated that they could create and confirm the passwords more quickly by utilizing the action of multi-touch. Moreover, it is visible that the standard deviation (SD) is further reduced in *Experiment2* than that in *Experiment1* (i.e., for the *Creation step*, SD 7.6 for *Experiment1* while SD 5.3 for *Experiment2*), which shows that participants can generally create their passwords more quickly in *Experiment2*.

In *Experiment3*, compared with the result in *Experiment2*, the average completion time is increased to 16.8 seconds, 11.2 seconds and 9.6 seconds for the *Creation step*, *Confirmation step* and *Login step* respectively. The reason is that participants should spend more time in single touching without the action of multi-touch. For example, selecting two clickable squares, we should use two single touches instead of a multi-touch. But similar to the situation regarding the *successes rate*, the results are still better than those in *Experiment1*, the main reason is that it is more convenient to use a touch gesture than a mouse-click for a participant.

The Number of Clicks. To further analyze the experimental results, we present the click information in Table 3. This table shows that in *Experiment1*, most participants prefer the number of 5 and 6 clicks with the percent of 32.6% and 30.7% respectively. For the number of 7 and 8 clicks, the percent of trails is 18.7% and 7.3%, and there is no participant click above 9 squares. The results in *Experiment3* is similar to the *Experiment1*, but there are 3.3% trails selecting 9 squares. The reason is that participants feel more convenient to use a touch gesture than a mouse-click.

In *Experiment2*, it is visible that most participants prefer to click 6 and 8 squares to construct their secrets with the percent of 36% and 24%. For the number of 7 clicks, the percent is 18.3%. Compared to *Experiment1*, there are about 6.7% and 3.3% of total trails in *Experiment2* clicking 9 and 10 squares whereas no participants choose to draw secrets with 4 clicks. The situation is similar when compared to *Experiment3* (i.e., there are 7% trails constructing passwords using only 4 squares and no trail selecting 10 squares in *Experiment3*). The major reason is that most participants prefer to create passwords using multi-touch on the Android phone in which a single click of multi-touch can select two squares. By means of only 4 multi-touch clicks, a participant can easily draw a secret with 8 squares.

Feedback Result. We present several questions used in the *feedback step* and corresponding scores in Table 4. The scores in the table are simply average values calculated by the recorded scores of all participants.

The scores in the No.2 and No.3 questions indicate that, on the same platform of mobile phones, two schemes are accepted by most participants while most participants feel more comfortable to create passwords using the *multi-touch enabled CD-GPS scheme*. In comparison, the No.1 question receives a lower score of 7.5 with regard to the platform of a PC. Similarly, for the No.4, No.5 and No.6 questions, the *multi-touch enabled CD-GPS scheme* obtains the highest score of 9.2. This means that most participants

Table 3. The number of selected squares in *Experiment1*, *Experiment2* and *Experiment3*

# of selected squares	Experiment1	Experiment2	Experiment3
4 squares	32/300 (10.7%)	0	21/300 (7.0%)
5 squares	98/300 (32.6%)	35/300 (11.7%)	101/300 (33.7%)
6 squares	92/300 (30.7%)	108/300 (36.0%)	98/300 (32.7%)
7 squares	56/300 (18.7%)	55/300 (18.3%)	45/300 (15.0%)
8 squares	22/300 (7.3%)	72/300 (24.0%)	25/300 (8.3%)
9 squares	0	20/300 (6.7%)	10/300 (3.3%)
10 squares	0	10/300 (3.3%)	0

Table 4. Several questions and relevant scores in the user study

Questions	Score (average)
1. I could easily create a password in the Experiment1	7.5
2. I could easily create a password in the Experiment2	8.9
3. I could easily create a password in the Experiment3	8.0
4. The time consumption in the Experiment1 is acceptable	6.7
5. The time consumption in the Experiment2 is acceptable	9.2
6. The time consumption in the Experiment3 is acceptable	7.9
7. I prefer to use multi-touch	9.5
8. I do not prefer to use multi-touch	2.1

feel multi-touch can reduce the time consumption since they can increase the speed of selecting squares by using several multi-touch clicks. Regarding the No.7 and No.8 questions, participants advocate to create a password by means of multi-touch with a higher score of 9.5 while the score of the opposition is only 2.1.

These results of the feedback show that utilizing the action of multi-touch can further enhance the graphical password in the aspect of usability. In addition, users can increase the password entropy by using several multi-touch clicks.

Usability and Security Discussion. For the usability, the scores regarding *Experiment2* and *Experiment3* (these two experiments were conducted on the same platform) indicate that most participants prefer the *multi-touch enabled CD-GPS scheme* in which they can use multi-touch to create passwords more quickly and comfortably. Back to Table 2, it is visible that participants indeed perform better in *Experiment2* by utilizing the multi-touch with regard to each step of creation, confirmation and login. Overall, these results show that the action of multi-touch can enhance the usability of the *CD-GPS scheme* by speeding up the password input.

For the security, as we analyzed in Section 3, by integrating the multi-touch with only 2 fingers, the password space can be enlarged by $\frac{K_i!}{2!}$ times (K_i means the number of clicked squares). As shown in Table 3, participants are likely to click more squares in *Experiment2* than *Experiment3*. For example, there are about 3.3% trails clicking 10 squares to construct passwords in *Experiment2* whereas no participant clicks 10 squares in *Experiment3*. Also, there are 24% trails clicking 8 squares in *Experiment2* but only 8.3% trails in *Experiment3*. In addition, no participant chooses 4 squares to create their passwords in *Experiment2* while up to 7% trails clicking 4 squares in *Experiment3*. In this case, if a participant select 8 squares by means of multi-touch, the password space can be enlarged by $\frac{8!}{2!} = 20160$ times compared to the original *CD-GPS scheme*. On the whole, these results indicate that the action of multi-touch can generally enhance the security of the *CD-GPS scheme* because users are more likely to select larger number of squares to construct their passwords through remembering less number of touches on touchscreen devices such as mobile phones.

6 Related Work

In recent years, a number of graphical password schemes have been proposed aiming to enhance the user authentication [20]. Blonder [2] first designed a click-based graphical password scheme that users could generate their passwords by clicking on several pre-defined locations on an image. For authentication, users are demanded to re-click on the same locations. Then, graphical password based authentication systems like *PassPoints* system [22], *Story* scheme [6], *DAS* (Draw-a-secret) scheme [10], Cued Click Points (CCP) [4] and *Qualitative DAS* scheme [13] are developed on a common computer.

With the rapid development of mobile computing, more work of designing graphical passwords has been studied on a mobile device. Dunphy *et al.* [8] presented different challenges such as shoulder surfing and intersection attack in the field of graphical passwords, and investigated the deployment of recognition-based graphical password mechanisms on a mobile device. Their experiments showed that user acceptance was often driven by convenience and login durations of approximately 20 seconds were unattractive to many users. Kim *et al.* [12] evaluated a number of novel tabletop authentication schemes that exploit the features of multi-touch interaction in order to inhibit shoulder surfing. Later, Oakley and Bianchi [18] presented the feasibility of constructing a graphical password with multi-touch, but their work did not give a detailed analysis. De Luca *et al.* [5] recently presented an implicit approach to improve user authentication based on the way they perform an action on current mobile devices by means of unlock patterns. However, they have not studied the impact of multi-touch on creating passwords. Several recent work about biometrics based authentication and potential attacks on touch-enabled mobile phones can be referred to [1,15,21,23].

Different from the above work, in this paper, we mainly focus on the platform of a touchscreen mobile phone and attempt to explore the impact of multi-touch on the click-draw based graphical passwords in the aspect of usability and security. In the user study with 60 participants, we find that the action of multi-touch can generally enhance the construction of graphical passwords.

7 Conclusion and Future Work

Graphical passwords have been developed as a promising alternative to traditional text-based passwords. In real-world applications, we find that the creation of graphical passwords may be different on a computer and on a touchscreen mobile phone. That is, users can use more actions like multi-touch on a mobile phone than on a common computer (e.g., desktop computer).

In this work, we therefore attempt to enhance the creation of graphical passwords by using the action of multi-touch. In particular, we conducted a study of using the click-draw based graphical passwords (*CD-GPS*) in the evaluation, which combines the current input types in the area of graphical passwords and we further developed an example system of *multi-touch enabled CD-GPS scheme* on a mobile phone. We begin by analyzing the potential impact of multi-touch on computing the password space of *CD-GPS* and we then conducted a user study that was composed of three major experiments (named *Experiment1*, *Experiment2* and *Experiment3*) with totally 60 participants. *Experiment1* was performed on a desktop computer, while *Experiment2* and *Experiment3* were conducted on an Android phone. We later give a detailed analysis of success rate, completion time, the number of clicks and users' feedback in these experiments. The experimental results show that by integrating the action of multi-touch, the construction of graphical passwords can be further improved in the aspect of both security and usability, and that users are more likely to generate more secure passwords by remembering less number of touches on a mobile phone.

Our work is an early work in discussing the impact of multi-touch on creating the *CD-GPS* graphical passwords. The future work could include performing a even larger user study with much more participants to validate the results obtained in this work (e.g., a more systematic experiment) and discussing the implications of multi-touch on shoulder-surfing and smudge attacks. In addition, future work could also include conducting a further analysis of password patterns generated by participants with different ages to explore the effect of multi-touch, and integrating and evaluating more actions (e.g., rotate, scrolling) in creating graphical passwords on a mobile device.

Acknowledgments. We would like to thank all participants for their hard work in the experiments and thank all anonymous reviewers for their helpful comments.

References

1. Angulo, J., Wästlund, E.: Exploring Touch-Screen Biometrics for User Identification on Smart Phones. In: Camenisch, J., Crispo, B., Fischer-Hübner, S., Leenes, R., Russello, G. (eds.) Privacy and Identity 2011. IFIP AICT, vol. 375, pp. 130–143. Springer, Heidelberg (2012)
2. Blonder, G.: Graphical Passwords. United States Paten 5559961, Lucent Technologies, Inc. (1996)
3. Chiasson, S., Biddle, R., van Oorschot, P.C.: A Second Look at the Usability of Click-based Graphical Passwords. In: Proceedings of the 3rd Symposium on Usable Privacy and Security (SOUPS), pp. 1–12. ACM, New York (2007)
4. Chiasson, S., van Oorschot, P.C., Biddle, R.: Graphical Password Authentication Using Cued Click Points. In: Biskup, J., López, J. (eds.) ESORICS 2007. LNCS, vol. 4734, pp. 359–374. Springer, Heidelberg (2007)
5. De Luca, A., Hang, A., Brudy, F., Lindner, C., Hussmann, H.: Touch Me Once and I Know It's You!: Implicit Authentication based on Touch Screen Patterns. In: Proceedings of the 2012 ACM Annual Conference on Human Factors in Computing Systems (CHI), pp. 987–996. ACM, New York (2012)

6. Davis, D., Monrose, F., Reiter, M.K.: On User Choice in Graphical Password Schemes. In: Proceedings of the 13th Conference on USENIX Security Symposium (SSYM), pp. 151–164. USENIX Association, Berkeley (2004)
7. Dirik, A.E., Memon, N., Birget, J.-C.: Modeling User Choice in the Passpoints Graphical Password Scheme. In: Proceedings of the 3rd Symposium on Usable Privacy and Security (SOUPS), pp. 20–28. ACM, New York (2007)
8. Dunphy, P., Heiner, A.P., Asokan, N.: A Closer Look at Recognition-based Graphical Passwords on Mobile Devices. In: Proceedings of the Sixth Symposium on Usable Privacy and Security (SOUPS), pp. 1–12. ACM, New York (2010)
9. Gołofit, K.: Click Passwords under Investigation. In: Biskup, J., López, J. (eds.) ESORICS 2007. LNCS, vol. 4734, pp. 343–358. Springer, Heidelberg (2007)
10. Jermyn, I., Mayer, A., Monrose, F., Reiter, M.K., Rubin, A.D.: The Design and Analysis of Graphical Passwords. In: Proceedings of the 8th Conference on USENIX Security Symposium (SSYM), pp. 1–14. USENIX Association, Berkeley (1999)
11. Karlson, A.K., Brush, A.B., Schechter, S.: Can I Borrow Your Phone?: Understanding Concerns when Sharing Mobile Phones. In: Proceedings of the 27th International Conference on Human Factors in Computing Systems (CHI), pp. 1647–1650. ACM, New York (2009)
12. Kim, D., Dunphy, P., Briggs, P., Hook, J., Nicholson, J.W., Nicholson, J., Olivier, P.: Multi-Touch Authentication on Tabletops. In: Proceedings of the SIGCHI Conference on Human Factors in Computing Systems (CHI), pp. 1093–1102. ACM, New York (2010)
13. Lin, D., Dunphy, P., Olivier, P., Yan, J.: Graphical Passwords & Qualitative Spatial Relations. In: Proceedings of the 3rd Symposium on Usable Privacy and Security (SOUPS), pp. 161–162. ACM, New York (2007)
14. Meng, Y.: Designing Click-Draw based Graphical Password Scheme for Better Authentication. In: Proceedings of IEEE International Conference on Networking, Architecture, and Storage (NAS), pp. 39–48 (2012)
15. Meng, Y., Wong, D.S., Schlegel, R., Kwok, L.-F.: Touch Gestures Based Biometric Authentication Scheme for Touchscreen Mobile Phones. In: Kutyłowski, M., Yung, M. (eds.) INSCRYPT 2012. LNCS, vol. 7763, pp. 331–350. Springer, Heidelberg (2013)
16. Millennial Media. Mobile mix: The mobile device index (September 2012), http://www.millennialmedia.com/research
17. Nelson, D.L., Reed, V.S., Walling, J.R.: Pictorial Superiority Effect. Journal of Experimental Psychology: Human Learning and Memory 2(5), 523–528 (1976)
18. Oakley, I., Bianchi, A.: Multi-Touch Passwords for Mobile Device Access. In: Proceedings of the 2012 ACM Conference on Ubiquitous Computing (UbiComp), pp. 611–612. ACM, New York (2012)
19. Shepard, R.N.: Recognition Memory for Words, Sentences, and Pictures. Journal of Verbal Learning and Verbal Behavior 6(1), 156–163 (1967)
20. Suo, X., Zhu, Y., Owen, G.S.: Graphical Passwords: A Survey. In: Proceedings of the 21st Annual Computer Security Applications Conference (ACSAC), pp. 463–472. IEEE Computer Society, USA (2005)
21. Trewin, S., Swart, C., Koved, L., Martino, J., Singh, K., Ben-David, S.: Biometric Authentication on A Mobile Device: A Study of User Effort, Error and Task Disruption. In: Proceedings of the 28th Annual Computer Security Applications Conference (ACSAC), pp. 159–168 (2012)
22. Wiedenbeck, S., Waters, J., Birget, J.-C., Brodskiy, A., Memon, N.: Passpoints: Design and Longitudinal Evaluation of A Graphical Password System. Int. J. Hum.-Comput. Stud. 63(1-2), 102–127 (2005)
23. Zhang, Y., Xia, P., Luo, J., Ling, Z., Liu, B., Fu, X.: Fingerprint Attack against Touch-enabled Devices. In: Proceedings of the 2nd ACM Workshop on Security and Privacy in Smartphones and Mobile Devices (SPSM), pp. 57–68 (2012)

Applying DAC Principles to the RDF Graph Data Model

Sabrina Kirrane[1,2], Alessandra Mileo[1], and Stefan Decker[1]

[1] Digital Enterprise Research Institute
National University of Ireland, Galway
http://www.deri.ie
firstname.lastname@deri.ie
[2] Storm Technology, Ireland
http://www.storm.ie

Abstract. In this paper we examine how Discretionary Access Control principles, that have been successfully applied to relational and XML data, can be applied to the Resource Description Framework (RDF) graph data model. The objective being to provide a baseline for the specification of a general authorisation framework for the RDF data model. Towards this end we provide a summary of access control requirements for graph data structures, based on the different characteristics of graph models compared to relational and tree data models. We subsequently focus on the RDF data model and identify a list of access rights based on SPARQL query operations; propose a layered approach to authorisation derivation based on the graph structure and RDFSchema; and demonstrate how SQL GRANT and REVOKE commands can be adapted to cater for delegation of privileges in SPARQL.

1 Introduction

A *Data Model* is an abstraction used to represent real world entities, the relationship between these entities and the operations that can be performed on the data. Database models can be broadly categorised as relational, tree and graph based. An important requirement for any of Database Management Systems (DBMSs) is the ability to protect data from unauthorised access. An *Access Control Model* is a blueprint for defining authorisations which restrict access to data. Discretionary Access Control (DAC), Mandatory Access Control (MAC) and Role Based Access Control (RBAC) are the predominant access control models both found in the literature and used in practice. In this paper we focus specifically on DAC and examine how it can be used to restrict access to RDF data. We base our work on the DAC model as: it has been successfully adopted by several relational DBMS vendors; because of its inherent flexibility; and its potential for handling context based authorisations in the future.

Several researchers have investigated how to add access control to RDF data. Existing approaches can be categorised as ontology based [9, 23], rules based and [15, 11, 18] and inference based [15, 20, 16, 21, 1]. In previous work, which would

L.J. Janczewski, H.B. Wolfe, and S. Shenoi (Eds.): SEC 2013, IFIP AICT 405, pp. 69–82, 2013.
© IFIP International Federation for Information Processing 2013

also be categorised as inference based, we demonstrated how Annotated RDF can be used to propagate permissions assigned to triples based on RDFSchema [19]. We proposed a number of rules that can be used for the derivation of access rights based on subject, access rights and resource hierarchies [22]. In this paper, we examine the specification, derivation and delegation of access control over RDF graph data guided by DAC principles and experiences applying these principles to the relational and tree based data models. Based on our analysis, we make the following contributions:(i) discuss how DAC principles can be used to restrict access to RDF data; (ii) describe how the graph structure can be used to derive implicit access rights; (iii) propose a set of rules that are necessary for derivation of authorisations based on RDFSchema; and (iv) demonstrate how SQL grant and revoke commands can be adapted to manage RDF authorisations. Together these contributions provide a solid building block for DAC policy enforcement for the RDF data model.

The remainder of the paper is structured as follows: In Section 4 we discuss related work. Section 2 describes how DAC is used to restrict access to relational and tree based data models. Issues applying DAC to graph data are discussed and possible handling mechanisms are proposed in Section 3. Finally, we conclude and outline directions for future work in Section 5.

2   Preliminaries

DAC policies limit access to data resources based on access rules stating the actions that can be performed by a subject. The term *subject* is an umbrella term used to collectively refer to users, roles, groups and attribute-value pairs. In DAC access to resources are constrained by a central access control policy, however users are allowed to override the central policy and can pass their access rights on to other users [25], known formally as delegation. Over the years the DAC model has been extended to consider: constraint based authorisations (e.g. time, location); access to groups of users, resources and permissions; support for both positive and negative authorisations; and conflict resolution mechanisms [24]. In this section we describe how DAC is used to protect relational and tree based data models.

2.1   Applying DAC to the Relational Model

In the relational model (Fig.1), data items are grouped into *n-ary relations*. A relation header is composed of a set of named data types known as *attributes*. The relation body is in turn made up of zero of more *tuples* i.e. sets of attribute values. A *primary key*, composed of one or more attributes which uniquely identifies each tuple, is defined for each relation. Relations are connected when one or more attributes (i.e. a *foreign key*) in a relation are linked to a primary key in another relation. Relations can be categorised as base relations or views. Base relations are actually stored in the database whereas views are virtual relations derived from other relations. Views are commonly used to: (i) provide access to

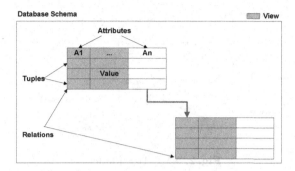

Fig. 1. Relational Data Model

information from multiple relations; (ii) restrict access to particular attributes or tuples; and (iii) derive data (e.g. sum, average, min and max).

In relational databases access is restricted both at a schema level (database, relations and attributes) and a data level (tuples and values). The access rights themselves are tightly coupled with database operations such as SELECT, INSERT, UPDATE, DELETE and DROP. In addition the GRANT privilege allows users to grant access to others based on their own privileges. Griffiths and Wade [14] describe how DAC is implemented in System R [3] an experimental DBMS developed to carry out research on the relational data model. Two of the underpinning principles of DAC are derivation of implicit authorisations from explicit authorisations and the delegation of access rights.

Authorisations explicitly defined at schema level are implicitly inherited by other database entities, for example (i) database authorisations are inherited by all database resources; (ii) relation authorisations are inherited by all tuples; and (iii) attribute authorisations are inherited by all attribute values. Aside from Schema level derivations Griffiths and Wade [14] describe how views can be used to implicitly grant access to one or more tables, attributes or tuples spanning multiple relations. Under DAC database users are granted sole ownership of the tables and views that they create. They can subsequently grant access rights to other database users. Griffiths and Wade [14] and Bertino et al. [8] discuss how the revocations process is complicated due to recursive delegation of permissions and propose algorithms which are used to revoke access rights.

2.2   Applying DAC to the Tree Model

In the tree model data is organised into a hierarchical structure with a single root *node*. Each data item, represented as a node, is composed of one or more *attributes*. Relations are connected via parent-child links: whereby each parent can have many children, however each child can have only one parent. Both object-oriented databases and the Extensible Markup Language (XML) are examples of the tree model. In the remainder of this section, we focus on XML however it is worth noting that the core derivation and delegation principles can also be applied to other instances of the tree data model.

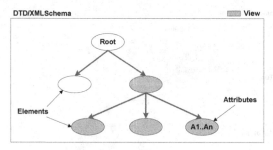

Fig. 2. XML Tree Model

In an XML data model (Fig.2) relations are represented as *elements* that can contain textual information and zero or more *attribute-value* pairs. Simple elements contain data values whereas complex data types are constructed from other elements and/or attributes giving XML it's hierarchical structure. A Document Type Definition (DTD) or an XMLSchema describe the structure of an XML document. In contrast to the relational model, XML data is not necessarily an instance of some schema.

Bertino et al. [6] describe how DAC is implemented in Author-X a prototype developed to demonstrate how access control policies can be applied to XML documents, that may or may not conform to a DTD/XMLSchema, exposed on the web. Similar to the relational model, tree based access control can also be specified at both schema and data levels. From a schema perspective access can be restricted based on the structure of the document/data item, a DTD or an XMLSchema. Whereas data level restrictions can be applied to specific elements and attributes. Similar to the relational model the access rights reflect the operations commonly performed on an XML document for example READ, APPEND, WRITE, DELETE and INSERT.

Propagation of authorisations based on the is-part-of relationship between documents, elements, sub-elements and attributes is one of the key features of DAC for XML [5]. Although implicit authorisations simplify access control administration, a knock on effect is that exceptions need to be catered for. In XML inheritance chains can be broken by explicitly specifying authorisations for leaf nodes. In addition, a combination of positive and negative authorisation can be used to grant access in the general case and deny access for specific instances. The introduction of negative authorisation brings with it the need for conflict resolution mechanisms (e.g. denial takes precedence). Gabillon [13] describes how delegation of privileges can be adapted to work for XML databases. The author defines a security policy language for XML which incorporates SQL GRANT and REVOKE commands.

3   Applying DAC to RDF

In this section we describe how the graph data model differs from the tree data model. We discuss how DAC can be applied to graph-based data and detail

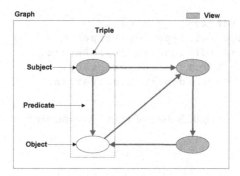

Fig. 3. RDF Graph Model

the implication such structural differences have on access control in general. Although in this paper we focus on RDF specifically a number of observations can be applied to other graph data models.

3.1 The RDF Data Model

The graph data model extends the tree model by allowing each *node* to have multiple parent relations, resulting in a generalized *graph* structure. Undirected and directed binary relationships between nodes are represented as *edges* and *arcs* respectively. In a directed graph the node from which an arc originates is called the *head* and the destination the *tail*. Graphs differ from trees in several aspects, for example: a graph doesn't have a top or bottom; a node can have more than one parent; a node can be its own ancestor; and multiple paths between nodes are permissible. The graph data model is often used where information about the graph topology is just as important as the data itself. An overview of several graph based models is provided by Angles and Gutierrez [2].

The RDF graph model is designed to represent knowledge in a distributed manner. RDF captures the semantics of data and presents it in a machine readable format. *Uniform Resource Identifiers* (URIs) in turn are used to uniquely identify data items. The fundamental building block of the RDF data model (Fig.3) is an RDF *triple* which constitutes a statement about the relationship between two nodes. An RDF triple is represented as a tuple $\langle S, P, O \rangle \in$ **UB** $\times$ **U** $\times$ **UBL** [1], where S is called the *subject*, P the *predicate*, and O the *object* and U, B and L, are used to represent **URIs**, **blank nodes** and **literals** respectively. The following triples represented using N3 [2] use the FOAF [3] vocabulary, a subset of which is presented in Fig. 4, to state that the JoeBloggs is a person who's first name is Joe and lastname is Bloggs:

```
entx:JoeBloggs rdf:type foaf:Person.
entx:JoeBloggs foaf:givenName "Joe".
entx:JoeBloggs foaf:lastName "Bloggs".
```

---

[1] For conciseness, we represent the union of sets simply by concatenating their names.
[2] http://www.w3.org/TeamSubmission/n3/
[3] FOAF Vocabulary Specification, http://xmlns.com/foaf/spec/

```
1   foaf:Person rdf:type rdfs:Class.
2   foaf:givenName rdf:type rdf:Property.
3   foaf:givenName rdfs:domain foaf:Person.
4   foaf:lastName rdf:type rdf:Property.
5   foaf:lastName rdfs:domain foaf:Person.
```

Fig. 4. Subset of FOAF Vocabulary

```
1    entx:G1 {
2      entx:salary rdf:type rdf:Property.
3      entx:salary rdfs:domain foaf:Person.
4      entx:JoeBloggs rdf:type foaf:Person.
5      entx:JoeBloggs foaf:givenName "Joe".
6      entx:JoeBloggs foaf:lastName "Bloggs".
7      entx:JoeBloggs entx:salary "40000".
8      entx:MayRyan rdf:type  foaf:Person.
9      entx:MayRyan foaf:givenName "May".
10     entx:MayRyan foaf:lastName "Ryan".
11     entx:MayRyan entx:salary "80000".
12   }
```

Fig. 5. Snapshot of Enterprise Employee Data

RDFSchema is a set of classes and properties used to describe RDF data. Unlike XMLSchema, RDFSchema does not describe the structure of an RDF graph. Instead RDFSchema provides a framework used by *vocabularies* (known formally as *ontologies*) to describe classes, properties and relations.

In RDF there is a tight coupling between the schema and instance data. Unlike the relational and XML data models classes, properties and instances cannot be identified based on the structure alone. Like XML, *Namespaces* are used to uniquely identify a collection of RDF resources. Prefixes are used as a shorthand notation for ontology Namespaces. In this paper, we use the following ontologies RDF, RDFSchema(RDFS), FOAF and a sample enterprise ontology:

```
@prefix rdf:  <http://www.w3.org/1999/02/22-rdf-syntax-ns#> .
@prefix rdfs: <http://www.w3.org/2000/01/rdf-schema#> .
@prefix foaf: <http://xmlns.com/foaf/0.1/> .
@prefix entx: <http://urq.deri.org/enterprisex#> .
```

An RDF *graph* is a finite set of RDF triples. *Named graphs* are used to collectively refer to a number of RDF statements. In this paper we use TriG [4], an extension of N3, which uses curly brackets to group triples into multiple graphs identifiable by a URI (Fig.5). In practice the triple and the named graph are stored as *quads*.

---

[4] http://www.w3.org/2010/01/Turtle/Trig/

3.2 Graph Based and Schema Based Authorisations

The first step in the identification of access control requirements for RDF data is to identify the resources that need to be protected and the access rights required. The graph data model alone is quite limiting when it comes to the management of access rights. Therefore in Section 3.3, we examine how RDFSchema can be used to define more expressive authorisations.

RDF Resources. From a data perspective access can be restricted to a node (subject or object), an arc (property), two connected nodes (triple), a collection of nodes and edges (multiple triples that share a common subject) or arbitrary views of the data (named graphs). Whereas from a schema perspective authorisations can be applied to classes and properties. Given the tight coupling between schema and data items, authorisations based on classes (e.g. `foaf:person`) and properties (e.g. `foaf:givenName`) would need to be derived using schematic vocabulary such as RDFSchema or Web Ontology Language (OWL) [5]. In Section 3.3, we examine how permissions can be derived based on both the graph structure and RDFSchema.

Access Rights. The access rights of both the relational and XML data models are very similar and differ primarily by vocabulary. SPARQL proposes several operations similar to ones that exist for relational and XML data (`SELECT`, `INSERT`, `DELETE/INSERT`, `DELETE` and `DROP`). However SPARQL also defines a number of additional query operations (`CONSTRUCT`, `ASK` and `DESCRIBE`) and a number of operations specifically for graph management (`CREATE`, `COPY`, `MOVE` and `ADD`). Notable omissions from the list of SPARQL operations are the `GRANT` and `REVOKE` commands which allows users to *grant access to* or *revoke access from* others access based on their own privileges. In Section 3.4 we discuss how the grant and revoke operations could be accommodated in SPARQL.

Access Control Policy. An *Access Control Policy* details the actual authorisations and access restrictions to be enforced. Each authorisation is represented as a quad $\langle Sub, Acc, Sign, Res \rangle$ where Sub denotes the *subject* (not to be confused with an RDF triple subject), Acc the *access rights*, $Sign$ indicates if the user is *granted* or *denied* access and Res represents the *resource* to be protected (i.e. rdf quad with optional variables, represented using a ? prefix, in any position). A matrix outlining the access rights that are appropriate for each operation (represented by an X) is provided in Table 1. For conciseness two connected nodes is abbreviated to *Con*, a collection of nodes and edges to *Col* and RDF properties to *Prop*. A sample access control policy is in turn presented in Table 2. Each authorisation is labelled (A_n) to ease referenceability. (A_1), (A_2) and (A_3) grant access rights SELECT, INSERT and DELETE to the graph *entx:G1*, (A_4) grants access to a particular class and (A_5) denies access to the salary property.

---

[5] http://www.w3.org/TR/owl2-overview/

Table 1. Relationship between Access Rights and Resources

Rights	Node	Arc	Con.	Col.	View		Prop.	Class
SELECT	X	X	X	X	X		X	X
CONSTRUCT	X	X	X	X	X		X	X
ASK	X	X	X	X	X		X	X
DESCRIBE	X	X	X	X	X		X	X
INSERT			X					
DELETE			X					
DROP					X			
CREATE					X			
COPY					X			
MOVE					X			
ADD					X			
GRANT			X		X		X	X
REVOKE			X		X		X	X
		Data Model					Schema	

Table 2. Sample Access Control Policy

	Sub	Rights	Sign	Res
(A_1)	Mgr	SELECT	+	`?S ?P ?O entx:G1`
(A_2)	Mgr	INSERT	+	`?S ?P ?O entx:G1`
(A_3)	Mgr	DELETE	+	`?S ?P ?O entx:G1`
(A_4)	Emp	SELECT	+	`?S rdf:type rdf:Class entx:G1`
(A_5)	Emp	SELECT	-	`entx:salary rdf:type rdf:Property entx:G1`

If no explicit or implicit policy exists it is possible to adopt either a closed policy (deny access by default) or an open policy (grant access by default).

3.3 Derivation of Authorisations

In both the relational model and the tree model authorisations can be derived based on the data schema. When it comes to the RDF data model similar derivations are highly desirable as they simplify authorisation administration. Existing RDF database vendors adopt a view based approach to derivation, organising triples into named graphs based on the access control requirements and granting access to the entire graph. Although similar to views in relational databases in this instance the graph is materialised. An alternative approach would be to derive permissions based on the graph structure. However as it isn't possible to distinguish between schema and instance data such an approach alone is quiet limited. Therefore we propose an additional layer of derivations based on a vocabulary such as RDFSchema to define rules that leverage the semantic relations between nodes and edges. In the following rules both the premises (above the line) and the conclusion (below the line) are represented as a 5 tuple

$\langle S, P, O, \gamma, \lambda \rangle$. Where: (i) S represents a *subject*, P a *predicate* and O an *object* (together they represent a triple); (ii) γ is used to denote a named graph (which may or may not be the same for each triple); and (iii) λ is used to represent permissions i.e. *authorisation subject*, *access rights* and *sign* attributes $\langle Sub, Acc, Sign \rangle$. By including the named graph in the derivation rules it is possible to constrain the derivation to a particular graph or alternatively to span multiple graphs. Such graphs in turn can be distributed across multiple data sources.

Derivation Based on the Graph Structure. Similar to the tree model we could assign permissions to a node and recursively derive authorisations for all nodes connected to it by arcs. Another approach would be to derive authorisations for all nodes along a particular path. Existing graph search algorithms, such as those proposed by Tarjan [26], could be used to recursively traverse the graph and assign permissions to the nodes. A thorough investigation into the application of graph traversal and access control is proposed in future work.

Derivation Based on RDFSchema. One limitation of the RDF data model is that it isn't possible to distinguish between schema and instances from the graph structure alone. For example to restrict access to attributes we would need a means to derive permissions for all instances of a particular property type. Likewise to restrict access to a relation we would need to derive permissions for all properties that are instances of a particular class. To accommodate schema based derivation a combined data approach to derivation is warranted. The following rules can be used to derive access rights based on the RDFSchema vocabulary.

Rule 1. Using this rule we can derive λ, which has been assigned to a class, for all instances of that class.

$$\frac{?X \; \texttt{rdf:type} \; \texttt{rdf:Class} \; \gamma \; \lambda, \; ?Z \; \texttt{rdf:type} \; ?X \; \gamma, \; ?Z \; ?Y \; ?A \; \gamma}{?Z \; ?Y \; ?A \; \gamma \; \lambda} \quad \text{(R1)}$$

Rule 2. In this rule, λ which has been assigned to a property of a class, is derived for all instances of that property.

$$\frac{\begin{array}{c} ?X \; \texttt{rdf:type} \; \texttt{rdf:Class} \; \gamma, \; ?Y \; \texttt{rdf:type} \; \texttt{rdf:Property} \; \gamma \; \lambda, \\ ?Y \; \texttt{rdfs:domain} \; ?X \; \gamma, \; ?Z \; ?Y \; ?A \; \gamma \end{array}}{?Z \; ?Y \; ?A \; \gamma \; \lambda} \quad \text{(R2)}$$

Rule 3. The following rule propagates λ, assigned to an instance of a class, to property values associated with that instance.

$$\frac{\begin{array}{c} ?X \; \texttt{rdf:type} \; \texttt{rdf:Class} \; \gamma, \; ?Z \; \texttt{rdf:type} \; ?X \; \gamma \; \lambda, \\ ?Y \; \texttt{rdfs:domain} \; ?X \; \gamma, \; ?Z \; ?Y \; ?A \; \gamma \end{array}}{?Z \; ?Y \; ?A \; \gamma \; \lambda} \quad \text{(R3)}$$

Table 3. Snapshot of Derived Authorisations

	Sub	Rights	Sign	Obj
(DA_1)	Emp	SELECT	+	`entx:JoeBloggs rdf:type foaf:Person entx:G1`
(DA_2)	Emp	SELECT	+	`entx:JoeBloggs foaf:givenName "Joe" entx:G1`
(DA_3)	Emp	SELECT	+	`entx:JoeBloggs foaf:lastName "Bloggs" entx:G1`
(DA_4)	Emp	SELECT	+	`entx:JoeBloggs entx:salary "40000" entx:G1`
(DA_5)	Emp	SELECT	+	`entx:MayRyan rdf:type foaf:Person entx:G1`
(DA_6)	Emp	SELECT	+	`entx:MayRyan foaf:givenName "May" entx:G1`
(DA_7)	Emp	SELECT	+	`entx:MayRyan foaf:lastName "Ryan" entx:G1`
(DA_8)	Emp	SELECT	+	`entx:MayRyan entx:salary "80000" entx:G1`
(DA_9)	Emp	SELECT	-	`entx:JoeBloggs entx:salary "40000" entx:G1`
(DA_{10})	Emp	SELECT	-	`entx:MayRyan entx:salary "80000" entx:G1`

Given a snapshot of the FOAF ontology (Fig. 4), a subset of an enterprise RDF dataset (Fig. 5) and a sample access control policy (Table. 2), we can derive additional authorisations such as those summarised in Table 3. (DA_1) to (DA_8) were derived by applying (R1) to (A_4). Whereas (DA_9) and (DA_{10}) were inferred from (R2) and (A_5).

Two additional rules which use the `rdfs:subclass` (R4) and `rdfs:subproperty` (R5) properties are proposed to demonstrate flexibility that can be gained from RDFSchema. More expressive rules based on richer vocabularies such as OWL could also be used. The database should be flexible enough to allow derivations to be turned on and off on a case by case basis.

Rule 4. In this rule we use the RSFSchema subclass inheritance mechanism to derive the permissions λ assigned to a class for all subclasses.

$$?X \text{ rdf:type rdf:Class } \gamma \ \lambda, \ ?Y \text{ rdf:type rdf:Class } \gamma, \ ?Y \text{ rdfs:subClassOf } ?X \ \gamma$$
$$?Y \text{ rdf:type rdf:Class } \gamma \ \lambda$$

$$(R4)$$

Rule 5. Similar to the above rule however in this instance we use the subproperty inheritance to derive the permissions λ assigned to a property for all subproperties.

$$?X \text{ rdf:type rdf:Property } \gamma \ \lambda, \ ?Y \text{ rdf:type rdf:Property } \gamma,$$
$$?Y \text{ rdfs:subPropertyOf } ?X \ \gamma$$
$$?Y \text{ rdf:type rdf:Property } \gamma \ \lambda$$

$$(R5)$$

3.4   Delegation of Access Rights

In both relational and XML databases GRANT and REVOKE commands are used to manage delegation of access rights. The SPARQL 1.1 update language does not currently support the GRANT and REVOKE commands. It thus needs to be extended to cater for authorisation administration and delegation of access rights. We propose an adapted version of the SQL GRANT (Def.1) and REVOKE (Def.2) commands that caters for named graphs. We adopt the USING NAMED clause from other SPARQL 1.1 operations.

```
( USING ( NAMED )? IRIref )*
```

In addition in keeping with standard SPARQL we adapt the syntax of the GRANT OPTION replacing surrounding [] with () and a ? which indicates cardinality.

```
(WITH GRANT OPTION)?
```

Privilege_name denotes the privileges identified in Section 3.1 (SELECT, CONSTRUCT, ASK, DESCRIBE, INSERT, DELETE/INSERT, DELETE, DROP, COPY, MOVE, ADD). Resource_name represents one or more instances of the following RDF resources (NAMED GRAPH, CLASS, PROPERTY, TRIPLE). User_name, role_name, attribute_value are used to identify users, roles and attributes respectively and a reserved word PUBLIC is used to assign access to all users. Finally the WITH GRANT OPTION is used to provide users with the ability to delegate the access right(s) to others.

Definition 1 (GRANT command).

```
GRANT privilege_name
( USING ( NAMED )? IRIref )*
ON resource_name
TO {user_name |PUBLIC |role_name |attribute_name}
(WITH GRANT OPTION)?;
```

Definition 2 (REVOKE command).

```
REVOKE privilege_name
( USING ( NAMED )? IRIref )*
ON resource_name
FROM {user_name |PUBLIC |role_name |attribute_value_pair}
```

As revocation is not dependent on the data model existing approaches, such as cascading [12, 14] and non-cascading [7], devised for relational databases would also work for rdf databases (datastores).

3.5 Conflict Resolution

Conflicts can occur as a result of inconsistent: explicit; derived; and delegated policies. Samarati [24] discusses the need for different conflict resolution depending on the situation. Earlier in this section, we proposed a number of derivation rules to ease RDF access control administration and stated that implicit authorisations should be overridden by explicit authorisations. It is important that the conflict resolution strategy proposed is in keeping with both the derivation rules and overriding mandate. In this paper, we propose three complementary approaches to conflict resolution that fit well with DAC: (i) *explicit policies override implicit policies* (ensures that positive explicit authorisations will always prevail over negative implicit authorisations); (ii) *most specific along a path takes precedence* (allows users to grant access in the general case and deny access for specific instances); and (iii) *denial takes precedence* (caters for scenarios where we have a conflict between two explicit or two implicit authorisations). In Section 3.3, we seen how derivation rules can result in conflicting authorisations, for example Table 3 (DA_4) and (DA_9) or (DA_8) and (DA_{10}). As both policies are implicit the *explicit policies override implicit policies* strategy is not applicable. In this instance the negative authorisation would prevail based on the *most specific along a path takes precedence*, as a policy assigned to a property is more specific than one applied to a class.

4 Related Work

Both Costabello et al. [9] and Sacco et al. [23] propose access control vocabularies and frameworks that can be used to enforce access control policies over RDF Data. In both instances the authors provide a filtered view of data using SPARQL ask queries. However the authors do not perform any reasoning over the access control policies they propose.

Other researchers adopt a rule based approach to access control. Dietzold and Auer [11] define access control requirements from a Semantic Wiki perspective. The authors propose a filtered data model using a combination of SPARQL queries and SWRL rules. Li et al. [18] also adopt a rule based approach providing users with a more intuitive way to specify access control policies. Both Dietzold and Auer [11] and Li et al. [18] use rules to give a more explicit meaning to the access control policies as opposed to authorisation derivation in our case.

Several reseachers Qin and Atluri [20], Javanmardi et al. [16], Ryutov et al. [21], Amini and Jalili [1] propose access control models for RDF graphs and focus on policy propagation and enforcement based on semantic relations. None of the authors examine access control from either a data model or a database perspective. Similar to us, Jain and Farkas [15] derive authorisations and propose conflict resolution mechanisms. They adopt a multilevel label-based approach to access control where policies are specified in terms of RDF patterns associated with an instance, a schema and a security classification. The derivations they propose are however limited to RDFSchema entailment rules.

Only Jain and Farkas [15] and Javanmardi et al. [16] actually mention DAC and even then they just describe DAC and do not examine how their approach compares or contrasts. A number of authors who use Semantic Technology for access control however do not apply their approach to the RDF data model, detail their support for DAC Kodali et al. [17], Damianou et al. [10], Berners-Lee et al. [4]. However to the best of our knowledge to date no one has investigated the application of DAC to the RDF data model. We fill this gap by examining how DAC has been used to protect the relational and tree data models and by proposing strategies that allow us to apply DAC to the RDF graph model. We identify the resources to be protected and the access rights required, based on the RDF data model and SPARQL [6] the predominant RDF query language respectively. In addition we propose mechanisms to assist with access control administration through derivation of authorisation, delegation of permissions and conflict resolution

5   Conclusions and Future Work

Although the RDF data model has been around for over a decade, little research has been conducted into the application of existing access control administration to RDF data. In this paper we discussed how the DAC model could be applied to RDF, a distributed graph based data model. We identified the resources to be protected and the access rights required based on the graph data model and SPARQL query operations respectively. We proposed a layered approach to authorisation derivation based on the graph structure and RDFSchema. We subsequently identified a number of rules that can be used to manage authorisations in an intuitive manner. Furthermore we demonstrated how SQL GRANT and REVOKE commands could be adapted to cater for authorisation administration over RDF data. As for future work, we propose to further investigate how enforcement of access control policies can be improved by exploiting the graph data structure and to examine complexity issues related to management of authorization over graph data.

Acknowledgements. This work is supported in part by the Science Foundation Ireland under Grant No. SFI/08/CE/I1380 (Lion-2), the Irish Research Council for Science, Engineering and Technology Enterprise Partnership Scheme and Storm Technology Ltd. We would like to thank Nuno Lopes and Aidan Hogan for their valuable comments on the paper.

References

1. Amini, M., Jalili, R.: Multi-level authorisation model and framework for distributed semantic-aware environments. IET Information Security 4(4), 301 (2010)
2. Angles, R., Gutierrez, C.: Survey of graph database models. Computing Surveys 1(212) (2008)
3. Astrahan, M.M., Blasgen, W., Chamberlin, D.D., Eswaran, K.P., Gray, J.N., Griffiths, P.P.: System R: Relational Management Approach to Database 1(2), 97–137 (1976)
4. Berners-Lee, T., Weitzner, D.J., Hendler, J.: Creating a Policy-Aware Web: Discretionary, Rule-based Access for the World Wide Web. Web and Information Security (2006)
5. Bertino, E., Sandhu, R.: Database security - concepts, approaches, and challenges. IEEE Transactions on Dependable and Secure Computing 2(1), 2–19 (2005)
6. Bertino, E., Castano, S., Ferrari, E.: Securing XML documents with Author-X. IEEE Internet Computing 5(3), 21–31 (2001)

---

[6] http://www.w3.org/TR/sparql11-update/

7. Bertino, E., Samarati, P., Jajodia, S.: Authorizations in relational database management systems. In: Proceedings of the 1st ACM Conference on Computer and Communications Security, CCS 1993, pp. 130–139 (1993)
8. Bertino, E., Samarati, P., Jajodia, S., Member, S.: An Extended Authorization Model for Relational Databases 9(1), 85–101 (1997)
9. Costabello, L., Villata, S., Delaforge, N.: Linked data access goes mobile: Context-aware authorization for graph stores. In: 5th WWW Workshop on Linked Data on the Web, LDOW (2012)
10. Damianou, N., Dulay, N., Lupu, E., Sloman, M.: The ponder policy specification language. In: Sloman, M., Lobo, J., Lupu, E. (eds.) POLICY 2001. LNCS, vol. 1995, pp. 18–38. Springer, Heidelberg (2001)
11. Dietzold, S., Auer, S.: Access control on RDF triple stores from a semantic wiki perspective. In: ESWC Workshop on Scripting for the Semantic Web (2006)
12. Fagin, R.: On an authorization mechanism. ACM Transactions on Database Systems (TODS) 3(3), 310–319 (1978)
13. Gabillon, A.: An authorization model for XML databases. In: Proceedings of the 2004 Workshop on Secure Web Service, SWS 2004, pp. 16–28 (2004)
14. Griffiths, P.P., Wade, B.W.: An authorization mechanism for a relational database system. ACM Transactions on Database Systems (TODS) 1(3), 242–255 (1976)
15. Jain, A., Farkas, C.: Secure resource description framework: an access control model. In: ACM SACMAT, pp. 121–129 (2006)
16. Javanmardi, S., Amini, M., Jalili, R., GanjiSaffar, Y.: SBAC: A Semantic Based Access Control Model. In: 11th Nordic Workshop on Secure IT-systems (NordSec 2006), Linkping, Sweden (2006)
17. Kodali, N., Farkas, C., Wijesekera, D.: Multimedia access control using RDF metadata (2003)
18. Li, H., Zhang, X., Wu, H., Qu, Y.: Design and application of rule based access control policies. In: Proc. of the Semantic Web and Policy Workshop, pp. 34–41 (2005)
19. Lopes, N., Kirrane, S., Zimmermann, A., Polleres, A., Mileo, A.: A Logic Programming approach for Access Control over RDF. In: Technical Communications of ICLP 2012 (2012)
20. Qin, L., Atluri, V.: Concept-level access control for the Semantic Web. In: Proceedings of the 2003 ACM Workshop on XML Security, XMLSEC 2003, p. 94. ACM Press (2003)
21. Ryutov, T., Kichkaylo, T., Neches, R.: Access Control Policies for Semantic Networks. In: 2009 IEEE International Symposium on Policies for Distributed Systems and Networks, pp. 150–157. IEEE (July 2009)
22. Kirrane, S., Lopes, N., Mileo, A., Decker, S.: Protect Your RDF Data! In: Proceedings of the 2nd Joint International Semantic Technology Conference (2012)
23. Sacco, O., Passant, A., Decker, S.: An Access Control Framework for the Web of Data. In: 10th International Conference on Trust, Security and Privacy in Computing and Communications (2011)
24. Samarati, P., de Capitani di Vimercati, S.: Access control: Policies, models, and mechanisms. In: Focardi, R., Gorrieri, R. (eds.) FOSAD 2000. LNCS, vol. 2171, pp. 137–196. Springer, Heidelberg (2001)
25. Sandhu, R.S., Samarati, P.: Access control: principle and practice. IEEE Communications Magazine (1994)
26. Tarjan, R.: Depth-First Search and Linear Graph Algorithms. SIAM Journal on Computing 1(2), 146–160 (1972)

A Lightweight Gait Authentication on Mobile Phone Regardless of Installation Error

Thang Hoang[1,3], Deokjai Choi[1], Viet Vo[1], Anh Nguyen[1], and Thuc Nguyen[2]

[1] ECE, Chonnam National University, Gwangju, South Korea
dchoi@jnu.ac.kr
[2] DKE, Ho Chi Minh University of Science, Ho Chi Minh City, Vietnam
ndthuc@fit.hcmus.edu.vn
[3] FIT, Saigon Technology University, Ho Chi Minh City, Vietnam
thang.hoangminh@stu.edu.vn

Abstract. In this paper, we propose a novel gait authentication mechanism by mining sensor resources on mobile phone. Unlike previous works, both built-in accelerometer and magnetometer are used to handle mobile installation issues, including but not limited to disorientation, and misplacement errors. The authentication performance is improved by executing deep examination at pre-processing steps. A novel and effective segmentation algorithm is also provided to segment signal into separate gait cycles with perfect accuracy. Subsequently, features are then extracted on both time and frequency domains. We aim to construct a lightweight but high reliable model; hence feature subsets selection algorithms are applied to optimize the dimension of the feature vectors as well as the processing time of classification tasks. Afterward, the optimal feature vector is classified using SVM with RBF kernel. Since there is no public dataset in this field to evaluate fairly the effectiveness of our mechanism, a realistic dataset containing the influence of mobile installation errors and footgear is also constructed with the participation of 38 volunteers (28 males, 10 females). We achieved the accuracy approximately 94.93% under identification mode, the FMR, FNMR of 0%, 3.89% and processing time of less than 4 seconds under authentication mode.

Keywords: gait authentication, identification, pattern recognition, behavioural biometric, mobile accelerometer, mobile security.

1 Introduction

The explosion of mobility nowadays is setting a new standard for information technology industry. Mobile devices sales skyrocketed over recent years. A survey on the mobile market[1] showed that there were six billion subscriptions by the end of 2011. Technology constantly evolves and creates more intelligent devices. Their abilities are not only limited in calling, or texting, but also cover a

---

[1] Report of the Wireless Intelligence Company [J. Gillet, "Wireless Intelligence: Global mobile connections surpass 6 billion by year-end", 2011].

L.J. Janczewski, H.B. Wolfe, and S. Shenoi (Eds.): SEC 2013, IFIP AICT 405, pp. 83–101, 2013.
© IFIP International Federation for Information Processing 2013

variety of utilities, including portable storage and business applications, such as e-commerce or m-banking [2].

However, misperceiving mobile devices as an absolutely safe repository to store critical information could make owners face up to security issues. Such devices can be easily lost, stolen, or illegally accessed [1], which makes sensitive or/and important information of mobile owners become vulnerable (see more [1]). Consequently, authentication settings have evolved to become a more priority issue. The most widely-used authentication methods in mobile currently are PINs, visual patterns, and passwords because of their ease in use and implementation. However, these methods are not always effective considering remembrance and security aspects [1]. Implementations on physiological biometric could overcome this issue completely [3]. However, it is hard to deploy them on mobile phone since existing mobile resources would not guarantee to acquire specialized data such as iris, fingerprint, etc. properly. Similar to other active authentications like PIN and password, physiological biometrics also cause time consuming which is one of the main obstacles preventing users from using these techniques. They forced us to pay attention and perform explicit gestures to be authenticated (e.g. typing passphrases, facing to the front camera, etc.). This causes obtrusiveness and inconvenience in frequent use.

Thus, a friendlier and reliable authentication mechanism which can operate implicitly without users awareness is desired to be found and aimed to ameliorate mobile security. Recently, a novel approach using wearable sensors to authenticate human gait has been introduced and achieved potential results [11, 13]. Accordingly, sensors are attached to human body in various positions such as pocket, waist and footgear to record physical locomotion. This approach takes advantage of modern mobile devices sensing capabilities including GPS, accelerometer, magnetometer, gyroscope sensor, etc. Moreover, devices are usually put in their owners' pockets for most of the day [1], so gaits can be authenticated implicitly and continuously by acquiring walking signals. For this reason, sensor-based gait authentication has a significant advantage in implementation on mobile. It will provide developers with an edge over improving various techniques in authentication.

The above potentialities of wearable sensor authentication motivated us to improve and establish a similar mechanism running on mobile. Since 2009, this study has been initiated on mobile and achieved encouraging results [8, 19]. However, they were still in early stages and methods were tried-out on ideal conditions in which mobiles were always installed at an exact position and orientation by tightening directly to equipment such as suite, footgear, or human body. Processing steps such as segmentation and noise elimination which could directly affect the recognition model were not analyzed in depth. Finally, there was no evaluation of the possibility of running authentication directly on mobile devices. Authentication tasks were assigned to powerful computers rather than mobile resources. An excessively complex model could face up to critical challenges when it is deployed under limited computational capabilities.

In this paper, we focus on finding solutions to deal with existing matters: (1) To handle mobile installation issues, we introduce a novel lightweight but effective calibration method by taking full advantage of existing sensors on modern mobile phone. (2) Gait preprocessing phases are investigated thoroughly to improve the effectiveness of authentication mechanism. A novel segmentation algorithm which could segment acquired data into well separated gait cycles is also presented. (3) To make sure the authentication model can run smoothly and independently under limited computational resources on mobile phone, we apply some techniques to reduce the processing time of learning algorithm. A scenario is also designed to construct a particular dataset under more realistic conditions to fairly evaluate our proposed model. We perform our study on both authentication and identification modes. The impacts of mobile installation errors and processing steps to the authentication model are analyzed deeply. Finally, the authentication is deployed directly on the mobile phone to experiment the possibility of running such model with limited computational resources. With promising results achieved from the experiment, solving installation issues and providing a novel lightweight reliable gait authentication are our main contributions.

The rest of this paper is organized into 4 sections. Section 2 presents state of the art in which we summarize typical previous studies related to sensor-based gait authentication. Section 3 presents our proposed authentication model. Section 4 summaries our experimental results. Finally, conclusions will be presented in Section 5.

2   State of the Art

Human gait has been considered as a particular style and manner of moving human feet and hence contains the information of identity authentication. In a more detailed level view, the mechanism of human gait involves synchronization between the skeletal, neurological and muscular system of human body [4]. In 2005, H. Ailisto et al. were the first to propose the gait authentication using wearable sensor [13] and this area was further expanded by Gafurov et al. [10]. In general, sensors are attached to various positions on human body to record locomotion signal. Various sensors are experimented including gyroscope, rotation sensor but acceleration sensor (or accelerometer) is the most commonly used. In this field, there are two typical approaches: (1) Template Matching (TM) and (2) Machine Learning (ML). In (1), acquired signal is preprocessed and then split into patterns. Best patterns which represent the most characteristics of the subject are considered as representative gait templates. They are then stored as referred templates corresponding to individual. Various distance metrics such as Dynamic Time Warping (DTW) [9, 14, 19], Euclidean distance [8, 9], autocorrelation [13], nearest neighbors [11] are used for calculating the similarity score between a given pattern and referred templates.

Second method is the most popular approach used in pattern recognition areas. In this approach, gait signal is segmented into patterns. On each pattern, features are extracted in time domain, frequency domain, and wavelet domain or by special techniques such as time delay embedding [18]. Extracted feature vectors are then classified using supervised classifiers like HMM [16], SVM [14, 15, 17, 18, 20], ANN [5], LDA [5]. Some other works propose hybrid approaches in which either distance metrics such as DTW [7], Euclidean [10, 12], are used to measure the similarity scores of features extracted in time and frequency domains, or similarity scores of gait templates can be considered as features which are used for classification [6].

In early stages, most of works used standalone sensors (SSs) have been implemented with a variety of success rate, they still have some restrictions. For example, SSs is relatively expensive and the interface of some special sensors needs to be developed separately. Thus, there is an increasing need to develop an easy-to-operate gait monitoring system within pervasive and ubiquitous environment. Recently, the developing of micro electromechanical (MEMs) technology helped such sensors to be miniaturized and integrated inside mobile devices (known as mobile sensors - MS). Gait authentication has been initially experimented on MS during recent years. In 2010, J. Frank et al. [18] used HTC G1 cell phone with built-in accelerometer attached at the trouser pocket position to collect gait signal. By using time-delay embedding combined with SVM classifier, they achieved a perfect recognition rate of 100%. In comparison to SSs, MSs are designed to be cheaper, simpler and as a result the quality is not guaranteed as SSs. For example, the sampling rate is low and unstable (<50Hz vs. >100Hz), the noise is rather high. Derawi et al. [19] pointed up that impact by redid Holien's work [21] using MS instead of SS and achieved EER of 20.1% compared to 12.9%. Table 1 summarized gait authentication approaches and their performances with various evaluation metrics such as Equal Error Rate (EER), Recognition Rate (RR), etc. on both SS and MS.

3   Methodology

We pay particular attention to the position of mobile device. It is put freely inside the trouser pocket. This position turns out to be the most appropriate for the mobile phone bearer [1]. The authentication method is implemented by machine learning approach. Acquired gait signal is precisely segmented into patterns containing a sequence of gait cycles using our segmentation algorithm. Features are then extracted in time and frequency domains. Subsequently, feature subset selection algorithms are applied to find the best feature subset giving the most accuracy rate as well as reducing feature dimension. Finally, Support Vector Machine (SVM) classifier is applied to obtain the last model. A detailed description of milestones in gait authentication will be explained in the following.

3.1   Data Acquisition

We perform our study on a Google Android HTC Nexus One mobile phone. The authentication mechanism is constructed based on gait signal acquired by a built -in accelerometer. Acceleration forces acting on the phone are measured in three

Table 1. State of the art gait authentication using Standalone (S) and Mobile sensor (M) including Accelerometer (A), Rotation Sensor (R) by approaches: Template Matching (TM), Machine Learning (ML) and Hybrid (H)

Previous Works	Sensor/ Sampling rate	Location	Methods	No. Subjects	Results
[14]	MA / 27Hz	T Pocket	TM, ML	11	79.1%, 92.7% RR
[6]	SA / 50Hz	Ankle	H	22 (16M 6F)	3.03% EER
[5]	9 SR	Body	ML (LDA)	30 (25M 5F)	100% RR
[15]	MA	T Pocket	ML (SVM)	36	HTER: 10.1%
[7]	SA / 40Hz	Ankle	H	22	3.27% EER
[16, 17]	MA / 120Hz	Hip	ML (HMM)	48 (30M 18F)	6.15% EER, 5.9%
	MA / 45Hz		ML (SVM)		FMR, 6.3%FNMR
[8]	SA / 100Hz	Ankle	TM (Euclidean)	10	20% EER
[18]	MA / 25 Hz	T Pocket	ML (SVM)	25	100% RR
[9]	SA / 100Hz	Hip	TM (PCA)	60(43M 17F)	1.6% EER
[19]	MA / 45Hz	Hip	TM (DTW)	51 (41M 10F)	20% EER
[20]	MA / 37Hz	Hip	ML (SVM)	6	90.3 3.2% RR
[10]	SA / 16Hz, 100Hz	Ankle	H (Euclidean)	21 (12M 9F)	5% EER
		Pocket	H (Manhattan)	100 (70M 30F)	7% EER
		Arm		50(33M 17F)	10% EER
		Hip		30 (23M 7 F)	13% EER
[11]	SA / 100Hz	Body	TM(NN)	30	96.7% RR
[12, 13]	SA / 256Hz	Waist	TM(cross-corr.), H (FFT, histogram)	36 (19M 17F)	6.4 %, 10%, 19% EER

spatial dimensions ($X, Y,$ and Z as illustrated in figure 1(a)) when subjects are walking. Based on the relationships between gravity, acceleration and motion, we present the output of accelerometer as 3-component vectors

$$A = [a_X, a_Y, a_Z] \tag{1}$$

where a_X, a_Y, a_Z represent the magnitude of the acceleration forces acting on three directions respectively.

Because of the accelerometers characteristics, its sensing is very sensitive to mobile installation. Normally in fact, it is impossible to ensure the phone will always be at a fixed orientation and position all the time without additional accessories. Two issues could occur concurrently: (1) misplacement and (2) disorientation errors (figure 1(b-d)). From our observation, the impact of misplacement does not significantly affect accelerometers sensing axes once it is put in the trouser pocket. It is easily solved without exploiting more information.

Looking into the case of disorientation error, as accelerometer senses acceleration forces acting on three dimensions of the phone, acquired signals will be contaminated if it is not always fixed correspondingly to its bearer. Acceleration vectors should always be represented in a constantly referred coordination system instead of an unstable one (mobile coordinate system in this case). To do this, an additional built-in magnetometer is used along with the accelerometer. In our study, Earth is considered as the referred context. A rotation matrix is calculated based on the yaw, pitch, and roll angles which represent the angle

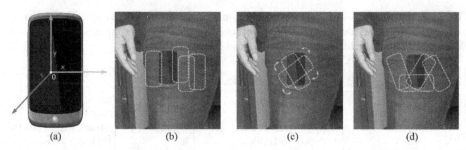

Fig. 1. (a) Mobile coordinate system, (b) misplacement error, (c) disorientation error and (d) both cases

changes between mobile and Earth coordinate system. These angles are determined by the combination of magnetometer and accelerometer.

In summary, two kinds of information are determined to construct an effective gait authentication model: (1) yaw, pitch and roll angles determined before users start to walk and (2) gait signal of individuals. A scenario to acquire these values is explained meticulously in section 4.2.

3.2   Data Pre-processing

Signal Transformation
As gait signals of individuals are acquired with arbitrary installations. Thus, the first step is standardizing raw signals to eliminate the impacts of disorientation and misplacement errors.

Disorientation Errors Elimination
Denote $A = [a_X \ a_Y \ a_Z]$ as the raw acceleration vector corresponding to mobile coordinate system. To transform the acceleration vector A to acceleration vector $A' = [a'_X \ a'_Y \ a'_Z]$ corresponding to the Earth coordinate system, we multiply A by a rotation matrix R as following

$$A' = A \cdot R \tag{2}$$

The rotation matrix R is calculated from yaw (α), pitch (β), roll (γ) angles, which represent three composed rotation that move an unstable frame C_M (mobile coordinate) to a given referred context C_E (Earth coordinate). In other words, α, β, γ angles denote the angles of rotating C_M about α, β, γ respectively. The rotation matrix R can be formulated as

$$R(\alpha, \beta, \gamma) = \begin{pmatrix} \cos\alpha\cos\beta & \cos\alpha\cos\beta\sin\gamma - \sin\alpha\cos\gamma & \cos\alpha\sin\beta\cos\gamma + \sin\alpha\sin\gamma \\ \sin\alpha\cos\beta & \sin\alpha\sin\beta\sin\gamma + \cos\alpha\cos\gamma & \sin\alpha\sin\beta\cos\gamma - \cos\alpha\sin\gamma \\ -\sin\beta & \cos\beta\sin\gamma & \cos\beta\cos\gamma \end{pmatrix} \tag{3}$$

Note that we assume once mobile device is fixed on a rigid body, its orientation is kept unchanged with respect to that of the rigid body during walking. This means the relative position between C_M and C_E is also unchanged. Thus, the three angles and R are constant.

Theoretically, the phone should be calibrated according to its bearers context. Its purpose aims to make sure accelerometer will precisely sense gait signals in 3 dimensions corresponding to subjects walking direction. However, it is such a challenge to determine the relative position of mobile phone and its bearer with limited existing mobile resources. There is a restriction when considering Earth coordinate system as the fixed context. In this method, mobile orientation is calibrated to make the phone always parallel to the ground. Its Z-axis points toward the sky and perpendiculars to the ground. Therefore, Z-axis coincides with bearers upright. X and Y axes are always tangential to the ground and point towards the East and the magnetic North Pole respectively (figure 2(a)). Acceleration forces acting on each X and Y axis will be sensed imperfectly.

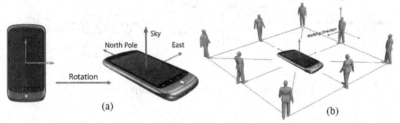

Fig. 2. (a) Mobile orientation after applying rotation matrix, (b) the relative position between the phone and its wearer

However, this minor limitation does not adversely affect our mechanism. We found that although the gait signals recorded at X or Y axis are imperfect, the total acceleration forces of these two axes are guaranteed to be accurate. Thus, calibrating Z-signal precisely is necessary and efficient in this step. The authentication is constructed regardless of discretely calibrating X and Y axis signals.

Misplacement Errors Elimination
When the phone is put in the subjects trouser pocket, it lays around his/her thigh. From our observation, walking is a slow activity with a moderate fluctuation. Consequently, any strong acceleration is likely to last no longer than a few tenths of a second. Furthermore, once the phone is placed close to a joint of the leg, output signals are dominated by gravitational signals [22]. The influence of misplacement in this case is not considerable and it can be reduced by applying a low-pass filter to eliminate detail components in the signal. This filter is described in the following section.

Time Interpolation and Noise Elimination
As the mobile accelerometer is power saving designed to be simpler than standalone sensors, its sampling rate is not stable and entirely depends on mobile OS. The time interval between two consecutive returned samples is not a constant. The sensor only outputs value when the forces acting on each dimension have a significant change. The sampling rate of our device is approximately 27 Hz. Therefore, acquired signal is interpolated to 32 Hz using linear interpolation to ensure that the time interval between two samplepoints will be fixed.

When accelerometer samples movement data by user walking, some noises will inevitably be collected. These additional noises came from various sources (e.g., idle orientation shifts, screen taps, bumps on the road while walking). Moreover, mobile accelerometer produces numerous noises compared with standalone sensors since its functionality is fully governed by mobile OS layer. A digital filter needs to be designed to eliminate noises and reduce the impact of misplacement error concurrently. Multi-level wavelet decomposition and reconstruction method are adopted to filter the signal.

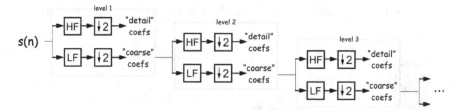

Fig. 3. Multi-level wavelet decomposition

According to figure 3, original signal is denoted by $S(n)$. High-pass filter and low-pass filter are denoted by HF and LF. Within each level, the outputs from high-pass filter are known as detail coefficients. On the other hand, low-pass filter outputs contain most of the information of the input signal. They are known as coarse coefficients. The signal is down-sampled by 2 at each level. Coefficients obtained from the low-pass filter are used as the original signal for the next level, and this process continues until the desired level is achieved.

In contrast, reconstruction is the reverse of decomposition process. To eliminate noises, we assign the detail coefficients to 0. The reconstruction of the signal is computed by concatenating the coefficients of high-frequency with low-frequency. In this study, the Daubechies orthogonal wavelet (Db6) with level 2 is adopted for reducing noise and eliminating the impact of misplacement error simultaneously.

3.3   Data Segmentation

Segmentation is the most important step that could directly affect to the quality of learning algorithms. As already stated, gait authentication is based on walking style of individuals. Meanwhile walking is a cyclic activity. Acquired signal should be segmented according to gait cycles instead of a fixed time interval (e.g. 5 or 10 seconds) like previous works [15–17].

Gait cycle is defined as the time interval between two successive occurrences of one of the repetitive events when walking [23]. In other words, two consecutive steps form a gait cycle. As shown in figure 4, the cycle starts with initial contact of the right heel, and then it will continue until the right heel contacts the ground again. The left goes through exactly the same series of events as the right, but displaced in time by half a cycle.

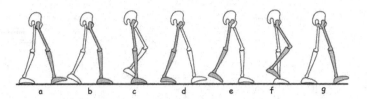

Fig. 4. Illustration of a gait cycle

When the subject walks, the movement of thigh will be from back to front. In addition, at the time the heel touches the ground in phase "a" or phase "g" as in figure 4, the association between ground reaction force and inertial force together make the transformed Z-axis signal strongly change and form negative peaks with absolute high magnitudes. These peaks are considered as marking points used to distinguish separated gait cycles. From our previous work [14], we designed an algorithm to detect these points. The algorithm filters noisy peaks based on a threshold calculated by mean and standard deviation. However, we recently observed that this threshold is not always robust especially in case subject walks with light steps. In this case, marking points are not displayed vividly. Thus, we improve the segmentation capability by applying an additional autocorrelation algorithm to estimate the approximate time gap tg between two consecutive gait cycles. Unlike previous works, tg is assumed to oscillate around a pre-defined fixed range [7, 19]. In fact, such range is not robust since user can walk with arbitrary velocities. tg should be dynamically calculated based on each characteristic of the gait signal.

First, the autocorrelation algorithm is applied to the transformed Z-axis data to determine the regularity of the signal.

$$A_m = \sum_{i=1}^{N-|m|} x_i x_{i+m} \tag{4}$$

where A_m is the autocorrelation coefficient, x_i is the time series data point, x_{i+m} is the time-lagged replication of the time series.

Then A_m is normalized to $[0,1]$ by dividing to A_0.

$$A_m = \frac{A_m}{A_0} \quad \text{with} \quad A_0 = \sum_{i=1}^{N} x_i^2 \tag{5}$$

Figure 5(a) illustrates autocorrelation coefficients A which represent the regularity of the walking signal. The approximate time gap of gait cycles is determined by the gap between two red peaks in which the first one correspond with A_0. The remaining A_k is detected by a designed peak detection algorithm.

$$tg = t(A_k) \tag{6}$$

where $t(i)$ is the time-lagged of point i.

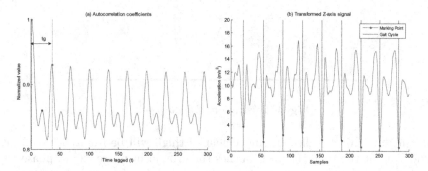

Fig. 5. (a) Auto-correlation coefficients with the estimated tg, (b) detected marking points in Z-signal

Algorithm 1. Gait Signal Segmentation

Input: Time series of transformed Z-axis gait signal S_Z, number of gait cycles (GCs) n per segment, number of overlapping gait cycles o with $n = ok, k \in \mathbb{N}$

Output: sets of separated segments M_i, M_i contains n consecutive GCs and overlaps o GCs with M_{i-1}

1. Extract set of negative peaks P using $T = \mu + k\sigma$ as described in [14] on S_Z.
2. Calculate the auto-correlation coefficients A_m of S_Z using Eq. 5
3. Find A_k and calculate the time gap t between gait cycles using Eq. 6
4. Filter unusual peaks in P based on their positions and values
for (each peak p in P) **do**
   if (position_of(p) − position_of($p − 1$) < αt) **then**
      if value_of(p) < value_of($p − 1$) **then**
         remove(p)
      else
         remove($p − 1$)
      end if
   else if (position_of(p) − position_of($p − 1$) < βt) **then**
      if position_of($p + 1$) − position_of(p) < γt **then**
         remove(p)
      else
         remove($p + 1$)
      end if
   else
      remove(p)
   end if
end for
5. Extract gait cycles GCs based on filtered P. $GC(i) = \langle S \rangle_{pos(p_i)}^{pos(p_{i+1})}$
6. Remove unusual GCs if their length is significant unlike t to obtain best gait cycles
7. Combine n consecutive GCs to form a segment
for ($i = 0, j = 0$; $j < length(GCs)n$; $i{+}{+}, j{+}{=}\,o$) **do**
   $M_i = \langle GC \rangle_j^{j+n}$
end for
return M_i

Denotes $P = p_i$ as the set of negative peaks[2] obtained when passing through a filter described in [14]. From Eq. 6, the distance between two marking points is estimated to be a definite amount of tg. Unusual peaks in P which do not fall to these positions are excluded to obtain the optimal set of marking points P' (figure 5(b)). The segmentation procedure is summarized as in Algorithm 1.

In this algorithm, user-defined values such as α, β, γ are estimated from experiment to precisely determine position of peaks representing the beginning of a gait cycle in all cases (e.g. $\alpha = 0.25, \beta = 0.75, \gamma = 0.16$ was used in our work). From our study, gait signal is segmented into separated patterns in which each pattern contains $n = 4$ consecutive gait cycles and overlap $n/2$ gait cycles from the previous one. Features are extracted in every separated pattern on both time and frequency domains to obtain feature vectors used for classification.

3.4   Feature Extraction and Classification

In this stage, three phases are investigated to obtain an optimal classification model: First, possible features on both time and frequency domains are extracted on 3 types of acceleration data including Z-axis signal a_Z, magnitude $m_{XYZ} = \sqrt{a_X^2 + a_Y^2 + a_Z^2}$ and sum of acceleration forces of $X - Y$ axes $m_{XY} = \sqrt{a_X^2 + a_Y^2}$. As discussed in section 3.2, $X - Y$ signals could not be distinguished with current limited resources on mobile devices. Hence, we consider the sum of forces acting simultaneously on both axes. Second, feature subset selection algorithms are applied for obtaining the best feature set. Feature subsets are selected based on the accuracy criterion of the learning algorithm. Finally, the best feature subsets are classified using Support Vector Machine (SVM) classifier with Radial Basis Function (RBF) kernel.

Time Domain Features
We extract features which can represent characteristics of gait signal in time domain including

- Average maximum acceleration
$$avg\_max = mean(\max(GC_i))_{i=0}^{n} \quad (7)$$

- Average minimum acceleration
$$avg\_min = mean(\min(GC_i))_{i=0}^{n} \quad (8)$$

- Average absolute difference
$$avg\_abs\_diff = \sum_{i=1}^{N} |x_i - \bar{x}| \quad (9)$$

- Root Mean Square
$$RMS = \frac{1}{N}\sum_{i=1}^{N} x_i^2 \quad (10)$$

- 10-bin histogram distribution
$$his\_dist = \langle n_j \rangle_0^9$$
with $n_j = \dfrac{\sum_i x_i}{size(bin_j)}$ where
$$\frac{j\Delta_j}{10} \leq x_i \in bin_j < \frac{(j+1)\Delta_j}{10}, \quad (11)$$
$$\Delta_j = \max - \min$$

- Standard deviation
$$\sigma = \sqrt{\frac{1}{N-1}\sum_{i=1}^{N} |x_i - \bar{x}|} \quad (12)$$

---

[2] Negative peaks are defined oppositely with peaks pre-defined in [14]. Negative peaks are data points that its value is lower than its predecessor and successor.

- Waveform length

$$wl = \sum_{i=1}^{N-1} |x_{i+1} - x_i| \qquad (13)$$

where x_i is the data point in time series of a segment, n is the number of gait cycles GC in the segment, N is the total number of data point in the segment.

These features above are extracted on 3 types of signal including a_Z, m_{XYZ} and m_{XY}

- Cadence period

$$T_{cad} = \frac{\sum_{i=1}^{n} l(GC_i)}{n} \qquad (14)$$

- Cadence frequency

$$f_{cad} = \frac{n}{\sum_{i=1}^{n} l(GC_i)} \qquad (15)$$

where $l(GC_i)$ is the length of gait cycle i.

Frequency Domain Feature

- 40 first FFT coefficients

$$fft = \langle X_k \rangle_{k=0}^{39} \quad \text{where} \quad X_k = \sum_{n=0}^{N-1} x_n e^{-\frac{j2\pi kn}{N}} \qquad (16)$$

- 40 first DCT coefficients

$$dct = \langle X_k \rangle_{k=0}^{39} \quad \text{where} \quad X_k = \frac{1}{2}x_0 + \sum_{n=1}^{N-1} x_n \cos\left[\frac{\pi}{N} n \left(k + \frac{1}{2}\right)\right] \qquad (17)$$

Similar to features on time domains, these coefficients are extracted on a_Z, m_{XYZ} and m_{XY}. As stated before, the walking speed of users in fact is not absolutely constant. Hence, the length of gait cycles is not stable. Calculating coefficients on frequency domain (e.g. FFT, DCT) requires window frames (or patterns) have the same fixed length. Meanwhile, the length of gait cycles fluctuates slightly around time gap tg calculated in section 3.3. As a result, the number of data points in every gait cycle needs to be normalized by using our proposed algorithm [14] to make sure the frequency coefficients are calculated properly.

Feature Subset Selection
Total 29 features are extracted in both time and frequency domains. However concatenating whole features to form a final feature vector whose dimension is grown up to be supreme not only require a lot of computational tasks but also return a suboptimal result. Only features that are highly discriminative between each individual should be selected. We applied algorithms using hill-climbing strategies to select the best feature subset from the feature pool.

Sequential Forward Selection (SFS) Algorithm
SFS algorithm was originally proposed by Whitney [25]. The idea of SFS algorithm is to determine the best feature from the feature pool which increases the most classification accuracy and concatenate it to the current feature vector at

Table 2. Feature subset(s) selection using SFS and SFFS algorithms

#	SFS Algorithm		SFFS Algorithm	
	Feature	Accuracy (%)	Feature	Accuracy (%)
1	dct_{XYZ}	75.27	dct_{XYZ}	75.27
2	dct_{XY}	88.67	dct_{XY}	88.67
3	his_dist_Z	90.86	his_dist_Z	90.86
4	wf_{XY}	92.52	fft_{XY}	91.70
5	wf_Z	93.29	fft_{XYZ}	93.62
6	avg_min_{XYZ}	93.43	$avg\_abs\_diff_{XYZ}$	94.01
7	dct_Z	93.50	dct_Z	94.25
8	T_{cad}	93.73	$avg\_abs\_diff_{XY}$	94.46
9	fft_{XY}	94.04	$avg\_abs\_diff_Z$	94.67
10	fft_{XYZ}	94.64	f_{cad}	94.69
11	$avg\_abs\_diff_{XYZ}$	94.78	avg_min_Z	94.81
12	avg_max_Z	94.90	avg_max_Z	94.85
13	——	——	wl_{XYZ}	94.92

each step. SFS algorithm performs a greedy optimization in the feature space. However, the main drawback of this algorithm is called "nesting effect" in which discarded features will not be picked anymore. Hence, a local maximum of the feature space is usually found only.

Sequential Floating Forward Selection (SFFS) Algorithm
SFFS algorithm [24] is the improvement of SFS to avoid nesting effect. In SFFS, a new feature is determined and concatenated to the current feature vector using the SFS strategy. Additionally, there is a backward phase to recheck to current feature vector after concatenating a new feature. Features in the selected set are conditionally excluded and moved back to feature pool until no improvement is achieved to the previous sets.

Table 2 illustrates the most significant feature subset selected by SFS and SFFS algorithms. The feature vector is initialized by empty. Each row represents a selected feature that increases the classification accuracy rate. By applying SFS and SFFS separately, the number of final feature subsets is reduced from 29 to 12 and 13 respectively. This is not only help to reduce processing time and computational tasks of learning and prediction but also ameliorate the classification accuracy. It will be shown more from our experiment.

4   Experiments

4.1   Data Collection Scenario

We experimented on data collected from built-in accelerometer and magnetometer in Google Nexus One mobile phone[3]. The sampling rate of both sensors is

---

[3] Access   http://www.gsmarena.com/htc_google_nexus_one-3069.php   for   its specification.

approximately 27 Hz by setting to SENSOR_DELAY_FASTED mode on Android SDK. In this study, we would like to construct a more realistic dataset. In reality, two main factors including the effect of footgear and mobile installation often occur that could significantly affect gait of individuals. Hence, a scenario is designed to construct the dataset in which acquired gaits are collected under the influence of such factors. During experiment process, each volunteer will wear all three types of footgear including sleeper, sandal and shoe. The scenario is designed as following:

- *Preparation* (1st) *phase:* Volunteers wear 1 of 3 footgear types and put the mobile phone in their trouser pocket according to any position and orientation. Subsequently, they will be asked to stand still for few seconds. During this time, the accelerometer and the magnetometer will be activated to collect values for determining yaw, pitch and roll angles. Subsequently, the rotation matrix will be calculated and stored inside mobile storage for acceleration vector transformation later.
- *Collection* (2nd) *phase:* After the rotation matrix is stored successfully, volunteers will perform walking activity around 36 seconds on the ground floor. They will be asked to walk as naturally as possible. During this time, accelerometer will be activated to collect gait signals.

A total of 38 volunteers including 28 males and 10 females with the average age from 24 to 28 participated to our dataset construction. Each volunteer will perform around 18 laps. Each lap includes two phases above. Before starting a new lap, they will change the footgear and install the mobile to another orientation and position. Note that since the transformation matrix is always estimated in the preparation phase before volunteers start walking. Hence we have a constraint that when volunteers perform walking, the mobile will not change its position and orientation. To ensure that, we ask volunteers to wear trousers having the narrow pocket (e.g. the jean trouser). Totally, we acquired 24624 seconds walk of 38 volunteers.

4.2   Overall Gait Identification Result

Total 8500 patterns are extracted from the dataset by using our segmentation algorithm. Around $\frac{8500}{38}$ patterns corresponding to each volunteer are split into two separated parts. The first part is used for training *(T-part)* and the remaining is used for prediction *(P-part)*. We used libsvm[4] [26] as the tool to perform SVM with RBF kernel. The performance of RBF kernel fully depends on selecting parameters (C, γ). In order to construct an optimal SVM model, we perform a strategy to find the good (C, γ) yielding the best classification result. Features described in section 3.4 are extracted on both *T-part* and *P-part*. To deal with over-fitting issue, 10-fold cross validation is applied on *T-part* with various (C, γ). The (C, γ) yielding the best cross validation accuracy will be selected. According to [26], we tried exponentially growing sequences of C and γ to identify the

---

[4] Software available at http://www.csie.ntu.edu.tw/~cjlin/libsvm

'coarse' pair first $C = 2^{-5}, 2^{-4}, 2^{-3}, \ldots, 2^{15}$ and $\gamma = 2^{-15}, 2^{-14}, 2^{-13}, \ldots, 2^{3}$. Subsequently, a more detailed search is performed to identify a finer (C_f, γ_f) yielding an optimal cross-validation accuracy. The best $(C_f, \gamma_f) = (2^{3.5}, 2^{-5.25})$ is identified at the cross-validation accuracy of 98.71%. Then, whole T-part is trained again using (C_f, γ_f) to obtain the final SVM model. An overall accuracy rate approximately 94.93% is achieved when using such model to predict T-part. Figure 6(a) illustrates the confusion matrix of prediction result.

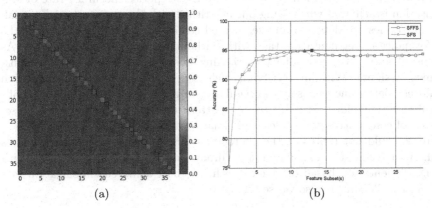

(a)   (b)

Fig. 6. (a) Confusion matrix of the gait recognition using SVM and RBF kernel with $C = 2^{3.5}, = 2^{-5.25}$, (b) the classification accuracy of various amounts of feature subsets by applying SFFS and SFS algorithm

Additionally, by applying the SFS and SFFS algorithm, the dimension of feature vectors is reduced and the classification accuracy is slightly increased as well. The processing time is also ameliorated significantly (table 3 and figure 6(b)). By applying SFFS, the prediction time only costs 411 ms per sample using mobile resources. In authentication mode, a task requires to predict on 9 consecutive samples (discussed in 4.3). It costs less than 4 seconds to make a decision. This is an acceptable level compared to original case ($\approx$ 20 seconds). Note that processing time is very important in mobile applications since we aim to deploy a lightweight authentication model running directly on mobile phone. Nowadays, it is likely to be optimized by its weight, power and size rather than computational power (e.g. CPU, memory). Hence reducing feature dimension will help the mobile device to perform classification task more quickly so that the interaction between the phone and its user is also improved.

Table 3. The performance of reducing feature dimension versus non-reducing case

	No. Subsets	Accucary	Loading Time	Prediction Time
Original	29	94.34%	205897 ms	2280 ms
SFS	12	94.90%	86799 ms	398 ms
SFFS	13	94.93%	84223 ms	411 ms

4.3   Impacts of Installation Error

Before discussing the impact of mobile installation, we first compare the performance of segmentation based on gait cycles against previous studies used fixed
size segmentation [15–17]. Since walking is a regularly cyclic activity, it is relatively easy to perceive that segmentation based on gait cycle always yields a
better classification result compared with based on a fixed length (table 4(a)).

Second, we analyze the impacts of installation errors to segmentation algorithm and the classification accuracy. Note that a perfect accuracy rate of segmentation is achieved when using our algorithm with the transformed Z-signal.
All gait cycles are detected and segmented correctly. Table 4(b) illustrates the
performance of segmentation task with/without fixing disorientation error. As
discussed above, the periodicity of walking is only represented well in transformed Z-signal. Without rectifying such issues, the segmentation algorithm
could not determine precisely the regularity of gait cycles caused by Z-signal's
instability. Therefore, each segmented pattern could not only represent a sequence of consecutive gait cycles well. That leads features extracted from these
patterns could not represent the characteristics of walking style of individuals
well. As a result, the classification accuracy rate is contaminated. Even with
using segmentation based on fixed length, the best achieved classification rate
at length = 3000ms is also worse (79.53%).

Table 4. (a) Improvements of segmentation based on gait cycles compared with fixed
length, (b) the influence of disorientation error to the effectiveness of classification
mode

(a)

Segmentation method		Accuracy
Fixed length	3000ms	87.88%
	6000ms	87.78%
	9000ms	84.73%
Gait cycle	2 gait cycles	92.26%
	4 gait cycles	94.93%
	8 gait cycles	90.94%

(b)

Segmentation method	Fixing dis-orientation	Accuracy
Fixed length	No	79.53%
Our algorithm	No	84.03 %
	Yes	94.93%

4.4   Authentication Result

The difference between authentication and identification is that authentication
performs binary classification tasks meanwhile identification performs multi-class
tasks. Based on the achieved results in identification, we also do an experiment
on authentication to determine how effective of our mechanism when it operates
under authentication mode. Since the unbalance of imposter vs. genuine data
(37 imposter vs. 1 genuine for each genuine person) could negatively affect the
performance of classification tasks [27]. Hence, we will rearrange the data to
make it fit to $\frac{3}{1}$ $\left(\frac{imposter\ data}{genuine\ data}\right)$ ratio corresponding to each genuine. To make a
fair evaluation, selecting imposter data will be based on ascending order of the

most misidentification in confusion matrix as shown in figure 6(a). For example, subject '1' is misidentified mostly with subjects '26', '2' and '24'. Hence, data of '26', '2' and '24' will be prior to be selected as imposters of subject 1 first. The remaining ones are selected randomly from the set of remaining subjects to achieve the ratio of 3:1.

As illustrated in figure 7, we achieved the False-Match-Rate (FMR) perfectly (0%). However, the False-Not-Match-Rate (FMNR) is still unacceptable (19.35%). In authentication, FMR and FMNR reflect the reliability and the friendliness of the system respectively. The problem that causes the high FMNR is the unbalance of imposter data vs. genuine data (3:1) issue. That would lead true genuine is recognized as imposter frequently. To reduce the FMNR without increasing FMR, we apply a scheme that is similar to [16]. From our dataset, we can extract n patterns from a lap of each subject. Instead of considering n as separated testing samples as usual, whole n patterns will be considered as genuine if there are m genuine patterns detected in n. That means each authentication task will perform on a sequences of n consecutive patterns to make a decision. From our experiment, we choose $m = 2$ and $n = 9$ which is significantly smaller than [16]. The achieved FMR and FNMR are 0% and 3.89% respectively which is remarkably comparative with other works [15–20].

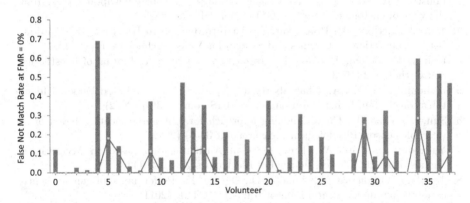

Fig. 7. FNMR of each 38 subjects at FMR=0% before (blue-columns) and after (red-line) applying voting scheme $m = 2, n = 12$

5   Conclusions

In this paper, we proposed a novel lightweight but highly reliable gait authentication on mobile phone. Although the quality of built-in sensors is low (the sampling rate is only 27Hz), the achieved results are very considerable. It reflects high potentials to deploy our mechanism to support current active mobile authentications such as PIN or password in reality. Since there is currently no public dataset in this field, the comparison between related works is only relative. Therefore, a more realistic dataset is also constructed to evaluate our mechanism fairly. Nevertheless, there is a minor unrealistic constraint in this study. We assumed that the phone is fixed at rigid body during walking phase. Furthermore, the influence of many environment factors such as human emotion, time effect, and ground materials to individual gait is not explored. Hence, such issues will be considered deeper in future. Moreover, since many excellent sensors are more and more integrated on modern mobiles nowadays (e.g. gyroscope, tilt sensor), mining all sensor resources to perfect a practical authentication model is our future road map.

Acknowledgments. "This research was supported by the MSIP (Ministry of Science, ICT&Future Planning), Korea, under the ITRC (Information Technology Research Center) support program (NIPA-2013-H0301-13-3005) supervised by the NIPA (National IT Industry Promotion Agency)"

References

1. Breitinger, F., Nickel, C.: User Survey on Phone Security and Usage. In: BIOSIG, vol. 164GI (2010)
2. Pousttchi, K., Schurig, M.: Assessment of todays mobile banking applications, from the view of customer requirements. In: 37th HICSS (2004)
3. Jain, A.K., Ross, A., Prabhakar, S.: An Introduction to Biometric Recognition. IEEE Transaction on Circuits and System for Video Technology 14(1) (2004)
4. Fish, D.J., Nielsen, J.: Clinical assessment of human gait. Journal of Prosthetics and Orthotics 2 (1993)
5. Mondal, S., Nandy, A., Chakraborty, P., Nandi, G.C.: Gait Based Personal Identification System Using Rotation Sensor. CIS Journal 3(3) (2012)
6. Sun, H., Yuao, T.: Curve Aligning approach for gait authentication based on a wearable sensor. Physiological Measurement 33(6) (2012)
7. Yuexiang, L., Xiabo, W., Feng, Q.: Gait Authentication Based on Acceleration Signals of Ankle. Chinese Journal of Electronics 20(3) (2011)
8. Terada, S., Enomoto, Y., Hanawa, D., Oguchi, K.: Performance of gait authentication using an acceleration sensor. In: 34th ICTSP (2011)
9. Bours, P., Shrestha, R.: Eigensteps: A giant leap for gait recognition. In: IWSCN (2010)
10. Gafurov, D., Snekkenes, E.: Gait Recognition Using Wearable Motion Recording Sensors. EURASIP Journal on Advances in Signal Processing 2009 (2009)
11. Pan, G., Zhang, Y., Wu, Z.: Accelerometer-based gait recognition via voting by signature points. IET Electronic Letters 45(22) (2009)
12. Mäntyjärvi, J., Lindholm, M., Vildjiounaite, E., Mäkelä, S.M., Ailisto, H.: Identifying Users of Portable Devices From Gait Pattern With Accelerometers. In: ICASSP (2005)
13. Ailisto, H., Lindholm, M., Mäntyjärvi, J., Vildjounaite, E., Mäkelä, S.M.: Identifying People from Gait Pattern with Accelerometers. In: Proceeding of SPIE 5779, Biometric Technology for Human Identification II (2005)
14. Thang, H.M., Viet, V.Q., Thuc, N.D., Choi, D.: Gait Identification Using Accelerometer on Mobile Phone. In: ICCAIS (2012)

15. Hestbek, M.R., Nickel, C., Busch, C.: Biometric Gait Recognition For Mobile Devices Using Wavelet Transform and Support Vector Machines. In: IWSSIP 2012 (2012)
16. Nickel, C., Busch, C.: Classifying Accelerometer Data via Hidden Markov Models to Authenticate People by the Way they Walk. In: 2011 IEEE ICCST (2011)
17. Nickel, C., Brandt, H., Busch, C.: Classificatoin of Acceleration Data for Biometric Gait Recognition on Mobile Devices. In: BIOSIG 2011 (2011)
18. Frank, F., Mannor, S., Precup, D.: Activity and Gait Recognition with Time-Delay Embeddings. In: 24th AAAI (2010)
19. Derawi, M.O., Nickel, C., Bours, P., Busch, C.: Unobtrusive User-Authentication on Mobile Phones using Biometric Gait Recoginition. In: 6th IIH-MSP (2010)
20. Sprager, S., Zazula, D.: A cumulant-based method for gait identification using accelerometer data with Principal Component Analysis and Support Vector Machine. Journal WSEAS Transactions on Signal Processing (2009)
21. Holien, K.: Gait Recoginition under non-standard circumstances. Master thesis, Gjøvik University College (2008)
22. Kern, N., Junker, H., Lukowicz, P., Schiele, B., Troster, G.: Wearable Sensing to Annotate Meeting Recordings. Journal Personal and Ubiquitous Computing 7(5) (October 2003)
23. Whittle, M.W.: Gait analysis an introduction, 4th edn. (2007)
24. Pudil, P., Novovicova, J., Kittler, J.: Float search methods in feature selection. Patter Recognition Letters 15 (1994)
25. Whitney, A.W.: A Direct Method of Nonparametric Measurement Selection. IEEE Transactions on Computers C-20(9) (1971)
26. Chang, C., Lin, C.J.: LIBSVM: a library for support vector machines. ACM Transactions on Intelligent Systems and Technology (2011)
27. Weiss, G.M., Provost, F.: Learning when training data are costly: The effect of class distribution on tree induction. Journal of Artificial Intelligence Research 19 (2003)

A Vulnerability in the Song Authentication Protocol for Low-Cost RFID Tags

Sarah Abughazalah, Konstantinos Markantonakis, and Keith Mayes

Smart Card Centre-Information Security Group (SCC-ISG)
Royal Holloway, University of London
Egham, Surrey, TW20 0EX, UK
{Sarah.AbuGhazalah.2012,K.Markantonakis,Keith.Mayes}@rhul.ac.uk

Abstract. In this paper, we describe a vulnerability against one of the most efficient authentication protocols for low-cost RFID tags proposed by Song. The protocol defines a weak attacker as an intruder which can manipulate the communication between a reader and tag without accessing the internal data of a tag. It has been claimed that the Song protocol is able to resist weak attacks, such as denial of service (DoS) attack; however, we found that a weak attacker is able to desynchronise a tag, which is one kind of DoS attack. Moreover, the database in the Song protocol must use a brute force search to retrieve the tag's records affecting the operational performance of the server. Finally, we propose an improved protocol which can prevent the security problems in Song protocol and enhance the server's scalability performance.

Keywords: RFID, mutual authentication, protocol, security, privacy.

1 Introduction

Radio frequency identification (RFID) technology is an identification technology that uses radio waves to identify objects such as products. An RFID system consists of three components, namely a tag, reader and server (database). An RFID tag is an identification device composed of an integrated circuit and antenna. It is designed to receive a radio signal and automatically transmit a reply to the reader. A passive RFID reader is a device that broadcasts a radio frequnecy (RF) signal through its antenna to power, communicate and receive data from tags. It is connected to the server to retrieve data associated with the connected tags. An RFID server is a database containing data related to the associated tags which it manages [1].

The major concerns of designing an RFID system are privacy and security [2]. Insecure communication between the reader and tag is inherently vulnerable to interception, modification, fabrication and replay attacks [2]. One of the problems that is encountered in designing an RFID system is a denial of service (DoS) attack. In a desynchronisation attack, which is one kind of DoS attack, the attacker tries to prevent both parties from receiving messages. For example, the attacker can block the exchanged message(s) from reaching the target causing

L.J. Janczewski, H.B. Wolfe, and S. Shenoi (Eds.): SEC 2013, IFIP AICT 405, pp. 102–110, 2013.

the tag and the server to be unable to update their information synchronously. Thus, the tag and back-end server cannot recognise each other in subsequent transactions [3].

Song et al. [4] proposed an efficient RFID authentication protocol for low-cost tags. This protocol uses the hash functions, message authentication code (MAC) and PRNG functions for authentication and updating purposes. Each tag stores only the hash of a secret namely (t), and the server stores the old and new values of the secret (s_{new}, s_{old}), the hashed secret (t_{new}, t_{old}) and the tag's information (D). This scheme uses a challenge-response protocol, where the server and tag generate random numbers to avoid replay attacks. However, Cai et al. [5] presented a paper showing that Song et al.'s protocol does not provide protection against a tag impersonation attack. Moreover, Rizomiliotis et al. [6] found that an attacker can impersonate the server even without accessing the internal data of a tag and launch a DoS attack.

As a result, a new version has been proposed in [7] (referred to here as the Song protocol). The Song protocol uses the same data and processes except that the construction of the exchanged message (M2 and M3) has been changed. In the new version of the Song protocol, Song claim that the proposed protocol resists DoS attack by storing the old and new values of the secret and the hashed secret, thus when the attacker blocks the transmitted message, the server still can use the recent old values to resynchronise with the tag.

In this paper, we focus on examining the new version of the Song protocol [7]. We discover that an attacker is able to desynchronise a tag without even compromising the internal data stored in the tag. Furthermore, this protocol is not scalable, as the server needs to perform a brute force search to retrieve the tag's records, which in turn affects the server performance, especially if it has to handle a large population of tags. After analysing the weaknesses of this protocol, we propose a revised protocol to eliminate these attacks with comparable computational requirements.

The rest of this paper is organised as follows: in Section 2, we present the Song protocol process in detail. In Section 3, the weaknesses of the Song protocol are illustrated. In Section 4, the revised protocol is presented. In Section 5, we analyse the proposed protocols with respect to informal analysis. In Section 6, we conclude and summarise the paper's contribution.

2   Review of the Song Protocol

This section reviews the Song protocol as shown in the original protocol [7]. Notation used in this paper are defined as follows:

- h: A hash function, h : $\{0, 1\}^* \rightarrow \{0, 1\}^l$
- f_k: A keyed hash function, $f_k : \{0, 1\}^* \times \{0, 1\}^l \rightarrow \{0, 1\}^l$ (a MAC algorithm)
- N: The number of tags
- l: The bit-length of a tag identifier
- T_i: The ith tag ($1 \leq i \leq N$)

- D_i: The detailed information associated with tag T_i
- s_i: A string of l bits assigned to i^{th} tag T_i
- t_i: T_i's identifier of l bits, which equals $h(s_i)$
- x_{new}: The new (refreshed) value of x
- x_{old}: The most recent value of x
- r: A random string of l bits
- ε: Error message
- $\oplus$: XOR operator
- $\|$: Concatenation operator
- $\leftarrow$: Substitution operator
- $x \gg k$: Right circular shift operator, which rotates all bits of x to the right by k bits, as if the left and right ends of x were joined.
- $x \ll k$: Left circular shift operator, which rotates all bits of x to the left by k bits, as if the left and right ends of x were joined.
- $\in_R$: The random choice operator, which randomly selects an element from a finite set using a uniform probability distribution

The Song protocol consists of two processes: the initialisation process, and the authentication process, which are summerised below:

2.1 Initialisation Process

This stage only occurs during manufacturing when the manufacturer assigns the initial values in the server and tag. The initialisation process is summarised below:

- An initiator (e.g. the tag manufacturer) assigns a string s_i of l bits to each tag T_i, computes $t_i = h(s_i)$, and stores t_i in the tag, where l should be large enough so that an exhaustive search to find the l-bit values t_i and s_i is computationally infeasible.
- The initiator stores the entries $[(s_i, t_i)_{new}, (s_i, t_i)_{old}, D_i]$ for every tag that it manages in the server. D_i is for the tag information (e.g., price, date, etc.). Initially $(s_i, t_i)_{new}$ is assigned the initial values of s_i and t_i, and $(s_i, t_i)_{old}$ is set to null.

2.2 Authentication Process

The authentication process is shown in Table 1 as presented in the new version of the protocol [7]:

Table 1. The authentication process of the Song protocol

1. Reader → Tag: $r1 \in_R \{0, 1\}^l$
2. Tag → Reader: $r2 \in_R \{0, 1\}^l$, $M1 = t_i \oplus r2$ and $M2 = f_{ti} (r1 \| r2)$
3. Reader → Server: $r1$, $M1 = t_i \oplus r2$ and $M2 = f_{ti} (r1 \| r2)$
4. Server → Reader: $M3 = s_i \oplus f_{ti} (r2 \| r1)$ and D_i
5. Reader → Tag: $M3 = s_i \oplus f_{ti} (r2 \| r1)$

1. Reader: A reader generates a random bit-string r1 $\in_R \{0, 1\}^l$ and sends it to the tag T_i.
2. Tag: The tag T_i generates a random bit-string r2 $\in_R \{0, 1\}^l$ as a temporary secret for the session, and computes M1 = $t_i \oplus$ r2 and M2 = f_{ti}(r1 $\|$ r2), then sends M1 and M2 to the reader.
3. Reader: The reader transmits M1, M2 and r1 to the server.
4. Server:
   (a) The server searches its database using M1, M2 and r1 as follows.
      i. It chooses t_i from amongst the values $t_{i(new)}$ or $t_{i(old)}$ stored in the database.
      ii. It computes M'2 $= f_{ti}$(r1 $\|$ (M1 $\oplus t_i$)).
      iii. If M'2 = M2, then it has identified and authenticated T_i. It then goes to step (b). Otherwise, it returns to step (i). If no match is found, the server sends ε to the reader and stops the session.
   (b) The server computes M3 = $s_i \oplus f_{ti}$ (r2 $\|$ r1) and sends it with D_i to the reader.
   (c) The server updates:

$$s_{i(old)} \leftarrow s_{i(new)}$$
$$s_{i(new)} \leftarrow (s_i \ll 1/4) \oplus (t_i \gg 1/4) \oplus \text{r1} \oplus \text{r2}$$
$$t_{i(old)} \leftarrow t_{i(new)}$$
$$t_{i(new)} \leftarrow h(s_{i(new)})$$

5. Reader: The reader forwards M3 to the tag T_i.
6. Tag: The tag T_i computes s_i = M3 $\oplus f_{ti}$(r2 $\|$ r1) and checks that h(s_i) = t_i. If the check fails, the tag keeps the current value of t_i unchanged. If the check succeeds, the tag has authenticated the server, and sets:

$$t_i \leftarrow h((s_i \ll 1/4) \oplus (t_i \gg 1/4) \oplus \text{r1} \oplus \text{r2})$$

3   Weaknesses of the Song Protocol

This section shows that the Song protocol suffers from DoS attack and database overloading.

3.1   DoS Attack

The Song protocol aims to meet some of the main security and privacy features. Resistance to DoS attack is one of the main security features. This is achieved by keeping the old values of the tag's secret (s_{old}) and hashed secret (t_{old}) in the server database just once; they are then renewed continuously once authentication is achieved. However, the Song protocol does not provide resistance to DoS attacks. Without knowing the secret value (t_i) which is stored in the tag, an adversary can easily cause synchronisation failure by twice intercepting the communication between the reader and the tag.

The protocol will fail if the attacker intercepts the communication in this way; if the server's message (M3) is intercepted, tampered or blocked up to twice, the server database will have no matching data to complete the mutual authentication, causing the DoS attack. For example, in the first access of the tag, the server's values (s_{old}, t_{old}) are set to null, while (s_{new}, t_{new}) values are set to specific values where (t_{new}) is equal to the tag's value (t_i). If the authentication succeeds, then (t_{new}) and (t_i) will be updated to the same value and (s_{old}, t_{old}) will take the previous values of (s_{new}, t_{new}). However, if the attacker blocks M3 from reaching the tag, then the server will update the server's data and the tag will be unable to update (t_i). In this situation, the value (t_i in the tag will have to match the value (t_{old}) in the database and mutual authentication can still be achieved. Now we suppose that the attacker blocks M3 for the second time; then the tag will also not update (t_i), while at that moment, (s_{old}, t_{old}) in the database have been renewed. As a result, the tag's data will not match the server's data, causing an authentication failure.

3.2   Database Overloading

The Song protocol claims that the server should be able to handle a large tag population without exhausting the server in identifying the tags. However, as shown in [7], the server needs to perform $[(k+2)*F]$ computations to authenticate the connected tag, where F is a relatively computationally complex function (such as a MAC or hash function) and k is an integer satisfying $1 \leq k \leq 2n$, where n is the number of tags. Hence, in every tag access, the server database has to run $[k*F]$ computations on all its records to find the matching record, thereby exhausting the server in the searching process and affecting operational performance.

4   Revised Protocol

We propose an improvement to the Song protocol by eliminating the two issues discussed in Section 3. In the Song protocol, if the authentication is achieved, the server's data will be updated even if the matching record is found in (s_{old}) and (t_{old}). In the revised protocol, we propose that the updating process should only take place when the authentication is achieved and the matching record is found in (s_{new}) and (t_{new}); otherwise, the data remains the same. The solution is based on Yeh et al.'s protocol [8] which was designed to avoid a DoS attack found in Chien et al.'s protocol [9].

In order to reduce the number of computations required by the server to authenticate the tag, we use the notion of indexing. This requires the server and tag to store another value to serve as an index. The server stores a new index (I_{new}) and an old index (I_{old}), where the tag stores an index value (I_i). The value of the index is assigned during manufacturing. In addition, the tag stores a flag value, which is kept as either 0 or 1 to show whether the tag has been authenticated by the server or not. Moreover, for calculating the index the server and tag need a new value (k) stored by both parties. We assume all the operations in the tag are atomic i.e. either all of the commands or none are processed.

In the revised protocol, we use the same notation as presented in the Song protocol. The initialisation and authentication processes are as follows:

4.1   Initialsation Process

This stage only occurs during manufacturing when the manufacturer assigns the initial values in the server and tag. The initialisation process is summarised below:

- The server assigns random values of L bits for each tag it manages to (s_{new}, t_{new}, k_{new}, I_{new}) in the server and (t_i, k_i, I_i) in the tag.
- Initially, (s_{old}, t_{old}, k_{old}, I_{old}) in the server is set to null.
- The Flag value in the tag is set to zero.

4.2   Authentication Process

The authentication process is summarised below:

- Reader: A reader generates a random bit-string r1 $\in_R \{0, 1\}^l$ and sends it to the tag T_i.
- Tag: A tag T_i generates a random bit-string r2 $\in_R \{0, 1\}^l$ as a temporary secret for the session, and computes M1 = $t_i \oplus$ r2 and M2 = f_{ti}(r1 ∥ r2). The tag then checks the value of the Flag:

  1. If Flag=0, which means the tag was authenticated successfully, the tag will use the new updated index which is equal to the server's value (I_{new}), and sends I_i, M1 and M2 to the reader. Finally, the tag sets Flag=1, and recomputes the value of an index I_i= h($k_i \oplus$ r2).
  2. If Flag=1, which means the tag has not been authenticated, the tag will use the value of the index computed in the former transaction (after setting Flag=1) which is equal to the server's value (I_{old}), then the tag transfers I_i, M1, and M2 to the reader. Finally, the tag sets Flag=1, and recomputes the value of an index I_i= h($k_i \oplus$ r2).

- Reader: The reader transmits M1, M2, I_i and r1 to the server.
- Server:

  1. The server searches the received value of (I_i) in (I_{new}) and (I_{old}) to find a match and retrieves the attached tag data. If there is a match in I_{new}, it retrieves (s_{new}, t_{new}, k_{new}) associated to (I_{new}). Then the server sets r2 ← M1 $\oplus$ t_{new}, and computes M'2 =f_{tnew}(r1 ∥ r2) to authenticate the tag. Then it marks x=new.
  2. If there is a match in I_{old}, the server retrieves the associated data (s_{old}, t_{old}, k_{old}), and computes M1 $\oplus$ t_{old} to obtain r2. The server computes M'2 =f_{told} (r1 ∥ r2). If M'2 = M2, then it has identified and authenticated T_i. Then it marks x=old.

3. The server computes $M3 = s_x \oplus f_{tx}(r2 \parallel r1)$ and sends it with D_i to the reader.
4. In case the index is found in I_{new}, the server sets:

$$s_{old} \leftarrow s_{new}$$
$$s_{new} \leftarrow (s_{new} \lll 1/4) \oplus (t_{new} \ggg 1/4) \oplus r1 \oplus r2$$
$$t_{old} \leftarrow t_{new}$$
$$t_{new} \leftarrow h(s_{new})$$
$$k_{old} \leftarrow k_{new}$$
$$k_{new} \leftarrow h(t_{new})$$
$$I_{old} \leftarrow h(k_{old} \oplus r2)$$
$$I_{new} \leftarrow h(k_{new} \oplus r2)$$

Otherwise, if I_i is found in I_{old}, the server keeps the data the same without any update except for:

$$I_{old} \leftarrow h(k_{old} \oplus r2)$$
$$I_{new} \leftarrow h(k_{new} \oplus r2)$$

- Reader: The reader forwards M3 to the tag T_i.
- Tag: The tag T_i computes $s_i = M3 \oplus f_{ti}(r2 \parallel r1)$ and checks that $h(s_i) = t_i$. If the check fails, the tag keeps the current values unchanged. If the check succeeds, the tag has authenticated the server, and sets:

$$t_i \leftarrow h((s_i \lll 1/4) \oplus (t_i \ggg 1/4) \oplus r1 \oplus r2)$$
$$k_i \leftarrow h(t_i)$$
$$I_i \leftarrow h(k_i \oplus r2)$$
$$\text{Flag} \leftarrow 0$$

5   Analysis

Due to the fact that the server updates its data after each successful authentication, the Song protocol cannot achieve resistance to a DoS attack. In this section, we analyse our revised protocol and show that it can provide immunity to several attacks including the DoS attack and at the same time improve the server performance. Although, the tag's storage, communication and computation costs will be higher than the Song protocol, but the revised protocol appears to meet stronger privacy and security requirements.

- DoS attack: We tend to use the old and new values of $(s_{new}, s_{old}, t_{new}, t_{old})$, as pointed in the Song protocol, to avoid DoS attack caused by M3 being intercepted. Moreover, in the proposed improved protocol, the server can still use $(s_{old}, t_{old}, I_{old})$ to identify a tag, even when the attacker blocks the message (M3) more than once, and thus can reach synchronisation.

Table 2. Computational requirements

		The Song protocol [7]	Our improved protocol Section 4	
Tag	Sending	MAC	MAC	
	Authenticating	MAC + H	MAC+ H	
	Updating	H	3H	
	Total	2MAC + 2H	2MAC + 4H	
			If x=new	If x=old
Server	Sending	MAC	MAC	MAC
	Authenticating	k*MAC	MAC	MAC
	Updating	H	4H	2H
	Total	(k+1)*MAC + H	2MAC +4H	2MAC +2H

n : The number of tags
k: An integer satisfying $1 \leq k \leq 2n$
x: The value kept as either new or old to show whether the tag uses the old or new values of the tag's record
H: Hash function
MAC: Message authentication code

- Database overloading: Table 2 demonstrates that the Song protocol needs to perform MAC functions on all the stored hashed secrets (t_{new}, t_{old}) until it finds the matched tag's record and authenticates the connected tag; in the improved protocol, on the other hand, the server can retrieve the associated tag's record directly according to the received value of index (I_i) and apply the MAC function only on the retrieved data.
- Tag location tracking: To prevent tracking the location of the tag's holder, the server's and tag's responses should be anonymous. In the proposed protocol, the server and tag update their data after each successful communication, so the exchanged values are changing continuously. Moreover, in the case the authentication failed, the attacker will still not be able to track the location.
- Tag impersonation attack: To impersonate the tag, the attacker must be able to compute a valid response $(I_i, M1, M2)$ to a server query. However, it is hard to compute such responses without the knowledge of $(t_i, k_i, r2)$. Moreover, the current values of M1, M2 and I_i are independent from the values sent previously due to the existence of fresh random numbers.
- Replay attack: The proposed protocol resists replay attack because it utilises challenge-response scheme. In each session the protocol uses a new pair of fresh random numbers (r1, r2), thus the messages cannot be reused in other sessions.
- Server impersonation attack: To impersonate the server, the attacker must be able to compute a valid response (M3). However, it is hard to compute such responses without knowledge of s_i, ID_i and r2.
- Traceability: All the messages transmitted by the tag are not static, they change continuously due to the existence of random numbers and the stored data are updated after each successful authentication. In addition, after the unsuccessful authentication, the tag's data will not change, however, M1 and M2 values still will be different in every session due to the existence of

random numbers (r2 and r2). Furthermore, the index of the tag is changed in both cases (successful authentication and unsuccessful authentication).

6   Conclusion

This paper showed that the Song protocol has a security problem and a performance issue, specifically a DoS attack and database overloading. To improve the Song protocol, we presented a revised protocol which can prevent the desynchronisation issues without violating any other security properties. Moreover, the newly proposed protocol enhances the overall performance, since it is based on using index values for retrieving the data associated to the connected tags.

References

1. Weis, S.: Security and privacy in Radio Frequency Identification devices. PhD thesis, Massachusetts Institute of Technology (2003)
2. Avoine, G.: Cryptography in Radio Frequency Identification and fair exchange protocols. PhD thesis, Ecole Polytechnique Federale de Lausanne, EPFL (2005)
3. Habibi, M., Gardeshi, M., Alaghband, M.: Practical attacks on a RFID authentication protocol conforming to EPC Class 1 Generation 2 standard. arXiv preprint arXiv:1102.0763 (2011)
4. Song, B., Mitchell, C.: RFID authentication protocol for low-cost tags. In: Proceedings of the First ACM Conference on Wireless Network Security, pp. 140–147. ACM (2008)
5. Cai, S., Li, Y., Li, T., Deng, R.: Attacks and improvements to an RIFD mutual authentication protocol and its extensions. In: Proceedings of the Second ACM Conference on Wireless Network Security, pp. 51–58. ACM (2009)
6. Rizomiliotis, P., Rekleitis, E., Gritzalis, S.: Security analysis of the Song-Mitchell authentication protocol for low-cost RFID tags. IEEE Communications Letters 13(4), 274–276 (2009)
7. Song, B.: RFID Authentication Protocols using Symmetric Cryptography. PhD thesis, Royal Holloway, University of London (2009)
8. Yeh, T., Wang, Y., Kuo, T., Wang, S.: Securing RFID systems conforming to EPC Class 1 Generation 2 Standard. Expert Systems with Applications 37(12), 7678–7683 (2010)
9. Chien, H., Chen, C.: Mutual authentication protocol for RFID conforming to EPC Class 1 Generation 2 Standards. Computer Standards Interfaces 29(2), 254–259 (2007)

Extraction of ABNF Rules from RFCs to Enable Automated Test Data Generation

Markus Gruber, Phillip Wieser, Stefan Nachtnebel,
Christian Schanes, and Thomas Grechenig

Research Group for Industrial Software, Vienna University of Technology,
1040 Vienna, Austria
{markus.gruber,phillip.wieser,stefan.nachtnebel,
christian.schanes,thomas.grechenig}@inso.tuwien.ac.at
http://security.inso.tuwien.ac.at/

Abstract. The complexity of IT systems and the criticality of robust IT systems is constantly increasing. Testing a system requires consideration of different protocols and interfaces, which makes testing hard and expensive. Test automation is required to improve the quality of systems without cost explosion. Many standards like HTML and FTP are semi–formally defined in RFCs, which makes a generic algorithm for test data generation based on RFC relevant. The proposed approach makes it possible to automatically generate test data for protocols defined as ABNF in RFCs for robustness tests. The introduced approach was shown in practice by generating SIP messages based on the RFC specification of SIP. This approach shows the possibility to generate data for any RFC that uses ABNF, and provides a solid foundation for further empirical evaluation and extension for software testing purposes.

1 Introduction

Security testing is an important and at the same time also expensive task for developing robust and secure systems. Costs of software testing increase due to the complexity and interconnection of modern software systems. Different interfaces, protocols and standards are used which requires much test effort to cover all aspects. Test automation can eliminate repetitive and time–consuming manual testing tasks and therefore reduce costs. Test data is required to test a System Under Test (SUT), and good test data might increase confidence in software quality, e.g., by testing more parts of the software [8].

Many Internet standards are commonly defined in a document called Request For Comments (RFC). The Internet Engineering Task Force (IETF) describes the purpose of RFC as:

"Memos in the RFC document series contain technical and organizational notes about the Internet. They cover many aspects of computer networking, including protocols, procedures, programs, and concepts, as well as meeting notes, opinions, and sometimes humor." [11]

Augmented Backus Naur Form (ABNF), a metalanguage to describe the syntax of parsable structures, is often used in RFCs to describe formal specifications,

L.J. Janczewski, H.B. Wolfe, and S. Shenoi (Eds.): SEC 2013, IFIP AICT 405, pp. 111–124, 2013.
© IFIP International Federation for Information Processing 2013

e.g., protocol specifications or flow definitions. These ABNF rules are usually hidden in informal descriptions.

Certain ABNF rules within an RFC are used to specify protocols or technologies. Examples are Hyper Text Transfer Protocol (HTTP) or Session Initiation Protocol (SIP), which are defined using ABNF rules. Based on these ABNF rules, test data can be generated in order to test different aspects of the interface, e.g., the conformance of a SUT to an RFC.

In this work, an approach to semi–automatically generate test data based on an RFC specification is presented. The process of extracting ABNF rules out of an RFC and the transformation from ABNF to XML Schema Definition (XSD) makes it possible to generate test data in Extensible Markup Language (XML) format. For test data generation, a number of existing frameworks and scientific test data generation algorithms can be used. XML is widely used in web applications and enables test data transformation to various other formats. The application of this approach is shown by generating test data for SIP messages based on the specification of SIP in RFC 3261 [20]. The possibility to semi–automatically generate test data based on an RFC might greatly reduce the time and effort needed to efficiently test a SUT.

Fenner [9] has developed a simple heuristic extractor as part of his ABNF parser. The solution proposed in this paper is based on this parser, but the workflow is adapted and additional features to generate a valid and self-contained set of ABNF rules are implemented. Valid and self-contained ABNF rulesets do not contain validation errors, e.g., syntax errors or missing rules. These rulesets can be validated by other ABNF parsers, e.g., Bill's ABNF Parser[1], to prove syntactic and semantic validity. Additionally, the ability to transform ABNF rules to XSD is introduced. For automated test data generation we use our approach presented in a previous work [21] which operates on an XSD model.

The remainder of this paper is structured as follows. An overview of related work is given in Sect. 2. Section 3 describes ABNF and the concept of ABNF model extraction. Section 4 covers test data generation based on transformation from ABNF rules to XSD. Section 5 covers the results and the lessons learned by developing and applying the approach for test data generation of SIP systems. The paper finishes with a conclusion and ideas for further work in Sect. 6.

2   Related Work

The IETF regularly publishes RFCs which describe Internet standards. Other organizations like International Organization for Standardization (ISO) and World Wide Web Consortium (W3C) publish standards in computer science as well.

ABNF is only one metalanguage to describe parsable structures, other widely used formal metalanguages are Backus Naur Form (BNF) [15], Wirth Syntax Notation (WSN) [25] or Extended Backus Naur Form (EBNF) [22].

Concerning test data generation, one can distinguish between random and dynamic test data generation [17]. Random data generation techniques do not

[1] https://code.google.com/p/bap/

require (but may take into account) an interface– or protocol specification of the SUT. While some authors state that random data generation produces test data efficiently [2], [12], others have come to the conclusion that most data is rejected by the SUT [16], [19]. Dynamic data generation approaches analyze the execution of test data against a SUT and try to generate new data based on the obtained knowledge. One approach tries to adapt test data so that critical software regions are tested more thoroughly [6], while another employs dynamic binary analysis [5].

The proposed approach generates data in the generic format XML. Several authors show the transformation of XML to other commonly used formats [24], [13], [10], [14]. Specific applications of test data generation from XSD have been proposed by several authors. A simple XML data generator based on defined rules has been proposed in [1]. Another software called TAXI generates XML documents based on an XSD [4], while ToxGene described in [3] is a template– based generator of synthetic XML documents. For the presented approach in this work our test data generation approach presented in [21] is used, which allows the generation of XML data based on XSD input.

3   Concept of ABNF Model Extraction from RFC

This section presents an introduction to the usage of ABNF in RFCs followed by the description of the process of the specification extraction approach. This is an iterative process of improving the quality of the extracted ruleset. This section also describes the ABNF error classes which can occur during this process.

3.1   Introduction to the Usage of ABNF in RFCs

ABNF is a metalanguage based on BNF and defined in RFC 5234 [7]. Both are notations for context–free grammars, used to describe the syntax of parsable structures, e.g., communication protocols. Most RFCs use ABNF to describe formal specifications. These ABNF rules, however, are usually embedded in informal descriptions, as seen in Fig. 1. In addition to the informal description at the top of this example, this ABNF rule consists of the rule name (HTTP-Version) and the rule definition on the right side. ABNF rules in one RFC can also reference ABNF rules in other RFCs. A mutual dependence of each ABNF rule can be described with a dependency tree, as shown in [23].

The version of an HTTP message is indicated by an
HTTP–Version field in the first line of the message.

        HTTP–Version   = "HTTP" "/" 1*DIGIT "." 1*DIGIT

Fig. 1. Example of an ABNF rule in RFC 2616

The ABNF specification is a set of derivation rules. These rules can be seen as a tree of rules and operators. Several options exist for creating this tree. One possible option is the *top–down parsing strategy*, which consists of taking a single element of interest, designating it as root of the tree and adding the dependent rules iteratively. Another possibility is the *bottom–up parsing strategy*. Here, all rules are considered and topologically sorted based on their dependencies, resulting in a tree with multiple roots. The approach presented in this paper follows the second approach, since it is more flexible and supports our goal to extract all ABNF rules, e.g., including referenced rules in other RFCs. A drawback of the second approach is, that the developer most likely will have to deal with rules that are not relevant, since only some rules (or a single rule including dependencies) are in scope of interest.

Special classes of ABNF rules are *prose rules, semantic pseudo rules* and *stub rules*. A prose rule is enclosed by < >. Prose rules are informal definitions of rules. Figure 2 shows an example of a prose rule in RFC.

LOALPHA = <any US–ASCII lowercase letter "a".."z">

Fig. 2. Example of a prose rule

Semantic pseudo rules use operators to describe semantic relations, which will lead to an ABNF syntax error. Figure 3 shows an example of a syntax error in an ABNF rule.

response_is_fresh = (freshness_lifetime > current_age)

Fig. 3. Example of a semantic pseudo rule, leading to a syntax error

Stub rules, in contrast to semantic pseudo rules, are semantically incorrect. Figure 4 shows an example of a stub rule, i.e., a Message Digest 5 (MD5) check-sum found in RFC 1864 [18]. It is very likely that this MD5 checksum will not represent a valid checksum of the generated sample.

md5–digest = "Q2hlY2sgSW50ZWdyaXR5IQ=="

Fig. 4. Example of a stub rule

3.2 Process of the Specification Extraction Approach

Based on the extractor developed by Fenner [9], additional features were implemented, e.g., namespacing, case escaping or detecting and separating prose rules, to *heuristically* extract all defined conditions from the RFC. Not all RFCs could be parsed automatically, because in some cases conflicts could not be resolved automatically in order to get semantically correct ABNF rulesets. To increase the quality of the approach, it was decided to use a semi–automatic approach to extract ABNF rules from RFCs.

Figure 5 describes our approach to extract a valid and self-contained ABNF ruleset of an RFC. The approach starts with the choosing of an arbitrary RFC, or multiple RFCs, one wants to have an ABNF ruleset for. After the initial configuration, it is an iterative process, fixing one problematic rule after another, until the full set of ABNF rules is generated.

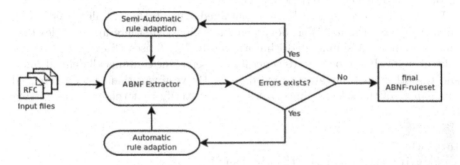

Fig. 5. Process of the ABNF extraction approach

The ABNF extractor automatically processes the following steps in order to get a final ruleset free of any errors:

1. Handle multiple input files as a single set of rules
2. Detect prose rules for semi–automatic processing
3. Expand # operators to valid constructs in ABNF syntax, because # is an originally unsupported rule in ABNF but defined later in some RFCs as #rule
4. Replace widely–used (but actually forbidden) characters "_" by "-" and "|" by "/"
5. Strip comments from rules
6. Unify the rules and remove redundancies
7. Replace rules that are defined multiple times (same name and same definition) by a single occurrence
8. Generate a dependency tree
9. Topologically sort rules based on the dependency tree

The topological sorting of rules is necessary, because if a rule is referenced before defined some parsers may throw errors. Additionally to the automatically processed tasks, the following rule adaption possibilities to clean the ABNF rules in order to get a valid and self-contained ruleset exist:

- Blacklist definitions for all rules which should be ignored
- Namespace transformations for rules with the same name in different RFCs

– Replace rule names with case–insensitive rule names
– Replace invalid rule definitions with customized rules

Our approach proposes a solution for each error, but the final choice of the rule adaption must be accomplished manually in order to avoid semantic errors.

3.3 Validating Validity and Self-Containedness of a Rule Set

The syntactic validity of ABNF rules can be tested using ABNF parsers, which throw an error if invalid ABNF syntax is used.

In order for a ruleset to be self-contained, all referenced rules need to be defined in the current ABNF document, meaning that there are no rules that are not defined. A simple algorithm as seen in Fig. 6 uses all extracted ABNF rules as input. It can be used to generate two sets: One contains all defined rules, and the other contains all referenced rules. By verifying that every referenced rule is part of the set of defined rules, one can verify that there are no missing rules.

```
for rule in rules
    defined_rules.insert(rule.name)
    for element in rule.body
        if typeof(element) is REFERENCE
            referenced_rules.insert(element)
    endfor
endfor
```

Fig. 6. Pseudocode: Constructing set of definitions and set of references

3.4 Error Classes of ABNF Generation

During the automated derivation of a model with the ABNF rules from one or more RFCs different problems can arise. The three main classes of problems are missing rule errors, syntax errors and double rule errors. By using multiple RFCs, e.g., referencing definitions in other RFCs, it can occur, that rules are defined more than once. If not all RFCs are given as input to the parser, missing rule errors can occur. Due to failures during the parsing process, syntax errors can arise, e.g., wrong definitions in the RFC or problems of parsing the ABNF rules from the RFC text. Figure 7 shows the errors which can occur during the extraction process.

Missing Rule Errors. A missing rule is a rule, that is referenced, but is not defined. For example the rules A and B are defined, rule A references rules B and C, but rule C is not defined. This could happen if a rule is defined as prose or defined in a referenced document.

If a rule may be referenced from another RFC, these references are informally defined either in a prose rule, or in the surrounding textual description. If this

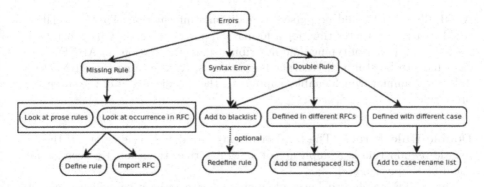

Fig. 7. Error Classes of ABNF Generation and Countermeasures

occurs, one can either import the complete referenced RFC or copy the specific rule. Another problem could occur, when some RFCs include some core rules (as defined in RFC 5234 [7]), while other core rules are missing. Core rules are basic rules that are in common use. Some authors include all ABNF core rules directly in implementations of scanners or parsers. For the sake of simplicity, it is suggested to include them in a separate file. Concerning duplicate – or missing – rules, they would be treated equally to extracted rules.

A special kind of errors are non–validation errors. A ruleset which contains non–validation errors contains valid ABNF syntax, but is semantically incorrect. Semantic errors can only be detected by so–called validating parsers (in contrast to non–validating parsers). One reason could be, that some rules are only stub rules. This issue can not be solved in ABNF, but only by some processor on a higher level that takes semantic aspects like data dependencies into account.

Another reason of non–validation errors could be *blind text* as part of a rule. Blind text is meant as additional information or description, but parsers may consider it part of the rule. An example of blind text in an ABNF rule can be seen in Fig. 8. Because of its indent, the blind text will be treated as part of the rule, which will result in a syntax error although the text is only meant as a comment.

```
credentials = auth-scheme #auth-param
   Note that many browsers will only recognize Basic and will↩
      require that it be the first auth-scheme presented. ↩
   Servers should only include Basic if it is minimally ↩
   acceptable.
```

Fig. 8. Example of blind text in an ABNF rule

Syntax Errors. The second error class are syntax errors. Mostly, semantic pseudo rules (as explained in Sect. 3.1) occur in addition to regular rule definitions, or are referenced by another semantic rule. Although it is not usable in

ABNF directly, it could be parsed as additional information. This information could be used at a later time for a format supporting it, e.g., XSD generation. Because of the lack of typing, and describing semantic relations in ABNF, these rules have to be stubbed. Another possibility is, transforming the ABNF to a different grammar, which enables supporting the specific aspect of the subjected prose rule.

Double Rule Errors. The third error class are double rule errors. If the semantic pseudo rule is a duplicate of a regular rule, the semantic pseudo rule could be simply ignored.

The ABNF standard defines rule names as case–insensitive, which is not always the case in RFCs. Sometimes, rules with the same name (and different casing) are intended to be different. The presented approach solves this by heuristically replacing the upper–cased letter with a lower–cased and some additional ABNF–compatible information tagging it as escaped. Figure 9 shows an example of escaping the upper–cased letters. This circumstance also often occurs, when importing referenced RFCs.

'Foo' would be escaped to '−−−f——oo'

Fig. 9. Example of escaped upper–case letter 'F'

Another case of double rule errors could occur when importing a referenced RFC, or processing multiple RFCs. Then, it may happen, that rules are defined in multiple RFCs. Similar rules with the same name and same body can be resolved by ignoring all duplicated rules. It may also happen, that the two rules mean two completely different things in the different scopes of the RFCs. In this case, it is required to namespace them in an ABNF–compatible fashion. One option would be to set a prefix to the affected rules to avoid duplicated rules.

4   Test Data Generation Based on Transformation from ABNF Rules to XSD

This section presents the approach of test data generation based on transformation from ABNF rules to XSD. An XSD file describes the structure of an XML document, and was introduced by the W3C. The reason for choosing XSD as the destination format is that test data generation in XML format, which is a generic format and can be transformed to many other formats, is easily possible and existing data generation algorithms can be used. Several differences and similarities of ABNF and XSD need to be taken into account, which are described in this section.

4.1   Differences Between ABNF and XSD

Each rule itself can be transformed to a valid XSD representation, but the result of the combination of the rules does not produce a valid XSD. In ABNF, literals, references and ranges may all be used as a part of the rule definition, but those constructs all need to be transformed to XSD differently.

Well–formed XSD documents are well–formed XML documents themselves. Not all characters are valid in XML, but it is required to be able to encode all bytes from 0x00 to 0xFF. Therefore one of the binary types had to be picked. The type *hexBinary* was chosen in favor of *base64Binary*, because it is easier to use with a regular expression pattern. When using hexBinary to encode a text, each letter is represented by two hexadecimal characters, and can be changed individually without the need to re–encode the rest of the string.

Literals, strings and ranges can be expressed either as patterns using a regular expression, or as an enumeration. It was decided to take the regular expression pattern approach, because the representation as regular expression is more compact and therefore in our opinion more readable. Especially when a large number of data instances are possible for an element, an enumeration is not a viable option. Existing regular expression parsers can be used to generate instances that conform to a regular expression.

Additionally a string literal in ABNF is case–insensitive. This means "foo" could produce "fOo", "FOo", etc. For the sake of simplicity, "foo" will only produce "foo" after transforming to XSD.

4.2   Mapping ABNF to XSD

To use our generic approach of data generation as described in our previous work [21], which allows the generation of XML data based on XSD input, an ABNF ruleset needs to be transformed to XSD. An example of the expected result, i.e., for the transformation of the DIGIT rule, is seen in Fig. 10.

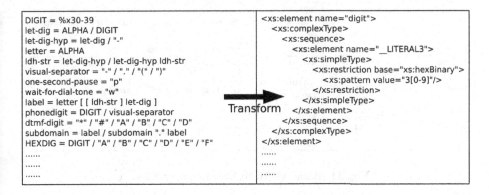

Fig. 10. Example of ABNF to XSD transformation

Our approach uses a transformation matrix, as seen in Fig. 11, from ABNF rules to XSD. These mapping rules require additional transformation logic to correctly generate a valid XSD element tree. The proposed approach derives transitions from ABNF rules to XSD elements by comparing the valid children of the enclosing element with the valid parents of an enclosed element, until a transition from the enclosing to the enclosed element is detected.

To reduce complexity, classes are combined, as defined in the first column of Fig. 11, of (in this case) compatible ABNF rules:

- $Choice, Group, Repetition \equiv CGR$
- $Literal, String, Range \equiv LSR$

A repetition is transformed to XSD using a (single–content) sequence with attributes minOccurs and maxOccurs. Therefore it is in the same class as group.

However, the following transformations are used to transform ABNF rule classes to XSD trees. XSD follows certain restrictions concerning element positioning in the tree, which need to be considered for the transformation.

1. $Rule \rightarrow CGR$
2. $Rule \rightarrow Reference$
3. $Rule \rightarrow LSR$
4. $CGR \rightarrow CGR$
5. $CGR \rightarrow Reference$
6. $CGR \rightarrow LSR$

Classes irrelevant to our approach have been omitted.

ABNF-Class	Operator	Parameter	XSD-Element

Rule	=
	=/
		name
		value
			`<element name="name">`
			    value
			`<\element>`

Choice	|	value []	`<choice> value [] <\choice>`
Group	( )	value []	`<sequence> value [] <\sequence>`
Repetition	n*m * [ ]	value min max	@minOccurs="min" @maxOccurs="max"
Reference		name	`<element ref="name" />`
Literal	"foo"	value	`<pattern value="someregex" />`
String	%xA.B...N %dA.B...N %bA.B...N	value type	`<pattern value="someregex" />`
Range	%xN–M %dN–M %bN–M	type min max	`<pattern value="someregex" />`

Fig. 11. Basic ABNF to XSD mapping rules

4.3   Description of XML Test Data Generation from XSD

After transformation of the ABNF rules to XSD, a generic data generation framework is used to generate the required test data in XML format. For this purpose, the test data generation features of an existing fuzzing framework called fuzzolution[2] were used, which are also described in [21].

The XSD document generated in the previous step serves as an input to the framework. Data is generated based on two features of the generated XSD, which are structural information and data–based restrictions.

Structural information is represented by elements like `choice`, `sequence` as well as attributes like `minOccurs`. The used framework takes these restrictions into account, and generates XML instances that conform to the given XSD. Data–based restrictions describe the data within the elements. In this example, hexadecimal values are generated for several elements based on the information available in the XSD.

Using the transformed XSD, the framework generates test data in XML format. These XML files contain the test data and might be used either directly by executing it against a SUT or by transforming it to another format first.

5   Experiences with Generation of Test Data for SIP Systems

In this section, the applicability of the proposed approach for a specific RFC is presented. For this purpose, test data for SIP messages as defined in RFC 3261 [20] is generated and validated. Since the number of Voice over IP (VoIP) systems and SIP users is constantly increasing, attackers have more incentive to attack SIP systems. This shows the necessity to automatically test SIP systems to find and resolve robustness errors.

5.1   Generation of SIP Test Data Based on the RFC

The process of generating test data in this approach can be summarized by these steps:

1. Generate ABNF rules out of the RFC using the presented ABNF extractor approach
2. Transform the ABNF ruleset to an XSD tree
3. Generate XML test data based on the XSD using the test data generation framework
4. Transform XML test data to SIP messages and validate them

Using the presented approach, a large amount of valid and invalid test data for SIP systems based on RFC 3261 could be generated. While the XSD contains restrictions which describe valid instances, invalid instances can be generated by

---

[2] http://security.inso.tuwien.ac.at/esse-projects/fuzzolution/

violating the constraints defined in the XSD, e.g., violating regular expression patterns or violating structural restrictions, e.g., omitting required elements.

To validate the generated valid data, a custom stand–alone tool was developed that transforms XML messages back to raw SIP messages. The resulting SIP messages were validated using APG[3], an ABNF parser. Part of the set of tools is a set of ABNF rules for SIP messages. These rules were used to show that the validity of the generated SIP messages. Provided that the external ABNF ruleset is valid, it was thus shown that the generated SIP messages are valid with respect to the RFC.

5.2   Learnings and Limitations of the Proposed Approach

Compared to the ABNF extraction of HTTP (RFC 2616), which needed a quite large amount of rule adaption iterations, SIP (RFC 3261) only needed a couple of iterations. As in RFC 2616, an informal note was parsed as part of one rule and had to be redefined. In contrast to RFC 2616 no syntactical errors were detected in rules. Also in contrast to RFC 2616, having quite a lot of dependencies, is was only necessary to import two other RFCs to fix missing rule errors. RFC 2806 could be imported directly, and RFC 1035 was written in BNF and had to be transformed to ABNF.

It was observed that the generated XSD file did not include all desired structural restrictions. A very specific example is that it is not possible to set required and optional message headers for different SIP methods (e.g., REGISTER and INVITE) individually. Instead, the message header elements and the SIP method are independent choice elements in XSD. This means that all permutations of those two groups are allowed. However, this is not a restriction of this approach, because the ABNF rules are not more restricted in the RFC.

5.3   Discussion of Test Data Generation from RFC

The framework used for data generation, fuzzolution, makes it possible to generate a large number of data files with little risk of memory shortages. The problem, however, lies in the large possibilities of combinations of possible test data instances.

The XSD file for the test data generation of SIP messages contains about 8000 lines of code. In its most basic configuration, the framework generates all possibilities, i.e. each combination of possible structural and data–related instances is generated. Because this schema file contains many choice indicators and optional elements, the number of possibilities of valid XML files is very large. Recursive structures are used (an element might contain itself), so it is not even possible to generate all instances because an infinite number of possibilities exists. All those problems are considered and resolved in our generic data generation approach [21] by configuration of the framework.

---

[3] http://www.coasttocoastresearch.com/apg

Missing ABNF rules have to be reviewed manually, deciding whether to import, stub or write the rule. This could be partially automated by parsing the text for referenced RFCs. The proposed approach includes fetching potentially interesting RFCs, searching the RFCs and ordering based on distance heuristics and importing of the top–rated RFC, with eventual user intervention.

6   Conclusion and Further Work

In this paper, an approach of generating test data from RFCs was presented. This is done by extracting an ABNF model from an existing RFC. Based on this model, an XSD file is generated, which in turn is the input for a data generation software which generates data in XML format. This test data might be used for testing a SUT. For the extraction of an ABNF model, a heuristic extractor by Fenner [9] is extended to get a valid and self-contained ruleset. Using the proposed approach makes it possible to semi–automatically generate test data based on an RFC. The application of the approach was shown using SIP and proved to be able to generate valid and invalid test data to test a system.

Future areas of work include the stateful representation of SIP in this approach, and the improvement of the transformation from ABNF to XSD in order to test more aspects of the system. In the SIP example, this means to make a distinction between allowed message headers for each allowed message.

The ABNF rules are only a small part of RFCs in comparison to the text length. They mostly consist of natural language descriptions discussing the field of interest. This information could be helpful constructing test data, or distinguish between valid and invalid variations. These include for example semantic relations, constraints, examples and references to other RFCs. The approach proposed in this paper might support additional research in implementing a parser looking for those natural language patterns.

With the presented approach, an automated extraction of a model for the generation of test data is possible. With the presentation of the transformation from ABNF to XSD, a generic data generation approach for different protocols is possible. This allows clear separation of concerns for test tools and a focus on a robust test generation logic.

References

1. Aboulnaga, A., Naughton, J.F., Zhang, C.: Generating synthetic complex-structured XML data. In: Proc. 4th Int. Workshop on the Web and Databases, WebDB 2001 (2001)
2. Arcuri, A., Iqbal, M.Z., Briand, L.: Random testing: Theoretical results and practical implications. IEEE Trans. Softw. Eng. 38(2), 258–277 (2012)
3. Barbosa, D., Mendelzon, A., Keenleyside, J., Lyons, K.: ToXgene: a template-based data generator for XML. In: SIGMOD 2002: Proceedings of the 2002 ACM SIGMOD International Conference on Management of Data, pp. 616–616. ACM, New York (2002)

4. Bertolino, A., Gao, J., Marchetti, E., Polini, A.: TAXI–a tool for XML-based testing. In: ICSE COMPANION 2007: Companion to the Proceedings of the 29th International Conference on Software Engineering, pp. 53–54. IEEE Computer Society, Washington, DC (2007)

5. Caballero, J., Yin, H., Liang, Z., Song, D.: Polyglot: automatic extraction of protocol message format using dynamic binary analysis. In: CCS 2007: Proceedings of the 14th ACM Conference on Computer and Communications Security, pp. 317–329. ACM, New York (2007)

6. Carbin, M., Rinard, M.C.: Automatically identifying critical input regions and code in applications. In: ISSTA, pp. 37–48 (2010)

7. Crocker, E., Overell, P.: Augmented bnf for syntax specifications: Abnf (2008)

8. Ebert, C., Dumke, R.: Software Measurement: Establish - Extract - Evaluate - Execute, 1st edn. Springer (August 2007)

9. Fenner, B.: Bill fenner's abnf extractor, http://code.google.com/p/bap/source/browse/trunk/aex (accessed: January 21, 2013)

10. Fong, J., Pang, F., Bloor, C.: Converting relational database into XML document, pp. 61–65 (2001)

11. I. E. T. Force. Overview of rfc decument series, http://www.rfc-editor.org/RFCoverview.html (accessed: January 26, 2013)

12. Gutjahr, W.: Partition testing vs. random testing: the influence of uncertainty. IEEE Transactions on Software Engineering 25(5), 661–674 (1999)

13. ITU-T. X.693 information technology ASN.1 encoding rules: XML encoding rules (XER). Identical standard: ISO/IEC 8825-4:2008 (Common) (November 2008)

14. Jacinto, M., Librelotto, G., Ramalho, J., Henriques, P.: Bidirectional conversion between XML documents and relational databases, pp. 437–443 (2002)

15. McCracken, D.D., Reilly, E.D.: Backus-naur form (bnf). In: Encyclopedia of Computer Science, pp. 129–131. John Wiley and Sons Ltd., Chichester

16. McMinn, P.: Search-based software test data generation: A survey. Software Testing, Verification and Reliability 14, 105–156 (2004)

17. Michael, C.C., McGraw, G., Schatz, M.A.: Generating software test data by evolution. IEEE Trans. Softw. Eng. 27(12), 1085–1110 (2001)

18. Myers, J., Rose, M.: The content-md5 header field (1995)

19. Ribeiro, J.C.B., Zenha-Rela, M.A., de Vega, F.F.: Test case evaluation and input domain reduction strategies for the evolutionary testing of object-oriented software. Information and Software Technology 51(11), 1534–1548 (2009)

20. Rosenberg, J., Schulzrinne, H., Camarillo, G., Johnston, A., Peterson, J., Sparks, R., Handley, M., Schooler, E.: RFC 3261: SIP - Session Initiation Protocol

21. Schanes, C., Fankhauser, F., Taber, S., Grechenig, T.: Generic data format approach for generation of security test data. In: The Third International Conference on Advances in System Testing and Validation Lifecycle, Barcelona, Spain. IEEE Computer Society Press, Los Alamitos (2011)

22. E. Standard. EBNF: ISO/IEC 14977: 1996 (E), http://www.cl.cam.ac.uk/mgk25/iso-14977.pdf

23. Stefanec, T., Skuliber, I.: Grammar-based sip parser implementation with performance optimizations. In: Proceedings of the 2011 11th International Conference on Telecommunications (ConTEL), pp. 81–86 (June 2011)

24. Van Deursen, D., Poppe, C., Martens, G., Mannens, E., Walle, R.: XML to RDF conversion: A generic approach, pp. 138–144 (November 2008)

25. Wirth, N.: What can we do about the unnecessary diversity of notation for syntactic definitions? Commun. ACM 20(11), 822–823 (1977)

Key Derivation Function: The SCKDF Scheme

Chai Wen Chuah, Edward Dawson, and Leonie Simpson

Queensland University of Technology
{chaiwen.chuah,e.dawson,lr.simpson}@qut.edu.au

Abstract. A key derivation function is used to generate one or more cryptographic keys from a private (secret) input value. This paper proposes a new method for constructing a generic stream cipher based key derivation function. We show that our proposed key derivation function based on stream ciphers is secure if the underlying stream cipher is secure. We simulate instances of this stream cipher based key derivation function using three eStream finalist: Trivium, Sosemanuk and Rabbit. The simulation results show these stream cipher based key derivation functions offer efficiency advantages over the more commonly used key derivation functions based on block ciphers and hash functions.

Keywords: Key derivation function, cryptographic key, stream cipher.

1 Introduction

A key derivation function (*KDF*) is a basic component of a cryptographic system. It is used to generate one or more cryptographic keys from a private input string; such as a password, Diffie-Hellman (DH) shared secret or non-uniformly random source material [12,13,16,24]. The derived cryptographic keys are then used for maintaining information security and protecting electronic data when it is stored or transmitted. To prevent an adversary gaining any useful information about the private string, it is essential that the cryptographic keys generated by the *KDF* are computationally indistinguishable from a binary random string [15]. That is, given a binary string the adversary may not be able to distinguish whether the string is the cryptographic key generated by the *KDF* or a random string of the same length.

For *KDF*s, the inputs consist of a private string and a public string. The public string consists of a random string or a concatenation of counter, session identifier or the identities of communicating parties. Where the cryptographic keys are obtained directly from the inputs without any intermediate step, this is refered to as a single phase *KDF* (see for example [1,7,14,23]). A more recent *KDF* design trend is the two phase *KDF* [9,15], where the phases consist of an extractor and an expander. The inputs to the extractor are the private string and a non-secret random string, while the inputs to the expander are the output from the extractor and the context information. In this design, the extractor and expander are two independent sub-functions, which can be designed and analysed separately. This permits mixing and matching of different types of extractor and

L.J. Janczewski, H.B. Wolfe, and S. Shenoi (Eds.): SEC 2013, IFIP AICT 405, pp. 125–138, 2013.
© IFIP International Federation for Information Processing 2013

expander functions to form good extract-then-expand *KDF* proposals, in terms of both security and/or performance.

Many existing *KDF* proposals (both single and two phase) are composed using either hash functions or block ciphers. Both hash functions and block ciphers divide the input into a series of equal-sized blocks, with some padding necessary if the last block input is not of the appropriate length. The input blocks are processed in sequence with a one-way compression function, and the output is a fixed block size. A *KDF* should be able to generate cryptographic keys of arbitrary length. Where the required length is not a multiple of the output block size, modification is necessary. Generally, the approach is to produce multiple output blocks until the required length has been obtained and to discard any bits in excess of the required length. This may be regarded as wasteful.

*KDF*s are widely used in Internet protocols [12,13,16,24]. Mobile devices like smartphones are increasingly used to access the Internet. These devices have low processing power, so efficiency is important. There is increasing interest in the design of more efficient *KDF*s for use in mobile devices or similar applications.

Stream ciphers are often used for encryption in resource constrained devices due to their speed and simplicity of implementation in hardware. Hash functions and block ciphers are often slower and require more resources than stream ciphers. Thus, a *KDF* based on stream ciphers may provide a more efficient alternative to the current block cipher or hash function based *KDF*s.

This paper proposes a new secure and efficient *KDF* based on the keystream generator of a stream cipher. We refer to this proposal as *SCKDF*. We present a generic model for a stream cipher based *KDF* which is secure if the underlying stream cipher is secure. We implement this generic *SCKDF* for three stream ciphers proposals: Trivium [6], Sosemanuk [4] and Rabbit [5]. The results show that the *SCKDF* is executes faster compared to existing *KDF*s based on hash functions and block ciphers.

This paper is organized as follows. We provide our notation and some background information on *KDF*s in Section 2. Section 3 reviews the properties of keystream generators. Our new proposal, a generic *SCKDF*, is presented in Section 4. The security proof for this construction is given in Section 5. Performance measurements to permit comparison of stream cipher, block cipher and hash function based *KDF*s for common applications scenarios are given in Section 6.

2   Backgroud for KDFs

Before we present the formal definition of a key derivation function, we recall the notion of min-entropy, as presented in [15].

Definition 1. *(min-entropy)[15]. A probability distribution $\mathcal{X}$ has min-entropy (at least) m if for all a in the support of $\mathcal{X}$ and for random variable X drawn according to $\mathcal{X}$, Prob(X=a) ≤ 2^{-m}.*

In our case, X is the random variable represented by the private string and $\mathcal{X}$ is the probability distribution for possible values of X.

Definition 2. *(Key derivation function). A key derivation function is defined as: $K \leftarrow KDF(p, s, c, n)$, where*

- *p is a private string, which is chosen from the space of all possible private strings PSPACE. We denote the length of p as pl.*
- *s is a salt, a public random string chosen from the salt space SSPACE. We denote the length of s as sl;*
- *c is a public context string chosen from a context space CSPACE. The length of c is cl.*
- *n is a positive integer that indicates the number of bits to be produced by the KDF;*
- *K is the derived n bit cryptographic key.*

The basic operation of a KDF is to transform the secret p and the public inputs (s and/or c) into an n bit string which can be used as a cryptographic key.

Note that all inputs are publicly known, except for the private string p. The salt is uniformly random and is used to create a large set of possible keys corresponding to a given p [23]. Context information is arbitrary but application specific data; for example, a session identifier or the identities of communicating parties [2,3]. Similar definition are used in other *KDF* proposals. See for example [1,7,14,23,9] and [15].

Definition 3. *A KDF function is called (t, q, ϵ)m-entropy secure if it is (t, q, ϵ)-secure with respect to all (computational)m-entropy sources, where the derived cryptographic key of the KDF from m-entropy sources is computationally indistinguishable from a binary random string. That is, when the adversary is given a limited number of queries (q in total) to polynomial time algorithm t, the adversary can distinguish between the cryptographic key derived from the KDF or a random string of the same length with negligible probability ϵ[15].*

2.1   Single Phase KDFs

A single phase *KDF* uses a pseudorandom function that takes the private input and public inputs and transforms these inputs directly into one or more variable length computationally indistinguishable cryptographic keys. Figure 1 depicts a single phase *KDF*.

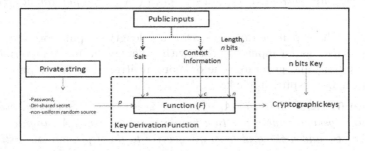

Fig. 1. Single phase model for KDFs

Definition 4. *(Single phase KDF). A KDF is a function of $F : \{0,1\}^{pl} \times \{0,1\}^{sl} \times \{0,1\}^{cl} \to \{0,1\}^*$ from a set $p \in_R PSPACE$ mapping to an arbitrary length of string $\{0,1\}^*$. The string should be indistinguishable from random strings of the same length in polynomial time.*

2.2   Two Phase KDFs

A two phase *KDF* is the composition of two subfunctions: an extractor (*Ext*) and an expander (*Exp*). Note that the output of the extractor is an input to the expander as shown in Figure 2. The typical construction of a two-phase *KDF* is: $KDF(p, s, c, n) = Exp\left(\{Ext\,(p\,,\,s)\}, c, n\right)$. We discuss each phase below.

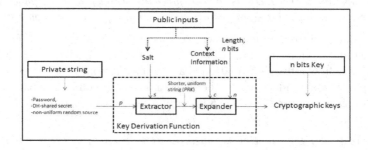

Fig. 2. Extract-then-expand model for KDFs

Extractor. The aim of the extractor is to transform the private input p into close to uniformly random output, which we denote as *PRK*. In this research, we generate the *PRK* from p using a computational extractor.

Definition 5. *(Computational extractor)[15]. Let PSPACE and SSPACE be set spaces of $\{0,1\}^{pl}$ and $\{0,1\}^{sl}$ respectively. A function $Ext : \{0,1\}^{pl} \times \{0,1\}^{sl} \to \{0,1\}^{kl}$ is called a (t_X, ϵ_X)-computational extractor if an adversary A running in polynomial time t_X can distinguish between PRK (derived from p) or a random string of the same length, with probability not larger than $(\frac{1}{2} + \epsilon_X)$ where p is chosen from $\{0,1\}^{pl}$ and s chosen from $\{0,1\}^{sl}$. If Ext is a (t_X, ϵ_X)-computational extractor with min-entropy m we call it a (m, t_X, ϵ_X)-computational extractor.*

Expander. The expander takes the arbitrary length output from the extractor phase, *PRK*, as an input together with other public input material (context information) and generates one or more arbitrary length computationally indistinguishable cryptographic key(s).

Definition 6. *(Expander)[15]. An expander is a (t_Y, q_Y, ϵ_Y)-secure variable-length-output pseudorandom function family if an adversary A running in polynomial time t_Y and making at most q_Y queries to the expander can distinguish the cryptographic key is generated by the expander or a random string of the same length with probability not larger than $(\frac{1}{2} + \epsilon_Y)$.*

2.3   The Security of *KDF*

The major security goal for a *KDF* is that the cryptographic keys generated by the *KDF* are indistinguishable from truly random binary strings of the same length, even when the public inputs are provided to the adversary. We follow the approach of Krawczyk [15] and define the *KDF* security through a distinguishing game played between a challenger C and an adversary A in polynomial time algorithm t. The *KDF* is considered secure if no A can win the distinguishing game with probability significantly greater than the probability of winning by guessing randomly.

The game runs in three major stages: the learning stage, the challenge stage and the adaptive stage as shown in Table 1. During the learning stage, A is allowed to interact with C to demand cryptographic keys corresponding to A's choice of public input c with p and s chosen by C. In this game, p is secret known only to C, while s is known by A. At the challenge stage, A is provided a challenge output K'. After receiving the challenge output, A is in the adaptive stage. A can continue the same process as in the learning stage, subject to the choice of public input (c) being different from the public input chosen in the challenge stage. Lastly, A has to distinguish whether the challenge output is the derived cryptographic key from the *KDF* or just a random string. We describe a *KDF* for which A cannot win this game with the probability not larger than $(\frac{1}{2} + \epsilon)$ as CCS-secure.

Definition 7. *(CCS-secure) The KDF is (t, q, ϵ) CCS-secure if for all probabilistic polynomial-time t adversaries A can make at most $q < |CSPACE|$ queries to the KDF who can win the following indistinguishability game with probability not larger than $(\frac{1}{2} + \epsilon)$.*

Table 1. CCS-secure

Learning stage	1. C chooses $p \leftarrow PSPACE$. 2. C chooses $s \xleftarrow{R} SSPACE$. 3. A is provided with the value s. 4. For $i = 1, \ldots, q' \leq q$,	(4.1) A chooses $c_i \leftarrow CSPACE$. (4.2) C computes $K_i = F(p, s, c_i, n)$. (4.3)A is provided the derived cryptographic key, K_i.
Challenge stage	1. A chooses $c \leftarrow CSPACE$ (subject to restriction $ctx \notin c_i, \ldots, c'_q$). 2. C chooses $b \xleftarrow{R} \{0, 1\}$.	(2.1) If $b = 0$, C outputs $K' = F(p, s, c, n)$, (2.2) else C outputs $K' \xleftarrow{R} \{0,1\}^n$.
	5. C sends K' to A.	
Adaptive stage	1. Step 4 in **Learning stage** is repeated for up to $q - q'$ queries (subject to restriction $c_i \neq c$). 2. A outputs $b' = 0$, if A believes that K' is cryptographic key, else outputs $b' = 1$. <center>A wins the game if $b' = b$.</center>	

In [15], Krawczyk showed the condition under which a two-phase *KDF* can be considered CCS-secure as follows in Theorem 1.

Theorem 1. *Let Ext be a (t_X, ϵ_X)-computational extractor with the respect to the private string p and Exp a (t_Y, q_Y, ϵ_Y)-secure variable-length-output pseudorandom function family, then the above extract-then-expand KDF scheme is $(min\{t_X, t_Y\}, q_Y, \epsilon_X + \epsilon_Y)$-CCS secure with the respect the private string p [15].*

2.4   Existing KDF Proposals

To date, both single phase and two-phase proposals of *KDF*s have been based on cryptographic hash functions[15] and block ciphers[8]. Hash functions are widely used for data authentication and block ciphers for data confidentiality. We describe two specific well-known two-phase *KDF* proposals, one based on hash functions and the other one based on block ciphers, in the remainder of this section.

Hash Functions. In [15], Krawczyk formalized a *KDF* using HMAC-SHA families (HKDF) and proved that HKDF is CCS-secure. The proposed HKDF consists of a computational extractor and a pseudorandom expander. The extractor function is $PRK \Leftarrow Ext_p(s) : F((s \oplus opad)\|F((s \oplus ipad)\|p))$, where F denotes a hash function, $\oplus$ denoter exclusive or (XOR), and $\|$ denoter concatenation.

The expander phase of the HKDF functions is $Exp_{PRK}(c, n) : K(1) \Leftarrow F(PRK \oplus opad)\|F((PRK \oplus ipad)\|c\|0)$ and F is the hash function. If $n > fl$, two or more iterations are necessary until the required length has been obtained: $K(i + 1) \Leftarrow F((PRK \oplus opad)\|F((PRK \oplus ipad)\|K(i)\|c\|i)), 1 \leq i < t$, where $t = \lceil \frac{n}{fl} \rceil$. The first n bits of the outputs $K(1)\|K(2)\|\dots\|K(t-1)$ are used as the cryptographic key, and the remaining bits are discarded.

Block Ciphers. The AES-CMAC based *KDF* is described in NIST SP800-108 [8]. The AES block cipher supports key sizes of 128, 192 and 256 bit and has an output size of 128 bits. The AES-CMAC based extractor can be either AES-128, 192 or 256, but the expander is fixed to use AES-128.

During the extraction phase, the input p is broken up into 128 bit blocks denoted as $D_i, 1 \leq i < t, t = \lceil \frac{pl}{128} \rceil$; and the salt s is used as the AES key. The D_i are processed sequentially by using AES. The process is $PRK_i = F_s(PRK_{i-1} \oplus D_i)$, where F is AES (128 or 192 or 256), $1 \leq i < t$ and $PRK_0 = 0^{128}$.

During the expansion, the PRK and c are the inputs to the expander phase, where c is broken into D_i blocks, $1 \leq i < t, t = \lceil \frac{cl}{128} \rceil$. PRK is used as the AES key. The extractor function is as below: $K(i) \Leftarrow F_{PRK}(K_{i-1} \oplus D_i)$ where F is AES-128, $1 \leq i < t$ and $K(0) = 0^{128}$. The last block of operation is $K(t) = F_{PRK}(K_{t-1} \oplus D_t \oplus K_b)$, $b \in \{1, 2\}$. If $n > 128$, more iterations are performed until the length of output obtained exceeds the required length. Then, the left-most n bits of the output are used as the cryptographic key and the remaining bits are discarded.

3   Keystream Generator

A pseudorandom keystream generator is one of the components of a stream cipher. The inputs to the pseudorandom keystream generator are a secret key and a known initial value (IV) and the output is a pseudorandom keystream as shown in Figure 3. The aim of the secure stream cipher is to use a pseudorandom keystream generator which approximate an ideal pseudorandom as defined in Definition 8 and Definition 9. Note that although the keystream output can be produced in bits, bytes or words, we consider the keystream as a binary string: $Z_1, Z_2, \ldots, Z_t$, where $Z_i \in \{0,1\}, i = 1, 2, \ldots, t$.

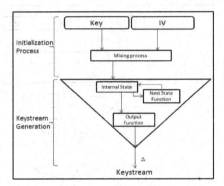

Fig. 3. Keystream Generator [22]

Definition 8. *(Keystream generator). Let KEYSPACE, IVSPACE, ISSPACE, ZSPACE be a set space over $\{0,1\}^k$, $\{0,1\}^i$, $\{0,1\}^{is}$ and $\{0,1\}^*$ respectively. A keystream generator is a pseudorandom generator (Definition 9) that takes the inputs key and IV and generates arbitrary length of keystream. Pseudorandom keystream generator: $\{0,1\}^k \times \{0,1\}^i \to \{0,1\}^{is} \to \{0,1\}^*$.*

Definition 9. *(Ideal pseudorandom generator) [17]. An ideal pseudorandom generator is said to pass all polynomial-time statistical tests if no polynomial-time algorithm can correctly distinguish between an output sequence of the generator and a truly random sequence of the same length with probability not larger than $\frac{1}{2} + \epsilon$, for some negligible value ϵ.*

4   Stream Cipher Based KDF

Our proposed *SCKDF* is a two-phase model where both the extractor and the expander are based on keystream generators for stream ciphers. For stream ciphers, the pseudorandom keystream generator takes two inputs: a key and an IV. In our *SCKDF*, we replace the pair of inputs to the pseudorandom keystream generator (key, IV) with the input pair (p, s) for the extractor phase and the input pair (PRK, c) for the expander phase. Detailed descriptions and specification for these phases are as follows.

4.1   Extractor

In this section, we propose an extractor based on the pseudorandom keystream generator for a stream cipher. The extractor takes p and s as the inputs and produces an output sequence PRK. Let v and w denote the key size and IV size respectively, for the stream cipher. Similarly, let r denote the key size of the stream cipher in the expander phase. (Note that is possible the same stream cipher may be used for both extractor phase and expander phase, but this is not necessary.) Figure 4 depicts our proposed stream cipher based extractor. The extractor process is as follows.

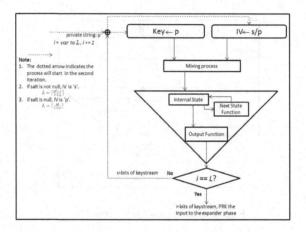

Fig. 4. Extractor based on stream ciphers

1. **Input:** p, s, pl, sl, r.
2. **Process:**
    (a) **If s is null**.
        i. Divide private string p into blocks, where each block is of length of $v + w$. Let D_i denote the ith block of p. The total number of blocks is $L = \lceil \frac{pl}{v+w} \rceil$. If the length of the last block D_L is less than $v + w$ bits, the block is padded with '0's. Go to Step 2c.
    (b) **Else (if s is not null)**. Public string s is proposed to have same length as w of pseudorandom keystream generator. However, if $sl < w$, set the remaining bits with '0's.
        i. **If $pl < v$**.
            A. Pad the remaining bits of p with '0's.
            B. Use the p as the key and s as the IV for the pseudorandom keystream generator.
            C. Generate r bits of keystream.
            D. **Proceed** to Step 3.
        ii. **Else, if $pl > v$**.
            A. Use the first v bits of p as the key and s as the IV for the pseudorandom keystream generator.

B. Generate $v + w$ bits of keystream.

C. The remaining bits of p are divided into blocks, where each block is of length of $v + w$. Let D_i denote the ith block of p. The total number of blocks is $L = \lceil \frac{pl-v}{v+w} \rceil$. If the length of the last block D_L is less than $v + w$ bits, the block is padded with '0's.

D. XOR the $v + w$ bits of keystream produced in Step 2(b)iiB with D_1 of p.

E. **Go** to Step 2c.

(c) For $i = 1$ to L, do the following:

    i. **If** $i = L$. Use the first v bits of D_i as the key and remaining w bits of D_i as the IV and generate r bits of keystream. **Proceed** to Step 3.

    ii. **Else, if** $i > L$.

        A. Use the first v bits of D_i as the key and remaining w bits of D_i as the IV for the pseudorandom keystream generator.

        B. Generate $v + w$ bits of keystream.

        C. The $v + w$ bits of keystream is XORed with D_{i+1} of p.

        D. $i := i + 1$.

3. **Output:**
   - An r-bit string, denoted PRK.

4.2   Expander

In this section, we describe a stream cipher based expander. This function takes inputs the output of extractor phase PRK, together with an arbitrary length binary string c, the context information. The expander output is a pseudorandom binary string. Let v and w denote the key size and IV size respectively for the stream cipher. Figure 5 illustrates our proposed stream cipher based expander. The expander process is as follows.

1. **Input:** PRK, c, cl, and n.
   - If c is null, then c is padded with '0's, $cl = w$.

2. **Process:**

(a) The context information c is divided into blocks, where each block size is of length of w. Let D_i denote the ith block of c. The total number of blocks is $L = \lceil \frac{cl}{w} \rceil$. If the length of the last block D_L is less than w bits, the block is padded with '0's.

    i. **If** $L = 1$.

        A. Use PRK (from the extractor phase) as the key and c as the IV for the pseudorandom keystream generator.

        B. Generate n bits of keystream.

        C. **Proceed** to Step 3.

    ii. **Else, if** $L > 1$.

        A. Use PRK (from the extractor phase) as the key and the first block D_1 as the IV for the pseudorandom keystream generator.

        B. Generate v bits of keystream.

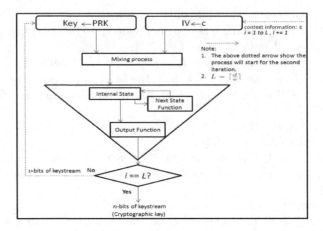

Fig. 5. Expander based on stream ciphers

   C. **Proceed** to Step 2b.
(b) For $i = 2$ to L, do the following:
   i. **If** $i = L$.
      A. Use v bits of keystream as the key and the D_i as the IV for the pseudorandom keystream generator.
      B. Generate n bits of keystream.
      C. **Proceed** to Step 3.
   ii. **Else, if** $i > L$.
      A. Use v bits of keystream as the key and the D_i the IV for the pseudorandom keystream generator.
      B. Generate v bits of keystream.
      C. $i := i + 1$.
3. **Output:** An n-bit binary string suitable for use as a cryptographic key.

5   The Security of SCKDF

Our proposed two-phase (extract then expand) *SCKDF* makes use of the pseudorandom keystream generator of a stream cipher in each phase. We assume this is an ideal keystream generator (satisfying Definition 8 and Definition 9 in Section 3). Note that, a similar assumption of an ideal primitive was also made by Krawczyk in proving Theorem 1 in [15].

For such a pseudorandom keystream generator the *SCKDF* proposed in Section 4 can be considered as CCS-secure.

Theorem 2. *Let pseudorandom keystream generator be a keystream generator from a family of pseudorandom keystream generator which satisfy Definition 8 and Definition 9. If an extract-then-expand SCKDF is built from the pseudorandom keystream generator, then the extract-then-expand SCKDF scheme is $(min\{t_X, t_Y\}, q_Y, \epsilon_X + \epsilon_Y)$-CCS secure with the respect to the private string p.*

Proof: To satisfy the conditions of Theorem 1, we need to show,

i The extractor is a (t_X, ϵ_X)-computational extractor.

ii The expander is a (t_Y, q_Y, ϵ_Y)-secure variable-length-output pseudorandom function family.

To prove (i) we assume that extractor is not a (t_X, ϵ_X)-computational extractor. This would imply that an adversary A has a polynomial time method to distinguish whether PRK is derived from p or a random string of the same length. For the underlying pseudorandom keystream generator this would then imply that the adversary has a polynomial time method to distinguish between PRK and a truly random string. This contradicts the assumption that pseudorandom keystream generator satisfies Definition 9. Hence (i) is true. Similarly, we can show (ii) is true. Hence by Theorem 1 the $SCKDF$ built from pseudorandom keystream generator is $(\min\{t_X, t_Y\}, q_Y, \epsilon_X + \epsilon_Y)$-CCS secure with the respect to the private string p. □

6   Performance Measurement

In order to compare the performance of stream cipher, hash function and block cipher based KDFs, we conducted experiments involving measuring the execution time taken to generate n bits of cryptographic key from p, s and c. The stream ciphers include the e-Stream finalists Trivium [6], Sosemanuk [4] and Rabbit [5]. It should be noted that to date these has been no significant security flaws discovered with any of these three stream ciphers. Hence any of these three stream ciphers seem to offer suitable pseudorandom keystream generator generators on which to build our $SCKDF$ model in Section 4. The hash functions are SHA families and block cipher used is AES128. The code of the stream ciphers, hash functions and block ciphers are retreived from [18], [10] and [21] respectively. The lengths of the four parameters (p, s, c and n) are taken from the applications below:

- **Application 1**: Host identity protocol version 2(HIPv2) is based on the DH shared secret key exchange protocol, which provides secure communications and maintains shared IP-layer state between two separate parties [13]. The cryptographic keys are generated using KDF and the inputs are as below:
  - Exp 1 : p = 128 bytes, s = 8 bytes, c= 32 bytes, n = 64 bytes
  - Exp 2 : p = 128 bytes, s = 8 bytes, c= 32 bytes, n = 192 bytes
  - Exp 3 : p = 256 bytes, s = 8 bytes, c= 32 bytes, n = 64 bytes
  - Exp 4 : p = 256 bytes, s = 8 bytes, c= 32 bytes, n = 192 bytes
- **Application 2**: PKINIT is applied in Kerberos protocol [24]. The inputs to the KDF are as below:
  - Exp 5 : p = 128 bytes, s = null, c= 64 bytes, n = 64 bytes
  - Exp 6 : p = 128 bytes, s = null, c= 64 bytes, n = 192 bytes
  - Exp 7 : p = 256 bytes, s = null, c= 64 bytes, n = 64 bytes
  - Exp 8 : p = 256 bytes, s = null, c= 64 bytes, n = 192 bytes

– **Application 3**: The tunneled extensible authentication method (TEAM) is a method that securing communication between peer and server by using transport layer security (TLS) to establish a mutually authenticated tunnel[12]. The inputs to the *KDF* are as below:
  • Exp 9 : p = 40 bytes, s = 32 bytes, c= null, n = 128 bytes

6.1 Software Performance

For all nine experiments the time is recorded for each of 100 trials. The average time (mean) and standard deviation for each experiment are presented in Table 2. The execution time was captured using CLOCK_MONOTONIC (which can be found in the programming language C library). All the simulations were performed at a machine with the following specifications: Intel (R) core (TM) 2 duo CPU E8400 @ 3.00GHz 2.99 GHz, 4GB RAM and in 64 bit OS.

Table 2 shows the software performance of *KDF*s based on three different cryptographic primitives. The three cryptographic primitives are stream cipher, hash function and block cipher. The execution time for Exp 9 was relatively faster compare with Exp 1-8 for all *KDF* proposals. This is due to the inputs length in Exp 9 being shorter than the input lengths for Exp 1-8. Overall, the execution time for all types of *KDF* increases, when the lengths of the inputs $(p, s, c$ or $n)$ increase.

Another observation from this table is the performance results show that all three stream cipher based *KDF*'s were significantly more efficient in software than either the hash function or block cipher based *KDF*'s. While, the most efficient *KDF* is the Trivium based *KDF* and the slowest *KDF* is block cipher based *KDF*.

Table 2. Software Performance of KDF

KDFs/Exp		Exp 1	Exp 2	Exp 3	Exp 4	Exp 5	Exp 6	Exp 7	Exp 8	Exp 9
Trivium	$\bar{x}$	12185.15	12886.61	19798.71	20623.36	14967.07	15829.43	21396.72	22628.53	4900.05
	S	1761.62	2575.09	1293.19	2178.31	1276.21	2605.27	219.91	4169.30	311.00
Sosemanuk	$\bar{x}$	18494.99	19237.54	30231.75	30153.16	20828.66	21714.94	33749.51	32449.32	8089.25
	S	2182.31	2040.69	5459.62	2906.47	2199.21	2547.35	8761.57	3162.79	165.06
Rabbit	$\bar{x}$	26307.11	26296.78	33691.33	36346.68	29845.23	31898.28	43679.73	43559.88	7825.69
	S	7024.60	1482.73	297.45	4245.17	277.67	1904.01	6523.79	3069.62	231.41
SHA1	$\bar{x}$	39583.75	79485.76	41267.27	83951.21	45068.91	96129.51	47816.59	99010.69	56364.39
	S	6129.62	1341.97	1422.08	2333.11	3489.43	1558.77	1429.24	712.13	5777.41
SHA224	$\bar{x}$	39327.14	77271.78	44264.8	82551.63	43258.77	80919.54	35060.03	74216.05	48076.72
	S	2453.69	1789.89	6180.79	16942.54	6144.87	1749.19	1519.05	668.50	1592.78
SHA256	$\bar{x}$	29756.25	68713.71	33140.46	72019.25	32685.35	72101.38	36264.51	75328.13	40487.08
	S	1581.87	2270.14	1384.51	1903.90	5763.42	4108.59	5491.55	3262.97	1540.99
SHA384	$\bar{x}$	82538.02	137821.08	84262.56	143402.09	83547.43	142936.8	89696.46	149876.24	96146.69
	S	3711.42	25900.93	1900.20	58864.25	1111.95	8541.55	1959.77	13847.19	556.55
SHA512	$\bar{x}$	54947.72	116787.15	60843.54	119729.85	59245.68	119497.2	60870.97	122340.7	74657.5
	S	1926.55	29908.35	1965.87	59220.04	5220.38	6334.94	2106.51	6051.33	1491.43
AES128	$\bar{x}$	236657.29	500199.78	330521.48	580804.49	322538.33	753565.93	410619.75	830594.7	148952.35
	S	12451.69	25568.83	41150.53	25316.09	10485.70	22020.28	21595.07	4468.46	52170.44

*Performance time is in nanosecond. $\bar{x}$ and S are sample mean and standard deviation respectively

6.2   Hardware Performance

This section presents hardware implementation and performance metrices for stream ciphers, hash functions and block ciphers. Note that, the hardware performance comparison is not the hardware performance of the actual *KDF* proposals. Rather it represents the hardware performance of the underlying cryptographic primitives obtained from existing literature. The result shows that Trivium requires less resource and has highest throughput, while SHA384 and SHA512 requires the highest resource in hardware. These results indicate that a hardware based *KDF* designed from Trivium using the *SCKDF* model would offer significant advantages over other designs in hardware.

Table 3. Hardware Performance of Hash Functions, Block Ciphers and Stream Ciphers

	Trivium x64	Sosemanuk	Rabbit	SHA1	SHA224	SHA256	SHA384	SHA512	AES	Better is:
Gates	4921	18819	28000	9859	15329	15329	27297	27297	5398	Lower
Throughputs (Mb/s)	22300	6062	473.6	2006	2370	2370	2909	2909	311.09	Higher
Technology	$0.13\mu m$	$0.13\mu m$	$0.18\mu m$	$0.13\mu m$	$0.13\mu m$	$0.13\mu m$	$0.13\mu m$	$0.13\mu m$	$0.11\mu m$	
Reference	[11]	[11]	[5]	[19]	[19]	[19]	[19]	[19]	[20]	

7   Conclusion

A *KDF* is an essential component in generating cryptographic keys for safe-guarding data storage and transmission over insecure channel. To be capable of working better on mobile devices such as smartphones, pocket PC and mobile phones, we proposed a lightweight *KDF* based on stream ciphers. Stream ciphers are often faster and require less resources which are suitable operated at low processing power and memory constrained devices, for example mobile devices. In this research, we have demonstrated that our newly proposed *KDF* based stream ciphers are secure if the underlying stream cipher are secure and more efficient compared to existing *KDF* proposals. From our analysis to date a *SCKDF* design based on Trivium cipher would be secure and efficient both in software and hardware.

References

1. Adams, C., Kramer, G., Mister, S., Zuccherato, R.: On the Security of Key Derivation Functions. Information Security 3225, 134–145 (2004)
2. X. ANSI. 9.42. American National Standard for Financial Services-Public Key Cryptography for the Financial Services Industry: Agreement of Symmetric Keys Using Discrete Logarithm Cryptography (2001)
3. Barker, E.B., Johnson, D., Smid, M.E.: SP 800-56A. Recommendation for Pair-Wise Key Establishment Schemes Using Discrete Logarithm Cryptography (Revised) (2007)
4. Berbain, C., et al.: SOSEMANUK, A fast software-oriented stream cipher. In: Robshaw, M., Billet, O. (eds.) New Stream Cipher Designs. LNCS, vol. 4986, pp. 98–118. Springer, Heidelberg (2008)

5. Boesgaard, M., Vesterager, M., Zenner, E.: The Rabbit stream cipher. In: Robshaw, M., Billet, O. (eds.) New Stream Cipher Designs. LNCS, vol. 4986, pp. 69–83. Springer, Heidelberg (2008)
6. Canniere, C.D., Preneel, B.: Trivium specifications (2005), citeseer.ist.psu.edu/734144.html
7. Chen, L.: Recommendations for Key Derivation Using Pseudorandom Functions. NIST Special Publication, 800:108 (2008)
8. Chen, L.: Recommendation for Key Derivation Using Pseudorandom Functions. NIST Special Publication, 800:108 (2009)
9. Chen, L.: SP 800-56C. Recommendation for Key Derivation through Extraction-then-Expansion (2011)
10. Eastlake, D., Hansen, T.: US secure hash algorithms (SHA and SHA-based HMAC and HKDF) (2011)
11. Good, T., Benaissa, M.: Hardware results for selected stream cipher candidates. In: State of the Art of Stream Ciphers, pp. 191–204 (2007)
12. Harkins, D.: Network Working Group G. Zorn Internet-Draft Network Zen Intended status: Standards Track Q. Wu Expires, Huawei (September 9, 2011)
13. Heer, T., Jokela, P., Henderson, T., Moskowitz, R.: Host Identity Protocol Version 2 (HIPv2) (2012)
14. Kaliski, B.: PKCS# 5: Password-based cryptography specification version 2.0. Technical report, RFC 2898, September 2000 (2000)
15. Krawczyk, H.: Cryptographic Extraction and Key Derivation: The HKDF Scheme. In: Rabin, T. (ed.) CRYPTO 2010. LNCS, vol. 6223, pp. 631–648. Springer, Heidelberg (2010)
16. McGrew, D., Weis, B.: Key Derivation Functions and Their Uses (2010), http://www.ietf.org/id/draft-irtf-cfrg-kdf-uses-00.txt
17. Menezes, A.J., Van Oorschot, P.C., Vanstone, S.A.: Handbook of applied cryptography. CRC (1997)
18. Robshaw, M.: The eSTREAM project. In: Robshaw, M., Billet, O. (eds.) New Stream Cipher Designs. LNCS, vol. 4986, pp. 1–6. Springer, Heidelberg (2008)
19. Satoh, A., Inoue, T.: ASIC-hardware-focused Comparison for Hash Functions MD5, RIPEMD-160, and SHS. INTEGRATION, The VLSI Journal 40(1), 3–10 (2007)
20. Satoh, A., Morioka, S., Takano, K., Munetoh, S.: A Compact Rijndael Hardware Architecture with S–box Optimization. In: Boyd, C. (ed.) ASIACRYPT 2001. LNCS, vol. 2248, pp. 239–254. Springer, Heidelberg (2001)
21. Song, J.H., Poovendran, R., Lee, J., Iwata, T.: INTERNET DRAFT Ibaraki University Expires: May 6, 2006, November 7, 2005 The AES-CMAC Algorithm draft-songlee-aes-cmac-02. txt (2005)
22. Stallings, W.: Cryptography and Network Security: Principles and Practices, 4th edn. Pearson Education India (2006)
23. Yao, F.F., Yin, Y.L.: Design and Analysis of Password-Based Key Derivation Functions. In: Menezes, A. (ed.) CT-RSA 2005. LNCS, vol. 3376, pp. 245–261. Springer, Heidelberg (2005)
24. Zhu, L., Wasserman, M., Astrand, L.H.: PKINIT Algorithm Agility (2012)

Sustainable Pseudo-random Number Generator

Zhu Huafei, Wee-Siong Ng, and See-Kiong Ng

USPO, I^2R, Singapore

Abstract. Barak and Halevi (BH) have proposed an efficient architecture for robust pseudorandom generators that ensure resilience in
the presence of attackers with partial knowledge or partial controls of
the generators' entropy resources. The BH scheme is constructed from
the Barak, Shaltiel and Tromer's randomness extractor and its security
is formalized in the simulation-based framework. The BH model however, does not address the scenario where an attacker completely controls the generators' entropy resources with no knowledge of the internal
state. Namely, the BH security model does not consider the security
of `bad-refresh` conditioned on `compromised = false`. The security of
such a case is interesting since if the output of the protocol conditioned
on `compromised = false` looks random to the attacker, then the proposed scheme is secure even if the attacker completely controls entropy
resources (recall that attackers with partial knowledge or partial controls of the generators' entropy resources in the BH model). The BH
scheme is called sustainable if the above mentioned security requirement
is guaranteed. This paper studies the sustainability of the BH pseudorandom generator and makes the following two contributions: in the first
fold, a new notion which we call sustainable pseudorandom generator
which extends the security definition of the BH's robust scheme is introduced and formalized in the simulation paradigm; in the second fold,
we show that the BH's robust scheme achieves the sustainability under the joint assumptions that the underlying stateless function G is a
cryptographic pseudorandom number generator and the output of the
underlying randomness extractor `extract()` is statistically close to the
uniform distribution.

Keywords: Provable security, Robust pseudo-random number generator, Sustainable pseudo-random number generator.

1 Introduction

Randomness is essential for security protocols and pseudorandom generators
are used to generate random bits from short random seeds [7,8]. A randomness
generator, usually is defined over a randomness extractor which in turn is defined
over certain mathematical assumptions (e.g., cryptographic hash functions and
one-way functions [5,13,4,3,9,12,2,1,14] and the references therein). The reality,
however is that procedures for cryptographic systems to obtain random strings
are often not well designed [10,6,11].

L.J. Janczewski, H.B. Wolfe, and S. Shenoi (Eds.): SEC 2013, IFIP AICT 405, pp. 139–147, 2013.
© IFIP International Federation for Information Processing 2013

Considering a scenario, where a Trusted Platform Module (TPM) is used to collect high-entropy resources so that randomness can be extracted from the generated high-entropy resource (notice that the assumption of high-entropy source is a necessary condition for extracting randomness. This is because one cannot extract m bits from a distribution source with min-entropy less than m). Let X be a random variable describing possible outputs of the TPM in a specified environment. Ideally, we would like the adversary not to be able to influence the distribution of X at all so that the original design for generating high-entropy resource is guaranteed. However, in a realistic setting an adversary may have some control over the environment in which the device operates, and it is possible that changes (e.g., temperature, voltage, frequency, timing, etc.) in this environment affect the distribution of random variable X.

Barak, Shaltiel and Tromer [4] formalized the mathematical mode for the adversary's influence on the source and then proposed an efficient construction of randomness extractors that aim to extract randomness from high entropy resources. They have shown that their randomness extractors work for all resources of sufficiently high-entropy, even the specified resources are correlated. Barak and Halevi [3] then presented formal models and architectures for robust pseudorandom generators (a pseudorandom generator is robust if it is resilient in the presence of attackers with partial knowledge or partial controls of the generators' entropy resources). The Barak and Halevi's (BH) pseudorandom generator consists of the following two algorithms

- A function next() that generates output r ($(r, s') \leftarrow$ next(s)) and then updates the state s' accordingly; The goal of this component is to ensure that if an attacker does not know the current state s then the output should be random form the point view of the attacker. Typically, next() is a deterministic algorithm given an initial state s_0. It is well-known that there exists no single deterministic randomness extractor for all high-entropy resources X and hence the design of next() function is a non-trivial task [4,3].
- A function refresh() that refreshes the current state s using some additional input x ($s' \leftarrow$ refresh(s, x)). The goal of this component is to ensure that if the input x is from a high-entropy resource then the resulting state is unknown to the attacker.

1.1   The Motivation Problem

The security of Barak and Halevi's robust pseudorandom generator is formalized in the simulation-based framework. The security game begins with the system player initializing $s = 0^m$ and compromised =true and then the attacker interacts with the system using the following interfaces:

- good-refresh(D) with D a distribution in high entropy source $\mathcal{H}$. The system resets compromised =false.
- bad-refresh(x) with a bit string x. If compromised = true then the system sets $s' =$ refresh(s, x) and updates the internal state to s'. Otherwise (if compromised = false) it does *nothing*;

- set-state(s') with an m-bit string s'. If compromised = true then the system returns to the attacker the current internal state s, and if compromised = false then it chooses a new random string $s' \leftarrow_R \{0,1\}^m$ and returns it to the attacker.
  Either way, the system also sets compromised = true and sets the new internal state to s'.
- next-bits(). If compromised = true then the system runs $(r, s') = \text{next}(s)$, replaces the internal state s by s' and returns to the attacker the m-bit string r. If compromised = false then the system chooses a new random string $r \leftarrow_R \{0,1\}^m$ and returns it to the attacker.

Recall that in the ideal world (in the BH model), when an attacker invokes bad-refresh conditioned on compromised = false, the system does *nothing* while in the real world scenario, even if the attacker invokes bad-refresh conditioned on compromised = false, the pseudorandom generator scheme will output a refresh statement $s' = \text{refresh}(s, x)$. If we consider the security of bad-refresh(x) conditioned on compromised = false, then there is a security gap between the real-world scenario and the ideal-world scenario in the BH model. Notice that this gap between the ideal world scenario and the real world sceario does not imply that the BH scheme is insecure since the security definition in the BH model does not encompass such a scenario.

1.2 This Work

At first glance, a formalization of sustainable pseudorandom generator is trivial since the state s of the current interface bad-refresh(x) conditioned on compromised = false is unknown to the attacker in the BH model. We however, aware that to define an output of bad-refresh(x) conditioned on compromised = false, the following scenarios must be carefully considered

- at least one invocation of good-refresh(D) with D in high entropy resource $\mathcal{H}$ has been called before the current invocation of the bad-refresh(x) with input x since the initial state of the BH system is 0^m which is publicly known and compromised =true.
- possible many invocations of next-bits() have been called since the flag defined in the BH model remains compromised = false in each next-bits() invocation.
- no set-state(s') with input s' is invoked between the latest good-refresh(D) invocation and the current bad-refresh(x) with input x and compromised = false invocation;

As a result, the output of bad-refresh(x) with input x and compromised = false from the point view of the adversary conditioned on the unknown of the current state s should be determined by the transcripts of invocations of the interfaces defined above. Before we define a possible output of bad-refresh(x), we would like first to consider the following interesting cases.

- Case 1: Suppose there are total l_1 calls of good-refresh(D). The transcript of the l_1 invocations can be expressed in the following form: $s_1 =$ refresh(s_0, x_0), $s_2 =$ refresh(s_1, x_1), $\cdots$, $s_{l_1} =$ refresh(s_{l_1-}, x_{l_1-1}), where s_0 is the initial state and $x_0, \ldots, x_{l_1}$ are selected from the high entropy source $\mathcal{H}$. Notice that $(s_1, \ldots, s_{l_1})$ are kept secret to the attacker.
- Case 2: Suppose there are total l_2 calls of next-bits(). We further consider the following two cases:
  Case 2.1: if compromised = true then the system runs $(r, s') =$ next(s), replaces the internal state s by s' and returns to the attacker the m-bit string (r, s'). More precisely, let s_0 be the initial state that is known to the attacker, then the transcript can be expressed in the following form: $(r_1, s_1) =$ next-bits(s_0), $(r_2, s_2) =$ next-bits(s_1), $\cdots$, $(r_{l_2}, s_{l_2}) =$ next-bits(s_{1_2-1}).
  Case 2.2: if compromised = false then the system runs $(r, s') =$ next(s), replaces the internal state s by s' and returns r but not s' to the attacker. More precisely, if s_0^* is unknown to the attacker (here we assume that s_0^* is obtained by invoking good-refresh(D) interface), then the transcript can be expressed in the following form: $(r_1, s_1) =$ next-bits(s_0^*), $(r_2, s_2) =$ next-bits(s_1), $\cdots$, $(r_{l_2}, s_{l_2}) =$ next-bits(s_{1_2-1}).

Notice that the transcripts useful to the attacker are those generated in Case 2.2 since the transcripts in Case 2.1 can be computed by the attacker itself while the transcripts in Case 1 reveal nothing other than notices of the activated executions. We will define an output of bad-refresh(x) conditioned on compromised = false a random string. This is because computational indistinguishability is preserved by efficient algorithms. The challenging task now is whether the BH's pseudorandom generator is sustainable? Luckily, we are able to show that the Barak and Halevi's robust pseudorandom generator is sustainable under the joint assumptions that the underlying stateless function G is a cryptographic pseudorandom number generator and the output of the underlying randomness extractor extract() is statistically close to the uniform distribution.

Road-Map: The rest of this paper is organized as follows: the notion of sustainable pseudorandom generator is first introduced and formalized in Section 2; We then show that the Barak and Halevi's robust pseudorandom generator is sustainable assuming the existence of cryptographic pseudorandom number generators and the t-resilient extractor and we conclude this work in Section 4.

2   Sustainable Pseudorandom Generators

In this section, we first recall the robust pseudorandom generator due to Barak and Halevi, and then provide a formal definition of sustainable pseudorandom generators

2.1   The Barak and Halevi's Construction

In the high level, Barak-Halevi's framework consists of two functions: next(s) that generates the next output and then updates the state accordingly; and refresh(s, x) that refreshes the current state s using some additional input x.

- A next function next takes as input a sate $s \in \{0,1\}^m$ to generate a pair (r, s'), where r is an l-bit string and s' is an m-bit state. next then outputs r and replaces s the internal state by the new state s'.
- A refresh function refresh takes as input (s, x) to generate a new state s', where $s \in \{0,1\}^m$ and $x \in \{0,1\}^n$. refresh then updates the state with s'.

Definition 1. *Given a collection $H = \{h_\lambda\}_{\lambda \in \Lambda}$ of functions h_λ: $\{0,1\}^n \rightarrow \{0,1\}^m$, we consider the probability space of choosing $\lambda \in_R \Lambda$. For every $x \in \{0,1\}^n$, we define the random variable $R_x = h_\lambda(x)$. We say that H is an l-wise independent family of hash functions if:*

- *for every x, R_x is uniformly distributed in $\{0,1\}^m$;*
- *$\{R_x\}_{x \in \{0,1\}^n}$ are l-wise independent.*

Lemma 1. *(due to Barak, Shaltiel and Tromer [4]) Let X be a random variable. Let $Pr[X = x]$ be the probability that X assigns to an element x. Let $H_\infty(X) = \log(\frac{1}{max_{x \in X} Pr[X=x]})$. Let $H = \{h_\lambda\}_{\lambda \in \Lambda}$ be a family of l-wise independent hash functions from n bits to m bits, $l \geq 2$. If $H_\infty(X) \geq k$, then for at least a $1 - 2^{-u}$ fraction of $\lambda \in \Lambda$, $h_\lambda(X)$ is ϵ-close to uniform for $u = \frac{l}{2}(k - m - 2\log(\frac{1}{\epsilon}) - \log(l) + 2) - m - 2)$.*

The function $h_\lambda(X)$ is called randomness extractor. To implement the next function next and refresh function refresh, Barak and Halevi first invoke the following standard cryptographic pseudorandom generator (PRG) [7] and a randomness extractor extract [4], where

- PRG is a stateless function G: $\{0,1\}^m \rightarrow \{0,1\}^{2m}$ such that $G(U_m)$ is computationally indistinguishable from U_{2m}, where m is a security parameter and U_m is the uniform distribution on $\{0,1\}^m$.
- An extractor is a function extract(): $\{0,1\}^{n \geq m} \times \Lambda \rightarrow \{0,1\}^m$ for some index set Λ (according to Theorem 1). The output $Ext(x, \lambda)$ is closed to the uniformly distributed, where $x \in \{0,1\}^n$ is the output of the high-entropy source and $\lambda \in \Lambda$.

The BH robust pseudorandom generator

Given an extractor extract(): $\{0,1\}^{n \geq m} \rightarrow \{0,1\}^m$ and a cryptographic non-robust PRG G: $\{0,1\}^m \rightarrow \{0,1\}^{2m}$, where m is a security parameter. By $(r, s') \leftarrow G(s)$, we denote that r is the first m bits in the output of $G(s)$ and s' is the last m bits and by $G'(s) = r$, we denote a function G' that on input $s \in \{0,1\}^m$ outputs only the first m bits of $G(s)$.

- refresh(s, x), returns $s' \leftarrow G'(s \oplus \text{extract}(x))$;
- next(s) returns $(r, s') \leftarrow G(s)$.

2.2 Definition of Sustainable Pseudorandom Generator

We follow the BH paradigm that models an attacker on the generator in the real world as an efficient procedure A that has four interfaces to the generator, namely good-refresh(), bad-refresh(), set-state() and next-bits(). The ideal-world game proceeds similarly to the real-world game, except that the calls that A makes to its interfaces are handled differently.

The real-World Game. The real world game begins with the system player initializing the internal state of the generator to null, i.e., $s = 0^m$ and then the attacker A interacts with the system using the following interfaces:

- good-refresh(D) with D a distribution in $\mathcal{H}$, called high entropy distributions. The system draws $x \leftarrow_R D$, sets $s' = \text{refresh}(s, x)$ and updates the internal state to s'.
- bad-refresh(x) with a bit string x. The system sets $s' = \text{refresh}(s, x)$ and updates the internal state to s'.
- set-state(s') with an m-bit string s'. The system returns to the attacker the current internal state s and then changes it to s'.
- next-bits(). The system runs $(r, s') \leftarrow \text{next}(s)$, replaces the internal state s by s' and returns to the attacker the m-bit string r.

The game continues in this fashion until the attacker decides to halt with some output in $0, 1$. For a particular construction PRG = (next, refresh), we let $Pr[A(m, H)^{\text{R(PRG)}} = 1]$ denote the probability that A outputs the bit 1 after interacting as above with the system that implements the generator PRG and with parameters m, H. Here R(PRG) stands for the real-world process from above.

The Ideal-World Game. Formally, the ideal-world game is parametrized by the same security parameter m and family of distribution $\mathcal{H}$ as before. The game begins with the system player initializing $s = 0^m$ and compromised =true and then the attacker interacts with the system using the following interfaces:

- good-refresh(D) with D a distribution in $\mathcal{H}$. The system resets compromised =false.
- bad-refresh(x) with a bit string x. If compromised = true then the system sets $s' = \text{refresh}(s, x)$ and updates the internal state to s'. Otherwise (if compromised = false) it outputs a random string s';
- set-state(s') with an m-bit string s'. If compromised = true then the system returns to the attacker the current internal state s, and if compromised = false then it chooses a new random string $s' \leftarrow_R \{0, 1\}^m$ and returns it to the attacker.
  Either way, the system also sets compromised = true and sets the new internal state to s'.

- next-bits(). If compromised = true then the system runs $(r, s') = $ next(s), replaces the internal state s by s' and returns to the attacker the m-bit string r. If compromised = false then the system chooses a new random string $r \leftarrow_R \{0, 1\}^m$ and returns it to the attacker.

The game continues in this fashion until the attacker decides to halt with some output in $\{0, 1\}$. For a particular construction PRG = (next, refresh), we let I(PRG) denote the ideal process and let $Pr[A(m, H)^{I(PRG)} = 1]$ denote the probability that A outputs the bit 1 after interacting as above with the system.

Definition 2. *We say that PRG = (next, refresh) is a sustainable pseudo-random generator (with respect to a family H of distributions) if for every probabilistic polynomial-time attacker algorithm A, the difference*

$$Pr[A(m, H)^{R(PRG)} = 1] - Pr[A(m, H)^{I(PRG)} = 1]$$

is negligible in the security parameter l, m and n.

3   The Proof of Security

Theorem 1. *The Barak and Halevi's robust pseudorandom generator is sustainable assuming that the underlying algorithm G is a cryptographic pseudorandom generator and randomness extractor extract with respect to the family H that is statistically close to the uniform distribution of $\{0, 1\}^m$.*

Proof. We consider the following experiments: Expr.R, an adversary A interacts with the real system; Expr.I, A interacts with the ideal process and Expr.H, a hybrid experiment which is defined below:

- good-refresh(D) with D a distribution in high entropy resource H. The system draws $d \leftarrow_R \{0, 1\}^m$, sets $s' = G'(d \oplus s)$, and updates the internal states to s'. The system resets compromised =false.
- bad-refresh(x) with a bit string $x \in \{0, 1\}^m$. The system sets $s' \leftarrow$ refresh($s \oplus$ extract(x)) and updates the internal states to s'.
- set-state(s') with an m-bit string s'. The system returns to the attacker the current internal state s. The system also sets compromised = true and sets the new internal state to s'.
- next-bits(s). The system runs $(r, s) = $ next(s) and replaces the internal state s by s' and returns to the attacker the m-bit string r.

One checks to see that the only difference between Expr.R and Expr.H is the definition of the good-refresh(D), $D \in H$. From the construction of randomness extractor [4], we know that the output of randomness extractor is statistically close to U_m. Also note that the output of good-refresh(D) with respect to high entropy source H is statistically close to U_m. As a result, the output of good-refresh(D) defined in Expr.R and that defined in Expr.R are statistically close (statistical closeness is preserved by any function [7]).

Next, we want to show that Expr.I and Expr.H are computationally close. Suppose that the view of A in Expr.I and that in Expr.H is distinguishable with non-negligible probability, we construct a challenger B such that given (r^*, s^*), it can distinguish whether it is an output of G for a random $s \leftarrow_R \{0,1\}^m$ or they are chosen at random and independently from $\{0,1\}^m$ with non-negligible property. The challenger B makes use of A as a subroutine and begins by choosing at random an index $i^* \leftarrow \{1, \ldots, q\}$ and setting $s \leftarrow 0^m$ and compromised = true. B's ith call of A is answered as follow

- good-refresh(D) with D a distribution in $\mathcal{H}$. If $i < i^*$, then the simulator chooses $s' \leftarrow_R \{0,1\}^m$ at random. If $i = i^*$, then the system sets $s' = s^*$, and if $i > i^*$, then the simulator draws $d \leftarrow_R \{0,1\}^m$, sets $s' = G'(d \oplus s)$, where s is the current internal state. Either way, the simulator updates the internal states to s' and resets compromised =false.
- bad-refresh(x) with a bit string x. If compromised = true, the simulator sets $s' \leftarrow$ refresh($s \oplus$ extract(x)). If compromised = false and $i < i^*$, the simulator sets $s' \leftarrow \{0,1\}^m$; and if compromised = false and $i = i^*$, then simulator sets $s' = s^*$ and updates the internal states to s'. If compromised = false and $i > i^*$, the simulator sets $s' \leftarrow$ refresh($s \oplus$ extract(x)).
- set-state(s') with an m-bit string s'. The simulator returns to the attacker A the current internal state s and sets compromised = true and the new internal state to s'.
- next-bits(). If compromised = true or $i > i^*$ then the simulator set $(r, s') \leftarrow G(s)$. If compromised = false and $i < i^*$ then simulator chooses $r, s' \leftarrow \{0,1\}^m$. If compromised = false and $i = i^*$, then the simulator sets $r = r^*$ and $s' = s^*$. Either way, the simulator replaces the internal state s by s' and returns to the attacker the m-bit string r.

Let q be a polynomial bounded on the total number of calls made by A to all of its interfaces. Consider the $(q + 1)$ experiments $H^{(i)}$, $i = 0, 1, \ldots, q$, where in experiment $H^{(i)}$, the first i calls of A to its interfaces are processed the way B processes queries for $i < i^*$ and the rest are processed the way B processes queries for $i > i^*$. We claim that $H^{(q)} =$ Expr.I and $H^{(0)} =$ Expr.R. Let $\Pr[\text{Dist}(H^{(0)}) = 1] = \delta_0$ and $\Pr[\text{Dist}(H^{(q)}) = 1] = \delta_q$

$$|\delta_0 - \delta_q| = |\sum_{i=1}^{q} \Pr[\text{Dist}(H^{(i)}) = 1] - \Pr[\text{Dist}(H^{(i-1)}) = 1]|$$

$$\leq \sum_{i=1}^{q} |\Pr[\text{Dist}(H^{(i)}) = 1] - \Pr[\text{Dist}(H^{(i-1)}) = 1]|$$

$$\leq q\varepsilon$$

This means that if the view of Expr.I and the view of Expr.R are distinguishable with non-negligible probability, then we are able to distinguish whether (r^*, s^*) is an output of G for a random $s \leftarrow_R \{0,1\}^m$ or they are chosen at random and independently from $\{0,1\}^m$ with non-negligible advantage.

4   Conclusion

In this paper, we have introduced and formalized the notion of sustainable pseudorandom generator which aims to fill the security gap between the ideal world and the real world in the BH robust pseudorandom generator. We have shown that the Barak and Halevi's construction is sustainable assuming that the underlying algorithm G is a cryptographic pseudorandom number generator and the output of the underlying randomness extractor is statistically close to the uniform distribution U_m.

References

1. De, A., Watson, T.: Extractors and Lower Bounds for Locally Samplable Sources. TOCT 4(1), 3 (2012)
2. Boldyreva, A., Kumar, V.: A New pseudorandom Generator from Collision-Resistant Hash Functions. In: Dunkelman, O. (ed.) CT-RSA 2012. LNCS, vol. 7178, pp. 187–202. Springer, Heidelberg (2012)
3. Barak, B., Halevi, S.: A model and architecture for pseudorandom generation with applications to /dev/random. In: ACM Conference on Computer and Communications Security, pp. 203–212 (2005)
4. Barak, B., Shaltiel, R., Tromer, E.: True Random Number Generators Secure in a Changing Environment. In: Walter, C.D., Koç, Ç.K., Paar, C. (eds.) CHES 2003. LNCS, vol. 2779, pp. 166–180. Springer, Heidelberg (2003)
5. Blum, M., Micali, S.: How to Generate Cryptographically Strong Sequences of Pseudo Random Bits. In: FOCS 1982, pp. 112–117 (1982)
6. Dorrendorf, L., Gutterman, Z., Pinkas, B.: Cryptanalysis of the windows random number generator. In: ACM Conference on Computer and Communications Security, pp. 476–485 (2007)
7. Goldreich, O.: Foundation of Cryptography, vol. I. Cambridge University Press (2001)
8. Goldreich, O.: Foundation of Cryptography, vol. II. Cambridge University Press (2004)
9. Goldreich, O., Izsak, R.: Monotone Circuits: One-Way Functions versus pseudorandom Generators. Electronic Colloquium on Computational Complexity (ECCC) 18, 121 (2011)
10. Gutterman, Z., Pinkas, B., Reinman, T.: Analysis of the Linux Random Number Generator. In: S&P 2006, pp. 371–385 (2006)
11. Goldberg, I., Wagner, D.: Randomness and the Netscape Browser. Dr. Dobb's Journal, 66–70 (1996)
12. Kamp, J., Rao, A., Vadhan, S.P., Zuckerman, D.: Deterministic extractors for small-space sources. J. Comput. Syst. Sci. 77(1), 191–220 (2011)
13. Yao, A.C.-C.: Theory and Applications of Trapdoor Functions (Extended Abstract). In: FOCS 1982, pp. 80–91 (1982)
14. Vadhan, S.P., Zheng, C.J.: Characterizing pseudoentropy and simplifying pseudorandom generator constructions. In: STOC 2012, pp. 817–836 (2012)

Improving Mobile Device Security with Operating System-Level Virtualization

Sascha Wessel, Frederic Stumpf, Ilja Herdt, and Claudia Eckert

Fraunhofer Research Institution AISEC, Munich, Germany
{sascha.wessel,frederic.stumpf,ilja.herdt,
claudia.eckert}@aisec.fraunhofer.de

Abstract. In this paper, we propose a lightweight mechanism to isolate one or more Android userland instances from a trustworthy and secure entity. This entity controls and manages the Android instances and provides an interface for remote administration and management of the device and its software. Our approach includes several security extensions for secure network access, integrity protection of data on storage devices, and secure access to the touchscreen. Our implementation requires only minimal modification to the software stack of a typical Android-based smartphone, which allows easy porting to other devices when compared to other virtualization techniques. Practical tests show the feasibility of our approach regarding runtime overhead and battery lifetime impact.

1 Introduction

Smartphones are already an omnipresent part of our everyday lives. They are used for various tasks with different security requirements like web browsing, banking, or business use cases. This results in an increased demand for isolated environments with different security levels for different tasks on a single device. Payment service providers want a secure environment to protect their applications for financial transactions. Companies want a corporate environment isolated from the private environment of a user and the possibility to manage the devices remotely. This especially includes the enforcement of various security policies, which cannot be enforced with a stock Android-based smartphone today, e.g., whitelisting and/or blacklisting of applications and versions of applications in case of known vulnerabilities.

In this contribution, we propose a lightweight isolation mechanism for Android based on operating system-level virtualization and access control policies to separate one or more Android userland instances from a trustworthy and secure environment. Furthermore, we propose several security extensions based on this environment to control and manage the Android instances and their input and output data. This includes secure network communication, integrity protection of data on storage devices, and secure access to the touchscreen, e.g., for password entry dialogs. Another important part of our security concept is the integration of a secure element (SE) (e.g., embedded into a microSD card) to store secret keys and data physically separated from the application processor of

L.J. Janczewski, H.B. Wolfe, and S. Shenoi (Eds.): SEC 2013, IFIP AICT 405, pp. 148–161, 2013.
© IFIP International Federation for Information Processing 2013

the smartphone. This is to ensure its protection even in case of hardware-based attacks. Furthermore, our concept aims at straightforward remote manageability for integration in IT infrastructures. This includes easy snapshot and recovery functionalities and, moreover, security updates independent of the smartphone manufacturer. The evaluation of our prototype implementation shows that our modifications introduce only a negligible performance overhead and reduce the battery lifetime by only 7.5 percent in the worst case.

This paper is organized as follows. In Section 2, we introduce our attacker model and in Section 3 an overview of virtualization techniques for Android is given, followed by a discussion of related work in Section 4. Section 5 introduces the basic concept of operating system-level virtualization for Android and our additional security mechanisms are described in Section 6. General implementation aspects are presented in Section 7 and our prototype is described in Section 8. Finally, we evaluate our results in Section 9 and conclude in Section 10.

2   Attacker Model

In our attacker model, we assume an attacker using common attack vectors on Android-based smartphones. This especially includes eavesdropping and modification of remote communication, installation of malicious applications on the device, and exploiting (known) vulnerabilities to gain access to higher privilege levels, typically root access. Besides remote attackers, we also consider local attackers with physical access to the device. However, it is not possible to protect the data and software running on the application processor against attacks using JTAG or similar mechanisms without modifications to the smartphone hardware, so such attacks are out of scope for this paper.

3   Virtualization Techniques for Android

Isolation mechanisms or rather virtualization techniques for Android can be classified in three groups, namely user-level isolation, operating system-level virtualization and system virtualization. Figure 1 shows these three basic concepts

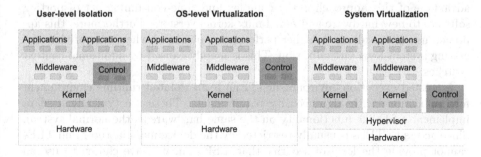

Fig. 1. Isolation and Virtualization Mechanisms for Android on three different Layers

for an example system with two isolated groups of applications and an additional control and management entity. By default, an Android system consists of an application layer, a middleware layer, and the kernel layer on top of the hardware. As shown in the figure, the main difference between the three concepts is which layers are shared by the isolated environments. Our concept is based on the architecture shown in the middle and is described in Section 5.

4   Related Work

The default Android security architecture uses different user identifiers (UIDs) per application group to implement a sandboxing mechanism. The communication between applications and core Android components is restricted based on permissions, which are requested during the installation of applications. It was shown that these mechanisms do not meet all security requirements [3,5], which led to a number of extensions to the Android architecture [4,11,10]. In contrast to our approach, these user-level isolation mechanisms usually require massive modifications to Android userspace components and introduce more complexity to the overall system.

Isolation based on operating system-level virtualization, as used in our approach, is a common concept of Unix-like operating systems today, especially on servers. In [2] *Cells* is introduced, a virtual mobile smartphone architecture, which utilizes Linux containers for isolation of two Android userspace instances running on one smartphone. In contrast to our approach, Cells does not focus on security. Specifically, it does not utilize access control policies and does not provide integrity protection or transparently encrypted and tunneled network connections.

Another approach to isolate runtime environments with different security requirements is system virtualization. System virtualization allows one to run multiple operating systems on one physical device using an additional software layer (a hypervisor [8] or microkernel [9]) as shown on the right side in Figure 1. This approach is also often used to add isolated security extensions to desktop or server systems [1,7,6]. Since current smartphone hardware does not provide hardware-assisted virtualization extensions, todays implementations usually require a paravirtualized kernel, like L4Android [9] for example. The main disadvantage of this approach is the complex and time-consuming act of porting software to new hardware and new Linux kernel versions. Furthermore, this approach usually results in a higher performance overhead when compared to operating system-level virtualization. This is mainly caused by additional context switches.

A trusted execution environment (TEE) is an isolated runtime environment for applications with high security requirements. These are typically used to implement a SE-like functionality on the same hardware as the normal system. Since access to TEEs is usually restricted by the device manufacturer and TEEs cannot provide the level of security that a SE can, we have chosen to use an external SE built into a microSD card for our prototype.

5   Lightweight Isolation Mechanism

Our concept is based on operating system-level virtualization, which provides userspace containers to isolate and control the resources of single applications or groups of applications running on top of one kernel as shown in the middle of Figure 1. This typically includes a unique hostname, process identifiers (PIDs), inter-process communications (IPCs), a filesystem, and network resources.

A trustworthy control and management environment is the first to run after boot and is the only component with full system access. Depending on the desired level of security, several Android userland instances are started from this environment or, alternatively, it ensures that only one additional Android userland instance is running at the same time. This means that processes are either frozen and not scheduled or stopped and removed from memory. In the following figures, we only depict a simplified system with one Android userspace instance.

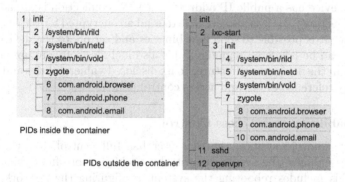

Fig. 2. Mapping of PIDs (Background Colors as in Figure 1)

Figure 2 shows the basic concept of operating system-level virtualization exemplarily for PIDs. From inside the container, only the processes corresponding to the particular container are visible. For an Android userland this looks like a process tree on a regular device. On the right side, the full system is shown including the processes 1, 2, 11 and 12 running outside of the container. The PIDs of the processes inside the container are mapped accordingly. Other resources are handled in a similar way.

A major advantage of this virtualization technique compared to system virtualization is that the isolation layer – here the kernel – has full control over all resources and can directly interfere at all processing layers and in all subsystems. This allows fine grained policy enforcement for system calls and integrity measurements of sensitive application groups at runtime. Additionally, for any input/output operation to devices, system call hooks can be used to add security extensions. We show four common implementation strategies of this approach in Section 7.

6   Integration of Security Mechanisms

In this section, we give an overview of security mechanisms and their integration in our basic concept. We systematically cover the three security aspects: isolation, communication, and storage. Most mechanisms are optional and can be applied to one or more containers if desired. The mechanisms are grouped into the following categories: remote management, capabilities and access control, network, storage, and display and user input.

6.1   Remote Management

A core component of our concept is a powerful remote management component. The trusted control and management component on the smartphone is isolated from the Android userspace through operating system-level virtualization as described in Section 5. It establishes a secure connection to a management server to fetch information. Alternatively, the management server can initiate the connection if the device has a public IP address or a VPN connection is already established (see Section 6.3). It is also possible to send an encrypted SMS to control the device. Since it is possible to send new binaries and scripts to the device, nearly everything can be triggered remotely. This also includes software updates independent from the device manufacturer to fix disclosed vulnerabilities and updates for integrity reference values and access control policies.

6.2   Capabilities and Access Control

On a stock Android system, the root user has full control over the system. Capabilities enhance the system security by enabling more fine-grained access control. This includes rebooting the system, configuring the network, loading kernel modules, and overriding file access permissions for example. Our concept ensures that all capabilities that are not necessary for an application to work properly are dropped systematically.

A similar approach is realized for access to devices, e.g., framebuffer, camera, network, and storage devices. So it is (remotely) configurable whether and when an Android container gets access to these devices.

To provide even more fine-grained access control, our concept provides access control for system calls based on well-known security models like mandatory access control (MAC) and access control lists (ACLs) as already utilized in other papers [11,13]. In our system, policies are typically configured by the administrator or automatically generated in learning mode or permissive mode. Another approach here is the automatic generation of policies on one reference smartphone, then slightly modified by an administrator, and finally the distribution to all managed devices.

6.3   Network and Telephony

A core component of our concept is the restriction of network and telephony services. Network filtering and routing can only be configured from the trustworthy environment. This includes the routing of all connections from and to an Android userland through an encrypted virtual private network (VPN) tunnel as shown in Figure 3. In this scenario, the Android userland accesses a virtual ethernet interface (veth0), which is bridged (br0) with a tunnel interface (tun0) of a VPN. The asymmetric keys are stored in the SE and the negotiation of a symmetric session key is handled entirely in the SE. The secret key never leaves the SE. Additionally, to prevent unauthorized access to the VPN, the SE is protected with a personal identification number (PIN) as described in Section 6.5. Besides the network routing, in Figure 3 a scenario is shown, in which the Android userland cannot configure or access the WLAN interface (wlan0). This is only possible from the trustworthy part of the system. The authentication for encrypted WLANs can be handled similar to the VPN authentication.

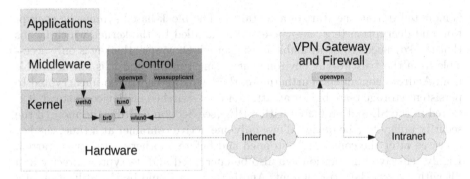

Fig. 3. Network with Transparent VPN

The second main communication channel to the outside world is the GSM/UMTS/LTE radio interface. Besides packet-based communication as described above, a common use case here are filter functions for SMS and calls. It is also possible to have separate phone numbers and connections for more than one Android container using VoIP for telephony as described in [2].

6.4 Storage

Virtualizing the root filesystem of the Android containers allows easy integration of snapshot and recovery functions and remote wipe functions as well as full and transparent root filesystem encryption. Furthermore, we apply integrity protection mechanisms to files as described in the following. Figure 4 shows a typical scenario with filesystem encryption and integrity protection controlled from the trustworthy control and management environment.

Encryption. Storage encryption can be integrated at the device level for a whole filesystem or at a per-file basis. Our default configuration uses an encrypted file system image, either in a single file or in a separate partition which

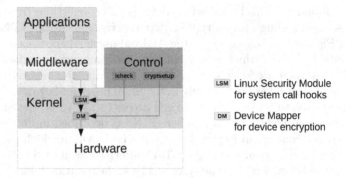

Fig. 4. Storage with Encryption and Integrity Protection

is mounted during the start of a container. The block-based symmetric encryption and decryption (e.g., aes-cbc-essiv) is handled by the kernel, which means that the key needs to be available in the kernel. Of course, the key is only accessible from the trustworthy environment during runtime and it is not accessible from Android containers. Furthermore, the key is never written unencrypted to persistent storage readable for an attacker on a switched off device. Instead, it is stored in the SE and protected with a PIN (see Section 6.5). Furthermore, if the security policy for the device allows only one active container at a time, the key is erased after the container is stopped and before another container is started. Highly sensitive information can also be encrypted and decrypted directly in a SE with a lower data throughput. Another option would be the utilization of a TEE-based implementation.

Integrity Protection. Basically, integrity protection can be enforced at the start of a container either on a whole filesystem or on a per file basis. This is especially useful after a recovery of the filesystem. Furthermore, our concept provides integrity protection of files while an Android container is running. Based on a whitelist or blacklist of file hashes, reading and/or writing to/from files is allowed or forbidden. This mechanism allows us to control which applications and system components are installed in the Android userland and to enforce that these applications and components fulfill certain requirements, like blacklisting of vulnerable versions of applications. It also allows blacklisting of known Malware. Our implementation for this mechanism is described in detail in Section 8. A similar approach could also be used for anomaly detection at runtime.

6.5 Display and User Input

A common problem for business and payment scenarios is the need for a trusted graphical user interface (GUI) for a secure password entry, e.g., to unlock a SE. Our concept uses a SE to store keys for several use cases and therefore also requires a secure password input dialog. Moreover, in our prototype switching from one Android container to another typically also requires a password.

To not introduce a performance impact, we usually give exclusive and full access rights to one Android container for the screen and touchscreen. To switch to the trustworthy environment, we use a hardware key (typically the power button). Additionally, we utilize the hardware LED of the device to indicate which environment receives the touchscreen events and which environment has access to the screen at the moment. Depending on the capabilities of the smartphone, different colors are associated to different containers (e.g., green for corporate, blue for private, red for guest and white for the trusted environment including the secure password entry). Of course, Android containers cannot directly access the LED driver any more.

7 Input and Output Hooks

In our concept, access to devices (like the LED) and other components needs to be restricted and sometimes virtualized to ensure the system's security. In this section, we give an overview of the generic approaches used in our implementation. Figure 5 shows four implementations to interfere with input and output operations to devices. Depicted are the data and control flow and the (un)modified components. The four implementation concepts are described in the following.

1. An unmodified Android userland component sends and receives data directly to/from a kernel component which has direct access to the hardware. The Android userspace has no permission to control the kernel component. This is reserved for the control and management environment. An example for this scenario is storage encryption, whereby the Android userland cannot set or get the encryption key (see Section 6.4).
2. An unmodified Android userland component sends and receives data directly to/from a kernel component which forwards this data to a trusted control component which itself forwards the data to a kernel component. This is typically used to implement a filter or access control mechanism in a trusted userspace component.

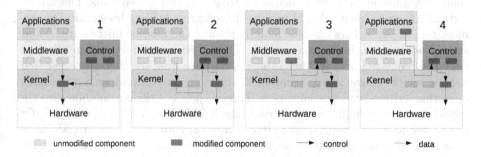

Fig. 5. Implementations to Interfere with Input and Output Operations of Containers

3. A paravirtualized Android userland component sends and receives data to/from a trusted userland component. The communication can be based on a shared memory segment or another IPC mechanism. For filtering purposes, this approach can provide already preprocessed data, which might be simpler to handle. An example for this scenario is the replacement of the rild or wpa_supplicant binaries in the Android userspace with stubs, if the Android userland does not have the permission to directly configure the radio modem and WLAN interface. On a device with more than one Android userland, this approach can also be used to share components between the Android userlands, e.g., the address book, or for multiplexing devices.

4. A special Android application communicates with a trusted component. This scenario can be used to allow an Android application to call a trusted dialog implemented in a trusted component outside the Android container, e.g., a password entry dialog. This can be useful for a modified Email application with SE-based S/MIME signatures.

8   Prototype Implementation

Our prototype implementation uses Debian GNU/Linux for the trusted control and management environment and to verify the portability of our approach, we used a rather old Android 2.3.5 on a *Google Nexus One* and a recent Android 4.0.4 on a *Samsung Galaxy S3* for the Android userspace instances. In both cases, the filesystems are stored on a microSD card. The stock kernel was modified to support Linux containers for operating system-level virtualization. This mainly includes resource isolation based on namespaces and resource control based on Linux kernel control groups (cgroups). Most capabilities are dropped for containers and access to devices etc. is restricted. Most of our additional concepts are implemented based on the generic approaches described in Section 7. However, one primary aspect of our approach is described in the following in more detail.

Our access control and integrity protection mechanisms are based on Linux Security Modules (LSM) [12], which provide lightweight, general support for access control by allowing modules to define security hooks for system calls. This allows a straightforward integration of task hooks, program loading hooks, IPC hooks, filesystem hooks, network hooks, module hooks (e.g., module initialization) and system hooks (e.g., hostname setting). The called hook function can allow or deny the requested access. This approach has also been used by other research papers, which utilize Linux Security Modules on an Android system without operating system-level virtualization. These typically utilize a module directly included in the mainline Linux kernel, like TOMOYO or SELinux [11,13]. Of course, without a container-based virtualization environment, all userspace components need to be included in the Android userspace. Here, we have a significant advantage in our virtualized system where the userspace components run in the trustworthy environment.

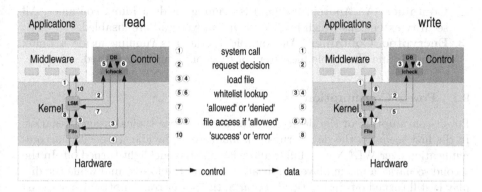

Fig. 6. Data and Control Flow for File-based Integrity Measurements

As an example, in Figure 4 a typical storage scenario with two security extensions is shown. First, we use the device mapper (DM) in the kernel for transparent encryption. It is controlled by the userspace tool *cryptsetup* running in the trustworthy environment. Second, for integrity protection, we use a LSM implementation controlled by our userspace daemon *icheck*. Figure 6 shows the control and data flow for file-based read (left side of the figure) and write (right side of the figure) operations. In our prototype implementation, this daemon calculates a SHA1 of files on file accesses and compares this hash with a whitelist of hashes stored in the trustworthy environment. If a hash is not found in the whitelist, access will be denied. The whitelist for system components is usually distributed with the system image and the whitelist of Android applications can either be distributed via the remote management interface or directly generated on the device by verifying and analyzing Android application packages (apk) including its cryptographic signatures.

9   Evaluation and Measurements

In this section, we present measurements regarding the performance impact, the power consumption, and the memory usage of our prototype implementation. The measurements show that our approach has a very limited impact on the performance of the system and especially the power consumption. Finally, a security evaluation is given.

All measurements were done for three Android environments running on a Google Nexus One with equal configuration parameters and with the same set of Android system services and applications running in the background:

1. **Default Android.** An Android userland is running directly on the system without operating system-level virtualization and without a trusted control and management entity. This is the reference value in the following figures (7, 8 and 9).

2. **Container.** An Android userland is running inside a Linux container. All security extensions which may result in an overhead are disabled.
3. **Encrypted Container.** An Android userland is running inside a Linux container and the whole filesystem of this container is encrypted.

9.1   Power Consumption

Power consumption of the device is measured in three typical usage scenarios. In the first scenario, the device runs continuously in the idle state without communication over WLAN or cellular and with display backlight turned off. In the second scenario, a music player application runs in the foreground while the display is still turned off. In the third scenario, the power consumption is measured during the usage of the web browser. Here, the display is turned on and user interaction is simulated every five minutes. Figure 7 shows our results.

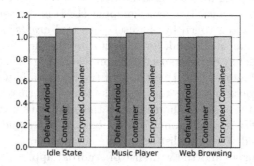

Fig. 7. Normalized Battery Overhead for Default Android and Containers

The highest impact on the power consumption was measured in the idle test scenario with 7.5 percent for the encrypted container and 7.1 percent for an Android container without storage encryption. For the music player scenario, the impact goes down to 4.0 and 3.6 percent and for the web browsing scenario it's below 1 percent for both containers. This increased power consumption is mainly a result of additional threads running outside the Android container in the trustworthy environment.

9.2   Performance

We run six Android benchmarks to measure the performance impact of our approach compared to a default Android userland without operating system-level virtualization. The results are shown in Figure 8.

Most benchmarks show less than 1 percent variation in performance overhead for Android containers. This shows that our approach provides nearly native performance for an Android userland running inside a Linux container. However, there are some values, which will be explained a little more closely.

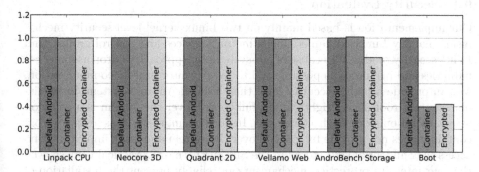

Fig. 8. Normalized Runtime Overhead for Default Android and Containers

The *AndroBench Storage* benchmark shows a higher performance for an Android container with encrypted root filesystem. This can be explained by an additional caching of the encrypted filesystem image, which cannot be prevented by the benchmark tool. Next, the boot procedure of an Android container is considerably faster due to different caching behavior, as shown in the next section.

9.3   Memory Usage

In Figure 9, the memory usage of the whole system is shown. A system with operating system-level virtualization naturally results in a slightly higher memory usage (depicted red). Noticeable here is the much higher amount of memory used for caching (depicted blue). For our measurements, we considered two system states. First, the memory usage of the system after the boot (depicted on the left) and second, the increase of memory usage after the start of additional applications (depicted on the right).

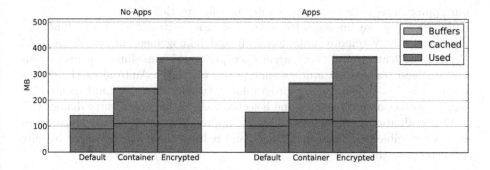

Fig. 9. Memory Usage for Default Android and Containers

9.4   Security Evaluation

Our implementation is based mainly on two Linux kernel-level security mechanisms, namely Linux containers including namespaces and control groups, and Linux security modules. Because of our systematic approach to drop as many capabilities and privileges as possible and to restrict inter process communication, we can provide a higher security level than a stock Android system. In particular, getting root access rights to get full control over the system is a common attack vector on stock Android systems. In our system, root access in an Android container does not provide full control over the system and more importantly no access to confidential keys stored in the SE. Furthermore, practical tests showed that our integrity protection mechanism can reliably prevent the installation of unknown and therefore possibly malicious applications. Finally, we prevented real attacks using exploits for the /dev/exynos-mem device security hole found in the stock Samsung Galaxy S3 firmware (CVE-2012-6422).

Comparing our approach to other virtualization techniques for Android as described in Section 3 indicates the following. On the one hand, our implementation has a smaller trusted computing base (TCB) compared to user-level isolation. Not sharing the middleware layer simply means that attacks on this layer, as described in [5], are not possible between Android containers. On the other hand, system virtualization with a focus on security (e.g., based on a microkernel) has a smaller TCB. However, this approach typically has practical disadvantages as already mentioned, but can be combined with our approach, e.g., in form of a TEE. To protect highly sensitive information in our prototype, we utilize a hardware SE to provide an even higher level of security including hardware-based attacks.

10   Conclusion

In this paper, we presented a lightweight mechanism to isolate one or more Android userland instances from a trustworthy control and management environment. In contrast to existing solutions based on full system virtualization, our approach requires no complex software modifications.

Additionally, we implemented several security extensions. A key functionality is the easy remote administration and management of mobile devices. Further key features are transparent encryption and tunneling of network connections and transparent storage encryption, where the Android userland does not have access to the used cryptographic keys. Moreover, we implemented integrity protection mechanisms and a secure GUI for password entry dialogs etc.

Our evaluation results show that our approach is practical and introduces only a negligible performance overhead and reduces the battery lifetime by only 7.5 percent in the worst case.

Acknowledgments. Parts of this work were supported by the German Federal Ministry of Education and Research (BMBF) under grant 01BY1011 within the project ASMONIA.

References

1. Alkassar, A., Scheibel, M., Stübel, M., Sadeghi, A.R., Winandy, M.: Security Architecture for Device Encryption and VPN. In: ISSE 2006 – Securing Electronic Busines Processes, pp. 54–63. Vieweg (2006)
2. Andrus, J., Dall, C., Hof, A.V., Laadan, O., Nieh, J.: Cells: A Virtual Mobile Smartphone Architecture. In: Proceedings of the 23rd ACM Symposium on Operating Systems Principles, SOSP 2011, pp. 173–187. ACM, New York (2011)
3. Barrera, D., Kayacik, H.G., van Oorschot, P.C., Somayaji, A.: A Methodology for Empirical Analysis of Permission-Based Security Models and its Application to Android. In: Proceedings of the 17th ACM Conference on Computer and Communications Security, CCS 2010, pp. 73–84. ACM, New York (2010)
4. Bugiel, S., Davi, L., Dmitrienko, A., Heuser, S., Sadeghi, A.-R., Shastry, B.: Practical and Lightweight Domain Isolation on Android. In: Proceedings of the 1st ACM Workshop on Security and Privacy in Smartphones and Mobile Devices, SPSM 2011, pp. 51–62. ACM, New York (2011)
5. Davi, L., Dmitrienko, A., Sadeghi, A.-R., Winandy, M.: Privilege Escalation Attacks on Android. In: Burmester, M., Tsudik, G., Magliveras, S., Ilić, I. (eds.) ISC 2010. LNCS, vol. 6531, pp. 346–360. Springer, Heidelberg (2011)
6. Garfinkel, T., Pfaff, B., Chow, J., Rosenblum, M., Boneh, D.: Terra: A Virtual Machine-Based Platform for Trusted Computing. In: Proceedings of the 19th ACM Symposium on Operating Systems Principles, SOSP 2003, pp. 193–206. ACM, New York (2003)
7. Hartig, H., Hohmuth, M., Feske, N., Helmuth, C., Lackorzynski, A., Mehnert, F., Peter, M.: The Nizza Secure-System Architecture. In: International Conference on Collaborative Computing: Networking, Applications and Worksharing (2005)
8. Hwang, J.Y., Suh, S.B., Heo, S.K., Park, C.J., Ryu, J.M., Park, S.Y., Kim, C.R.: Xen on ARM: System Virtualization Using Xen Hypervisor for ARM-Based Secure Mobile Phones. In: 5th IEEE Consumer Communications and Networking Conference, CCNC 2008, pp. 257–261 (2008)
9. Lange, M., Liebergeld, S., Lackorzynski, A., Warg, A., Peter, M.: L4Android: A Generic Operating System Framework for Secure Smartphones. In: Proceedings of the 1st ACM Workshop on Security and Privacy in Smartphones and Mobile Devices, SPSM 2011, pp. 39–50. ACM, New York (2011)
10. Ongtang, M., Butler, K., McDaniel, P.: Porscha: Policy Oriented Secure Content Handling in Android. In: Proceedings of the 26th Annual Computer Security Applications Conference, ACSAC 2010, pp. 221–230. ACM, New York (2010)
11. Shabtai, A., Fledel, Y., Elovici, Y.: Securing Android-Powered Mobile Devices Using SELinux. IEEE Security and Privacy 8(3), 36–44 (2010)
12. Wright, C., Cowan, C., Smalley, S., Morris, J., Kroah-Hartman, G.: Linux Security Modules: General Security Support for the Linux Kernel. In: Proceedings of the 11th USENIX Security Symposium, pp. 17–31. USENIX Association, Berkeley (2002)
13. Zhang, X., Aciicmez, O., Seifert, J.P.: A Trusted Mobile Phone Reference Architecture via Secure Kernel. In: Proceedings of the 2007 ACM Workshop on Scalable Trusted Computing, STC 2007, pp. 7–14. ACM, New York (2007)

Generating Realistic Application Workloads for Mix-Based Systems for Controllable, Repeatable and Usable Experimentation

Karl-Peter Fuchs, Dominik Herrmann, and Hannes Federrath

University of Hamburg, Computer Science Department, Germany

Abstract. Evaluating and improving the performance of anonymity systems in a real-world setting is critical to foster their adoption. However, current research in this field mostly employs unrealistic models for evaluation purposes. Moreover, previously documented results are often difficult to reproduce. We propose two complementary workload models that operate on network traces in order to improve the evaluation of anonymity systems. In comparison to other approaches our workload models are more realistic, as they derive characteristics from trace files recorded in real networks and preserve dependencies of the flows of individual hosts. We also describe our ready-to-use open source evaluation suite that implements our models. Given our tools, researchers can easily create and re-use well-defined workload sets for evaluation purposes. Finally, we demonstrate the importance of realistic workload models by evaluating a well-known dummy traffic scheme with our tools.

1 Introduction

Mix-based anonymity systems have become an important technology to protect the privacy of users on the Internet. Since the original proposal by David Chaum in 1981 [9] a large number of mixing schemes for various application areas has been published. Especially low-latency anonymity services like Tor [11] and JAP (JonDonym) [7] have found widespread adoption.

The security and performance evaluation of such systems is challenging because of their complex construction and dynamic nature: Typically they consist of multiple nodes distributed on the Internet, which interact with each other, with a set of clients and (usually) a set of servers. Analytically derived statements obtained by mathematical proofs or queuing theory serve as an important foundation in this field. However, analytical results cannot reliably predict the behaviour and performance of a system once real users adopt it in practice. Simulations with realistic traffic are essential to obtain significant results.

Nevertheless, we observe that some researchers in the privacy-enhancing technologies (PET) community struggle with the evaluation of their proposals: On the one hand, some publications lack an evaluation in a practical setting, and, on the other hand, practically deployed systems such as Tor are sometimes evaluated with quite unrealistic traffic models. Moreover, different datasets are used

L.J. Janczewski, H.B. Wolfe, and S. Shenoi (Eds.): SEC 2013, IFIP AICT 405, pp. 162–175, 2013.
© IFIP International Federation for Information Processing 2013

for evaluation and some papers lack important details regarding the employed preprocessing or sampling technique.

We believe these deficiencies are mainly due to the lack of *appropriate standard workload models* and the fact that there is no *easily accessible, well-established evaluation procedure* in the PET research area. As a consequence there is a huge gap between theory and practice and published results are difficult to compare to each other. The **contribution of this paper** is threefold: **Firstly**, we propose a dependency-preserving model for workload extraction from Internet trace files that is suitable for the evaluation of low-latency anonymity systems (DPE Model). **Secondly**, we propose a replay and feedback model for traffic generation that takes into account the latencies of the evaluated system (R&F Model). **Thirdly**, we describe our workload generation tool that allows researchers to create or reproduce well-defined evaluation scenarios (Reproducible Scenario Builder). We have integrated these three components into an evaluation suite that has been released as open source software under the GPLv3 at https://www.informatik.uni-hamburg.de/SVS/gmix/.

The rest of this paper is structured as follows: In Sect. 2 we review related work before we outline our design goals and the construction of our workload model in Sect. 3. In Sect. 4 we describe our evaluation suite, which includes implementations of the DPE and R&F models as well as the Reproducible Scenario Builder. Finally, in Sect. 5 we present results from empirical evaluations that indicate that our models generate realistic traffic. We also demonstrate the importance of realistic workload models, before we conclude in Sect. 6.

2 Fundamentals and Related Work

Our contribution, a trace-driven workload model for the evaluation of anonymity systems, relates to two fields, *network research* and *privacy-enhancing technologies*. In this section we review the most relevant efforts from these two areas. We also identify shortcomings of the existing approaches that motivate our work.

2.1 Evaluation of Distributed Systems

Figure 1 sketches the components needed for the evaluation of a distributed system. The evaluation can be performed with different levels of abstraction: (1) studying a proposed system *analytically* (e. g., via mathematical proofs or queuing theory), (2) modelling (parts of) the proposed system and its environment and validating the analytical results within *simulations*, and (3) implementing the proposal and measuring its performance in an *emulated network* or a *real-world setting*. In each case *models* can be used to control certain aspects of the proposed system or certain influence factors of the environment.

The *network research community* has brought up several mature and approved models and implementations, e. g., the network simulators ns-2, ns-3, SSF, OPNET and OMNeT++ (providing models for Components A, B and C in Fig. 1), the virtual network emulators Modelnet and Emulab (Components B and C) or the workload generation tools Tmix and Swing (Component A).

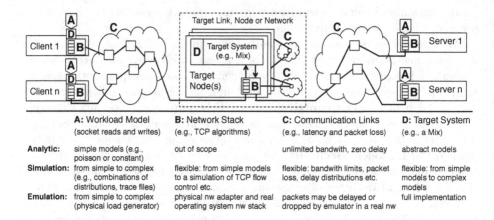

A: Workload Model (socket reads and writes)	**B: Network Stack** (e.g., TCP algorithms)	**C: Communication Links** (e.g., latency and packet loss)	**D: Target System** (e.g., a Mix)
Analytic: simple models (e.g., poisson or constant)	out of scope	unlimited bandwith, zero delay	abstract models
Simulation: from simple to complex (e.g., combinations of distributions, trace files)	flexible: from simple models to a simulation of TCP flow control etc.	flexible: bandwith limits, packet loss, delay distributions etc.	flexible: from simple models to complex models
Emulation: from simple to complex (physical load generator)	physical nw adapter and real operating system nw stack	packets may be delayed or dropped by emulator in a real nw	full implementation

Fig. 1. Models typically involved in evaluation of distributed systems

2.2   Existing Approaches for the Evaluation of PETs

The *PET community* has started to adapt and extend these solutions for the evaluation of anonymity systems. Noticeable examples are the network simulator *Shadow* [17] and the emulation testbed *ExperimenTor* [5]. Both systems try to accurately model the topology and routing mechanism (Component *C*) of the Tor network [11], which is the most popular anonymity system at the moment. Shadow employs realistic models for the network stack (Component *B*), and ExperimenTor even uses physical hardware for this part. Both approaches make use of the actual Tor implementation for experimentation (Component *D*). In [14] we have introduced the *gMix framework* that focuses on the implementation of Component *D*, i. e., it facilitates building customized anonymity systems from ready-to-use implementations (plug-ins) of previously suggested mix concepts. Like ExperimenTor, gMix can be used in conjunction with a virtual network emulator. Additionally, it provides a basic discrete-event network simulator for abstract but fast evaluations (Components *B* and *C*).

Workload Models. The approaches mentioned in the previous paragraph make use of quite sophisticated models for Components *B*, *C* and *D*. However, they employ only very basic workload models (Component *A*): The gMix framework only supports basic statistical distributions, and recent studies using Shadow and ExperimenTor rely on a simple *on–off* workload model: In *on* phases, clients retrieve files of different size in varying intervals. File sizes are chosen to match typical web page sizes [20,23]. Intervals are drawn from a distribution obtained in a 2003 study [15,17] or at random with an upper bound of 11 seconds [23]. Others (cf. [25]) simply *pick up* HTTP flows from a trace file and replay them successively for each client (simplex, *open loop* [13]).

These workload models are a strong simplification of the actual events taking place when a user browses through the WWW, which is one of the most popular applications anonymity systems are used for [18,27]. Actually, downloading a typical web page requires the web browser to handle multiple request–response pairs and parallel connections (a more detailed description follows in Sect. 3.4). In contrast to real-world implementations, the simplistic workload models used in these studies assume that web pages are retrieved within a single roundtrip or within a single TCP connection. Note that this discrepancy does not necessarily mean that the results obtained in [17,23,25] are wrong (the authors do consider the limitations of their models when drawing conclusions). As we strive for more realistic evaluations and we want to validate and compare the results obtained in previous studies, we have designed a more comprehensive and accurate traffic model which will be described in the next section.

3 Designing a Workload Model for Anonymity Systems

Performance evaluations consist of observing the system under test while it handles a specific workload. In their seminal paper Agrawala et al. [1] describe the application of workload models for the evaluation of the performance of computers. Instead of live workloads, workload models are used to generate synthetic workloads that can be replayed multiple times. A realistic **workload model** is supposed to capture both the behaviour of the users that are issuing requests to a system as well as the load these requests induce on the system under test. Today, workload models play an important role to analyse distributed systems. Creating realistic network traffic for experimentation is a well-studied subject in the network research community. However, the applicability of these models and tools for the context of anonymity systems is diverging.

Our workload model consists of two complementary parts: the "Dependency-Preserving Extraction (DPE) Model" and the "Replay and Feedback (R&F) Model". The DPE Model is used to extract flows in a dependency-preserving manner from trace files. Moreover, it captures behavioral characteristics of the individual hosts. The R&F Model determines how traffic is replayed during evaluation, taking into account feedback from the system under test.

In Sect. 3.1 we review the structure of the system under test we are interested in, namely low-latency anonymity systems. In Sects. 3.2 and 3.3 we outline the overall goals that motivated our design decisions for our workload model. After that we will describe our two complementary workload models, the DPE Model (Sect. 3.4) and the R&F model (Sect. 3.5).

3.1 Characteristics of Anonymity Systems

Figure 2 shows the typical architecture of an anonymity service (cf. [7,11,14]). Mixes and clients form an overlay network. Connections of user applications (e. g., web browsers) are multiplexed and routed via several mix nodes before they are forwarded to their destinations (e. g., to a web server). Clients apply a layer of encryption for each mix to assert bitwise unlinkability. Mix servers are distributed across the Internet and communicate via TCP or UDP.

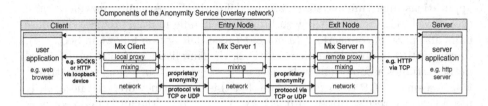

Fig. 2. Typical architecture of an anonymity service

Mixes delay messages to build an anonymity set (*output strategy*, cf. [9,14]). Congestion causes further delays in deployed anonymity systems (cf. [10]). The typical delay is on the order of a few seconds (cf. [10,27]). Given a certain level of privacy, maximizing throughput and minimizing user-perceived latency are the primary objectives during the design of anonymity systems.

Workload modelling for anonymity systems differs fundamentally from the objectives typically encountered in network research, where the goal is often to create realistic workloads for a single server or a realistic (background) traffic mix for a single target link (so-called *dumbbell topology*) on the packet level (cf., for instance, [22]). As a result, most tools from the network community cannot be used for the evaluation of PETs without modification. However, the traffic modelling approaches codified in those tools may still be applicable, though.

3.2 Design Goals

Our contribution has been guided by the following goals. Our main objective is to provide a more **realistic** workload model (in comparison to the models used by the PET community at the moment, cf. Sect. 2.2). Researchers should be able to adapt our model to their needs (**control**) and choose from different levels of abstraction (**flexibility**). Moreover, easy access and high **usability** are critical factors for the adoption of any new proposal. Therefore, we aim for a solution that requires little time for setup and parameterisation. Furthermore, we want to facilitate the **repeatability** of experiments i. e., it should be easy for researchers to share their experimental setups with the scientific community. Since there is no ultimate evaluation platform (cf. Sect. 2) and we cannot implement our proposal for all platforms, we want to assert easy **adaptability**.

3.3 Selecting a Suitable Workload Modelling Approach

Traffic generators can be classified according to their insertion level into application-level, flow-level (TCP) and packet-level (IP) generators. We find **application-level generators** to be the most appropriate: Packet generators (probably the most common type) and flow generators are not as appropriate because anonymity networks do not directly forward IP packets or TCP flows for both performance (overhead for establishing channels) and security reasons (hiding the number of real connections). Among the application-level workload models, we considered **two common approaches** for our solution: **Application-Specific Models** (ASM, cf., e. g., [4,8]), which try to model user or application behaviour itself (e. g., via state machines) and **Extraction-Based Models** (EBM), that try to extract application behaviour from packet header traces recorded in real networks (cf., for instance, [2,16,26]).

While **ASMs** provide a higher level of control and accuracy, they also require a separate model for each application of interest (increasing complexity) and they require adaptation when application behaviour changes, e. g., when new protocols like [6] gain currency (diminishing flexibility). Moreover, the experimenter has to choose realistic values or distributions for several parameters (flexibility vs. usability). Those values are typically derived from trace files or previous studies. **EBMs** are more flexible as they are not tailored to a single application's behaviour. The level of detail achievable with EBMs is lower, though, since the packet traces required by these models (and provided by different research institutes, e. g., [21,24]) are typically truncated after the transport layer header for anonymity and storage reasons. Therefore, some details, like whether a transmitted data block contains a single HTTP response or several HTTP responses sent within a short time frame, cannot be reconstructed (reducing accuracy). However, EBMs provide better usability, as most parameters that have to be configured by the experimenter in ASMs can be automatically derived from the source trace files in EBMs.

Due to usability advantages and implicit support for different applications, we decided to implement an EBM for our purposes.

3.4   The Dependency-Preserving Extraction Model

To extract an application-neutral characterisation of host behaviour from a packet header trace, both **models for individual flows** and **models for the relations between flows** are required. For this purpose we extend the *A-B-T Model*, the standard model of ns-2 and ns-3 [26].

The basic idea of the *A-B-T Model* is to *reverse-engineer* the read and write operations of applications from a packet header trace. To this end, an analysis of the sequence and acknowledgement numbers of TCP packets is performed to infer the size of data units transferred on the application layer (Application Data Units, ADUs). This information is stored in so-called *connection vectors*. Each vector consists of n epochs. An epoch is a triplet of a request size A, a reply size B and a delay T between epochs (cf. Fig. 3). The payload length of consecutive packets is interpreted as a single ADU until a packet in the opposite direction is received (starting a new epoch). The delay is derived from packet timestamps.

One problem with the *A-B-T Model* for our purposes is the fact that it assumes the simulation to replay ADUs with an accurate model of the TCP stack, including the simulation of the TCP feedback loop (congestion avoidance algorithms). While this approach offers a high level of detail, it also results in a strong increase of complexity for both experimental setup and runtime and may prevent medium or large scale experiments. Since we want to give experimenters the choice to simulate all individual connections or to preserve

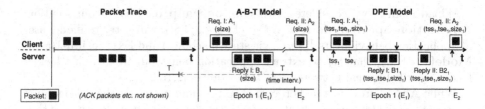

Fig. 3. From packet header trace files to the *A-B-T* and *DPE* representation

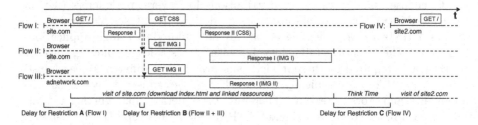

Fig. 4. Relations between the flows of a host (for the case of HTTP)

the transfer durations of the source trace (cf. Sect. 3.5), we extend the A-B-T model to **store timestamps** for the start (tss_j) and end (tse_j) of each ADU and further regard consecutive packets with a distance of more than $\tau = 1\,\text{ms}$ as individual ADUs (cf. Fig. 3). The actual value of τ can be changed by the experimenter. More formally, an epoch e in our model may contain i replies (instead of the single reply size B in the A-B-T model), represented by the triplet $r_i = (\text{tss}_i, \text{tse}_i, \text{size}_i)$. T is no longer present in our model as it (as well as all other delays between ADUs) can be computed from the absolute timestamps.

The **second problem** with the *A-B-T Model* is that it does not capture **relations between flows** [26]. Figure 4 illustrates this issue for the example of HTTP. When a modern web browser downloads a web page, it will open a single connection to request the root (HTML) document. After the arrival of the document, the browser will typically open additional connections to download referenced objects like images or CSS files. In order to preserve relations between flows, we store source and destination addresses of the hosts involved and use the absolute timestamps of our extended epoch representation (see above) to calculate restrictions between flows of the same host.

A **restriction** is bound to a flow and contains a *target event* and a *delay*. A flow may not be replayed in the testbed before the *target event* occurred in the simulation and the additional *delay* has passed. If several flows are open at the same time, the *target event* will be the latest finished reply of a parallel flow, as the new flow might have been established due to that reply (cf. *Restriction B* in Fig. 4). If no open flows have received a reply yet, the *target event* will be the end of the latest finished flow (*Restriction C* in Fig. 4) or the start of the trace file if no flows are finished yet (*Restriction A*). The *delay* is simply the offset of the flow in question from the *target event* as observed in the source trace.

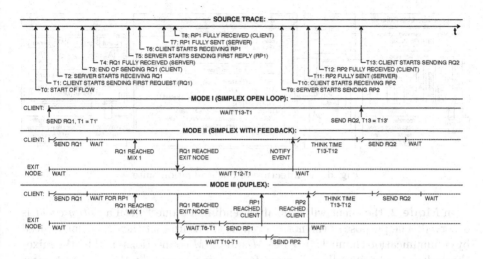

Fig. 5. Replay modes of the R&F Model

3.5   The Replay and Feedback (R&F) Model for Load Generation

The R&F Model determines how the flows extracted by the DPE Model are replayed. It supports different levels of detail that affect realism, control and complexity. One of **three replay modes** (two simplex and one duplex mode) can be selected. We will explain each mode for the example of a transaction between a client and a server via HTTP (cf. Fig. 5).

Mode 1 simply replays requests in an **open simplex loop**, i. e., the simulated clients use a fixed schedule and send each request at the same simulated time (T1' and T13' in Fig. 5) as in the source trace (T1 and T13), i. e., T1 = T1' and T13 = T13'. This mode is used in [25] and reflects common assumptions of analytic evaluations. *Mode 1* is useful to understand the basic properties of the object of study as results are not blurred by other effects. These properties as well as correlations between involved parameters are difficult to derive from more detailed and realistic evaluations. However, using Mode 1 will still be more realistic than, for instance, modelling the arrival of messages by a poisson process.

Mode 1 has two significant limitations: It should only be used when connections are modelled with *unlimited bandwidth* as otherwise the connections between clients and first mix (*C–M*, cf. Fig. 2) may become the bottleneck, which reduces the burstiness of flows (sending buffers of clients will most or all of the time be filled with requests) [13]. Even with unlimited bandwidth, requests that are dependent on previous replies (e. g., RQ2 at T13 in Fig. 5 might have been caused by RP1 at T12) might be replayed before the reply in question has reached the simulated server, i. e., the delay introduced by the anonymity system does not affect the simulated sending behaviour of clients.

The remaining two replay modes take feedback from the system under test into account to prevent these effects (*closed loop*). All modes assert that the *think time* (T13 − T12) between requests is always preserved.

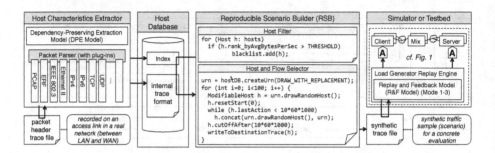

Fig. 6. Architecture of our evaluation suite

In **Mode 2**, the client will wait after sending a request until a *notify event* is observed. The purpose of the notify event is to ensure that the delays introduced by communication channels (e. g., *C–M* and *M–M* connections) and by the mixes themselves can be modelled. The *notify event* is triggered by the *Exit Node* after it has received all replies for the client's request (*Exit Nodes* run a proxy that requests data from servers on client's behalf (cf. Fig. 2). The client will send its next request (RQ2 in Fig. 5) only after the *notify event* has been observed and the additional think time has passed. The **assumption** in this model is, that servers are able to answer requests in the same time as observed in the original trace. While this is a simplifying assumption, its effect on accuracy should be small as the delay introduced inside the anonymity network (through delaying messages to build an anonymity set or congestion) is usually the bottleneck, i. e., *Exit Nodes* will typically be able to receive data from servers much faster than they can forward them through the anonymous reply channels to clients.

In **Mode 3** (duplex mode) clients will wait after sending a request until they receive the corresponding reply (or replies) and (after the additional think time) send the next request (RQ2 in Fig. 5). In this mode the delays introduced by communication channels and mixes can be modelled for both requests and replies. *Exit Nodes* will start forwarding replies to clients as soon as they receive the first bytes (of theses replies) from the corresponding servers (T6 − T1 and T10 − T1 in Fig. 5). As in *Mode 2*, delays for these incoming replies on *Exit Nodes* are recreated as in the original trace. *Mode 3* offers the highest level of detail among the three modes and allows predictions about user-perceived quality of service attributes (e. g., RTT and throughput).

4   Implementation of Our Workload Model

We have implemented the DPE and R&F workload models described in Sect. 3 and integrated them into an evaluation suite that can be re-used by others. The evaluation suite (cf. Fig. 6) consists of **four main components**: the Host Characteristics Extractor, the Host Database, the Reproducible Scenario Builder, and a Simulator or Testbed.

The **Host Characteristics Extractor (HCE)** is the implementation of the DPE Model. Its input consists of a packet header trace file recorded in a real network. The HCE uses packet parsers (e. g., for PCAP and ERF and higher-level protocols) to extract an application-level characterisation for each host from the trace file that consists of flows and restrictions according to the DPE Model. Additionally, aggregated statistics (see below) are recorded for each host. The output of the HCE is stored in an intermediate format in the Host Database.

Building workload models typically involves selecting a portion of hosts that meet some desired criteria from the raw trace files. This is problematic as the size of suitable trace files is typically much higher than the available RAM (e. g., we use a 23 GB sample from the 2009 "Auckland 10" data set [24] for our evaluation in Sect. 5). The **Host Database** is an efficient solution for that task. Compared to the approach typically encountered in the network research community, namely iteratively traversing the whole trace with packet filters [3], our solution is faster and more flexible: During parsing the HCE records *aggregated statistics* for various behavioral characteristics for each host and stores them in the Host Database. Inspired by *Information Retrieval* systems the Host Database creates an *index* that allows for fast selection of the traffic of those hosts that meet certain selection criteria for a concrete experiment. At the moment the index contains about 30 statistics, among them the average sending rate and number of flows for each host. Furthermore, it contains the ranks of hosts for each attribute. As a result, it is easy to perform data cleansing (e. g., blacklisting the 5 % hosts with the highest sending rate) and to select adequate hosts for a realistic test scenario. The Host Database is used by the Reproducible Scenario Builder to create synthetic trace files that represent concrete evaluation scenarios based on the sending and receiving behaviour of hosts.

The **Reproducible Scenario Builder (RSB)** allows researchers to create or re-create traffic traces used for replay during simulation. This involves the selection of appropriate hosts from the *Host Database* as well as data cleansing tasks. As there is no one-fits-all approach for these tasks, we require the experimenter to specify his decisions by implementing a **Host and Flow Selector**. A typical selector fits into (much) less than 100 lines of code and can be implemented in a few minutes. Figure 6 shows a code example. Thus the effort for implementing the selector should be almost negligible compared to the decision process required to define an adequate scenario (usability). If an experimenter publishes his extractor and states his input trace file, other scientists can recreate the same synthetic output trace file (repeatability). We include several *standard selectors* that address typical evaluation scenarios, e. g., selectors that choose n random hosts that are continuously online for a duration of m minutes, selectors that only take into account specific protocol mixes (e. g., HTTP and HTTPs only), as well as selectors for x hosts with a *high* sending rate and y hosts with a *low* sending rate.

The RSB can create both *unmodified* and *re-composed* workload sets. While unmodified replay of host characteristics is preferable in terms of realism and accuracy, re-composed workload sets allow for more control and may be more suitable to identify, understand and verify correlations. To this end, selectors may make use of several methods that allow to change the characteristics of a host. For instance, *offline phases* (i. e., periods without data transfer with a minimum length of y ms) may be removed and flows of different hosts can be concatenated or cut off. Furthermore, various random samples, e. g., think times, can be drawn from the index. While re-composed workloads cannot offer the same level of control as analytical or probabilistic traffic models, they offer a noticeable increase of flexibility compared to unmodified extraction from traces.

The synthetic trace files generated by the RSB are used as input for the Load Generator of the Simulator or Testbed component, in which the experiments are carried out. Based on the application-level characterisation stored in the synthetic trace the **Load Generator** simulates individual clients (implementing the R&F Model). It interacts with a **Simulator or Testbed** that represents the system under test. Typical experiments supported by the evaluation suite include: (1) evaluations of the overhead introduced by a certain anonymity system against a baseline, i. e., the quality of service attributes measured in the source trace, (2) comparisons of the performance of different anonymity system proposals, (3) validations of the severity of different traffic analysis attacks [19], and (4) finding the suitable parameters for an anonymity system proposal.

In principle, our evaluation suite can be used to evaluate any low-latency anonymity system. We provide an implementation for the discrete-event network simulator of *gMix* (cf. Sect. 1), because it is available as open source software and already includes abstract models for several mix types. However, we expect easy adaptability for other platforms (cf. Sect. 2) as solely a replay engine capable of parsing our synthetic trace files is required (only a small fraction of the 10,000 SLOC in total). The HCE, the Host Database and the RSB can be re-used.

5   Evaluation

Our evaluation serves two purposes: firstly, we validate the accuracy of our two complementary models and their implementations, and secondly, in order to show the importance of realistic workload models for anonymity systems, we compare characteristics of the traffic created by our dependency-preserving workload model with the traffic created by the more simplistic extraction technique used in [25]. All source code and configuration files can be downloaded from the project website (cf. Sect. 1), including details on how to reproduce our results.

In order to **validate the accuracy** of our workload model we collect traffic characteristics in the source trace files and compare the obtained values with the values computed for traffic being replayed in a simulation. A similar methodology has been used for the evaluation of the A-B-T model [16]. As we focus our attention on the workload model in this experiment, the measurements are performed for a simulated anonymity system that introduces no delay with all connections having unlimited bandwidth. We used Mode 3 of the R&F Model (duplex) for this evaluation. Figure 7 (left-hand side) shows the resulting cumulative distribution function of the characteristic "ADU sizes" for two samples

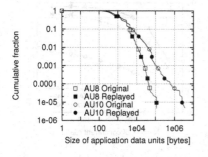 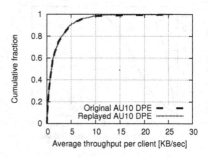

Fig. 7. Evaluation of the accuracy of our workload model

from the data sets, "Auckland 8" (2003) and "Auckland 10" (2009). Figure 7 (right-hand side) displays results for the characteristic "average throughput per client". According to these (and several other, not shown) measurements, traffic replayed using our workload model does not exhibit any significant differences in comparison to the source traces.

Finally, we illustrate the **relevance of realistic workload models** for the prediction of the behaviour of anonymity systems. For this purpose we present a case study in which we evaluate the behaviour of the DLPA dummy traffic scheme [25] for two different workload models, namely, *DPE* (our model) and *DLPAE*. DLPAE implements the extractor used in [25]: this extractor simply *picks up* and concatenates flows from the source trace for each client. Figure 8 (left-hand side) shows that the average throughput per client generated by DL-PAE is considerably higher than the throughput generated by DPE. This result is due to the fact that traffic formed by concatenating flows is not as bursty as the real traffic. In the case of DPE, periods of inactivity (*think times*, cf. Sect. 4) reduce the average throughput.

The DLPA dummy traffic scheme has been only assessed with DLPAE so far [25]. As the efficiency of a dummy traffic scheme depends on the sending behaviour of the clients, its suitability for real-world, bursty traffic is questionable. We have investigated this hypothesis by measuring the amount of dummy messages that is output by a DLPA node (mix). The simulated mix exerts a maximum processing delay of $\Delta = 1$ second. We find that for 100 users 86 % of the output messages are dummies when traffic is modelled with DLPAE (cf. graph on the right-hand side of Fig. 8). With the more realistic traffic generated by our DPE/R&F Model, only 10 concurrent users can be handled by the mix to achieve a similar efficiency. This difference can be explained by the think times that dominate the real client behaviour. Accordingly, the efficiency of DLPA can be expected to be significantly worse in practice than estimated previously.

While we have only demonstrated the importance of realistic workload modelling for the DLPA, it is certainly of interest for other low-latency anonymity systems as well. Our models and tools can be used to reduce the complexity of this task. We hope that our contribution motivates other researchers to evaluate existing and novel proposals with realistic workloads.

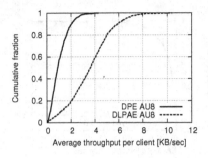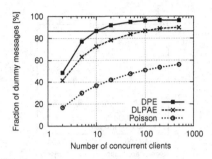

Fig. 8. Comparison of our workload model with previous work

6   Conclusion

Evaluating a distributed system thoroughly is a laborious task, which entails many critical decisions. Nevertheless, an empirical evaluation of anonymity systems is essential to understand the factors that influence their performance in practice. Unfortunately, for many proposed and practical systems there has been little work on comparable, repeatable and realistic evaluations so far.

Our work serves two purposes: Firstly, we strive to provide a usable, more realistic workload model that can be employed in simulations to predict the attainable performance of a system in a real-world setting. In contrast to previous work, we ensure that dependencies between flows are maintained during the simulation, which allows us to mimic the real behaviour of applications more closely. Secondly, we want to work towards a standardised evaluation methodology for the evaluation of anonymity systems that reduces upfront efforts and ensures repeatability of experiments. We believe our evaluation suite and the included scenario builder are first steps in that direction.

Acknowledgments. We thank our colleague Andrey Kolesnikov (Telecommunications and Computer Networks Group) for insightful discussions regarding workload modelling in the network research community.

References

1. Agrawala, A., Mohr, J., Bryant, R.: An Approach to the Workload Characterization Problem. Computer 9(6), 18–32 (1976)
2. Alcock, S., Lawson, D., Nelson, R.: Extracting Application Objects from TCP Packet Traces. In: Australasian Telecommunication Networks and Applications Conference, pp. 151–156 (2007)
3. Alcock, S., Lorier, P., Nelson, R.: Libtrace: A Packet Capture and Analysis library. SIGCOMM Comput. Commun. Rev. 42(2), 42–48 (2012)
4. Barford, P., Crovella, M.: Generating Representative Web Workloads for Network and Server Performance Evaluation. In: SIGMETRICS, pp. 151–160 (1998)
5. Bauer, K., Sherr, M., McCoy, D., Grunwald, D.: ExperimenTor: A Testbed for Safe Realistic Tor Experimentation. In: Workshop on Cyber Security Experimentation and Test (2011)

6. Belshe, M., Peon, R., Thomson, M., Melnikov, A.: SPDY Protocol. Internet Draft (2012), http://tools.ietf.org/html/draft-ietf-httpbis-http2-00
7. Berthold, O., Federrath, H., Köpsell, S.: Web MIXes: A System for Anonymous and Unobservable Internet Access. In: Federrath [12], pp. 115–129
8. Cao, J., Cleveland, W.S., Gao, Y., Jeffay, K., Smith, F.D., Weigle, M.C.: Stochastic Models for Generating Synthetic HTTP Source Traffic. In: INFOCOM (2004)
9. Chaum, D.: Untraceable Electronic Mail, Return Addresses, and Digital Pseudonyms. Communications of the ACM 24(2), 84–90 (1981)
10. Dhungel, P., Steiner, M., Rimac, I., Hilt, V., Ross, K.W.: Waiting for Anonymity: Understanding Delays in the Tor Overlay. In: Peer-to-Peer Computing, pp. 1–4. IEEE (2010)
11. Dingledine, R., Mathewson, N., Syverson, P.: Tor: The Second-Generation Onion Router. In: 13th USENIX Security Symposium, pp. 303–320 (2004)
12. Federrath, H. (ed.): Designing Privacy Enhancing Technologies. LNCS, vol. 2009. Springer, Heidelberg (2001)
13. Floyd, S., Paxson, V.: Difficulties in Simulating the Internet. IEEE/ACM Trans. Netw. 9(4), 392–403 (2001)
14. Fuchs, K.-P., Herrmann, D., Federrath, H.: Introducing the gMix Open Source Framework for Mix Implementations. In: Foresti, S., Yung, M., Martinelli, F. (eds.) ESORICS 2012. LNCS, vol. 7459, pp. 487–504. Springer, Heidelberg (2012)
15. Hernández-Campos, F., Jeffay, K., Smith, F.D.: Tracking the Evolution of Web Traffic: 1995–2003. In: MASCOTS, pp. 16–25. IEEE (2003)
16. Hernández-Campos, F., Smith, F.D., Jeffay, K.: Generating Realistic TCP Workloads. In: Int. CMG Conference, pp. 273–284 (2004)
17. Jansen, R., Hopper, N.: Shadow: Running Tor in a Box for Accurate and Efficient Experimentation. In: Proceedings of the Network and Distributed System Security Symposium (NDSS 2012). Internet Society (2012)
18. McCoy, D., Bauer, K., Grunwald, D., Kohno, T., Sicker, D.: Shining Light in Dark Places: Understanding the Tor Network. In: Borisov, N., Goldberg, I. (eds.) PETS 2008. LNCS, vol. 5134, pp. 63–76. Springer, Heidelberg (2008)
19. Raymond, J.F.: Traffic Analysis: Protocols, Attacks, Design Issues, and Open Problems. In: Federrath [12], pp. 10–29
20. Ramachandran, S.: Web metrics: Size and number of resources (May 2010), https://developers.google.com/speed/articles/web-metrics
21. The Cooperative Association for Internet Data Analysis, http://www.caida.org/
22. Vishwanath, K.V., Vahdat, A.: Swing: Realistic and Responsive Network Traffic Generation. IEEE/ACM Trans. Netw. 17(3), 712–725 (2009)
23. Wacek, C., Tan, H., Bauer, K., Sherr, M.: An Empirical Evaluation of Relay Selection in Tor. In: Proceedings of the Network and Distributed System Security Symposium (NDSS 2013). Internet Society (2013)
24. WAND Network Research Group, http://www.wand.net.nz/wits/
25. Wang, W., Motani, M., Srinivasan, V.: Dependent Link Padding Algorithms for Low Latency Anonymity Systems. In: Ning, P., Syverson, P.F., Jha, S. (eds.) ACM Conference on Computer and Communications Security, pp. 323–332. ACM (2008)
26. Weigle, M.C., Adurthi, P., Hernández-Campos, F., Jeffay, K., Smith, F.D.: Tmix: A Tool for Generating Realistic TCP Application Workloads in ns-2. Computer Communication Review 36(3), 65–76 (2006)
27. Wendolsky, R., Herrmann, D., Federrath, H.: Performance Comparison of Low-Latency Anonymisation Services from a User Perspective. In: Borisov, N., Golle, P. (eds.) PET 2007. LNCS, vol. 4776, pp. 233–253. Springer, Heidelberg (2007)

An Empirical Evaluation of the Android Security Framework[*]

Alessandro Armando[1,2], Alessio Merlo[1,3,**], and Luca Verderame[1]

[1] DIBRIS, Università degli Studi di Genova, Italy
name.surname@unige.it
[2] Security & Trust Unit, FBK-irst, Trento, Italy
armando@fbk.eu
[3] Università e-Campus, Italy
alessio.merlo@uniecampus.it

Abstract. The Android OS consists of a Java stack built on top of a native Linux kernel. A number of recently discovered vulnerabilities suggests that some security issues may be hidden in the interplay between the Java stack and the Linux kernel. We have conducted an empirical security evaluation of the interaction among layers. Our experiments indicate that the Android Security Framework (ASF) does not discriminate the caller of invocations targeted to the Linux kernel, thereby allowing Android applications to directly interact with the Linux kernel. We also show that this trait lets malicious applications adversely affect the user's privacy as well as the usability of the device. Finally, we propose an enhancement in the ASF that allows for the detection and prevention of direct kernel invocations from applications.

1 Introduction

Android is the most widely deployed operating system for smartphones and recent estimates [11] indicate that it will continue to remain so in next years. Roughly speaking it consists of a Java stack built on top of a native Linux kernel. Services and functionalities are achieved through the interplay of components living at different layers of the operating system by means of suitable calls.

Security in Android is granted by a set of cross-layers security solutions combining basic Linux security mechanisms (e.g. Discretionary Access Control) with Java native (JVM isolation) and Android-specific (e.g. the Android permission system) mechanisms. These solutions collectively constitute the Android Security Framework (ASF). The ASF supervises the cross-layer interplay among components in order to detect malicious or unwanted interactions and intervene if necessary.

Recently, the security offered by the ASF has been challenged by the discovery of a number of vulnerabilities involving different layers of the Android stack and the corresponding interplay (see, e.g., [1,8,7]). By analyzing interplay-related vulnerabilities, two peculiarities arise:

[*] This work has been partially founded by EU project FP7-257876 SPaCIoS.
[**] Corresponding author.

L.J. Janczewski, H.B. Wolfe, and S. Shenoi (Eds.): SEC 2013, IFIP AICT 405, pp. 176–189, 2013.
© IFIP International Federation for Information Processing 2013

- the security mechanisms of the Android stack (both Java native and Android-specific) are not completely integrated with those in the Linux kernel, thus potentially allowing for insecure interplay;
- malicious and unprivileged Android applications can force the execution of insecure interplay, thereby by-passing the controls performed by the ASF.

For instance, the Zygote vulnerability reported in [1] allows a malicious application to force the Linux kernel to fork an unbounded number of processes thereby making the device totally unresponsive. In this case, the problem is due to the fact that the ASF is not able to discriminate between a legal interplay (performed by trusted Android services) and an insecure one (executed by applications), thereby permitting the direct invocation of a critical kernel functionality (i.e. the fork operation) by any application. This is basically due to a lack of control on Linux system calls involved in the launch of the new application.

An interesting question is whether such lack of control between the Android stack and the Linux kernel is limited to some type of calls only or else it is a more general issue in the ASF. To ascertain this, we have defined and carried out an empirical assessment on the interplay between the Android stack and the Linux kernel. To this end we have implemented a new kernel module, called *Monitoring Kernel Module*. The Monitoring Kernel Module once installed captures all the invocations targeted to the Linux kernel. We then implemented an Android application (i.e. *KernelCallTester*) that systematically tries to replicate all the calls captured by the Monitoring Kernel Module. This has allowed us to assess to which extent the ASF is able to discriminate between trusted and untrusted invocations of core system functionalities. Our tests—executed involving a number of actual smartphone users—show that very little control is exercised by the ASF and that malicious applications may force and exploit insecure interplays. To show this, we have semi-automatically analyzed all logs produced by the Monitoring Kernel Module. This has led to the discovery of two interplays that adversely affect the user's privacy as well as the usability of the device. We have then implemented and tested two malicious applications (i.e. *WriteTest* and *CacheHooker*)) that execute the malicious interplays. Our experiments on our testbeds showed also in this case that the ASF does not prevent the leakage of private information nor the unavailability of the device. Finally, we designed and implemented an improvement of the ASF (i.e. the *Kernel Call Controller* module) that recognizes and rules the insecure interplays between the Android stack and the Linux kernel we have identified. Again, we tested the effectiveness of the proposed improvement by using our experimental setup (that involves a number of actual users and devices).

Structure of the Paper. In Sect. 2 we briefly introduce the architecture and the interplay of Android, while in Sect. 3 we discuss peculiarities and limitations of the ASF. In Sect. 4 we describe the setup and the implementation of the *Monitoring Kernel Module* and the *KernelCallTester* application. In Sect. 5 we analyze the testing phase and the experimental results. In Sect. 6 we describe the development and the testing of two malicious applications (i.e. *WriteTest* and *CacheHooker*) able to exploit the lack of control in the ASF. Then, in Sect. 7

we propose an improvement in the ASF able to solve the problem. In Sect. 8 we discuss the related work and we conclude in Sect. 9 with some final remarks and future directions.

2   Android in a Nutshell

The Android Architecture consists of 5 layers. The Linux kernel lives in the bottom layer (henceforth the *Linux kernel*). The remaining four layers are Android-specific and we therefore collectively call them *the Android stack*:

Application Layer (A). Applications are at the top of the stack and comprise both user and system applications that have been installed and execute on the device. Each application is made of a set of components each performing a different role in the logic of the application (see [2] for further details).

Application Framework Layer (AF). The Application Framework provides the main services of the platform that are exposed to applications as a set of APIs. This layer provides the System Server, that is a process containing Android core components [1].

Android Runtime Layer (AR). This layer consists of the Dalvik Virtual Machine (Dalvik VM, for short), i.e. the Android runtime core component that executes application files built in the Dalvik Executable format (.dex).

Libraries Layer (L). The Libraries layer contains a set of C/C++ libraries that support the direct invocation of basic kernel functionalities. They are widely used by Application Framework services to interact with the Linux kernel and to access data stored on the device. Examples of libraries are the *Bionic libc*, a custom implementation of libc for Android, and *SQLite*, a self-contained and transactional database engine.

Kernel Layer (K). Android relies on the Linux kernel version 2.6 for core system functionalities. These functionalities include *i)* the access to physical resource (i.e. device peripherals, memory, file system) and *ii)* the Inter-Process Communication (IPC). Device peripherals (e.g. GPS antenna, Bluetooth/Wireless/3G modules, camera, accelerometer) are accessed through Linux drivers installed as kernel modules. Triggering peripheral drivers, as well as accessing file system and memory are achieved by means of *system calls* (e.g. open, read and write for files management). IPC may be carried out through the use of the Binder driver or by reading from/writing on native Unix Domain Sockets. Binder driver is activated through *binder* calls (i.e. ioctl) , while sockets are accessed through *socket calls* (e.g. connect, bind, sendmsg).

2.1   Notes on the Interplay in Android

Operations in Android are carried out through interactions among layers. Such interactions constitute the interplay of Android and are implemented through

---

[1] http://events.linuxfoundation.org/slides/2011/abs/abs2011_yaghmour_internals.pdf for a comprehensive list of such service components.

6 kinds of calls (namely, *function, dynamic load, jni, system, binder,* and *socket* calls) involving distinct subsets of layers and libraries (see [2] for details on calls). As previously discussed, *system, binder,* and *socket* calls allow to trigger directly the Linux kernel functionalities. Hereafter, we refer to these kinds of calls as *kernel calls.* Android provides OS functionalities to applications by means of combinations of calls. For instance, the launch of a new application in Android is normally provided by the following interplay:

1. a requesting application (i.e. the home screen of the device) executes a *binder call* to the Activity Manager Service (AMS) at the Application Framework layer to start the launching process.
2. The AMS checks the permissions of the requesting application and, in case they are sufficient, executes a set of *socket calls* (i.e. `connect`, `sendmsg`, `listen`) to the Zygote socket at K layer for writing down a command aimed at requesting the launch of a new application. The command contains information related to the application to launch.
3. The controlling process of the Zygote socket (i.e. the Zygote process) parses the command and invokes a *JNI call* to load a proper library function at L layer for accessing kernel functionalities.
4. The invoked function directly executes a `fork` *system call* at K layer, building a new Linux process that will host the launching application. If something goes wrong, the command provided by the AMS to the Zygote socket forces the kernel to destroy the created process, otherwise a new Dalvik VM with the code of the launching application is bound to the process and the execution starts.

Interplay in Android is poorly documented and not standardized. As a matter of fact, the interplay of only a few operations is discussed in the official literature ([4]) and the interplay related to the launch of a new application is not documented. The above description (borrowed from [1]) has been inferred by systematically analyzing Android source code. Moreover, the lack of documentation and standardization implies that the same functionalities could be potentially carried out through different interplay, some of which may lead to security flaws. To prevent this, the Android Security Framework discriminates whether an interplay is secure or not, according to the permissions of applications and the basic Android security policy. We introduce in the following the basis of the ASF and then we reason about its limitations related to the analysis of the interplay.

3   The Android Security Framework

The Android Security Framework (ASF) provides a cross-layer security solution (i.e. sandboxing) built by combining native per-layer security mechanisms. Each layer in the Android stack (except the Libraries layer) comes with its own security mechanisms:

- **Application layer (Android Permissions)**. Each application comes with a file named `AndroidManifest.xml` that contains the permissions that the application may require during execution. During installation the user is asked to grant all the permissions specified in the manifest.
- **Application Framework (Permission Enforcement)**. Services at this layer enforce the permissions specified in the manifest and granted by the user during installation.
- **Runtime (VM Isolation)**. Each application is executed in a separate Dalvik VM machine. This ensures isolation among applications.
- **Linux (Access Control)**. As in any Linux kernel, resources are mapped into files (e.g. sockets, drivers). The Linux Discretionary Access Control (DAC) model associates each file with an owner and a group. Then, DAC model allows the owner to assign an access control list (i.e. read, write, and/or execute) on each file to the owner itself (UID), the owner's group (GID) and other users.

Sandboxing is a cross-layer solution adopted in Android to provide strong isolation among applications. In detail, Android achieves sandboxing of the applications by binding each Android application to a separate user at K layer, thereby combining the native separation due to the execution of applications on different Dalvik VMs with the isolation provided by native Linux access control.

Once an application is installed on the device (i.e. the user accepts all required permissions in the `AndroidManifest.xml` file) a new user at the Linux layer is created and the corresponding user id (UID) is bound to the installed application. As stated in the previous section, once the application is launched, a new process, with such UID, and a novel Dalvik VM are created in order to execute the application.

This solution forces any non privileged UID to have at most one process running (i.e. the one containing the running application). Rarely, more than one active process for the same UID can be allowed if explicitly requested in the `AndroidManifest.xml`. However, the maximum number of active processes is upper-bounded by the number of components composing the application.

At runtime, sandboxing and other per-layer security mechanisms are expected to avoid illegal interplay. For instance, if an application tries to invoke a `kill` system call on the process hosting another application, the sandboxing is violated (i.e. a Linux user tries to kill a process belonging to another user) and the system call is blocked.

3.1   Security Considerations on the Android Security Framework

Some recent vulnerabilities indicate that the integration of the Android-specific security mechanisms with those provided by Linux may suffer from unknown security flaws.

For instance, as shown in [1] in the launching flow presented in Sect. 2.1 an application can invoke *socket calls* directly and send an ad-hoc command through the Zygote socket, thereby by-passing the Activity Manager Service. The ASF identifies such interplay as legal, since it is not able to notice that an application is invoking calls targeted to the Linux kernel instead of a trusted service in the Application Framework layer. More in detail, each running application, as well as any trusted service, is hosted in an unprivileged process at Linux layer due to *sandboxing*; this makes hard for the Linux kernel to discriminate whether a socket or system call comes from an application rather than a trusted server; this impersonation should be noticed by security mechanisms in the Android stack. However, in the specific case no mechanism recognizes the unexpected caller, thus allowing the malicious interplay. Furthermore, such an interplay can be repeated an arbitrary number of times by the malicious application until the device becomes totally unresponsive [1].

Other vulnerabilities suggest that security breaches can be hidden in the communications among applications. For instance, single messages exchanged among applications (by means of *binder calls*) can be individually compliant with the applications permissions and hence permitted by the ASF; however, some maliciously crafted interplay can lead to undetected privilege escalation [8] or attacks on legal applications [7].

We argue that at the above problems are due to a lack of control on:

- the identification of the caller for direct kernel invocations (i.e. *binder*, *socket* and *system calls*) that may allow malicious applications to operate undetected on the Kernel instead of legal Android services;
- the monitoring of cross-layer interplay, that may allow malicious interactions if single calls do no violate any system policy or the sandboxing;
- the identification of repeated interplay, that can make the OS weak against Denial-of-Service attacks.

In the following, we substantiate our claims by means of an empirical evaluation carried out on the Android platform.

4   Assessing the ASF on Kernel Calls

As discussed, the Zygote vulnerability is basically due to a lack of control on the identity of the components invoking a *socket call* targeted to the Kernel layer that is normally expected to be executed by trusted services in the Application Framework layer. However, the same problem may affect other calls normally invoked by the same trusted services.

Unfortunately, due to a very limited documentation on this topic, it is impossible to rely exclusively on current technical and research literature to retrieve reliable information on the set of kernel calls invoked by trusted services. To this aim, static analysis techniques could help (they are widely adopted to retrieve models of Android applications from the Dalvik code). However, due to the complexity and the size of the Android source code, static analysis can be complex and cumbersome. Hence, we opted for an empirical approach with the two-fold aim of i) relating trusted services with the kernel calls they invoke, and ii) verifying whether the ASF is able to recognize that an execution of a kernel call, as well as it is invoked by a legal service, is invoked by a malicious application instead.

To this aim, we set up the experiment into two steps: we implemented 1) a *Monitoring Kernel Module* (MKM) able to intercept kernel calls invoked by the whole *Android stack* and 2) a tester application (*KernelCallTester*) that is able to replicate the calls intercepted by the MKM. Then, we set up the MKM to intercept kernel calls executed by trusted services in the AF layer and the *KernelCallTester* application to reproduce each kernel call as soon as it has been intercepted (see Fig.1), in order to assess whether the ASF recognizes such attempt as malicious.

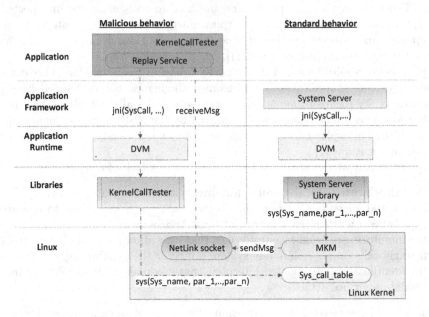

Fig. 1. Interaction between the MKM and the `KernelCallTester`

The MKM is a kernel module which customizes the way in which kernel calls are invoked. Upon installation, the MKM retrieves the kernel call prototypes from `systemcalls.h` and the kernel calls numbers from `unistd.h`. Then, it modifies each entry in the `sys_call_table` structure, which contains the kernel calls routines; in particular, the MKM substitutes each routine in the table with a customized one. Each customized routine gets the calling thread name and process pid (using the Linux macro `current`) as well as the optional parameters passed to the call and, then, it executes the normal routine. At runtime, the MKM creates a *netlink socket* in order to store the intercepted kernel calls and the corresponding parameters. Each time the MKM intercepts a kernel call, the custom routine writes a message on the netlink socket.

KernelCallTester has been designed to replicate kernel calls invocations intercepted by the MKM and stored on the netlink socket. For each kernel call invocation, *KernelCallTester* tries to replicate it a random number of times. *KernelCallTester* is composed by a a broadcast receiver, an Android service (called `Replay Service`), running on the device in background, and a C++

pre-compiled library. The broadcast receiver is in charge to launch the `Replay Service` once the device completes the boot. The `Replay Service` connects to the netlink socket created by the MKM and parses data contained on it. For each invocation stored on the socket, the `Replay Service`, by means of a *jni* call to the *KernelCallTester* library, starts replicating the corresponding kernel call with the same parameters as the original one. Depending on the kind of kernel calls, the `Replay Service` may also execute other ad-hoc calls. For instance, if a `read` call is invoked on a file, the `Replay Service` tries to execute an `open` on the same file before invoking the `read`. After replicating the call, `Replay Service` removes the entry from the socket. The `Replay Service` keeps track in proper log files of the success/failure of each replication attempt. Besides, error messages for failed invocations are stored.

4.1   Deploying and Configuring MKM and *KernelCallTester*.

We deployed the MKM and the *KernelCallTester* into two Android builds, namely v. 2.3.3 (API 10) and v. 4.0.3 (API 15), as the most representative distributions currently available on commercial devices[2], respectively for entry-level and top-notch smartphones.

Since the ability to load modules is natively disabled in the Linux kernel deployed in Android, we enabled such feature by recompiling the kernel for a generic ARM architecture. Such modification does not alter any kernel functionality, thus the behavior of the recompiled kernel is equivalent to the original one. Moreover, we have developed a custom `rc.module` script, executed as a service in the `init.rc`, which installs the MKM automatically at startup.

We configured the MKM to intercept kernel calls executed by trusted services and to keep track of a subset of the most representative kernel calls[3], including core system calls (e.g. for I/O and process management: `open`, `close`, `read`, `write`, `lseek`, `mkdir`, `rmdir`, `exit_group`, `exit`, `getpid`, `gettid`, `kill`, `lstat64`, `prctl`, `setuid`, `setgid`, `waitid`, `shutdown`, `gettuid`, `geteuid`, `getgid`, `mount`, `umount`), socket calls (`bind`, `connect`, `sendmsg`, `sendto`, `socket`, `recvfrom`, `recvmsg`, `listen`) and binder calls (which rely on the `ioctl` system call).

This selection covers a wide range of Android security relevant operations, like file management, Internet connection, IPC communication and launch of new applications. The motivation of reducing the subset of monitored kernel calls is to limit the overhead generated by both the MKM and *KernelCallTester* on the testing devices.

5   Testing and Experimental Results

We installed the two customized Android builds presented in Sect.4.1 into a set of ten smartphones. In particular, we deployed the Android build v.2.3.3 to five smartphones (i.e. HTC Desire HD, LG Optimus One p550, LG Optimus 3D,

---

[2] http://developer.android.com/about/dashboards/index.html
[3] https://github.com/android/platform_bionic/blob/master/libc/SYSCALLS.TXT

LG Optimus L3, Galaxy Next GT-S5570) and the Android build v.4.0.3 to other
five smartphones (i.e. Galaxy Nexus, HTC Sensation XL, Motorola Droid RAZR
MAXX, Galaxy Tab 7.1, HTC Vivid). Then, we delivered the smartphones to
a heterogeneous set of users (i.e. university students, teenagers, professors and
clerks) for normal use for two weeks. Users have been left free to install and use
every kind of application.

During the testing period the execution of applications had forced services in
the AF layer to invoke kernel calls to provide functionalities to applications. By
analyzing the MKM logs from different smarpthones, which reported more than
100.000 kernel call invocations, we were able to relate services in the AF layer
with the kernel calls they invoke. Results are presented in Table 1.

Table 1. Kernel calls invoked by services in the AF layer

AF service	Kernel calls
Alarm Manager	getpid, ioctl, open
Activity Manager	close, getpid, gettid, ioctl, lseek, mkdir, open, prctl, read, write
Audio Service	-
BatteryStats	close, exit, gettid, open
GpsLocationProvider	getpid, ioctl
Location Manager Service	getpid, ioctl, lseek, open, read
Package Manager	close, getpid, gettid, ioctl, lstat64, open, sendmsg, write
Power Manager Service	getpid, ioctl, open, read, write
ServerThread	close, connect, getpid, gettid, ioctl, lseek, lstat64, open, prctl, read, recvmsg, sendmsg, sendto, socket, write
ThrottleService	close, exit_group, getpid, gettid, ioctl, open, prctl, read, sendmsg, write
VoldConnector	getpid, gettid, ioctl, open, recvmsg, write
Window Manager	close, getpid, gettid, ioctl, open, read, write

Furthermore, 28 out of 33 (85%) of the kernel call types intercepted by the
MKM have been successfully replicated by the *KernelCallTester* both on Android v. 2.3.3 and v. 4.0.3. Only 5 calls (15%) failed due to Linux permissions
errors or wrong parameters. More in detail:

System Calls. System calls reproduced by *KernelCallTester* can be divided
into file management and process management system calls.
   – **File Management System Calls.** The MKM intercepts system calls
   related to files management as well as the parameters used (e.g. the data
   written and absolute path of the file opened). Since files are accessed in
   Linux by means of *file descriptors*, whenever a file system call occurs,
   KernelCallTester tries to reopen the targeted files, then reproduces the
   corresponding operation (write, read or lseek). Moreover, *KernelCall-
   Tester* handles mkdir and rmdir system calls. In all tests executions,

we noticed that possible failures are only due to Linux permission errors (e.g. *KernelCallTester* is not in the owner group of a certain file).
  - **Process Management System Calls.** *KernelCallTester* is also able to reproduce successfully process management system calls like `gettid`, `getpid` or `exit_group`. Only the `kill` call cannot be reproduced because an unprivileged user is authorized to kill only process she owns.
Socket Calls. Since sockets are mapped on files, *KernelCallTester* firstly tries to `connect` to the socket before reproducing socket calls like `recvmsg` or `sendmsg`. Failure is again only due to insufficient Linux access permissions (e.g. sockets owned by *root* with permissions set to *660*) or unaccepted parameters (e.g. `bind` fails because the targeted socket is already bound).
Binder Calls. Binder calls rely on `ioctl` system call which allows sending simple commands and data to a file descriptor. Regarding IPC, the sender process performs a `ioctl` call to the Binder, specifying the addressee and including the data of the message. The Binder, which handles the passing mechanism, reads incoming messages and routes them to the appropriate destinations. *KernelCallTester* is not able to reproduce exactly the same call since one of the arguments is the pointer to the data sent which is located within addresser's memory space, causing a *Bad Address* failure.

Above all, our tests show that **every kernel call invoked by trusted services in the AF layer can be reproduced by any unprivileged application.** More specifically, our experiments show that the ASF never intervenes whether a kernel call invocation is attempted by an application in stead of a trusted service, revealing that Android does not perform any discrimination according to the caller of a kernel call. Moreover, no intervention is performed on repeated (and suspicious) invocation of the same kernel call; in particular, each attempts to replicate (also 10K times in a few seconds) the same kernel call has never been recognized as suspicious by the ASF.

Thus, the possibility to properly forge and directly execute kernel calls from the A layer may allow any application to take advantage of the kernel functionalities for malicious purposes. To this aim, in the next section we show two interplays that a malicious application can execute to reduce the performance of the device and to violate the privacy of the user.

6   Kernel Calls and Malicious Interplay

A central design point of the Android security architecture is that applications cannot adversely impact other applications and the operating system, or the user [4]. Such statement represents the final goal of the ASF, according to the official Android documentation. Starting from this statement, we identified two security goals that should be obliviously granted:
  - an application cannot exhaust system resources;
  - an application cannot access data of another application.

---

[4] `https://developer.android.com/guide/topics/security/security.html`

186   A. Armando, A. Merlo, and L. Verderame

Then, we analyzed all logs produced by the MKM during the testing phase in order to find potential vulnerabilities that, if exploited, allow to violate the previous security goals. The analysis has been carried out with both manual and automatic inspection of whole set of logs. The analysis activity allowed to infer that:

- file system operations with proper parameters and sufficient permissions are unbounded;
- files located in /data/data/com.android.browser/cache/webviewCache, containing the cache (e.g. images, javascript codes, web pages accessed by the user) of installed browsers, can be read by any application.

Thus, we implemented two malicious applications, namely *WriteTest* (requiring no privileges upon installation) and *CacheHooker* (requiring only the INTERNET permission) that exploit such characteristics to perform attacks by means of kernel calls.

WriteTest repeatedly execute an open, a write and a close system call at different periods of time. Each interplay create a dummy file of 4 MB in the internal memory of the phone.

CacheHooker cyclically invokes a read on the cache file, followed by a write on its data folder. Moreover it connects (using socket and connect calls) and sends (relying on sendmsg call) every copied file to a remote server. The connecting operation exploits the android.permission.INTERNET permission.

We installed both applications to the testing smartphones, so that they execute as services in background after a random period of time after the boot completion. Users reported that other applications had started to crash or to terminate at launch, and that Android provides back pop-ups on the exhaustion of the phone memory. Uninstalling other applications did not solve the problem. Only very few users was able to identify the *WriteTest* application and solve the problem by flashing the device. Furthermore, during the testing period *CacheHooker* has successfully and silently grabbed users browsing data delivering them to the remote server.

7   Enhancing the ASF

We argue that malicious interplay related to kernel calls may be limited by providing the ASF with the possibility to identify the caller of a kernel call. To this aim, we propose an improvement to the ASF requiring the modification of the *Bionic Libc* and the development of a kernel call evaluation module, called *Kernel Call Controller* (KCC). KCC, placed at the Library layer, exposes a set of options for evaluating a kernel call, which can be set by the *Activity Manager* at the AF layer:

Application Kernel Call Restriction. It allows to deny/permit kernel call invocations performed by the Application layer (i.e. caller with PID greater than 10000).

Kernel Call Frequency Restriction. It allows to upper-bound the number of calls of a given type (also with different parameters) that can be invoked by a single caller in an amount of time (i.e. 1, 10 or 60 seconds).

Bionic Libc is a derivation of the standard C implementation for a mobile environment. In Android, this library is included in each Linux process and it performs the actual invocation of the kernel calls. Each call is implemented by a different tiny assembler source fragment (called *syscall stub*), which is responsible for executing the corresponding kernel code. Syscall stubs are generated automatically by a Python script (i.e. *gensyscalls.py*).

We extended the Bionic Libc by modifying the syscall stubs, i.e. changing the script that generates them. In particular, before executing the kernel code of the call, the modified stub invokes the main routine of KCC , which is able to i) identify the PID of the caller, ii) calculate the frequency of each invocation, and then iii) assess whether the behavior is compliant with the KCC settings, allowing/denying the execution of the call accordingly. Furthermore, information collected by the KCC are stored in the */data* folder as a text file for offline analysis.

The idea of hooking the system call procedures has been also adopted by SEAndroid[5]. However, the adoption of SEAndroid has a considerable impact on the system architecture. In fact, whereas our patch involves only a modification of the Bionic Libc, SEAndroid requires a deep customization of some parts of the Android Framework and the recompilation of the Linux Kernel.

We deployed KCC as well as *WriteTest* and *CacheHooker* in our two Android builds and then installed them into the ten smartphones. Then, we repeated the same test described in Sect. 5, providing users with devices. We configured KCC disabling the invocations of kernel calls from the A layer and limiting the number of allowed calls to 10 per second. KCC was able to block unexpected direct kernel calls invocations from *WriteTest* and *CacheHooker* applications, thus fully preventing the memory exhaustion and the web cache privacy leak (i.e. no data has been sent to the remote server).

During the testing phase, no user reported any visible performance issue or unexpected behavior. Such results, although limited to a small subset of all available Android applications, indicate that applications may not need to perform direct kernel call invocations to work properly. However, further analysis should be carried out on a more comprehensive set of applications.

8   Related Work

Literature on Android security has considerably spread in recent years, including general surveys, like [15] and [9], vulnerabilities, tools and formal methods to enhance both the Android architecture and the corresponding security model. Regarding vulnerabilities, recent works show that the Android platform may suffer from DoS attacks [1], covert channels [14], web attacks [12] and privilege

---

[5] http://selinuxproject.org/page/SEAndroid

escalation attacks [8]. The same works underline that such vulnerabilities affect each Android build.

Several authors underline the limitation of the current Android security model, thus proposing methodologies and tools to extend the native Android security solutions. For instance, in [13] authors propose an extension to the basic Android permission systems and corresponding new policies, while in [16] authors suggest new privacy-related security policies for addressing security problems related to users' personal data. Other tools are devoted to malware detection (e.g. XMan-Droid [5] and Crowdroid [6]) and application certification (e.g. Scandroid [10] and Comdroid [7]).

However, none of such solutions takes into consideration interplay between the Android stack and the Linux kernel, focusing on interplay related to the Android stack only.

Monitoring of system calls in Android is discussed by Blasing et al. [3]. They propose an Android Application Sandbox (AASandbox) which is able to perform both static and dynamic analysis in a fully isolated environment. AASandbox relies on a loadable kernel module which monitors system calls, although such approach is particularly different from the one proposed in this paper for a two-fold reason. First, the kernel module is able to log only the return value of each system call, without logging the parameters. Furthermore, authors do not provide any security assessment regarding Android system calls, neither suggest any solution that could mitigate possible malicious interplay.

To the best of our knowledge, our work is the first attempt to empirically investigate correlations and security issues related to the interplay among the Android layers and the Linux kernel.

9   Conclusions

In this paper, we empirically demonstrated that Android allows applications to directly invoke Kernel functionalities. We built an ad-hoc kernel module (i.e. the *Monitoring Kernel Module*) and an application (i.e. *KernelCallTester*) to capture and replicate all kernel calls invoked by trusted services in AF layer. We demonstrated that this trait may lead to undermine the security of the system as well as the privacy of the user; we proved it by means of two malicious applications (i.e. *WriteTest* and *CacheHooker*) implemented after analyzing the logs of the MKM. However, other potential vulnerabilities may be hidden in the logs produced by the MKM. Nevertheless, the discovery of vulnerabilities in Android is far from being automated and exhaustive. In order to achieve such results in the near future, we argue that two problems must be tackled. First, it is currently difficult to assess whether a specific behavior (e.g. connecting to a system socket) violates the Android Security policy, since the same policy is very informally defined. For this, we argue that proper languages for formally stating the expected security properties and behavior of an Android build should be investigated. Then, new techniques for automatically/semi-automatically search for vulnerabilities in Android builds should be identified.

References

1. Armando, A., Merlo, A., Migliardi, M., Verderame, L.: Would you mind forking this process? A denial of service attack on Android (and some countermeasures). In: Gritzalis, D., Furnell, S., Theoharidou, M. (eds.) SEC 2012. IFIP AICT, vol. 376, pp. 13–24. Springer, Heidelberg (2012)
2. Armando, A., Merlo, A., Migliardi, M., Verderame, L.: Breaking and fixing the android launching flow. Elsevier Computer and Security (2013)
3. Blasing, T., Batyuk, L., Schmidt, A.-D., Camtepe, S., Albayrak, S.: An android application sandbox system for suspicious software detection. In: 2010 5th International Conference on Malicious and Unwanted Software (MALWARE), pp. 55–62 (2010)
4. Brady, P.: Anatomy and physiology of an android. Google I/O (2008)
5. Bugiel, S., Davi, L., Dmitrienko, A., Fischer, T., Sadeghi, A.-R.: Xmandroid: A new android evolution to mitigate privilege escalation attacks. Technical Report TR-2011-04, Technische Univ. Darmstadt (April 2011)
6. Burguera, I., Zurutuza, U., Nadjm-Therani, S.: Crowdroid: behavior-based malware detection system for android. In: Proceedings of the 1st ACM Workshop on Security and Privacy in Smartphones and Mobile Devices, SPSM 2011 (2011)
7. Chin, E., Felt, A.P., Greenwood, K., Wagner, D.: Analyzing inter-application communication in Android. In: Proceedings of the 9th International Conference on Mobile Systems, Applications, and Services, MobiSys 2011, pp. 239–252. ACM, New York (2011)
8. Davi, L., Dmitrienko, A., Sadeghi, A.-R., Winandy, M.: Privilege escalation attacks on android. In: Burmester, M., Tsudik, G., Magliveras, S., Ilić, I. (eds.) ISC 2010. LNCS, vol. 6531, pp. 346–360. Springer, Heidelberg (2011)
9. Enck, W., Ongtang, M., McDaniel, P.: Understanding Android Security. Security & Privacy 7(1), 50–57 (2009)
10. Fuchs, A.P., Chaudhuri, A., Foster, J.S.: Scandroid: Automated security certification of android applications. Technical report (2009)
11. Gartner Group. Press Release (August 2012), http://www.gartner.com/it/page.jsp?id=2120015
12. Luo, T., Hao, H., Du, W., Wang, Y., Yin, H.: Attacks on webview in the android system. In: Proceedings of the 27th Annual Computer Security Applications Conference, ACSAC 2011, pp. 343–352. ACM, New York (2011)
13. Nauman, M., Khan, S., Zhang, X.: Apex: extending android permission model and enforcement with user-defined runtime constraints. In: Proceedings of the 5th ACM Symposium on Information, Computer and Communications Security, ASIACCS 2010, pp. 328–332. ACM, New York (2010)
14. Schlegel, R., Zhang, K., Zhou, X., Intwala, M., Kapadia, A., Wang, X.: Soundcomber: A Stealthy and Context-Aware Sound Trojan for Smartphones. In: Proceedings of the 18th Annual Network & Distributed System Security Symposium (NDSS) (February 2011)
15. Shabtai, A., Fledel, Y., Kanonov, U., Elovici, Y., Dolev, S., Glezer, C.: Google android: A comprehensive security assessment. IEEE Security Privacy 8(2), 35–44 (2010)
16. Zhou, Y., Zhang, X., Jiang, X., Freeh, V.W.: Taming information-stealing smartphone applications (on android). In: McCune, J.M., Balacheff, B., Perrig, A., Sadeghi, A.-R., Sasse, A., Beres, Y. (eds.) Trust 2011. LNCS, vol. 6740, pp. 93–107. Springer, Heidelberg (2011)

A Security Engineering Process Approach for the Future Development of Complex Aircraft Cabin Systems

Hartmut Hintze, Benjamin Wiegraefe, and Ralf God

TUHH, Institute of Aircraft Cabin Systems, Hamburg, Germany
{hartmut.hintze,benjamin.wiegraefe,ralf.god}@tuhh.de

Abstract. Due to increasing functionality associated with rising complexity of aircraft cabin systems which are used by cabin crew, passengers, maintenance staff and other stakeholders, security engineering has to become an integral part of the system engineering process in aviation industry. This paper deals with a security engineering process approach for the development of complex aircraft systems, which is fully integrated into the development process. As an appropriate process model we introduce the so called three-V-model, which represents the governing system engineering process (SEP) associated with the safety engineering process (SafEP) and the security engineering process (SecEP). All three processes are pursued concurrently and are interacting reciprocally on each development level with the predominant SEP. We describe in detail involved security engineering activities and finally demonstrate how the interaction between the SEP and the SecEP is improved and optimized by the use of so called security context parameters (SCPs).

Keywords: Security, Aircraft Cabin Systems, Complex Systems, Development Process, Three-V-Model, Security Context Parameters.

1 Introduction

The cabin management system takes on a central role for all tasks to operate the aircraft cabin. Primary functions are communication, indication, control, monitoring and configuration of other cabin systems. For this reason it represents a complex system characterized by a large amount of interactions between a plurality of aircraft cabin systems. To achieve the objectives of SAE ARP-4754 [1] for certification of highly integrated and complex aircraft systems, the development process is following a process model which is called the V-model. The development of the system functions is supported by the safety assessment process [1-2], which follows a V-model as well and has to ensure the reliability of the system functions. The combination of the functional V-model and the safety V-model is known in literature as the Two-V-Model [3]. To cover security requirements which are related to the system functions, the recent EUROCAE / RTCA documents [4] provides guidance material for a security engineering process. This process will become mandatory for the development of aircraft cabin functions and related systems. In this paper we take up this approach, refine it and integrate it as a 'third V' to end up with an appropriate and

L.J. Janczewski, H.B. Wolfe, and S. Shenoi (Eds.): SEC 2013, IFIP AICT 405, pp. 190–202, 2013.

comprehensive new process model for the development process in aircraft industry. The resulting Three-V-Model is intended to be used as the baseline for the development of future aircraft cabin systems and will consider the system engineering process (SEP) associated with the safety engineering process (SafEP) and the security engineering process (SecEP) at the same time. Furthermore the interactions between the SEP and the SecEP are improved via the introduction of so called security context parameters (SCPs). Theses parameters help to quantify and transfer required information for security management from the SEP to the SecEP and vice versa. This approach avoids time consuming information filtering work at SecEP side and thus provides the opportunity for speeding up the overall development process.

2   System Security in the Development of Cabin Management Systems

2.1   Historical Overview

Within the past 20th century engineering work in commercial aviation was focused on improving the performance parameters for higher payload, extended range, higher speed and more comfort for the passengers. Important milestones were reached by major achievements in aircraft design, engine technology and by the use of pressurized cabins for higher cruise altitude.

The use of electronics within passenger aircraft started with engine control in the 1950s and then in the 1970s was extended to electronic flight control. A peak was reached in 1988 when Airbus introduced its fully digital fly-by-wire technology in the A320. With this aircraft, Airbus completely discarded the use of analog primary flight controls and replaced them by fully computer-controlled digital signaling via an avionics data communication network to control hydraulic actuators at the flight-control surfaces.

Today, in the 21st century the focus has moved to the aircraft cabin with its complex systems. The cabin is the central element within air travel and the business card of the airline. The primary transport service of an airline comes along with a fierce competition for customers and forces the airline to deal intensively with passenger's future travel requirements. The cabin management system with its various service functionalities plays a central role in this struggle for customer satisfaction. Electronics and data network of the cabin management system have continuously been refined over the past 25 years. This on-going evolution led to a mature and sophisticated system. However a still increasing range of cabin functions, maintenance tasks and passenger services and a related growing amount of processes are now culminating in a challenging situation where the existing architecture needs to be reconsidered and reworked in terms of flexibility and scalability to be fit for the future.

Preferred types of architectures for next-generation cabin management systems are based on the concept of distributed systems with wireless communication links e.g. for ad-hoc-sensor networks, mobile PCs and other mobile devices to satisfy the needs of the various stakeholders in the cabin [5-6]. These novel architecture principles aboard passenger aircraft place special emphasis on the aspects of security. In the past, security was mostly handled by physical security mechanisms: the hardware was physically separated, software was encapsulated and communication paths were regulated and secured. But for distributed architectures with wireless communication interfaces the means of physical security mechanism is no longer sufficient. Hence, it is necessary to establish logical security mechanisms, i.e. security mechanisms against unauthorized access to communication networks, software, information and data of a system. Furthermore, the unauthorized execution of activities within the system has to be prohibited. Logical security in aircraft is becoming more and more a challenge and therefore has to be considered from the very beginning when developing a new aircraft.

2.2   The Need for a Change

A closer look into today's cabin management systems proves that an evolutionary system extension led to the involvement of new stakeholders, an integration of a multitude of functionalities to deal with novel use cases and to an extension of data intercommunication to infrastructures outside of the cabin as described in [6]. This progression was mainly achieved on a system level and thus can be considered to be a bottom-up approach in the development process. In consequence the emerging security issues were predominately handled on a system level as well. This strategy has led to a substantial workload dealing with security at a late engineering stage during the overall aircraft development process. According to systems engineering principles [7] it is feared that this strategy can negatively influence development timelines and development cost and may even lead to imperfect or unsatisfying technical solutions.

To cope with these potentially adverse effects there is the need for a change in the development strategy which relocates a significant part of security engineering activities to the first development level, i.e. the aircraft level, and thus enables a favored top-down approach. This top-down approach for security management is feasible when an optimized and standardized communication starts already on an aircraft development level. Further refinement on subsequent development levels will then be reached with reduced effort and in a more directed manner.

Such type of top-down approach for a security engineering process is generally applicable, e.g. in automotive and railway industry or for nuclear power plants and electric power utilities. Due to our specific work in aircraft industry and security, we have tailored this approach to the development of a next-generation cabin management system. The above mentioned means of logical security coming along with novel system architectures in the cabin will be considered.

2.3   The Three-V-Model

Figure 1 shows our so called Three-V-Model. The first V represents the fundamental system engineering process (SEP) for the development of aircraft functions according to literature [1]. The two branches of this V are symbolizing the three major phases of system design, implementation and system integration. The second V accompanies and supports the basic SEP and represents the safety engineering process (SafEP). This process is well known from literature [2] and focuses on system safety requirements and airworthiness design, i.e. reliability and fault tolerance topics.

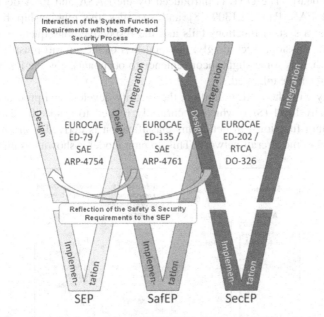

Fig. 1. The Three-V-Model derived from EUROCAE, SAE and RTCA guidelines [1-2, 4] for the systems engineering process (SEP), the safety engineering process (SafEP) and the security engineering process (SecEP)

To make sure that for novel aircraft system architectures the security requirements are visualized and encountered more comprehensively and at an early stage during the development process we introduce an accompanying and supporting third V, which represents the security engineering process (SecEP). A generic specification for a SecEP is given in [4]. To cope with all particular guidelines of the aircraft development process we further on refer to this Three-V-Model as a comprehensive process model. In this model the SEP for the development of system functions, the SafEP covering system reliability and the SecEP to protect the system from attack and misuse are pursued in a concurrent way.

Figure 1 additionally illustrates, that the requirements for the system functions in the SEP are governing the respective safety and security requirements and these requirements reciprocally affect the system functions. The Three-V-Model ensures that for the design of future cabin management architectures the security aspects are encountered right from the beginning. This will guarantee that the required security level (SL) can be finally reached and security can serve as an enabler for the intended system functions.

2.4 The Aircraft Domain Model

Within the well-established safety engineering process (SafEP), i.e. the 'second V', the so called design assurance level (DAL) is defined at an early stage during the development phase. The DAL is introduced by the EASA and FAA documents CS 25.1309 and FAR Part 25.1309 [8] and specifies the relationship between the likelihood that a system functions fails and the respective consequences for the aircraft within its mission. Accordingly, the total loss of the aircraft must be extremely improbable whereas some slight inconvenience to occupants, e.g. the loss of in-flight entertainment, can be tolerated.

By analogy with the DAL definition, the security development process (SecEP) is using a security level (SL), which is currently related to a specific categorization of aircraft cabin functions. In detail this classification is derived from the so called domain model of the aircraft network. This domain model is shown in Figure 2.

Aicraft Control Domain ACD	Airline Information & Services Domain AISD	Passenger Information & Entertainment Services Domain PIESD	Passenger-Owned Devices Domain PODD
Flight & Embedded Control Functions	Administrative Functions	Embedded IFE Functions	Usage of Passenger Notebooks
Cabin Core Functions	Cabin Operation	Passenger Device Interface	Connection of Passenger Mobile Phones
	Flight Support	Flight Support	
	Cabin Maintenance	Onboard Passenger Web	
Control of the Aircraft	Operations of the Airline	Entertain the Passenger	

Fig. 2. The aircraft domain model

The domain model of the global aircraft network architecture which is specified by the ARINC report 664P5 [9] comprises four different domains and is depicted in Figure 2. The ARINC report 811 [10] refers to these four aircraft domains for a classification of security domains. The first domain, the aircraft control domain (ACD), represents the highest criticality level and hosts all flight relevant and embedded control functions. Furthermore, basic cabin safety functions are located within the ACD as well. The airline information and services domain (AISD) contains all global functions for cabin operation and maintenance purposes which are not safety critical. This implies that the AISD has a lower SL than the ACD. An even lower SL is assigned to the passenger information and entertainment services domain (PIESD) with its adjacent passenger owned devices domain (PODD) at lowest SL. These two domains host information and entertainment functions and deliver interfaces to connect passenger notebooks or other mobile devices to the aircraft.

However it must be taken into account that a sustainable and more generic approach for a security engineering process must be applicable to all existing and prospective cabin functions and nevertheless should be in accordance with the nowa-days defined domain allocation. Therefore a top-down approach for the security man-agement process which matches with the conventions of the past and allows an efficient handling of challenges in the future has to be ensured. The next chapter de-scribes such type of a top-down approach, i.e. a generic security engineering process.

3   A Generic Security Engineering Process Approach

There are three major objectives for a generic and efficient security engineering process in aircraft development. The first is a top-down approach, i.e. security engi-neering has to start at the very beginning of the development and to follow the overall process. The second is a global applicability to existing and prospectively expected aircraft functions and the third is an enhanced communication between engineering departments by using a standardized information transfer for security topics on all development levels. The subsequent four sections will provide an elucidation of an approach which is able to comply with these three major objectives:

1. Execute SEP and SecEP concurrently and on all development levels
2. Define the links for process interaction and synchronization
3. Specify the SecEP objectives at a particular development level
4. Use security context parameters (SCPs) for standardized communication

3.1   Execute SEP and SecEP Concurrently and on All Development Levels

The Three-V-Model in Figure 1 suggests three concurrent processes during system development, i.e. the system engineering process (SEP), the safety engineering process (SafEP) and the security engineering process (SecEP). The SafEP and the SecEP are interacting reciprocally with the governing SEP. Figure 3 provides a more detailed view to dedicated development levels.

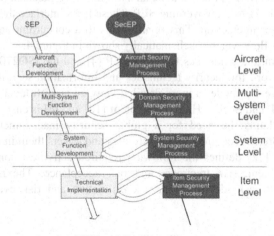

Fig. 3. Development levels of SEP and SecEP and interactions during the design phase

The illustration focuses on the simultaneous execution of the SEP and the SecEP during the functional development of the system, i.e. the system design phase which is represented by the left branch of the V-model. Note, that the established SafEP will not be considered hereafter.

Due to the high complexity of aircraft, the design phase is subdivided into four development levels (cf. Figure 3): the aircraft level, the multi-system level, the system level and finally the item level. Each development level refines the higher level information to an appropriate granularity until the design process reaches the lowest development level, which is the item level. The aircraft level, system level and the item level are defined and described in [1]. The inserted multi-system level is deduced from EUROCAE ED-202 [4], which proposes a security management process for all development levels and points out the need to additionally consider the aircraft domain model (cf. section 2.4) for the risk management within the SecEP. This prerequisite can be referred to a treatment on a multi-system development level. Unfortunately the SEP, as it is today, does not address a multi-system development level. This is due to the fact that still today aircraft functions are grouped and developed hierarchically according to historically defined ATA chapters [11] which do not sufficiently consider system interactions and crosscutting aircraft functions. Hence we have introduced and inserted an implied multi-system level between the aircraft level and system level to consider the aircraft domain model.

3.2   Define the Links for Process Interaction and Synchronization

In order to perform security management within the SecEP the current proposal in EOROCAE and SAE documents [2] is to have an information transfer from the established SafEP to the prospective SecEP. In contrast to this proposal we advocate a direct information link in-between the leading SEP and the parallel and equal SecEP. This is because the complexity of future aircraft systems with progressive logical security considerations requires a security management process, which is no longer a derived subset of the SafEP, but has to be an autonomously executed process and thus has to have direct links to the governing SEP. These links interlace the SecEP and the SEP by peer-to-peer interaction. This finally leads to a concurrent and continuously interacting process flow which is schematically shown in Figure 4.

In line with both, the guidelines for the SecEP [4] and the ISO27005 information technology framework for security techniques and information security management systems [12] Figure 4 provides a more detailed view on aircraft level to the synchronization of the SEP and SecEP. Harmonization of [12] and [4] is ensured, because the latter one only claims the need for a global security management process and [12] explicitly expresses required SecEP activities and covers them in detail. The ISO 27005 framework [12] defines the following required activities: concept establishment, risk assessment, risk treatment and risk acceptance. The risk assessment is further split into risk identification, risk estimation and risk evaluation as per definition of [12].

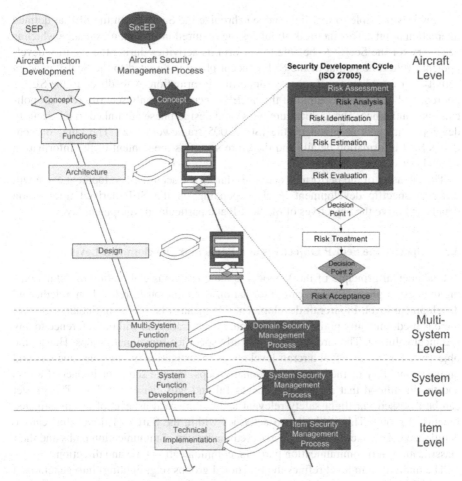

Fig. 4. Particularized SecEP activities at aircraft level interacting with the governing SEP

A comparable refinement of the SEP activities on aircraft level can be deduced from the system development lifecycle according to [1] which defines the four development phases of concept, functions, architecture and design. During concept phase the SEP gathers general and supportive information which is prerequisite for the development of an aircraft. This information might be the operational environment of the considered aircraft including stakeholders, requirements and experience from the development of aircraft in the past. On the next stage follows the elicitation of functions by using the information acquired during the concept phase. During the subsequent architecture phase, the defined functions together with functional requirements are then used to draft the architecture, which assigns the interaction of all pre-defined stakeholders and functions. The subsequent design phase may particularize the proposed architecture, e.g. by a further refinement of functions and assigned stakeholders. However depending on a specific development level the realization of a design phase is optional.

Now it is possible to interlink and synchronize the SecEP with the SEP at defined interaction points. This interlink stipulates the required information exchange which is necessary for the SecEP to be able to perform its activities during the security development cycle. The output of the SEP concept phase is directed to the SecEP concept activity, for establishing all process supporting information. A feedback to the SEP is not required because the output of the SecEP concept is mainly security relevant policies and guidelines. The architecture phase and design phase are linked to the security development cycle as given by the ISO 27005 framework [12]. The latter one enquires SEP information details and therefore specifies the content of the information which has to be exchanged.

The intensity of the performed activities during the security development cycle will differ at specific development levels depending on the SEP derived information details and drive the objectives of the SecEP at a particular development level.

3.3   Specify the SecEP Objectives at a Particular Development Level

A fundamental principle of the V-model is the continuous elaboration of details during the design phase. Engineering information is continuously refined on a dedicated development level. In aircraft development this means that on the initial aircraft level there is predominantly notional information, i.e. abstract data without reference to any technical solution. The aircraft level basically specifies functional groups. Hence, the objectives for the SecEP at aircraft level are an investigation on the consequences and on the probability of the loss of functional groups, i.e. the scope or impact of a loss and the likelihood that an attack is successful and will cause such loss. The impact can be assessed via flight safety relevant and commercial aspects of an investigated functional group. This is similar to activities within the SafEP [13] and thus can be parallelized. The likelihood can be assessed via known communication paths and their classification into communication partners, communication type and direction.

The multi-system level refines the functional groups (e.g. lighting) into generalized aircraft functions (e.g. cabin lighting, emergency lighting and exterior lighting) and allocates them within the aircraft domain model. Thus, major objectives on multi-system level are an impact analysis of the loss of generalized functions on multi-system level, an estimation of the likelihood of an attack, an assignment of attack paths and a security domain allocation. Again the impact can be assessed via flight safety relevant and commercial aspects of a generalized function. On multi-system level the likelihood can be assessed via a known communication partner, a communication direction, the type of information and the purpose of received information. The assessment of these parameters provides additional information on a possible attack path and enables the allocation within the aircraft domain model.

The definition of objectives on an aircraft and multi-system level leads directly to a consistent top-down approach, which can be seamlessly used as a superstructure for nowadays performed security activities on the system level. This generic SecEP approach provides the advantage of filtering out non-security relevant function groups and generalized functions at earlier development levels. This avoids costly and time-consuming work on later development levels, e.g. the system level. The subsequent section will show how a straightforward and standardized exchange of pre-defined information in-between SEP and SecEP can be achieved by introducing security context parameters (SCPs).

3.4 Use Security Context Parameters (SCPs) for Standardized Communication

The security context parameters are introduced to extract the beforehand identified security relevant information from the SEP in a standardized and simple way. Keeping it short and simple is beneficial, because the system designer in the SEP usually has less knowledge about security management issues and therefore needs to be guided and supported by experts from the SecEP. Standardization can be accomplished by implementing and using predefined security context parameters (SCPs) comprised of parameter types and valid values. Due to a specific level of detail during aircraft development, the parameter types and values are dependent on a specific development level. Parameter types and values representing the aircraft level are given in Table 1.

Table 1. Security context parameters (SCPs) on aircraft development level

Parameter Type	Valid Values
Function Group Name	[aircraft function group name]
Communication Partner	[stakeholder, aircraft function group]
Communication Direction	[bidirectional, unidirectional (send), unidirectional (receive)]
Type of Communication	[variable data, pre-defined discrete information]

Referring to [12] the function group name assigns a considered asset. For each function group the possible communication partners are specified to address the likelihood and to identify possible attack paths.

A more detailed description of communication requires the communication direction and the type of communication. Valid values for the communication direction are bidirectional or unidirectional. The communication type distinguishes between variable data or pre-defined discrete information. As a result the communication direction and type of communication allows determining the likelihood of an attack of a function group. In spite of this simplicity the SCPs allow to achieve the defined SecEP objective at aircraft level, i.e. to differentiate between security and non-security relevant function groups.

Analogously, parameter types and values representing the multi-system level are given in Table 2. Due to a higher level of detail during the multi-system development phase, these parameter types and values are more specific.

Table 2. Security context parameters (SCPs) on multi-system development level

Parameter Type	Valid Values
Function Name	[multi-system function name]
Communication Partner	[stakeholder, multi-system function]
Communication Interface	[ethernet, AFDX, ARINC 429, serial, discrete]
Communication Direction	[send, receive]
Type of Information for each Direction	[control data, information data]
Purpose of Use for Received Information	[forwarding, using, processing, executing]

Description of values:

Control data is data, which sent or received for remote control of a function by another function, e.g. turn on/off the whole entertainment function by the cabin crew management function.
Information data is data, which can be stored or displayed, but is not used for any kind of system or function control, e.g. a function which is monitored by another function provides such type of data to the monitoring function.

Forwarding information means piping the received information to other functions without using or processing it.
Using information means utilizing the received information without processing it, e.g. displaying video or audio information.
Processing information means converting and forwarding information to other functions, e.g. information is compressed, decompressed or checked and forwarding it.
Executing information means to use received information for the execution of connected functions, e.g. remote control of a function by another function.

Referring to [12] at multi-system level the function name assigns a more detailed asset. Consequently the communication partners are particularized stakeholders and more fine-grained functions, which now elaborate the likelihood and a possible attack path.

Furthermore the SCPs at this level address the interface type in a more specific way. The interface is the basis of every risk analysis because it defines the possibility that a system is attackable at all. Without any interface a system would not be attackable from an information security point of view. Defining the type of an interface as early as possible provides the opportunity to suspend specific threat scenarios.

An industry-specific interface could for instance prevent attacks of a standard malware like the worm Conficker [14] but would still be vulnerable to a specifically developed and complex malware like the worm Stuxnet [15]. Therefore an industry-specific interface like ARINC 429 which is used in the aircraft industry decreases the risk for a standard malware attack. This finally implies that the interface type allows a meaningful evaluation of the risk at this level.

At multi-system level the communication directions of each communication partner are divided into send and receive. The type of information which is exchanged, i.e. control data or information data, is assigned separately to each communication direction. The purpose of use for received information, which is detailed to forwarding, using, executing and processing information, allows a more explicit assessment of the likelihood. Additionally an allocation of possible attack paths is enabled. The defined SecEP objectives on multi-system level, i.e. to differentiate between security and non-security relevant functions, are finally achieved.

Having defined security context parameters at aircraft and multi-system level, the next step is an SCP definition at system level. At system level there is previous work on security management activities from other groups [16]. A way straightforward is to use these earlier results for structuring the SecEP at the system level. After synchronizing with the governing SEP and defining SecEP objectives at system level the SCPs can be elaborated and used analogously at the system level. This approach is fully compatible with previous work at a system level. However it resolves the challenge of a top-down approach which is globally applicable to aircraft functions and which enables standardized information exchange for security management issues across all development levels by the use of SCPs.

4   Summary and Conclusion

Increasing functionality and a rising complexity of aircraft systems leads to a complex aircraft communication network with various communication paths and partners. This progression in aircraft industry requires a reconsideration of the established systems engineering approach with emphasis to security engineering and management. To cope with the challenge of security management we have introduced the Three-V-Model representing three concurrent and interacting processes, i.e. the system engineering process (SEP), the safety engineering process (SafEP) and, for the first time, the security engineering process (SecEP). Compliant with existing guidelines and compatible to the established aircraft development process we execute the SecEP across all development levels and simultaneously to the SEP and SafEP. Defining process links and synchronizing processes on particular development levels enables an equal treatment of the SecEP. Information exchange in-between the processes is achieved by using security context parameters (SCPs). SCPs were introduced to realize a standardized communication of engineering departments and to guarantee a top-down approach for security management starting at aircraft level.

In practice, this approach enables filtering of security and non-security relevant functional information starting at the highest development level, i.e. the aircraft level and thus reduces workload on the subsequent development levels. This top-down approach using standardized communication via SCPs facilitates the collaboration of the engineering departments and clearly separates competences and work shares of neighboring departments. Moreover, this approach will particularly enable the parametric assignment of security relevant information using the model based requirements engineering methodology [17] which fosters a consistent tracking and tracing of changes during the overall development process and across all development levels.

References

1. EUROCAE / SAE: Certification considerations for highly-integrated or complex aircraft systems. EUROCAE ED-79 / SAE ARP-4754 (1996)
2. EUROCAE / SAE: Guidelines and methods for conducting the safety assessment process on civil airborne systems. EUROCAE ED-135 / SAE ARP-4761 (1996)
3. Benz, S.: Eine Entwicklungsmethodik für sicherheitsrelevante Elektroniksysteme im Automobil. PhD thesis, Universität Karlsruhe, Karlsruhe (2004)
4. EUROCAE / RTCA: Airworthiness security process specification. EUROCAE ED-202 / RTCA DO-326 (2010)
5. Hintze, H., Tolksdorf, A., God, R.: Cabin core system - A next generation platform for combined electrical power and data services. In: Proceedings of 3rd International Workshop on Aircraft System Technologies, AST 2011, Hamburg, 221-231 (2011)
6. Rosenberg, B.: Cabin Management Systems. Avionics Magazine, 26–30 (2010)
7. Ebert, C.: Systematisches Requirements Engineering, 3rd edn. dpunkt.verlag, Heidelberg (2010)
8. EASA / FAA: Equipment, systems, and installations. EASA Certification Standards 25.1309 / FAA Federal Aviation Regulations 25.1309
9. ARINC: Network domain characteristics and interconnection. ARINC 664P5 – Aircraft data network part 5 (2005)
10. ARINC: Commercial aircraft information security concepts of operation and process framework. ARINC Report 811 (2005)
11. Air Transport Association: Information Standards for Aviation Maintenance. ATA Spec 2200 (2010)
12. ISO/IEC: Information technology – Security techniques – Information security risk management. ISO/IEC 27005:2008 (2008)
13. Blanquart, J.-P., Bieber, P., Descargues, G., Hazane, E., Julien, M., Léonardon, L.: Similarities and dissimilarities between safety levels and security levels. In: Embedded Real Time Software and Systems, ERTS 2012 (2012),
   http://www.erts2012.org/site/0P2RUC89/8A-2.pdf
14. Nahorney, B.: The Downadup Codex - A comprehensive guide to the threat's mechanics. In: Symantec - Security Response (2009),
   http://www.whitepapersdb.com/whitepapers/download/1207
15. Falliere, N., OMurchu, L., Chien, E.: W32.Stuxnet Dossier. In: Symantec - Security Response (2011),
   http://www.wired.com/images_blogs/threatlevel/2011/02/Symantec-Stuxnet-Update-Feb-2011.pdf
16. Bieber, P., Blanquart, J.-P., Descargues, G., Dulucq, M., Fourastier, Y., Hazane, E., Julien, M., Léonardon, L.: Security and Safety Assurance for Aerospace Embedded Systems. In: Embedded Real Time Software and Systems, ERTS 2012 (2012),
   http://www.erts2012.org/site/0P2RUC89/8A-1.pdf
17. Hintze, H., God, R.: A model-based security engineering process approach for the development of next generation cabin management systems (2013) (unpublished results)

Mobile Device Encryption Systems

Peter Teufl, Thomas Zefferer, and Christof Stromberger

IAIK, Graz University of Technology
Inffeldgasse 16a, 8010 Graz, Austria
{peter.teufl,thomas.zefferer}@iaik.tugraz.at,
stromberger@student.tugraz.at

Abstract. The initially consumer oriented iOS and Android platforms, and the newly available Windows Phone 8 platform start to play an important role within business related areas. Within the business context, the devices are typically deployed via mobile device management (MDM) solutions, or within the bring-your-own-device (BYOD) context. In both scenarios, the security depends on many platform security functions, such as permission systems, management capabilities, screen locks, low-level malware protection systems, and access and data protection systems. Especially, the latter play a crucial rule for the security of stored data. While the access protection part is related to the typically used passcodes that protect the smartphone from unauthorized tempering, the data protection facility is used to encrypt the core assets – the application data and credentials. The applied encryption protects the data when access to the smartphone is gained either through theft or malicious software. While all of the current platforms support these systems and market these features extensively within the business context, there are huge differences in the implemented systems that need to be considered for deployment scenarios that require high security levels. Even under the assumption, that the underlying encryption systems are implemented correctly, the heterogeneity of the systems allows for a wide range of attacks that exploit various issues related to deployment, development and configuration of the different systems.

In order to address this situation, this paper presents an analysis of the access and data protection systems of the currently most popular platforms. Due to the important influence of the developer on the security of the iOS Data Protection system, we also present a tool that supports administrators in evaluating the right choice of data protection classes in arbitrary iOS applications.

1   Introduction

The recent success story of smartphones and tablets, which will be referred to as mobile devices for the remainder of this document[1], was mainly fueled by user-friendly and consumer-oriented devices introduced by Apple and Google in 2007

---

[1] Due to restricting the analysis to iOS and Android devices, a distinction between smartphones and tablets is not required.

L.J. Janczewski, H.B. Wolfe, and S. Shenoi (Eds.): SEC 2013, IFIP AICT 405, pp. 203–216, 2013.

and 2008. For the past years, Apple's iOS platform and Google's Android platform have been dominating the market. During this time, both companies have introduced a wide range of security related features for their smartphone platforms in order to make their platforms ready for business applications. Recently, the market power of iOS and Android has been challenged by a new Windows Phone 8 release[2] and a new version of RIM's BlackBerry platform. For all major smartphone platforms, encryption represents a core feature that is advertised for its strong security[3],[4],[5]. However, encryption systems of smartphone platforms differ in various security related aspects. For instance, different platforms rely on different approaches to encrypt data (file based encryption vs. file-system based encryption) and implement different methods to derive required encryption keys from user input (e.g. PIN or passcodes). Furthermore, different platforms offer both developers and end users different options to use and configure provided encryption features. The choice of these parameters also significantly influences the security of provided encryption systems.

As a consequence of these differences, a direct comparison of different platforms is difficult. However, understanding capabilities and limitations of encryption systems provided by smartphone platforms is crucial when deploying these platforms in security-critical areas and allowing mobile devices to access confidential data. While general security assessments of smartphone platforms have already been presented in literature [4] [11] [9], no in-depth assessment and comparison of different encryption-systems is available so far. Such an assessment could serve as a basis of decision-making and help administrators in charge to choose the platform that best meets the given requirements.

To bridge this gap, we propose an abstract assessment model for encryption systems provided by smartphone platforms. Based on experience gained during the development of a security-critical application[6], the proposed assessment model defines generic properties of encryption systems provided by nowadays smartphone platforms. The proposed abstract model can be applied to arbitrary smartphone platforms in order to assess and compare capabilities of their encryption systems. In this paper, we use the proposed model to assess and compare the encryption systems of Apple iOS and Google Android. These platforms have been chosen due to their predominating market share and their growing importance for business applications. The Windows Phone 8 and BlackBerry platforms have not been considered so far, since detailed information on the platforms' encryption systems has not been made publicly available so far. As soon as this information is published, the proposed assessment model can be

---

[2] Due to the lack of its business related features, such as mobile-device-management and encryption, Windows Phone 7 is not considered here.

[3] http://www.apple.com/ipad/business/ios/

[4] http://www.samsung.com/global/business/mobile/product/smartphone/GT-I9300MBDXSP-features

[5] http://www.windowsphone.com/en-us/business/for-business

[6] SecureSend for iOS
https://itunes.apple.com/us/app/secure-send/id560086616?mt=8,   Android and Windows Phone versions are currently under development.

applied to these platforms as well. For the time being, this paper focuses on Apple iOS and Google Android and provides an detailed assessment of these platforms' encryption systems.

2   Related Work

Due to their growing relevance for security-critical applications, the security of Google Android and Apple iOS is also of increasing interest for the scientific community. A general comparison between Google Android and Apple iOS is for instance given by Goadrich et al. in [5]. However, their work focuses rather on differences in application development between these two platforms than on security issues. Security aspects of application development under Android have been discussed in more detail by Enck et al. in [4]. More general assessments of Android's security features have been provided by Shabtai et al. [11] and by Pacatilu in [8]. Similar to the Android platform, also the security of the iOS platform has been discussed in literature. A comprehensive analysis of possible attacks on the iOS platform has for instance been provided by Pandya in [9].

Most of the above mentioned publications have discussed, analyzed, and assessed the security of Google Android and Apple iOS on a rather general level. For our contribution, related work dealing with encryption systems for mobile devices is of special interest. Indeed, various authors have approached this topic from different perspectives so far. The relevance of encryption solutions on mobile devices and possible implications on jurisdiction have been discussed by Paul et al. in [10]. Proprietary encryption solutions for smartphone platforms have for instance been proposed in [12] and [3].

Interestingly, most related work on encryption systems on mobile devices focuses on the development of proprietary solutions. From a application developer's point of view, it is however more convenient to rely on encryption functionality provided by the underlying smartphone platform instead of implementing own encryption systems. Furthermore, implementing own encryption solutions carries the risk of making implementation errors that again can compromise security. Due to these reasons, relying on integrated encryption systems provided by the underlying smartphone platform can be advantageous in most cases. However, reliance on provided encryption systems requires detailed knowledge of their capabilities and limitations. We propose an abstract and platform-agnostic assessment model for the evaluation of encryption systems provided by smartphone platforms in the next section.

3   Assessment Model

Several architectural and conceptual differences between encryption systems of different smartphone platforms render systematic assessments and direct comparisons difficult. In order to allow for systematic assessments, we therefore extract common properties of nowadays systems and combine them with generic security considerations. This way, we first derive a platform-agnostic encryption model and identify common assets and threats of encryption systems for mobile devices. From the identified threats, generic attack scenarios are then derived. The proposed abstract encryption model and the derived generic attack scenarios can finally be used to systematically assess and compare specific encryption systems of arbitrary smartphone platforms.

Figure 1 shows an abstract and platform-agnostic model that covers typical capabilities of nowadays smartphone platforms' encryption systems.

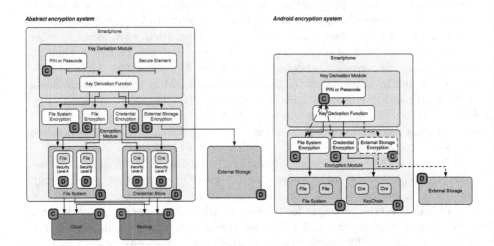

Fig. 1. Abstract encryption model (left), Android encryption system (right)

As shown in Figure 1, mobile devices typically provide three different locations to store data. Data can either be stored in the local *file system*, in a dedicated *credential store* provided by the platform, or in an *external storage* such as a microSD card. To encrypt data being stored at these locations, smartphone platforms feature some kind of *encryption module*. Depending on the smartphone platform, the encryption module contains one or more submodules to completely encrypt an entire storage location, or to encrypt specific files and credentials residing at a certain storage location. The different encryption modules need to be supplied with appropriate encryption keys. These keys are provided by the *key derivation module*. This module implements a key derivation function that derives required encryption keys from different inputs. Potential inputs are PINs or passcodes defined and entered by the user, or master keys stored in secure elements. The platform-agnostic model shown in Figure 1 also includes further external components such as *backup* and *cloud* components. These external components also need to be considered when assessing encryption systems, as data is potentially transferred to these external entities.

However, the security of data and/or credentials stored on mobile devices does not solely depend on the components of the smartphone's encryption system. Additionally, configuration options defined by administrators or users, and decisions made by application developers on how to use functionality provided by the given encryption system can also influence the capabilities of encryption systems and hence the security and confidentiality of data stored on mobile devices.

Components of the encryption system that are subject to configuration options (C) and developer decisions (D) are marked accordingly in Figure 1. The user and/or administrator influences the strength of the used PIN or passcode, and enables or disables file system encryption and encryption of external storages manually or via mobile device management (MDM) solutions. Also, application developers need to decide where to store data (file system, credential store, external storage). Additionally, developers can choose to rely on a file based encryption of data and are responsible to select appropriate security levels for encrypted files. Finally, developers can also decide whether data is transferred to external cloud or backup components.

3.1 Assets and Threats

From the platform-agnostic encryption model shown in Figure 1, general assets and threats can be derived. In general, encryption systems are developed and used to assure the confidentiality of data. Hence, data represents the primary assets that needs to be considered for systematic assessments of encryption systems on smartphone platforms. The security of encryption systems on smartphone platforms and the confidentiality of the asset data can be compromised by different threats. Due to their mobility and their broad support for third-party applications, *theft* and *malware* represent the main threats for mobile devices. Hence, encryption systems for mobile devices need to be designed such that encrypted data stored on the smartphone cannot be decrypted by an illegitimate user or by malware running on the mobile device.

3.2 Assumptions

Based on the two basic threats *theft* and *malware*, we define assumptions that define the scope of the conducted security assessment. In particular, the conducted assessments are based on the following three assumptions.

First, our assessments are based on the assumption that all cryptographic algorithms used by the assessed encryption systems are correctly implemented by the smartphone platform. The goal of this assessment is not to evaluate the correct implementation of particular algorithms but to analyze weaknesses of the respective encryption systems that can be exploited by an attacker to gain access to the asset data. **Second**, we assume that an attacker steals a smartphone with the intention to gain access to data stored on the device. We further assume that the attacker is an expert who knows the deployed encryption system and its weaknesses, and thus is capable of either circumventing the encryption system or mounting brute-force attacks on the passcode. In case of theft, we assume that the smartphone is locked via a PIN or passcode. **Finally**, malware is only considered in this paper within the scope of jailbreaking a locked (or switched off) stolen mobile device. Other types of malware that are used to attack a user directly without stealing the mobile device is not considered for the following reasons: Malicious software that uses root exploits to gain access the the operating system is not limited in its capabilities and can attack the data directly on the smartphone. Another category of malicious software only relies on provided system APIs without exploiting a security vulnerability to gather pre-attack information about the passcode (e.g. via phishing, or retrieving information about the passcode complexity). This information can then be used when the device is stolen by an attacker. However, this type of malware is also not considered in this work, since a detailed description of such attacks would be beyond the scope of this work.

3.3 Attack Scenarios

Based on the defined assets, threats, and assumptions, a set of generic attack scenarios can be derived from the platform-agnostic encryption model shown in Figure 1.

Attacks on the encryption system include attacks on properties of the encryption system and its integration into the platform. The following specific attacks need to be considered here: (1) Circumventing the encryption system by utilizing *jailbreaking/rooting* on a stolen smartphone, (2) *attacking backups* that are either stored on disk or in the cloud, and (3) *attacking cloud storage* that is provided by the platform for data-synchronization purposes.

Under the assumptions that the encryption system is implemented correctly, **attacks on key derivation** are considered to be the most likely attacks: (1) Some encryption systems do not use the user's passcode to derive encryption keys, which enables *jailbreaking/rooting* attacks, (2) even when the passcode is used for deriving encryption keys, the system is still susceptible to *brute-force attacks* on the passcode. The time required to carry out such attacks primarily depends on the employed key derivation function, and the inclusion of a secure element in the key derivation process.

Finally, **attacks on user configurations or developer decisions** need to be considered due to the various properties and parameters that can be influenced by the administrators, the users and the developers. Depending on the specific properties of the system (e.g. brute-force times on the passcode), appropriate passcodes must be chosen, or the system might not be enabled by default (*poor configuration option*). Application developers can influence the way, in which smartphone applications make use of available security features. Depending on the particular platform, an application developer can decide where to store data, which security level to use, and whether data is transmitted to external backup and cloud components. If *poor developer decisions* are made, attacks can potentially circumvent integrated security features.

In this section, we map the abstract encryption model and the generic attack scenarios defined above to the Google Android platform (version 4.2). Figure 1 shows the result of this mapping process and illustrates relevant components of Android's encryption system. In contrast to the iOS system, the Android backup system (Google Backup) is not considered in this analysis due to two reasons:

It is not activated per default and local backups, which play an important role for stolen devices, are not available in the raw Android version by Google.

3.4   Encryption System

Android uses a file-system based encryption system based on the dm-crypt transparent disk-encryption system[7] that has been available in the Linux kernel since version 2.6. By using the Linux kernels's device-mapper functionality, the encryption layer can be added between the file-system and the actual block-device that stores the raw data.

Android derives the keys for the file-encryption system from the PIN/passcode of the user during system startup. In contrast to other platforms such as iOS, no secure element is involved in this key-derivation procedure. For more detailed information on the Android encryption system and design considerations the reader is referred to the Android documentation[8].

In addition to this system, an additional system for the secure storage of private cryptographic keys is provided by Android. This secure storage is called Android KeyChain and is publicly accessible to third-party applications since Android 4.0. Keys stored in the Android KeyChain are encrypted with AES. The encryption key is derived from the user's PIN or passcode that is used to unlock the smartphone.

In general, external storage on Android devices (e.g. microSD cards) are not protected by the Android file-encryption system. Furthermore, there is no access control on these areas beyond the permissions, which are required to read or write to this storage. Some smartphone vendors have extended the functionality of Android to support encryption of external storage media. However, a detailed analysis of these vendor-specific approaches is beyond the scope of this paper.

As all used encryption keys for file-system encryption and KeyChain are derived from the user's PIN/passcode, these encryption systems are not vulnerable to **jailbreaking/rooting**. Even if an attacker gains root access to the smartphone, the user's PIN/passcode that is required to derive encryption keys remains unknown.

3.5   Key Derivation

As briefly mentioned above, the key derivation on Android is based on the PIN/passcode of the user. For the encryption and decryption process, the password of the user is combined with a salt value that is stored in the encryption footer of the file system. The resulting value is then used as input for the PBKDF2 function, which basically applies SHA1 repeatedly. The result represents a 128 bit AES key, that is used to decrypt the 128 bit AES master key for file-system encryption and for the protection of KeyChain entries.

---

[7] http://code.google.com/p/cryptsetup/wiki/DMCrypt
[8] http://source.android.com/tech/encryption/android_crypto_implementation. html

Since Android does not include a secure element, the user's PIN/passcode is the only unknown in the key-derivation process. Thus, the key-derivation process is not bound to the mobile device and can also be out-sourced to external more powerful entities. This significantly facilitates the accomplishment of **brute-force attacks** on the user's PIN/passcode and potentially decreases the security of Android's key-derivation method.

3.6   Configuration Options and Developer Decisions

The security of Android's encryption system heavily depends on the configuration chosen by the user or a mobile device management (MDM) system. On Android, the file-system encryption is not enabled by default and must either be activated by the user or by the respective policy of the MDM system. Before the encryption system is activated, a password needs to be defined by the user. The security of the whole system primarily depends on the length and quality of this password. In general, the user has the choice to enter a simple numerical PIN code or a more secure alpha-numeric passcode. In managed envrionments, a minimum quality of the user's PIN or passcode can be enforced by appropriate MDM policies.

Beside the user, also application developers can influence the security and confidentiality of data being stored on smartphones. First of all, a developer needs to decide where to store confidential data. Depending on the chosen storage location, different encryption schemes are applied to the stored data. As discussed above, the availability of encryption systems on Android also depends on user configurations. Hence, application developers must not assume that certain encryption features such as file-system encryption are enabled on the target device.

4   iOS Analysis

The analysis of the iOS system is more complex than the Android analysis, because there are three systems (Figure 2) that need to be considered for data and credentials protection (two, when external backups are not counted). Especially, the file-based data protection system offers a high level of security due to the inclusion of a secure element. However, this high level of security can only be achieved when the right configuration and developer choices are made. The information in the subsequent analysis is based on Apple documentation [1], third-party analysis [6], [13], and our own analysis within the context of secure application development and external consulting projects.

4.1   Encryption System

The first **file-system encryption system** – depicted in the left part of Figure 2 – is available since the iPhone 3gs (iOS 3.x) and encrypts the whole file-system. The file system key (EMF key) is randomly created when the device is started

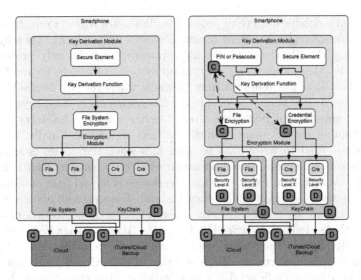

Fig. 2. iOS encryption systems: The always-on file-system based system is shown in the left part, the file-based data protection system is depicted on the right

for the very first time. It is stored in the so-called *Effaceable Storage*, which is a part in the flash memory that can be wiped very fast. This capability is employed for fast remote wiping, which only deletes the cryptographic keys instead of the whole file-system. The EMF key itself is encrypted by the unique device identifier (UID) AES key, which is stored within a secure element. The employment of a secure element eliminates the possibility to gain access to file-system images that are either gained by cloning or ripping out the flash memory. In other words, any attack must be executed on an iOS device due to the presence of the secure element.

The system can easily be attacked via **Jailbreaking/Rooting**, which concentrates on the weakest point of the file-system based encryption system: The protection of the EMF key for encrypting the file-system is not based on the passcode of the user, but relies only on the integrated secure element. Thus, even when a passcode is set on the device, the application of a jailbreak enables the attacker to gain root access to the operating system, which decrypts the data with the EMF key. Thus, an attacker can gain access to all data without knowing the encryption keys. Due to the availability of jailbreaks for almost all iOS versions[9], the execution of such an attack does neither require in-depth knowledge nor sophisticated resources.

The second system – the **Data Protection API** – has been introduced with iOS 4 for protecting individual files and credentials. The system is based on various protection classes that need to be defined by the developer for stored files and credentials. These protection classes define when the respective file-system encryption keys are available and can be used for decrypting the protected

---

[9] A good overview is given at: http://www.apfelzone.at/jailbreak-ubersicht/

files. The four available data (file) protection classes are *NSFileProtection{None, Complete, UntilFirstUserAuthentication, CompleteUnlessOpen}*. Thereby, *None* indicates that the file is not specifically protected and the only protection is offered by the file-system based encryption system. *Complete* means that the file-encryption keys are removed from memory whenever the device is locked. *UntilFirstUserAuthentication* decrypts the file-system encryption keys when the passcode is entered the first time after a device reboot. The decrypted keys are then kept in device memory until the next shutdown. Finally, *Complete-UnlessOpen* is used to write data to open files when the device is locked and in addition offers a system based on asymmetric cryptography that is used for encrypting data which is received while the device is locked (e.g. emails).

iOS offers the KeyChain which encrypts and stores credentials, such as private keys, passwords, certificates etc. There are similar protection classes for protecting these credentials: *kSecAttrAccessible{Always, WhenUnlocked, After-FirstUnlock}*. Thereby, their functionality corresponds to the first three data protection classes. An important difference is that the KeyChain protection classes also exist in a *DeviceOnly* version which indicates that the credentials cannot be transferred off-device via iCloud or iTunes backups. A detailed discussion of these protection classes the reader is referred to [2]. The most important aspect is that for the protection classes other than *None, Always* the keys required for decryption are derived by utilizing the secure element *and* the user's passcode.

Considering **Jailbreaking/Rooting** the following conclusions can be drawn: When the *None, Always* protection classes are employed, the protection is equal to that offered by the file-system based encryption system and can easily be circumvented by applying a jailbreak to the system. The problem is extensively discussed in [6].

4.2   Key Derivation

Strictly speaking the term "key derivation" is not adequate for the description of the **file-system encryption system**. The reason is, that the UID key within the secure element is used to encrypt/decrypt the actual file-encryption master key (EMF key). Thus, there is no typical key-derivation function involved. Since, the previously described jailbreaking/rooting attack can easily be deployed to gain access to the file-system, a specific attack on this "key derivation" system is not necessary, and thus not further considered.

The **Data Protection system** employs the standardized *Password Based Key Derivation Function 2* (PBKDF2)[1], which is specified in PKCS#5[7] as key derivation function. The user's passcode is tangled with the UID key stored in the secure element and combined with a salt. The resulting value is then used as input for the key derivation function with an iteration count of 10,000. The gained key is used to encrypt and decrypt the aforementioned protection class keys.

When applying a jailbreak to the iOS device, which is protected by the Data Protection system, the attacker has access to the file-system. However, the files and credentials that use the correct protection classes (other than *None* for files,

Always for KeyChain entries) cannot be decrypted without knowing the passcode. Under the assumption, that this passcode is not known to the attacker the only remaining option for the attacker is the application of a **brute-force attack**. Due to usability issues with long and complex passcodes, the attacker can assume that only rather short ones are utilized. Although, this reduces the number of possible passcodes, the presence of the secure element and the PBKDF2 key derivation function significantly slows down the brute-force attack. Due to the high iteration count of PBKDF2, the derivation of an AES key from the passcode takes roughly 90 ms[10]. This delay can be used as a basis for calculating the worst-case brute-force attack times when choosing a password. Also, and probably even more important, the brute-force attack must be carried out on the device, since the secure element is also involved in the key derivation process. Thus, the brute-force attack cannot be sped up by using external processing resources and must be carried out on the device. The described attack is implemented by a forensic toolkit offered by the UK based company Elcomsoft[11].

Although the **backup encryption system** is technically not a part of the mobile device, it still plays an important role for the security of the data and the credentials. On iOS, the backup can either be made via an iTunes installation, or to the Apple based iCloud solution. Thereby, the iTunes backup can either be stored in plain text or be encrypted with a key derived from a user based password. This key derivation is also based on the PBKDF2 function. However, and this is the most important difference, due to the lack of a secure element on the PC/laptop where iTunes is installed, the key derivation subsystem is less protected than its counterpart on the iOS device.

The backup on an iTunes device can be attacked via different techniques. (1) in case of unencrypted backups the attacker can just copy the whole backup and get access to all of the files that are marked for backup by the installed iOS applications (see below). (2) in case of an encrypted backup, the attacker can carry out a **brute-force attack** on the encryption password. Due to the lack of a secure element, the attacker can use external processing resources to speed up the brute-force attack. This scenario is basically identical to the brute-force attack on the Android encryption system.

4.3   Configuration/Developer

The *file-system* based encryption system of iOS cannot be configured, since it is enabled per-default and cannot be deactivated. The *data protection* system is activated as soon as device passcode is set, *and* if the developer has chosen the correct protection classes for the application files. Since, the required protection classes can neither be configured by the user nor the administrator (MDM), the most important configuration options are the password properties, such as length, complexity class and the automated screen lock functionality and the

[10] http://www.securitylearn.net/tag/iphone-data-recovery-on-ios-5/
[11] http://www.elcomsoft.co.uk/eift.html

related timeout values[12]. The user/administrator is capable of configuring the options for the third system – the *backup functionality*. Here, the configuration options are related to storing encrypted or plain backups on iTunes, and activating/deactivating the backup functionality for iTunes and iCloud respectively. Especially the encrypted iTunes backup and the iCloud backup depend on the properties of the chosen passcodes. Thereby, the iTunes passcode is chosen by the user on the laptop/PC where the backup is stored. For iCloud backups the security of the password for the required iCloud account is considered as vital.

Poor configuration options are especially critical in the unmanaged scenario where the user selects the passcode, the attacker can base an attack on the data protection system and the backups on the following assumptions: (1) Due to usability issues related to passcode length and complexity class the user will typically not use a passcode or select a rather short one. (2) Since the default setting for PIN locks on an iOS device uses 4-character numerical PIN codes, which can easily be verified by the attacker when looking at the type of used lock screen, a brute-force attack might be feasible. (3) For the iTunes related backup the administrator/user choice regarding the activation/deactivation of the backup, and the user's choice of the backup encryption password play an important role within security. (4) The user/administrator also decides whether the iCloud-based system is allowed. In case of its availability a weak password of the associated iCloud account, can used as an attack path by an attacker do gain access to the backups.

On iOS, the developer influences some vital aspects of the encryption system security. (1) The developer specifies the protection classes for specific files or KeyChain entries. When the wrong classes (especially *None* and *Always*) are chosen by the developer the security is reduced to that of the file-system based encryption, which can easily be circumvented. (2) The developer also decides whether a file is included in iTunes/iCloud backups. Critical files that should not be included in backups, must be explicitly marked by the flag *kCFURLIsExcludedFromBackupKey*. Unfortunately, neither the protection classes of application files nor the backup flag can directly be inspected by the user/administrator. This opens a critical security issue, that could easily be exploited by an attacker. Assuming an application (e.g. the Apple mail) application uses the right protection classes, further assuming a user opens an attachment (e.g. a PDF file) in an external application that employs the *None* protection class for storing the file, then an attacker does not need to apply a brute-force attack on the passcode in order to get access to the email with the PDF document. Instead, the attacker can simply apply a jailbreak and extract the file form the external application that was used to view/edit the PDF file.

In order to mitigate of the threat, we have created a simple Java based tool[13] for determining the protection classes of the installed applications. The tool ex-

---

[12] The available setting can be seen in the Apple Configuration Application, if no MDM-system is used. https://itunes.apple.com/en/app/apple-configurator/id434433123?mt=12

[13] https://github.com/ciso/ios-dataprotection/

tracts the protection classes of each file on the iOS system from an existing iTunes backup, and thus allows the user/administrator evaluate the security of the installed applications. Obviously, the protection classes can only be determined for those files that are included in an iTunes backup.

Attack	Brute-force attacks	Jailbreak/Rooting	Poor developer's choice	Poor configuration options
Applies to	Key Derivation	Encryption System	Developer	Configuration
Android				
File System	off-device	brute-force required	no influence	default: off
KeyChain	off-device	brute-force required		passcode is mandatory
External storage				
iOS				
File system			always on	no influence
Data protection (files, KeyChain)	on-device	brute-force required		
External storage	NA	NA	NA	NA

Fig. 3. Comparision between iOS and Android encryption systems. The black, light-grey and white cells indicate critical, medium, and minor issues. The dark-grey cells indicate that the attack is not relevant for the given property or the analyzed platform.

5   Conclusions

The conducted analysis shows, that although encryption systems are present on all current platforms, their heterogeneity causes security issues that need to be considered when deploying a mobile device platform. When looking at iOS and Android, the following summary can be given. Due to the strong key derivation function based on the user's passcode and the device's secure element, the iOS systems offer a good level of protection. However, this level can only be achieved when the developer as well as the user/administrator make the right decisions. Since, there are multiple systems that need to be considered, an in-depth knowledge is required by the developer and the user/administrator. One of the most disturbing facts is that neither the user nor the administrator can verify whether an application uses the appropriate protection classes. We have addressed this problem by creating a backup analysis tool that extracts the protection classes of application files, which can then be used to asses the security of application data. On Android, the employed encryption system is much simpler than that on iOS. The main advantage is that the the file-system based encryption system requires a passcode during boot-up which offers an adequate protection against jailbreak attacks that require a system reboot. On the other hand, due to the lack of a secure element, brute-force attacks on the user's passcode can be executed off-device and speed up by utilising external processing resources.

References

1. Apple: iOS Security. Tech. Rep. May, Apple Inc. (2012),
   http://images.apple.com/ipad/business/docs/iOS_Security_May12.pdf
2. Belenko, A., Sklyarov, D.: Evolution of iOS Data Protection and iPhone Forensics:
   from iPhone OS to iOS 5 (2011)
3. Chen, Y.C.Y., Ku, W.S.K.W.S.: Self-Encryption Scheme for Data Security in Mobile Devices (2009),
   http://ieeexplore.ieee.org/lpdocs/epic03/wrapper.htm?arnumber=4784733
4. Enck, W., Ongtang, M., McDaniel, P.: Understanding Android Security (2009),
   http://ieeexplore.ieee.org/lpdocs/epic03/wrapper.htm?arnumber=4768655
5. Goadrich, M.H., Rogers, M.P.: Smart Smartphone Development: iOS versus Android. Science Education, 607–612 (2011),
   http://dl.acm.org/citation.cfm?id=1953330
6. Heider, J., Khayari, R.E.: iOS Keychain Weakness FAQ - Further Information on
   iOS Password Protection (2012),
   http://sit.sit.fraunhofer.de/studies/en/sc-iphone-passwords-faq.pdf
7. Kaliski, B.: PKCS #5: Password-Based Cryptography Specification Version 2.0
   (2000), http://www.ietf.org/rfc/rfc2898.txt
8. Pacatilu, P.: Android Applications Security. Informatica Economica 15(3), 163–171
   (2011),   http://search.ebscohost.com/login.aspx?direct=true&db=bth&AN=
   69706020&site=ehost-live
9. Pandya, V.R.: Iphone Security Analysis. Journal of Information Security 1, 74–87
   (2008),
   http://www.scirp.org/journal/PaperDownload.aspx?
   DOI=10.4236/jis.2010.12009
10. Paul, M., Chauhan, N.S., Saxena, A.: A security analysis of smartphone data flow
    and feasible solutions for lawful interception (2011),
    http://ieeexplore.ieee.org/lpdocs/epic03/wrapper.htm?arnumber=6122788
11. Shabtai, A., Fledel, Y., Kanonov, U., Elovici, Y., Dolev, S., Glezer, C.: Google
    Android: A Comprehensive Security Assessment (2010),
    http://ieeexplore.ieee.org/lpdocs/epic03/wrapper.htm?arnumber=5396322
12. Shurui, L.S.L., Jie, L.J.L., Ru, Z.R.Z., Cong, W.C.W.: A Modified AES Algorithm
    for the Platform of Smartphone (2010),
    http://ieeexplore.ieee.org/lpdocs/epic03/wrapper.htm?arnumber=5636941
13. Zovi, D.A.D.: Apple iOS 4 Security Evaluation (2011),
    http://www.trailofbits.com/resources/ios4_security_evaluation_
    paper.pdf

Smartphone Volatile Memory Acquisition for Security Analysis and Forensics Investigation

Vrizlynn L.L. Thing and Zheng-Leong Chua

Cybercrime & Security Intelligence (CSI) Department
Institute for Infocomm Research, Singapore
vriz@i2r.a-star.edu.sg

Abstract. In this paper, we first identify the need to be equipped with the capability to perform raw volatile memory data acquisition from live smartphones. We then investigate and discuss the potential of different approaches to achieve this task on Symbian smartphones. Based on our initial analysis, we propose a simple, flexible and portable approach which can have a full-coverage view of the memory space, to acquire the raw volatile memory data from commercial Symbian smartphones. We develop the tool to conduct the proof-of-concept experiments on the phones, and are able to acquire the volatile memory data successfully. A discussion on the problems we have encountered, the solutions we have proposed and the observations we have made in this research is provided. With the acquired data, we conduct an analysis on the memory images of the identified memory regions of interest, and propose a methodology for the purpose of in-depth malware security and forensics analysis.

Keywords: Symbian, mobile devices, smartphones, volatile memory data acquisition, malware security and forensics analysis.

1 Introduction

Mobile phones are becoming increasingly prevalent and sophisticated. They are continuously evolving into "smarter" devices (i.e. smartphones with higher processing power and enhanced features) to cater to the needs of users to stay connected anytime, anywhere, with information readily available. Due to the connection and processing capability of smartphones, illegal access to a wealth of information (for example, contacts list, emails, messages, downloaded confidential documents from email attachments) belonging to the users can be acquired from their smartphones with the appropriate technologies (for example, information theft malwares [1], or mobile forensics tools). Therefore, the capabilities to perform in-depth security analysis to prevent and detect attacks, and forensics investigation to acquire evidence from these devices are essential.

Current mobile phone forensics tools are restricted to the acquisition and analysis of active files and data (i.e. logical data acquisition) from the Subscriber Identity Module (SIM), memory cards and the internal flash memory [2–8]. There exists research work focusing on the low-level physical accquisition

L.J. Janczewski, H.B. Wolfe, and S. Shenoi (Eds.): SEC 2013, IFIP AICT 405, pp. 217–230, 2013.

of raw data from the mobile phones' non-volatile memories [9–12], to support in-depth forensics investigations and evidence analysis, but did not take the volatile memories into consideration.

On the other hand, to support smartphones volatile application data acquisition, loaded malware driver detection, malware behaviour and analysis, it is necessary to have the capability to perform raw volatile memory data acquisition from mobile devices. The ability to acquire the raw volatile memory data from a live device provides security analysts and forensics investigators with a complete picture and insight of the operational states of the live device. However, current anti-virus and anti-malware tools [1, 13–16] for smartphones are limited to the scanning of programs and files in the non-volatile storage space to carry out signature based virus detection.

In this paper, we propose a method to acquire raw volatile memory data from live Symbian smartphones and the methodology to analyse the acquired data to facilitate security analysis and forensics investigations. We develop the tools to conduct the proof-of-concept experiments on commercial Symbian smartphones. There are two main reasons for the choice on the Symbian OS in this research:

1. Even as Android and iOS is rising fast to become the most popular mobile OSes, with Android holding a market share of 52.5%, according to a mobile OS market share survey by Gartner [17, 18], Symbian still holds 16.9% of the market share and is the second most widely used OS in mobile phones. In addition, based on the statistics provided by StatCounter [19], Symbian is observed to be the top smartphones used for the purpose of mobile web browsing.
2. Nonetheless, little has been done on the research of Symbian smartphones live memory security and forensics analysis yet. The reason is that most modern mobile OSes (including Symbian), like generic computer system OSes, use a layer of abstraction such as the virtual memory instead of operating directly on the physical memory. This abstraction layer provides the ability to sandbox each process into its own memory space for security protection. Therefore, with this memory protection in place, a raw volatile memory acquisition tool would have to reside in the kernel space to gain access to the entire memory space [20, 21]. However, in Android, a process memory is exposed to the user-side through the procfs filesystem and this mechanism can be utilized to achieve the live volatile memory acquisition from smartphones running Android OS [22]. On the other hand, Symbian OS does not provide any such mechanism to be leveraged on. As such, it is necessary to investigate and devise a method for conducting a live volatile memory data acquisition pertaining to Symbian smartphones.

The rest of the paper is organised as follow. In Section 2, we present an overview of the existing work on mobile phone forensics research. In Section 3, we present the historical account of mobile forensics research specific to the Symbian smartphones. In Section 4, we present our investigation on the potential approaches to achieve a raw volatile memory data acquisition from commercial Symbian smartphones. We describe the design and the implementation of our live Symbian volatile memory acquisition tool, the problems we encountered and the solutions we devised, in Section 5. The experiments are described in Section 6. We also proposed the analysis methodology in Section 6. Conclusions follow in Section 7.

2   Mobile Phone Forensics Research

In this section, we present an overview of the existing mobile forensics work in general.

In an early work in 2003, Willassen [2] researched on the forensic investigation of GSM phones. The author presented the types of data of forensic relevance, which can exist on the phones, the SIM and the core network, and emphasized the need for more sound mobile forensics procedures and tools.

In 2006, Willassen [9] proposed extracting the physical image of the mobile phone's internal flash memory by desoldering the memory chip and reading it from a device programmer. However, this method is too invasive and brings with it a high risk of chip damage if the extraction is not performed with high precision and care. Another proposed method was to read the memory through the boundary-scan (JTAG) test pins. The extracted memory was examined to detect the presence of deleted file contents. However, the test pins are usually not prominently shown and labelled. In this case, attempting to identify them may be very challenging and time consuming. There is also the possibility that these pins on the commercial smartphones are not accessible to users.

In the same year (2006), Casadei et al. [3] presented their SIMbrush tool developed for both the Linux and Windows platforms. The tool relied on the PCSC library and supported the acquisition of the entire file system, including the non standard files, on the SIM. However, files with restricted read access conditions could not be extracted.

In 2007, Kim et al. [4] presented a tool to acquire the data from a Korea CDMA mobile phone's internal flash memory. The tool communicated with the phone through the RS-232C serial interface and was able to acquire the existing files on the phone using the underlying Qualcomm Mobile Station Modem diagnostic mode protocol.

In the same year (2007), Al-Zarouni [10] studied the mobile phone flasher devices and considered their applicability in mobile phone forensics. Flasher devices were originally used to perform SIM unlocking and firmware flashing. Therefore, they offered access to the phone's flash memory. As they did not need installation on the phone, they were deemed to be forensically sound. However, their operations were not well-documented and since they were designed to write to the memory, the effect of evidence altering while performing a read was also unknown. Their reading capability and memory access range also varied for phones of different brands and models.

In 2008, Jansen et al. [7] proposed a phone manager protocol filtering technique by intercepting the data between the phone and the phone manager. The objective was to address the latency in the coverage of newly available phone models by existing forensic tools. The authors also proposed an identity module programming technique, to populate the phone's SIM with reference test data, so as to provide a baseline for the validation of SIM forensic tools.

In 2008, Zdziarski [23] published a book on iPhone forensics which contains information on how to conduct forensic analysis of iPhone, iPhone 3G, and iPod Touch. The book covers information on the type of data that can be stored on an iPhone, the procedure to build a custom recovery toolkit, the recovery of the raw user disk partition, and the application of data carving techniques to recover deleted voicemail, images, emails, etc. from the phone.

In 2009, Hoog [8] presented the existing forensic evidence acquisition tools for Android phones. The Android Debug Bridge (ADB) enabled interaction with the phone over the USB connection. Therefore, active files on the phone can be retrieved through the "adb pull" command. Other tools such as the Nandroid backup and Paraben Device Seizure also supported the extraction of files residing on the phone.

In 2010, Thing et al. [22] proposed a method to acquire live volatile memory data from Android smartphones. In Android, the process memory is exposed to the user-side through the procfs filesystem. The authors proposed utilizing the process tracing (ptrace) system call to suspend the target process, acquire a snapshot of its memory, and then resume its execution. A study and analysis of the dynamic characteristics of volatile data in the process memory was then carried out.

In 2011, Hoog and Strzempka [24] published a book on iPhone and iOS forensics. The book covers information on the techniques to acquire evidentiary data from the iPhone, iPad and other iOS devices. It also provides practical advise on the securing of the devices, and the data and applications residing on them.

3   History of Symbian Smartphone Forensics

In 2007, Mokhonoana and Olivier [5] proposed an on-phone forensic tool to acquire the active files from a Symbian OS version 7 phone and store it on the removable media. Instead of interfacing with the PC connectivity services, the tool interacts with the operating system to perform a logical copy of the files. Experiments were conducted on the Sony Ericcson P800 phone. The main limitation of the tool is that files in use could not be copied (e.g. call logs, contacts).

In 2008, Distefano et al. [6] proposed a mobile phone internal acquisition technique on the Symbian OS version 8 phones. The mobile phone data is acquired using a tool residing on the removable media, instead of the PC/mobile phone USB connection based approach. The tool utilizes the Symbian S60 File Server API in the read-only mode. The authors carried out experiments comparing the tool with Paraben Device Seizure (USB connection to phone) [25] and P3nfs (Remote access through Bluetooth) [26]. The tool took a longer time to perform the acquisition but managed to acquire more data compared to the P3nfs. When compared with the Paraben Device Seizure, lesser data was acquired. However, the authors observed that the larger data size from Paraben was due to the additional information from its acquired data management.

In 2012, Thing and Tan [11] proposed a method to acquire privacy-protected data from Symbian OS version 9.3 and version 9.4 phones. The authors bypass the Symbian platform security (introduced from Symbian OS version 9.1) to obtain an unrestricted read access to the entire filesystem on the phone. Based on the obtained privilege, the authors retrieve the files relevant to SMS messages from the Nokia E72 and N97 phones (running Symbian OS version 9.3 and version 9.4, respectively). Reverse-engineering work is then carried out to derive the various SMS storage formats on the files and to recover both active and deleted SMSes previously stored on the phones' flash memory.

In the same year (2012), Thing and Chua [12] proposed a low-level linear bitwise data acquisition technique for the Symbian OS version 9.4 phones to support evidentiary file carving. A study and analysis of how files are stored and fragmented on the Symbian smartphone flash memory was also carried out.

However, there is no existing work on the live volatile memory data acquisition pertaining to Symbian smartphones. To the best of our knowledge, this is the first work that aims to investigate and devise a method for conducting a live volatile memory data acquisition from Symbian smartphones.

4   Investigation of Potential Live Symbian Volatile Memory Data Acquisition Approaches

In Symbian, debugging APIs are provided for its programmers. They are typically used during Symbian application development to debug and investigate program efficiency problems. We investigate the potential usefulness of these APIs in live raw volatile memory data acquisition from the commercial Symbian smartphones.

4.1   Run-Mode Debugging

The run-mode debugging APIs are applicable in accessing the process memory of a running application. This type of debuggers is target-resident based and focus primarily in debugging applications and middleware. A process or thread identifier is required in order to access a relevant target specific memory region. However, they are restricted in capability and do not have a deep insight in the kernel-mode software and device drivers. For malwares and rootkits to obtain privileged functionalities, they must be able to execute in the supervisor mode and the way to achieve this is through the use of drivers or kernel modules. Therefore, the acquisition tool must be able to obtain a deep insight into the kernel space modules. In addition, memory not committed to any process at the acquisition point in time will not be accessible.

4.2   Stop-Mode Debugging

The stop-mode debugging APIs are able to "freeze" the processes on the device and acquire a snapshot of its current memory state. However, they are required to be hardware-assisted by utilizing (or tapping onto) the JTAG boundary-scan test pins [9, 27, 28] on the device. This hardware based approach works by accessing the debug ports used by the embedded device processors. JTAG is then switched between the extest or debug mode so as to produce an image dump of the memory. However, the test pins are usually not prominently shown and labelled. In this case, attempting to identify them is known to be very challenging and time consuming. On the commercial smartphones, these pins are commonly removed to prevent access by users.

4.3   Kernel Module

Instead of relying on the existing Symbian drivers or APIs, we can instead write our own kernel space driver for the purpose of memory acquisition. The driver can be a logical device driver that utilizes a logical channel to interact with the user-side application. The driver can then receive specific arguments such as the address of the memory to acquire, and send the acquired data to the user-side application to be stored on the non-volatile memory or to be transmitted out from the phone through a network connection such as 3G or Wifi. Upon receiving the memory address, we intend to perform direct de-referencing of the address to obtain the corresponding memory data and pass it back to the user-side calling application. The idea of the direct de-referencing of the address method is simple. It also provides a flexible way of accessing the memory on the device. Since it utilizes the basic de-reference operator, it should theoretically work across Symbian smartphones with different CPU architectures and/or memory models since the kernel shields us from the effect of these different implementations.

From the absence of relevant prior art, we observed that the live volatile memory data acquisition from Symbian smartphones remains a challenging task. However, we have identified a potential Symbian kernel space driver approach which could achieve a successful acquisition. In this paper, we propose a methodology and discuss the challenges we faced when devising the tool to perform the live volatile memory data acquisition. We also look into the security analysis and forensics investigation of Symbian smartphones based on the acquired data and discuss the observations we have made.

5   The Proposed Acquisition Approach

The live volatile memory data acquisition tool that we have designed, composes of two parts. It consists of a user-side component and a kernel-side component. The user-side component is responsible for loading the kernel-side component, initializing the client side of the logical channel (to support the subsequent communication with the kernel-side component during operation), passing in the addresses to be de-referenced and storing the returned data onto the non-volatile memory. The kernel-side component is a logical device driver which is responsible for setting up the logical channel with the user-side component to support communication during operation, and to return the acquired data from the de-referenced address (which is passed in by the user-side component). We named

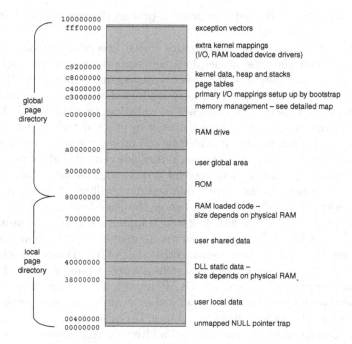

Fig. 1. Symbian Multiple Model Memory Map

the kernel-side component the "Live Volatile Memory Data Acquisiton" driver or "Lamda", and referred to the user-side component as the "LamdaLoader".

Figure 1 shows the Symbian multiple model memory map [20]. With the multiple memory model, Symbian has the concept of a local page directory and a global page directory. The memory region from 0x00000000 to 0x7FFFFFFF is translated via the local page directory while the memory region from 0x80000000 to 0xFFFFFFFF is translated via the global page directory. The global page directory memory regions is accessible by any process while the local page directory memory region is restricted to the current process.

The regions of memory that we are interested in is the global page directory region. Specifically, we are interested in the memory address region from 0xC9200000 to 0xFFEFFFFF (that is, the extra kernel mappings for the I/O and RAM loaded device drivers) and from 0xC8000000 to 0xC91FFFFF (that is, the kernel data, heap and stacks, which contain the kernel objects for the loaded drivers).

Even though we have identified the regions of the memory to perform acquisition, we tested our tool by trying to acquire the entire memory region, starting from the address 0x00000000, from a commercial Nokia N97 smartphone running Symbian OS version 9.4, S60 5th Edition. Upon execution, the smartphone returns a KERN-EXEC 3 panic result and causes it to reboot. Referring to the memory map, we noticed that the address that we sent in is in the region of unmapped NULL pointer traps. The KERN-EXEC 3 panic is caused by an untrapped page fault and since the offending process is a kernel thread, it causes the smartphone to reboot.

The encountered page fault during this initial execution matches the documented behaviour that the kernel does not support on-demand paging [20]. However, upon investigation of the memory management unit (MMU) code in the Symbian product development kit, we realized that demand paging is actually implemented. This information leads us to believe that the KERN-EXEC 3 panic was not caused solely by a page fault but by other underlying mechanisms. We refer to the documentation provided by the product development kit which describes the impacts of demand page on kernel-side code. The document reveals that demand paging is not implemented for kernel code and data. Therefore, any page fault experienced in the kernel code and data will result in an unhandled fault. We decide to modify the tool to handle the page fault gracefully.

In Symbian, the exception handling and trapping mechanism is provided in the form of the XTRAP/XTRAPD macros (to enable the exception trapping). The difference between the two macros is that the XTRAPD macro declares the result variable whereas the XTRAP macro uses a pre-existing variable. They behave in a similar way as the user-side TRAP/leave(), but instead, they can catch hardware exceptions such as those generated by a faulty memory access. In addition, we utilize the TPhysAddr Epoc::LinearToPhysical(TLinAddr aLinAddr) function in Lamda to return the physical address corresponding to the virtual address passed in by the LamdaLoader. We then check the returned value before de-referencing the virtual address as an additional safety net. If KPhysAddrInvalid (defined in kernel/kern_priv.h) is returned, it indicates that the specific virtual address is unmapped. If the returned value is not KPhysAddrInvalid, we proceed to carry out address de-referencing. It is also important to note that even when a virtual address is mapped to a valid physical address, there are instances when the CPU is not permitted to access a page as it does not satisfy the access policy for the page currently. This could also result in a fault. Hence, the exception trapping is useful in this scenario even with the valid mapping check function in place.

6   Experiments and Analysis

In this section, we use our tool to perform the acquisition of the ROM shadow region (0x80000000 to 0x8FFFFFFF) for verification purpose, and the extra kernel mapping (I/O, RAM loaded device drivers) region (0xC9200000 to 0xFF-EFFFFF) and the kernel data, heap and stacks region (0xC8000000 to 0xC91FF-FFF) of the N97 smartphone's volatile memory for further analysis.

6.1   ROM Shadow Image

We acquired the ROM shadow images from three different experiments; one from a N97 smartphone, another from the same smartphone after a hard-reset was performed, and the third from another N97 smartphone with the same version of the ROM flash image. We performed a bitwise comparison and verified that the acquired memory images are identical and therefore, proved that they indeed contain the same version of the ROM image. Next, we analyse the image to identify an approach to facilitate integrity checks of the drivers provided in the ROM flash image on the smartphones originating from the manufactors.

Symbian drivers are binary files and should contain certain specific header information. In Symbian, its E32Image files contain a 12-byte UID (unique identifier and composes of a set of UID1, UID2 and UID3) data that indicate the file type and identify the particular file object. A 4-byte UID1 value of 0x1000007A indicates that the file is of an executable type. Therefore, a logical driver has a UID1 value of 0x1000007A as it is a DLL executable file. In addition, it has a 4-byte UID2 value of 0x100000AF to indicate that it is a logical device driver (LDD). The 4-byte UID3 value is used to identify a particular object (for example, a particular executable file). As the data is stored in little-endian format, the data pattern for searching and extracting the device driver binaries from the ROM memory image is (79 00 00 10 AF 00 00 10). On further analysis, we also discovered that the binary header structure of the detected driver within this memory image is that of the TRomImageHeader structure, as shown in Fig. 2.

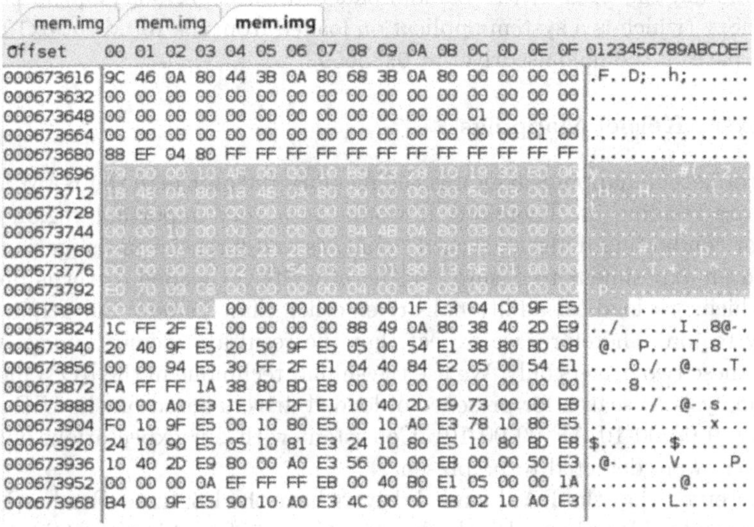

Fig. 2. TRomImageHeader

6.2   Kernel Data, Heap, Stacks

In this region of the memory, we are able to detect the presence of the loaded executables and libraries as their paths are clearly shown in this memory region. Therefore, known malware executables, loaded dynamic libraries and driver names can be easily detected by performing a simple search. As shown in Fig. 3, we observed that the path for the loaded sisadriver is at offset 0x855890.

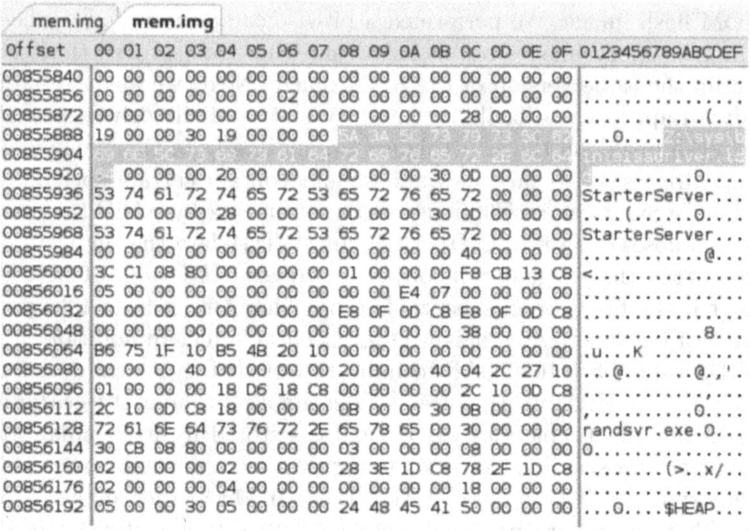

```
mem.img  mem.img
Offset  00 01 02 03 04 05 06 07 08 09 0A 0B 0C 0D 0E 0F  0123456789ABCDEF
00855840 00 00 00 00 00 00 00 00 00 00 00 00 00 00 00 00  ................
00855856 00 00 00 00 00 00 02 00 00 00 00 00 00 00 00 00  ................
00855872 00 00 00 00 00 00 00 00 00 00 00 00 28 00 00 00  ............(...
00855888 19 00 00 30 19 00 00 00                          ...0....
00855904
00855920    00 00 00 20 00 00 00 00 00 00 00 30 0D 00 00 00  ... ...0....
00855936 53 74 61 72 74 65 72 53 65 72 76 65 72 00 00 00  StarterServer...
00855952 00 00 00 00 28 00 00 00 0D 00 00 30 0D 00 00 00  ....(......0....
00855968 53 74 61 72 74 65 72 53 65 72 76 65 72 00 00 00  StarterServer...
00855984 00 00 00 00 00 00 00 00 00 00 00 00 40 00 00 00  ............@...
00856000 3C C1 08 80 00 00 00 00 01 00 00 00 F8 CB 13 C8  <...............
00856016 05 00 00 00 00 00 00 00 00 00 00 00 E4 07 00 00 00  ................
00856032 00 00 00 00 00 00 00 00 00 E8 0F 0D C8 E8 0F 0D C8  ................
00856048 00 00 00 00 00 00 00 00 00 00 00 00 38 00 00 00  ............8...
00856064 B6 75 1F 10 B5 4B 20 10 00 00 00 00 00 00 00 00  .u...K .........
00856080 00 00 00 40 00 00 00 00 20 00 00 40 04 2C 27 10  ...@.... ..@.,'.
00856096 01 00 00 00 18 D6 18 C8 00 00 00 00 2C 10 0D C8  ............,...
00856112 2C 10 0D C8 18 00 00 00 0B 00 00 30 0B 00 00 00  ,..........0....
00856128 72 61 6E 64 73 76 72 2E 65 78 65 00 30 00 00 00  randsvr.exe.0...
00856144 30 CB 08 80 00 00 00 00 03 00 00 00 08 00 00 00  0...............
00856160 02 00 00 00 02 00 00 00 28 3E 1D C8 78 2F 1D C8  ........(>..x/..
00856176 02 00 00 00 04 00 00 00 00 00 00 00 18 00 00 00  ................
00856192 05 00 00 30 05 00 00 00 24 48 45 41 50 00 00 00  ...0....$HEAP...
```

Fig. 3. LDD Path in Kernel Data

We also found the path of the LamdaLoader at offset 0x1903456, the path to AknIconSrv (which is a system application loaded from the ROM) at 0x1920464 and the path of the nokiaiscdriver at 0x856592.

6.3   Extra Kernel Mappings

The extra kernel mappings region is the memory region where the RAM loaded drivers are residing in. Therefore, it would be a very important region of interest for conducting malware security analysis and forensics investigations. We designed an experiment to ensure that no other RAM loaded driver is present. After which, we load an additional driver other than Lamda and acquire this memory region. Therefore, we expect that the resultant memory image would contain these two drivers only. We use the similar technique in the ROM memory image analysis to search for presence of loaded drivers based on the UID string pattern (79 00 00 10 AF 00 00 10). Consistent with our expectation, only the two drivers were detected to be present.

We observed that the RAM loaded drivers have the E32ImageHeader (Fig. 4) rather than the TRomImageHeader header structure found in the ROM drivers. The difference is due to the way these two types of drivers were compiled differently in Symbian. Unlike the previous case of ROM drivers integrity check, where simple matching can be performed, the actual extraction of the RAM drivers has to be conducted to facilitate further security and forensics analysis. Therefore, to do so, we have to first determine the size of the driver.

Our first attempt is to use the TUint32 iUncompressedSize field in the E32ImageHeaderComp. However, this field could not be utilized as the loaded driver found in the RAM is in a compressed form and the size is (expectedly) different from its provided uncompressed driver size. We attempted to calculate the

```
mem.img
Offset     00 01 02 03 04 05 06 07 08 09 0A 0B 0C 0D 0E 0F 0123456789ABCDEF
124788928  8D 00 00 00 01 00 00 00 00 00 00 00 6E 00 00 00 ............n...
124788944  07 00 00 00 44 72 69 76 65 72 31 00 00 00 00 00 ....Driver1.....
124788960  07 00 00 00 44 72 69 76 65 72 31 00 14 DF FF 7F ....Driver1.....
124788976  01 00 00 00 01 00 00 00 78 00 90 D0 F8 00 60 00 ........x.....`.
124788992  0C 00 00 00 00 00 00 00 03 03 03 03 B0 08 00 00 ................
124789008  A3 08 00 00                            AF 17 8F E5 .....        ....
124789024  C1 5E 56 70 45 50 4F 43 ED EC B7 38 00 00 0A 00 .^VpEPOC...8....
124789040  FC 7A 1F 10 02 00 02 02 40 E5 2B DB 10 95 E1 00 .z......@.+.....
124789056  2B 00 00 12 60 14 00 00 00 00 00 00 10 00 00 00 +...`..........
124789072  00 00 10 00 00 20 00 00 00 00 00 00 0C 0A 00 00 .....  .........
124789088  00 80 00 00 00 00 00 00 01 00 00 00 F8 14 00 00 ................
124789104  01 00 00 00 60 14 00 00 9C 00 00 00 00 00 00 00 ....`...........
124789120  FC 14 00 00 E0 15 00 00 00 00 00 00 5E 01 01 20 ............^..
124789136  9C 15 00 00 AF 17 8F E5 00 00 00 00 FF FF 0F 00 ................
124789152  00 00 00 00 00 00 00 00 00 00 00 00 00 00 00 00 ................
124789168  DE BB 9E BE 37 E6 9F 39 97 39 57 BE 1D 6E F3 30 ....7..9.9W..n.0
124789184  CC D9 78 5B 7A 6F 33 79 94 5E 1C 1B CA 5E 93 37 ..x[zo3y.^...^.7
124789200  98 29 6C CD 4B 97 5D A5 CB 1D E3 46 B9 5B AD 5B .)l.K.]....F.[.[
124789216  45 AD 2D 72 F3 4B CE 63 39 B5 4C CB 4B 2A 83 A3 E.-r.K.c9.L.K*..
124789232  5D BA D5 CC 30 C7 04 2D 33 12 B6 A4 CB 5C B5 D4 ]...0..-3....\..
124789248  CD B5 AA 15 CE 2E 75 B5 9B 41 B1 42 A8 DC F7 E5 ......u..A.B....
124789264  F9 6E F7 B6 F4 D5 7B F4 3E AC 1E E9 F3 BE 66 AF .n....{.>.....f.
124789280  7E 79 89 4A 85 6A B1 54 56 5E 73 65 33 47 CB 29 ~y.J.j.TV^se3G.)
```

Fig. 4. UID String with E32ImageHeader Signature 'EPOC'

size by utilizing the fields such as the iCodeSize and iTextSize, but as expected, these attempts proved futile as these offsets are based on the uncompressed code.

We hypothesize that the compressed driver size information must exist within the header or within range of the located driver as the Loader Server has to be able to determine the size of the driver in order to decompress or load it. Through further analysis on a few examples of RAM loaded drivers in the memory image, we observe that the 4 bytes preceding the UID value hold the actual file size of the driver. With that information, we are able to extract the exact RAM loaded drivers from the memory image programmatically. The extracted compressed drivers can then be uncompressed and analysed offline.

As mentioned, the extra kernel mappings not only hold the RAM loaded device drivers but also the I/O information. While searching for the RAM loaded binary drivers, we came across an entire region of memory which corresponds to the content of the address map at offset 0x34525696. Offset 0x34525696 points to the user local data region in the local page directory. Therefore, our initial hypothesis is that this is the region which the kernel mapped for use as the I/O buffer. Since most I/O operations are buffered for performance benefits, this would imply that when an application requests for an input from the user (for example, a password), the input will first be buffered before being read by the application. The reverse is also true such as when an application needs to write data to a file. Therefore, further work can be done to research on the feasibility of monitoring the I/O buffer in order to intercept the information.

As such, since the framebuffer might be on the RAM, there is also a possibility that the current active screen of the device can be found in the image. Furthermore, for processes that have ended, traces of them may still be residing in the RAM since a deallocation of the memory does not result in the RAM being cleared. The reverse may also be true. However, for Symbian, when an unit of memory is allocated, it is initialized to zero.

Considering these characteristics of memory allocations and deallocations, we may be able to extract information such as the phone numbers, call logs, SMSes, recently opened files and even the plaintext version of the encrypted files; since in order to process an encrypted file, it must first be decrypted into the RAM.

6.4   Further Experiment: Page Tables Error

We have attempted to acquired the entire memory space from 0x00000000 to 0xFFFFFFFF without any unexpected error except during the acquisition of the page tables region from 0xC4000000 to 0xC8000000. A smooth process of non-disrupted successful acquisition of the page tables memory region is only possible from 0xC4000000 to 0xC6024599. When the tool tries to resolve the address at 0xC6024600, the smartphone was rebooted. We attempted the experiment a few times and the faulting point is consistent. This is an anomoly as we know that we already have the exception handling mechanism in place and this reboot must be caused by something else.

Unfortunately, we are unable to trace the system as tracing is disabled on commercial phones. Therefore, we are unable to identify the exact cause of this error. Our implemented solution is to skip this unaccessible memory and go to the next address. We then observed that after this faulting address at 0xC6024600, there are several interleaved regions of unaccessible memory.

A hypothesis that requires further investigation to verify in our future work is that this error could be caused by implementation differences on commercial phones. For example, Nokia, which is the manufacturer of N97, could have chosen to map a smaller memory range instead of that indicated by Symbian. It is therefore necessary to investigate where the manufacturer actually output the debug trace to. Possible investigative approaches could target the JTAG, Serial, or other ports on the phone.

7   Conclusions

With the prevalence of smartphones and the increasing amount of important information they are holding and storing, it is necessary to be equipped with the capability to conduct an in-depth security analysis and forensics investigations of smartphone information theft malwares. Therefore, in this paper, we identified the need for a memory acquisition technology or tool to conduct raw volatile memory acquisition from live Symbian smartphones. We investigated the different potential approaches to achieve this task and concluded that the kernel space driver approach to perform address de-referencing is the simplest, and most flexible and portable way to achieve the acquisition of raw volatile memory data from the live Symbian smartphones. This approach is also able to obtain a full-coverage view of the entire memory space. We designed and developed the tool for the purpose of performing the acquisition. Along the way, we also solved the problems relating to exception handling and detection of unmapped addresses by enhancing the tool.

In addition, we identified the relevant memory regions of interest to facilitate further in-depth security analysis and forensics investigations of malwares. Subsequently, we analysed the ROM memory image, the kernel data, heap and stacks memory image, and the extra kernel mappings (I/O, RAM loaded device drivers) to identify ways and devise methods to detect and extract useful information (for examples, the identification and matching of the ROM drivers, the identification and extraction of the RAM loaded device drivers, and the identification of the pathnames of the loaded executables) to support further analysis. Some interesting observations with regard to the I/O buffer region and corresponding information in the user local data memory region in the local page directory, were made.

With this research work, we hope that it provides more insights into the Symbian operational environment and an understanding of how more in-depth anti-malware tools and forensics acquisition and analysis tools can be designed and developed.

References

1. Thing, V.L.L., Subramaniam, P., Tsai, F., Chua, T.-W.: Mobile phone anomalous behaviour detection for real-time information theft tracking. In: International Conference on Technical and Legal Aspects of the e-Society (February 2011)
2. Willassen, S.: Forensics and the GSM mobile telephone system. International Journal of Digital Evidence 2(1), 1–17 (2003)
3. Casadei, F., Savoldi, A., Gubian, P.: Forensics and SIM cards: an overview. International Journal of Digital Evidence 5(1), 1–21 (2006)
4. Kim, K., Hong, D., Chung, K., Ryou, J.-C.: Data acquisition from cell phone using logical approach. In: Proceedings of World Academy of Science, Engineering and Technology, vol. 26 (December 2007)
5. Mokhonoana, P.M., Olivier, M.S.: Acquisition of a Symbian smart phone's content with an on-phone forensic tool. Department of Computer Science, University of Pretoria (2007)
6. Distefano, A., Me, G.: An overall assessment of mobile internal acquisition tool. In: Proceedings of the 8th Digital Forensics Research Conference (DFRWS), Digital Investigation, vol. 5(1), pp. S121–S127 (September 2008)
7. Jansen, W., Delaitre, A., Moenner, L.: Overcoming impediments to cell phone forensics. In: Proceedings of the 41st Hawaii International Conference on System Sciences (2008)
8. Hoog, A.: Android forensics. Presented at Mobile Forensics World 2009 (May 2009)
9. Willassen, S.: Forensic analysis of mobile phone internal memory. In: Pollitt, M., Shenoi, S. (eds.) Advances in Digital Forensics. IFIP, vol. 194, pp. 191–204. Springer, Boston (2006)
10. Al-Zarouni, M.: Introduction to mobile phone flasher devices and considerations for their use in mobile phone forensics. In: Proceedings of the 5th Australian Digital Forensics Conference (December 2007)
11. Thing, V.L.L., Tan, D.J.J.: Symbian smartphone forensics and security: Recovery of privacy-protected deleted data. In: Chim, T.W., Yuen, T.H. (eds.) ICICS 2012. LNCS, vol. 7618, pp. 240–251. Springer, Heidelberg (2012)

12. Thing, V.L.L., Chua, T.-W.: Symbian smartphone forensics: Linear bitwise data acquisition and fragmentation analysis. In: International Conference on Security Technology (November 2012)
13. AVG, Mobilation (May 2012), http://www.avg.com
14. Robota, Anti-virus scanner for symbian mobile phones (May 2012), http://www.robota.nl
15. Dr.Web, Mobile security suite (May 2012), http://www.drweb.com
16. Lookout, Mobile security (May 2012), https://www.mylookout.com
17. Gartner: Market Share: mobile communication devices by region and country, 3q11 (November 2011), http://www.gartner.com
18. Gartner: Gartner says sales of mobile devices grew 5.6 percent in third quarter of 2011; smartphone sales increased 42 percent, (November 2011), http://www.gartner.com/it/page.jsp?id=1848514
19. Statcounter, Top 8 mobile operating systems (February 2012), http://gs.statcounter.com/#mobile_os-ww-monthly-201202-201202-bar
20. Sales, J.: Symbian os internals: Real-time kernel programming (January 2006)
21. Vomel, S., Freiling, F.C.: A survey of main memory acquisition and analysis techniques for the windows operating system. Digital Investigation 8(1), 3–22 (2011)
22. Thing, V.L.L., Ng, K.-Y., Chang, E.-C.: Live memory forensics of mobile phones. Digital Investigation 7, S114–S120 (2010)
23. Zdziarski, J.: iPhone forensics. OI'Reilly Media (September 2008)
24. Hoog, A., Strzempka, K.: iPhone and iOS forensics. Syngress (June 2011)
25. Paraben: Device seizure, http://www.paraben.com/
26. Sourceforge, P3nfs, http://sourceforge.net/projects/p3nfs.berlios/
27. Breeuwsma, I.M.F.: Forensic imaging of embedded systems using jtag (boundary-scan). Digital Investigation 3(1), 32–42 (2006)
28. Savoldi, A., Gubian, P.: Symbian forensics: An overview. In: IEEE International Conference on Intelligent Information Hiding and Multimedia Signal Processing, pp. 529–533 (August 2008)

Program Transformation for Non-interference Verification on Programs with Pointers

Mounir Assaf[1], Julien Signoles[1], Frédéric Tronel[2], and Éric Totel[2]

[1] CEA, LIST, Software Reliability Laboratory, PC 174, 91191 Gif-sur-Yvette France
firstname.lastname@cea.fr
[2] Supelec, CIDre, Rennes France
firstname.lastname@supelec.fr

Abstract. Novel approaches for dynamic information flow monitoring are promising since they enable permissive (accepting a large subset of executions) yet sound (rejecting all unsecure executions) enforcement of non-interference. In this paper, we present a dynamic information flow monitor for a language supporting pointers. Our flow-sensitive monitor relies on prior static analysis in order to soundly enforce non-interference. We also propose a program transformation that preserves the behavior of initial programs and soundly inlines our security monitor. This program transformation enables both dynamic and static verification of non-interference.

1 Introduction

Information security is usually enforced through access control security policies. Those security policies, implemented at the OS level, can authorize or deny information flows at a coarse-grained subject/object level. Information flow control (IFC) mechanisms, occuring at the application level, offer more granularity to enforce precise flow policies.

The seminal work in IFC has been initiated by Denning and Denning [1]. They proposed a static analysis to verify that information is propagated inside programs securely with respect to a flow policy. For instance, a simple flow policy disallows leakage of secret variables into public ones, hence ensuring confidentiality. This notion has been generalized by Goguen and Meseguer [2] as non-interference. Non-interference, precisely its termination-insensitive formulation (TINI), has been widely adopted in IFC as a security policy [3,4,5]. Informally, it states that, when changing only secret inputs, terminating executions of a program must deliver the same public outputs.

Volpano et al. [3] formalize a Denning-style static analysis as a type system for a simple imperative language. Volpano's work provides the first soundness proof stating that a typable program is secure with respect to TINI. However, Volpano's type system lacks flow-sensitivity since security labels associated to variables are not allowed to change during analysis. For example, the program $public = secret; public = 0$ is secure because the final content of variable $public$ is overridden. Still, this program is not typable by Volpano's type system because of flow-insensitivity.

Hunt and Sands [6] extend Volpano's type system with flow-sensitivity, hence permitting security labels to change in order to reflect the precise security level of their

L.J. Janczewski, H.B. Wolfe, and S. Shenoi (Eds.): SEC 2013, IFIP AICT 405, pp. 231–244, 2013.

contents. Introducing flow-sensitivity to security type systems contributes to more permissive security analyses. Hunt and Sands prove the soundness of their type system with respect to TINI, while typing a larger subset of secure programs in comparison with Volpano's type system.

Dynamic monitoring of information flows is also known to provide more permissiveness [7,5] (accepting a large subset of executions). Unlike static analyses which enforce TINI for all possible execution paths, dynamic monitoring ensures that a single execution path is secure. However, permissiveness through the combination of both dynamic monitoring and flow-sensitivity requires careful examination. Indeed, Russo and Sabelfeld [5] prove that flow-sensitivity in purely dynamic IFC introduces covert channels leaking information. The main idea behind this result is that a purely dynamic monitor ignores non-executed conditional branches, missing at the same time information flows they produce. Therefore, a flow-sensitive dynamic monitor must rely on static analyses for sound (rejecting all unsecure executions) IFC.

Contributions. In this paper, we investigate **permissive yet sound flow-sensitive** IFC for programs handling pointers. Our contributions are:

- We formalize a hybrid information flow monitor for an imperative language with pointers and aliasing, by relying on a semantics built upon the Clight [8] semantics. This semantics is especially used in the CompCert [9] provably correct compiler. We prove the soundness of our monitor with respect to TINI.
- We also propose a **sound program transformation** which inlines our information flow monitor. For languages that are compiled directly into native machine code as it is the case for the C language, inlining is necessary to ensure fine-grained information flow monitoring. To our knowledge, our program transformation is the first proven **sound inlining approach for dynamic monitors handling pointers**.
- Assuming the implementation of security labels and their join operator, TINI can be enforced by running the self-monitoring transformed program. This **dynamic approach** has the advantage of being permissive since it soundly monitors a single execution path, ignoring possible unsecure paths that are not executed. The program transformation T also enables the verification of TINI by static analysis for free. Such a **static approach** computes an over-approximation of the transformed program semantics, enforcing TINI for all execution paths.

Outline. Section 2 introduces information flow background. Section 3 formalizes our information flow monitor for a simple imperative language handling pointers and aliasing. Section 4 defines a program transformation inlining our information flow monitor. We discuss related work in Section 5 and future work in Section 6.

2   Background

Non-interference. Our attacker model assumes that attackers know the source code of analyzed programs. It also supposes that attackers can only modify public inputs and read public outputs. A program is non-interferent if two terminating executions which differ only on secret inputs deliver the same public outputs. This notion of non-interference [2] formalizes independence of public outputs from secret inputs.

Information flows. Explicit and implicit flows [1] are generally taken into account when enforcing TINI. Explicit flows are produced from any source variable y assigned to a destination variable x. Implicit flows are produced whenever an affectation occurs in conditional branches. For instance, the following program if $(secret)$ $x = 1$ $else$ $skip$ generates an implicit flow from $secret$ to x, whatever the executed branch is. Even if x is not assigned, an attacker could learn that $secret$ is false if x is different from 1. As one generally enforces a sound approximation of TINI, we suppose that assignments inside conditionals always produce implicit flows from the guards to assigned variables.

Additional information flows arise in the presence of pointers. Consider for example, the program if $(secret)$ $\{x = \&a\}$ $else$ $\{x = \&b\}$ $print$ $*x$. An attacker, knowing the initial values of a and b, may learn information about the value of variable $secret$ whenever $*x$ is output : there is an information flow from $secret$ to $*x$. There are actually two different kinds of information flows involved in this case. The first one is an implicit flow from $secret$ to x because of assignments inside a conditional depending on $secret$. The second one, due to pointer aliasing and dereferencing, is from x to $*x$. Thus, by transitivity, there is an information flow from $secret$ to x.

Similarly, the program if $(secret)$ $\{x = \&a\}$ $else$ $\{x = \&b\}$ $*x = 1$ exposes pointer-induced flows from $secret$ to variables a and b. An attacker having access to either variables a or b after the assignment $*x = 1$, may learn information about variable $secret$. It is worth noting that even if a (resp. b) is not assigned by instruction $*x = 1$, an information flow from $secret$ to a (resp. b) is still produced. In fact, this pointer-induced information flow involves all variables that could have been written by $*x = 1$ (here, both variables a and b).

As we are aiming at enforcing TINI, we ignore in this paper all covert channels due to diverging runs and timing channels. Hence, a program like $while$ $(secret)$ $skip$; could leak information about variable $secret$. Yet, this is acceptable since even in the presence of outputs, Askarov et al. [4] have proved that an attacker could not know the secret in polynomial time in the size of the secret.

3   Information Flow Monitoring Semantics

Language overview. Figure 1 presents the abstract syntax of our language. It is a simple imperative language handling basic types (κ) like integers and pointers ($ptr(\tau)$). It handles aliasing but no pointer arithmetics: binary operators do not take pointers as arguments. The semantics of this language is inspired by the Clight semantics [8]. Clight is formalized in the context of the CompCert verified compiler for C programs [9].

A simplified version of the Clight big-step operational semantics considers an environment E and a memory M. $E : Var \rightharpoonup Loc$ maps variables to statically allocated locations. $M : Loc \rightharpoonup \mathbb{V}$ maps locations to values of type τ. The evaluation of an instruction c in an environment E and a memory M, denoted by $E \vdash c, M \Rightarrow M'$, results in a new memory M'. Expressions can be evaluated as either left-values or right-values depending on the position in which they occur. Only expressions having the form id or $*a$ can occur in l-value positions such as the left-hand side of assignments, whereas any expression can occur in right-value position.

As illustrated by Figure 2, l-value evaluation of expression a_1 in environment E and memory M ($E \vdash a_1, M \Leftarrow l$) provides the location l where a_1 is stored, whereas r-value

Types: $\tau ::= \kappa \mid ptr(\tau)$

Expressions: $a ::= n \mid id \mid uop\, a \mid a_1\, bop\, a_2$

$ \mid *a \mid \&a$

Instructions: $c ::= skip \mid a_1 = a_2 \mid c_1;\, c_2$

$ \mid if\, (a)\, c_1\, else\, c_2 \mid while\, (a)\, c$

Declarations: $dcl ::= (\tau\, id)^*$

Programs: $P ::= dcl;\, c$

$$(Assign)\quad \frac{\begin{array}{c} E \vdash a_1, M \Leftarrow l \\ E \vdash a_2, M \Rightarrow v \\ M' = M[l \mapsto v] \end{array}}{E \vdash a_1 = a_2, M \Rightarrow M'}$$

Fig. 1. Abstract syntax of our language

Fig. 2. Assignment semantics in Clight

evaluation of a_2 ($E \vdash a_2, M \Rightarrow v$) provides the value v of expression a_2. The assignment rule then maps the value v to the location l in the new memory M'.

In order to extend Clight's three judgment rules with the information flow monitor semantics, we consider a lattice $\mathbb{S} = (SC, \sqsubseteq)$ where $public \in SC$ is the minimal element of $\mathbb{S}$. We note $\sqcup$ the associated join operator. We also consider a new kind of memory $\Gamma : Loc \rightharpoonup \mathbb{S}$, which maps locations to security labels. Informally, security memory Γ tracks the security level of locations content through tainting. For example, an assignment $x = y + z$ generates an information flow from y and z to x. Thus, Γ maps to $E(x)$ (*i.e.* the location associated to x) the security label $\Gamma(E(y)) \sqcup \Gamma(E(z))$.

Expressions. Both Clight's r-value and l-value evaluations of expressions are extended to support the propagation of security labels, as illustrated in Figure 3: the evaluation of expressions yields both a value $v \in \mathbb{V}$ and a security label $s \in \mathbb{S}$. If the pair (l, s_l) is the result of l-value evaluation of expression a, then the security label s_l captures pointer-induced flows produced by possible dereferences occurring in a, whereas $s_r = \Gamma(l)$ captures explicit flows produced by reading the value $M(l)$ of a. Therefore, the r-value evaluation of a produces a value $v = M(l)$ and a security label $s = s_l \sqcup s_r$ taking into account both explicit and pointer-induced flows through the join operator (rule *RV*). Note that the semantics of Clight expressions can be obtained from Figure 3 by ignoring all the monitor related operations.

The security label associated to the r-value of a defines the label associated to the l-value of $*a$ (rule LV_{MEM}), hence taking into account the pointer-induced information flow from a to $*a$. R-values of constants are labeled as *public* because attackers are supposed to know the source code. Since the locations of variables are at known offsets from the base pointer, we associate *public* to the l-values of variables (rule LV_{ID}). The label of the l-value of a defines the label associated to the r-value of $\&a$ (rule RV_{REF}). The security label associated to the r-value of a is propagated to the r-value of $uop\, a$ (rule RV_{UOP}). Likewise, the security label associated to the r-value of $a_1\, bop\, a_2$ takes into account both a_1 and a_2 r-values security labels through the join operator.

Figure 4 illustrates an example of the r-value evaluation of $*x$. Supposing that x is stored at location l_x and points to a variable a stored at location l_a, the r-value evaluation of $*x$ takes into account both pointer-induced and explicit flows since both s_x (the security label of x) and s_a (the security label of a) affect the resulting security label s.

$$LV_{ID} \quad \dfrac{E(id) = l}{E \vdash id, M, \Gamma \Leftarrow l, public}$$

$$LV_{MEM} \quad \dfrac{E \vdash a, M, \Gamma \Rightarrow ptr(l), s}{E \vdash *a, M, \Gamma \Leftarrow l, s}$$

$$RV_{CONST} \quad E \vdash n, M, \Gamma \Rightarrow n, public$$

$$RV \quad \dfrac{E \vdash a, M, \Gamma \Leftarrow l, s_l \quad M(l) = v \quad s_r = \Gamma(l) \quad s = s_l \sqcup s_r}{E \vdash a, M, \Gamma \Rightarrow v, s}$$

$$RV_{REF} \quad \dfrac{E \vdash a, M, \Gamma \Leftarrow l, s}{E \vdash \&a, M, \Gamma \Rightarrow ptr(l), s}$$

$$RV_{UOP} \quad \dfrac{E \vdash a, M, \Gamma \Rightarrow v, s \quad uop \; v = v'}{E \vdash uop \; a, M, \Gamma \Rightarrow v', s}$$

$$RV_{BOP} \quad \dfrac{E \vdash a_1, M, \Gamma \Rightarrow v_1, s_1 \quad E \vdash a_2, M, \Gamma \Rightarrow v_2, s_2 \quad v_1 \; bop \; v_2 = v \quad s_1 \sqcup s_2 = s}{E \vdash a_1 \; bop \; a_2, M, \Gamma \Rightarrow v, s}$$

Fig. 3. Information flow monitor big-step semantics of expressions

$$LV_{MEM} \quad RV \quad \dfrac{LV_{ID} \; \dfrac{E(x) = l_x}{E \vdash x, M, \Gamma \Leftarrow l_x, public} \quad \begin{array}{c} M(l_x) = ptr(l_a) \\ \Gamma(l_x) = s_x \quad s_x = public \sqcup s_x \\ \hline E \vdash x, M, \Gamma \Rightarrow ptr(l_a), s_x \end{array}}{E \vdash *x, M, \Gamma \Leftarrow l_a, s_x} \quad M(l_a) = v \quad \Gamma(l_a) = s_a \quad s = s_a \sqcup s_x$$

$$RV \quad \dfrac{}{E \vdash *x, M, \Gamma \Rightarrow v, s}$$

Fig. 4. An example of expression $*x$ evaluation

One consequence of rules LV_{ID} and RV_{REF} is that addresses of variables are labeled as *public*. Thus, they can be accessed by attackers and used to bypass security measures such as ASLR (Address Space Layout Randomization). In fact, this kind of information leaks is out of scope for our analysis since addresses of variables are not secret inputs of programs. Furthermore, mapping any security label s other than *public* to the l-value of variables id would taint all data accessed through dereferences of id, causing a label creep problem [10].

Instructions. The semantics of instructions is presented in Figure 5. It is a combination of dynamic monitoring and static analysis through the use of $S_P(c)$, the set of locations that may have been written by instruction c of program P. The statically computed set $S_P(c)$ is fed to the semantics whenever a call to the *update* operator occurs. We also introduce a new meta-variable pc to capture implicit flows. pc can be viewed as the security label of the program counter. Each time a program enters a conditional, pc is updated with the guard security label in order to reflect generated implicit flows. Therefore, evaluation of instructions occurs in a memory Γ, an execution context pc in addition to a memory M and an environment E. It produces new memories Γ' and M'.

For assignment $a_1 = a_2$ (rule *Assign*), the join of three security labels are mapped to the location of a_1. First, s_1 takes into account pointer-induced flows from the l-

$$(Assign) \quad \frac{\begin{array}{c} E \vdash a_1, M, \Gamma \Leftarrow l_1, s_1 \quad E \vdash a_2, M, \Gamma \Rightarrow v_2, s_2 \\ s = s_1 \sqcup s_2 \sqcup \underline{pc} \quad s' = s_1 \sqcup \underline{pc} \quad M' = M[l_1 \mapsto v_2] \\ \Gamma'' = \Gamma[l_1 \mapsto s] \quad \Gamma' = update(a_1 = a_2, s', \Gamma'') \end{array}}{E \vdash a_1 = a_2, M, \Gamma, \underline{pc} \Rightarrow M', \Gamma'}$$

$$(Comp) \quad \frac{\begin{array}{c} E \vdash c_1, M, \Gamma, \underline{pc} \Rightarrow M_1, \Gamma_1 \\ E \vdash c_2, M_1, \Gamma_1, \underline{pc} \Rightarrow M_2, \Gamma_2 \end{array}}{E \vdash c_1; c_2, M, \Gamma, \underline{pc} \Rightarrow M_2, \Gamma_2}$$

$$(If_{tt}) \quad \frac{\begin{array}{c} E \vdash a, M, \Gamma \Rightarrow v, s \ \ istrue(v) \\ \underline{pc}' = s \sqcup \underline{pc} \quad E \vdash c_1, M, \Gamma, \underline{pc}' \Rightarrow M_1, \Gamma_1 \\ \Gamma_1' = update(c_2, \underline{pc}', \Gamma_1) \end{array}}{E \vdash if \ (a) \ c_1 \ else \ c_2, M, \Gamma, \underline{pc} \Rightarrow M_1, \Gamma_1'}$$

$$(W_{ff}) \quad \frac{\begin{array}{c} E \vdash a, M, \Gamma \Rightarrow v, s \ \ isfalse(v) \\ \underline{pc}' = s \sqcup \underline{pc} \quad \Gamma' = update(c, \underline{pc}', \Gamma) \end{array}}{E \vdash while \ (a) \ c, M, \Gamma, \underline{pc} \Rightarrow M, \Gamma'}$$

$$(If_{fff}) \quad \frac{\begin{array}{c} E \vdash a, M, \Gamma \Rightarrow v, s \ \ isfalse(v) \\ \underline{pc}' = s \sqcup \underline{pc} \quad E \vdash c_2, M, \Gamma, \underline{pc}' \Rightarrow M_2, \Gamma_2 \\ \Gamma_2' = update(c_1, \underline{pc}', \Gamma_2) \end{array}}{E \vdash if \ (a) \ c_1 \ else \ c_2, M, \Gamma, \underline{pc} \Rightarrow M_2, \Gamma_2'}$$

$$(W_{tt}) \quad \frac{\begin{array}{c} E \vdash a, M, \Gamma \Rightarrow v, s \ \ istrue(v) \\ \underline{pc}' = s \sqcup \underline{pc} \\ E \vdash c, M, \Gamma, \underline{pc}' \Rightarrow M', \Gamma' \\ E \vdash while \ (a) \ c, M', \Gamma', \underline{pc} \Rightarrow M'', \Gamma'' \end{array}}{E \vdash while \ (a) \ c, M, \Gamma, \underline{pc} \Rightarrow M'', \Gamma''}$$

$$(Skip) \ E \vdash skip, M, \Gamma, \underline{pc} \Rightarrow M, \Gamma \qquad update(c, s, \Gamma) \triangleq \begin{cases} \Gamma(l) & \forall l \notin S_P(c) \\ \Gamma(l) \sqcup s & \forall l \in S_P(c) \end{cases}$$

Fig. 5. Information flow monitor big-step semantics of instructions

value of a_1. Second, s_2 considers explicit flows from the r-value of a_2. Third, $\underline{pc}$ captures the implicit flows generated by conditionals. Additionally, assignments generate pointer-induced flows from the l-value of a_1 to the set of possibly written locations. Consequently, the *update* operator propagates the union of $\underline{pc}$ and s_1 to $S_p(a_1 = a_2)$. Assuming that x points to a variable a stored at location l_a, Figure 6 illustrates the evaluation of instruction $*x = 1$. The security label s_x (resp. $\underline{pc}$) affects the security label of variable a in order to take into account pointer-induced flows (resp. implicit flows). Finally, the *update* operator propagates the security label s' to the set $S_P(*x = 1)$ to capture pointer-induced flows due to the assignment $*x = 1$.

$$(Assign) \quad \frac{\begin{array}{c} E \vdash *x, M, \Gamma \Leftarrow l_a, s_x \quad E \vdash 1, M, \Gamma \Rightarrow 1, public \quad s = s_x \sqcup public \sqcup \underline{pc} \\ s' = s_x \sqcup \underline{pc} \quad M' = M[l_a \mapsto 1] \quad \Gamma'' = \Gamma[l_a \mapsto s] \quad \Gamma' = update(*x = 1, s', \Gamma'') \end{array}}{E \vdash *x = 1, M, \Gamma, \underline{pc} \Rightarrow M', \Gamma'}$$

Fig. 6. An example of instruction $*x = 1$ evaluation

For conditionals (rules If_{tt} and If_{ff}), a new context of execution $\underline{pc}'$ takes into account implicit flows generated by the conditional guard a. When a is evaluated to *true* (rule If_{tt}, the other one is symmetrical), the resulting security memory takes into account the implicit flows induced by both the executed branch c_1 and the non-executed one c_2. Implicit flows in c_1 are computed by the evaluation of c_1 in $\underline{pc}'$, whereas the *update* operator handles the ones from c_2 by propagating $\underline{pc}'$ to the set $S_P(c_2)$. Rules W_{tt} and W_{ff} are similar to conditional rules. Finally, a sequence of instructions $c_1; c_2$ is executed in the same execution context (rule *Comp*).

Soundness. In order to formalize TINI, Definition 1 introduces an equivalence relation for memories: two memories M_1 and M_2 are s-equivalent if they are equal for the set of locations l whose label $\Gamma(l)$ is at most s.

Definition 1 (Equivalence relation $\sim_\Gamma^s$). *For all Γ, $s \in \mathbb{S}$, M_1, M_2,*
  M_1 and M_2 are s-equivalent $(M_1 \sim_\Gamma^s M_2)$ if and only if

$$\forall l \in Loc, \Gamma(l) \sqsubseteq s \implies M_1(l) = M_2(l).$$

Non-interference, by Definition 2, ensures that an attacker knowing only inputs and outputs up to a security level s cannot gain any knowledge of inputs whose security levels are strictly higher than s.

Definition 2 (Termination-insensitive non-interference).
For all $c, E, \Gamma, M_1, M_1', M_2, M_2', s, \underline{pc} \in \mathbb{S}$, such that
$E \vdash c, M_1, \Gamma, \underline{pc} \Rightarrow M_1', \Gamma_1'$ *and* $E \vdash c, M_2, \Gamma, \underline{pc} \Rightarrow M_2', \Gamma_2'$,

$$M_1 \sim_\Gamma^s M_2 \implies \Gamma_2' = \Gamma_1' = \Gamma' \text{ and } M_1' \sim_{\Gamma'}^s M_2'.$$

This definition of non-interference is termination-insensitive since it ignores behaviors of diverging runs, including information leaks due to the attacker ability to observe (non-)termination of programs. Definition 2 is equivalent to the definitions of TINI in the literature [3,4,6,11]. Moreover, our definition of non-interference is equivalent to what Askarov et al. [4] call batch job TINI, since attackers are not allowed to know intermediate results of computation through outputs.

Theorem 1 (Soundness). *The information flow-extended semantics is sound with respect to termination-insensitive non-interference as defined in 2.*

Theorem 1 proves that our monitor semantics is sound with respect to TINI. The proof, by induction on instructions evaluation $\Rightarrow$, relies on the fact that both l-value and r-value evaluations of expressions in s-equivalent memories yield the same result for expressions whose label is below s. This theorem also proves that attackers cannot learn information by observing the behavior of our monitor since it ensures that both output security memories are equal. Full details of our proofs can be found in the technical report [12].

4   Program Transformation

This section presents an inlining approach for our monitoring semantics as a program transformation. This approach has the benefits of enabling both static and dynamic analysis since both analyses can be considered depending on the required level of confidence. The former would focus on soundness by ensuring that all execution paths of the analysed program are secure. The latter would emphasize on permissiveness by enforcing non-interference for the execution path of a single run.

Informally, the program transformation maps a shadow variable —a security label— to each variable of $Var(P)$, the set of variables of the initial program P. Inlining our monitor then consists of propagating those security labels with respect to the monitor semantics. For this reason, types of our language are extended with a type τ_s representing security labels. Expressions are extended with security labels denoted s and a join operator $\sqcup$ on security labels. The range of memories M is also extended to $\mathbb{V} \cup \mathbb{S}$.

In order to handle pointers, we introduce in Definitions 3 and 4 the depth $\mathscr{D}(id)$ of a variable id and a bijection $\Lambda(id,k)$, with $k \in [0, \mathscr{D}(id)]$. $\mathscr{D}(id)$ is the number of dereferences such that $*^{\mathscr{D}(id)}id$ yields a basic type κ, whereas Λ maps each initial variable id to $\mathscr{D}(id)$ different shadow variables. Basically, $*^k\Lambda(id,k)$ is the security label of $*^k id$.

Definition 3 (Depth $\mathscr{D}(x)$ of variable x).

Let τ_x be the type of variable $x \in Var(P)$. $\mathscr{D}(x) = \mathscr{D}(\tau) = \begin{cases} 0 & \text{if } \tau = \kappa \\ 1 + \mathscr{D}(\tau') & \text{if } \tau = ptr(\tau') \end{cases}$

Definition 4 (Bijection Λ).
$\Lambda : \{(x,k) : x \in Var(P) \text{ and } k \in [0, \mathscr{D}(x)]\} \rightarrow Var'$ *such that* $Var' \subset Var \setminus Var(P)$ *is a bijection mapping to each initial variable x exactly $\mathscr{D}(x)$ shadow variables, denoted $\Lambda(x,k)$, such that $\Lambda(x,k)$ has a type $ptr^{(k)}(\tau_s)$.*

We extend Λ to all l-value expressions $(\Lambda(*^r x,k) \triangleq *^r \Lambda(x,k+r))$ such that $\Lambda(*^k id,0)$ is equal to $*^k\Lambda(id,k)$. Hence $\Lambda(*^k id,0)$ also captures the security label of $*^k id$.

Our program transformation, denoted T, maintains a pointer-related invariant in order to correctly handle aliasing. Essentially, if x points to an integer variable a, shadow variable $\Lambda(x,1)$ also points to $\Lambda(a,0)$. This way, whenever we read (or write) the same integer through $*x$ or a, we also read (or write) the same security label through either $*\Lambda(x,1)$ or $\Lambda(a,0)$. Listings 1 and 2 illustrate an example of our program transformation. Instruction 3 in Listing 1 is transformed into instructions 3, 4, 5 and 6 in Listing 2. Instructions 3, 5 and 6 of the transformed program reproduce the semantics of *Assign* rules as defined in the monitoring semantics (Figure 5), whereas instruction 4 maintains the aliasing invariant. Thanks to instructions 4 and 9 of the transformed program, instruction 13 updates the correct security label during execution.

Listing 1. The initial program.

```
1   // SP(c3)=SP(c5)={E(x)}
2   if (secret)
3     x = &a ;
4   else
5     x = &b ;
6   // SP(c7)={E(a),E(b)}
7   *x = 1
```

Listing 2. The transformed program.

```
1   pc'=pc⊔Λ(secret,0);
2   if (secret) {
3     Λ(x,0) = public;
4     Λ(x,1) = &Λ(a,0);
5     Λ(x,0) = Λ(x,0)⊔pc';
6     x = &a ;
7   } else {
8     Λ(x,0) = public;
9     Λ(x,1) = &Λ(b,0);
10    Λ(x,0) = Λ(x,0)⊔pc';
11    x = &b ;
12  }
13  *Λ(x,1) = Λ(x,0)⊔public;
14  Λ(a,0) = Λ(x,0)⊔pc;
15  Λ(b,0) = Λ(x,0)⊔pc;
16  *x = 1
```

As in Definition 5, two expressions are aliased in memory M if their l-value evaluation yields the same location. Hence, the aliasing invariant, stated as Lemma 1, ensures that two l-value expressions are aliased iff their shadow variables are aliased.

Definition 5 (Aliasing equivalence relation $\sim_{lval}^{M}$).
For all $a_1, a_2 \in Exp$, for all E, M such that $E \vdash a_1, M \Leftarrow l_1$ and $E \vdash a_2, M \Leftarrow l_2$.

$$a_1 \sim_{lval}^{M} a_2 \iff l_1 = l_2$$

Lemma 1 (Aliasing invariant).

For all $E, c, M, M', \Gamma, \Gamma', \underline{pc}, pc$ such that $E \vdash T[c, pc], M, \Gamma, \underline{pc} \Rightarrow M', \Gamma'$.

Let the predicate $\Omega(M) \triangleq \forall x, y \in Var(P)$, for all $r \in [0, \mathscr{D}(y)]$,

$$x \sim_{lval}^{M} *^{r} y$$

$$\iff \forall k \in [0, \mathscr{D}(x)], \Lambda(x, k) \sim_{lval}^{M} \Lambda(*^{r}y, k)$$

Then $\Omega(M) \implies \Omega(M')$.

Transformation T relies on Definition 6 of operators $\mathcal{L}_L$, $\mathcal{L}_R$ and $\mathcal{L}$ which express security labels of expressions in terms of shadow variables. They respectively capture the label of the l-value of a, the label of the r-value of a, and $\Gamma(l_a)$, where l_a is the location of a. They accurately reproduce the monitoring semantics for expressions as defined in Figure 3.

Definition 6 (Operators $\mathcal{L}_L$, $\mathcal{L}_R$ and $\mathcal{L}$).

$$\mathcal{L}_R(n) \triangleq public \qquad \mathcal{L}_R(uop\ a) \triangleq \mathcal{L}_R(a) \qquad \mathcal{L}_R(\&a) \triangleq \mathcal{L}_L(a)$$

$$\mathcal{L}_R(a_1\ bop\ a_2) \triangleq \mathcal{L}_R(a_1) \sqcup \mathcal{L}_R(a_2) \qquad \mathcal{L}_R(a) \triangleq \mathcal{L}_L(a) \sqcup \mathcal{L}(a) \qquad \mathcal{L}(a) \triangleq \Lambda(a, 0)$$

$$\mathcal{L}_L(id) \triangleq public \qquad \mathcal{L}_L(*a) \triangleq \mathcal{L}_R(a)$$

The l-values of a variable id is associated with the security label *public* (rule LV_{ID}), so does $\mathcal{L}_L(id)$. $\mathcal{L}_L(*a)$, the security label associated to the l-value $*a$, is defined as $\mathcal{L}_R(a)$, the security label associated to the r-value of a (rule LV_{MEM}). As for r-values (rule RV_{CONST}), the security label of constant integers $\mathcal{L}_R(n)$ is defined as *public*. The security label of r-values expressions $\mathcal{L}_R(a)$ is defined as the join of their l-value label $\mathcal{L}_L(a)$ and the label of their content $\mathcal{L}(a)$ (rule RV) in order to take into account both pointer-induced and explicit flows. $\mathcal{L}_R(\&a)$, the label of r-value expressions $\&a$ is defined as $\mathcal{L}_L(a)$, the label of the l-value a (rule RV_{REF}). $\mathcal{L}_R(uop\ a)$ and $\mathcal{L}_R(a_1\ bop\ a_2)$ are respectively defined according to rules RV_{UOP} and RV_{BOP}. Finally, the label $\mathcal{L}(a)$ associated to the content of a is defined as $\Lambda(a, 0)$, which represents $\Gamma(l_a)$ in the monitoring semantics. Figure 7 illustrates the computation of the label associated to a r-value $*x$. Intuitively, for the transformation to be correct, we must ensure that the evaluation of $\Lambda(x, 0)$ and $*\Lambda(x, 1)$ in M respectively results in $s_x = \Gamma(l_x)$ and $s_a = \Gamma(l_a)$.

$$\mathcal{L}_R(*x) = \mathcal{L}_L(*x) \sqcup \mathcal{L}(*x) = \mathcal{L}_R(x) \sqcup \Lambda(*x, 0) = \mathcal{L}_L(x) \sqcup \mathcal{L}(x) \sqcup *\Lambda(x, 1)$$
$$= public \sqcup \Lambda(x, 0) \sqcup *\Lambda(x, 1)$$

Fig. 7. An example of security label computation by both semantics and transformation T

We present the program transformation rules in Figure 8. For brevity, $c_k; \forall k \in [0, n]$ denotes the sequence of instructions $c_0; c_1; \ldots c_n$. Since the transformation T must maintain the execution context and must propagate it to all possibly written locations in non-executed branches, it creates for each conditional and loop a new shadow variable of type τ_s, denoted pc'. Variable pc' captures the new execution context $\underline{pc'}$ defined in the semantics. The transformation then parameterizes the branches with the new shadow variable pc'. It also uses the inverse of environment E, denoted E^{-1}, in order to find the set of variables corresponding to the locations $l \in S_P(c)$. Then it propagates the execution context pc' to all the corresponding shadow variables. This way, the program transformation reproduces the semantics of the *update* operator for conditionals and loops. Note that E^{-1} is well defined since each location has only one corresponding declared variable. We are confident that even for further extensions including dynamically allocated locations, we should be able to find a corresponding shadow expression if there is an expression pointing to that location.

$$T[skip, pc] \mapsto skip \qquad T[c_1; \; c_2, pc] \mapsto T[c_1, pc]; \; T[c_2, pc]$$

$$T[a_1 = a_2, pc] \mapsto \begin{cases} \Lambda(a_1, 0) = \mathcal{L}_L(a_1) \sqcup \mathcal{L}_R(a_2) \sqcup pc; \\ \Lambda(a_1, k) = \Lambda(a_2, k); \forall k \in [1, \mathscr{D}(a_1)] \\ \Lambda(E^{-1}(l), 0) = \Lambda(E^{-1}(l), 0) \sqcup \mathcal{L}_L(a_1) \sqcup pc; \forall l \in S_P(a_1 = a_2) \\ a_1 = a_2; \end{cases}$$

$$T[if \; (a) \; c_1 \; else \; c_2, pc] \mapsto \begin{cases} pc' = \mathcal{L}_R(a) \sqcup pc; \\ if \; (a) \; \{ \\ \quad T[c_1, pc'] \\ \quad \Lambda(E^{-1}(l), 0) = \Lambda(E^{-1}(l), 0) \sqcup pc'; \forall l \in S_P(c_2) \\ \} \; else \; \{ \\ \quad T[c_2, pc']; \\ \quad \Lambda(E^{-1}(l), 0) = \Lambda(E^{-1}(l), 0) \sqcup pc'; \forall l \in S_P(c_1) \\ \} \end{cases}$$

$$T[while \; (a) \; c, pc] \mapsto \begin{cases} while \; (a) \; \{ \\ \quad pc' = \mathcal{L}_R(a) \sqcup pc; \\ \quad T[c, pc']; \\ \} \\ pc' = \mathcal{L}_R(a) \sqcup pc; \\ \Lambda(E^{-1}(l), 0) = \Lambda(E^{-1}(l), 0) \sqcup pc'; \forall l \in S_P(c) \end{cases}$$

Fig. 8. Program transformation semantics

For assignments $a_1 = a_2$, the program transformation propagates three security labels to the shadow expression of a_1 according the monitor semantics. Since assignments create new aliasing relations, transformation T also generates $\mathscr{D}(a_1)$ assignments to maintain the aliasing invariant stated in Lemma 1. Finally, T uses E^{-1} and Λ to find shadow variables corresponding to locations in $S_P(c)$ and taints them with the security label $\mathcal{L}_L(a_1) \sqcup pc$.

The transformed program $T(P)$ is behaviourally equivalent to the initial program P. Let $E|_{var(P)}$ (resp. $M|_{Loc(P)}$ and $\Gamma|_{Loc(P)}$) be the restriction of environment E (resp.

of memory M and Γ) to the set $Var(P)$ of initial variables (resp. to the set $Loc(P)$ of initial locations). More precisely, Theorem 2 states that for any terminating run, executions of P and $T(P)$ in equal input memories for initial locations $Loc(P)$ result in equal memories for those same locations. The proof by induction on instructions evaluation relies on the fact that program transformation T introduces only assignments handling shadow variables. Hence, those additional assignments do not modify neither values nor security labels associated to the set $Loc(P)$ of initial locations.

Theorem 2 (Initial semantics preservation). *For all c, E, M, Γ, pc, pc such that:*
$$E|_{Var(P)} \vdash c, M|_{Loc(P)}, \Gamma|_{Loc(P)}, \underline{pc} \Rightarrow M_1, \Gamma_1 \text{ and } E \vdash T[c, pc], \overline{M, \Gamma}, \underline{pc} \Rightarrow M_2, \Gamma_2.$$

Then, $M_2|_{Loc(P)} = M_1$ and $\Gamma_2|_{Loc(P)} = \Gamma_1$.

Theorem 3 proves the soundness of the transformation T with respect to the monitor semantics presented in Figure 5. Informally, the theorem supposes that values of shadow variables (resp. execution context variable pc) are initialized according to the initial security memory Γ (resp. execution context pc). Then after the execution of the transformed instructions, it states that the values of shadow variables capture the exact values of the output security memory.

Theorem 3 (Sound monitoring of information flows). *Let c, for all $E, M, \Gamma, M', \Gamma'$ such that $E \vdash T[c, pc], M, \Gamma, \underline{pc} \Rightarrow M', \Gamma'$.*

Let us define the predicate $\Upsilon(E, M, \Gamma) \triangleq$ for all $x \in Var(P)$, for all $k \in [0, \mathscr{D}(x)]$, $E \vdash *^k x, M \Leftarrow l_{xk}$ and $\Gamma(l_{xk}) = s_{xk} \implies E \vdash *^k \Lambda(x, k), M \Rightarrow s_{xk}$.

The following result holds: $\Upsilon(E, M, \Gamma)$ and $E \vdash pc, M \Rightarrow \underline{pc} \implies \Upsilon(E, M', \Gamma')$.

As the program transformation is sound with respect to our information flow monitor semantics, it is also sound wrt. TINI. Therefore, we can soundly reason about information flows through security labels defined by this program transformation. To our knowledge, that is the first proof of soundness for inlining information flow monitors handling pointers with aliasing. The proof, by induction on instructions evaluation $\Rightarrow$, heavily relies on the aliasing invariant stated in Lemma 1.

TINI verification. Figure 9 shows that the program transformation T can be used to verify TINI through both dynamic and static analysis. Assuming the implementation of security labels and their join operator, running the self-monitoring program $T(P)$ enforces TINI dynamically —actually, this is a hybrid approach since the monitor relies on a prior static analysis S_P— for single execution paths. This dynamic approach has the advantage of being permissive since it ignores possible unsecure paths that are not executed. It also enables dynamic loading of security policies [13], taking into account eventual updates. The transformation T also enables the verification of TINI by static analysis: for instance, off-the-shelf abstract interpretation tools can compute an over-approximation of $T(P)$ semantics for all execution paths, without implementing new abstract domains. While still being more permissive than traditional type systems, such an approach freezes the enforced security policy. Yet, it enhances our confidence in the analyzed program. It also completely lifts the burden of runtime overhead.

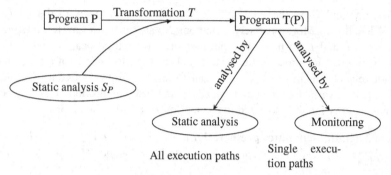

Fig. 9. Non-interference verification using the program transformation T

5   Related Work

Information flow monitors. Le Guernic et al. [7] formalize a sound flow-sensitive monitor for a simple imperative language with outputs. Le Guernic's monitor combines both static and dynamic analysis in order to enforce TINI. It is based on edit automata [14], which are monitors enforcing a security policy by modifying program actions, namely changing secret outputs to default values in Le Guernic's monitor. Extending our approach with outputs is straightforward. Le Guernic et al. suggest that their monitor can be implemented as a program transformation or a virtual machine (VM).

Russo and Sabelfeld [5] parameterize their hybrid monitor for a simple imperative language by different enforcement actions (default, failstop or suppress). They also prove the necessity to rely on static analysis to soundly monitor information flows while still being more permissive than Hunt-Sands-style [3] flow-sensitive type systems. Unlike monitors based on Russo and Sabelfeld's one, we use a big-step semantics. Hence, we neither need to maintain a stack of security labels for execution contexts, nor insert instructions to notify the monitor at the immediate postdominator of each conditional.

Moore and Chong [15] extend the VM-like monitor of Russo and Sabelfeld with dynamically allocated references, allowing different sound memory abstractions. In our semantics, we use the most precise instantiation of their memory abstraction where each concrete location correspond to one abstract location. While it is undecidable in the general case to determine which locations might be updated by an instruction, we argue that, for the sake of permissiveness, it is necessary to be as precise as possible at least for the set of finite statically allocated locations.

Austin and Flanagan [11] investigate a purely dynamic monitor for a λ-calculus language with references. Their monitor supports a limited flow-sensitivity since it implements a conservative no-sensitive upgrade policy; the monitor stops the execution when assigning a public variable in a secret context. Thus, their monitor is proven sound without having to rely on static analyses. Austin and Flanagan [16] also enhance their monitor by a permissive-upgrade approach; their monitor labels public data that is assigned in secret contexts as partially leaked, then soundly forbid branching on those data. Our monitor is fully flow-sensitive, hence more permissive.

Sound inlining. Chudnov and Naumann [17] design a sound monitor inlining approach based on Russo and Sabelfeld's monitor. As they aim at monitoring information flows for Javascript, they argue that VM monitors are impractical because of just-in-time compilation. Their language supports output instructions but no references. We also believe that inlining is necessary when the language is compiled rather than interpreted.

Magazinius et al. [18] investigate sound inlining of security monitors for an imperative language supporting dynamic code evaluation but no references. Their monitor is purely dynamic since it uses a no-sensitive upgrade policy as in Austin and Flanagan [11]. Our program transformation approach can also be applied for such a policy in order to soundly monitor information flows for richer languages, including pointers.

6   Conclusion and Future Work

We have formalized a sound flow-sensitive information flow monitor handling pointers and aliasing. We have also inlined our monitor through a program transformation proven sound with respect to our monitor semantics, hence with TINI. Our program transformation enables permissive yet sound enforcement of TINI by both dynamic and static analyses. Our monitor semantics ignores diverging runs since it is inspired by a simple version of the Clight big-step semantics stripped of coinduction [8]. As pointed by Le Guernic [7], this is not problematic when dealing with TINI because we ignore non-termination covert channels.

As we aim to support a large subset of the C language, we plan on extending both the semantics and the program transformation with richer C constructs. We are currently implementing our program transformation as a Frama-C plug-in, an open-source tool for modular analysis of C programs [19]. Frama-C enables the design of powerful analyses relying on the collaboration of off-the-shelf plug-ins. We are going to rely on Value Analysis [20], an abstract interpretation plug-in of Frama-C, in order to compute a correct approximation $S_P(c)$, of the set of locations that might be updated by an instruction c. Frama-C also supports ACSL [21], a formal specification language for C programs. This language can allow us to handle declassification annotations.

Acknowledgement.   We would like to thank Sébastien Bardin for his valuable comments.

References

1. Denning, D., Denning, P.: Certification of Programs for Secure Information Flow. Communications of the ACM 20(7), 504–513 (1977)
2. Goguen, J., Meseguer, J.: Security Policies and Security Models. In: IEEE Symposium on Research in Security and Privacy (1982)
3. Volpano, D., Irvine, C., Smith, G.: A Sound Type System for Secure Flow Analysis. Journal in Computer Security 4(2-3), 167–187 (1996)
4. Askarov, A., Hunt, S., Sabelfeld, A., Sands, D.: Termination-Insensitive Noninterference Leaks More Than Just a Bit. In: Jajodia, S., Lopez, J. (eds.) ESORICS 2008. LNCS, vol. 5283, pp. 333–348. Springer, Heidelberg (2008)

 5. Russo, A., Sabelfeld, A.: Dynamic vs. Static Flow-Sensitive Security Analysis. In: Computer Security Foundations Symposium, pp. 186–199. IEEE (2010)
 6. Hunt, S., Sands, D.: On Flow-Sensitive Security Types. In: Conference Record of the 33rd ACM SIGPLAN-SIGACT Symposium on Principles of Programming Languages, vol. 41, pp. 79–90. ACM (2006)
 7. Le Guernic, G., Banerjee, A., Jensen, T., Schmidt, D.A.: Automata-Based Confidentiality Monitoring. In: Okada, M., Satoh, I. (eds.) ASIAN 2006. LNCS, vol. 4435, pp. 75–89. Springer, Heidelberg (2008)
 8. Blazy, S., Leroy, X.: Mechanized Semantics for the Clight Subset of the C Language. Journal of Automated Reasoning 43(3), 263–288 (2009)
 9. Leroy, X.: Formal Verification of a Realistic Compiler. Communications of the ACM 52(7), 107–115 (2009)
10. Sabelfeld, A., Myers, A.: Language-Based Information-Flow Security. IEEE Journal on Selected Areas in Communications 21(1), 5–19 (2003)
11. Austin, T., Flanagan, C.: Efficient Purely-Dynamic Information Flow Analysis. ACM Sigplan Notices 44(8), 20–31 (2009)
12. Assaf, M., Signoles, J., Tronel, F., Totel, E.: Program Transformation for Non-interference Verification on Programs with Pointers. Research report RR-8284, INRIA (April 2013), http://hal.inria.fr/hal-00814671
13. Chandra, D., Franz, M.: Fine-Grained Information Flow Analysis and Enforcement in a Java Virtual Machine. In: Twenty-Third Annual Computer Security Applications Conference, ACSAC 2007, pp. 463–475. IEEE (2007)
14. Ligatti, J., Bauer, L., Walker, D.: Edit Automata: Enforcement Mechanisms for Run-time Security Policies. International Journal of Information Security 4(1), 2–16 (2005)
15. Moore, S., Chong, S.: Static Analysis for Efficient Hybrid Information-Flow Control. In: 2011 IEEE 24th Computer Security Foundations Symposium (CSF), pp. 146–160. IEEE (2011)
16. Austin, T.H., Flanagan, C.: Permissive Dynamic Information Flow Analysis. In: PLAS 2010: Proceedings of the 5th ACM SIGPLAN Workshop on Programming Languages and Analysis for Security, pp. 1–12. ACM (2010)
17. Chudnov, A., Naumann, D.: Information Flow Monitor Inlining. In: 2010 23rd IEEE Computer Security Foundations Symposium (CSF), pp. 200–214. IEEE (2010)
18. Magazinius, J., Russo, A., Sabelfeld, A.: On-the-fly Inlining of Dynamic Security Monitors. Computers & Security (2011)
19. Cuoq, P., Kirchner, F., Kosmatov, N., Prevosto, V., Signoles, J., Yakobowski, B.: Frama-C: A Program Analysis Perspective. In: Eleftherakis, G., Hinchey, M., Holcombe, M. (eds.) SEFM 2012. LNCS, vol. 7504, pp. 233–247. Springer, Heidelberg (2012)
20. Cuoq, P., Prevosto, V., Yakobowski, B.: Frama-C's Value Analysis Plug-in (September 2012), http://frama-c.com/download/frama-c-value-analysis.pdf
21. Baudin, P., Filliâtre, J.C., Hubert, T., Marché, C., Monate, B., Moy, Y., Prevosto, V.: ACSL: ANSI/ISO C Specification Language (September 2012), http://frama-c.cea.fr/acsl.html

A Viable System Model for Information Security Governance: Establishing a Baseline of the Current Information Security Operations System

Ezzat Alqurashi*, Gary Wills, and Lester Gilbert

Electronics and Computer Science, University of Southampton, United Kingdom
{eha1r10,gbw,L.H.Gilbert}@soton.ac.uk

Abstract. The academic literature offers many different frameworks and models of Information Security Governance (ISG). Considerable advancements have been made in identifying the components and principles of ISG. However, the current research has not identified the viability principles and components of ISG that ensure business continuity. This paper proposes a systemic model of ISG using the principles and systems of cybernetics as embodied in Stafford Beer's Viable System Model (VSM). It also establishes a baseline of the current information security operations system by adopting and simulating the BS ISO/IEC 27035 and shows the results of the simulation. Adopting the proposed viable system model of information security governance helps organizations not only in ensuring the effectiveness of internal controls but also in ensuring business continuity.

Keywords: information security governance, viable system model, business continuity, BS ISO/IEC 27035.

1 Introduction

Information security has evolved in step with the increasing complexity of its diverse environments. During the last decade, Information Security Governance (ISG) has emerged as a new information security discipline in response to new laws and regulations aiming to counter evolving security challenges (Von Solms, 2006). Boards of directors and executive management have become accountable for the effectiveness of the internal controls of their corporation's information security. Adopting a framework is considered an essential starting point in securing information systems, complying with regulations, and increasing the efficiency of business processes (Entrust, 2004). Therefore, corporations and organizations need a framework to govern their information security (Corporate Governance Task Force, 2004; Entrust, 2004; Posthumus & von Solms, 2004).

Against this background, a number of researchers and organizations have proposed various ISG frameworks and models. The Corporate Governance Task Force (2004) has provided guidance in the development and implementation of an organizational ISG structure including recommendations for the responsibilities of members of

L.J. Janczewski, H.B. Wolfe, and S. Shenoi (Eds.): SEC 2013, IFIP AICT 405, pp. 245–256, 2013.

organizations. Posthumus and Von Solms (2004) have defined two structure levels—information security governance and information security management—for dealing with business information risk at a corporate governance level. Von Solms and von Solms (2006) have proposed an ISG model based on the principle of Direct-Control Cycle over three levels of structure: governance, management, and operation. The Information Technology Governance Institute (ITGI, 2006) has provided guidance for boards of directors and executives on the development and maintenance of information security programs. Da Veiga and Eloff (2007) have identified a list of information security components mapped to three levels of structure: strategic, managerial and operational, and technical in order to approach ISG through a holistic perspective. Recently, Ohki et al. (2009) have identified functions and interfaces of ISG between stakeholders, auditors, executives, and managers.

Vinnakota (2011) stated that there is a growing emphasis on the need for systemic models of ISG to deal with the dynamic nature of today's changes and organizations' complexity. The Viable System Model (VSM) provides a promising route for exploration to counter the increasing level of threats and to meet the need for rapid response at the organizational level (Gokhale, 2002). Although much work has been done to date, more studies need to be conducted to define the viability components of the ISG.

The purpose of this paper is to present a VSM of ISG (VSMISG) to address the current shortcomings. In more detail, in this paper we extend the state of the art in the following ways. 1) We provide viability principles to ISG: autonomy, feedback, recursion, requisite variety, and viability. 2) We suggest systems to ISG: information security operations, coordination, control and compliance monitoring, planning, and policy. 3) We introduce an ISG model based on the redefined principles and suggested systems. 4) We establish a baseline of the current information security operations system.

The rest of this paper is organized as follows. In section 2 we present a background on ISG frameworks and models. In section 3 we describe the VSM. Section 4 contains a description of our model, while in section 5 we describe the modeling and simulation process. In section 6 we define the research method, in section 7 we show the simulation results, and then we conclude in section 8.

2   Information Security Governance: Frameworks and Models

Before we proceed to proposing our VSMISG, we give a brief description of the current ISG frameworks and models.

2.1   ISG Framework by the CGTF

The Corporate Governance Task Force (CGTF) was formed in 2003 to develop a governance framework to drive implementation of effective information security programs. It defined a framework which covers the following areas:

- The roles and responsibilities of the board of directors/trustees
- The roles and responsibilities of the senior executives
- The roles and responsibilities of the executive team members
- The roles and responsibilities of senior managers
- Responsibilities of all employees and users
- Organizational unit security program
- Organizational unit reporting
- Information security program evaluation.

The framework provides recommendations on members' roles and responsibilities in all organizational levels. It specifies that every organizational unit should develop and evaluate its own security program and report its effectiveness to top management (Corporate Governance Task Force, 2004).

2.2 Governance and Management Strategy for Dealing with Business Information Risks

This framework is composed of two levels: ISG and Information Security Management (ISM). The ISG side, including the board of directors and executive management, directs the organization by formulating the strategy, mission, vision, and policy of information security. It controls the information security efforts by requiring periodic reports from various department heads to show the effectiveness of their security plans. The ISM side is concerned with how to meet the security requirements with assistance of conventional security codes of practice such as BS 7799 (1999). The framework identifies internal and external factors that may have impacts on information security such as business issues, IT infrastructure, standards, best practices and legal and regulatory matters (Posthumus & Von Solms, 2004).

2.3 Guidance for Boards of Directors and Executive Management

The Information Technology Governance Institute (ITGI, 2006) proposed a framework to guide the development and maintenance of a comprehensive information security program. It identified eight components for achieving effective ISG:

1. Organizational security structure
2. Business and IT security strategy
3. Risk management methodology
4. Information value security strategy
5. Security policies
6. Security standards
7. Monitoring processes
8. Continuous evaluation process.

2.4   ISG Framework Based on Direct-Control Cycle

This is a model based on two principles required for governing information security. The first principle identifies three actions—direct, execute, and control—while the second principle identifies three management levels: strategic, tactical, and operational. The strategic level starts the direct process by defining the importance of protecting information assets in its vision. The tactical level should align to the strategic vision of information security by formulating appropriate information security policies, organization standards, and procedures that meet that vision. The operational level defines administrative guidelines and procedures.

The control process depends on the characteristic of "measurability": that is, any statement of information security policies or strategic directives should not be formulated unless it is measurable. The operational level collects measurement data electronically from log files of various resources, and then reports them to the tactical level. Other data that cannot be collected electronically are collected through questionnaires, interviews, and inspections. The tactical level then integrates all the received data to determine the level of compliance against the defined policies, standards, and procedures. Then, the strategic level receives the compliance reports to relevant directives that need to reflect relevant risk situations (Von Solms & Von Solms, 2006).

2.5   ISG Framework Based on a Holistic Perspective

This framework is based on evaluation of four approaches in order to define a holistic perspective toward ISG. The framework is composed of the common components identified from these approaches. The identified components are arranged into six categorizations. The framework consists of three levels of management: strategic, managerial and operational, and technical. Every level consists of one or more of the six categorizations. It includes change management as it influences all the identified components in the framework that it needs to consider when implementing any of these components (da Veiga & Eloff, 2007).

2.6   ISG Framework Based on Functions and Interfaces

This framework identifies five ISG functions: direct, monitor, evaluate, report, and oversee. It also identifies four interfaces between stakeholders, auditors, executives, and managers. Executives perform the first four functions and the auditors perform the overseeing. Executives direct the management of information security, monitor the information security management practice and security incidents, evaluate results against defined goals, and report security issues and activities to stakeholders. Auditors oversee executives' information security related activities (Ohki, Harada, Kawaguchi, Shiozaki, & Kagaya, 2009).

3   The Viable System Model (VSM)

Stafford Beer introduced the VSM as a blueprint for designing the communication and control aspects of viable systems. Beer described the VSM in his book *Brain of the Firm* (1972), and then developed it in the books *The Heart of Enterprise* (1979) and *Diagnosing the System for Organizations* (1985). The VSM is a model for organizational structure that is based on the structure of the human nervous system (Beer, 1981).

Beer claimed that an organization can be viable if it is constructed around five main management systems: operations, coordination, control, planning (intelligence), and policy. He labeled these systems from 1 to 5 respectively. Beer defined a function of the control system to monitor the performance of the operations system known as compliance monitoring. The systems are interconnected together by communication channels or information flows. In addition, Beer argued that an organization can be viable if it is based on 5 principles: autonomy, direct feedback, recursion, requisite variety, and viability. These are described in the next section.

4   The Viable System Model of Information Security Governance (VSMISG)

In this section we propose a Viable System Model for ISG (VSMISG) based on the Viable System Model. First, we present the principles followed by the systems of the VSMISG.

4.1   The Principles

The VSMISG is based on five principles: autonomy, feedback, recursion, requisite variety, and viability of the VSM. We define these principles in the following sections (Beer, 1981; Lewis, 1997; Schwaninger, 2006).

Autonomy
The adaptation to dynamic changes in diverse information security environments necessitates that organizations must be autonomous. This means that individuals need to possess the authority and the knowledge to be able to make necessary immediate actions. Autonomy does not mean separation but the freedom to act within a clear accountability. Autonomous information security operations deploy resources with minimal reference to senior managers, enabling the quick adaptation to dynamic changes in related environments. The large ellipse to the left in Fig. 1 represents the environment in which the organization is embedded. The operations system has its own environment within the organizational environment. In fact, every unit in the operations system has its own environment that it needs to deal with in the operations environment.

Direct Feedback

Information security events are communicated between the information security systems through reliable communication channels. The communication channels connect all the information security systems and functions, as well as connect corporations or organizations with their diverse information security environments. For instance, when the information security operations system (S1) can not cope with the changes in its related environments, it will seek the intervention of the information security control system (S3) through the communication channels between them. If no proper response is received within a defined timeframe, then S1 will directly escalate the situation (direct feedback) to the information security policy system (S5) to immediately intervene through exceptionally designed communication channels known as algedonic channels which are indicated by red lines in Fig. 1. The system (S5) must eventually receive the urgent information and "alarm signals" from the lower systems (Skyttner, 2005). The presence of effective communication channels and the proper design of information flow and reliable information systems are essential elements behind the feedback principle.

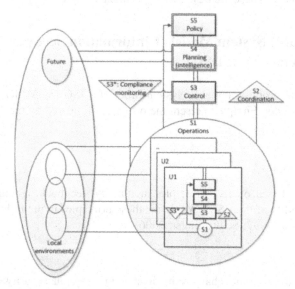

Fig. 1. The Viable System Model for Information Security Governance (VSMISG)

Recursion

Viable systems are recursive; that is, a viable system contains and is contained in a viable system (Beer, 1979). For example, the information security operations system and its units are viable systems in their own right, and the operations system is embedded within an organization which is also a viable system. Furthermore, the organization is embedded within an industry which is also a viable system. The recursion principle is depicted in Fig. 1 by the viable systems inside the units (U1, U2, etc.) which are contained in the viable operations system. The recursion principle enables organizations to cope with complexity within their diverse information security environments by creating as many levels of controlling systems as required.

Requisite Variety
In order for system S1 to cope with the dynamic changes in its environments, it must possess the necessary capabilities to control the changes in these environments. And in order for S3 to absorb the changes of S1, it must be able to contain its changes. Also, system S4 must possess the necessary capabilities to absorb the strategic changes in its environment depicted by the large ellipse in Fig. 1. The capabilities of the controlling system must absorb the uncertainties of the controlled system (Skyttner, 2005) to maintain the balance of the whole system.

Viability
A viable system is defined as one that is able to maintain a separate existence by surviving on its own (Beer, 1979). However, "survival" should not be understood as being able to merely exist. Coping with dynamic changes in diverse information security environments can only be maintained by learning, adapting, and growing (Beer, 1984). It is a key principle for arranging and managing the structure of organizational systems in a way that they merge with defined systems and interrelationships. The clear definitions of the systems, their internal sub-systems, and their intra- and interrelationships are essential to the continuity of business systems.

4.2   The Systems

The VSMISG consists of five systems and one function which are grouped into three groups as follows:

Information Security: Operations System (S1) and Coordination System (S2)
The information security operations system (S1) is where the organization's works to protect its information. The system continuously deals with and controls dynamic changes in various information security environments. To be able to cope with these changes, it needs to make decisions without delay. The operations system (S1) must depend on other systems to keep decisions to a minimum. It must be autonomous to effectively respond and control its relevant environments. Being autonomous does not mean complete separation from the organizational system; rather, it is within an accountability framework. The information security coordination system (S2) coordinates the Units (U1, U2, etc.) of S1 to resolve possible conflicts and ensure stability and harmony. It dampens uncontrolled oscillations between the units of S1. The coordination system (S2) consists of the information security systems necessary for decentralized decision making (Skyttner, 2005) that the autonomy of S1 is based on.

Information Security: Control System (S3) and Compliance Monitoring Function (S3*)
The information security operations system (S1) includes one or more specialized units (Fig. 1) that deal with and control the dynamic changes in its information security environments. To do that, the specialized units require various resources.

Sometimes these requirements conflict. The information security control system (S3) provides the required resources in a way that enables the units of S1 to accomplish their objectives. S3 is concerned with the "inside and now" world of corporations and organizations. It regulates the current information security activities and requirements of S1 for consistence with defined future requirements. S3 ensures through the compliance monitoring (S3*) function that current information security activities of S1 comply with defined information security policies and that current activities of S2 ensure a proper coordination between the units of S1.

Information Security: Planning (Intelligence) System (S4) and Policy System (S5)
The information security planning (intelligence) system (S4), which represents the ISG part in organizations, is responsible for the research and development of a strategic information security plan. Various information security environments such as risks, competition, clients, regulations, standards, and partners exist around the boundary of the organization system. S4 needs to interact with and adapt to the changes in these environments. It needs to direct the system toward achieving the goals of information security and to securely position the corporate system. S4 collects the necessary information about relevant strategic environments and analyzes them to formulate a suitable information security plan with defined requirements. The control system (S3) must implement this plan and maintain cohesion inside the corporate or organizational system. S4 is concerned with the "outside and future" world of the corporate system. It models and monitors the system and relevant strategic environments and makes predictions on future trends of information security environments.

The information security policy system (S5) sets the information security policy and defines the information security identity of the corporate or organizational system which is based on defined purposes. S5 establishes the basis for the development of information security guidelines, and makes final decisions regarding long-term information security directions.

5   Modeling and Simulation

This section introduces the information security operations system model that is adopted in this research for establishing the baseline. The International Organization for Standardization (ISO) and the International Electrotechnical Commission (IEC) published an information security incident management model embodied in BS ISO/IEC 27035 (2011). The standard is intended to simulate information security incident management for large and medium-sized organizations. It provides guidance on managing information security incidents and vulnerabilities. The operational side of the model, which is the focus of our study, is composed of three phases: detection and reporting, assessment and decision, and response. The activities of the model are grouped under these phases, described, and simulated below.

Detection and Reporting

1. Detection: events are detected by detection systems or by users.
2. Reporting: events are reported by reporting systems or by users.

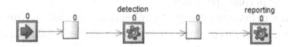

Fig. 2. Detection and reporting phase simulation

In Figs. 2, 3, and 4, the squares with green arrows represent input entry points, the gray arrows represent routing, the white squares represent queues (storage), the squares with pinions represent activities, and the squares with check signs represent the end of work.

Assessment and Decision

1. Information collection by a Point of Contact (PoC): the (PoC) collects the required information related to a reported information security event.
2. PoC assessment: the PoC assesses the event to decide whether it is a false positive or a possible incident.
3. Information collection by Information Security Incident Response Team (ISIRT): the ISIRT collects the required information related to a possible incident received from the PoC. It also collects reports of information security incidents and alarms of abnormality or anomaly.
4. ISIRT assessment: the ISIRT assesses possible incidents, reports of incidents, and alarms to decide if they are false positives or confirmed incidents.

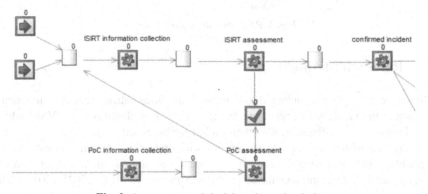

Fig. 3. Assessment and decision phase simulation

Response

1. Immediate response: the ISIRT provides an immediate response to a confirmed incident which could include the activation of recovery procedures.

2. Incident categorization and severity classification: mapping an information security incident into relevant categorizations and determining the severity of the incident to the business.
3. Later response: other related effects to operations systems may need further responses to restore normal operations.
4. Digital evidence collection: The ISIRT collects digital evidence for information security forensic analysis to manage information security incident and for legal challenges.
5. Communication: the ISIRT communicates with stakeholders and the press to inform them about a confirmed incident.
6. Responses to crisis situation: activated when the ISIRT determines an information security incident is not under control and requires escalation to crisis situation.

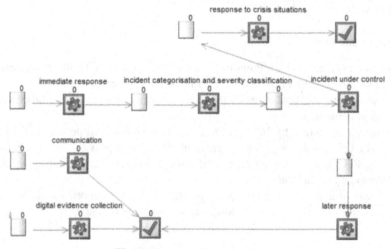

Fig. 4. Response phase simulation

6   Research Method

A literature review was conducted to determine the information security components that ensure the viability of organizations. This has led to identifying the VSM which was adopted to be the theoretical background of the proposed model.

A baseline of the current information security operations system was established by adopting and simulating the current state of the operational side of the information security incident management model embodied in BS ISO/IEC 27035 (2011). The data used in the simulation came from two sources. The first source was from a case study undertaken by HP Laboratories (2012) and from an information security expert using a questionnaire. The simulation software package employed in this study is the discrete event simulator SIMUL8, which allows the creation of a visual model of the system under study by directly drawing animated objects on the display.

All the entry inputs, queues, routing arrows, activities, and outputs of the model were visualized by using the objects of the SIMUL8. The number of exponential distributed inputs that were entered into the simulation (detected) is 1000 cases, including information security events, alarms, and reports at intervals of 19.2 (m), 68.55 (m), and 60 (m) respectively. The Poisson distribution was used for the queuing time of the model's activities. It is assumed that the Poisson distribution is the proper distribution used to describe random arrival rates over a period of time for models based on queuing theory (Black, 2009).

7   Results

The purpose of this section is to report the simulation parameters which constitute the baseline of the current information security operations system. The simulation parameters are shown in Table 1.

Table 1. The simulation parameters

No.	Activity	Distribution type	Expected average queuing time (m)	Actual average queuing time (m)	Std. Dev.
1.	Reporting		11	8	13
2.	PoC information collection		506	505	226
3.	PoC assessment		566	568	228
4.	ISIRT information collection		1282	1277	609
5.	ISIRT assessment		578	578	226
6.	Immediate response	Poisson	1111	1120	476
7.	Communication		280	286	133
8.	Digital evidence collection		278	284	128
9.	Incident categorization and severity classification		294	300	120
10.	Later response		1502	1501	480
11.	Response to crisis situation		6643	6666	3717

Table 1 shows the activities of the simulation model, the statistical distribution of queuing time, the expected and actual average queuing time, and the standard deviation. The detection activity was not listed in the table since it defines the rate of inputs entered into the simulation; hence one of the input's entry points was used for this purpose. The response to crisis situation activity shows the longest queuing time. This is because it includes the time of reporting and remediating a crisis situation as defined by HP Laboratories (2012).

8   Conclusion

The adoption of the VSM from the cybernetics literature provides the principles and systems of viability to ISG. We conducted a simulation to establish a baseline of the current information security operations system as defined in BS ISO/IEC 27035 (2011). The results reported are comparable to those defined in the HP case study.

The current operations system is the only VSMISG component that the established baseline represents. Our future work will focus on demonstrating the importance of the direct feedback principle by simulating the information security policy system and connecting it to the current operations system through the direct feedback channels.

References

1. Beer, S.: Brain of the Firm, 2nd edn. Wiley, Chichester (1981)
2. Beer, S.: The viable system model: its provenance, development, metho-dology and pathology. Journal of the Operational Research Society 35(1), 7–25 (1984),
   http://www.jstor.org/stable/2581927 (retrieved)
3. Beer, S.: The Heart of Enterprise. Classic Beer Series, p. 596. Wiley (1979)
4. Black, K.: Business Statistics: Contemporary Decision Making, p. 836. John Wiley & Sons (2009),   http://books.google.com/books?id=KQ25WExx5usC&pgis=1 (retrieved)
5. BS ISO/IEC 27035, BSI Standards Publication Information technology — Security techniques — Information security incident management (2011)
6. Corporate Governance Task Force, Information security governance: a call to action. National Cyber Security Summit Task Force 1(3) (2004)
7. da Veiga, A., Eloff, J.: An information security governance framework. Information Systems Management 24(4), 361–372 (2007)
8. Entrust, Information Security Governance (ISG): An Essential Element of Corporate Governance (April 2004)
9. Gokhale, G.B.: Organisational Information Security: A Viable System Perspective. Information Security & Threats System 17799 (2002)
10. HP Laboratories (2012), Security Analytics: Risk Analysis for an Organisation's Incident Management Process,
    http://www.hpl.hp.com/techreports/2012/HPL-2012-206.html (retrieved)
11. ITGI, Information security governance: guidance for boards of directors and executive management. Corporate Governance. Isaca (2006)
12. Lewis, G.: A cybernetic view of environmental management: The impli-cations for business organizations. Business Strategy and the Environment 6, 264–275 (1997)
13. Ohki, E., Harada, Y., Kawaguchi, S., Shiozaki, T., Kagaya, T.: Infor-mation security governance framework. In: Proceedings of the First ACM Workshop on Information Security Governance - WISG 2009, vol. 1 (2009)
14. Posthumus, S., Von Solms, R.: A framework for the governance of information security. Computers & Security 23(8), 638–646 (2004)
15. Schwaninger, M.: Theories of viability: a comparison. Systems Research and Behavioral Science 347, 337–347 (2006)
16. Skyttner, L.: General systems theory: problems, perspectives, practice (2005)
17. Vinnakota, T.: Systems approach to Information Security Governance: An imperative need for sustainability of enterprises. In: 2011 Annual IEEE India Conference, pp. 1–8 (2011), doi:10.1109/INDCON.2011.6139620
18. Von Solms: Information Security – The Fourth Wave. Computers & Security 25(3), 165–168 (2006)
19. Von Solms, R., Von Solms, S.: Information security governance: A model based on the direct-control cycle. Computers & Security 25(6), 408–412 (2006)

A Review of the Theory of Planned Behaviour in the Context of Information Security Policy Compliance

Teodor Sommestad and Jonas Hallberg

Swedish Defence Research Agency
Olaus Magnus väg 42, Linköping, Sweden
{Teodor.Sommestad,Jonas.Hallberg}@foi.se

Abstract. The behaviour of employees influences information security in virtually all organisations. To inform the employees regarding what constitutes desirable behaviour, an information security policy can be formulated and communicated. However, not all employees comply with the information security policy. This paper reviews and synthesises 16 studies related to the theory of planned behaviour. The objective is to investigate 1) to what extent the theory explains information security policy compliance and violation and 2) whether reasonable explanations can be found when the results of the studies diverge. It can be concluded that the theory explains information security policy compliance and violation approximately as well as it explains other behaviours. Some potential explanations can be found for why the results of the identified studies diverge. However, many of the differences in results are left unexplained.

Keywords: information security, security policy, security rule, policy compliance, policy violation, computer misuse, theory of planned behavior.

1   Introduction

In virtually all organisations, the behaviour of the employees significantly influences information security. A common practice, which is intended to lower the information security risk, is to establish an information security policy. Information security policies describe, for instance, the consequences of security policy violation, the acceptable use of computer resources, the responsibilities regarding information security, and the type of training that employees should have. As described in [1], the objective of an information security policy is "to provide management direction and support for information security". Thus, one of the central themes of an information security policy is to describe suitable and unsuitable behaviours. Assuming an adequate information security policy, it follows that compliance with the policy is desirable. Unfortunately, not all employees comply with the information security policy.

A meta-analysis of different variables' influence on information security policy compliance and violation can be found in [2]. This paper extends the results in [2] with the results from additional studies and a deeper analysis of those parts that are related to the *theory of planned behaviour* (TPB) [3]. The TPB is one of the most well

L.J. Janczewski, H.B. Wolfe, and S. Shenoi (Eds.): SEC 2013, IFIP AICT 405, pp. 257–271, 2013.

established theories in the behavioural sciences, and the relationships described in the TPB are among the most frequently tested in models of information security policy compliance and violation behaviour. Although several prediction models for information security policy compliance and violation share theory with the TPB, there have been few attempts to test the TPB on its own in the information security context. In most studies that involve variables and relationships drawn from the TPB, the tested model includes variables from several theories. For instance, the variables from the TPB are combined with the variables from protection motivation theory in the model used by Ifinedo [4].

In this paper, we try to assemble the pieces and cues from previous work related to (but not necessarily exclusively addressing) the TPB in the context of information security policy compliance and violation. Two research questions are investigated:

1. How well does the TPB explain information security policy compliance and violation?
2. When divergent results are reported, can a reasonable explanation be made?

The outline is as follows. In section 2, the TPB is briefly described. In section 3, the review method is presented. In section 4, the synthesis of the extracted results is presented and the research questions are addressed. In section 5, the reliability of the answers to the research questions and their implications for practitioners and researchers are discussed. In section 5, the results are discussed and recommendations for practitioners and future research are provided. The paper is concluded in section 6.

2   The Theory of Planned Behaviour

The TPB [3] and its predecessor, the theory of reasoned action [5], has attracted considerable attention within the behavioural research community. An indicator of its popularity is the number of citations made to the original article (i.e., [3]) for the TPB (more than 23,000 citations in Google Scholar as of January 2013). The core variables and relationships of the TPB are outlined in Figure 1.

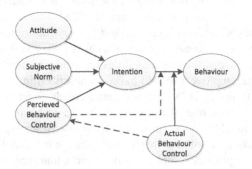

Fig. 1. The theory of planned behaviour (adapted from [6])

According to the theory, behaviour is influenced by intentions related to the behaviour and by actual behaviour control, which moderates the effect of intentions on behaviour. Although actual behaviour control is what really moderates the effect of intentions, most applications use perceived behaviour control (PBC) as a proxy because of the difficulties associated with measuring actual behaviour control. The use of PBC as a proxy is advocated by Ajzen [3], one of the originators of the TPB.

The TPB states that intentions (INT) are influenced by attitude (ATT), subjective norms (SN), and perceived behaviour control (PBC). The influences are assumed to be linear, i.e., the effects can be modelled using additive models. Whereas the theory claims that these three constructs are sufficient to explain the intentions concerning a behaviour in question, there is no universal ordering of their importance. On the contrary, the relative importance of the constructs differs among populations and behaviours. For instance, for behaviours for which there is complete volitional control, perceived behaviour control is of little value because it is equal for all respondents [3].

ATT, SN, and PBC are the results of the beliefs of the individual in question and the strength of these beliefs. ATT is determined by behavioural beliefs, SN is determined by normative beliefs, and PBC is determined by control beliefs. The theory describes how the assessments of the underlying beliefs should be aggregated into ATT, SN, and PBC. However, in studies concerning predicting intentions and behaviours (and not with explaining the underlying beliefs that form them), these three constructs are often assessed directly.

Through the large number of applications, tests, and reviews of the TPB, a considerable amount of knowledge concerning the theory in general has been accumulated. Fishbein and Ajzen [6] and Ajzen [7] discuss caveats, extensions, and competing theories and contest the relevance and implications of many of the findings. For example, Fishbein and Ajzen [6] think that the reason that *self-identity* predicts *intentions* is that the questions that measure *self-identity* are in fact questions regarding *intentions*, and Fishbein and Ajzen [6] find little difference between the constructs PBC and *self-efficacy*.

3   The Theory of Planned Behaviour and Studies Regarding Information Security Policy Compliance and Violation

As noted in the introduction, the TPB has been applied in several studies of compliance and direct incompliance with information security policies. The following steps were performed to answer the two research questions: 1) identify studies related to the TPB and information security policy compliance and violation, 2) extract data from the studies and synthesise the results, and 3) identify and test possible explanations for divergent results.

3.1   Studies Included

The aim of this review is to include all quantitative studies of security policy compliance and violation that investigate variable relationships described by the TPB. This systematic review based its search process on the search process performed (and described) in [2]. The systematic review of [2] surveyed quantitative peer-reviewed research regarding security policy compliance and violation published until early 2012. It used structured phrases in Scopus, Inspec, and Complendex, which were complemented with manual searches on the Internet and in databases and review of citations made in the identified studies. The structured search phrases yielded 461 publications, manual searches yielded 6 publications, and reviews of citations yielded 5 publications. These results were filtered by four reviewers to identify the studies that met the well-defined inclusion criteria; i.e., they should (1) explicitly study security policy compliance behaviour, (2) present quantitative results, and (3) be peer-reviewed. The four reviewers found 29 studies that satisfied these criteria [2].

Of the 29 studies included in [2], 14 studies included relationships associated with the TPB and were therefore included in this review. The authors of this paper also reiterated the search procedure performed in [2] during January 2013 to identify recent contributions related to the TPB and security policy compliance and violation. Two additional studies ([8] and [9, 10]) were found from the structured search queries. Table 1 includes information about the consequence studied (Compliance or Violation), the TPB variables included, other variables included, and the sample size (N).

3.2   Data Extraction and Synthesis of Results

Only one of the identified studies covered all the relationships described by the TPB, and only eight studies included all the antecedents of intentions. The models used in 16 studies are thus incomplete with respect to the TPB. The aim is to synthesise the results of the studies to answer the two research questions based on approximations of the overall effectiveness of the TPB. It should be noted that although the variable *descriptive norm* is currently included in SN of the TPB [6], it is treated as an external variable in our analysis to allow straightforward synthesis and comparison among the studies (only one study, [12], includes the variable descriptive norm).

Variables used as dependent and independent variables must share similar definitions and measurements scales for a synthesised result to be meaningful. The authors reviewed the measurement scales used in the different studies to assess their similarity. For the 16 studies, the scales are judged sufficiently similar to motivate a synthesis, although differences do exist. The possible influence of differences in definitions on measurement scales are addressed as part of the answer to research question 2, whether reasonable explanations for divergent results can be determined.

A common and practical effect size to use when results of multiple studies are synthesised is the Pearson correlation between variables. If correlation coefficients were missing in the papers, the authors were contacted and the coefficients or the raw data of the study were requested. Seppo Pahnila kindly provided us with additional data from [11] and explained the dependencies between the studies reported in [15] and [11]. Unfortunately, none of the other authors contacted were able to complement their results with correlation coefficients because they did not retain the data.

Table 1. Studies and the variables used in their models

Reference	Consequence	Year of publication	Antecedents of intention			Antecedents of behaviour		Other antecedents included in the model	N
			ATT	SN	PBC	INT	PBC		
[9, 10]	C	2012	•	•	•	•	•	none	106
[11]	C	2010	•	•	•	•	•	response efficacy, visibility, threat appraisal, deterrences, rewards	904 to 908
[12]	C	2009	•	•	•			descriptive norm, organisational commitment, punishment severity, punishment certainty	312
[13]	C	2010	•	•	•			None	464
[14]	V	2007	•	•	•			None	113
[15]	C	2007	•	•	•			habits, sanctions, information quality, rewards	240
[16]	C	2009	•	•	•			perceived security protection mechanism	176
[4]	C	2012	•	•	•			perceived vulnerability, perceived severity, response efficacy, response cost	124
[8]	C	2012	•	•	•			none	148
[17]	V	2011	•	•				identity match	306
[18]	C	2010	•	•				detection probability, sanction severity, security risk, perceived benefits	246
[19]	C	2010	•					none	275
[20]	C	2010			•			vulnerability, perceived severity, rewards, response efficacy, response cost	210
[21]	V	2004				•		self-defence intention	162
[22]	C	2005					•	perceptions of information security climate	104
[23]	C	2011					•	deterrent certainty, deterrent severity, legitimacy, value congruence,	602

To offer a more complete review and be able to include all results obtained, the regression coefficients were also synthesised. All studies used linear regression models to test the modelled relationships and, consequently, reported the regression coefficients. However, using simple mean values for regression coefficients is only meaningful if the regression models they come from are sufficiently similar to avoid the bias due to multicollinearity, i.e., if two correlated variables are included as predictors in a regression model, their regression coefficients will be different than if each of them were included in separate models. Many of the regression models included additional variables and relationships that are not included in the TPB, and many lacked variables of the TPB. For instance, the model used by Herath and Rao [12] includes variables drawn from deterrence theory [24] and social control theory [25]. Thus, there is an apparent risk of bias due to differences in the regression models.

The importance of differences between regression models is, however, unclear [26]. The use of mean values is considered reasonable for models with low numbers of variables and relationships, such as those included in this review [26]. Consequently, although the mean values of regression coefficients are less reliable than the mean values of the correlation coefficients, they are meaningful indicators of the strength of the relationships and serve as a complement to the correlation coefficients.

The regression coefficients and correlation coefficients were aggregated as unweighted mean values and mean values weighted by sample size. The correlation coefficients were rescaled via the Fisher transformation before the mean values were calculated. No dramatic differences existed between these aggregates (cf. Table 2, Table 3, and Table 4). We will therefore only address the unweighted means in the discussions.

A potential issue in systematic reviews is the publication bias, i.e., the general tendency to publish significant and positive results more often than insignificant or negative results. A Funnel plot was created over the studies sample size and correlation coefficients. The studies did not appear to be biased because large samples (i.e., those with small variance) are close to the average correlation coefficients and studies with small samples (i.e., those with large variance) have more varied results.

3.3   Identification of Possible Explanations for Divergent Results

There are a great number of possible reasons to expect that the included studies have attained different results. For instance, the samples are from different cultures, the measurement instruments (questions) differ among the studies, and the actual behaviours studied differ to some extent. All the applications, tests, and reviews made of the TPB provide a considerable amount of knowledge concerning the theory in general and how it performs under different conditions. To identify factors that are known to influence or bias the results when the TPB is applied, overviews and meta-analyses [3, 5–7, 27–35] of the theory were reviewed. There is additional relevant literature that postulates factors of relevance to TPB applications. However, the authors believe that the reviewed literature sufficed to identify the most established factors. How these factors were treated in the studies was assessed using the information available in the reviewed papers (e.g., concerning how the questions were formulated).

4   The Explanation Offered by the Theory of Planned Behaviour

Attempts to answer the two research questions are provided below. Section 4.1 attempts to answer the first research question, i.e., how well the theory explains information security policy compliance and violation. Section 4.2 tries to answer the second research question, i.e., whether divergent results can be explained in a reasonable manner.

4.1 How Well Does the Theory of Planned Behaviour Explain Information Security Policy Compliance and Violation?

The TPB proposes that three variables (ATN, SN, and PBC) determine intentions and that intentions and PBC determine actual behaviour. Thus, it should be possible to explain the variance in intentions and actual behaviour with these variables.

Table 2 includes the regression and correlation coefficients for the antecedents of intentions; Table 3 includes the antecedents of behaviour. The last three rows of Table 2 provide the unweighted and sample-weighted means for the regression coefficients and the correlation coefficients in addition to the combined sample size (N) for the studies that include the corresponding coefficient.

Table 2. Regression coefficients and correlation coefficients for the antecedents to intentions

Study	Regression coefficients			Correlations coefficients		
	ATT	SN	PBC	ATT	SN	PBC
[9, 10]	0.12	0.73	0.15	0.29	0.82	0.54
[11]	Unav.	0.45	0.17	0.51	0.59	0.40
[12]	0.07	0.31	0.17	0.38	0.59	0.51
[13]	0.25	0.29	0.22	0.48	0.49	0.40
[14]	0.20	0.47	0.15	0.49	0.61	0.22
[15]	0.54	0.25	-	Unav.	Unav.	-
[16]	0.18	0.02	0.43	0.36	0.21	0.49
[4]	0.48	0.19	0.17	0.69	0.50	0.32
[8]	0.20	0.37	0.36	0.30	0.60	0.60
[17]	0.67	0.22	-	0.61	0.53	-
[18]	0.34	-0.09	-	0.37	-0.04	-
[19]	0.64	-	-	Unav.	-	-
[20]	-	-	0.34	-	-	0.47
Unweighted mean	0.34	0.29	0.24	0.48	0.47	0.43
Sample-weighted mean	0.34	0.29	0.24	0.48	0.52	0.45
Number of respondents (N)	2510	2912	2570	2900	2900	2452

Table 3. Regression coefficients and correlation coefficients for the antecedents to behaviour

Study	Regression coefficients		Correlation coefficients	
	INT	PBC	INT	PBC
[9, 10]	0.35	0.22	0.47	0.40
[11]	0.40	Unav.	0.85	0.42
[21]	0.29	-	Unav.	-
[15]	0.87	-	-	Unav.
[22]	-	0.33	-	0.40
[23]	-	0.19	-	0.23
Unweighted mean	0.48	0.25	0.85	0.35
Sample-weighted mean	0.46	0.21	0.83	0.35
Number of respondents (N)	1173	812	1011	1717

Table 4. Explained variance in intentions

Study	Consequence	R^2
[9, 10]	Compliance	0.71
[12]	Compliance	0.41
[13]	Compliance	0.35
[14]	Violation	0.43
[16]	Compliance	0.26
[4]	Compliance	0.60
[8]	Compliance	0.51
Unweighted mean		0.47
Sample-weighted mean		0.42
Number of respondents (N)		1443

Eight studies measured intentions and all its antecedents according to the TPB. Table 4 presents the explained variance (coefficient of determination, R^2) for seven of these studies. The values are calculated based on the cross-correlation matrixes reported from the studies (the correlation between predictors is missing in [11]).

The ability of the TPB to explain information security policy compliance and violation is perhaps best judged by considering how well the TPB explains behaviours in general (i.e., behaviours in other fields). In the meta analysis by Armitage and Conner [29], which covered a total of 154 studies based on the TPB, the mean explained variance in intentions was 0.39. Rivis and Sheeran [33] were able to explain variance of 0.39 in data from 5,810 samples. In a recent meta-analysis of 237 prospective studies regarding health behaviours, McEachan et al. [31] found that the theory, on average, explained variance of 0.44. The explained variance in information security policy compliance and violation intentions suggests that the efficacy of the TPB is similar for information security intentions/behaviours and intentions/behaviours in general. The magnitude of the regression coefficients also supports this conclusion. The median regression coefficients reported in [36] for 30 different behaviours (ATT=0.26, SN=0.36, and PBC=0.29), the mean regression coefficients reported in [33] (ATT=0.40, SN=0.16, and PBC=0.11), and the mean regressions coefficients reported in [37] for 23 studies of condom use (ATT=0.47, SN=0.21, and PBC=0.20) are of the same magnitude as the means in Table 2.

Only Cox [9, 10] and Siponen et al. [11] included both antecedents to behaviour and cross correlations and thereby enable calculation of the explained variance in behaviour. The explained variance (R^2) in behaviour reported in [9] is 0.25, and the explained variance offered by [11] is 0.31. These results can be compared with the result of Armitage and Conner [29] and McEachan et al. [31] (R^2 of 0.27 and 0.19). The mean values of the correlations found (I=0.85 and PBC=0.35) should be compared with those found in the broader reviews of [29] (I=0.47 and PBC=0.18) and [31] (I=0.43 and PBC=0.31). Overall, the influence of both Intentions and PBC on behaviour appears to be stronger for information security policy compliance and violation than what is reported in broader reviews.

4.2   When Divergent Results Are Reported, Can a Reasonable Explanation Be Made?

The aim of this section is to answer the following question: *when divergent results are reported, can a reasonable explanation be made?* In general, one should expect that the errors of results produced with surveys are caused by the measurement instrument (i.e., the questionnaire), the sampling method (i.e., the sampling frame and responses), the internal validity of the model (in this case, the TPB), and the statistical conclusion errors [38].

A general reflection is that statistical conclusion errors appear unlikely considering that all surveys have more respondents than the recommended minimum according to [38]. However, there are several other possible explanations. As mentioned in section 3.3, this paper does not aspire to be exhaustive with regard to observing divergent results and analysing possible causes for them. It only aspires to cover some of the more obvious divergences and the most frequently discussed causes for such divergent results when the TPB is used.

Table 5 lists seven observations of results that diverge together with a possible cause for this divergence and a schematic analysis to assess whether this cause contributes to the observed divergence.

Table 5. Observed divergent results and attempts to explain them

Observation	Possible cause	Analysis
In some studies, PBC has little effect on intentions.	The behaviour is more volitional in the studies in which PBC has little effect [6].	Likely. The study investigating PBC and violation intention (which is arguably more volitional than compliance) has the lowest regression coefficient of 0.15 (the mean of the regression coefficient for compliance intention is 0.25). The correlation coefficients point in the same direction, with 0.22 for violation vs. 0.46 for compliance.
In some studies, the effects of ATT and SN seem small.	The theory is used for beliefs concerning an object or goal and not behaviour with an "action element" [6].	Likely. When the questions clearly concern behaviour (in [8–10, 14, 17, 19]), the unweighted mean correlation coefficients (ATT=0.43 and SN=0.66) are greater than when the questions concern the goal or state "compliance" (in [11–13, 18]) (ATT=0.41 and SN=0.37). The regression coefficients have the same tendency, (ATT=0.37 and SN=0.45) vs. (ATT=0.22 and SN=0.24).
In some studies, the SN is comparably important.	Violation (i.e., risky behaviour) is modelled instead of compliance (healthy behaviour). [33, 39]	Likely. SN has a stronger mean correlation in the two studies of violation (r=0.57) than in the other studies that report correlations (r=0.47). Also, the mean regression coefficient is greater for violation (β=0.35) than for compliance (β=0.30).
The influence of antecedents on security policy compliance is high compared with other behaviours (e.g., health-related).	Self-reports, rather than objective observations or predictions of future behaviour, are used to measure behaviour. Or/and the predicted behaviour is measured at the same occasion, not on a future occasion. [6]	Likely. All studies used self-reports of behaviour, and all studies collected these self-reports at the same time that the other variables were assessed. Thus, relative to the average application of TPB, the importance of intention and PBC may be inflated in the present studies because of how behaviour was measured.

Table 5. *(Continued)*

Varying regression coefficients for TPB variables.	The regression coefficients are weakened because of multicollinearity and inclusion of many variables. The regression coefficients are inflated because of multicollinearity and because TPB variables are omitted from the model.	Likely. Large regression coefficients are reported by studies with few variables ([17, 19]). However, studies with correlated variables (e.g., habits in [15]) also report large regression coefficients. Furthermore, neither [13] nor [14] included additional variables, but they produced comparably small regression coefficients.
In some studies, PBC has little effect on intentions and behaviour.	Self-efficacy is measured, and this operationalisation excludes external sources [30] or perceived autonomy [6].	Possible. Studies that used PBC (i.e., [8–10, 14, 16]) yielded greater coefficients on intentions than studies that used self-efficacy, (β=0.27 and r=0.47) vs. (β=0.21 and r=0.42). However, for regression coefficients, PBC seems to have less influence on behaviour than self-efficacy.
In some studies, the antecedents of intentions seem less important	The "principle of compatibility" is not fulfilled, i.e., the action, target, context and time should be the same when all variables are measured [6, 32, 35, 40]	Unlikely. In [4], a mix of questions regarding general security behaviour and compliance behaviour is used; in [9, 10], following rules and taking precautions are mixed; and in [12], technology questions are mixed with questions regarding compliance behaviour. Their unweighted correlation coefficients (ATT=0.47, SN=0.66, and PBC=0.46) are even greater than the correlation coefficients of those with compatible questions (ATT=0.47, SN=0.48, and PBC=0.43). The regression coefficients point in different directions.

5 Discussion

As indicated above, it is non-trivial to interpret the results of studies related to the TPB or its variables. Validity issues associated with the analyses are discussed in section 5. Section 5.2 presents recommendations for decision makers concerned with information security management. Section 5.3 offers recommendations for security researchers.

5.1 Issues When Interpreting the Puzzle Left by Mixed Models and Adaptations

It is fair to say that the TPB has not been the focus of quantitative studies on information security policy compliance and violation despite its immense popularity in the behaviour sciences. This review was only able to identify 15 quantitative surveys that investigated one or more variables included in the TPB. Two studies (namely [9, 10] and [11]) included all the TPB variables, and other (potentially correlated) variables are included in most of the tested regression models.

Furthermore, many of the studies did not follow the guidelines, caveats, and recommendations regarding how the TPB should be applied and tested (e.g., concerning the measurement instruments), most likely because the TPB was not the focus of these studies. Fishbein and Ajzen [6] find that *"[e]ven though virtually hundreds of studies have tested variations of our theory, we were able to find only relatively few that contained all the elements required for a complete and valid test"*. Our conclusion is that this also applies to the studies that apply the TPB to information security policy compliance and violation. In our view, no study followed all the guidelines completely.

The implication of these two factors (incomplete models and incompliance with guidelines) is that the results should be interpreted cautiously. When other variables are mixed with the TPB variables, the regression coefficients can be influenced. When departures are made from established guidelines, caveats, and recommendations, it should be expected that this theory's efficacy will be influenced. In Table 5, some other possible explanations for differences in the results were explored, but no crystal clear explanations could be found. A larger sample of studies regarding the TPB and differences related to individuals' security behaviours (e.g., sampling differences) may explain the divergent results better.

5.2   Recommendations for Practitioners and Decision Makers

The TPB is one of the most-researched theories in the behavioural sciences. However, despite its value to and use in other domains (e.g., dieting, drug use, exercise, and marketing) it has not been widely proposed or used as a basis for ideas on how security behaviour should be influenced or controlled. Bits and pieces of the theory are used, and ideas coupled to the TPB can be found in the practitioner-oriented security literature. For instance, NIST's handbook about computer security [41] explains that *"changing attitudes is just one step toward changing behaviour"*. However, it is surprisingly difficult to find references to the theory by name or cases in which the whole theory (i.e., all the variables and relationships in it) has been used within the practitioner-oriented information security literature (textbooks, white papers, and guidelines, for example). Despite this lack of references, the authors' experiences suggest that decision makers in the information security field often make predictions following the reasoning of the TPB, but they are presumably unaware of the fact that the TPB has formalised their reasoning.

Although it uses a small number of predictor variables, the TPB has a considerable ability to explain human intentions and behaviour compared with its alternatives [6]. The results of this study indicate that the TPB is approximately as meaningful for information security behaviour as it is for behaviours on average. Thus, it is reasonable to expect that decision-making and interventions (e.g., education programs) would benefit from using the TPB as a basis, as decision-making and interventions in other domains already do.

5.3   Recommendations for Researchers and for Future Work

The TPB is a theory with impressive merits, and the results of this review clearly demonstrate that it is valid for the behaviours related to information security policy compliance and violation. Our opinion is that researchers should consider conducting studies focusing explicitly on the TPB to further explore and establish its efficacy for predicting and explaining information security behaviour before mixing multiple theories (and essentially creating new theories). Studies regarding the TPB can aim at establishing the relative importance of its variables, identifying its explanatory power under different circumstances and for different behaviours, and exploring extensions that are of particular relevance to inform security behaviour.

To correctly appraise the relevance, accuracy, and importance of the TPB and its variables, researchers should attempt to follow the provided guidelines, caveats, and recommendations. For instance, clear guidelines concerning the design of question-naires are provided on Azjen's website [28], and the relevance of many theoretical ideas are discussed in [6]. These ideas may offer inspiration for research regarding the circumstances and behaviour-types that are relevant for exploration.

The originators of the theory are (and have been) open to include additional va-riables in their theoretical framework if the proposed addition is (1) behaviour-specific, (2) possible to conceive as a causal factor of behaviour, (3) conceptually different from existing predictors, (4) applicable to a wide range of behaviours studied by social scientists, and (5) explains a sufficient amount of additional variance [6, 7]. Several additions have been proposed and dismissed on the basis of these require-ments (see [6, 7]). For instance, habits are not considered to fulfil (2) because past behaviour (which is used to measure habit) is not itself a causal factor [3]. Whereas many proposals have been dismissed on fair grounds, there may be extensions or adaptations that are especially suitable and meaningful for information security beha-viours. Thus, extensions that comply with all requirements except for (4) may be rele-vant for the security community to explore. For instance, meaningful and promising ideas for extensions can be sought in literature regarding security economics and the human aspects of information security.

6   Conclusions

This review sought the answer to two research questions by synthesising the reports from 16 empirical studies that address the TPB or its variables in relation to informa-tion security policy compliance and violation. The answer to the first research ques-tion is that the TPB has approximately the same explanatory power for information security policy compliance and violation as it has for behaviours on average. Approx-imately 0.4 of the variance in intentions can be explained, and the correlations and regression coefficients for variables that influence behaviour are also similar to those found in other domains. The answer to the second research question is that some po-tential explanations for why the results of the identified studies diverge can be found. However, many of the differences in the results are left unexplained.

Acknowledgments. The authors would like to thank the following researchers for responding to our inquiries: Prof. Merril Warkentin, Dr. Allen Johnston, Dr. Sang M. Lee, Dr. Sang-Gun Lee, Prof. Mikko Siponen and, in particular, Dr. Seppo Pahnila. This research is sponsored by the Swedish Civil Contingencies Agency (MSB).

References

1. ISO/IEC: Information technology – Security techniques – Information security management measurements, ISO/IEC 27004, Geneva, Switzerland (2009)
2. Sommestad, T., Hallberg, J., Lundholm, K., Bengtsson, J.: Variables influencing information security policy compliance: a systematic review of quantitative studies. Under review
3. Ajzen, I.: The theory of planned behavior. Organizational Behavior and Human Decision Processes 50, 179–211 (1991)
4. Ifinedo, P.: Understanding information systems security policy compliance: An integration of the theory of planned behavior and the protection motivation theory. Computers and Security, 83–95 (2012)
5. Fishbein, M.: A theory of reasoned action: Some applications and implications (1979)
6. Fishbein, M., Ajzen, I.: Predicting and Changing Behavior: The Reasoned Action Approach. Psychology Press, New York (2010)
7. Ajzen, I.: The theory of planned behaviour: reactions and reflections. Psychology & Health 26, 1113–1127 (2011)
8. Hu, Q., Dinev, T., Hart, P., Cooke, D.: Managing Employee Compliance with Information Security Policies: The Critical Role of Top Management and Organizational Culture. Decision Sciences 43, 615–660 (2012)
9. Cox, J.: Information systems user security: A structured model of the knowing–doing gap. Computers in Human Behavior 28, 1849–1858 (2012)
10. Cox, J.: Organizational narcissism as a factor in information security: A structured model of the user knowing-doing gap (2012)
11. Siponen, M., Pahnila, S., Mahmood, A.: Compliance with Information Security Policies: An Empirical Investigation. Computer 43, 64–71 (2010)
12. Herath, T., Rao, H.R.: Protection motivation and deterrence: A framework for security policy compliance in organisations. European Journal of Information Systems 18, 106–125 (2009)
13. Bulgurcu, B., Cavusoglu, H., Benbasat, I.: Information security policy compliance: An empirical study of rationality-based beliefs and information security awareness. MIS Quarterly: Management Information Systems 34, 523–548 (2010)
14. Dugo, T.M.: The insider threat to organizational information security: a sturctural model and empirical test (2007), http://etd.auburn.edu/etd/handle/10415/1345
15. Pahnila, S., Siponen, M., Mahmood, A.: Employees' behavior towards IS security policy compliance. In: Proceedings of the Annual Hawaii International Conference on System Sciences, Big Island, HI, p. 10 (2007)
16. Zhang, J., Reithel, B.J., Li, H.: Impact of perceived technical protection on security behaviors. Information Management and Computer Security 17, 330–340 (2009)
17. Guo, K.H., Yuan, Y., Archer, N.P., Connelly, C.E.: Understanding nonmalicious security violations in the workplace: A composite behavior model. Journal of Management Information Systems 28, 203–236 (2011)
18. Li, H., Zhang, J., Sarathy, R.: Understanding compliance with internet use policy from the perspective of rational choice theory. Decision Support Systems 48, 635–645 (2010)
19. Johnston, A.C., Warkentin, M.: The Influence of Perceived Source Credibility on End User Attitudes and Intentions to Comply with Recommended IT Actions. Journal of Organizational and End User Computing 22, 1–21 (2010)

20. Vance, A.: Motivating IS Security Compliance: Insights from Habit and Protection Motivation Theory. Why do employees violate is security policies? Insights from multiple theoretical perspectives. pp. 93–110. Faculty of Science, Department of Information Processing Science, University of Oulu, Oulu, Finland (2010)

21. Lee, S.M., Lee, S.-G., Yoo, S.: An integrative model of computer abuse based on social control and general deterrence theories. Information & Management 41, 707–718 (2004)

22. Chan, M., Woon, I.: Perceptions of information security in the workplace: linking information security climate to compliant behavior. Journal of Information Privacy and Security 1, 18–41 (2005)

23. Son, J.-Y.: Out of fear or desire? Toward a better understanding of employees' motivation to follow IS security policies. Information and Management 48, 296–302 (2011)

24. Gibbs, J.P.: Crime, Punishment, and Deterrence, New York (1975)

25. Hirschi, T.: Causes of Delinquency. Unveristy of California Press, Berkeley (1969)

26. Becker, B.J., Wu, M.-J.: The Synthesis of Regression Slopes in Meta-Analysis. Statistical Science 22, 414–429 (2007)

27. Ajzen, I.: The theory of planned behavior. Organizational Behavior and Human Decision Processes 50, 179–211 (1991)

28. Ajzen, I.: Theory of Planned Behavior,
    http://people.umass.edu/aizen/tpb.html

29. Armitage, C.J., Conner, M.: Efficacy of the Theory of Planned Behaviour: a meta-analytic review. The British Journal of Social Psychology / the British Psychological Society 40, 471–499 (2001)

30. Conner, M., Armitage, C.J.: Extending the Theory of Planned Behavior: A Review and Avenues for Further Research. Journal of Applied Social Psychology 28, 1429–1464 (1998)

31. McEachan, R.R.C., Conner, M., Taylor, N.J., Lawton, R.J.: Prospective prediction of health-related behaviours with the Theory of Planned Behaviour: a meta-analysis. Health Psychology Review 5, 97–144 (2011)

32. Montano, D.E., Kasprzyk, D.: Theory of reasoned action, theory of planned behavior, and the integrated behavioral model. In: Glanz, K., Rimer, B., Viswanath, K. (eds.) Health Behavior and Health Education: Theory Research, and Practice, pp. 68–96. United States of America (2008)

33. Rivis, A., Sheeran, P.: Descriptive Norms as an Additional Predictor in the Theory of Planned. Current Psycology: Developmental, Learning, Personality, Scoial 22, 218–233 (2003)

34. Sheppard, B., Hartwick, J., Warshaw, P.: The theory of reasoned action: A meta-analysis of past research with recommendations for modifications and future research. Journal of Consumer Research 15, 325–343 (1988)

35. Trafimow, D.: Distinctions Pertaining to Fishbein and Ajzen's Theory of Reasoned Action. In: Ajzen, I., Albarracin, D., Hornik, R. (eds.) Prediction and Change of Health Behavior: Applying the Reasoned Action Approach, Erlbaum, Hillsdale (2007)

36. Sheeran, P., Trafimow, D., Finlay, K., Norman, P.: Evidence that the type of person affects the strength of the perceived behavioural control-intention relationship. The British Journal of Social Psychology / the British Psychological Society 41, 253–270 (2002)

37. Albarracín, D., Johnson, B.T., Fishbein, M., Muellerleile, P.A.: Theories of reasoned action and planned behavior as models of condom use: a meta-analysis. Psychological Bulletin 127, 142–161 (2001)

38. Malhotra, M., Grover, V.: An assessment of survey research in POM: from constructs to theory. Journal of Operations Management 16, 407–425 (1998)
39. Hooker, K., Kaus, C.R.: Health-related possible selves in young and middle adulthood. Psychology and Aging 9, 126–133 (1994)
40. Ajzen, I., Albarracin, D.: Predicting and Changing Behavior. In: Ajzen, I., Albarracin, D., Hornik, R. (eds.) Prediction and Change of Health Behavior: Applying the Reasoned Action Approach. Erlbaum, Hillsdale (2007)
41. NIST: An introduction to computer security: The NIST Handbook. Nist Special Publications. 800 (1995)

Enforcement of Privacy Requirements

Padmanabhan Krishnan[1] and Kostyantyn Vorobyov[2]

[1] paddykrishnan@ieee.org
[2] Centre for Software Assurance
Bond University, Gold Coast, Queensland, 4229, Australia
kvorobyo@bond.edu.au

Abstract. Enterprises collect and use private information for various purposes. Access control can limit who can obtain such data. However, the purpose of their use is not clear. In this paper we focus on the purpose of data access and demonstrate that dynamic role-based access control (RBAC) mechanism is not sufficient for enforcement of privacy requirements. To achieve this we extend RBAC with monitoring capability and describe a formal approach to determining whether access control policies actually implement privacy requirements based on the behaviour of the system. We demonstrate the advantages of our approach using various examples and describe the prototype implementation of our technique.

Keywords: Privacy protection, Access control, Formal analysis.

1 Introduction

Organisations collect, store and share information with individuals and other organisations. They need to respect the privacy of the entities they interact with and comply with legislative requirements. Privacy policies are used to specify how organisations handle the data in their interactions. These policies can also be shown to be compliant with legislation.

Privacy, especially privacy enhancing technologies (PETs), is focused on protecting an individual's information. Thus, issues such as identity management, user consent, data anonymisation and retention have been the focus of PETs. These issues have implications for enterprises, as they collect data from individuals and use it for various purposes. While access control can limit who can obtain the information, it is not clear (especially to an individual) how an enterprise restricts the use of data. This affects both, individuals (who may be reluctant to transact with an enterprise) and enterprises (which may be inadvertently breaching various privacy guarantees).

While technologies, such as encryption, access control and authorisation can be used to implement a policy, it is important to capture the privacy requirements. The policy then has to be developed from the requirements and finally one can develop enforcement mechanisms.

Policy authoring and enforcement are challenging issues. As it is not possible to anticipate all possible uses of data, it is difficult for designers to indicate the

L.J. Janczewski, H.B. Wolfe, and S. Shenoi (Eds.): SEC 2013, IFIP AICT 405, pp. 272–285, 2013.
© IFIP International Federation for Information Processing 2013

appropriate policy. Thus, policies are often changed when inappropriate usage (i.e., a breach) is detected. Consequently, it is easier to specify what happens when a breach occurs [1]. The difficulty of writing privacy policies is increased as privacy does not have a standard meaning. Each person is likely to have a different interpretation, which could also depend on the application domain [2]. Additionally, privacy is context dependent and would depend on the user and also the queries handled by the system [3]. Finally, it is important for policies not to impede normal behaviour [4].

The purpose of data access [5,6] has attracted attention, especially as there are often conflicting issues between organisations and individuals. For instance, in health systems the importance of surveillance indicates that not all personal information may be private. In general, the purpose for which data is used is important in privacy. Users give permission to enterprises for specific tasks (and they assume that the data will not be used for other tasks). For example, Facebook's privacy policy states that they can use the information they receive for any services they provide including making suggestions of new connections. This is a very broad policy, as anything can be viewed as a service. Amazon allows users to opt out of receiving promotional offers. However, it is not clear if the user's information is not used in creating such offers. Amazon also states that they will not share personally identifiable information to third party providers. But what is personally identifiable is not clearly stated.

Personally identifiable information could include name, date-of-birth, address and national identity number. The chances of identifying an individual from a collection depends on the data. For example, a commonly occurring name or a specific date-of-birth in a census data is unlikely to identify an individual. However, by combining various data types personal information can be identified. Thus, it is important to control the collection of accesses rather than only a single data access.

The main contribution of this paper is a formal approach to determining if access control policies actually implement privacy requirements given a behaviour. We show how a dynamic access control mechanism is not sufficient to enforce privacy requirements. We need to extend the access control mechanism with some monitoring capability.

A prototype implementation that supports this approach is also described. The usefulness of this approach is demonstrated via various examples. In Section 2 we present the formal details. In Section 3 we give some simple examples that illustrate our approach and in Section 4 we give a description of a proof-of-concept implementation of our technique. Section 5 presents a review of the related work. Finally, we draw some conclusions and describe future directions in Section 6.

2 Framework

A specific system in our framework consists of an automaton that represents the behaviour (such as gathering and using the gathered information) and an automaton that represents a controller (including access control). For the behaviour automaton we do not separate individuals into separate automata. We have a single automaton where the label on the transition has the action as well as the individual (and role) who performs the action. The controller can observe actions exhibited by the behaviour automaton, but can also prevent certain actions. This is achieved using dynamic role based access control (RBAC) [7] and a simple semantics of purpose.

Before we describe the formal details, especially of the access control part, we present a motivating example. Assume that Alice releases some personal information. This information can be used for internal purposes, but cannot be used for marketing purposes. Assume Bob can access this information and can decide how to use it. But Bob has to be prevented from using it for marketing purposes. One way is to force Bob to assume different roles for each use. This, however, could increase the number of roles. Also, then there is no difference between purpose (which is a semantic concept) and roles (which is an enforcement concept). Furthermore, the access control mechanism will have to permit and then withdraw the role being assumed. Therefore, it is better to tag certain actions with predicates that represent purposes. The access control entity now either permits or disallows actions. This can be viewed as a mixture of access control and workflow transition enabling.

Thus the control automaton's alphabet will consist of normal actions, access control actions (i.e., permitting and withdrawing roles) and purpose related actions.

We define a composition operator that combines the behaviour automaton with the controller. The composition is based on synchronisation on common actions. However, the access control automaton cannot prevent behaviour purely via the synchronisation requirements. Hence, the composition operator allows actions to occur when the access control automaton cannot exhibit an action.

2.1   Formal Details

The main focus of the formalism is to describe the interactions between behaviour, access control and privacy policies.

We assume a set of atomic access control actions indicated by $\mathcal{A}$. These actions correspond to operations on data elements. We also assume a set of individuals $\mathcal{I}$ and a set of roles $\mathcal{R}$.

The set of behavioural actions (say Λ) that are performed by individuals assuming a particular role is defined by the set $\mathcal{A} \times \mathcal{I} \times \mathcal{R}$. A typical element of this set is indicated by α or by $\langle a, i, r \rangle$ where a is an action (element of $\mathcal{A}$), i an individual (element of $\mathcal{I}$) and r is a role (element of $\mathcal{R}$). We define projection functions act, $indiv$ and $role$ which identify the action, the individual and the role respectively. That is, $act(\langle a, i, r \rangle) = a$, $indiv(\langle a, i, r \rangle) = i$ and $role(\langle a, i, r \rangle) = r$.

The dynamic access control system uses the set of behavioural actions of the form $\langle a, i, r \rangle$, $\langle i, +r \rangle$ or $\langle i, -r \rangle$. The access control uses actions belonging to Λ to observe the evolution of behaviour. The access control process can keep track of the behaviour and change the permission accordingly. For instance, if an individual has accessed a data item, the access control process can withdraw access to other data items so that the privacy requirements are met.

The action $\langle i, +r \rangle$ indicates that user i can assume role r while the action $\langle i, -r \rangle$ indicates that user i can no longer assume role r. This will be extended with actions related to the semantics of purposes.

To capture the semantics of purposes, we assume P to be a set of atomic predicates (where a typical element is denoted by p). That is, each element of P represents a specific purpose. We use subsets of P to mark behaviours as a particular behaviour could correspond to many purposes.

We use finite state automata to describe the possible behaviours and access control actions. A behaviour automaton (denoted by $\mathcal{A}_B$) is of the form $(Q_B, \Lambda, \longrightarrow_B, q_{B_0})$, while an access control (denoted by $\mathcal{A}_C$) automaton is of the form $(Q_C, \Lambda_C, \longrightarrow_C, q_{C_0})$.

Here Q_B and Q_C are the sets of states, Λ and Λ_C the alphabets (or transition labels), $\longrightarrow_B$ and $\longrightarrow_C$ the transition relations and q_{B_0} and q_{C_0} the initial states of the respective automata. We do not have any notion of accepting states as behaviours are *valid*. For the sake of simplicity, we will assume that the automata are deterministic and hence the transition relations are functions.

Given a behaviour automaton, a purpose map is a function from the transition function to a subset of P. We let $\mathcal{M}_P = \{f \mid f : \longrightarrow_B \rightarrow \mathcal{P}(P)\}$ be the set of all possible purpose maps. Functions in $\mathcal{M}_P$ mark each transition in the behavioural automaton with a set of purposes.

Formally the labels of the control automaton are drawn from the set (which was denoted by Λ_C) $\Lambda \cup (\mathcal{I} \times \{+, -\} \times \mathcal{R}) \cup \mathcal{P}(P)$. That is, it can observe actions of the behaviour automaton, can change role permissions and allow or deny purpose related action. We will use β to indicate a typical element of this set.

To define the semantics of how the access control process influences or controls the exhibited behaviour, we need to keep track of the roles that can be assumed by the individuals. That is, we need to track the potential role assignments that are currently permitted. This set of possibilities is denoted by the set $\mathcal{S}$ which is the set of all functions from individuals to a subset of roles (i.e., $\mathcal{I} \rightarrow \mathcal{P}(\mathcal{R})$). We use ρ to represent a typical element of $\mathcal{S}$.

Given a specific role assignment, we define if a behavovioral action α is permitted only if the individual performing the action can assume the required rule. The formal definition is given below.

Definition 1. *The predicate $permit(\rho, \alpha)$ is true if and only if $role(\alpha) \in \rho(indiv(\alpha))$ is true.*

We define the ready set of the access control automaton in a given state as the set of actions it can potentially exhibit at the state. The standard definition is given below.

Definition 2. *For a state q_c belonging to Q_c, we define $ready(q_c)$ as follows.*

$$ready(q_c) = \{\beta \mid exists \ q_c' \ such \ that \ q_c \xrightarrow{\beta}_C q_c'\}$$

In order to ensure that the access control system can indeed control the behaviour, we introduce a notion of stability. Essentially we want a system to evolve only after the access control process has finished making all the access control changes.

Definition 3. *An access control automaton is stable in state q_c, written as stable(q_c), if and only if ready$(q_c) \subseteq \Lambda$.*

An access control automaton is stable when it can only observe behaviour actions and cannot exhibit any action that can change the role assignment.

This implies that a state that has both observable and access control transitions is not stable.

To define the semantics of the joint behaviour of the behavioural and access control automata, we define the set of possible states of the overall computation.

Definition 4. *The set of possible system states is the $S \times Q_B \times Q_C$.*

A particular state of the computation is represented by a triple denoted by $\lceil \rho, q_B, q_C \rceil$ where $\rho \in S$, $q_B \in Q_B$ and $q_c \in Q_C$.

The transition relation of the automaton obtained by composing the behaviour and access control automata indicated by $\parallel$ is defined as follows. For this, we assume a specific purpose map m.

Definition 5. $\mathcal{A}_B \parallel \mathcal{A}_C = (S \times Q_B \times Q_C, \Lambda_C, (f_\emptyset, q_0^B, q_0^C), \longrightarrow)$ *where* $\longrightarrow$ *is defined by the following rules.*

1. $\lceil \rho, q_b, q_c \rceil \xrightarrow{\alpha} \lceil \rho, q_b', q_c' \rceil$ *if* $q_b \xrightarrow{\alpha} q_b'$, $q_c \xrightarrow{\alpha} q_c'$ *provided stable(q_c), permit(ρ, α) and $m(q_b \xrightarrow{\alpha} q_b') = \emptyset$.*

2. $\lceil \rho, q_b, q_c \rceil \xrightarrow{\alpha} \lceil \rho, q_b', q_c \rceil$ *if* $q_b \xrightarrow{\alpha} q_b'$ *provided stable(q_c), $\alpha \notin$ ready(q_c), permit(ρ, α) and $m(q_b \xrightarrow{\alpha} q_b') = \emptyset$*

3. $\lceil \rho, q_b, q_c \rceil \xrightarrow{\epsilon} \lceil \rho', q_b, q_c' \rceil$ *if* $q_c \xrightarrow{i,+r} q_c'$ *where* $\rho'(j) = \rho(j)$ *if* $i \neq j$ *and* $\rho'(i) = \rho(i) \cup \{r\}$ *otherwise.*

4. $\lceil \rho, q_b, q_c \rceil \xrightarrow{\epsilon} \lceil \rho', q_b, q_c' \rceil$ *if* $q_c \xrightarrow{i,-r} q_c'$ *where* $\rho'(j) = \rho(j)$ *if* $i \neq j$ *and* $\rho'(i) = \rho(i) \setminus \{r\}$ *otherwise.*

5. $\lceil \rho, q_b, q_c \rceil \xrightarrow{\alpha} \lceil \rho, q_b', q_c' \rceil$ *if* $q_b \xrightarrow{\alpha} q_b'$, $q_c \xrightarrow{ps} q_c'$ *provided stable(q_c) and $m(q_b \xrightarrow{\alpha} q_b') \subset ps$.*

The first two rules specify permitted behaviour. This requires the action to be permitted in the current state. Furthermore, the access control automaton must be in a stable state and the transition has no specific purpose. Note, that if an action has the right permissions, it cannot be prevented by the access control automaton. That is, there is no need for the behaviour automaton to synchronise on all common actions. The third and fourth rules describe the access control automaton changing the current permissions. Thus, the behaviour automaton does not change its local state. The last rule enforces the required semantics of purpose. If the transition of the behaviour automaton has a purpose related marking, it is permitted only if the controller allows all the purposes present in the marking.

We write $\lceil \rho, q_b, q_c \rceil \overset{\alpha}{\dashrightarrow} \lceil \rho', q_b', q_c' \rceil$ if there is a sequence of transitons $\lceil \rho, q_b, q_c \rceil \overset{\epsilon}{\longrightarrow} \lceil \rho^1, q_b^1, q_c^1 \rceil \overset{\epsilon}{\longrightarrow} \cdots \lceil \rho^k, q_b^k, q_c^k \rceil \overset{\alpha}{\longrightarrow} \lceil \rho^{k+1}, q_b^{k+1}, q_c^{k+1} \rceil \overset{\epsilon}{\longrightarrow} \cdots$ $\lceil \rho', q_b', q_c' \rceil$. That is, there is a sequence of "internal" moves (indicated by the ϵ transitions) around a transition exhibiting α. We write this as the triple $(\sigma, \alpha, \sigma')$ where σ is $\lceil \rho, q_b, q_c \rceil$ and σ' is $\lceil \rho', q_b', q_c' \rceil$.

Before we present a few simple examples, we make some observations about the structure of the access control automaton.

At any state if the automaton has a transition of the form $\langle a, i, r \rangle$ and $\langle j, +r \rangle$ or $\langle j, -r \rangle$, the transition with the label $\langle a, i, r \rangle$ can be removed without affecting the overall semantics. This is because of the definition of stability; the transition with the label $\langle a, i, r \rangle$ will never be taken. Similarly, if there is no transition of the form $\langle i, +r \rangle$ from the initial state of the access control automaton, the joint behaviour will not exhibit any action.

For the behaviour automaton, any state that has transitions of the form $\langle a, i, r \rangle$ and $\langle b, i, r \rangle$ can exhibit neither or both actions unless there is a purpose that distinguishes the two transitions.

2.2 Privacy Requirements

We use linear time temporal logic (LTL) to encode the requirements, including privacy, on the behaviour of the composed system. We define two types of atomic predicates. The first is $occurs(\langle a, i, r \rangle)$ which is true at a given state if there is a transition with the label $\langle a, i, r \rangle$. We also define abbreviations where we can leave one of the fields blank. This implicitly implies universal quantification. For instance, $occurs(\langle a, -, r \rangle)$ is an abbreviation for $\forall i \in \mathcal{I} : occurs(\langle a, i, r \rangle)$.

The second is $occurs(p)$ where p is a purpose and is true if there is a transition marked with a set that contains p. As usual we take runs of the composed automata to define satisfaction. More precisely, $(\sigma_0, \alpha_0, \sigma_1), (\sigma_1, \alpha_1, \sigma_2), \cdots, i \models occurs(\alpha)$ iff $\alpha_i = \alpha$. Similarly, $(\sigma_0, \alpha_0, \sigma_1), (\sigma_1, \alpha_1, \sigma_2), \cdots, i \models occurs(p)$ iff one of the transitions in $(\sigma_i, \alpha_i, \sigma_{i+1})$ has a marking that contains p.

To express LTL properties we use standard logical and LTL operators, such as $\lor, \land, \neg, \rightarrow$(for implies), $\mathcal{U}, \square$ and $\diamond$.

3   Examples

In this section we present some simple examples that illustrate our approach.

The first example is of a user, say Alice, who writes a blog and also applies for the job. The interviewer (which is a role) is allowed to read the job application and once they have read the application they can not read the blog.

To model the behaviour we use the following abbreviations:

$\alpha_1 = \langle blogWrite, Alice, user \rangle,$
$\alpha_2 = \langle apply, Alice, user \rangle,$
$\alpha_3 = \langle readApplication, Bob, interviewer \rangle,$
$\alpha_4 = \langle readBlog, Bob, interviewer \rangle,$

This requirement can be written·as

$$occurs(\langle readApplication, -, interviewer \rangle) \rightarrow \Box\neg(occurs(\langle readBlog, -, interviewer \rangle).$$

If the behaviour automaton had the following structure,

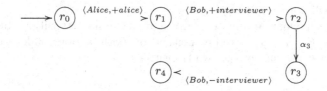

the following automaton can enforce the above requirement:

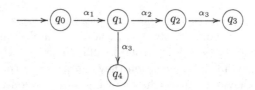

This is because after Bob has read Alice's application (α_3), he cannot assume the role of an interviewer. Note, that the stability requirements on the access control automaton means that α_4 is not enabled until the transition from r_3 to r_4 is executed. But once this transition is executed, α_4 cannot be exhibited as the *permit* predicate will evaluate to false.

The second example is when Alice generates some data item and Bob can access it only after it is made anonymous. To model this we let:

α_1 be $\langle dataWrite, Alice, generator \rangle,$
α_2 be $\langle dataAnonimise, Alice, generator \rangle,$
α_3 be $\langle dataAccess, Bob, accessor \rangle.$

The privacy requirement is captured by the formula

$$\neg\ occurs(\alpha_3)\ \mathcal{U}\ occurs(\alpha_2)$$

The behaviour can be represented by

Then, the enforcement automaton is as follows.

In this case the access control automaton gives Bob the permission to assume the role of *accessor* only after observing α_2. Hence, the behaviour automaton cannot perform exhibit α_3 in state q_1. This is very similar to classical discrete event control systems where the controller can observe certain actions before enabling other actions.

Our final example is from [8].

Sometimes a patient needs to be transferred to another unit. This is normally permitted unless the patient opts out. Also a patient's treatment can be used for training purpose. This, however, requires explicit permission from the patient.

For the sake of simplicity we assume there is only one patient *Pat* who can assume the patient's role (*pat*) and one doctor *Doc* who can assume the doctor's role *doc*.

The abbreviation α_1 stands for $\langle optOut, Pat, pat \rangle$ which indicates that the patient wants to opt out of the transfer scheme; while the abbreviation α_2 denotes $\langle signPerm, Pat, pat \rangle$ which indicates that the patient is happy for the treatment information can be used for training.

The actions α_3: $\langle diagnosis, Doc, doc \rangle$ and α_4: $\langle treat, Doc, doc \rangle$ are part of the normal medical process.

The action α_5: $\langle move, Doc, doc \rangle$ indicates the patient being transferred while the action α_6: $\langle useTrain, Doc, doc \rangle$ indicates the treatment being used in the training process.

We use the predicates *forTraining* and *transfer* as the set of purposes.

The privacy requirements are:

$\neg occurs(\alpha_6) \; \mathcal{U} \; occurs(forTraining) \lor \Box(\neg occurs(forTraining))$, and
$\Box(occurs(\alpha_1) \rightarrow \Box(\neg occurs(transfer)))$

Consider the following behaviour.

Let the transition $q_2 \xrightarrow{\alpha_6} q_2$ be marked with the purpose *forTraining* and the transition $q_2 \xrightarrow{\alpha_5} q_3$ be marked with the purpose *transfer*.

Consider the following access control automaton.

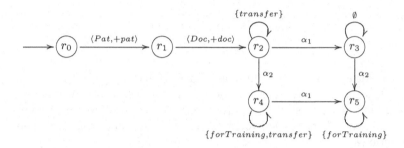

The joint behaviour ensures that whenever the patient selects to opt out (indicated by the action α_1), the access control removes the option of the *transfer* purpose (in this case the ability to exhibit α_5). When the patients gives permission (indicated by the action α_2), the action α_6 can be exhibited. Note, that all these actions are executed by the medical staff (indicated by role *doc*) and hence dynamic RBAC by itself cannot enforce such requirements.

4   Prototype Implementation

We now describe the proof-of-concept implementation of our approach.

The prototype implementation consists of two parts: the front-end (a graphical user interface (Figure 1)) and the back-end (a code generator).

The graphical interface allows a user to specify atomic elements of a system, which includes individuals, access control actions, roles, predicates and states. Using these elements one can construct two labelled transition systems (LTS) that describe behavioural and enforcement automata. Additionally, a user is provided with the interface for specification of properties in LTL.

LTS specified via the front-end are used to generate a specification in the SAL [9] language. The generated specification consists of two modules that represent behaviour and enforcement automata and SAL properties, which, depending on the user's intent, should or should not hold in a system with enforced privacy requirements.

We now explain how we generate SAL specifications. At the SAL level we remove the notion of users, roles and access control actions, replacing behavioural actions with predicates. Actions observed by enforcement automaton (i.e. $\langle a, i, r \rangle$, $a \in \mathcal{A}$, $i \in \mathcal{I}$, $r \in \mathcal{R}$) are mapped to boolean variables, which indicate whether a particular behavioural action was observed (*true*) or not (*false*). Similarly, the set of roles, permitted or forbidden for individuals, is mapped to the set of boolean variables, such that a user can assume a particular role, if the respective variable is set to *true* and can not otherwise. Finally, a label in the behavioural LTS may be associated with a set of predicates which represent purposes. Values of purposes are specified by the user.

Generated modules are composed into an asynchronous system synchronised as follows:

- A transition in an enforcement LTS with a label of the form $\langle i, \oplus, r \rangle$, $i \in \mathcal{A}$, $\oplus \in \{+, -\}$, $r \in \mathcal{R}$ is executed unconditionally and sets a boolean variable (say p_1) that allows or forbids an individual i to assume some role r to *true* or *false* respectively.
- A transition in a behaviour LTS with a label of the form $\langle a, i, r \rangle$, $a \in \mathcal{A}$, $i \in \mathcal{I}$, $r \in \mathcal{R}$ is executed if and only if permitted by p_1 (i.e., the value of p_1 is *true* – an individual i can assume role r) set by enforcement automaton. That is, a given user can perform an action assuming a particular role only if that is permitted by privacy requirements. This, in turn, sets to *true* a boolean variable (say a_1), which indicates that some action a, performed by the individual i, assuming the role r was observed via the enforcement LTS.
- A transition in an enforcement LTS with a label of the form $\langle a, i, r \rangle$, $a \in \mathcal{A}$, $i \in \mathcal{I}$, $r \in \mathcal{R}$, is executed if and only if permitted by a_1 (set by the behaviour LTS). This indicates that some action action a, performed by the individual i, assuming the role r was observed by the behaviour LTS.

```
TRANSITION [
    behaviour_state = q0 AND GeneratorAlice = true
        -->
    behaviour_state' = q1; a1' = true;
    []
    behaviour_state = q1 AND GeneratorAlice = true
        -->
    behaviour_state' = q2; a2' = true;
    []
    behaviour_state = q1 AND AccessorBob = true
        -->
    behaviour_state' = q4; a3 = true;
    []
    behaviour_state = q2 AND AccessorBob = true
        -->
    behaviour_state' = q3; a3 = true;
]
```

Listing 1. Example 2. Behaviour LTS

```
TRANSITION [
    enforcement_state   = r0
        -->
    enforcement_state' = r1;
    []
    enforcement_state   = r1
        -->
    enforcement_state' = r2; GeneratorAlice' = true;
    []
    enforcement_state   = r2 AND a2 = true
        -->
    enforcement_state' = r3;
    []
    enforcement_state   = r3
        -->
    enforcement_state' = r3; AccessorBob' = true;
]
```

Listing 2. Example 2. Enforcement LTS

Code listings 1 and 2 depict SAL representation of enforcement and behaviour LTS based on example 2. Variables `enforcement_state` and `behavior_state` represent enforcement and behavioral automata states, booleans `AccessorBob` and `GeneratorAlice` forbid or allow individuals to assume roles and boolean variables `a1`, `a2`, `a3` represent observed actions α_1, α_2 and α_3 respectively. States `r0 ... r3` of the enforcement transition system and `q0 ... q4` of the behaviour LTS refer to states $r_0, ..., r_3$ and $q_0, ..., q_4$ of the enforcement and behaviour automata in example 2.

Note how enforcement automaton prevents privacy violation (i.e., a transition from q_1 to q_4). The transition is executed only if Bob can assume the role of accessor (i.e., `AccessorBob` is *true*), which is set to *true* only when action α_2 is observed (i.e., `a2` is *true*), which is only possible if data is made anonymous. That is, transition $q_1 \rightarrow q_4$ is eliminated by the enforcement LTS, which prevents a privacy violation.

Finally, the generated SAL specification can be checked with `sal-smc` (SAL symbolic model checker) using LTL properties specified by the user via front-end. For example, one can check whether privacy requirements are indeed enforced or whether the enforcement of privacy requirements does not impede system's behaviour, i.e., a particular state in the behaviour transition system is reached or a particular action is executed. For instance, in the above example, one can specify a property `G(not q4)` (state q_4, which constitutes a privacy violation, is never reached) to verify that generated system does prevent the violation of privacy.

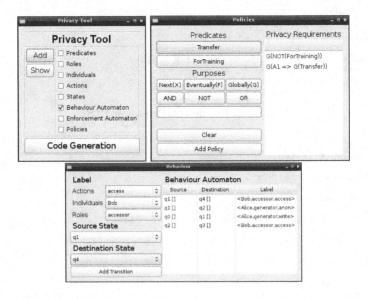

Fig. 1. User Interface of Prototype Implementation

5   Related Work

Our semantic framework is based on parallel composition of finite state automata. Our composition operator is derived from the classical controller [10] for discrete event systems and synchronisation on common actions [11].

The precise semantics of the different uses of purposes in the privacy policies are not clear. The data-purpose algebra [12] shows how data can be used at each stage in the computation. They use a set of atomic values to indicate purpose. These atomic values are associated with data items indicating if the data can be used for a specific purpose. The semantics in [13] is to support automatic auditing. It is also based on Markov decision processes. Conditional purpose using a hierarchical structure and compliance is presented in [5]. The meaning of purpose via an action is presented in [6]. Semantics of intention [14] provides another look at purpose. Johnson et al. [15] present the concepts of template author, policy authors and policy implementers. But it is more about managing privacy policies rather than semantics of the policies themselves.

RBAC [16] and its extensions [17] are very common forms of access control. They can be used to specify who has access to data and also what role they need to assume. One can verify if an implementation technique actually satisfies the policies specified in RBAC. The link between access control and workflow [18] is used to verify designs. The formalism is based on Petri nets. Our access control automaton describes a much simpler semantics. However, our requirements are also limited.

There is also need to model dynamic behaviour. Denotic logic [19] and modal logic [6] have been used to give a semantics to purpose. [3] also develop a notion of privacy where portions of data can be protected.

6   Conclusions

In this paper we have described a formal approach to determining whether access control policies implement privacy requirements given a system's behaviour. This is achieved by extending dynamic role-based access control mechanism with monitoring capability. We represent a specific system using two automata, such that first, behaviour automaton, represents behaviour (e.g. gathering and using the gathered data) and second, controller automaton, captures privacy requirements of the system (including access control). Enforcement of privacy requirements is achieved via a synchronised composition of the two, such that the controller grants access permissions, observes actions exhibited by the behaviour automaton and prevents actions which may violate privacy. In this paper we show how access control may fail to detect privacy violations and demonstrate the applicability of our approach using various examples. We have implemented our approach in a prototype tool, which provides a simple interface for specification of the system's behaviour and privacy requirements and can automatically generate a specification in the SAL language. One can then model check the generated specification against an arbitrary set LTL properties using SAL symbolic model checker.

Acknowledgements. The first author was affiliated with Bond University where most of this work was done. He is currently affiliated with Oracle Labs. The second author was supported by a VC grant from Bond University.

References

1. Ayres, L.T., Curtin, C.M., Ng, T.A.: Standardizing Breach Incident Reporting: Introduction of a Key for Hierarchical Classification. In: Proceedings of The 5th IEEE International Workshop on Systematic Approaches to Digital Forensic Engineering, pp. 79–83. IEEE Computer Society (2010)
2. Cate, F.H.: The limits of notice and choice. IEEE Security & Privacy 8(2), 59–62 (2010)
3. Farnan, N.L., Lee, A.J., Chrysanthis, P.K., Yu, T.: Don't reveal my intension: Protecting user privacy using declarative preferences during distributed query processing. In: Atluri, V., Diaz, C. (eds.) ESORICS 2011. LNCS, vol. 6879, pp. 628–647. Springer, Heidelberg (2011)
4. Antón, A.I., Earp, J.B., Carter, R.A.: Precluding incongruous behavior by aligning software requirements with security and privacy policies. Information & Software Technology 45(14), 967–977 (2003)
5. Kabir, M.E., Wang, H., Bertino, E.: A conditional purpose-based access control model with dynamic roles. Expert Systems with Applications 38(3), 1482–1489 (2011)
6. Jafari, M., Fong, P.W.L., Safavi-Naini, R., Barker, K., Sheppard, N.P.: Towards defining semantic foundations for purpose-based privacy policies. In: Proceedings of the 1st ACM Conference on Data and Application Security and Privacy, pp. 213–224. ACM (February 2011)
7. Ferraiolo, D.F., Kuhn, D.R.: Role-based access controls. In: Proceedings of the National Computer Security Conference, U.S. Department of Commerce, Gaithersburg, Md. 20899 USA, NSA/NIST, pp. 554–563. Elsevier Advanced Technology Publications (October 1992)
8. LeBlanc, M.: Physiotherapists' privacy requirements in Ontario. Technical report, College of Physiotherapists of Ontario (2004)
9. de Moura, L., Owre, S., Rueß, H., Rushby, J., Shankar, N., Sorea, M., Tiwari, A.: SAL 2. In: Alur, R., Peled, D.A. (eds.) CAV 2004. LNCS, vol. 3114, pp. 496–500. Springer, Heidelberg (2004)
10. Wonham, W., Ramadge, P.: Modular supervisory control of discrete-event systems. Mathematics of Control, Signals and Systems 1, 13–30 (1988)
11. Zielonka, W.: Notes on finite asynchronous automata. Theoretical Informatics and Applications 21(2), 99–135 (1987)
12. Hanson, C., Berners-Lee, T., Kagal, L., Sussman, G.J., Weitzner, D.J.: Data-purpose algebra: Modeling data usage policies. In: Proceedings of the 8th IEEE International Workshop on Policies for Distributed Systems and Networks, pp. 173–177. IEEE Computer Society (June 2007)
13. Tschantz, M.C., Datta, A., Wing, J.M.: On the semantics of purpose requirements in privacy policies. The Computing Research Repository abs/1102.4326 (2011)
14. Kagal, L., Pato, J.: Preserving privacy based on semantic policy tools. IEEE Security & Privacy 8(4), 25–30 (2010)

15. Johnson, M., Karat, J., Karat, C., Grueneberg, K.: Optimizing a policy authoring framework for security and privacy policies. In: Proceedings of the 6th Symposium on Usable Privacy and Security. ACM International Conference Proceeding Series, vol. 485. ACM (2010)

16. Jha, S., Li, N., Tripunitara, M.V., Wang, Q., Winsborough, W.H.: Towards formal verification of role-based access control policies. IEEE Transactions on Dependable and Secure Computing 5(4), 242–255 (2008)

17. Fong, P.W.L., Siahaan, I.: Relationship-based access control policies and their policy languages. In: Proceedings of the 16th ACM Symposium on Access Control Models and Technologies, pp. 51–60. ACM (2011)

18. Barletta, M., Calvi, A., Ranise, S., Viganò, L., Zanetti, L.: Workflow and access control reloaded: a declarative specification framework for the automated analysis of web services. Scalable Computing: Practice and Experience 12(1) (2011)

19. Piolle, G., Demazeau, Y.: Representing privacy regulations with deontico-temporal operators. Web Intelligence and Agent Systems 9(3), 209–226 (2011)

Towards Security-Enhanced and Privacy-Preserving Mashup Compositions

Heidelinde Hobel[1], Johannes Heurix[2], Amin Anjomshoaa[2], and Edgar Weippl[1]

[1] SBA Research, Vienna, Austria
{hhobel,eweippl}@sba-research.org
http://www.sba-research.org
[2] Institute of Software Technology and Interactive Systems,
Vienna University of Technology, Austria
{heurix,anjomshoaa}@ifs.tuwien.ac.at
http://www.tuwien.ac.at

Abstract. In recent years, there has been an emerging trend towards people building their own sophisticated applications to automate their daily tasks without specialized programming knowledge. Enterprise mash-ups facilitate end users' development of applications in a business context autonomously or with minimal support from the software engineering staff. Hence, mashup solutions are aimed at exploiting the full potential of end users' software development. However, the use of mashup solutions for business tasks gives rise to several security and privacy-related questions, since sensitive data records could be created even with simple procedures. In this paper, we propose an approach where security rules for mashup compositions can be defined, and submitted mashups are automatically evaluated for compliance with the respective policies.

Keywords: Enterprise Mashups, Semantics, Security, Privacy, Usability.

1 Introduction

Web 2.0 comprises a set of new technologies as well as behavior models of end users [1]. One of these technologies is known as *mashup*, which is also becoming popular in an enterprise context as *Enterprise Mashups*. According to [2], Enterprise Mashups are defined as

> "... a Web-based resource that combines existing resources, be it content, data or application functionality, from more than one resource by empowering the end users to create and adapt individual information centric and situational applications."

The basic idea is that existing resources, such as data and services, are used to create a new resource in such a way that even users with limited programming skills are able to fulfill this task. The mashup development is based on mashup editors such as JackBe Mashup [3] or IBM Mashup Center [4] by providing

L.J. Janczewski, H.B. Wolfe, and S. Shenoi (Eds.): SEC 2013, IFIP AICT 405, pp. 286–299, 2013.
© IFIP International Federation for Information Processing 2013

an integrated development environment (IDE), where programming is accomplished by simple drag-and-drop operations of predefined modules (basically the mashup's operations) and connecting them. Google's Blockly [5] has similar objectives, providing a graphical programming editor that allows programming by puzzling blocks together.

Hence, the application of mashups facilitates *"short-time, situational, ad-hoc, tactical, and individual"* [6] software development and has great potential for various application fields, especially for businesses [7]. However, by shifting the responsibility of application development into end users' hands, several security and privacy-related questions arise, as the end user is given the opportunity to access the enterprise's data and process that data without regulations. In traditional software development, the security of applications is guaranteed by the skill of the software developers, sophisticated test-mechanisms, and reviews. However, these measures are not applicable for mashup solutions, as the expense is usually not considered justifiable due to the short-lived and individual nature of mashups.

In this paper we propose a platform-based approach for establishing rules for mashup design in order to prevent data leakage and distribution of data to unauthorized people and mitigate semantic aggregation, thus empowering enterprises to regain authority over end users' mashup development. This is required since in the last instance, the enterprise is responsible for its own security and for the privacy of owners of the records stored in its databases.

The contributions of this paper are as follows:

- We introduced a platform-based security architecture for designing and enforcing policies for composing mashups in an organizational context.
- We formulated the modeling of mashup compositions in our own notation.
- We implemented a prototype as proof of concept and provided a case study in order to illustrate the usability of the system.

The paper is structured as follows: In Section 2 we provide an overview of the potential of mashup solutions in a business context and the related security and privacy issues, followed by Section 3, where we introduce our platform-based approach for security-enhanced and privacy-preserving mashup compositions. Section 4 evaluates the prototype implementation and a case study, followed by the discussion (Section 5), related work (Section 6), and conclusion (Section 7).

2 Background

According to [6,8], mashup solutions are the answer to the common problem that only 20% of the required software solutions can be satisfied by the software development staff of a company; the remaining 80%, comprising all *"situational, ad-hoc, tactical, and individual software solutions"* [6], are neglected due to insufficient resources. Mashup solutions aim to solve this shortage by involving the end users in software development, supported by SOA, Web Services, and lightweight compositions [8].

The major advantage is that an end user can easily implement a completely suitable application for any task in a short time. However, this also implies that typical software quality and security measures, such as the skill of the developers, test mechanisms, reviews, and audits, cannot be applied to mashups, as they would be very costly for this kind of development where software is developed in a short time and for every task, leading to the emergence of new bottlenecks.

Anjomshoaa et al. [9] summarized the security, privacy and trust issues that arise with the mashup technology and data processing application: *"(1) Resource Trustworthiness, (2) Content and Feed Copyright Issues, (3) Information Leakage, (4) Distribution to unknown or unauthorized users, (5) Distribution of sensitive information, and (6) Creation of sensitive information through aggregation"*. *Information leakage* refers to the mashup's nature of facilitating data processing and publishing, and sensitive information that is not allowed to cross organizational borders, and thus organizations must be prepared to ensure that only permitted data is generated by mashup solutions and published publicly. *Distribution of (sensitive) data to unknown or unauthorized users* means that internal borders within organizations also have to be considered in data distribution that is facilitated by mashup solutions. Sensitive information refers to data that contains personal information or information about companies that could be used against the company itself, resulting in a security breach and ultimately affecting the company's competitiveness. *Creation of sensitive information through aggregation* is an intrinsic issue of the mashup technology enabling sophisticated data processing possibilities. Without appropriate regulations on how data may be processed, mashup solutions can be used to process huge amounts of data with the result of disclosing valuable personal or organizational information in an unauthorized way or for malicious purposes. [9]

Hence, the application of mashup solutions requires new measures for secure and privacy-preserving data handling in an enterprise context, where we have to concentrate on data processing rather than access rights.

3   A Platform for Security-Enhanced and Privacy-Preserving Mashup Compositions

In traditional Enterprise/Web Applications, the functionality is provided by the software engineering staff in the form of methods or functions, where a great part of these methods/functions access the enterprise's data and transform the data according to the implemented logic. We have to consider that the implemented logic is developed by skilled developers by considering organizational policies and weaving them into their implementations. With mashups, the task of implementing functionality is shifted from skilled developers to other end users. However, as allowing end-users unrestricted data transformations may compromise the organization's security integrity, we propose the extension of traditional enterprise or Web platforms by an additional vertical layer that is responsible for validating the security and privacy-preserving characteristics of end users' mashups and server-side execution of accepted mashups to protect the security and privacy of the enterprise's data.

3.1 System Architecture

The system architecture of the proposed approach is based on the fundamental Enterprise/Web Architecture and extends the existing functionality by a module that (i) validates mashups based on a ruleset and (ii) allows the server-side execution of accepted mashups. While making use of matured and well-engineered security mechanisms of traditional platforms, we can concentrate on mashup validation mechanisms that ensure that the mashups' provided functionality is compliant with the enterprise's policies.

As illustrated in Figure 1, the existing platform is extended with the mashup validation and execution module, where the traditional enterprise functions are granted access to the company's data on demand, as these functions are considered trustworthy.

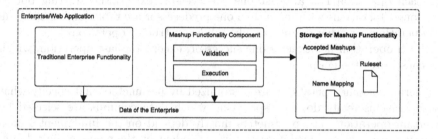

Fig. 1. Proposed architecture of the platform-based approach

In order for mashup functionality to be executed on the system, the mashup has to pass the validation mechanism of the system, which is based on a ruleset. Additional name mapping is used to map domain-specific names to the naming convention that is used in the ruleset. Accepted mashups are stored in the system, and only these mashup solutions are allowed to be executed and to access data. Other required functionalities are an interface for submitting or designing a mashup solution and an interface for displaying violated rules so that the mashup designer can correct unapproved mashup compositions.

3.2 Mashup Validation

Mashup characteristics are validated by a specific ruleset that defines how the mashups need to be composed. The ruleset incorporates the policies of the enterprise, defining what has to be done, what can be done, and what must not be done. As the names of concepts used depend on the actual domain and there are different mashup languages, a flexible mapping system is required to map the domain and mashup language-dependent names to the naming convention used in the ruleset.

Ruleset Design. A mashup solution is basically a composition of predefined operations, i.e., a set of operations with a specific sequence. In order to validate the mashup's characteristics, we formalize a mashup composition as a directed graph and thus, $M = (O, A)$ where

- M is a mashup solution/graph,
- O is the set of operations/nodes $\{op_1, ..., op_k\}$ that are used in mashup solutions,
- A is the set of directed edges or arrows respectively connecting the operations and determining the successor of a node.

A typical graph that represents a mashup solution is restricted by the following two characteristics:

1. Each operation has at least one predecessor, except the starting operations. Operations with more than one predecessor are table joining/merging operations or other operations like table constructor operations.
2. Each operation has exactly one successor, except the last operation, which constitutes the endpoint.

Furthermore, some operations are customized by parameters that specify what the operations really do, e.g., specifying which data columns are selected by a certain operation. The parameters mostly depend on the fundamental data structure, e.g., the specified operation is dependent on the name of the column, and thus we formalize operations with parameters as: `op[P]`, where P is the set of usable parameters. Concluding, we formalize a specific mashup solution M_i as a graph with the set O notated in the following form

$$M_i := \{op[P_1]_1, op[P_2]_2, \ldots, op[P_n]_n\}$$

and the set A as the sequence of operations. Other context information also has to be considered in the ruleset, such as the role of the user who is the designer and executor of the mashup. The enterprise platform can be used to derive such context information and can therefore be included in the ruleset.

Based on the definitions given above, it can be concluded that the graph of every mashup solution results in a tree structure, more precisely an in-tree, where

- The root node holds the solution, i.e., the endpoint of the mashup.
- The leaf nodes constitute the operations fetching data from the source tables.
- The inner nodes constitute the actual data transforming operations.

The ruleset aims to restrict the relationships between the defined concepts, such as the type and sequence of operations, the relationship between an operation and a specific context, etc. For the implementation of the ruleset checker, there are several equivalent possibilities such as Object Constraint Language (OCL), rule-based systems, ontologies, etc. In the case of ontologies, we propose the following general relations: (1) Operation `hasParameter` Parameter, and (2)

Operation **hasSuccessor** Operation. Obviously, in most cases the role of the user will be important in the execution of the operation, and thus we define the following relation: Executor **performs** Operation. These and other specified relations are restricted afterwards based on the determined effect of the rule. With sophisticated ontologies we can use property, hasValue, and cardinality constraints to achieve the intended effect.

Validation Workflow. The actual implementation of the validation process depends on the technology used for the ruleset design. We illustrate the workflow implementation with an ontology-based core system, as shown in Figure 3.2:

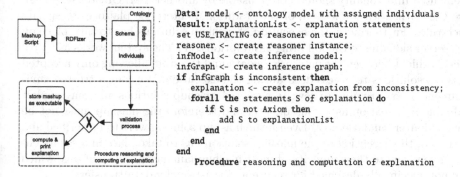

```
Data: model <- ontology model with assigned individuals
Result: explanationList <- explanation statements
set USE_TRACING of reasoner on true;
reasoner <- create reasoner instance;
infModel <- create inference model;
infGraph <- create inference graph;
if infGraph is inconsistent then
    explanation <- create explanation from inconsistency;
    forall the statements S of explanation do
        if S is not Axiom then
            add S to explanationList
        end
    end
end
Procedure reasoning and computation of explanation
```

Fig. 2. Activity diagram and pseudocode of the validation process with an ontology-based core system

The **mashup script** to be analyzed is parsed for operations, parameters, and the sequence of the operations. This is done by a dedicated **RDFizer** (cf. [10]), which creates individuals from the parsed information and maps them to the **schema** incorporating classes and relations in order to provide machine-understandable meaning for the individuals. The **rules** are implemented by logical restrictions based on the relations of the ontology. The inference model of the ontology is created in the **validation process** and is the result of applying the reasoner to the fundamental ontology. It contains all entailed knowledge about the ontology, e.g., subclass relationships that are inferred from defined classes. In the last step, the reasoner automatically checks whether the inference model of the ontology is consistent. If a predefined rule is violated, the reasoner iterates over the axioms in order to find statements that do not comply with the predefined axioms. However, only the individuals that do not comply with the restrictions and their relations should be printed as explanation for the user, as we consider all axioms to be correct, although certainly, failures in the ontology design could also occur that require manual examination of the rules. Finally, all statements that concern individuals have to be prepared in human-readable form. If the reasoner identifies no inconsistency, the submitted mashup solution is persisted and can afterwards be executed by an end user with the role and other dependencies that are identical to the submitter of the mashup solution.

We used Pellet [11] as reasoner engine due to its ability to reason in an inconsistent state. The pseudocode for the procedure for creating an inference model, consistency verification, and the computation of the explanation (see Figure 3.2) was derived from a Java implementation with the Pellet [11] reasoner.

3.3   Execution

Some of the rules are dependent on the actual context, and thus a mashup solution may only be executed in the context in which it was validated. For instance, the rules for a mashup are often dependent on the role of the user, and the implemented functionality should not be usable by another user. Obviously, we can use the authentication system of the traditional enterprise platform to specify such rules. Furthermore, the execution of mashup solutions has to take place on the server side due to the following assumptions: (1) The system works as a protection shield between the enterprise's data and the staff, allowing only accepted mashup solutions to access data during the execution. Without a trusted environment, users are able to rewrite accepted mashup solutions and may exploit valuable information as a consequence, and therefore the mashup must not be changed after validation. (2) Even if the mashup solution were to be verified and accepted, the execution of the mashup solution has to take place in a secure environment due to the simplicity of most mashup languages and solutions, which are not specifically designed for secure and trustworthy data transfers.

4   Evaluation

We identified the healthcare sector as a suitable domain for an application example, as it uses highly sensitive data and is a major research field of privacy-preserving data publishing (PPDP) [12]. We evaluated our proposed approach by implementing a prototype, an implementation of a specific ruleset for a fictional healthcare application field, and used this to discuss an application example in the form of a case study where doctors are able to write mashups solutions to analyze data for their research by following the privacy rules of the hospital.

4.1   Prototype Implementation

As proof of concept, we implemented a Web application platform using Java for the business logic and the Apache Wicket Framework for the front-end. We did not use existing functionality methods, considering them as independent from our approach, and concentrated on the implementation of the mashup functionality module. The validation mechanism is implemented based on the proposed workflow for ontology concepts due to their adaptability and characteristics of semantic solutions, using the Web Ontology Language (OWL) to model the security rules. We limited ourselves in that only mashup scripts written in the Enterprise Mashup Markup Language (EMML) [13] could be validated and, if accepted, executed on the EMML Reference Runtime Engine. The embedded ontology that comprises the ruleset was designed with Protege [14].

The handling of the prototype for the execution of mashups works as follows: A user can access the platform with a browser of her/his choice and upload mashup code using a form. Despite the proposed approach to store only accepted mashups, we stored them as persistent for test purposes so that the user can access her/his uploaded mashup scripts and validate them on demand. If the mashup script adheres to the embedded rules, it is executed and the output of the mashup is displayed, otherwise the violated rule is displayed together with the respective mashup's relations (see Section 3.2, Ruleset Design) that have been computed from the validation system.

4.2 Design of the Ruleset

For the healthcare example, we defined two basic policies for mashup design:

1. A user has to anonymize the transformed data before it is displayed for privacy reasons.
2. A user may only filter the fundamental data according to **Birth**, **ZIP**, or **Sex** of patients.

The set of usable parameters P for the domain comprises the attributes **Name**, **Birth**, **ZIP**, **Sex**, and **Disease**. Furthermore, for our domain we defined the following three usable mashup operations, constituting the operations of the set O for the domain of our case study:

- **Fetch:** This operation fetches a data table. We neglect the resource address for our examples, assuming that only one available data table exists, provided by a Web Service.
- **Filter[P]:** A usual filter operation uses an expression such as *Attribute = Value*. However, we simplify the expression by taking only the column into account. As we are using EMML, the mapping system has to decompose the XPath expression.
- **Anonymize:** A Web Service predefined by the development staff anonymizing a data table according to a privacy model.

For evaluation purposes we restricted ourselves to the following mashup formalization:

$$M_i := \{\mathsf{op}[\mathsf{P}_1]_{(1)} \mapsto \mathsf{op}[\mathsf{P}_2]_{(2)} \mapsto \ldots \mapsto \mathsf{op}[\mathsf{P}_n]_{(n)}\}$$

which is possible by excluding operations like joining/merging tables from consideration, resulting in each operation having only a single predecessor. Therefore, the above informal notation of a mashup solution should be interpreted as an abbreviation of an ordered n-tupel.

We implemented the policies for mashup solutions with the following three restrictions (cf. Description Logic), determining the sequence of operations (cf. Equation (1)-(3)), the attributes that can be used for filtering (cf. Equation (4)), and that in every case an anonymization operation has to be called by the user (cf. Equation (5); in case of $\exists$ please remember to define a contradiction due to the fact that ontologies work with the Open World Assumption (OWA)):

$$\texttt{Fetch} \sqsubseteq \forall \texttt{hasSuccessor.(Filter or Anonymize)} \tag{1}$$

$$\texttt{Filter} \sqsubseteq \forall \texttt{hasSuccessor.(Filter or Anonymize)} \tag{2}$$

$$\texttt{Anonymize} \sqsubseteq \forall \texttt{hasSuccessor.Nothing} \tag{3}$$

$$\texttt{Filter} \sqsubseteq \forall \texttt{hasParameter.(Birth or ZIP or Sex)} \tag{4}$$

$$\texttt{Executor} \sqsubseteq \exists \texttt{performs.Anonymize} \tag{5}$$

4.3 Validation

Alice is a fictional doctor in the hospital, well-educated in healthcare and interested in research and publication of her results. She is using the hospital's mashup functionality to design personalized mashup solutions for data transformations, facilitating analysis of enormous amounts of data.

In the first case, she just wants to know which effect the date of birth has on a disease and implements the mashup $M_1 := \{\texttt{Fetch} \mapsto \texttt{Filter[Birth]}\}$. In this case, the platform computes an inconsistency due to the missing operation **Anonymization** (cf. Equation (5)) and provides the following notification as failure message along with some type of information about the naming conventions used: **Failure: Executor not performs Anonymization**.

Hence, Alice knows that she has to perform an Anonymization operation. In the next mashup solution, she inserts the operation in the following way: $M_2 := \{\texttt{Fetch} \mapsto \texttt{Anonymization} \mapsto \texttt{Filter[Birth]}\}$, whereupon the platform rejects the submitted mashup solution according to Equation (3) with the following notification: **Failure: Anonymization hasSuccessor Filter**.

Finally, she changes the implementation of the mashup to the following: $M_3 := \{\texttt{Fetch} \mapsto \texttt{Filter[Birth]} \mapsto \texttt{Anonymization}\}$, and the results of the implemented logic are displayed on the screen. Furthermore, as Alice is unfamiliar with the security policies of the enterprise concerning data transformations, she tries to implement a mashup that filters for a specific name: $M_4 := \{\texttt{Fetch} \mapsto \texttt{Filter[Name]} \mapsto \texttt{Anonymization}\}$. However, as it is not her task to establish a link between a patient's name and disease, which might circumvent the security mechanism of the anonymization operation, the system forbids the mashup according to Equation (4) and displays the following notification: **Failure: Filter hasParameter Name**.

A possible and useful enhancement of the restrictions shown here would be the application of another ruleset that controls data published to another research center, so that Alice cannot release datasets that are not approved by the authority.

Due to paper length limitations, we cannot provide a more in-depth use case example, but we believe the basic approach should be clear from our explanations. We also defined more complex use cases, using the full graph of our mashup notation and several operation types as well as parameters. Furthermore, we implemented our system for more than one application domain and used different reasoning engines for evaluation. Due to Pellet's ability to reason in an inconsistent state, we used it for the main part of evaluation. Additionally, we used our formal notation to define objects, enabling us to simulate mashup scripts as test objects and use automated tests to validate their compliance with the defined policies. With automated tests, we were able to test permutations of defined operations, parameters, and sequences, and we analyzed the results of the reasoning system automatically as well as manually in a single review process.

The drawback of our solution is that the formulation and restriction of mashup compositions can be a time-consuming task and it is hard to formulate proper rules for security and privacy purposes in advance. We believe that the best approach is to begin with a small domain. For instance, platforms such as Web-based time-management platforms, where staff members have to enter their working hours, could be enhanced if different users could design their own mashup solutions for personalized statistical evaluations. Of course, trying to model the entire data structure of an enterprise and using mashup solutions for each use case would be a daunting task. The data-processing patterns should be kept as simple as possible. For instance, data aggregations have to take place at the beginning and then it will be stated which operations have to be executed so that the data is cleaned up afterwards before further tasks can be performed on the aggregated set of data.

In our evaluation we neglected performance aspects of reasoning since it is closely related to the reasoner used. Furthermore, we limited ourselves to the in-tree definition of mashup solutions and left mashup solutions with cyclic architecture out of consideration.

5   Discussion

We illustrated our approach on the example of an ontology-based core implementation that is based on pure logic and deductive reasoning and therefore fully comprehensible by machines as well as humans. The proposed platform is designed to return the authority over data-processing to the enterprise, so that the enterprise is able to regulate how and under which circumstances data is accessed and processed by specifying patterns that are modeled in the embedded ruleset. In this section, we analyze our approach at multiple levels.

5.1   Advantages of the Mashup Formalization

As we consider the mashup as an in-tree, where we have sequential $\{op_i\} \mapsto \{op_j\}$ relations and joining/merging $\{op_1, \ldots, op_n\} \mapsto \{op_r\}$ relations, we can divide the whole tree into sub-problems and concentrate on analyzing the single operations, sequences of operations, and joining/merging problems. Testing single operations means validating their parameters and context $\{\texttt{context}\} \mapsto \{\texttt{op[P]}_\ell\}$, testing sequences of operations means validating against malicious aggregation (e.g., SUM, MAX, etc.) $\{\texttt{op}_i\} \mapsto \{\texttt{op}_j\}$, and testing joining/merging operations means validating that culminating previous results does not constitute a possible threat $\{\texttt{op}_1, \ldots, \texttt{op}_n\} \mapsto \{\texttt{op}_r\}$. Furthermore, we can categorize single operations as well as sequences of operations, facilitating that each category can be assigned a specific threat level. The explained sub-problem characteristics together with the usage of categories facilitate a flexible ruleset that allows the end user to program individual and personalized software without the administrator having to adapt the ruleset for each use case.

5.2 Security and Privacy Issues

In the following, we will discuss the effects of our system on security and privacy issues that are introduced in Section 2.

Information Leakage and Distribution of Data/Sensitive Information to Unknown or Unauthorized Users: We extended a traditional enterprise platform with our security architecture for mashup functionality. As we verify mashup functionality based on a ruleset where the role of the user can be modeled as well, we can protect the enterprise's data from arbitrary access and transformation. Thus, we can define that only authorized people may execute mashup scripts, which must be compliant with the enterprise's data transformation policies. However, as several browser-related attacks exist and the platform implementation acts as trusted environment, the platform has to be secured by appropriate security measures, which go beyond the scope of this work. Furthermore, there is no way to ensure that staff members who have access to the platform do not forward information to unauthorized people.

An important advantage of the proposed security architecture is the adaptive system structure, providing only additional security measures that are independent from other measures, such as regulations for database security. Especially in the case of mashups, it is important that we distinguish between access rights of data and transformation rights, as mashups are aimed to freely access data and process them according to the needs of the user, and we therefore have to concentrate on transformation rules in mashup security. We believe that access rights are not within the scope of mashup security and should be covered by other well-known security measures (see [15]).

Creation of Sensitive Information through Aggregation: Establishing rules that forbid the creation of sensitive information is actually possible, but in reality it is hard to cover all possibilities of sensitive aggregation procedures. However, the enterprise has the option of enforcing data processing patterns, thereby mitigating the threat of sensitive aggregation. An example is our case study in Section 5, where we illustrated rules that permit only a selection of attributes that are allowed to customize a filter operation, thus determining the permitted aggregation methods.

Extracting Information by Inference Attacks: One attack often neglected in security evaluation lies in the extraction of sensitive data by inferencing several well-anonymized data sets. In the case of mashups this could be achieved by generating suitable mashups, where each strictly adheres to the defined rules regarding privacy protection, but the resulting data sets may be linked by unprotected data columns. Since this is an aspect of the anonymization engine in use and is completely independent from the solution proposed in this paper, depending on the anonymization method in use, be it k-anonymity, differential privacy, or other privacy models [12], the problem must be solved there. One solution could be to log what data has been accessed by a single user through mashups and prohibiting additional mashups if the combination with old mashups would be sensitive regarding inference. Still, this may reduce the value of the overall mashup solution drastically.

5.3   Scalability & Performance

The proposed approach can be used on new systems as well as systems that are already in place. Only the ruleset and mapping implementations have to be adapted for the actual domain. The proposed mapping and ruleset-based design that builds the fundamental vocabulary as well as the basis for the definition of the composition restrictions is going to grow rapidly if it is used in large companies. In order to keep track of the dependencies and restrictions, the ruleset can be divided into fine granular classes so that a separate file is loaded for each context that only includes the mashup restrictions for the respective context. Additionally, we have to consider that for security and privacy reasons, the mashups have to be executed on the server side. However, a layered architecture of the proposed platform allows the use of a redundant server structure, and thus it is possible to distribute the workload on several machines.

6   Related Work

To the best of our knowledge, there are only a few publications on security aspects of mashups due to the novelty of the mashup technology. Below, we discuss the works most related to our topic and approach.

Enterprise mashups have great potential for creating value, but the following papers, among others, motivated us to invest time and effort in our proposed approach. In [9], the authors discuss the security, trust, and privacy problems that come with the mashup's architecture and classify the security threats (cf. Section 2). In [7], the authors explain the shift from the purely casual sector to business-supporting applications. In [16], the enterprise mashup technology is introduced in the business domain for improving individual work processes and as the answer to the ever-changing requirements. In [17], the authors give a market overview of different mashup tools and state that although non-commercial tools provide some predefined security solutions, there are still unfulfilled requirements.

The following papers are related to our work in that they propose security-enhancing and privacy-preserving solutions for composition-based application development. In [18], the authors discuss accountability for mashup services and propose a framework to facilitate trust and the resolution of legal requirements. Their proposed framework has an ontology-based approach. The paper proposes models that are meant for information systems developers to understand the entities in mashup service solutions. In [19], the authors propose a privacy-preserving approach for mashup data Web services by using ontologies, metadata, and ontology queries. Their approach is based on rewriting mashup queries to fulfill privacy constraints and modify them for available data Web services. Following these steps, the composition of the mashup in question is computed and, in contrast to our proposed approach, meant for automatically suggested mashup patterns. Instead of computing patterns, our approach is meant for compliance checking so that the enterprise retains the authority over mashup development but allows end users to design their own solutions. In [20], the authors discuss a composability pattern for general service or modular software development that is based on Language-integrated Query (LINQ). The authors explain how specific operations are divided into higher-ordered classes, so that developing is limited to merely chaining together those operations, and building complex applications is accomplished by forming trees of operations.

7 Conclusion

Mashup solutions offer great potential for end users' software development; however, due to their nature, they give rise to several security and privacy-related issues. The security measures on which we rely in traditional software development are insufficient for mashup solutions, which is why we have presented a novel approach in this paper that empowers enterprises to assume authority over end users' mashup development.

We designed and implemented a security architecture where mashup design policies can be defined and enforced. The proposed platform-based approach is designed to be flexible in such a way that only the ruleset and the domain mapping have to be adapted to the actual application system. We used an example to illustrate how security-enhancing and privacy-preserving policies can be modeled and discussed the security-enhancing effects of the proposed security architecture for mashups in an enterprise context, as well as threats suggested in literature that are a consequence of the nature of mashups.

Future work could possibly deal with providing a top level domain for the patterns, thus allowing the users to reuse and extend their customized domain conventions and requirements.

Acknowledgements. The research was funded by COMET K1 and FEMtech 836740, FFG - Austrian Research Promotion Agency.

References

1. Murugesan, S.: Understanding Web 2.0. IT Professional 9(4), 34–41 (2007)
2. Hoyer, V., Stanoevska-Slabeva, K.: The changing role of IT departments in enterprise mashup environments. In: Feuerlicht, G., Lamersdorf, W. (eds.) ICSOC 2008. LNCS, vol. 5472, pp. 148–154. Springer, Heidelberg (2009)
3. JackBe - Presto Mashup Composers, http://www.jackbe.com/products/composers.php
4. IBM Mashup Center, http://www-01.ibm.com/software/info/mashup-center
5. Google Blockly - A visual programming editor, http://code.google.com/p/blockly/
6. Hoyer, V., Stanoesvka-Slabeva, K., Janner, T., Schroth, C.: Enterprise mashups: Design principles towards the long tail of user needs. In: IEEE International Conference on Services Computing, SCC 2008, vol. 2, pp. 601–602 (2008)
7. Anjomshoaa, A., Bader, G., Tjoa, A.M.: Exploiting Mashup Architecture in Business Use Cases. In: 2009 International Conference on Network-Based Information Systems, pp. xx–xxvii. IEEE (2009)
8. Ogrinz, M.: Mashup Patterns: Designs and Examples for the Modern Enterprise, 1st edn. Addison-Wesley Professional (2009)
9. Bader, G., Anjomshoaa, A., Tjoa, A.M.: Privacy Aspects of Mashup Architecture. In: Proceedings of the 2010 IEEE Second International Conference on Social Computing, pp. 1141–1146. IEEE Computer Society (2010)
10. RDFizers, http://simile.mit.edu/wiki/RDFizers
11. Pellet: OWL 2 Reasoner for Java, http://clarkparsia.com/pellet/
12. Fung, B.C.M., Wang, K., Chen, R., Yu, P.S.: Privacy-preserving data publishing: A survey of recent developments. ACM Comput. Surv., 14:1–14:53 (June 2010)
13. Open Mashup Alliance (OMA) - EMML Documentation, http://www.openmashup.org
14. Protege, http://protege.stanford.edu/
15. Bertino, E., Sandhu, R.: Database security - concepts, approaches, and challenges. IEEE Transactions on Dependable and Secure Computing 2(1), 2–19 (2005)
16. Pahlke, I., Beck, R., Wolf, M.: Enterprise Mashup Systems as Platform for Situational Applications. Business Information Systems Engineering, 305–315 (2010)
17. Hoyer, V., Fischer, M.: Market Overview of Enterprise Mashup Tools. In: Bouguettaya, A., Krueger, I., Margaria, T. (eds.) ICSOC 2008. LNCS, vol. 5364, pp. 708–721. Springer, Heidelberg (2008)
18. Zou, J., Pavlovski, C.J.: Towards Accountable Enterprise Mashup Services. In: Proceedings of the IEEE International Conference on e-Business Engineering, ICEBE 2007, pp. 205–212. IEEE Computer Society, Washington, DC (2007)
19. Barhamgi, M., Benslimane, D., Ghedira, C., Gancarski, A.: Privacy-preserving data mashup. In: 2011 IEEE International Conference on Advanced Information Networking and Applications (AINA), pp. 467–474 (2011)
20. Beckman, B.: Why LINQ Matters: Cloud Composability Guaranteed. Queue 10, 20:20–20:31 (2012)

On Privacy-Preserving Ways to Porting the Austrian eID System to the Public Cloud

Bernd Zwattendorfer and Daniel Slamanig

Institute for Applied Information Processing and Communications (IAIK),
Graz University of Technology (TUG), Inffeldgasse 16a, 8010 Graz, Austria
{bernd.zwattendorfer,daniel.slamanig}@iaik.tugraz.at

Abstract. Secure authentication and unique identification of Austrian citizens are the main functions of the Austrian eID system. To facilitate the adoption of this eID system at online applications, the open source module MOA-ID has been developed, which manages identification and authentication based on the Austrian citizen card (the official Austrian eID) for service providers. Currently, the Austrian eID system treats MOA-ID as a trusted entity, which is locally deployed in every service provider's domain. While this model has indeed some benefits, in some situations a centralized deployment approach of MOA-ID may be preferable. In this paper, we therefore propose a centralized deployment approach of MOA-ID in the public cloud. However, the move of a trusted service into the public cloud brings up new obstacles since the cloud can not be considered trustworthy. We encounter these obstacles by introducing and evaluating three distinct approaches, thereby retaining the workflow of the current Austrian eID system and preserving citizens' privacy when assuming that MOA-ID acts honest but curious.

1 Introduction

The Austrian eID system constitutes one major building block within the Austrian e-Government strategy. Secure authentication and unique identification of Austrian citizens – by still preserving citizens' privacy – are the main functions of the Austrian eID system. The basic building block for secure authentication and unique identification in the Austrian eID system is the Austrian citizen card [10], the official eID in Austria.

To facilitate the adoption of this eID concept at online applications, the open source module MOA-ID has been developed. Basically, MOA-ID manages the identification and authentication process based on the Austrian citizen card for various service providers. Currently, the Austrian eID concept treats MOA-ID as a trusted entity, which is deployed locally in every service provider's domain. While this model has indeed some benefits, in some situations a centralized deployment approach of MOA-ID may be preferable. For instance, a centralized MOA-ID can save service providers a lot of operational and maintenance costs. However, in terms of scalability – theoretically the whole Austrian population could use this central service for identification and authentication at service providers – the existing approach is advantageous.

L.J. Janczewski, H.B. Wolfe, and S. Shenoi (Eds.): SEC 2013, IFIP AICT 405, pp. 300–314, 2013.
© IFIP International Federation for Information Processing 2013

To bypass the issue of scalability, in this paper, we propose a centralized deployment approach of MOA-ID in the public cloud. The public cloud is able to provide nearly unlimited computing resources and hence the scalability problem can easily be compensated. However, the move of a trusted service into the public cloud brings up new obstacles. In particular, MOA-ID, since now running in the public cloud, can no longer be considered a trustworthy entity. We encounter these obstacles by introducing three different approaches, each describing how the current Austrian eID system can be securely migrated into the public cloud. All approaches retain the workflow of the current Austrian eID system and preserve citizens' privacy when assuming that MOA-ID acts honest but curious. The first approach uses both proxy re-encryption and redactable signatures, the second one relies on anonymous credentials, and the third one sets up on fully homomorphic encryption.

2   The Current Austrian eID System

In the following subsections we describe the basic ideas of the Austrian eID concept by presenting involved components and processes.

2.1   The Austrian Citizen Card Concept

Unique identification and secure authentication are essential processes in e-Government. Particularly, unique identification is essential when a large amount of users comes into play, such as the population of a whole country. In such a huge population, identification of citizens based on first name, last name, and date of birth may be ambiguous. To mitigate this problem, each Austrian citizen is registered in a central register and is assigned a unique identification number. Furthermore, another unique identifier is computed from this number and stored on each citizen card. This so-called sourcePIN is created by a trusted entity, the so-called SourcePIN Register Authority (SRA), and can be used for unique citizen identification at online applications. However, the sourcePIN requires special protection as it is forbidden by law to permanently store the sourcePIN outside the citizen card. Therefore, the Austrian eID concept uses a sector-specific model for identification at online applications. In this sector-specific model, the sourcePIN is used to derive unique sector-specific identifiers, so called sector-specific PINs (ssPINs) for every different governmental sector, e.g., tax, finance, etc. Thereby, citizens' privacy is assured as the sourcePIN cannot be derived from a given ssPIN and different ssPINs of one citizen cannot be linked together.

The key element of the Austrian eID concept constitutes the Austrian citizen card [10], which is basically an abstract definition of a secure eID token possessed by every Austrian citizen. Due to this abstract definition, the Austrian citizen card is a technology-neutral concept, which allows for different implementations. Currently, implementations based on smart cards and mobile phones are in use. In general, the main functions of the Austrian citizen card are 1) *identification and authentication of citizens* and 2) *secure and qualified electronic signature creation.* Citizen identification is based on a special data structure (the *Identity Link*), which is solely stored on the Austrian citizen card. This special data structure contains the citizen's first name, last name, date of birth, a unique identifier (sourcePIN), and the citizen's qualified signature certificate. To guarantee its integrity and authenticity, the *Identity Link* is digitally signed by the SourcePIN Register Authority at issuance. Citizen authentication is carried out by creating a qualified electronic signature according to the EU Signature Directive.

2.2   Identification and Authentication at Online Services

To facilitate the integration of the citizen card's identification and authentication functionality into online services, the open source module MOA-ID is available. The current Austrian eID system relies on a local deployment model, where MOA-ID is deployed and operated in basically every service provider's domain. Due to that fact, MOA-ID is assumed to be trusted, i.e., it will not leak sensitive information such as the citizen's sourcePIN. Figure 1 illustrates in an abstract way the typical identification and authentication scenario of Austrian citizens using MOA-ID.

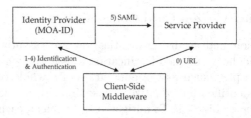

Fig. 1. Simplified illustration of MOA-ID based authentication

Service Provider: The service provider usually provides web-based services, which require unique identification and secure authentication by using the Austrian citizen card. This organization can be either a public authority or a private sector company.

Client-Side Middleware: The Austrian eID concept foresees an abstract and generic access layer to the citizen card, irrespective of its implementation. The client-side middleware implements this interface, which provides online applications easy access to citizen card functionality without the need of knowing any citizen card specifics. The identity provider MOA-ID uses this interface for accessing diverse citizen card functions.

Identity Provider (MOA-ID): MOA-ID represents an identity provider for governmental or private sector service providers. On the one hand, MOA-ID manages the communication with the citizen and her citizen card and, on the other hand, MOA-ID provides specific and authentic citizen card attributes to the service provider for further processing.

In the following we briefly explain an authentication process flow at online services, whereas steps 1 and 2 represent the identification and steps 3 and 4 the authentication process of the Austrian citizen.

Setup: The SRA as trusted entity is responsible for managing citizens' Identity Links. Identity Links can be stored on smart card-based citizen card implementations or server-based (in a hardware security module) using the Austrian Mobile Phone Signature.

Citizen registration: All Austrian citizens are registered in a central register. In order to activate the citizen card, a citizen must prove her identity, e.g. by using a personal ID. This can be done through various channels, either proving the identity personally in a registration office or via certified mail.

Service provider registration: Governmental service providers can be identified either by a special domain ending ("gv.at") or by including a specific object identifier in the service provider's SSL certificate.

Authentication at online services:

1 *Reading and verifying citizen's Identity Link:* After having received an authentication request from the service provider, MOA-ID starts the citizen identification process by requesting the citizen's *Identity Link* through the citizen's client-side middleware. After that, MOA-ID verifies the signature of the returned *Identity Link* to check its integrity and authenticity.

2 *Calculation of the citizen's ssPIN according to the Austrian eID concept:* MOA-ID calculates the ssPIN by applying a cryptographic hash function H (SHA-1) to the concatenation of the sourcePIN and a sector-specific identifier s of the service provider, i.e., ssPIN $= H(\text{sourcePIN}\|\text{s})$.

3 *Requesting the generation of a qualified electronic signature of the citizen:* MOA-ID requests a qualified electronic signature from the citizen through her client-side middleware. By signing a specific message, the citizen gives her consent that she is willing to authenticate at the respective service provider.

4 *Verification of the citizen signature:* MOA-ID verifies the citizen's qualified signature.

5 *Assembling citizen identification and authentication data in a structured way and providing it to the service provider:* MOA-ID assembles a special data structure including authentic identity information of the citizen from the *Identity Link*. These data are structured according to the specifications of the Security Assertion Markup Language (SAML, http://saml.xml.org) and are delivered to the authentication requesting service provider using a SAML defined protocol, thereby ensuring integrity and authenticity of the data transfer.

3   Cryptographic Building Blocks

In this section we introduce the cryptographic building blocks. We note that we do not provide an explicit description of a conventional digital signature scheme (DSS) since this should be clear from the other signature primitives.

3.1   Redactable Signatures

A conventional digital signature does not allow for alterations of a signed document without invalidating the signature. However, there are scenarios where it would be valuable to have the possibility to replace or remove (specified) parts of a message after signature creation such that the original signature stays valid (and no interaction with the original signer is required). Signature schemes which allow *removal* of content (replacement by some special symbol ⊥) by *any* party are called redactable [8], while signature schemes which allow (arbitrary) *replacements* of *admissible* parts by a *designated* party are called sanitizable signature schemes [2]. Below, we present an abstract definition of redactable signatures:

RS.KeyGen: This probabilistic key generation algorithm takes a security parameter and produces and outputs a public (verification) key pk and a private (signing) key sk.

RS.Sign: This (probabilistic) signing algorithm gets as input the signing key sk and a message $m = (m[1], \ldots, m[\ell])$, $m[i] \in \{0, 1\}^*$ and outputs a signature $\sigma = \text{RS.Sign}(sk, m)$.

RS.Verify: This deterministic signature verification algorithm gets as input a public key pk, a message $m = (m[1], \ldots, m[\ell])$, $m[i] \in \{0, 1\}^*$, and a signature σ and outputs a single bit $b = \text{RS.Verify}(pk, m, \sigma)$, $b \in \{\text{true}, \text{false}\}$, indicating whether σ is a valid signature for m.

RS.Redact: This probabilistic redaction algorithm takes as input a message $m = (m[1], \ldots, m[\ell])$, $m[i] \in \{0, 1\}^*$, the public key pk, a signature σ, and a list MOD of indices of blocks to be redacted. It returns a modified message and signature pair $(\hat{m}, \hat{\sigma}) = \text{RS.Redact}(m, pk, \sigma, \text{MOD})$ or an error. Note that for any such signature $(\hat{m}, \hat{\sigma})$ we have $\text{RS.Verify}(pk, \hat{m}, \hat{\sigma}) = \text{true}$

3.2 Anonymous Signatures

Anonymous signature schemes allow group members to issue signatures on behalf of a group, while hiding for each signature which group member actually produced it. There are several flavors of anonymous signatures: *Group signatures* [1] which involve a dedicated entity (the group manager), who runs a setup and an explicit join protocol for every group member to create the respective members signing key. Furthermore, the group manager is able to open signatures issued by group members to identify the respective signer.

Ring signatures [11] are conceptually similar to group signatures, but there is no group manager and the anonymity provided is unconditional. They are "ad-hoc", meaning that a user may take an arbitrary set (ring) of valid public keys to construct a ring signature and the ring represents the anonymity set. We choose to use ring signatures for one of our approaches and present an abstract definition of this signature scheme below, where the key generation is that of a standard digital signature scheme (DSS) and hence omitted here:

AS.Sign: This (probabilistic) signing algorithm gets as input the signing key sk_i s.t. $pk_i \in R$, a ring of public keys $R = (pk_1, \ldots, pk_n)$, a message m and outputs a signature $\sigma = \text{AS.Sign}(sk_i, R, m)$.

AS.Verify: This deterministic signature verification algorithm gets as input a ring of public keys $R = (pk_1, \ldots, pk_n)$, a message m, and a signature σ and outputs a single bit $b = \text{AS.Verify}(R, m, \sigma)$, $b \in \{\text{true}, \text{false}\}$, indicating whether σ is a valid signature for m under R.

3.3 Proxy Re-Encryption

Proxy re-encryption is a public key encryption paradigm where a semi-trusted proxy can transform a message encrypted under the key of party A into another ciphertext, containing the initial plaintext, such that another party B can decrypt with its key. Although the proxy can perform this re-encryption operation, it neither gets access to the plaintext nor to the decryption keys. According to the direction of this re-encryption, such schemes can be classified into bidirectional, i.e., the proxy can transform from A to B and vice versa, and unidirectional, i.e., the proxy can convert in one direction only, schemes. Furthermore, one can distinguish between multi-use schemes, i.e., the ciphertext can be transformed from A to B to C etc., and single-use schemes, i.e., the ciphertext can be transformed only once. We use the unidirectional single-use identity-based proxy re-encryption scheme of [7], but note that we could also use non-identity-based ones.

RE.Setup: This probabilistic algorithm gets a security parameter and a value MaxLevel indicating the maximum number of consecutive re-encryptions permitted by the scheme (in case of single-use we set MaxLevel=2). It outputs the master public parameters $params$, which are distributed to users, and the master private key msk, which is kept private.

RE.KeyGen: This probabilistic key generation algorithm gets $params$, the master private key msk, and an identity $id \in \{0,1\}^*$ and outputs a private key sk_{id} corresponding to that identity.

RE.Enc: This probabilistic encryption algorithm gets $params$, an identity $id \in \{0,1\}^*$, and a plaintext m and outputs $c_{id} = \mathsf{RE.Enc}(params, id, m)$.

RE.RKGen: This probabilistic re-encryption key generation algorithm gets $params$, a private key sk_{id_1} (derived via RE.KeyGen), and two identities $(id_1, id_2) \in \{0,1\}^*$ and outputs a re-encryption key $rk_{id_1 \to id_2} = \mathsf{RE.RKGen}(params, sk_{id_1}, id_1, id_2)$.

RE.ReEnc: This (probabilistic) re-encryption algorithm gets as input a ciphertext c_{id_1} under identity id_1 and a re-encryption key $rk_{id_1 \to id_2}$ (generated by RE.RKGen) and outputs a re-encrypted ciphertext $c_{id_2} = \mathsf{RE.ReEnc}(c_{id_1}, rk_{id_1 \to id_2})$.

RE.Dec: This decryption algorithm gets $params$, a private key sk_{id}, and a ciphertext c_{id} and outputs $m = \mathsf{RE.Dec}(params, sk_{id}, c_{id})$ or an error.

3.4 Anonymous Credentials

Anonymous credential systems [3,4] enable anonymous attribute-based authentication, i.e., they hide the identity of the credential's owner. Multi-show approaches support unlinkability, i.e., different showings of a credential remain unlinkable and are unlinkable to the issuing [4], while others are one-show [3]. Anonymous credentials are very expressive since they allow to encode arbitrary attributes into the credential. Additonally, during the proof of possession of a credential a user can selectively reveal values of attributes or prove that certain relations among attributes hold, without revealing the attribute values. We use an abstract definition of an anonymous credential system as follows:

AC.KeyGen: This probabilistic key generation algorithm is run by an authority and takes a security parameter and produces and outputs a public key pk and a private key sk.

AC.Issue: This interactive algorithm is run between a user U and an authority A. U has as input a list of attributes with corresponding values $\mathtt{attr}$ and wants to obtain a credential for $\mathtt{attr}$ (U may also have as input a long term secret). U executes the credential issuing protocol for $\mathtt{attr}$ with A by using U's input $\mathtt{attr}$ and A has as input it's private key sk. Both algorithms have as input pk and at the end of this interaction U obtains a credential $\mathtt{Cred}$ corresponding to $\mathtt{attr}$.

AC.Prove: This interactive algorithm is run between a user U and a verifier V. U proves the possession of $\mathtt{Cred}$ for $\mathtt{attr'}$, which represents some subset of $\mathtt{attr}$, to a verifier V. At the end of the protocol, V outputs $\mathtt{accept}$ if U has a valid credential $\mathtt{Cred}$ for $\mathtt{attr'}$, otherwise V outputs $\mathtt{reject}$.

We note that the Prove algorithm may also be non-interactive, i.e., the credential holder produces a signature of knowledge which can then be given to the verifier to check the validity of the proof locally.

3.5 Fully Homomorphic Encryption

Fully homomorphic encryption (FHE) schemes are semantically secure (public-key) encryption schemes which allow arbitrary functions to be evaluated on ciphertexts given the (public) key and the ciphertext. Gentry [5] provided the first construction along with a general blue-print to construct (bootstrap) such schemes from less powerful ones. Since then lots of improvements and alternate approaches have been proposed (cf. [12]). However, it seems to require some more years of research to make them practical in general [6]. A fully homomorphic (public-key) encryption scheme is defined by the following efficient algorithms.

FHE.KeyGen: This probabilistic key generation algorithm takes a security parameter and produces and outputs a public-key pk, a public evaluation key evk, and a private key sk.

FHE.Enc: This probabilistic encryption algorithm takes a message $m \in \{0,1\}^n$ and a public-key pk and outputs a ciphertext $c = \mathsf{FHE.Enc}(m, pk)$.

FHE.Dec: This deterministic algorithm takes a ciphertext c and a private key sk and outputs $m = \mathsf{FHE.Dec}(c, sk)$.

FHE.Eval: This homomorphic evaluation algorithm takes an evaluation key evk, a function $f : \{0,1\}^n \to \{0,1\}$ and k ciphertexts and outputs a ciphertext $c_f = \mathsf{FHE.Eval}(f, c_1, \ldots, c_k, evk)$.

In this definition messages are bits, but this can easily be generalized to larger spaces. Let us consider arbitrary message spaces in the following. For one approach we need to assume that FHE schemes exists which are "key-homomorphic". Loosely speaking, this means that for each pair of public keys pk_1 and pk_2 one can derive $f_{1,2}$ and $evk_{1,2}$ such that

$$m = \mathsf{FHE.Dec}(\mathsf{FHE.Eval}(f_{1,2}, \mathsf{FHE.Enc}(m, pk_1), evk_{1,2}), sk_2).$$

This means that by using $f_{1,2}$ one performs a "re-encryption" of m encrypted under pk_1 to another ciphertext under pk_2, which can then be decrypted using sk_2. Such a scheme can trivially be realized using any FHE scheme by letting $f_{1,2}$ represent the circuit, which firstly decrypts the ciphertext c using sk_1 obtaining m and then encrypts m using pk_2 and $evk_{1,2} = evk_1$. However, since now sk_1 would be explicitly wired in the circuit, this would reveal the secret key which is clearly undesirable. Since we are currently not aware of an FHE construction which supports this (loosely defined) property, we need to assume that such a scheme will be available in the future.

4   Porting the Austrian eID System to the Public Cloud

The current local deployment model of MOA-ID has some benefits in terms of end-to-end security or scalability, but still some issues can be identified compared to a centralized deployment model of MOA-ID. The adoption of a centralized model may have the following advantages and disadvantages:

On the one hand, the use of one single and central instance of MOA-ID has a clear advantage for citizens as they only need to trust one specific identity provider. In addition, users could benefit from a comfortable single sign-on (SSO). On the other hand, especially service providers can save a lot of costs because they do not need to operate and maintain a separate MOA-ID installation. Nevertheless, still some disadvantages can be identified. Namely, a single instance of MOA-ID constitutes a single point of failure or attack. Particularly, scalability may be an issue as all citizen authentications will run through this centralized system. This is probably the main issue, as theoretically the whole

Austrian population could use this service for identification and authentication at service providers. However, the issue on scalability can be tackled by moving MOA-ID into a public cloud, which is able to theoretically provide unlimited computing resources. Needless to say, a move of a trusted service into the public cloud, however, brings up some new obstacles.

In order to make a migration of the Austrian eID system and MOA-ID into the public cloud possible, we have identified three approaches to adapt the existing Austrian eID system for running it in the public cloud. The adapted Austrian eID system of the respective solution will provide all functions of MOA-ID (identification, ssPIN generation, and authentication) as in the current status, but protects citizen's privacy with respect to the cloud provider. For providing compact descriptions, we denote the SourcePIN Register Authority by SRA and the Identity Link by $\mathcal{I} = ((A_1, a_1), \ldots, (A_k, a_k))$ as a sequence of attribute labels and attribute values. Let the set of citizens be $C = \{C_1, \ldots, C_n\}$ and the set of service providers be $S = \{S_1, \ldots, S_\ell\}$ as well as the citizen's client-side middleware be denoted as M. Moreover, let us assume that Citizen C_i wants to authenticate at service provider S_j who requires the set of attributes $\mathcal{A}_j$ from $\mathcal{I}$ and exactly one "pseudonym", i.e., the ssPIN for the sector s the service provider S_j is associated to. Additionally, recall that every citizen C_i has a signing key sk_{C_i} stored on the card and the public key pk_{C_i} is publicly available.

4.1 Using Proxy Re-Encryption and Redactable Signatures

Here, the Identity Link $\mathcal{I}$ is modified in a way that it does not include the sourcePIN, but additionally all ssPINs according to all possible governmental sectors. In this augmented Identity Link $\mathcal{I}'$, every attribute a_i is encrypted using an uni-directional single-use proxy re-encryption scheme under a public key (the identity of MOA-ID) such that the corresponding private key is *not* available to MOA-ID and is only known to the SRA. Furthermore, instead of using a conventional digital signature scheme, $\mathcal{I}'$ is signed by the SRA using a redactable signature scheme such that every a_i from $\mathcal{I}'$ can be redacted. The public verification key is available to MOA-ID. Every service provider S_j obtains a key pair for the proxy re-encryption scheme when registering at the SRA. The latter entity produces a re-encryption key, which allows to re-encrypt ciphertexts intended for MOA-ID to S_j, and gives it to MOA-ID. Below we present the detailed workflow:

Setup: SRA generates $(pk_{\mathrm{SRA}}, sk_{\mathrm{SRA}}) = \mathsf{RS.KeyGen}(\kappa)$, $(params_{\mathrm{RE}}, msk_{\mathrm{RE}}) = \mathsf{RE.Setup}(\kappa, 1)$ as well as $sk_{\mathrm{MOA\text{-}ID}} = \mathsf{RE.KeyGen}(params_{\mathrm{RE}}, msk_{\mathrm{RE}}, id_{\mathrm{MOA\text{-}ID}})$. It keeps secret $(sk_{\mathrm{RS}}, msk_{\mathrm{RE}}, sk_{\mathrm{MOA\text{-}ID}})$ and publishes $params_{\mathrm{RE}}$ as well as pk_{RS}.

Citizen registration: The registration of a citizen C_i at the SRA works as it is done now with the exception that $\mathcal{I}'$ includes additional attributes $a_{k+1}, \ldots, a_m$ representing ssPINs for all sectors. Furthermore, for every $(A_i, a_i) \in \mathcal{I}'$ the SRA replaces a_i by $c_{a_i} = \mathsf{RE.Enc}(params, a_i, id_{\mathrm{MOA\text{-}ID}})$ and produces a redactable signature $\sigma_{\mathcal{I}'} = \mathsf{RS.Sign}(sk_{\mathrm{SRA}}, \mathcal{I}')$. Then, $(\sigma_{\mathcal{I}'}, \mathcal{I}')$ is stored on C_i's citizen card.

Service provider registration: The registration for service provider S_j at the SRA works as follows. SRA produces a private key $sk_{S_j} = \mathsf{RE.KeyGen}(params_{\mathrm{RE}}, msk_{\mathrm{RE}}, id_{S_j})$ for S_j and a re-encryption key $rk_{\mathrm{MOA\text{-}ID} \to S_j} = \mathsf{RE.RKGen}(params, sk_{\mathrm{MOA\text{-}ID}}, \mathrm{MOA\text{-}ID}, S_j)$ and gives sk_{S_j} to S_j and $rk_{\mathrm{MOA\text{-}ID} \to S_j}$ to MOA-ID respectively.

Authentication at online services:

1 & 2: After having received an authentication request from S_j, MOA-ID starts the citizen identification process by requesting C_i's Identity Link $\mathcal{I}'$ through M. Thereby, we have two possibilities:

    1. If MOA-ID tells M which attributes $\mathcal{A}_j$ are required by S_j, then M runs $(\hat{\mathcal{I}}', \sigma_{\hat{\mathcal{I}}'}) =$ RS.Redact$(\mathcal{I}', pk_{\mathsf{RS}}, \sigma_{\mathcal{I}'}, \mathsf{MOD})$ wheres MOD contains all the indices of c_{a_i} from $\mathcal{I}'$ with exception of $\mathcal{A}_j$ (including the ssPIN required by S_j). Then, M sends $(\hat{\mathcal{I}}', \sigma_{\hat{\mathcal{I}}'})$ to MOA-ID which runs $b = $ RS.Verify$(pk_{\mathsf{RS}}, \hat{\mathcal{I}}', \sigma_{\hat{\mathcal{I}}'})$ and proceeds if $b = \mathtt{true}$ and aborts otherwise.

    2. M sends $(\mathcal{I}', \sigma_{\mathcal{I}'})$ to MOA-ID which runs $b = $ RS.Verify$(pk_{\mathsf{RS}}, \mathcal{I}', \sigma_{\mathcal{I}'})$ and proceeds if $b = \mathtt{true}$ and aborts otherwise. Then, MOA-ID runs $(\hat{\mathcal{I}}', \sigma_{\hat{\mathcal{I}}'}) = $ RS.Redact$(\mathcal{I}', pk_{\mathsf{RS}}, \sigma_{\mathcal{I}'}, \mathsf{MOD})$, whereas MOD contains the indices of all attributes in $\mathcal{I}'$ with exception of $\mathcal{A}_j$ (including the ssPIN required by S_j).

3: In this step, MOA-ID usually requests the generation of a qualified electronic signature from C_i. Here we have the following possibilities:

    1. MOA-ID requests no signature, since $\mathcal{I}'$ is signed and only available to C_i.

    2. M produces a standard signature $\sigma = $ DSS.Sign(sk_{C_i}, m^*) for a special message m^* on behalf of C_i (which, however, allows unique identification of C_i by MOA-ID).

    3. M produces a ring signature $\sigma = $ AS.Sign(sk_{C_i}, R, m^*) for a special message m^* on behalf of ring R including pk_{C_i}.

4: MOA-ID verifies the validity of signature σ either by running $b = $ DSS.Verify(pk_{C_i}, m^*, σ) or $b = $ AS.Verify(R, m^*, σ) (note that due to $\sigma_{\mathcal{I}'}$ and it's potentially redacted version can always be linked together, it is advisable that every citizen C_i uses a fixed ring all the time, i.e., all citizens in R use the same ring, since otherwise, e.g., when they are sampled uniform at random, then intersection attacks on the rings will soon reveal C_i.).

5: MOA-ID takes all remaining attributes c_{a_i} from $\mathcal{I}'$ (or $\hat{\mathcal{I}}'$) and computes for every such attribute $c'_{a_i} = $ RE.ReEnc$(c_{a_i}, rk_{\mathsf{MOA\text{-}ID}\to S_j})$ and assembles all these resulting c'_{a_i} into the SAML structure, which is then communicated to S_j. S_j can then decrypt all the attributes using sk_{S_j}.

4.2   Using Anonymous Credentials

The Identity Link $\mathcal{I}$ is augmented to $\mathcal{I}'$ in a way that it does not include the sourcePIN, but additionally all ssPIN's. Now, the SRA issues an anonymous credential Cred to every citizen for attr being all attributes in $\mathcal{I}'$. Essentially, a citizen then authenticates to a service provider by proving to MOA-ID the possession of a valid credential, i.e., MOA-ID checks whether the credential has been revoked or not. Note that for one show credentials, if the entire credential Cred is shown to MOA-ID, this amounts to a simple lookup in a blacklist. If the credential is not revoked, MOA-ID signs the credential to confirm that it is not revoked and the citizen performs via M a (non-interactive) proof by revealing the necessary attributes $\mathcal{A}_j$ including the required ssPIN to S_j, who can then in turn verify the proof(s) as well as MOA-ID's signature.

Setup: SRA generates $(pk_{\mathrm{SRA}}, sk_{\mathrm{SRA}}) = $ AC.KeyGen(κ) and keeps secret sk_{SRA} and publishes pk_{SRA}. Furthermore, MOA-ID produces a key pair for a digital signature scheme $(pk_{\mathrm{MOA\text{-}ID}}, sk_{\mathrm{MOA\text{-}ID}}) = $ DSS.KeyGen(κ) and publishes $pk_{\mathrm{MOA\text{-}ID}}$.

Citizen registration: At registration of citizen C_i at the SRA a modified Identity Link $\mathcal{I}'$ is generated, which includes additional attributes $a_{k+1}, \ldots, a_m$ representing ssPINs for all sectors and other citizen attributes. Then, SRA and C_i run AC.Issue and the resulting credential Cred is stored on C_i's Citizen Card.

Service provider registration: The registration for service provider S_j works as it is done now.

Authentication at online services:

1, 2 & 3: After having received an authentication request from S_j, MOA-ID starts the citizen identification process by requesting C_i's credential Cred and checks whether Cred has not been revoked. If Cred has not been revoked MOA-ID produces a signature $\sigma =$ DSS.Sign($sk_{\text{MOA-ID}}$, Cred, σ) and sends σ along with a description of $\mathcal{A}_j$ to M.

4: M runs $b =$ DSS.Verify($pk_{\text{MOA-ID}}$, Cred, σ) and if $b =$ true produces a non-interactive proof π which opens all attribute values of $\mathcal{A}_j$ including the ssPIN required by S_j and sends (Cred, π, σ) to S_j. Otherwise, M aborts.

5: S_j computes $b =$ DSS.Verify($pk_{\text{MOA-ID}}$, Cred, σ) and if $b =$ true verifies the proof π. If both checks verify, C_i is authenticated, otherwise S_j aborts.

Note that in this approach Cred is shown to MOA-ID, which however does not reveal the attribute values but makes revocation easier, since it only requires blacklist lookups. One could also use multi-show credentials, whereas M would then have to perform a proof with MOA-ID which convinces MOA-ID that the credentials are not revoked [9], which provides stronger privacy guarantees.

4.3 Using Fully Homomorphic Encryption

This approach is a rather theoretic one and requires an FHE scheme which is also "key-homomorphic" as already discussed before. The idea for this approach is the following: The Identity Link $\mathcal{I}$ of a citizen holds the same attributes as now (and in particular the sourcePIN), but every attribute a_i is encrypted using an FHE scheme with the above described property under MOA-ID's public key for which MOA-ID does *not* hold the private key. Furthermore, this resulting $\mathcal{I}'$ is conventionally signed by the SRA. Then, for authentication at S_j, the resulting $\mathcal{I}'$ and the signature σ are sent to MOA-ID who checks the signature and homomorphically computes the respective ssPIN from the encrypted sourcePIN (without learning neither sourcePIN nor ssPIN). Then, for all encrypted attributes required by S_j (including the afore computed encrypted ssPIN), MOA-ID performs the "FHE re-encryption" to S_j's public key. On receiving the respective information from MOA-ID, the service provider can decrypt all attribute values.

Setup: SRA generates ($pk_{\text{MOA-ID}}$, $evk_{\text{MOA-ID}}$, $sk_{\text{MOA-ID}}$) = FEH.KeyGen(κ) and keeps secret $sk_{\text{MOA-ID}}$ and publishes ($pk_{\text{MOA-ID}}$, $evk_{\text{MOA-ID}}$). Furthermore, SRA produces a key pair for a digital signature scheme (pk_{SRA}, sk_{SRA}) = DSS.KeyGen(κ) and publishes pk_{SRA}.

Citizen registration: During registration of citizen C_i at the SRA, for every $(A_i, a_i) \in \mathcal{I}$ SRA replaces a_i by $c_{a_i} =$ FHE.Enc(a_i, $pk_{\text{MOA-ID}}$) and produces a signature $\sigma_{\mathcal{I}'} =$ DSS.Sign(sk_{SRA}, $\mathcal{I}'$). Then, ($\sigma_{\mathcal{I}'}$, $\mathcal{I}'$) is stored on C_i's citizen card.

Service provider registration: For the registration of service provider S_j, SRA computes (pk_{S_j}, evk_{S_j}, sk_{S_j}) = FEH.KeyGen(κ) as well as $evk_{\text{MOA-ID},S_j}$ and $f_{\text{MOA-ID},S_j}$, and gives sk_{S_j} to S_j as well as $evk_{\text{MOA-ID},S_j}$ and $f_{\text{MOA-ID},S_j}$ to MOA-ID.

Authentication at online services:

1 & 2: After having received an authentication request from S_j, MOA-ID starts the citizen identification process by requesting C_i's Identity Link $\mathcal{I}'$ and its corresponding signature $\sigma_{\mathcal{I}'}$. MOA-ID runs $b =$ DSS.Verify(pk_{SRA}, $\mathcal{I}'$, $\sigma_{\mathcal{I}'}$) and proceeds if $b =$ true and aborts otherwise. Let c_{a_k} be the encrypted sourcePIN, then MOA-ID computes $c'_{a_k} =$ FHE.Eval(f_H, c_{a_k} ‖FHE.Enc(s_j, $pk_{\text{MOA-ID}}$), $evk_{\text{MOA-ID}}$) where s_j is the sector specific identifier required by S_j and f_H is a circuit representing the evaluation of the SHA-1 hash function, which is used for ssPIN generation.

3: In this step MOA-ID requests the generation of a qualified electronic signature from C_i. Here we have the following possibilities:

1. MOA-ID requests no signature, since $\mathcal{I}'$ is signed and only available to C_i.
2. M produces a standard signature $\sigma = \mathsf{DSS.Sign}(sk_{C_i}, m^*)$ for a special message m^* on behalf of C_i (which, however, allows unique identification of C_i by MOA-ID).
3. M produces a ring signature $\sigma = \mathsf{AS.Sign}(sk_{C_i}, R, m^*)$ for a special message m^* on behalf of ring R including pk_{C_i}.

4: MOA-ID verifies the validity of signature σ either by running $b = \mathsf{DSS.Verify}(pk_{C_i}, m^*, \sigma)$ or $b = \mathsf{AS.Verify}(R, m^*, \sigma)$.

5: MOA-ID takes all attributes c_{a_i} in $\mathcal{A}_j$ from $\mathcal{I}'$ including c_{a_k} and computes for every such attribute $\hat{c}_{a_i} = \mathsf{FHE.Eval}(f_{\mathrm{MOA\text{-}ID}, S_j}, c_{a_i}, evk_{\mathrm{MOA\text{-}ID}, S_j})$, thus performing a re-encryption to pk_{S_j}, and assembles all these resulting $\hat{c}_{a_i}$ into the SAML structure, which is then communicated to S_j. S_j can now decrypt all attributes using sk_{S_j}.

5   Evaluation

In this section we evaluate the different approaches based on selected criteria targeting several aspects, e.g. evaluating the overall architecture or aspects

Table 1. Evaluation of the various approaches. We use $\checkmark$ to indicate as the criterion being full applicable, $\times$ as not applicable, and $\approx$ as partly applicable. For quantitative criteria we use L for *low*, M for *medium*, and H for *high*.

Re-use of existing infrastructure: How much of the existing infrastructure of the Austrian eID system can be re-used or do a lot of parts need to be exchanged or modified?

Conformance to current workflow: Is the authentication process flow of the approach conform to the existing citizen card authentication process flow?

Scalability: Is the approach applicable in a large scale or not?

Practicability: Can the authentication process be carried out within a reasonable time frame?

Extensibility: Is the applied infrastructure of the approach easily extensible to new requirements, e.g., adding new sectors and thus requiring new ssPINs?

Middleware complexity: Does the approach require high complexity or computational power from the client-side middleware?

Service provider effort: How much effort is required by the service provider adopting a particular approach?

Trust in MOA-ID: Does the approach require MOA-ID being trusted?

Anonymity: Does the approach support citizens to be anonymous with respect to MOA-ID?

Unlinkability: Are users unlinkable to MOA-ID, i.e., can different authentications of one citizen be linked together?

Authentication without prior registration: The current Austrian eID system allows registration-less authentications. Hence, is this feature still possible or not?

Criterion	Approach 1	Approach 2	Approach 3
Re-use of existing infrastructure	$\approx$	$\approx$	$\approx$
Conformance to current workflow	$\checkmark$	$\approx$	$\checkmark$
Scalability	$\checkmark$	$\checkmark, \approx$	$\checkmark$
Practicability	$\checkmark$	$\checkmark, \approx$	$\times$
Extensibility	$\times$	$\approx$	$\checkmark$
Middleware complexity	L	L, H	L
Service provider effort	L	M	H
Trust in MOA-ID	L	L	L
Anonymity	$\times, \checkmark$	$\checkmark$	$\times, \checkmark$
Unlinkability	$\times$	$\times, \checkmark$	$\times$
Authentication without prior registration	$\checkmark$	$\checkmark$	$\checkmark$

regarding the individual entities. We briefly describe the selected criteria for evaluation below and Table 1 shows a comparison of our three approaches.

In the following, we give some explanations why specific criteria could be fulfilled, partly fulfilled, or not-fulfilled by the respective approach.

Re-Use of Existing Infrastructure: This criterion can only be partly fulfilled by all approaches since all approaches require some modification of the existing Austrian eID infrastructure. Approach 1 and 3 require some kind of additional governance structure, as proxy re-encryption keys for service providers have to be generated and managed by SRA. Additionally, the attribute values of the existing Identity Link structure must be exchanged by encrypted values and the Identity Link needs to be augmented. For approach 1, the conventional signature of the Identity Link must also be exchanged by a redactable signature. In contrast to that, Approach 2 using anonymous credentials requires a complete re-structuring of the Identity Link. However, all approaches can still rely on the same basic architectural concept of the Austrian eID infrastructure, using MOA-ID as identity provider.

Conformance to Current Workflow: Approach 1 and 3 fully comply with the current citizen card authentication process flow, hence they follow the steps identification, ssPIN provision, and authentication. Approach 2 is slightly different, as MOA-ID just checks if a provided credential is not revoked. The actual verification of the credential is carried out directly at the service provider.

Scalability: Basically, all approaches can be adopted in a large scale. Approach 1 and 3 are similar to the existing Austrian eID system, as only a few attributes need to be exchanged within the Identity Link and the computational requirements for the middleware remain low. For approach 2, it must be distinguished whether one-show or multi-show anonymous credentials will be used. For one-show credentials, revocation checking is a very light-weight process and hence easy adoptable. In contrast to that, revocation for multi-show credentials is much more complex and not easily applicable for a large amount of users such as the Austrian population. Finally, any scalability doubts concerning MOA-ID can be neglected as it is running in a public cloud providing nearly unlimited resources.

Practicability: Approach 1 and 2 seem to be to date the most promising practical approaches. Approach 1 relies only on cryptographic mechanisms, which can already efficiently implemented. For approach 2, again we must distinguish between one-show and multi-show credentials. For one-show credentials, proof generation requires moderate effort. For multi-show credentials, proof generation for non-revocation proofs is complex and computational expensive. This gives a lot of load to the client-side middleware, which makes approach 2 using multi-show credentials quite impracticable. For approach 3, the assumptions we made for FHE still require further research activities and are far away from any implementation. Although we rely on public clouds, FHE is currently not practicable.

Extensibility: For adding new sectors, approach 1 would require a full exchange of the Identity Link, as it must be re-signed when adding a new encrypted ssPIN. The same issue holds for approach 2, since a new credential incorporating the new ssPIN must be stored on the citzen card with exception when using scope-exclusive pseudonyms as proposed in ABC4Trust (https://abc4trust.eu). In approach 3, ssPIN's are computed from the encrypted version of the sourcePIN and no modifications of the Identity Link are required.

Middleware Complexity: In approach 1, client-side middleware complexity is low as only redaction of the Identity Link is required. Middleware complexity in approach 2 depends on the type of anonymous credentials used. Proof computation of multi-show credentials is computational expensive, which would impose a significant computational burden on M [9] when taking into account that the system covers all citizens of Austria. For approach 3, middleware complexity is low again as its functionality is equal to current middleware implementations.

Service Provider Effort: The effort for service providers adopting approach 1 is low. Service providers just need to verify the data received by MOA-ID and do some decryption operations. For approach 2, the effort is slightly higher because service providers need to set up appropriate verification mechanisms for the claims provided by the user. The effort for service providers in approach 3 is the highest as FHE decryption is currently still computationally expensive.

Trust in MOA-ID: Since no sensitive citizen data such as the sourcePIN or any ssPIN are revealed to MOA-ID, no trust is required. In approach 1 and 3 MOA-ID only sees encrypted citizen data. In approach 2 MOA-ID does only see the credential but non of its attribute values. However, some trust assumptions are required that MOA-ID works correctly.

Anonymity: For approach 2, anonymity is obvious as the whole approach sets up on anonymous credentials. Achieving anonymity in approach 1 and 3 depends on the sub-processes to be chosen for citizen authentication (signature creation). Both approaches 1 and 3 rely on three similar alternative sub-processes. Sub-process 1 does not request a citizen signature and fully relies on the Identity Link's signature for citizen authentication, as the Identity Link is only available to the citizen. In this case, the citizen stays fully anonymous in the face of MOA-ID. In sub-process 2, citizen signature creation is requested by MOA-ID for citizen authentication. In this case, citizens are uniquely identifiable by MOA-ID due to pk_{C_i}. Finally, within sub-process 3 ring signatures are created and enable citizen anonymity with respect to the defined ring.

Unlinkability: For our approaches, it is very hard to achieve unlinkability with respect to MOA-ID. In approach 1 and 3 citizens are linkable because they always present the same Identity Link and corresponding signature. Citizens could only be unlinkable in approach 2, where one-show credentials provide linkability and multi-show credentials provide unlinkability.

Authentication without Prior Registration: This criterion can still be fulfilled by all of our approaches.

6 Conclusions

Based on the results of our evaluation, we conclude that all approaches might be feasible but not all of them might be really practical when considering an implementation of a cloud-based approach instead of the current Austrian eID system. Approach 1 might be the best as it could be quickly realized and requires less effort for the client-side middleware and the service provider. However, linkability and higher efforts for extensions are the drawbacks of this approach. Depending on the type of anonymous credential system, approach 2 might also be practicable and possible to implement. Although it provides more complexity and efforts for the client-side middleware, compared to approach 1 it could provide full anonymity and unlinkability. Finally, although approach 3 has its advantages, e.g., in terms of extensibility, and would be promising for the future, it is currently not practicable. Implementations of fully homomorphic encryption schemes are currently still in the early stages which definitely hinder a fast adoption of this approach.

Acknowledgements. We would like to thank the anonymous reviewers for their valuable suggestions. The second author has been supported by the European Commission through project FP7-FutureID, grant agreement number 318424.

References

1. Ateniese, G., Camenisch, J.L., Joye, M., Tsudik, G.: A Practical and Provably Secure Coalition-Resistant Group Signature Scheme. In: Bellare, M. (ed.) CRYPTO 2000. LNCS, vol. 1880, pp. 255–270. Springer, Heidelberg (2000)
2. Ateniese, G., Chou, D.H., de Medeiros, B., Tsudik, G.: Sanitizable Signatures. In: de Capitani di Vimercati, S., Syverson, P.F., Gollmann, D. (eds.) ESORICS 2005. LNCS, vol. 3679, pp. 159–177. Springer, Heidelberg (2005)
3. Brands, S.: Rethinking Public Key Infrastructures and Digital Certificates: Building in Privacy. MIT Press (2000)
4. Camenisch, J., Lysyanskaya, A.: An Efficient System for Non-transferable Anonymous Credentials with Optional Anonymity Revocation. In: Pfitzmann, B. (ed.) EUROCRYPT 2001. LNCS, vol. 2045, pp. 93–118. Springer, Heidelberg (2001)
5. Gentry, C.: Fully Homomorphic Encryption using Ideal Lattices. In: ACM STOC 2009, pp. 169–178. ACM (2009)
6. Gentry, C., Halevi, S., Smart, N.P.: Homomorphic evaluation of the AES circuit. In: Safavi-Naini, R. (ed.) CRYPTO 2012. LNCS, vol. 7417, pp. 850–867. Springer, Heidelberg (2012)
7. Green, M., Ateniese, G.: Identity-Based Proxy Re-encryption. In: Katz, J., Yung, M. (eds.) ACNS 2007. LNCS, vol. 4521, pp. 288–306. Springer, Heidelberg (2007)
8. Johnson, R., Molnar, D., Song, D., Wagner, D.: Homomorphic Signature Schemes. In: Preneel, B. (ed.) CT-RSA 2002. LNCS, vol. 2271, pp. 244–262. Springer, Heidelberg (2002)

9. Lapon, J., Kohlweiss, M., De Decker, B., Naessens, V.: Analysis of Revocation Strategies for Anonymous Idemix Credentials. In: De Decker, B., Lapon, J., Naessens, V., Uhl, A. (eds.) CMS 2011. LNCS, vol. 7025, pp. 3–17. Springer, Heidelberg (2011)
10. Leitold, H., Hollosi, A., Posch, R.: Security Architecture of the Austrian Citizen Card Concept. In: ACSAC 2002, pp. 391–402 (2002)
11. Rivest, R.L., Shamir, A., Tauman, Y.: How to leak a secret: Theory and applications of ring signatures. In: Boyd, C. (ed.) ASIACRYPT 2001. LNCS, vol. 2248, pp. 552–565. Springer, Heidelberg (2001)
12. Vaikuntanathan, V.: Computing Blindfolded: New Developments in Fully Homomorphic Encryption. In: IEEE FOCS 2011, pp. 5–16 (2011)

Using the Conflicting Incentives Risk Analysis Method

Lisa Rajbhandari and Einar Snekkenes

Norwegian Information Security Laboratory, Gjøvik University College, Norway
firstname.lastname@hig.no

Abstract. Risk is usually expressed as a combination of likelihood and consequence but obtaining credible likelihood estimates is difficult. The Conflicting Incentives Risk Analysis (CIRA) method uses an alternative notion of risk. In CIRA, risk is modeled in terms of conflicting incentives between the risk owner and other stakeholders in regards to the execution of actions. However, very little has been published regarding how CIRA performs in non-trivial settings. This paper addresses this issue by applying CIRA to an Identity Management System (IdMS) similar to the eGovernment IdMS of Norway. To reduce sensitivity and confidentiality issues the study uses the Case Study Role Play (CSRP) method. In CSRP, data is collected from the individuals playing the role of fictitious characters rather than from an operational setting. The study highlights several risk issues and has helped in identifying areas where CIRA can be improved.

Keywords: Risk analysis, risk, privacy, conflicting incentives.

1   Introduction

Risk is usually expressed as a combination of likelihood and consequence but obtaining credible likelihood estimates is difficult. Thus, there is a need to improve the predictability and the coverage of the risk identification process. This challenge is a consequence of limited availability of representative historic data relevant for new and emerging systems. Besides, people are not well calibrated at estimating probabilities [20]. Furthermore, to improve the efficiency of the identification process, there is a need to identify issues that are key to risk discovery, and avoid activities that shed little or no light on potential problem areas. The Conflicting Incentives Risk Analysis (CIRA) [19] method addresses these issues by using an alternative notion of risk. In CIRA, risk is modeled in terms of conflicting incentives between the risk owner and other stakeholders in regards to the execution of actions. However, little evidence exists to suggest that CIRA is feasible to analyze risk in non-trivial settings.

In this paper, we explore to what extent CIRA is feasible for analyzing risk in non-trivial settings. We look into the feasibility of CIRA for analyzing privacy risks in a case study of an identity management system. Privacy is "too complicated a concept to be boiled down to a single essence" [21]. We agree with

L.J. Janczewski, H.B. Wolfe, and S. Shenoi (Eds.): SEC 2013, IFIP AICT 405, pp. 315–329, 2013.

the view of Solove [21] that it is important to understand the socially recognized activities that cause privacy problems to an individual in order to protect it. As the data collected using CIRA will be sensitive and confidential, data is collected through Case Study Role Play (CSRP). CSRP is developed from the integration of case study [26], persona [6] and role play [25]. Personas are "hypothetical archetypes of actual users" and embody their goals [6]. Each role as described in the persona is played by a real person. Using CSRP, data is collected from the individuals playing the role of fictitious characters rather than from an operational setting. In this paper, we have extended the previous work on CIRA by (1) improving the data collection and analysis phase, and (2) showing that it is feasible to use CIRA in non-trivial settings. Our work has contributed to the development of CIRA and helped to identify practical problems that can be addressed in future research.

The rest of the paper is organized as follows. Related work is given in Sect. 2 followed by a description of the case in Sect. 3. In Sect. 4, we present the analysis of the case. We further present and discuss the result of our analysis in Sect. 5. Sect. 6 concludes the paper.

2   Related Work

There are many classical risk management approaches and guidelines. Usually, in these approaches, risk is specified as a combination of likelihood and consequence. The ISO/IEC 27005 [13] standard (its new version ISO/IEC 27005:2011), the ISO 31000 [12] standard (that supersedes AS/NZS 4360:2004 [2]) and NIST 800-39 [16] provide the guidance on the entire risk management process. NIST 800-39 [16] supersedes NIST SP 800-30 [22]; its revised version NIST 800-30 Rev. 1 [17] is a supporting document to NIST 800-39. CORAS [15] is a model based method that uses Unified Modeling Language (UML) for security risk analysis. ISRAM [14] is a survey based model to analyze risk in information security; surveys are conducted for gathering probability and consequence. In Risk IT [10] framework (which is integrated into COBIT 5 [11]), risk is estimated as the combination of frequency (rate by which an event occurs over a given period of time) and magnitude of IT risk scenarios. In RAMCAP [1] (its updated version RAMCAP Plus), risk is estimated as the combination of threat, vulnerability and consequence. Cox has shown the limitations of estimating risk as the combination of threat, vulnerability and consequence [7].

There are several methods that specifically look into privacy risks, and are usually called Privacy Impact Assessment (PIA). For instance, there are Privacy Impact Guidelines of the Treasury Board of Canada Secretariat [18] and PIA of the Information Commissioner's Office, United Kingdom [9]. PIA is a "systematic process for evaluating the potential effects on privacy of a project, initiative, or proposed system or scheme" [24]. It helps to identify and manage privacy risks for an organization that deals with personal data of its stakeholders. However, these methods usually do not attribute the events to people. Wright [24] states that PIA should be integrated into risk management along with other strategic planning tools.

The CIRA Method [19] identifies stakeholders, their actions and consequences of actions in terms of perceived value changes to the utility factors that characterize the risk situation. The idea being that risk is the combination of the strength of the force that motivates the stakeholder that is in the position to trigger the action to send the risk owner to an undesirable state and the magnitude of this undesirability. Risk magnitude is related to the degree of change to perceived utility caused by potential state changes.

3 Case Description: NorgID Identity Management System

The case description is fictitious but the design of the system is inspired by MinID [8]. The Identity Management System (IdMS) helps to manage the partial identities of end-users. IdMS usually consists of three class of stakeholders: End-user, Identity Provider (IdP) and Service Provider (SP). IdP is the organization that issues the credentials/ electronic identity to the end-user. SP is the organization that provides services to end-user after verifying their identities.

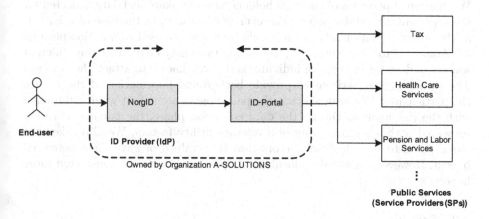

Fig. 1. NorgID Identity Management System

A-SOLUTIONS is an organization with 20 employees that manages a federated IdMS. It developed an authentication system called NorgID and a portal (ID-Portal). Their goal is to provide secure access to digital public services. NorgID is one of the IdPs which provides authentication for logging on to a federation called 'ID-portal' as shown in Fig. 1. It provides the end-user cross-domain Single Sign-On (SSO), i.e. the end-user needs to authenticate only once and can gain access to many services by using the portal such as tax, health care, pension, labor and other eGovernment services. The end-user can log on to the ID-portal using NorgID, by providing his personal ID, a password and a one-time PIN code. NorgID uses two databases: (a) for storing personal data about the users and (b) for storing logs containing usage of IdMS for each user (the details regarding the collected information are not mentioned in the privacy policy). The personal information collected includes his social security number, PIN-codes, password, email address, telephone number and address. NorgID has been quickly and widely adopted because of its easy access and features that have convinced enough people to use the application.

4   Analyzing Privacy Risks Using CIRA

In this section, we first provide the assumptions and considerations, along with the scoping for the risk analysis activity. We provide a brief summary of the method along with the steps for data collection (1-9) and analysis (10-13). We then implement the procedure on the given case of an IdMS. The analysis focuses on the risks faced by an end-user.

4.1   Assumptions and Considerations

For investigating the case, we used the Case Study Role Play (CSRP) method. We developed personas of the stakeholders based on empirical data collected for the representative stakeholders. However, for instance, in the case of a hacker, as the empirical data might not be easily elicitable, we used assumption persona [3]. According to Atzeni et al. [3], the assumptions may be derived from different sources of data for the type of individuals that are known to attack the systems. The scenarios were written to provide background information of the role to the participants. We assumed that the participants are honest when interacting with the risk analyst. During the data collection phase, the participants were presented with a set consisting of 3 relevant utility factors. We also asked the participants to provide other factors that they valued or gave them perceived benefit. However, for the simplification of the case we have not considered those factors.

4.2   Scoping

Scoping consists of the activities used to determine the boundary for the risk analysis activity. We (as the risk analyst) assumed that the system is in a certain initial state. Moreover, we focused on privacy risk events that are caused by the intentional behavior of a stakeholder.

4.3   Summary of CIRA

CIRA identifies stakeholders, actions and perceived expected consequences that characterize the risk situation. In CIRA, a stakeholder is an individual (i.e. physical person) that has some interest in the outcome of actions that are taking place within the scope of significance. There are two classes of stakeholders: the strategy owner and the risk owner. Strategy owner is the stakeholder who is capable of triggering an action to increase his perceived benefit. Typically, each stakeholder has associated a collection of actions that he owns. The risk owner is the stakeholder whose perspective we consider when performing the risk analysis, i.e., he is the stakeholder at risk. By utility, we mean the benefit as perceived by the corresponding stakeholder. Utility comprises of utility factors. Chule et. al. [4] identify the utility factors relevant for our work. Each factor captures a specific aspect of utility e.g. prospect of wealth, reputation, social relationship. The procedure is as given in Table 1 along with the approximate time required for each of the steps when implementing the NorgID case study (the required time will be further explained in Sect. 5).

Table 1. Procedure in CIRA with approximate time required for each step when implementing NorgID IdMS

Steps	Time (mins)
1. Identify the risk owner (includes development of persona)	30
2. Identify the risk owners' key utility factors	30
3. Given an intuition of the scope/ system- identify the kind of strategies/ operations which can potentially influence the above utility factors	30
4. Identify roles/ functions that may have the opportunities and capabilities to perform these operations	60
5. Identify the named strategy owner(s) that can take on this role (includes development of persona)	90
6. Identify the utility factors of interest to this strategy owner(s)	90
7. Determine how the utility factors can be operationalized	240
8. Determine how the utility factors are weighted by each of the stakeholders	120
9. Determine how the various operations result in changes to the utility factors for each of the stakeholders	280
10. Estimate the utility for each stakeholder	20
11. Compute the incentives	15
12. Determine risk	15
13. Evaluate risk	210

4.4 Implementing the CIRA Procedure

The application of CIRA to the NorgID IdMS is presented below.

1. Identify the risk owner. At first we need to determine the risk owner. The user (Bob) is the risk owner. We assume he represents the general users of NorgID. The persona of Bob is given in Table. 2.

2. Identify the risk owners' key utility factors. This step consists of determining the key utility factors for the risk owner.

We presented Bob with three utility factors: privacy, satisfaction from the service and usability along with the explanation for each. We collected his opinion on whether he thought (as a user of NorgID), these factors are important and would give him perceived benefit.

3. Given an intuition of the scope/ system- identify the kind/ classes of operations/ strategies which can potentially influence the above utility factors. For determining the strategies, we look into the taxonomy of activities that cause privacy problems as provided by Solove [21]. The strategies that we considered are:

- Secondary use of Bob's information (**SecUse**): It is related with using Bob's information for another purpose than that is mentioned in the policy without getting his consent.
- Breach of confidentiality of Bob's information: It is "breaking a promise to keep a person's information confidential" [21]. We consider two strategies that can lead to breach of confidentiality: Sharing credentials (**ShareCred**) and Stealing Information (**StealInfo**).

4. Identify the roles/ functions that may have the opportunities and capabilities to perform these operations. There can be many strategy owners capable of executing these strategies. However, for this paper we consider only three stakeholders as the objective is to show the feasibility of the CIRA method. The stakeholders are CEO and System Administrator of A-SOLUTIONS, and a hacker capable of executing SecUse, ShareCred and StealInfo operations respectively.

5. Identify the named strategy owner(s) that can take on this role. In this step, we pin point the strategy owner(s) that are in the position of executing the above strategies. We consider the stakeholders: John (CEO), Nora (System Admin) and X (Hacker). Their personas are provided in Table 2.

6. Identify the utility factors of interest to this strategy owner(s). In CIRA, as we consider the perception of an individual, each relevant stakeholder is an expert. Like before, we provided a list of utility factors for John, Nora and Hacker X to choose from. For the hacker, we identified his utility factors from the existing literature [23]. The identified utility factors for John (CEO): privacy reputation, wealth for business continuity, compliance; for Nora (System Admin): availability, trust, free time and for X (Hacker): wealth, status, ego.

7. Determine how the utility factors can be operationalized. For each identified utility factor, we determine the scale, measurement procedure, semantics of values and explain the underlying assumptions, if any. The brief explantion

Table 2. Personas of risk owner and strategy owners

Role	Name	Description
End-user	Bob	30 years old, local school teacher, regular user of NorgID with general IT knowledge; aware of some privacy issues mainly due to the media coverage of data breaches (associated with services such as social networking and health care).
CEO	John	50 years old, ensures the overall development and relationship with its stakeholders; has motivation to increase the company's service delivery capacity.
System Admin	Nora	29 years old, known for her friendly behavior and highly trusts her co-workers; ensures both the NorgID and ID-Portal are functioning properly and secure; manages the access permission for internal staff to the server; in her absence, to assure that co-workers get proper system function, she usually lets them access servers and even shares important credentials to the server.
Hacker	X	28 years old, skilled in computing and interested in new challenges; to pursue his interest he left his job a year ago and now completely spends his time by gathering knowledge through first-hand experience; wants to earn money and also build status for himself in the so-called hackers' community.

of the metrics presented in Table 3 and Table 4 are a flavor of the metric we used in the analysis for the stakeholders Bob (User) and John (CEO). It is to be noted that different flavors of the metric exist and can be used according to the context. Due to space constraint, we leave out the details of the metrics for the utility factors of Nora (System Admin) and X (Hacker).

8. Determine how the utility factors are weighted by each of the stakeholders. We asked Bob to rank the utility factors based on its importance. Then, for collecting the weights for the utility factors the following question was asked- "Given that you have assigned a weight of 100 to utility factor #1, how much would you assign to utility factor #2, #3 and so on (on a scale of 0-99)?". Bob ranked and assigned weights of 100, 80, 70 to the utility factors privacy, satisfaction and usability respectively as given in Table 5.

Similarly, the weights of the utility factors according to their ranking for each of the strategy owners were also collected. John (CEO) assigned weights of 100, 80 and 50 to the utility factors compliance, privacy reputation and wealth respectively. Nora (System Admin) assigned weights of 100, 80 and 78 to the utility factors service availability, free time and trust respectively. X (Hacker) assigned weights of 100, 90 and 85 to the utility factors wealth, ego and status respectively.

9. Determine how the various operations result in changes to the utility factors for each of the stakeholders (start with risk owner). We assume the system/ environment to be in a fixed initial state and all the players

Table 3. Metrics for the utility factors of the risk owner Bob (User)

Utility factor	Definition	Measurement Procedure
Privacy(%)	It refers to the extent to which you have control over your personal information. Defined by $$1/(1+N) \qquad (1)$$ where N- expected/ projected number of incidents per month.	N is obtained from the analysis of the scenario directly or indirectly caused by the events triggered by various stakeholders [19]. If $N = 0$, the value of privacy is 100%; if $N = 1$, the value of privacy decreases to 50% and so on. That is with increasing number of incidents, the value of privacy decreases.
Satisfaction(%)	It refers to the extent to which you perceive the continuance usage of the portal to access services based on your experience. Model as expectation fulfillment relating to function: service availability, support(reponsiveness (scale: %), effectiveness (scale: %)) and service completeness.	Service availability is the number of interactions with a response time of less than 1 second divided by the total number of interactions. Responsiveness is given as $$1/(1+t) \qquad (2)$$ where t is the average time in mins required to 'solve' a problem reported by the user. Effectiveness is the 'extent' to which the problem is solved. Service completeness relates to the number of features that the service actually delivers divided by the number of features that the user could reasonably expect (see [19]).
Usability(%)	It refers to the extent to which a user perceives the ease of interaction with the portal. Model as user's past experience with using the service.	The value can be obtained by doing the survey. A scale of 0 to 100% is used, a value of 0 denotes it takes more than 30 mins to get acquainted with the service; 25% denotes it can be done within 20-30 mins; 50% denotes it takes 10-20 mins; 75% it takes less than 10 mins; 100% denotes it takes less than 5 mins.

Table 4. Metrics for the utility factors of the strategy owner John (CEO)

Utility factor	Definition	Measurement Procedure
Privacy Reputation(%)	It refers to the reputation of the company with respect to privacy incidents (e.g. loss, misuse or breach of personal information). Model as user's expectation relating to future behavior of the company in terms of: experience of others and own experience; both defined by $$1/(1+P) \qquad (3)$$ where P is the number of privacy incidents.	P is obtained from the survey. If $P = 0$, the value of reputation is 100%; if $P = 1$, the value decreases to 50% and so on. That is with increasing number of incidents, the value of reputation decreases (see [19]).
Wealth(Million €)	The unit for wealth is currency units. The weight for wealth will then specify how much utility each currency unit will give.	It is obtained from the investigation of the entity by the risk analyst.
Compliance(%)	It refers to the extent to which you think the company would benefit by following the rules and regulations. This demonstrates willingness of the company to take necessary steps to protect the personal information of its stakeholders. Model as percent of compliance with legislation (e.g. Data Protection Act, EU directive).	At first the risk analyst needs to gather the the rules that needs to be followed by the company. A value of 0 means that no rules are followed; 25% means that 1/4 of thoes rules are followed; 50% means that half of those rules are followed; 75% means 3/4 of the rules are followed and 100% means all rules are followed.

Table 5. Utility factors for Bob (User)

Rank	Utility factors	Weights
1	Privacy	100
2	Satisfaction	80
3	Usability	70

are utility optimizing. By utility optimizing, we mean that they are optimizing their behavior relative to the weighted sum of the elements in their utility factor vector. For each of the identified utility factors, we determine the initial and final values after the strategies of the players are executed (for the utility factors' valuation, we utilize the metrics explained above). We use the additive utility function of MAUT to estimate the utility. The additive utility function for a given player is defined to be the weighted average of its individual utility functions [5] given as:

$$U = \sum_{k=1}^{m} w_k \cdot u(a_k) \qquad (4)$$

where, m is the number of utility factors of the player, w_k is the assigned weight of utility factor a_k and $\sum_{k=1}^{m} w_k = 1$, and $u(a_k)$ is the utility function for the utility factor 'a_k'.

Table 6. Final Values of the Utility Factors after the Strategy of the Strategy Owners are Executed

Stakeholders	Utility Factors	Wts	IV	Final Values		
				John SecUse	Nora ShareCred	X-Hacker StealInfo
Bob(User)	Privacy(%)	0.40	100	8	17	5
	Satisfaction(%)	0.32	72	74	74	74
	Availability (%)	0.33	85	87	87	87
	Support (%)	0.33	52	55	55	55
	Responsiveness (%)	0.50	14	17	17	17
	Effectiveness (%)	0.50	90	92	92	92
	Service Completeness(%)	0.33	80	82	82	82
	Usability(%)	0.28	80	80	80	80
John(CEO)	Compliance(%)	0.43	80	60		
	Privacy Reputation(%)	0.35	67	15		
	Experience of others(%)	0.50	33	9		
	Own experience(%)	0.50	100	20		
	Wealth(Million €)	0.22	5	25		
Nora(Sys Adm)	Service Availability(%)	0.39	85		87	
	Free time(%)	0.31	0		30	
	Trust(%)	0.30	50		90	
X(Hacker)	Wealth(Thousand €)	0.36	0			50
	Ego(%)	0.33	40			95
	Status (%)	0.31	50			85

For our case study, Table 6 depicts the normalized weights (for the assigned weights in Step 8) for the utility factors, its initial value (IV) and its final values, if the strategies of the stakeholders were to be executed. For the other elements comprising the utility factors, we make the assumption that the stakeholders perceive each of these to be equally important. The values for the metrics are obtained either based on our investigation or by conducting interviews/surveys with the participants. Usually, the individual utility functions (i.e. utility factors in our case) are assigned values in the interval of 0 (worst) to 1 (best) when using MAUT. For instance, in our case, we can easily compress the wealth to the interval 0 to 1. However, this would not be particularly helpful as most of the values will be clustered right at the end. Thus, it is more intuitive to utilize the given scales for the utility factors' valuation. Moreover, the units of the weights are such that the utility is unit less. Next, the values for each of the stakeholders are determined.

For Bob (User). We determine the values of the first two utility factors for Bob from our investigation and the last one (usability) is based on the survey. To determine the value of privacy to the user, we investigated the number of privacy incidents at each state. Our findings are based on several studies on issues such as how secondary usage of data and breach of confidentiality will impact the end-user. Based on our study, $N = 0$ per month at the initial state. $N = 11$, $N = 5$ and $N = 20$ when John, Nora and Hacker X use their respective strategies. By instantiating (1) with the value of N, we obtain the IV of privacy as 100% and its final values as 8%, 17% and 5% respectively.

Note that the values for satisfaction are obtained using the techniques borrowed from MAUT and from our investigation. For support (an element of satisfaction), the values for the responsiveness are obtained after instantiating (2) with $t = 6$ at the initial state and $t = 5$ when the other strategies of the stakeholders are executed. Thus, responsiveness increased from the IV of 14% to 17% for all three strategies. Besides, it was determined that effectiveness also increased from 90% to 92% when the three strategies of the stakeholders are executed. We then evaluate the values for support instantiating (4) with the obtained values of responsiveness and effectiveness: for the IV as 0.50*14+0.50*90 = 52%. Similarly, the final values for the three strategies are evaluated as 55%. The following values were determined for the other elements of satisfaction: availability increases from 85% to 87% and service completeness increases from 80% to 82% after the three strategies are executed. Thus, using (4) and the values determined for the other elements comprising our satisfaction utility factor, the obtained IV is 72% and the final values for the other strategies are evaluated as 74%. The value of usability as obtained from Bob was 80% for all cases.

Due to lack of space, we leave out the details of the computations of changes to the utility factors belonging to the other stakeholders. The results can be found in Table 6.

10. Estimate the utility. We again use the techniques from MAUT to estimate the utility for each of the strategies for each player using (4). We make the

Table 7. Matrix of Utilities and Change in Utilities w.r.t. Strategy of the Strategy Owners

Stakeholders	IV	Utilities			Changes in Utilities (Δ)		
		SecUse	ShareCred	StealInfo	SecUse	ShareCred	StealInfo
Bob(User)	85	49	53	48	-36	-32	-37
John(CEO)	59	37			-22		
Nora(Sys Admin)	48		70			22	
X(Hacker)	29			76			47

simplifying assumption that utility is linear. For our case study, we use (4) to compute the utilities for the stakeholders with the values given in Table 6. In the initial state, the utilities are given as follows:

For Bob (User): $0.40 \cdot 100 + 0.32 \cdot 72 + 0.28 \cdot 80 = 85$
For John (CEO): $0.43 \cdot 80 + 0.35 \cdot 67 + 0.22 \cdot 5 = 59$

Similarly, for other stakeholders, the utilities are obtained as given in Table 7.

11. Compute the incentives. We need to compute the incentives (i.e. changes in utilities) for each of the strategies for each player. The change in utility Δ is the difference between the utility of the player in the state resulting from strategy use and the initial state. In our case study, from Table 7, when John uses the SecUse option, Δ for Bob and himself are -36 and -22 respectively. When Nora uses the ShareCred option, the Δ for Bob and herself are -32 and 22 respectively. In addition, when the hacker uses the StealInfo operation, the Δ for Bob and himself are -37 and 47 respectively.

12. Determine risk. This can be achieved by investigating each of the strategies with respect to sign and magnitude of the changes determined in the previous step. In our case study, when John uses the SecUse option, it results in a negative change in utility for both the players (falls in the third quadrant in the incentive graph as shown in Fig. 2). Thus, we know it is an undesirable situation for both the players and they both want to move out of this quadrant. Thus, this might result in co-operation. However, Nora's degree of desirability to play the ShareCred is slightly more as it leads her to a better position with a gain of 22. In this case, 22 is the strength of the force that motivates Nora to send Bob to an undesirable state and -32 is the magnitude of this undesirability and the combination of these is the risk (-32, 22). Similarly, it is clear that the Hacker X's degree of desirability to play the StealInfo is high as it leads him to a better position with a gain of 47 and -37 is the magnitude of the undesirability faced by Bob, which results in the risk (-37, 47).

13. Evaluate risk. We identity the risk acceptance and rejection criteria for the risk owner to determine whether a specified level of risk is acceptable or not. In our model, we make the simplifying assumption that all strategy owners will need the same time to act if they have the same magnitude of incentive.

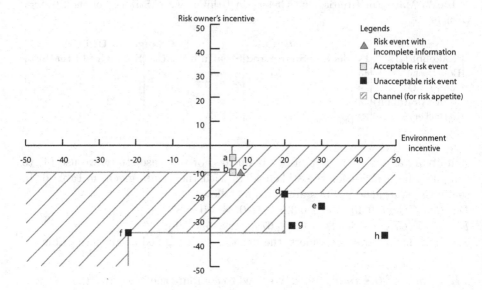

Fig. 2. The Incentive graph

Strategies will be executed in decreasing order of utility as perceived by each of the strategy owners.

We presented Bob with following risk pairs: a. (-5,6), b. (-11, 6), c. (-11, 8), d. (-20,20), e. (-28, 30) along with the ones determined in Step 12, which are f. (-36,-22), g. (-32,22) and h. (-37, 47) obtained when the strategy owners execute the strategies SecUse, ShareCred and StealInfo respectively. The risk pairs are represented by (C, I_i) where C is the consequence for the risk owner and I refers to how strong is strategy owner i's incentive to make the first move or the magnitude of incentive. For instance, for the risk pair 'b', Bob gets the value of C as -11 when the final values for privacy, satisfaction and usability in the execution of any of the strategies would be 95%, 70% and 50% respectively (keeping the weights of the utility factors and their initial values as obtained before). Note that this is one of the several possible combinations that gives Bob the consequence of -11. Nora has an incentive of 6, when the final values for availability, freedom and trust are 90%, 10% and 53% respectively. Similarly for other stakeholders the possible combinations can be determined.

To determine the risk acceptance criteria, we asked Bob (User): 'How strong a temptation is it acceptable to give a strategy owner to execute the strategy, so as to cause him (i.e. Bob) a given loss?'. From the above risk pairs, he accepted the risk pairs a and b (represented by the light gray square) as shown in Fig. 2. However, for the risk pair, c he was willing to accept the risk only if Nora was in the position of executing the strategy (represented by the triangle) and unsure in case other strategy owners executed their strategy. The remaining risk pairs were not acceptable to him (represented by the black square).

5   Results and Discussion

Our findings can be grouped in the following categories: (1) application of CIRA to NorgID IdMS, (2) feasibility of CIRA in terms of its complexity and risk analyst effort required, (3) improvements made and (4) some limitations of CIRA that require further work. Application of CIRA to NorgID IdMS, resulted in the determination of risks faced by the risk owner. We were further able to represent acceptable/ unacceptable risk events by means of an incentive graph which was easy to communicate to the risk owner.

Assuming we have n stakeholders, each stakeholder owns s strategies and has u utility factors that go into the computation of his utility, then the effort of the various tasks can be estimated as follows: The total number of strategies to be considered will be $n*s$. The total number of utility factors to be considered will be $n*u$. However, in practice, it is expected that utility factors will be taken from a limited set. To determine the risk acceptance criteria, it will suffice to ask the risk owner $n*s$ yes/no (i.e. accept/reject) questions. Thus the complexity of CIRA in terms of human effort will be in the order of

$$n * (u + s) \qquad (5)$$

By instantiating (5) with the value of $n = 4$, $s = 1$ and $u = 3$ as in the NorgID case study, we obtain the estimate of complexity as 16. Furthermore, the effort in terms of total amount of time spent in doing the case study was determined to be approximately 27 hrs (which includes the time given in Table 1 along with the time for initial preparation (1 hr), scenario construction to provide the background information of the role to the participants (2 hrs), role play selection and guidance (2 hrs) and documentation (1.5 hrs)). The given hours are approximate values; the values were jotted down only after the actual process was completed. It is clear that steps for determining the changes to the utility factors with respect to the operations (Step 9) and the operationalization of utility factors (Step 7) required the highest amount of time i.e. approximately 280 and 240 mins respectively. When the problem space grows, for instance the values of $n = 8$, $s = 10$ and $u = 5$, we would expect that the risk analyst would have to spend in the order of 200 hours to complete the analysis. Note that the elapsed time may be longer. CIRA is still in development phase and the steps will be optimized. For e.g. a comprehensive library of utility factors will be developed. It is expected that this library will speed up the data collection phase. Moreover, tools will be developed to support the risk analyst.

Learning from the case study, we discovered the following issues that resulted in improvements: the procedure was updated to ease the data collection process and the data collection manual was developed for the risk analyst. Interviews/ survey responses indicated that it was essential that the risk analyst and the participants have the same understanding of the concepts (e.g. utility factors) used during the data collection phase. Thus, even though a lot of resources were required for instance, in the operationalization of the metrics for the utility factors and also determining their value, we focused on these key issues in order to improve data quality.

The following limitations of CIRA were identified: (1) We have assumed that all the participants are honest when interacting with the risk analyst. However, the fact that they might be reluctant to provide information or give wrong information during the interview/ survey needs further investigation. (2) As metrics have always been a challenge in information security, for some of the utility factors it was difficult to formulate the metrics. Hence, we need to collect definitions of utility factors and perform their validation. (3) To determine whether an obtained set of utility factors represents the complete set for a particular stakeholder in a given context requires further work. (4) More work is also needed in capturing the uncertainties in relation to estimates using interval arithmetic or bounded probabilities instead of point values. (5) When assigning weights, the same scale is used for all the stakeholders. The mapping of scale of one stakeholder with another also needs further investigation. (6) Finally, CIRA tool support.

6   Conclusion

In this paper, we have explored the feasibility of CIRA to analyze risk in a non-trivial setting. The CIRA method is still at an early stage of development. However, the results from our case study suggests that it is possible to use CIRA in such settings, and that the method helps the analyst to get a better understanding of the risks. Our work has contributed to the development of CIRA and helped to identify practical problems that can be addressed in future research.

Acknowledgement. The work reported in this paper is part of the PETweb II project sponsored by The Research Council of Norway under grant 193030/S10. We would like to thank the anonymous reviewers for their valuable comments.

References

[1] ASME Innovative Technologies Institute (ASME-ITI). RAMCAP(Risk Analysis and Management for Critical Asset Protection) Framework, Version 2.0 (May 2006)

[2] AS/NZS 4360. Risk management. AS/NZS (2004)

[3] Atzeni, A., Cameroni, C., Faily, S., Lyle, J., Flechais, I.: Here's Johnny: A Methodology for Developing Attacker Personas. In: ARES, pp. 722–727 (2011)

[4] Chulef, A.S., Read, S.J., Walsh, D.A.: A Hierarchical Taxonomy of Human Goals. Motivation and Emotion 25(3), 191–232 (2001)

[5] Clemen, R.T.: Making Hard Decision: An Introduction to Decision Analysis, 2nd edn. Duxbury (1996)

[6] Cooper, A.: The Inmates are Running the Asylum. Macmillan Publishing Co., Inc., Indianapolis (1999)

[7] Cox Jr., L.A.: Some limitations of "Risk = Threat x Vulnerability x Consequence" for risk analysis of terrorist attacks. Risk Analysis 28(6), 1749–1761 (2008)

[8] Difi (Direktoratet for forvaltning og IKT). MinID,
     http://minid.difi.no/minid/minid.php?lang=en (online accessed: November
     2012)
[9] Information Commissioner's Office (ICO). Privacy Impact Assessment Handbook,
     Version 2.0 (2009),
     http://www.ico.org.uk/pia_handbook_html_v2/files/PIAhandbookV2.pdf
     (online accessed: May 2013)
[10] ISACA, Rolling Meadows. The Risk IT Framework (2009)
[11] ISACA. COBIT 5: A Business Framework for the Governance and Management
     of Enterprise IT. IT Governance Institute (2012)
[12] ISO 31000. Risk Management – Principles and Guidelines (2009)
[13] ISO/IEC 27005. Information technology -Security techniques -Information secu-
     rity risk management. ISO/IEC, 1st edn. (2008)
[14] Karabacak, B., Sogukpinar, I.: ISRAM: information security risk analysis method.
     Computers & Security 24(2), 147–159 (2005)
[15] Lund, M.S., Solhaug, B., Stølen, K.: A Guided Tour of the CORAS Method. In:
     Model-Driven Risk Analysis, pp. 23–43. Springer, Heidelberg (2011)
[16] NIST. NIST SP 800-39, Managing Information Security Risk - Organization, Mis-
     sion, and Information System View (2011)
[17] NIST. NIST SP 800-30 Revision 1, Guide for Conducting Risk Assessments
     (September 2012)
[18] Treasury Board of Canada Secretariat. Privacy Impact Assessment Guidelines: A
     Framework to Manage Privacy Risks Guidelines (April 2012),
     http://www.tbs-sct.gc.ca (online accessed: January 2013)
[19] Rajbhandari, L., Snekkenes, E.: Intended Actions: Risk Is Conflicting Incentives.
     In: Gollmann, D., Freiling, F.C. (eds.) ISC 2012. LNCS, vol. 7483, pp. 370–386.
     Springer, Heidelberg (2012)
[20] Shanteau, J., Stewart, T.R.: Why study expert decision making? Some histor-
     ical perspectives and comments. Organizational Behavior and Human Decision
     Processes 53(2), 95–106 (1992)
[21] Solove, D.J.: A Taxonomy of Privacy. University of Pennsylvania Law Re-
     view 154(3), 477 (2006); GWU Law School Public Law Research Paper No. 129
[22] Stoneburner, G., Goguen, A., Feringa, A.: NIST SP 800-30, Risk Management
     Guide for Information Technology. NIST (July 2002)
[23] The Honeynet Project. Know Your Enemy, 2nd edn. Addison-Wesley (2004)
[24] Wright, D.: Should privacy impact assessments be mandatory? Commun.
     ACM 54(8), 121–131 (2011)
[25] Yardley-Matwiejczuk, K.M.: Role play: theory and practice. Sage Publications
     Limited (1997)
[26] Yin, R.K.: Case Study Research: Design and Methods, 4th edn. Applied Social
     Research Method Series, vol. 5. Sage (2009)

Performance Analysis of Scalable Attack Representation Models

Jin B. Hong and Dong Seong Kim

Computer Science and Software Engineering,
University of Canterbury,
Christchurch,
New Zealand
jho102@uclive.ac.nz, dongseong.kim@canterbury.ac.nz

Abstract. Attack graphs (AGs) have been widely used for security analysis. The construction of the graph-based attack models including the AG have been studied, but the security evaluation considering the full attack paths cannot be computed using existing attack models due to the scalability problem. To solve this, we propose to use hierarchical attack representation models (HARMs). First, we formulate key questions that need to be answered to compare the scalability of existing attack models. We show the scalability of the HARMs via simulations, by taking into account practical attack scenario based on various network topologies.

Keywords: Attack Graph, Attack Tree, Complexity Analysis, Security Model, Scalability.

1 Introduction

Attack models are used to evaluate the security of networked systems and to provide countermeasures to enhance the security [1–9]. Previous studies showed that the graph-based attack models (e.g., attack graph (AG) [10], multiple prerequisite graph (MPG) [11], two-layered attack graph (TLAG) [4]) have a scalability problem if full attack paths are considered [10–14]. The tree-based attack models (e.g., attack tree (AT) [15], attack countermeasure tree (ACT) [16]) can be constructed and evaluated in a scalable manner depending on their structures. Methods to construct tree-based attack models are described as either decomposition of the attack goal [7], computing min-cuts from the networked system with an assumed attacker and the target [8], or drawn by security experts manually. As far as we know, there is no automated generation method that captures all possible attack paths in tree-based attack models.

There are phases in the lifecycle of the attack models [17]. The pre-processing phase gathers the network and security information, the construction phase generates the attack model, the evaluation phase processes the security analysis using security metrics, and the modification phase captures any updated events in the networked system and modifies the attack model accordingly.

Previous researchers proposed various attack model structures that improved the scalability in the construction phase, and heuristic methods, such as graph simplifications, are used to avoid the scalability problem in the evaluation phase [4, 5, 11].

L.J. Janczewski, H.B. Wolfe, and S. Shenoi (Eds.): SEC 2013, IFIP AICT 405, pp. 330–343, 2013.

Full attack paths contain all possible attack scenarios, and analysing full attack paths can drive one to find out the optimal security solution. But as far as we know, computing full attack paths to evaluate the security of networked systems is scoped to small networks only, because of the scalability problem. Existing attack models are not scalable to compute the full attack paths in the networked system, because there are many attack paths in a general networked system (e.g., a networked system with fully connected components). Therefore, we require a general solution to the scalability problem for the attack models.

We proposed hierarchical attack representation models (HARMs) to improve the scalability problem [17]. Our previous study shows that the HARMs have better or equal complexities in three phases of the attack models, such as construction, evaluation and modification, compared with an AG and an AT. It is important that the attack models are scalable for all network topologies (e.g., mesh, star, complete), so that all types of the networked systems can be modelled, analysed and secured (e.g., smart grids, sensor networks, ad hoc networks). However, our previous study only considered the worst case analysis using the system where nodes are fully connected.

We denote an AG that only represents the network structure (i.e., the full attack paths information is not expressed) as a simplified AG. The simplified AG representation is used in the layers of the HARMs, compared with the simplified AG in the phases of construction and evaluation. The simulation considered different network topologies and variable number of vulnerabilities to improve the limitations of simulations observed in previous works. We consider the evaluation phase to compute the full attack paths. The contributions of this paper are:

- To list key questions to compute the scalability, and identify unanswered questions for existing attack models;
- To simulate the attack model's construction and evaluation phases, and compare the scalability considering multiple vulnerabilities and various network topologies using a practical network system

The rest of the paper is as organised as follows. In Section 2, related work is introduced. In Section 3, the HARMs and existing attack models are compared using five key questions. Section 4 represents the simulation result, and discussion is given in Section 5. Finally, section 6 concludes this paper.

2   Related Work

Over the last decade, many attack models have been proposed. There are no general tree-based attack model construction methods that avoid the scalability problem. Hence, we will consider graph-based attack models to compare the performance in the phases of attack models. Sheyner [10] used a full attack graph, but it had a scalability problem. Many researchers presented efficient methods of the AG construction and evaluation. To improve the efficiency of the attack models, researchers considered improvements on the full AG [18–20], or proposed new graph-based attack model structures [4,5,11].

Ou *et al.* [5] used a logical attack graph (LAG), and the construction of the LAG can be done in a time of polynomial complexity. However, evaluation method and its complexity analysis are not mentioned. The simulation for the construction phase assumed that each host has same vulnerabilities, but in real systems we can expect various number of vulnerabilities for different hosts with different services and applications. Moreover, exploiting vulnerability does not necessarily give the root privilege, as assumed in their work. Ingols *et al.* [11] used a predictive graph to avoid the scalability problem of the AG. Later, they proposed a multiple prerequisite graph (MPG), more scalable than the predictive graph. They reported the scalability of the MPG has the size complexity of $O(n \log n)$, where n is the number of hosts in the networked system. They used heuristic methods to simply the MPG to evaluate the network security. A direct attack was used for the attack scenario in the simulation. Although they used more than one type of vulnerabilities, the number of vulnerabilities was fixed. Xie *et al.* [4] used a two-layer attack graph (TLAG), where the upper layer captured the host reachability, and the lower layer captured the vulnerability information. There are similarities between the HARMs and the TLAG, but the TLAG stores the lower level information in each edge (i.e., construct the vulnerability attack graph between host pairs), but the HARMs store the lower level information in each host. As a result, less memory space is required for the HARMs than the TLAG, as well as construction and evaluation times in general. The network structure was described, but the simulation did not perform the scalability test, and the vulnerability information was not given.

We compare the structure of the HARMs, which are designed to use any attack models in their layers, with simplified AG, LAG, MPG, and TLAG in terms of scalability by taking into account the worst case performance.

3   Model Comparisons

Existing attack models and their studies lack in comparative studies to show how well their models scale in various environments and attack scenarios. We listed five key questions to compare the scalability of attack models:

Q1. Was the computational complexity analysis performed?
Q2. Compared against other attack models?
Q3. Different network topologies have been considered?
Q4. The Effect of variable number of vulnerabilities for hosts is considered?
Q5. Different types of vulnerabilities (user/root) are considered?

To compare the scalability of the HARMs, we will consider different graph-based attack models (simplified AG, LAG, MPG, and TLAG) and compare their scalability in the construction and the evaluation phase by inspecting their model structures and features. We assume the reachability information is given as in [11]. Also, we assume that other information (e.g., credentials, interfaces, ports) is abstracted in the attack model, as they are linearly proportional to the number of hosts and vulnerabilities. The HARMs will consider the simplified AG model in both the upper and the lower layer. In the evaluation phase, we will consider the calculation of the full attack paths. We will only consider the number of hosts and vulnerabilities of each attack model to compare the scalability, because they are the major variable factors for the scalability among many others.

3.1 The Construction Phase

Studies on existing attack models have failed to answer some of the key questions when analysing the scalability of attack models. The answers for the key questions considering the construction phase are given in Table 1. Moreover, the corresponding attack model is required to be modified if there is a change in a networked system. The existing attack models that are not in a hierarchical representation require inspecting all attack model components to make modifications accordingly. However, attack models using the hierarchical representation (e.g., the HARMs and the TLAG) may apply modifications in the required layer only.

Table 1. Studies covered for the construction phase

Attack models	TLAG [4]	LAG [5]	MPG [11]	HARMs [17]
Q1	Yes	Yes	Yes	Yes
Q2	No	Yes	Yes	Yes
Q3	No	Yes	No	Yes
Q4	No	Yes	No	Yes
Q5	No	No	Yes	Yes

The construction phase of the attack model is required to retrieve the network information and connecting the network components specific to the attack model requirements (e.g., connecting a vulnerability node to its subsequent vulnerabilities or hosts based on the reachability, application and port information). We assume that the vulnerabilities of each host can be exploited based on the reachability information only. The analysis is focused on answering the key questions, and identifying key features of each attack model.

The construction of the full AG requires the calculation of full attack paths in the construction phase, which has a scalability problem that is impractical for a large (sized) networked system [12]. Instead, a simplified AG can be constructed, which is a simplified version of the full AG that only captures the network properties. There are other simplified versions of the full AG, which are modified to fit their usage [21]. The connections between vulnerabilities and hosts are independent in the simplified AG, so there are more edges in the simplified AG than the HARMs. However, the computational complexity of the construction phase of simplified AG and the HARMs is equivalent [17].

The LAG has a construction complexity of $O(\delta N)$, where N is the number of hosts in the networked system and δ is the time to find the host in the lookup table [5]. However, they assumed all vulnerabilities are the same (remote to exploits). Since each derivation node is an *AND* node, repeated nodes are required for each exploit if there are multiple sources it could be exploited from. If we allow the derivation nodes to be *OR* nodes, the number of repeated nodes will be reduced.

The MPG graph has the number of components linearly proportional to the number of hosts and vulnerabilities in the networked system [11]. Their performance in the simulation showed almost linear relationship between the computational time and the number of hosts. Also, they use *prerequisite* nodes in the model. This reduces the number of independent connections between hosts and vulnerabilities. But in the worst case, there will only be a single reachability group without the number of edges reduced. Moreover, they reported that even after 99% reduction in the graph size, they still had a problem representing the MPG because of complex relationship between hosts and vulnerabilities. In work [6], they described the client-side attacks using the reverse reachability calculations as an additional function.

The TLAG divides the network into two layers, where the upper layer captured the host reachability and the lower layer captured the vulnerability information between each host pair [4]. The main representation is simplified AG for both the upper and the lower layer. The analysis on the computational cost was given as $O(n^2)$, where n is the number of hosts in the network. The number of vulnerabilities is not assessed in the complexity analysis. They assumed that only the user level access is enough to compromise the host, and they did not take into account super-user (i.e., the root privilege). The lower level construction is based on host pairs. If the network consists of many edges between hosts, then the number of lower layer models increases proportional to the number of edges, which can be up to $O(n^2)$ number of edges. However, if the lower layer models in the TLAG are identical between different host pairs, they can share the same lower layer model. In the optimal case, where a host will have the same exploit sequence from any source, the number of lower layer models is linearly proportional to the number of hosts in the TLAG. Only the optimal case will show the same number of lower layer models with the HARMs. However, the TLAG requires that every edge has a reference to its lower layer information, whereas the HARMs only require the reachability information.

3.2   The Evaluation Phase

The evaluation process is a critical part in the security analysis, but due to the structural design, some attack models lack in efficient security analysis (e.g., scalability problem). Studies on existing attack models only answered a few of key questions listed. This is shown in Table 2.

Table 2. Studies covered for the evaluation phase

Attack models	TLAG [4]	LAG [5]	MPG [11]	HARMs [17]
Q1	Yes	No	Estimated	Yes
Q2	No	No	Yes	Yes
Q3	No	No	No	Yes
Q4	No	No	No	Yes
Q5	No	No	Yes	Yes

We consider the evaluation phase to compute the full attack paths (i.e., all possible attack sequences). Existing attack models use simplifications and heuristic methods (e.g., graph simplification [11]) to evaluate the network security, but they only consider specific attack scenarios and subset of all possible attacks. Matrix evaluation can be used to compute the overall security of the networked system, but it lacks in detailed analysis of the individual attack path. To improve these limitations, we compute the full attack paths.

Security analysis using the LAG is not available [5]. We estimate the evaluation complexity for the LAG is equivalent to the simplified AG, because each fact node (or also known as a host node with a given privilege) makes an independent connection to derivation nodes (or also known as vulnerability nodes). The number of paths from each fact node increases exponentially as the number of choices increases in the attack path, which are the same characteristics found in the simplified AG.

The evaluation of the MPG is to simplify the graph, then analyse the security. The evaluation complexity is estimated from the trend observed in their simulation. However, we will consider computing the full attack paths. The number of edges in the MPG depends on the number of reachability groups. If we consider the worst case (i.e., a complete graph), the performance of the MPG is equivalent to the simplified AG with a single prerequisite node (i.e., a single reachability group). If there are multiple prerequisite nodes, then connections between hosts and vulnerabilities are grouped by the prerequisite nodes, and it reduces the complexity in the evaluation. The optimal number of reachability groups is not analysed. Their analysis or simulation did not consider different network topologies or variable number of vulnerabilities.

The evaluation of the TLAG considered the overall security using the probability of an attack. But this evaluation method lacks in assessing different attack paths and their effects. The number of host-pair attack graphs (i.e., lower layer information) was not linearly proportional to the number of hosts. The analysis did not consider different network topologies, variable number of vulnerabilities in their analyses and simulations, and vulnerabilities giving different privileges when exploited.

The evaluation of the HARMs was obtained using the simplified AG in both the upper and the lower layer, but we observe that the computational complexity in both construction and evaluation phase have improved in comparison to the simplified AG. The improvements achieved using the HARMs compared with the simplified AG will be shown in the next section.

4 Simulation Result

The HARMs improve the efficiency of the attack model by reducing the number of independent connections between hosts and vulnerabilities. We investigate the improvements achieved using the HARMs through simulations. Our simulation setup used identical hosts, so that the scalability of the HARMs and the TLAG will be identical. We will consider a network with heterogeneous nodes in our future work to compare the scalability of the HARMs and TLAG.

The result of the simulation must be credible using appropriate quantification methods. For our simulations, we used an automated network simulation tool named *Akaroa2*, which produces credible stochastic simulation results with statistical analysis [22, 23]. All simulation results were obtained with the confidence level of 0.95, and the relative error of 0.05. The simulation program was coded using Python, and it was conducted in a Linux environment with Intel(R) Core2 Quad CPU 2.66GHz with 3.24GB of RAM.

4.1   A Practical Network Structure

In our previous study [17], we considered a fully connected system for the complexity analysis. The attack scenario used in the simulation is similar to that in the experiment conducted by Ingols *et al.* [11]. The networked system used in the simulation is shown in Figure 1. A network in our simulation setup used four sites, with each site consisting of five DMZ hosts, five administrative LAN hosts, and ten internal subnets. Each subnet has a bus topology to connect all hosts. The port information and the firewall rules are abstracted. We assigned ten remote-to-other vulnerabilities to half of hosts in each subnet, and the other half with one remote-to-root and nine remote-to-other vulnerabilities. The attack scenario was to compromise a host in the DMZ, an administrative LAN host, and all hosts in the network that has a remote-to-root vulnerability. Hosts that were not directly reachable from the attacker were compromised using other hosts as a stepping stones. The number of hosts in each subnet was increased to compare the scalability between the simplified AG and the HARMs. The scalability comparison is shown in Figure 2 for construction, and 3 for evaluation.

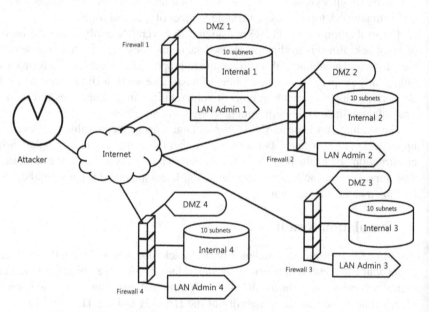

Fig. 1. A Networked System Configuration for Simulation

Figure 2 shows the performances of the simplified AG and the HARMs in the construction phase. Only Ingols *et al.* [11] and our work considered different types of vulnerabilities in the simulation. The simulation result shows that the number of edges in the simplified AG increases more rapidly than the HARMs. However, construction times for the simplified AG and the HARMs do not have a significant difference. This indicates that the number of edges has a little influence on the construction time.

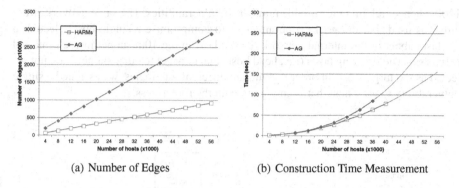

(a) Number of Edges

(b) Construction Time Measurement

Fig. 2. A Comparison between AG and HARMs in the Construction Phase

Both attack models have linear growth of the edge numbers, but the number of edges for the HARMs was always less than that of the simplified AG.

The trend observed from the simulation is comparable with the simulation result of the MPG [11]. The time comparison shows that the time for the evaluation increases rapidly for the simplified AG, but almost linearly does for the HARMs as shown in Figure 3(b). In contrast, the number of nodes computed in the HARMs is much greater than that of the simplified AG. The simplified AG constructs the attack paths using vulnerability sequences only, but the HARMs also analyse the sequence of hosts. Therefore, we require extra space of memory to store the information.

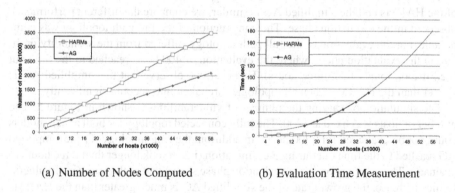

(a) Number of Nodes Computed

(b) Evaluation Time Measurement

Fig. 3. A Comparison between AG and HARMs in the Evaluation Phase

4.2 Network Topologies and Vulnerabilities

We use various network topologies and variable number of vulnerabilities in our second simulation and compare it with the performance of the simplified AG. We incorporate bus, ring, and star topologies to connect hosts in each internal network, and the number of vulnerabilities for each host is varied from 10 to 150. The number of hosts is fixed at

1200 when simulating the variable number of vulnerabilities. The same network structure was used, but the goal of the attack is to compromise a single host selected in the last subnet in the internal network (e.g., a host in the 10th subnet in each internal networks). The bridging hosts (i.e., head hosts that connect to other subnets) are not selected as the target host. In order to simulate different topologies, we assigned a single vulnerability to each host that is enough to gain the root access.

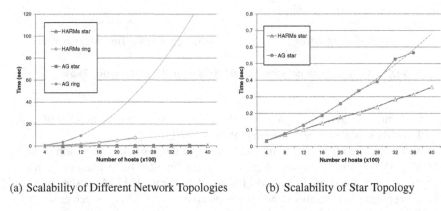

(a) Scalability of Different Network Topologies   (b) Scalability of Star Topology

Fig. 4. Scalability Difference of Network Topologies in the Evaluation Phase

The simulation of different topologies is shown in Figure 4. Since the construction of the HARMs and the simplified AG is similar, we compare the different performance observed in the evaluation phase. The construction of the full path topology was computable, but the evaluation of the full path topology suffered from the scalability problem in the evaluation phase, where the evaluation of 400 hosts reached to the time out (i.e., it took longer than three hours). However, we observe that the simplified AG is slower than the HARMs when all topologies are taken into account significantly.

The simulation of varying the number of vulnerabilities is shown in Figure 5. The number of hosts was fixed at 1200. The fully connected topology for both attack models could not be evaluated for 1200 hosts. In addition, the ring topology for the simplified AG reached to the time out during the simulation (i.e., it took longer than three hours to evaluate). The comparison in the evaluation phase shows that as the number of vulnerabilities increase, the growth rate of the simplified AG is much greater than the HARMs for all network topologies. The trend for the simplified AG showed a quadratic increase, whereas the trend for the HARMs showed a linear increase in time. The slopes are almost linear for all topologies of HARMs, indicating the number of vulnerabilities is also a constant factor in the evaluation phase.

We simulated the performance of the simplified AG and the HARMs considering practical attack scenarios, various network topologies and variable number of vulnerabilities. Both attack models were built and analysed using the same networked system in the simulation. The same method to construct the attack model was applied to both the simplified AG and the HARMs, and the result shows that the time measurement for

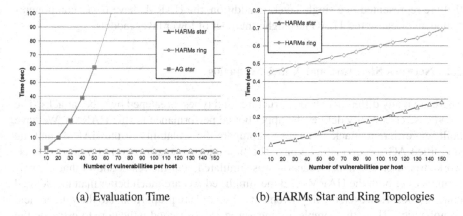

(a) Evaluation Time   (b) HARMs Star and Ring Topologies

Fig. 5. Scalability Difference with Varying Number of Vulnerabilities

the construction phase is similar. The same algorithm was used to compute the full attack paths, but we observe that the HARMs improved the performance in the evaluation
phase dramatically.

5 Discussion

The efficiency of the HARMs is shown through comparisons with existing attack models and simulations. We listed some key questions to compare the scalability of attack
models. The simulation shows that the scalability of the HARMs, and was compared
with the simplified AG to show the efficiency of the HARMs in the construction and the
evaluation phases. However, to improve the usability of the HARMs, we must consider
the modification phase in case of update events in the networked system.

5.1 Scalability of Attack Model Phases

The simplified AG suffered the scalability problem due to independent connections
between the model components. The representation of the simplified AG had more
edges compared with the HARMs. The number of nodes was the same, but the number
of edges was greater in the simplified AG. However, the construction time shows that
there is only a little difference between the HARMs and the simplified AG.

A few existing attack models compared the performance against the simplified AG
in the construction and the evaluation phases. None of the attack models considered an
update event in the networked system, and how their models are updated. The similarity
between the simplified AG, LAG, and the MPG is that they are represented as a single
layer in an attack model. Those attack models suffer from a scalability problem in the
representation, and also the modification may affect all nodes in the attack model in
the worst case. However, hierarchical models, such as the HARMs and the TLAG, have
less structural changes as they have less relationship between nodes than attack models

that are represented in a single layer. In addition, the HARMs have fewer components to update, because the TLAG has higher number of lower layer models.

5.2 Network Structure and Attack Scenarios

There are many different network structures and types threatened by cyber attacks. The worst case complexity defines the upper bound performance for the HARMs. We have built two different attack scenarios to compare the scalability of the HARMs and the simplified AG through simulations. The first attack scenario covered a practical network structure. The attack scenario was simulated, and the result shows that the performances of both the HARMs and the simplified AG are much better than the defined complexities. However, the improvements observed are proportional to their theoretical complexities. Thus, the complexity measurements are good indicators to estimate the performance of the HARMs. The efficiency of the HARMs is shown in the evaluation phase, where the HARMs outperform the simplified AG. The simulation study showed a clear benefit of using the HARMs.

The second simulation compares the scalability of different network topologies, and how much the scalability is affected when the number of vulnerabilities increased. The results were comparable with some of the existing attack models and their analyses [5, 11]. The comparison between the HARMs and the simplified AG shows the performance of the HARMs was always better than the simplified AG. The quadratic growth trend of the simplified AG in the evaluation phase was comparable against the HARMs, where the growth trend was almost linear. However, we only considered a single network topology for each simulation. The networked system consists of different network topologies, but this is not modelled in our study. To accurately measure the expected performance of the networked system and its attack models, combinations of network topologies need to be modelled and simulated.

The variation of vulnerabilities affected the simplified AG significantly, showing an almost exponential growth in the evaluation phase. However, the HARMs showed a linear growth of the evaluation time, which is practically computable for a large number of vulnerabilities. Because the underlying algorithms are the same (e.g., construction algorithm, full path search algorithm), the improvement of scalability comes from the structural advantages of the HARMs.

The performance between the HARMs and the TLAG is not compared in the simulation because identical hosts were used. A network with homogeneous hosts will result in HARMs and TLAG having the same number of upper and the lower layer components. A further comparison is required using a network with heterogeneous hosts to distinguish the HARMs and the TLAG performances.

Since our focus was on comparing the scalability of current attack representation models, we have not considered a real system because we have assumed that the complexity in each host is linearly proportional to the number of hosts (i.e., a constant factor). However, the complexities in real systems are difficult to represent in a simulation, and various network protocols and services may affect how the network traffic flows, such that considering the time in the security analysis may vary the result. We will consider a real system in our future works.

5.3   The Simplified AG and the HARMs

The simulation demonstrated the improvements of existing attack models using the same underlying attack model and algorithms. The time measurement for the construction phase was similar, but the simplified AG showed that it created more edges than the HARMs. Consequently, the performance of the evaluation phase shows that the evaluation time for the simplified AG has increased more rapidly compared with the HARMs, where the growth of the HARMs evaluation time was almost linear. The underlying algorithm to compute the attack paths was the same, but we observe that the performance of the HARMs is more efficient than the simplified AG. The structure of the HARMs reduces the total number of edges in the attack model, so we require fewer computations during the evaluation phase.

In the evaluation process, the number of nodes used in the computations was captured in the simulation. The simulation showed that the number of nodes in the HARMs is greater than the simplified AG, because the upper layer components of the HARMs are also evaluated. As a result, more memory space is required for the HARMs. However, if we allocate the memory space efficiently (e.g., by freeing spaces used by the lower layer calculations when finished), we can reduce the extra memory required by the HARMs. Also, if the lower layer information has been changed, only the lower layer calculations are affected. As a result, the complexity of the HARMs is not largely affected. In contrast, the evaluation time for the simplified AG may fluctuate depending on the changes in the lower layer. In addition, we observed that the number of nodes is only one of the factors that affect the time complexity in the evaluation phase. The clustering of nodes can reduce the time complexity dramatically, as shown in the simulation.

6   Conclusion

Attack models have evolved over the last decade to evaluate the network security. They can also provide countermeasures to enhance the security. The major hurdle of evaluating the network security considering the full attack paths is the scalability problem, where the number of possible attack scenarios grows exponentially as the number of hosts and vulnerabilities increase. Improvements to the full AG have been developed, and new types of attack models (e.g., LAG, MPG and TLAG) have been proposed to address the scalability problem. The HARMs are described and compared with some of the existing attack models to show the scalability improvements.

The efficiency of the HARMs is demonstrated through the simulation, where the underlying algorithms and models were the same to evaluate the full attack paths, but we observe that the performance of the HARMs was better than the simplified AG in the simulation. Moreover, the HARMs have better performance than computational complexities when a practical network scenario is considered.

References

1. Ammann, P., Wijesekera, D., Kaushik, S.: Scalable, graph-based network vulnerability analysis. In: Proc. of the 9th ACM Conference on Computer and Communications Security (CCS 2002), pp. 217–224. ACM, New York (2002)

2. Dewri, R., Poolsappasit, N., Ray, I., Whitley, D.: Optimal security hardening using multi-objective optimization on attack tree models of networks. In: Proc. of ACM Conference on Computer and Communications Security (CCS 2007), pp. 204–213. ACM, New York (2007)
3. Gupta, S., Winstead, J.: Using Attack Graphs to Design Systems. IEEE Security and Privacy 5(4), 80–83 (2007)
4. Xie, A., Cai, Z., Tang, C., Hu, J., Chen, Z.: Evaluating network security with two-layer attack graphs. In: Proc. of Computer Security Applications Conference, ACSAC 2009 (2009)
5. Ou, X., Boyer, W., McQueen, M.: A scalable approach to attack graph generation. In: Proc. of the 13th ACM Conference on Computer and Communications Security (CCS 2006), pp. 336–345. ACM (2006)
6. Ingols, K., Chu, M., Lippmann, R., Webster, S., Boyer, S.: Modeling modern network attacks and countermeasures using attack graphs. In: Proc. of Annual Computer Security Applications Conference (ACSAC 2009), pp. 117–126. IEEE (2009)
7. Saini, V., Duan, Q., Paruchuri, V.: Threat modeling using attack trees. J. Comput. Sci. Coll. 23(4), 124–131 (2008)
8. Dawkins, J., Hale, J.: A systematic approach to multi-stage network attack analysis. In: Proc. of Second IEEE International Information Assurance Workshop (IWIA 2004), pp. 48–56 (2004)
9. Edge, K.: A Framework for Analyzing and Mitigating the Vulnerabilities of Complex Systems via Attack and Protection Trees. PhD thesis, Air Force Institute of Technology (2007)
10. Sheyner, O., Haines, J., Jha, S., Lippmann, R., Wing, J.: Automated generation and analysis of attack graphs. Technical report, CMU (May 2002)
11. Ingols, K., Lippmann, R., Piwowarski, K.: Practical attack graph generation for network defense. In: Proc. of Computer Security Applications Conference (ACSAC 2006), pp. 121–130 (2006)
12. Lippmann, R., Ingols, K.: An Annotated Review of Past Papers on Attack Graphs. ESC-TR-2005-054 (2005)
13. Noel, S., Jajodia, S.: Managing attack graph complexity through visual hierarchical aggregation. In: Proc. of the 2004 ACM Workshop on Visualization and Data Mining for Computer Security (VizSec 2004), pp. 109–118. ACM (2004)
14. Chen, F., Liu, D., Zhang, Y., Su, J.: A scalable approach to analyzing network security using compact attack graphs. Journal of Networks 5(5) (2010)
15. Schneier, B.: Secrets and Lies: Digital Security in a Networked World. John Wiley and Sons Inc. (2000)
16. Roy, A., Kim, D., Trivedi, K.: Attack Countermeasure Trees (ACT): towards unifying the constructs of attack and defense trees. Security and Communication Networks 5(8), 929–943 (2012)
17. Hong, J., Kim, D.: HARMs: Hierarchical Attack Representation Models for Network Security Analysis. In: Proc. of the 10th Australian Information Security Management Conference in SECAU Security Congress, SECAU 2012 (2012)
18. Sawilla, R.E., Ou, X.: Identifying critical attack assets in dependency attack graphs. In: Jajodia, S., Lopez, J. (eds.) ESORICS 2008. LNCS, vol. 5283, pp. 18–34. Springer, Heidelberg (2008)
19. Noel, S., Jajodia, S.: Understanding complex network attack graphs through clustered adjacency matrices. In: Proc. of the 21st Annual Computer Security Applications Conference (ACSAC 2005), vol. 10, pp. 160–169 (2005)

20. Hewett, R., Kijsanayothin, P.: Host-centric model checking for network vulnerability analysis. In: Proc. Annual Computer Security Applications Conference (ACSAC 2008), pp. 225–234 (2008)
21. Albanese, M., Jajodia, S., Noel, S.: Time-efficient and cost-effective network hardening using attack graphs. In: Proc. Dependable Systems and Networks (DSN 2012). IEEE Computer Society, Los Alamitos (2012)
22. Pawlikowski, K., Jeong, H., Lee, J.: On credibility of simulation studies of telecommunication networks. IEEE Communications Magazine 40(1), 132–139 (2002)
23. Ewing, G., Pawlikowski, K., McNickle, D.: Akaroa-2: Exploiting network computing by distributing stochastic simulation. In: Proc. European Simulation Multiconference (ISCS 1999), pp. 175–181 (1999)

ADAPT: A Game Inspired Attack-Defense
and Performance Metric Taxonomy

Chris B. Simmons, Sajjan G. Shiva, Harkeerat Singh Bedi, and Vivek Shandilya

University of Memphis, Computer Science Department, Memphis, Tennessee
{cbsmmons,sshiva,hsbedi,v.shandilya}@memphis.edu

Abstract. Game theory has been researched extensively in network security demonstrating an advantage of modeling the interactions between attackers and defenders. Game theoretic defense solutions have continuously evolved in most recent years. One of the pressing issues in composing a game theoretic defense system is the development of consistent quantifiable metrics to select the best game theoretic defense model. We survey existing game theoretic defense, information assurance, and risk assessment frameworks that provide metrics for information and network security and performance assessment. Coupling these frameworks, we propose a game theoretic approach to attack-defense and performance metric taxonomy (ADAPT). ADAPT uses three classifications of metrics: (i) Attacker, (ii) Defender (iii) Performance. We proffer ADAPT with an attempt to aid game theoretic performance metrics. We further propose a game decision system (GDS) that uses ADAPT to compare competing game models. We demonstrate our approach using a distributed denial of service (DDoS) attack scenario.

Keywords: Game Theory, Taxonomy, Security Management.

1   Introduction

Game theory has received increased attention from network security researchers, investigating defense solutions. The game theory approach has the advantage of modeling the interactions between attackers and defenders, where players have the ability to analyze other player's behavior. This may enable an administrator to develop better strategic defenses for the system. For instance, when there are many actions available to the attacker and defender, it becomes difficult to develop solution strategies. Hamilton, et al. [1] outlined the areas of game theory which are relevant to information warfare using course of actions with predicted outcomes and what-if scenarios. Jiang, et al. [2] proposed an attack-defense stochastic game model to predict the next actions of an attacker using the interactions between an attacker and defender. Therefore, it is vital to provide a network administrator the capability to compare multiple strategies using the appropriate metrics to optimize the network.

In this work we consider various metrics for game theoretic models. Bellovin [3] inferred that designing proper metrics for security measurement is a tough problem that should not be underestimated. Current research is lacking in terms of providing

L.J. Janczewski, H.B. Wolfe, and S. Shenoi (Eds.): SEC 2013, IFIP AICT 405, pp. 344–365, 2013.
© IFIP International Federation for Information Processing 2013

information a system administrator can use in determining metrics to quantify performance of diverse game theoretic defense models. One of the problems faced by research pertaining to security games is how to evaluate different network security game models, in terms of performance, accuracy, and effectiveness. The Institute for Information and Infrastructure Protection (I3P) has identified security metrics as priority for current research and development [4]. We extend this notion to provide a comprehensive taxonomy to aid in assessing the overall performance and quality of a game theoretic model. Prior game theoretic research mainly focused on classifying metrics based on a distribution of games across various game types and models. Further, the game theoretic defense mechanisms in literature are arbitrary and ad hoc in nature. This makes game theoretic defense models very complex and designed towards application specific scenarios [5]. We propose an alternative real world approach by classifying our metrics based on a real world distributed denial of service (DDoS) scenario.

In this paper, we attempt to address limitations in research through the proposed game theoretic attack-defense and performance metric taxonomy (ADAPT), which is a taxonomy of game related metrics. We define a game as the interactions between two players with conflicting goals. In our case these players are the attacker (hacker) and system administrator (defender). Game metrics are a set of tools which are used to measure the various kinds of impact a game model has on each of its players. We classify these game metrics based on their impact on attacker, defender, and the performance of the game model on the system which is being run. Prior research has shown, with the use of game theory, how the interaction should take place based on the strategy and the strategy selected from the game model. In this traditional scenario one game model is assessed relative to a particular attack. He, et al. [6] proposed a Game Theoretical Attack-Defense Model (GTADM), similar to ADAPT, that quantifies the probability of threats in constructing a risk assessment framework. We extend these general game theory steps and concepts proposed in He, et al. [6] with the use of ADAPT being able to assess competing game models and select the game model which is suitable for defense. This provides a defender with a preliminary view of multiple game models associated to a particular attack.

This research is composed of attack attributes and associated metrics that can be used to assess and compare competing game models. Thus, ADAPT provides a metric-centric approach to selecting the optimal game model. A game model is to evaluate the security level, performance, and quality of a system that will aid in selecting the appropriate game defense model at a specific time of the game. These metrics belong to different game theoretic defense models, information assurance, and risk assessment frameworks. Prior work towards developing a security metric taxonomy focuses on three core relationships of metric classifications involving organization, operation, and technical [7, 8, 9]. In proposing ADAPT, we focus on metrics with technical association.

This paper is organized as follows: In section 2 we provide a motivating scenario and in section 3 we define characteristics for good security metrics followed by our proposed metric taxonomy. In section 4 we define the metrics used in a game inspired attack-defense and performance metric taxonomy. In section 5 we introduce a game model comparing system based on ADAPT and the methodology used to map metrics within ADAPT, followed by ADAPT applied within the Game Inspired Defense Architecture (GIDA). In section 6 we provide a brief literature review on performance and security metrics. In section 7, we conclude our paper and highlight future work.

2   Motivating Scenario

In this section we start with a brief overview of game theory concepts and provide a motivating example, which highlight the relationship to the proposed metrics that will assess game defense models. There are four basic concepts of Game Theory : (i) *A player* is the basic entity of a game who decides to perform a particular action (ii) *A game* is a precise description of the strategic interaction that includes the constraints of, and payoffs for, actions that the players can take, but does not correspond to actual actions taken (iii) *A strategy* for a player is a complete plan of actions in all possible situations throughout the game (iv) *A Nash equilibrium* is a solution concept that describes a steady state condition of the game; no player would prefer to change his strategy as that would lower his payoffs given that all other players are adhering to the prescribed strategy. Roy, et al. [10] surveyed existing game theoretic solutions designed to enhance network security. They emphasized that Game Theory has the advantage of treating explicitly intelligent decision makers having divergent interests.

Now, let us consider a scenario, in which a DDoS attack is taking place. There are multiple game models to choose for defense, but the defender is unsure which model has performed the best historically to make a determination. The defender can view the strategy spaces of all the games associated to the DDoS attack; however it will take the defender a significant amount of time to select the best game available. In modeling such player strategies, the DDoS attack presents a challenging scenario, which has increased in sophistication [11] and motivates our research in this paper. Although research has evolved relative to the DDoS attack, it is continuously a scenario that deserves much attention due to its simplicity and dominate nature of coordinated botnet use [12] to cause an enormous amount of damage. Moreover, the punishment relative to a DDoS attack is minimal to non-existent. Typically, when a DDoS attack takes place in the real world, attackers lease nodes to conduct an attack against a target, or set of targets. Once the attack is complete, the leased nodes are returned to the pool; where another party will lease those nodes allowing a constant change in IP addresses. Due to the nature of the DDoS attack, the most common defense against DDoS attacks is to block nodes. Parameswaran, et al. [13] utilized blocklist as a defense mechanism in a spammer's game theoretic model. Majority of the DDoS attacks are just blocked, which does not sustain a punitive cost and punishment by legal action is rare.

Therefore, in this work the DDoS example is considered by and large a static one shot game to provide an intuitive example of how the proposed taxonomy can be implemented within a system. When we look at network attacks in general, there are fundamental components that are likely present in a DDoS attack. Mirkovic and Reihner [11] echoed this point by placing emphasis on crucial features of an attack to comprehend the detailed differences. Hence, we believe the network has some tangible attack components that will allow experiential knowledge mapping to ADAPT metrics. The goal is to produce a summary of metrics, which will in turn be used to determine the best game model pursuant to the metrics selected within the ADAPT framework. Thus answering the question from Mirkovic and Reihner [11], how would two different defense models perform under a given attack? We represent a generalization of how each attribute will be mapped to the attacker, defender, and the performance of the target system. The scope of this work investigates metrics selected based on experiential knowledge, as opposed to metrics autonomously selected by the system.

Continuing our scenario, an attacker initiating a DDoS attack acquires a number of nodes to conduct the attack. This increases the amount of bandwidth consumed by the attacker and introduces an increase in the attacker's probability of being caught by the defender. We observe by generalizing attack components and associating them to game inspired metrics, where we are able to provide an overview of game model performance. This enables the defender to select the optimal game model for defense. We further illustrate our scenario in section 5.

3   Characteristics of Game Inspired Metrics

We use characteristics of security metrics to further assist with evaluating metrics for game theoretic defense models. A performance study requires a set of metrics to be chosen for analysis [7]. Performance analysis requires comparing two or more systems and finding the best among them [7]. We extend this to game theoretic defense models, where the network administrator has the ability to select the best game suitable for optimal defense at a specific time. With a dynamic selection process of the best game permits a network administrator to systematically choose a defense solution applicable for defense. The game selection is based on the knowledge of how well a game model represents the considered security situation. Our methodology of game model selection is highlighted in section 5.

There is increased research involving the development of taxonomy for security metrics, where characteristics are provided to ensure organizations understand the metrics when quantifying and evaluating security. Understanding the metrics require a distinction between metric and measurement. Metrics are the resultant of a comparison of two or more baseline measurement over time, whereas measurement is a single point in time view of specific factors [14]. Swanson [15] defined a metric as tools designed to facilitate the appropriate decision for a specific situation, improve performance and accountability through collection, analysis, and reporting of pertinent performance information.

In the Federal Plan for Cyber security and Information Assurance Research and Development of 2006, the National Science and Technology Council (NSTC) has recommended developing information assurance metrics as a priority in federal agencies [16]. Vaughn et al. [17] described one of the pressing issues involving security engineering is the adoption of measures or metrics that can reliably depict hardware and software system assurance. Research has suggested the characteristics of good metrics [7, 8, 14, 15, 17]. We encompass a list of metric characteristics from literature that provides a foundation to develop comprehensive game theoretic defense taxonomy. Wesner [9] introduced the concept of a metric being S.M.A.R.T.(specific, measurable, actionable, relevant, timely). Manadathata and Wing [18] described a system action can potentially be part of an attack, and hence contributes to attack surface, which also includes the contribution of system resources. We use the notion for validation of our game theoretic defense architecture to measure which game is providing a higher level of security compared to another.

Applying relevant metric characteristics from research illustrates our proposed game inspired approach to an attack-defense and performance metric taxonomy ADAPT (Figure 1). As mentioned earlier, it utilizes three classifications of metrics: attacker, defender, and performance. ADAPT enables a network administrator to view and apply pertinent metrics to evaluate performance in multiple security games.

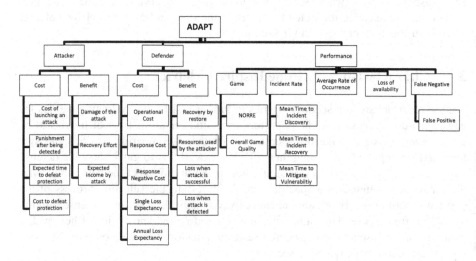

Fig. 1. Attack-Defense and Performance metric Taxonomy (ADAPT)

4   Adapt: Attack-Defense and Performance Metric Taxonomy

As seen from (Figure 1), ADAPT produces relevant metrics to assign values to the components of the attack-defense cost and benefit as well as the performance. These metrics and their calculations are determined based on a review of literature. We utilized these metrics from literature being the same domain in which relevance is closely related to cyber security. An information security measurement standard provides insight to how well a system is performing and analyze whether investments, in information security, are beneficial. Potential benefits include increasing information security performance and providing quantifiable inputs for investment.

We identify, in ADAPT, the following three classifiers: (i) Attacker, (ii) Defender (iii) Performance. We assume that these metrics are generic and not specific for a particular game. The attacker and defender metrics have relation to the game models. The performance metrics are used separately from the defender metrics, mainly because the performance metrics have association to the performance of the game model as a whole. Furthermore, the performance metrics relate to the performance of the system in which the game model is run. Its classification provides additional information associated to the game that will assist a defender in selecting the optimal competing game models for defense.

4.1   Attacker Metrics

In this section we provide insight into the metrics selected regarding the cost and benefit from the perspective of the attacker.

Cost of Attacker. The cost of an attacker to attack a specific target can be divided into the following metrics.

He et al. [6] used cost of launching an attack and punishment to the attacker as metrics to define the cost of attack.

- **Cost of launching attack (COLA):** Consists of money and time that an attacker can pay in order to launch an attack against a target.
- **Punishment after being detected (PABD):** Consists of the legal loss of the attacker, which involves one of the metrics used to define the cost of an attacker.

He et al. [6] used four instances in game scenarios involving non-cooperative non-zero-sum static game with complete information, where the relations between Strategy Profile and attacker cost are:

    o   When the attacker and defender both take actions:

$$Cost\ of\ attacker = COLA + P \times PABD \tag{1}$$

    P is the detection rate of attacks.

    o   When the attacker takes an action and the defender does not:

$$Cost\ of\ attacker = COLA \tag{2}$$

    o   When the attacker does not take an action and the defender takes an action:

$$Cost\ of\ attacker = 0 \tag{3}$$

    o   When the attacker and defender do not take an action:

$$Cost\ of\ attacker = 0 \tag{4}$$

Carin et al. [19] proposed the following metrics to cyber risk assessment evaluating the Attack/Protect Model. These metrics are based on generating a probability distribution for cost, in terms of time, of successfully defeating the protections applied to critical intellectual property (IP).

- **Expected cost of defeating a protection (ECDP):** Involves the cost in man hours an attacker would exhibit to successfully defeat the protection. The probability distribution (Pr) is based on historical data of successfully attacking the IP. The cost of the ith man-hour in the attack is denoted by (c_i).

$$\sum_{i=0}^{\infty} c_i \, Pr(i) \tag{5}$$

- **Expected time to defeat the protection (ETDP):** Involves the hours an attacker contributes to successfully defeat the protection. The probability distribution (Pr) is based on historical data of successfully attacking the IP.

$$\sum_{i=0}^{\infty} i \, Pr(i) \tag{6}$$

Benefit of Attacker. Benefit of attacker entails the benefit the attacker receives when implementing an attack against a specific target (i.e. Fame or Monetary Value). Below we provide various metrics from literature assessing benefit of attacker.

Lye [20] divided the benefit of an attacker into the following metrics. Although the parameters used calculate the benefit, it can be inferred with an example (e.g. the damage can involve the reduced bandwidth of a system due to a DoS attack, whereas the recovery effort a network administrator puts forth in the amount of time to bring the system to its original state prior to the attack).

- **Damage of the attack (DOA):** Consists of the degree of damage in which the attacker is able to cause on the target system.
- **Recovery effort (time) required by defender (RERD):** Involves the time it takes for a defender to bring the system to a safe state of execution.
- **Expected income by the attacker (EIBA):** Involves the monetary value received by the attacker when an attack is successful. This value can be computed using the amount of effort exhibited by the defender in terms of time to bring the system to a safe state prior to the attack.

He et al. [6] indicated the benefit of an attacker is based on the loss of defending a system. The damage of defender when the attack action is undetected by the IDS (SD) as:

$$SD = Con_p \times Con_v + Int_p \times Int_v + Ava_p \times Ava_v \tag{7}$$

Con_p, Int_p, Ava_p are the damage degrees the attack action has made on the attack object respectively in Confidentiality, Integrity and Availability. Con_v, Int_v, Ava_v are the objects assets in Confidentiality, Integrity and Availability. These values are not constants, and they can be set by the network administrator.

The damage when the attack is detected (FD) is defined as:

$$FD = (Con_p \times Con_v + Int_p \times Int_v + Ava_p \times Ava_v) - Restore \tag{8}$$

Restore is the recovery on the attack action.

$$Restore = Con_p^r \times Con_v + Int_p^r \times Int_v + Ava_p^r \times Ava_v \tag{9}$$

As with the benefit of attacker, He et al. [6] uses four instances in the case of non-cooperative non-zero-sum static game with complete information, the relations between Strategy Profile and attacker benefit are:

- o When the attacker and defender take an action:

$$Benefit\ of\ attacker = (SD) \times (1 - P) + (FD) \times P \qquad (10)$$

- o When the attacker takes an action and the defender does not:

$$Benefit\ of\ attacker = SD \qquad (11)$$

- o When the attacker fails take an action and the defender takes an action:

$$Benefit\ of\ attacker = 0 \qquad (12)$$

- o When the attacker and defender do not take an action:

$$Benefit\ of\ attacker = 0 \qquad (13)$$

Plainly stated, the benefit of the attacker is based on the loss of defending the system.

$$Benefit\ of\ attacker = -Benfit\ of\ Defender \qquad (14)$$

Cremonini and Nizovtsev [21] defined the benefit of attacker in terms of the amount of effort, measured by time, put by an attacker into an attack. They provide the below calculation.

$$Benefit\ of\ attacker = E\big(B(x)\big) \qquad (15)$$

x: The amount of effort placed in the attack.

$$E\big(B(x)\big) = \pi(x) \times G \qquad (16)$$

$\pi(x)$: Probability of success of attack given the amount of effort put into attack.
G: One time payoff the attacker receives in the case of successful attack.

4.2   Defender Metrics

In this section we provide insight into the metrics selected involving the cost and benefit from the perspective of the defender.

Cost of Defender. The cost of defender involves the cost of a defender to defend a system against an attack. Below we incorporate literature applying cost of defense.

He et al. [6] indicated the cost of a defender consists of Operational Cost, Response Cost and Response Negative.

- **Operational Cost (OC):** Can be derived from the risk assessment knowledge library.
- **Response Negative Cost (RNC):** Can be derived using the following formula:

$$RNC = -P_a \times Ava_v \qquad (17)$$

P_a is in [0, 1] being the damage degree to the availability of the system caused by response actions.

- **Response Cost (RC):** Involves the values derived from the Attack-defense Knowledge Library.

He et al. [6] also provided four instances in relation between the Strategy Profile and defender costs in the case of non-cooperative non-zero-sum static game with complete information, which are:

o When the attacker and defender take an action:

$$Cost\ of\ defender = -(RC + P_a \times Ava) \times P \tag{18}$$

o When the attacker takes an action and the defender decides to not defend:

$$Cost\ of\ defender = 0 \tag{19}$$

o When the attacker doesn't take any action and the defender takes an action:

$$Cost\ of\ defender = -(RC + P_a \times Ava) \times P_m \tag{20}$$

o When the attacker doesn't take any action nor the defender:

$$Cost\ of\ defender = 0 \tag{21}$$

P_m: False detection rate of the IDS.

You and Shiyong [22] provided metrics that help compute the cost and payoff of an attacker and defender. Using the performance metrics of exposure factor and average rate of occurrence, we compute single loss expectancy and annual loss expectancy.

- **Single Loss Expectancy (SLE):** Involves the dollar amount associated to a single asset, which is computed using the Asset Value (dollar amount assigned by the network administrator) and the exposure factor (retrieved from a performance metric).

$$SLE = Asset\ Value \times Exposure\ Factor \tag{22}$$

- **Annual Loss Expectancy (ALE):** Involves the dollar amount or time associated to an asset over a particular period of time. The single loss expectancy used above and average rate of occurrence (retrieved from a performance metric) to compute ALE.

$$ALE = SLE \times ARO \tag{23}$$

Benefit of Defender. Benefit of defender involves the benefit of a defender to defend a system against an attack, either prior to or following an attack. Below we provide research assessing benefit of defense.

- **Recovery by Restore (RBR):** Involves the ability for the defender to recover a target system to its original state from an attack action.
- **Resources used by the attacker (RUBA):** Involves quantitatively reflecting the number of nodes used by the attacker, which is m.

$$(RUBA) = m \qquad (24)$$

He, et al. [6] defined the benefit of a defender based on damage of defender when attack is successful (SD), damage of defender when attack is detected (FD) and Restore, as explained in the previous section of Benefit of Attacker.

In the case of non-cooperative non-zero-sum static game with complete information, He, et al. [6] uses four instances to describe the relations between Strategy Profile and defender benefit as:

- o The attacker and defender both take actions:

$$Benefit\ of\ defender = (SD) \times (1 - P) + (FD) \times P \qquad (25)$$

- o When the attacker takes an action and the defender does not:

$$Benefit\ of\ defender = -(SD) \qquad (26)$$

- o The attacker does not take an action and the defender takes an action:

$$Benefit\ of\ defender = 0 \qquad (27)$$

- o When the attacker and defender do not take an action:

$$Benefit\ of\ attacker = 0 \qquad (28)$$

- **Loss When Attack is Successful (LWAS):** Involves the degree of damage in which the attacker is able to cause on the target system. This metric is a negative benefit to the attacker, capturing the historical data to improve a defender's incentive to defend.
- **Loss When Attack is Detected (LWAD):** Involves the ability for the defender to recover a target system to a non-compromising state from an attack action. This metric is a positive benefit to the attacker, capturing the historical data to improve a defender's incentive to defend.

4.3 Performance Metrics

Performance metrics entail the assessment of the system performance and evaluation of unlike game theoretic defense models. Typically, the payoff metrics in game models are used to gauge the cost-benefit analysis between the attacker and defender. This alone is not sufficient to measure and validate a particular game model. Therefore, the attacker and defender metrics represent the game, whereas the additional metrics provided under the performance classification represent asset performance towards selecting the best competing game models for defense. The premise involving the performance metrics gives further insight into the knowledge of the attack relative to the asset.

Performance metrics use cost-benefit assessment of attack and defense, risk assessment, and a game theoretic approach to construct an assessment of performance. This will support a network administrator view appropriate metrics when analyzing and selecting a particular game theoretic defense model. Initially the performance metrics are computed using the attack information received, then updated with each attack instance using ADAPT and the defending system. For instance, items such as, false positive (FP) or mean time to incident discovery (MTTID) are set to zero, once computed by the initial attack, these values are updated to provide asset performance relative to the game models. This performance assessment relative to game models provides contribution to existing taxonomies.

In this section we list various performance metrics from literature that can be applied to game theoretic defense models and used for model assessment.

- **Number of rounds to reach Nash Equilibrium (NORRE):** Burke [23] proposed a metric which provides the number of rounds to reach a Nash Equilibrium, in order to evaluate a game theory model of information warfare, based upon the repeated games of incomplete information model. Burke [23] stated equilibrium provides the ability to analyze a game theory model's predictive power, which is evaluated in terms of accuracy and performance.

$$NORRE = Count(actions\ played\ until\ nash\ equilibrium) - 1 \qquad (29)$$

- **Overall Game Quality (OGQ):** Jansen [24] stated qualitative assignments can be used to represent quantitative measures of security properties (e.g., vulnerabilities found). We define a metric overall game quality, where the game model is determined based on the availability of the system (e.g. percentage of available bandwidth), the performance of the game (e.g. average NORRE), and the quality of the system (e.g. false positive rate). This metric is based on the overall equipment effectiveness, where game theory parameters are applied to measure the efficiency of various games [25]. Other works utilized false positive rate as a part the actual game model [26]. This metric is resilient to both options of the false positive rate when determining the overall game quality.

$$OGQ = Availability \times Performance \times Quality \qquad (30)$$

- **Exposure Factor (EF):** Exposure factor represents the percentage of loss a threat may have on a particular asset. Exposure factor with a combination of other metrics will provide insight to the level of importance a system may have in the event of an attack.

$$EF = \frac{Asset\ Loss}{Tot.Asset\ Level} \qquad (31)$$

- **Average Rate of Occurrence (ARO):** Average Rate of Occurrence is an estimate of the frequency of attack probability. Average Rate of Occurrence can assist with determining defense strategies of a specific asset. Minimizing the ARO provides insight to how well a game theoretic defense solution is performing.

$$ARO = \frac{Count\ (Occurrences)}{Time\ Interval} \qquad (32)$$

- **Loss of Availability (LOA):** Loss of availability refers to the loss of resource which is currently unavailable to the legitimate requesting processes. The higher the value of this metric incurs an increased loss.

$$LOA = \frac{Count\ (Unavailable\ Resources)}{Tot.No.of\ Legitimate\ Requesting\ Processes} \qquad (33)$$

- **Incident Rate (IR):** Incident Rate indicates the number of detected security breaches a system or asset experienced during an allotted time period. Using incident rate, with a combination of other metrics, can indicate the level of threats, effectiveness of security controls, or attack detection capabilities [27].

$$IR = Count(Incidents) \qquad (34)$$

- **Mean Time to Incident Discovery (MTTID):** Mean-Time-To-Incident-Discovery characterizes the efficiency of detecting attacks, by computing the average elapsed time between the initial occurrence of an incident and its subsequent discovery. The MTTID metric also serves as a leading indicator of flexibility in system or administrator's ability to defend as it measures detection of attacks from known and unknown vectors [27].

$$MTTID = \frac{Date_{of\ Discovery} - Date_{of\ Occurrence}}{Count(Incidents)} \qquad (35)$$

- **Mean Time to Incident Recovery (MTTIR):** Mean Time to Incident Recovery measures the effectiveness of recovering from an attack. The more responsive a system or administrator is, the less impact the attack may have on the asset [27].

$$MTTIR = \frac{Date_{of\ Recovery} - Date_{of\ Occurrence}}{Count(Incidents)} \qquad (36)$$

- **Mean Time to Mitigate Vulnerability (MTTMV):** Mean time to mitigate vulnerabilities measures the average time exhibited to mitigate identified vulnerabilities in a particular asset. This metric indicates a system or administrator's ability to patch and/or mitigate a known vulnerability to reduce exploitation risk [27].

$$MTTMV = \frac{Date_{of\ Mitigation} - Date_{of\ Detection}}{Count(Mitigated_{Vulnerabilities})} \qquad (37)$$

- **False Negative Rate (FNR):** The frequency in which the system fails to report malicious activity occurs. It involves the number of incidents that are not detected, which are present within the system [28].

$$FNR = \frac{(Missed\ Incidents)}{Count(Incidents)} \qquad (38)$$

- **False Positive Rate (FPR):** The frequency in which the system reports a malicious activity in error. It involves the number of incidents that were detected and upon further discovery produced a false incident [10].

$$FPR = \frac{(False\ Positives)}{Count(Incidents)} \qquad (39)$$

5   A Game Model Comparing System Based on Adapt

In this section we describe the process in which ADAPT will be used to compare game models followed by a scenario of its application using a distributed denial of service (DDoS) attack. Lastly, we highlight ADAPT's application to the Game Inspired Defense Architecture (GIDA), wherein a game decision system (GDS) uses ADAPT to compare competing game models. The GDS facilitates selecting the optimal game theoretic defense model.

5.1   Methodology

In this section we present the method to compare the candidate game models relevant to an identified attack using metrics in ADAPT. The identified attack is resolved into attack vectors, which is used to locate the relevant metrics within ADAPT. Using these metrics the game models are compared to select the game model most suitable for defense.

In a given attack scenario a certain set of anomalies are identified. Those anomalies are used to identify the attack using the AVOIDIT taxonomy proposed in Simmons, et al. [29]. This identified attack is resolved into "attack components". These attack components are parameters indicating some aspect of the system, albeit malfunction and/or failure, affected by the attack. They are composed of various anomalies which are observed by sensors such as Firewalls, IDS, and their values indicate their severity. Using these attack components a set of metrics that fittingly quantize the system's current security state are identified in ADAPT. Using these metrics the game models with their respective game model components which correspond to these metrics in their interaction modeling in terms of actions-payoff of players are selected. These models are compared with each other to pick the one, which corresponds/maps best to the selected metrics.

The present experiment had a simple case. To achieve the above flow we used the following 5 steps.

1. Given an attack, A, and a target system T, we identify a set of attack components AC.
2. We map the attack components AC_n with its respective ADAPT metric, AM_n.
3. Given the game model and the game model components we provide the Boolean value (0 or 1) to all the metrics. If a game model component corresponds to a selected metric then the component gets a value 1 else a 0. This is done for all the game model components of each of the competing game models.
4. All values associated with each game model component of a game model are summed to give a total score of evaluation of the competing game models.
5. The game model with the highest score is selected as being the most relevant for defense, which is appropriate for instantiation.

In a given model, temporal consideration is not parameterized separately. In terms of actions at a given state of the game and how and when the game transits between the states is considered as the mode to keep track of the time. For more complex scenarios time must be taken into consideration in more explicit ways in the modeling. In the future work we intend to exhibit temporal considerations and improve the evaluation based on weighted values and not just 0/1 for greater precision.

The ADAPT taxonomy is constructed in a way to evaluate the holistic view of a game model, along with its respective system. It requires some resources to instantiate each game model to run a game. The metrics in the performance branch evaluate the overhead of instantiating a game model. The attacker/defender branch metrics evaluate the parameters which affect the attacker/defender payoff. The next section illustrates the ADAPT methodology using a zero-sum game scenario where the game model components correspond to a benefit to the defender, thus correspond to the cost of the attacker and vice versa. Due to space constrains, the reader is encouraged to refer to Bedi, et al. [30] for an elaborate discussion.

5.2   A Case Study: DDoS Attack Scenario

We continue our example from section 2, wherein we analyze a DDoS attack and ADAPT's applicability to discern the main features of the attack. This offers the framework for game model selection with a relevant set of metrics. We focus on the bandwidth reduction where multiple attacking nodes attempt to push their packets to exhaust limited bandwidth of a link in the network. The attacker's strategy is to maximize either the botnet size or the sending rate to flood the pipe. We will call this strategy a flood strategy by the attacker, as he is not concerned with detection, but to overwhelm its target. Whereas the defender's strategy is to implement the optimal firewall setting which will allow legitimate flows and block malicious flows. This defense strategy is simply to defend or not defend.

Experiential knowledge is used to evaluate the crucial features of our DDoS attack example to capture the appropriate attack components for analysis. We illustrate these components with an example. This example is based on prior work in this domain [31, 32].

Attack Components

In our example scenario, the attack is a network based DDoS and it consists of the following attack components:

- v_b: Average bandwidth used by the attacker,
- v_n: Ratio of the number of lost legitimate users to the total number of legitimate users,
- v_c: Number of nodes used by the attacker to launch an attack

The values of these components define the impact of the attack over a target system. In this example, the attacker's goal is to increase v_b and v_n, which are the rewards. An assumption is made on the attacker's cost v_c is linearly proportional to the number of attacking nodes employed and $v_c = m$.

Continuing our DDoS example, the IDS captures a fixed number of properties to begin facilitating situational analysis for decision making, whereas the firewall has a default drop threshold set. Various sources provide input properties used by ADAPT.

It is assumed the mapping is preset, which is initially performed manually via expert knowledge and keywords. The initial input properties to ADAPT for the DDoS example are: (a) total bit rate, (b) total number of flows, (c) drop rate, and (d) number of flows dropped.

A legitimate flow is one in which the network bandwidth is used in a fair manner, being the flow per node being less than or equal to the ratio of total bandwidth to the number of nodes. The loss of legitimate flows is used in this example to determine if the flow is negatively impacted. This provides a way to distinguish attacker flows.

The bitrates sum is computed per IP address. The IPs which consume above the amount of bandwidth than their predefined share are considered malicious nodes. For example, for the attacker to break the initial threshold set by the defender there must be a minimum number of unfriendly nodes required to drop at least one friendly (legitimate) node. If the defender initiates a response to the attack, an incurred cost to the defender, is accounted in terms of resources and time.

Similarly, the following attack components, which are used in our example, are mapped to corresponding attacker, defender, and performance metrics.

The first component v_b, being the average bandwidth used by the attacker maps to the following metrics:

(a) The **SLE** metric in ADAPT is classified under the cost of defender. It captures the dollar amount associated to a single asset, which is computed using the Asset value and the Exposure factor. In our scenario, the asset is the bandwidth of the pipe and its value can be determined by the network administrator. We associate the Exposure Factor as the ability of the attacker to access and exploit the asset.
(b) The **EIBA** metric in ADAPT is classified under the benefit of attacker. In our DDoS example, this is associated to the zero-sum game to express the attacker's monetary success.
(c) The **EF** metric in ADAPT is classified under performance. In our example, this metrics is associated with the percentage of loss on the bandwidth.

The second component v_c, being the number of nodes used by the attacker to launch an attack maps the following metrics:

(a) The **RNC** metric in ADAPT is classified under the cost of defender. In our example, this metric is associated with the damage the attack was able to accomplish considering the defender's response.
(b) The **DOA** metric in ADAPT is classified under the benefit of attacker. It involves the monetary value received by the attacker when an attack is successful
(c) The **LOA** metric in ADAPT is classified under performance. It represents the percentage of loss a threat may have on a particular asset.

The third component v_n, being the ratio of the number of lost legitimate users to the total number of legitimate users maps to the following metrics:

(a) The **RUBA** metric in ADAPT is classified under the cost of defender. It relates to quantitatively reflecting the number of nodes used by the attacker

(b) The **COLA** metric in ADAPT is classified under the benefit of attacker. It involves the cost incurred by the attacker when an attack is launched.

(c) The **IR** metric in ADAPT is classified under performance. It represents the incident rate associated to the target system.

Table 1 highlights a visual representation of the attack components we use to map metrics with ADAPT. The column titled "ADAPT Metrics" contain the metrics mapped using the attacker, defender, and performance classifiers. Each component gets mapped to either cost or benefit (but not both) for each of the players; attacker and defender. Also, a component corresponding to the cost (or benefit) of a defender cannot correspond to the cost (or benefit) of the attacker.

Table 1. Attack Components Correlation with ADAPT Metrics

DDoS Attack Components	ADAPT Metrics				
	Defender		Attacker		Performance
	Cost	Benefit	Cost	Benefit	
v_b	SLE	X	X	EIBA	EF
v_n	RNC	X	X	DOA	LOA
v_c	X	RUBA	COLA	X	IR

Table 1 illustrates the ADAPT metrics, which depicts the player and performance related metrics for mapping. Using the described game scenario the defender is able to use ADAPT to systematically retrieve potential game models suitable for defense based on the attack components received and its metric mapping. The scenario has to be evaluated with respect to these three factors, which the metrics in ADAPT capture. Once this is done a relationship between the quantified components of the game governing equations as discussed in the example are evaluated. This makes the game model involving the obtained attack components best depicting the scenario, will be chosen to be the game model that best suits the present scenario. The metrics in ADAPT quantifies the parameters of the scenario. Using these values, the correlation of a model can be evaluated using a suitable algorithm as described in Bedi, et al [30]. As with any sensor, there are instances where false positives occur, in which human intervention is required for the improvement of those sensors. For the purpose of this paper, we assume the attack has a relevant game model in the repository, where human intervention and expert knowledge is required to update the repository for increased accuracy of an ADAPT based system. In future work, we are developing a frame work for constructing game models, which facilitate dynamic analyses of imperfect information and respond with changes in the strategies dynamically for optimum response in real world scenarios. This future work is based on our prior work [26] where we recommend game theoretic defense strategies to network security problems assuming imperfect sensory information.

In our example the strategy of the attacker and defender does not change. For the sake of discussion, let us consider an instance in which the strategy of the attacker changes, by increasing or decreasing the number of nodes exhibited in the DDoS attack. Also, let us consider, the defender is able to change its strategy, as well.

In both cases, of the attacker and defender, ADAPT is resilient to the change, as the generalized metrics remain mapped within the taxonomy. Paruchuri, et al. [30] proposed an efficient heuristic approach for security against multiple adversaries where the attacker is unknown to the defender. This work is in line with our DDoS example, due to its unknown nature of the true attacker.

5.3   ADAPT in the Game Inspired Defense Architecture

The Game Inspired Defense Architecture (GIDA) is foreseen as a holistic approach designed to counter cyber-attacks [26, 30, 34, 35]. GIDA (Figure 2) focuses on the concept of offering defense strategies against probable and committed attacks by modeling situations as multi-player game scenarios. The attack-defense analysis is done by ADAPT. GIDA provides security by operating in the following fashion: Identification of attack, Extraction of game models relevant to the identified attack, and Assessment of candidate game models and execution of the one which is most relevant to present attack.

GIDA consists of three components, namely, ADAPT (our taxonomy), a Knowledge Base (KB), and a Game Decision System (GDS). The GDS is a preventative system, within the GIDA framework, to collect input from various sources for continuous attack information updates relative to game models.

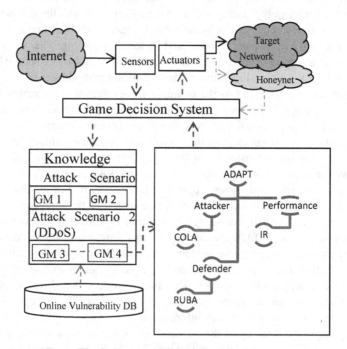

Fig. 2. Game Inspired Defense Architecture

The knowledge base (KB) consists of game models mapped to the types of attacks identified and additional attack related data. The GDS operates in a preventative fashion through the assessment of candidate game models respective to a particular attack and executes the game model which is best among them. ADAPT provides the metrics to be mapped to the components, and evaluate them in terms of different aspects of the player's payoffs, and the game's performance. This gives the GDS the specific set of game metrics defining the ongoing attack. The GDS acts as the brain with provisions to process input information and take the appropriate action.

One implementation of our proposed defense architecture is depicted (Figure 2). Our network topology consists of a Target Network which our architecture aims to protect. This network is connected to the Internet through a series of Sensors and Actuators. Currently, GIDA uses an intrusion detection system (IDS) as the sensor and a firewall as the actuator. The topology also includes a honeynet, which is a network of honeypots. The honeypot is primarily used as a virtual implementation of the target network for analyzing traffic and gathering additional information from the attacker.

Once an attack is identified against a target, the sensors feed information to the GDS. The GDS contains an attack identification mechanism, which forwards the suspected attack to the KB. The KB is searched for additional attack related information and candidate game models which can defend against the identified attack. In this present case (Figure 2), the knowledge base provides two game models: GM 3 and GM 4. These suggested game models are then sent to ADAPT to assess the attack, defender, and performance metrics for selection of the optimal game model.

The depiction of ADAPT (Figure 2) highlights how ADAPT uses its knowledge of the two game models to classify each component of an attack with the game metrics. Due to space constraints, we provide a single example of a component's selection process using the tree structure of ADAPT (Figure 2). ADAPT navigates its tree for each component of the attack to capture the metrics from the identified attack for analysis. These metrics are used to evaluate the computed cumulative score of the selected game models. The GDS uses ADAPT to select the model which possesses greater relevance to the present observed attack based on each attack components impact to the attacker, defender, and the performance of the system during the game. Once a game model is selected, the GDS executes the game model by sending the proposed defense actions to the respective sensor or actuator. Updated information is obtained via the KB's ability to access vulnerability databases such as National Vulnerability Database (NVD), MITRE Corporation's Common Vulnerabilities and Exposures (CVE) list, etc.

We envision this process of attack identification and defense to be iterative in nature where sensors like IDS constantly provide input to GIDA. Based on these inputs, the GDS, ADAPT, and the KB reevaluates their findings to further improve the proposed defense measures. This process continues until the attack is subdued. It should be noted that GIDA has an option of playing a selected game. Simple games such as firewall setting changes may be performed automatically, however defender interaction may be required for complex games. Nagaraja and Anderson [36] provided insight into discovering the effectiveness of iterated attack and defense operations through a proposed framework using evolutionary game theory.

Moreover, there are various types of plausible attacks on any given target system. GIDA uses the GDS to address attacks before they reach fruition to observe and attempt to make a decision on the optimal game model for defense. This gives GDS the ability to operate in a reactive manner, as well, considering attacker initiates. We anticipate certain attacks to be continuous in nature and the intention is to impede any or further damage to its respective target, hence the GIDA framework is proactive to prevent damage on a monitored network.

6   Related Work

There are several recent efforts which consider security games evaluation, involving performance and security metrics. In this section we provide an overview of literature relative to game theory defense models and performance metrics.

He, et al. [6] proposed a novel Game Theoretical Attack-Defense Model (GTADM) which quantifies the probability of threats in order to construct a risk assessment framework. They focus on the computation of the attack probability according to the cost-benefit of the attacker and the defender, and defined relevant metrics to quantify the payoff matrix.

Alpcan and Basar [25] proposed a game theoretic analysis of intrusion detection in an access control environment. They provided several common metrics that were used to help identify the performance of the Intrusion Detection System IDS. Using the metrics they provided, simulation was used to determine the costs and actions of the attacker and IDS.

Bloem, et al. [37] proposed an intrusion response as a resource allocation problem, where the resources being used were the IDS and network administrator. They provided insightful metrics regarding the response time of an IDS and its ability to respond without the administrator's involvement. Also, they used an administrator response time metric to determine the time of effort used to compute administrator involvement after an alert from the IDS. This metric can prove beneficial in determining how well a system is able to successfully respond against attacks while minimizing the administrator's involvement.

Liu, et al. [38] proposed an incentive based modeling and inference of attacker intent, objectives, and strategies. They provided several examples that compute the bandwidth before, during, and after an attack. They specified metrics to compute the absolute impact and relative availability to determine the system degradation. These metrics are used to distinguish how well the system was able to capitalize on the attack, as well as how well the attacker was able to succeed in reducing the bandwidth.

You and Shiyoung [22] proposed a network security behavior model based on game theory. They provide a framework for assessing security using the Nash equilibrium. In assessing the security, they also provide metrics used to analyze the payoff and cost of an attacker and defender using the exposure factor, average rate of occurrence, single loss expectancy, and annual loss expectancy.

Savola [8] surveyed emerging security metrics approaches in various organizations and provided a taxonomy of metrics as applicable to information security. His taxonomy provided a high level approach to classifying security metrics for security management involving organization, operational, and technical aspects. He also included high level classification for metrics involving security, dependability, and trust for products, systems, and services. The metrics provided are all high level, with a lack of specific metrics used for each category, but he provides a good starting point to organizations needing to begin analyzing various security metrics within their organization.

Fink et al. [39] proposed a metrics-based approach to IDS evaluation for distributed real-time systems. They provided a set of metrics to aid administrators of distributed real-time systems to select the best IDS system for their particular organization. They presented valuable information needed to gather the requirements of an organization in order to capture the importance, and use the requirements to successfully measure the performance according to requirements imposed by the organization.

7   Conclusion and Future Work

Game theoretic models continue to present information and analysis to initiate defense solutions against an attack for a network administrator. This paper is an attempt to provide an intuitive game theoretic metric taxonomy that a defender can use to synthesize how well a particular game model is performing in a network. We assume the collected metrics are generic and can be used regardless of the type of game theoretic model used for defense. We believe providing a list of metrics for a game inspired defense architecture will provide an administrator with the appropriate information to make an intelligent decision in game theoretic defense analysis. This assumption is not approved through real experiences.

Creative metrics are necessary to enhance a network administrator's ability to compare various defense schemes. We propose a game theory inspired Attack-Defense And Performance metric Taxonomy (ADAPT) to help a network administrator view pertinent metrics during a game theoretic model analysis. Although this work provides game related model selection, alternative solutions of ADAPT can be used without a game theoretic aspect.

Future work involves demonstrating the usefulness of ADAPT through the implementation of the game decision system (GDS), which assists a game inspired defense architecture with model selection. We are currently in progress towards developing the game decision system based on ADAPT using an open source knowledge base to store metrics associated to particular attack and game models. The game strategies will be assessed using a weighted score ranking between models which will assist with selecting the game with the most relevance to the identified attack. The use of ADAPT in this system will have knowledge of the attack and its target to assess the proposed game decision strategies to defend against the attack. In the event an attack is not mapped, we will construct game models to handle such scenarios. We intend to implement the model described within He, et al. [6], as well as others, to compare results with an ADAPT based system. Furthermore, an enhancement to the taxonomy may be considered with an additional game theoretic defense model classification distinguishing the various game models. We foresee using an ADAPT based system as a comprehensive solution to optimal game selection.

References

1. Hamilton, S.N., Miller, W.L., Ott, A., Saydjari, O.S.: The role of game theory in information warfare. In: Proceedings of the 4th Information Survivability Workshop, ISW-2001/2002 (2002)
2. Jiang, W., Tian, Z., Zhang, H., Song, X.: A Stochastic Game Theoretic Approach to Attack Prediction and Optimal Active Defense Strategy Decision. In: IEEE International Conference on Networking, Sensing and Control, pp. 648–653 (April 2008)
3. Bellovin, S.: On the Brittleness of Software and the Infeasibility of Security Metrics. IEEE Security and Privacy 4(4) (July-August 2006)
4. National Cyber Security Research and Development Challenges Related to Economics, Physical Infrastructure and Human Behavior: An Industry, Academic and Government Perspective, The Institute for Information Infrastructure Protection, I3P (2009), http://www.thei3p.org/docs/publications/i3pnationalcybersecurity.pdf
5. Gopalakrishnan, J., Marden, R., Wierman, A.: An architectural view of game theoretic control. ACM SIGMETRICS Performance Evaluation Review 38(3) (2011)
6. He, W., Xia, C., Wang, H., Zhang, C., Ji, Y.: A Game Theoretical Attack-Defense Model Oriented to Network Security Risk Assessment. In: Proceedings of the 2008 International Conference on Computer Science and Software Engineering, vol. 3 (2008)
7. Bryant, A.R.: Developing a framework for evaluating organizational information assurance metrics programs. Thesis, Airforce Institute of Technology, Defense Technical Information Center (2007)
8. Savola, R.: A Novel Security Metrics Taxonomy for R&D Organizations. In: Proceedings of the 7th Annual Information Security Conference (2008)
9. Wesner, J.W.: Winning with quality: Applying quality principles in product development. Addison-Wesley, New York (1994)
10. Roy, S., Ellis, C., Shiva, S., Dasgupta, D., Shandilya, V., Wu, Q.: A Survey of Game Theory as Applied to Network Security. In: HICSS43 Hawaii International Conference on System Sciences (2009)
11. Mirkovic, J., Reiher, P.: A Taxonomy of DDoS Attack and DDoS Defense Mechanisms. In: ACM CCR (April 2004)
12. Li, Z., Goyal, A., Chen, Y., Paxson, V.: Automating analysis of large-scale botnet probing events. In: ASIACCS 2009 (2009)
13. Parameswaran, M., Rui, H., Sayin, S.: A game theoretic model and empirical analysis of spammer strategies. In: Collaboration, Electronic Messaging, AntiAbuse and Spam Conf., vol. 7 (2010)
14. Payne, S.: A Guide to Security Metrics. SANS Institute (June 2006)
15. Swanson, M.: NIST Special Publication 800-55: Security Metrics Guide for Information Technology Systems (2003)
16. The National Science and Technology Council. Federal plan for cyber security and information assurance research and development (2006)
17. Vaughn, R., Henning, R., Siraj, A.: Information Assurance Measures and Metrics: State of Practice and Proposed Taxonomy. In: Proceedings of 36th Hawaii International Conference on System Science, HICSS 2003 (2003)
18. Manadhata, J., Wing, P.: An attack surface metric. Technical Report CMU-CS-05-155 (2005)
19. Carin, L., Cybenko, G., Hughes, J.: Quantitative Evaluation of Risk for Investment Efficient Strategies in Cyber security: The QuERIES Methodology. IEEE Computer (2008)

20. Lye, K., Wing, J.: Game strategies in network security. In: Proceedings of the Foundations of Computer Security (2002)
21. Cremonini, M., Nizovtsev, D.: Understanding and Influencing Attackers Decisions: Implications for Security Investment Strategies. In: 5th Workshop on the Economics of Information Security (June 2006)
22. You, X., Shiyong, Z.: A kind of network security behavior model based on game theory. In: Proceedings of the Fourth International Conference on Parallel and Distributed Computing, Applications and Technologies (2003)
23. Burke, D.A.: Towards a game theory model of information warfare. Master Thesis, Air Force Institute of Technology, USA (1999)
24. Jansen, W.: Directions in Security Metrics Research. NISTIR 7564 (March 2009)
25. Alpcan, T., Baser, T.: A game theoretic analysis of intrusion detection in access control systems. In: Proc. of the 43rd IEEE Conference on Decision and Control (2004)
26. Shiva, S., Roy, S., Bedi, H., Dasgupta, D., Wu, Q.: An Imperfect Information Stochastic Game Model for Cyber Security. In: The 5th Intnl. Conference on i-Warfare and Security (2010)
27. Center for Internet Security. "The CIS Security Metrics" (May 2009),
    https://www.cissecurity.org/tools2/metrics/
    CIS_Security_Metricsv1.0.0.pdf
28. McGraw, G.: Software Security: Building Security. Addison-Wesley (2006)
29. Simmons, C., Shiva, S., Dasgupta, D., Wu., Q.: AVOIDIT: A cyber attack taxonomy. Technical Report: CS-09-003, University of Memphis (August 2009)
30. Bedi, H., Shiva, S., Simmons, C., Shandilya, V.: A Game Inspired Defense Architecture. In: GameSec 2012 (Poster), Conference on Decision and Game Theory for Security (2012)
31. Wu, Q., Shiva, S., Roy, S., Ellis, C., Datla, V.: On Modeling and Simulation of Game Theory-based Defense Mechanisms against DoS and DDoS Attacks. SpringSim (2010)
32. Bedi, H., Roy, S., Shiva, S.: Game Theory-based Defense Mechanisms against DDoS Attacks on TCP/TCP-friendly Flows. In: IEEE Symposium on Computational Intelligence in Cyber Security, Paris, France (2011)
33. Paruchuri, P., Pearce, J.P., Tambe, M., Ordonez, F., Kraus, S.: An Efficient Heuristic Approach for Security Against Multiple Adversaries. In: AAMAS (2007)
34. Shiva, S., Roy, S., Dasgupta, D.: Game Theory for Cyber Security. In: 6th Cyber Security and Information Intelligence Research Workshop (April 2010)
35. Shiva, S., Bedi, H.S., Simmons, C.B., Fisher II, M., Dharam, R.: A Holistic Game Inspired Defense Architecture. In: Gaol, F.L. (ed.) Recent Progress in DEIT, Vol. 2. LNEE, vol. 157, pp. 471–476. Springer, Heidelberg (2012)
36. Nagaraja, S., Anderson, R.: The topology of covert conflict. In: Proceedings of the 5th Workshop on The Economics of Information Security, WEIS 2006 (2006)
37. Bloem, M., Alpcan, T., Basar, T.: Intrusion response as a resource allocation problem. In: IEEE Conference on Decision and Control (2006)
38. Liu, P., Zang, W., Yu, M.: Incentive-based modeling and inference of attacker intent, objectives, and strategies. ACM Transactions on Information and System Security, TISSEC (2005)
39. Fink, G., Chappell, B., Turner, T., O'Donoghue, K.: A metrics-based approach to intrusion detection system evaluation for distributed real-time systems. In: Proceedings of the 16th International Parallel and Distributed Processing Symposium, Fort Lauderdale, FL, USA (April 2002)

Phishing for the Truth: A Scenario-Based Experiment of Users' Behavioural Response to Emails

Kathryn Parsons[1,*], Agata McCormac[1], Malcolm Pattinson[2],
Marcus Butavicius[1], and Cate Jerram[2]

[1] Defence Science and Technology Organisation
PO Box 1500, Edinburgh, SA, 5111, Australia
{Kathryn.Parsons,Agata.Mccormac,
Marcus.Butavicius}@dsto.defence.gov.au
[2] Business School, The University of Adelaide
10 Pulteney Street, Adelaide, SA, 5005, Australia
{Malcolm.Pattinson,Cate.Jerram}@adelaide.edu.au

Abstract. Using a role play scenario experiment, 117 participants were asked to manage 50 emails. To test whether the knowledge that participants are undertaking a phishing study impacts on their decisions, only half of the participants were informed that the study was assessing the ability to identify phishing emails. Results indicated that the participants who were informed that they were undertaking a phishing study were significantly better at correctly managing phishing emails and took longer to make decisions. This was not caused by a bias towards judging an email as a phishing attack, but instead, an increase in the ability to discriminate between phishing and real emails. Interestingly, participants who had formal training in information systems performed more poorly overall. Our results have implications for the interpretation of previous phishing studies, the design of future studies and for training and education campaigns, as it suggests that when people are primed about phishing risks, they adopt a more diligent screening approach to emails.

Keywords: phishing, information security, security behaviours, email security, security training.

1   Introduction

Phishing is a term that describes an attempt to deceptively acquire personal and financial information via electronic communication with malicious intent. Social engineering strategies in conjunction with computer knowledge are used to gather usernames, passwords, and bank account and credit card details (Anti-Phishing Working Group, 2010). Phishing attacks are commonly committed via email, and victims are often directed to fraudulent websites that appear legitimate (Moore & Clayton, 2007). Such breaches can have serious consequences, including direct consequences, such as

---

[*] Corresponding author.

L.J. Janczewski, H.B. Wolfe, and S. Shenoi (Eds.): SEC 2013, IFIP AICT 405, pp. 366–378, 2013.
© IFIP International Federation for Information Processing 2013

financial loss if a phisher obtains access to a bank account, and indirect consequences, such as damaged reputation (Tam, Glassman & Vandenwauver, 2010).

Although there is a growing body of phishing studies, there is a lack of research examining the impact of the cognitive bias known as the subject expectancy effect (Anandpara, Dingman, Jakobsson, Liu & Roinestad, 2007). Essentially, studies where participants know they are participating in a phishing study have been criticised because they lack real world validity. This criticism is based on the assumption that individuals who are aware that they are taking part in a phishing study may be more suspicious, and this may therefore result in a bias towards 'phishing' decisions (Anandpara et al., 2007). It is unlikely that individuals would have this level of suspicion when checking their personal inboxes (Furnell, 2007).

In response to the possible influence of the subject expectancy effect, researchers have begun incorporating a role play scenario into the design of their phishing studies. This approach aims to minimise the bias caused by the subject expectancy effect, because participants are not informed that they are participating specifically in a phishing study. A study of this nature was conducted by Downs, Holbrook and Cranor (2007). Participants were informed that they were participating in a study about computer use, not computer security. They were given the identity of 'Pat Jones' and were shown images of emails from 'Pat's' inbox. Some emails were legitimate and some were phishing emails and participants were given options about how they would respond to each email. Downs et al. (2007) found that participants who were more knowledgeable and experienced with the internet environment were less susceptible to phishing attacks. They also found that participants' perceptions of the consequences of emails did not reliably predict their behaviour (2007). This study used only five email screen shots, which limits the ability to generalise these findings to other types of emails.

Downs, Holbrook and Cranor (2006) conducted a similar study that used a role play design and also incorporated qualitative interviews on computer security and trust. The study focused on decision strategies and susceptibility to phishing and concluded that participants were most likely to use subjective cues, such as relying on the text within an email, to determine the trustworthiness of emails, rather than relying on more objective cues, such as using information contained within URLs and links (Downs et al., 2006). They also found that participants were more vulnerable to unfamiliar phishing scams, and were generally less susceptible to scams they had seen previously. However, the authors acknowledge that their findings were significantly limited by a small sample size of only 20 participants (Downs et al., 2006), which, once again, limits the generalisability of findings.

The limitations and shortcomings of these previous studies provided the incentive for this current study, which was designed to address these issues, and further the vital work in the area of electronic mail fraud. For example, this is the first study that we are aware of that tested the influence of the subject expectancy effect on participants' response to phishing emails. This was achieved by using a role play design where, although all of the participants were aware they were participating in a study about email, only half of the participants were informed they were participating in a *phishing* study. This will therefore reveal whether the knowledge that participants are participating in a phishing study influences their decisions. Our examination of the influence of the subject expectancy effect may highlight the need to reevaluate or interpret the findings of all previous phishing studies in light of the effect. This study will therefore provide vital knowledge regarding the design of future studies.

Participants in the current study were also exposed to a comparatively larger number of emails than in the previous studies, and these emails varied widely. Furthermore, to better understand what makes some people more susceptible to phishing emails than others, this study included a demographics questionnaire and a measure of impulsivity. This provided a more comprehensive assessment of individual differences than the previous research.

2   Methodology

2.1   Participants

A total of 117 students from the University of Adelaide were recruited via email and participated in the study. Of the 117 participants, 27 were male and 90 were female. The majority of participants were first year students (93), there were also 19 second year and 4 third year students, and 1 participant was completing post-graduate studies. Most participants were 25 years of age and younger (108) and only 5 participants were over the age of 30. Participants received $25 cash for their participation.

2.2   Materials

2.2.1   Emails

The study consisted of 50 images of emails; half of these images were genuine emails, and half were phishing emails. The selected emails were comprised of 'actual' real and phishing emails that were either received by the authors, or found online. A range of emails, including banking, shopping and social networking emails were utilised to ensure that they were representative of the types of topics that would be expected in a typical inbox. An example of a phishing email can be seen in Figure 1, and an example of a real email used in the experiment can be seen in Figure 2.

A fictitious character, by the name of 'Sally Jones' was created, and the original emails that contained personal information were altered to include her details as if she was the intended recipient. Participants were informed that they were viewing emails from the inbox of 'Sally Jones', and were asked to make a decision regarding how they would manage each email. They were not provided with any other information regarding the persona of Sally Jones.

2.2.2   Measures of Individual Differences

A number of demographics were collected including information about gender and education level. The Cognitive Reflection Test (CRT), which is a very quick and

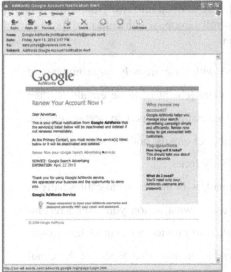 

Fig. 1. Example of a phishing email. Email containing logo reprinted with permission from Google.

Fig. 2. Example of a real email. Email containing logo reprinted with permission from Google.

efficient measure of impulsivity (Frederick, 2005), was also utilised. The test includes three questions and the most obvious response is not correct. To answer correctly, participants should stop and consider the question before providing an answer. A higher score on this test relates to a better ability to control impulsivity. This particular test was selected because findings indicate that the predictive validity of this measure was equal or above other cognitive measures (Frederick, 2005).

It is hypothesised that individuals who are better able to effectively manage impulsivity may be less susceptible to phishing emails, as they may be more likely to thoroughly deliberate the legitimacy of the email. This hypothesis was tested in a study by Kumaraguru and colleagues (2007). Participants with higher CRT scores were less likely to click on the phishing emails, but the results were not statistically significant. This may be due to the small number of phishing emails in the experiment, and the relatively small number of participants. The current study will retest this hypothesis with a larger number of emails and participants.

2.3   Method

Participants were informed that they were completing an experiment on how people manage emails. They were told that they would be required to view images of 50 emails, taken from the inbox of Sally Jones. In order to test the influence of the subject expectancy effect, the participants were divided into two groups, the 'Control' Group and the 'Alerted' Group. The 'Control' Group, which consisted of 59 participants, were given the following description:

> "Managers are often inundated with an extremely large number of emails on a daily basis, and the management of these emails is often very difficult. We're interested in assessing how people manage emails. You will be presented with a number of emails, both personal and work related, taken from the inbox of 'Sally Jones'.
>
> Your job is to examine each email, with the aim of assisting Sally to process her Inbox. You will be asked what action you would recommend to her. You will also be asked to provide a rating of how confident you are with your recommendation, and what aspect of the email most influenced your recommendation."

The 'Alerted' Group, which consisted of 58 participants, were informed that they were participating in a phishing study and were given the same description with the following sentence added to the end:

> "We are specifically interested in assessing the ability to identify 'phishing' emails. These are fraudulent email messages that are used to obtain personal information for the purposes of identity theft."

The research assistant also gave a verbal description of what phishing emails are to be sure that all participants had this knowledge.

For each of the 50 emails, all participants were asked to respond to the question, "How would you manage this email?" with one of four replies: a) leave the email in the inbox and flag for follow up; b) leave the email in the inbox; c) delete the email; or d) delete the email and block the sender. For each email, participants were also asked, "What aspect of this email influenced your decision?"

After responding to all 50 emails, participants were required to complete the demographics questionnaire and the cognitive test. The logic of this process ensured that the demographic questions could not alert the participants in the 'Control' Group that they were participating in a phishing study until after they had completed the main task.

3   Results

3.1   Phishing Emails

As shown in Figure 3, when responding to phishing emails, participants in the 'Control' Group most frequently responded with 'Flag for follow up' (37%), whereas the participants in the 'Alerted' Group were mostly likely to respond with 'Delete' (38%). The pie chart below also indicates that participants in the 'Alerted' Group were far more likely to respond with 'Delete and block' (11% of 'Control' Group responses versus 23% of 'Alerted' Group responses).

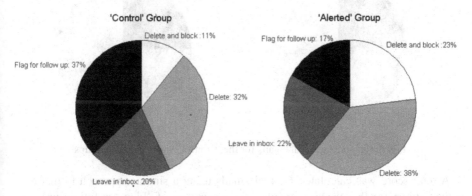

Fig. 3. Responses to phishing emails for the 'Control' and 'Alerted' Groups

For the phishing emails, a response of 'Delete and block' was considered most appropriate, and a response of 'Flag for follow up' was deemed least appropriate. A total score was calculated for phishing emails, where a response of 'Delete and block' was assigned a score of 4, a response of 'Delete' was assigned a score of 3, a response of 'Leave in inbox' was assigned a score of 2, and a response of 'Flag for follow up' was assigned a score of 1. This assignment was such that the more appropriate the action when faced with a phishing email, the higher the values assigned to it.

A Mann-Whitney U-test was used to compare the ranks for the participants in the 'Control' Group and the 'Alerted' Group. The results indicated that there was a statistically significant difference, $U(116) = 2644.00$, $Z = 5.089$, $p < .001$. Participants in the 'Control' Group had a mean rank of 43.19, while participants in the 'Alerted' Group had a mean rank of 75.09. This means that the participants in the 'Alerted' Group were significantly better at correctly managing the phishing emails, indicating that knowledge that participants were undertaking a phishing study tended to improve performance.

3.2   Real Emails

Interestingly, for the real emails, there was very little difference between the groups in regards to the frequency of both 'Delete and block' and 'Flag for follow up'

responses. Instead, as shown in Figure 4, the percentage of responses in those categories was very similar, and the groups differed in regards to the responses, 'Leave in
inbox' and 'Delete'. When responding to real emails, the participants in the 'Control'
Group were far more likely to respond with 'Delete' (37%), whereas the participants
in the 'Alerted' Group were most likely to respond with 'Leave in inbox' (44%).

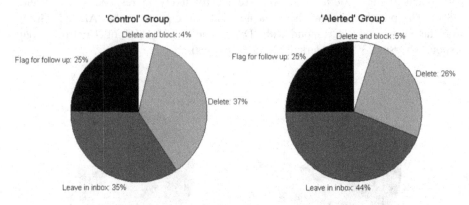

Fig. 4. Responses to real emails for the 'Control' and 'Alerted' Groups

A total score was calculated for real emails using a similar approach to that employed above for the phishing emails, i.e., a response of 'Flag for follow up' was
assigned a score of 4, a response of 'Leave in inbox' was assigned a score of 3, a
response of 'Delete' was assigned a score of 2, and a response of 'Delete and block'
was assigned a score of 1.

A Mann-Whitney U-test was used to compare the ranks for the participants in the
'Control' Group and the 'Alerted' Group. There were no statistically significant differences between the groups, $U(116) = 2008.50$, $Z = 1.624$, $p = .104$, with a mean
rank for participants in the 'Control' Group of 53.96, and a mean rank for participants
in the 'Alerted' Group of 64.13. Although the difference was not statistically significant, the participants who were alerted that they would be viewing some phishing
emails were more likely to correctly manage the real emails.

3.3   Bias and Discrimination

To further examine the nature of any subject expectancy effect, the signal detection
theory measures of discrimination and bias were calculated from the data (Green and
Swets, 1966). In this context, discrimination refers to the ability of a participant to
distinguish real from phishing emails while bias refers to an overall tendency to keep
or delete emails in the inbox. A' and B'' were used as measures of discrimination and
bias respectively (refer to Stanislaw and Todorov, 1999). These non-parametric
measures are calculated directly from the commonly used measures 'Hit Rate' (HR)
and 'False Alarm Rate' (FAR):

The HR refers to the probability that a phishing email is met with a phishing decision and the FAR refers to the probability that the participant responded with a phishing decision when it was a real email. For the purposes of this analysis, when faced with phishing emails, responses of 'Delete' or 'Delete and block' were deemed to be 'hits', and responses of 'Flag for follow up' or 'Leave in inbox' were deemed to be 'misses'. When faced with real emails, responses of 'Delete' or 'Delete and block' were deemed to be 'false alarms', and responses of 'Flag for follow up' or 'Leave in inbox' were deemed to be 'true misses'.

An A' value of 1 equates to perfect discrimination, and a value of 0.5 indicates that the respondent could not distinguish phishing emails from the real emails. A B" value of zero indicates that there was no bias in the responses, a value of -1 indicates an extreme bias towards 'phishing' decisions, and a value of 1 indicates an extreme bias towards 'real' decisions.

The results indicated that the participants in the 'Alerted' Group were better able to discriminate between the phishing and real emails than the participants in the 'Control' Group ($A'_{Control} = 0.52$, $CI_{95\%} = [0.48, 0.56]$; $A'_{Alerted} = 0.72$, $CI_{95\%} = [0.68, 0.76]$). Furthermore, the results showed that participants in both the 'Control' and 'Alerted' Group had a very small response bias ($B"_{Control} = 0.07$, $CI_{95\%} = [0.01, 0.13]$; $B"_{Alerted} = 0.04$, $CI_{95\%} = [-0.04, 0.13]$), indicating that this study did not find evidence of the subject expectancy effect.

3.4   Time Taken

An independent-samples t-test demonstrated a significant difference between the time taken to manage emails between the two groups, $t(116) = 4.093$, $p < .001$. The participants in the 'Control' Group ($M = 21.47$, $SD = 5.83$) took significantly less time to make their decisions than the participants in the 'Alerted' Group ($M = 27.05$, $SD = 8.67$). The eta squared statistic (.13) indicated a large effect size. This therefore suggests that informing participants that they were completing a phishing study may have resulted in an increase in diligence and vigilance.

3.5   Individual Differences

Since the manner in which participants managed emails is best captured via the four response categories, the mean ranks for phishing and real emails were used, and a series of Kruskal-Wallis and Mann-Whitney U-tests were conducted. The aim was to examine the influence of these variables on the mean ranks for phishing and real emails for the 'Control' Group and 'Alerted' Group.

3.5.1   Gender and Age

Contrary to the findings of Jagatic et al. (2005) and Sheng, Holbrook, Kumaraguru, Cranor and Downs (2010), who found that females and participants aged below 25 years were most vulnerable, the current study found no evidence of a relationship between either gender or age and the ability to correctly manage emails. However, of the 117 participants in this study, 90 were female and 108 were under 26 years of age. Because of this bias in our population, we can not discount the findings of Jagatic et al. (2005) and Sheng et al. (2010), and this is an issue worthy of further research.

3.5.2   Level of Education and Knowledge

After ranking the total phishing scores, a Kruskal-Wallis test was used to evaluate any association between performance in managing emails and participants' level of education. When participants were not told that they were conducting a phishing study, the participants with a higher level of education were significantly better at correctly managing phishing emails, $\chi^2 = 8.186$ (2, $N = 59$), $p = .017$ (Mean ranks; 'Year 12 or equivalent' = 27.33, 'Bachelor Degree' = 32.07, 'Honours Degree' = 56.17). However, there was no difference in the ability to correctly manage phishing emails when people were informed that they were completing a phishing study. This therefore suggests that people with more education were more likely to think about security without being prompted.

However, contrary to expectations, results indicated that the participants in the 'Control' Group who had completed a course in the area of information systems or information technology were less accurate in their ability to correctly manage phishing emails. A Mann-Whitney U-test revealed a mean rank of 21.50 for the n = 17 participants who had completed a course in the area of information systems or information technology, and a mean rank of 33.44 for the n = 42 who had not completed such a course, U(58) = 501.50, Z = 2.421, p = .015.

3.5.3   Employment Experience

A Kruskal-Wallis test revealed that, for the participants in the 'Alerted' Group, those who were currently employed (mean rank = 34.48) or had previous employment experience (mean rank = 30.69) were significantly better at identifying phishing emails than those without any employment experience (mean rank = 17.18), $\chi^2 = 7.817$ (2, N = 58), $p = .02$. Interestingly, this was only true for the participants who were informed that they were conducting a phishing study.

3.5.4   Cognitive Impulsivity

For participants in the 'Control' Group, those who obtained a higher score on the test of cognitive impulsivity (and were therefore better able to control impulsivity) were significantly better at identifying phishing emails, $\chi^2 = 8.241$ (3, N = 59), $p = .041$. The mean rank for the participants who obtained a score of three, which was the maximum possible score, was 48.92, which is significantly higher than the mean rank obtained by participants with the other possible scores (mean ranks; '0' = 27.89, '1' = 27.11, '2' = 29.79). This is consistent with our hypothesis. However, there were no significant differences for the participants in the 'Alerted' Group, which suggests that, once participants knew they were undertaking a phishing study, they were more likely to stop and consider their response, regardless of whether they were usually more impulsive.

3.6   Qualitative Content Analysis

Participants' responses to the question, *"What aspect of this email influenced your decision?"* were analysed using content analysis. An analysis of the participants' responses to the open-ended question in conjunction with their response to the multiple choice question supported the hypothesis that participants were more likely to 'Delete' or 'Delete and block' emails when they were suspicious of their legitimacy. In a minority of cases, participants flagged an email for follow up to alert 'Sally' of a possible security threat that she should report to the purported organisation. However, this reasoning was rare, and an examination of these cases revealed that re-categorising them would not impact on the statistical significance of the results reported above.

The justification of decisions supported the findings of Furnell, Tsaganidi and Phippen (2008), that participants were influenced by their perception of trust. This was based on the perceived trustworthiness of the company that the email appeared to originate from. For example, participants responded with statements such as *"[Company name] is a trusted chat program used all over the world, so emails from it would be legit"*. These participants did not appear to question whether the email actually did originate from that company, but rather, appeared to decide based solely on the face validity of the email.

Many participants also mentioned the visual presentation of emails. For example, many participants deleted a real email from a telephone company because it did not contain any company logos, and therefore concluded that it seemed suspicious. This is consistent with the findings of Everard and Galletta (2006), who found the perceived quality of an online Web site was strongly influenced by the style of the Web site, and poor style was associated with low perceived quality.

Another common justification was based on incentives within emails. Participants were more susceptible to phishing emails when the email promised a financial reward. For example, two survey requests with a financial incentive for participation resulted in responses such as *"the $100 monetary compensation is a great incentive for me to participate in this survey"*. Hence, potential incentives may limit participants' ability to make valid and considered security decisions. It should be noted that participants were paid $25 for their participation, and therefore, may have been more susceptible to offers of financial reward.

Other commonly cited reasons for decisions included spelling and grammatical errors, the personalisation of the email, and the perceived legitimacy of the URL. As also found by Furnell (2007), although these were cues that could conceivably prove useful, they often failed to assist participants in making the correct decisions concerning the legitimacy of an email. In support of previous research, which indicated that participants do not notice security indicators (Herzberg, 2009, Schechter et al., 2007), only one participant in our study used 'HTTPS' as a justification for their decision.

4   Discussion

This study provides further evidence that people are poor at identifying phishing emails. Overall, approximately 42% of all emails were incorrectly classified in this experiment. Participants who knew they were undertaking a phishing study were better able to make the distinction between real and phishing emails, which means that this study found no evidence of the subject expectancy effect. Participants in the 'Alerted' Group were not simply biased towards 'phishing' decisions, but were instead more likely to correctly manage all emails. Although the improved ability to correctly manage the real emails was not statistically significant, they were still more likely to correctly manage the real emails than the participants in the 'Control' Group. Evidence suggests that priming participants with the notion of phishing may have resulted in more diligent decision making, as the participants in the 'Alerted' Group took significantly longer to complete the experiment.

The influence of the different instructions provided to the two groups in our experiment may be explained by the general phenomenon known as framing (Tversky & Kahneman, 1981). In other words, it was the context in which the task was presented which influenced their decision making processes. Unlike the 'Control' group, the participants in the 'Alerted' group were specifically informed that the study was testing how well they could detect phishing emails and this had a positive influence on their decision-making. As discussed in the context of Signal Detection Theory (Green and Swets, 1966), this change was not in decision bias towards classifying an email as phishing but instead reflected an improvement in discrimination ability. Framing the task as one of detecting phishing emails may have caused participants to focus more on cues in the stimuli that better distinguished real from phishing emails. This has important implications for training and education programs, as it suggests that when people were primed to think about phishing, they were better able to identify phishing emails, and hence, less susceptible to phishing attacks.

The findings in regards to individual differences also have important implications for education and training programs. Participants who had attended an information systems or technology course were, in fact, less likely to correctly manage emails. This may suggest that knowledge in this area could lead to complacency. Instead, actual security behaviours (such as using spam filters and adjusting security preferences) were better predictors of the ability to deal with phishing emails. In addition, when the task was framed as a phishing test, participants with employment experience performed better, possibly as a result of more experience in dealing with categorising emails in a work environment. Our results also indicated that participants who were better able to control impulsivity were better at managing phishing emails. This suggests that it may be more effective to emphasise the importance of stopping and thinking before responding to any email rather than exclusively teaching security rules. This is supported by the training literature, which indicates that it is more effective to emphasise specific behaviours rather than rules (Parsons, McCormac, Butavicius & Ferguson, 2010).

Our findings also have implications for the research literature on users' susceptibility to phishing emails. Previous studies should be interpreted in the light of the 'framing' effect identified in this study and future research should carefully consider how the task is presented to the user. Critically, the discovery of the framing effect suggests that the risk of phishing may, on the whole, be underestimated in previous literature. Specifically, in our study the inferior results of the 'Control' Group, who were not informed that they were undertaking a phishing study, better represent the performance of real-world users. This is because in real life the frequency with which people are reminded about the risks of phishing emails is generally low.

It is, however, important to highlight the fact that phishing studies such as ours do not directly measure actual susceptibility. In our experiment, participants were not required to click on any of the links or provide personal information, and it is therefore possible that, in a real world situation, participants may have become suspicious before succumbing to any of the phishing attacks. This study was also a role play, and the manner in which participants deal with emails in an experimental environment may not relate precisely to how participants would deal with actual emails received in their personal inboxes. Furthermore, in this study, participants did not know which sites 'Sally' subscribes to, and therefore their ability to make context dependent decisions was limited. In a real life situation, whether someone is a member of a particular bank or social networking site is likely to influence the decision to delete or keep an email. Future research should investigate how to more accurately replicate these variables in an experimental context.

References

Anandpara, V., Dingman, A., Jakobsson, M., Liu, D., Roinestad, H.: Phishing IQ tests measure fear, not ability. In: Proceedings of the 11th International Conference on Financial Cryptography and 1st International Conference on Usable Security, Scarborough, Trinidad, Tobago, pp. 362–366 (2007)

Anti-Phishing Working Group. Global Phishing Survey: Trends and Domain Name Use in 2H2009 (May 2010), http://www.antiphishing.org

Downs, J.S., Holbrook, M.B., Cranor, L.: Decision strategies and susceptibility to phishing. In: Proceedings of the Second Symposium on Usable Privacy and Security, Pittsburgh, PA, USA, pp. 79–90 (2006)

Downs, J.S., Holbrook, M., Cranor, L.: Behavioral response to phishing risk. In: Proceedings of the Anti-Phishing Working Groups 2nd Annual eCrime Researchers Summit, Pitsburgh, PA, USA, pp. 37–44 (2007)

Frederick, S.: Cognitive reflection and decision making. Journal of Economic Perspectives 16(4), 25–42 (2005)

Furnell, S.: Phishing: can we spot the signs? Computer Fraud & Security 3, 10–15 (2007)

Furnell, S., Tsaganidi, V., Phippen, A.: Security beliefs and barriers for novice Internet users. Computers & Security 27, 235–240 (2008)

Green, D.M., Swets, J.: Signal Detection Theory and Psychophysics. Wiley, New York (1966)

Herzberg, A.: Why Johnny can't surf (safely)? Attacks and defenses for web users. Computers & Security 28, 63–71 (2009)

Jagatic, T.N., Johnson, N.A., Jakobsson, M., Menczer, F.: Social phishing. Communications of the ACM 50(10), 94–100 (2007)

John, O.P., Donahue, E.M., Kentle, R.: The Big Five Inventory–Versions 4a and 54. University of California, Berkeley, Institute of Personality and Social Research, Berkeley (1991)

John, O.P., Naumann, L.P., Soto, C.J.: Paradigm shift to the integrative big-five trait taxonomy: History, measurement, and conceptual issues. In: John, O.P., Robins, R.W., Pervin, L.A. (eds.) Handbook of Personality: Theory and Research, 3rd edn., pp. 114–158. Guilford Press, New York (2008)

John, O.P., Srivastava, S.: The big-five trait taxonomy: History, measurement, and theoretical perspectives. In: Pervin, L.A., John, O.P. (eds.) Handbook of Personality: Theory and Research, 2nd edn., pp. 102–139. Guilford Press, New York (1999)

Kumaraguru, P., Rhee, Y., Sheng, S., Hasan, S., Acquisti, A., Cranor, L.F., Hong, J.: Getting users to pay attention to anti-phishing education: Evaluation of retention and transfer. In: Proceedings of the 2nd Annual eCrime Researchers Summit, Pittsburgh, PA, pp. 70–81 (2007)

Moore, T., Clayton, R.: An empirical analysis of the current state of phishing attack and defence. In: Proceedings of the Sixth Workshop on the Economics of Information Security, Pittsburgh, PA, USA, pp. 1–20 (2007)

Parsons, K., McCormac, A., Butavicius, M., Ferguson, L.: Human Factors and Information Security: Individual, Culture and Security Environment. DSTO Technical Report, DSTO-TR2484 (2010)

Sheng, S., Holbrook, M., Kumaraguru, P., Cranor, L., Downs, J.: Who falls for phish? A demographic analysis of phishing susceptibility and effectiveness of interventions. In: Proceedings of the 28th International Conference on Human Factors in Computing Systems, Atlanta, Georgia, USA, pp. 373–382 (2010)

Stanislaw, H., Todorov, N.: Calculation of signal detection theory measures. Behavior Research Methods Instruments & Computers 31(1), 137–149 (1999)

Tam, L., Glassman, M., Vandenwauver, M.: The psychology of password management: a tradeoff between security and convenience. Behaviour & Information Technology 29(3), 233–244 (2010)

Tversky, A., Kahneman, D.: The framing of decisions and the psychology of choice. Science 185, 453–458 (1981)

Phishing and Organisational Learning

Wayne D. Kearney and Hennie A. Kruger

School of Computer, Statistical and Mathematical Sciences,
North-West University, Private Bag X6001, Potchefstroom, 2520
South Africa
Kearneys@iinet.net.au, Hennie.Kruger@nwu.ac.za

Abstract. The importance of addressing the human aspect in information security has grown over the past few years. One of the most frequent techniques used to obtain private or confidential information from humans is phishing. One way to combat these phishing scams is to have proper security awareness programs in place. In order to enhance the awareness and educational value of information security awareness programs, it is suggested that an organisational learning model, characterised by so called single-loop and double-loop learning, be considered. This paper describes a practical phishing experiment that was conducted at a large organisation and shows how a learning process was initiated and how security incidents such as phishing can be used successfully for both single and double-loop learning.

Keywords: Phishing, Social engineering, Information security awareness, Organisational learning.

1 Introduction

Traditionally the mitigation of information security risks was addressed using a variety of technical controls. It is however widely accepted and recognised that technology on its own cannot deliver complete solutions to the security problem and that the human aspect of security should receive more attention [1], [2], [3]. One way of addressing the human side of security is to focus on awareness and educational activities [4] making use of some form of an awareness program.

An information security awareness program normally focuses on a number of issues related to the correct security behaviour of users. In some instances it may also concentrate on one area such as social engineering which is one of the most serious threats to information security as criminals keep on focussing on deceptive techniques to attack computer users and organisations [5]. Phishing, which is one of the social engineering techniques, occurs when people are manipulated by deception into giving out information [6] and is one of the major threats to modern organisations and information technology users in general. It requires an ongoing awareness not to become a victim of a phishing scam and various researchers have completed studies related to phishing experiments and awareness levels of users [5], [7], [8].

A popular technique to improve user awareness pertaining to phishing scams is to conduct unannounced phishing tests in order to evaluate users' propensity to respond

L.J. Janczewski, H.B. Wolfe, and S. Shenoi (Eds.): SEC 2013, IFIP AICT 405, pp. 379–390, 2013.
© IFIP International Federation for Information Processing 2013

to an attack [5], [9]. Albrechtsen [10] contend that these type of incidents and experiments present great opportunities to learn and improve information security. To ensure that learning does take place Van Niekerk and Von Solms [3] suggested that an organisational learning model be used.

This paper describes a practical phishing exercise that was conducted in industry and shows how organisational learning took place as a result. The remainder of the paper is organised as follows. Section 2 presents the background to the study as well as appropriate references to related work. In section 3 the methodology used is discussed while section 4 details the results. Concluding remarks are presented in section 5.

2 · Background and Related Work

Organisational learning theories deal with the idea of how organizations learn and adapting its behaviour [3]. This concept has been subjected to a wide and growing variety of researchers and a number of definitions have been suggested in the literature [11], [12]. Despite all these definitions the concept of organizational learning is by no means an unambiguous concept, as no one irrefutable definition has emerged in literature [13]. Organisational learning originated from the work by Argyris and Schon during the 1970s and one of the definitions suggested by them will be assumed in this study. The definition is formulated as follows. Organisational learning occurs when individuals within an organisation experience a problematic situation and enquire into it on the organisational behalf [14].

In an effort to enhance organisational learning, Buckler [15] proposed that an actual learning process, as depicted in figure 1, occurs in organisations. Buckler then argues that individuals will move through the different learning stages driven by their inherent individual motivations to learn. Associated with these motivational forces, there will be certain barriers to the learning process, and where the motivational restraining (barrier) forces are matched, learning will not take place. In order for organisational learning to result in performance improvement, the enactment stage (see figure 1) of the learning

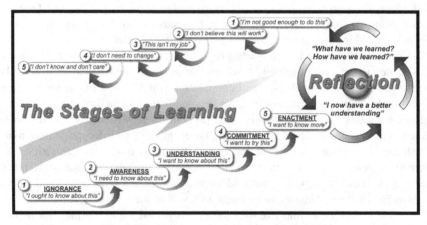

Fig. 1. The learning process (adapted from [15])

process needs to be achieved – this will imply behavioural change which is a requirement for successful organisational learning. To assess the effectiveness of the behavioural changes, the reflection stage should be entered.

There are various applications of learning processes but in general three types of learning can be categorised. These three types are summarized by Kennedy [13] as follows.

- Single-loop learning, which occurs when errors are detected and corrected and organisations continue with the present status quo without modifying present policies and goals. In essence, single-loop learning focuses on improving the status quo through small incremental changes in how organisations functions. An example in the area of information security could be a case of unauthorized access by a user to privileged data. A single-loop response would be to simply deny future access to this specific user. The status quo is maintained and present policies and/or goals are not modified.
- Double-loop learning challenges, and possibly makes changes to the status quo and the existing assumptions and conditions. It means that the organisation questions and modifies its existing norms, policies, procedures and objectives and it can lead to transformational change that radically alters the status quo. In the information security example mentioned, a double-loop response may be to investigate the circumstances and reasons for the unauthorized access. Double-loop learning may then occur when a decision is taken to improve (change) the process of allocating access rights in order to minimize future unauthorized access risks.
- Deutero learning involves focusing on the learning process itself. This type of learning seeks to improve how organisations perform single and double-loop learning. It can be described as "learning how to learn" and it occurs when organisations learn how to perform both single and double-loop learning.

Due to the focus on long term goals and the more complex nature of double-loop learning, most companies focus only on single-loop learning [16]. According to Van Niekerk and Von Solms [3] this is also true in the information security discipline. They pointed out that generative, or double-loop learning, emphasizes continuous experimentation and feedback.

Although there are a large number of studies on organisational learning, there are not particularly many studies that relate organisational learning to information security. Even so, the studies that have been conducted in this area prove that information security is an important area that offered ample opportunities, linked to organisational learning, that can make a significant contribution to organisations and their performance. Examples of studies where organisational learning and information security were explored include the following.

Van Niekerk and Von Solms [3] investigated, amongst other models, the use of an organisational learning model for information security education. Their aim was to ensure that adequate attention is given to behavioural theories in information security education programs. Albrechtsen [10] conducted a comprehensive study into the barriers that exist and that prohibit productive organisational learning from information security incidents while Ahmat *et al* [16] suggested that the practice of incident response may lead to organisational learning. They proposed a double-loop learning model for security incident learning to address potential systemic corrective action. An interesting and authoritative study was conducted by Pfleeger and Caputo [2] where it was argued that blending behavioural sciences and cyber security may lead to the mitigation of cyber security risks. Although organisational learning was not specifically mentioned, the study strongly supports the idea that behavioural sciences (of which organisational learning is at least a sub-section) is relevant to information security in general. To further motivate this idea, Thomson and Van Niekerk [4] also contend that employee apathy towards information security can be addressed through the use of existing theory from the social sciences.

There are also a number of studies where the focus is not on information security per se but rather on how information technology in general relates to organisational learning. These studies usually concentrate on computer systems necessary to facilitate organisational learning and knowledge transfer [17], [18].

In the context of this paper, where it is claimed that a phishing exercise may lead to organisational learning, the next few paragraphs will briefly refer to the phishing concept and examples of studies related to it.

The basic idea of phishing is when someone attempts to fraudulently acquire sensitive information from a victim by impersonating a trustworthy entity [8]. A more formal definition can be obtained from the Oxford English Dictionary [19] where phishing is defined as *the fraudulent practice of sending e-mails purporting to be from reputable companies in order to induce individuals to reveal personal information, such as passwords and credit card numbers, online.*

Phishing attacks are on the increase and successful attacks may have devastating effects on both enterprises and individuals. The Symantec Intelligence Report [20] of June 2012 reported that one out of every 170.9 e-mails sent during the month of June 2012, in South Africa, was a phishing scam. In the Netherlands the figure for June 2012 was one out of every 54.4 e-mails. Considering the billions of e-mail messages that are transmitted worldwide during a specific month, it becomes clear to what extend phishing attacks form part of the day to day electronic communication activities. With this in mind it becomes more and more important to implement the right and effective countermeasures to mitigate or prevent phishing attacks. One way of dealing with this growing number of phishing incidents is to implement security awareness and training programs where users are made aware of phishing scams. The use of practical tests seems to be a popular and effective way of making people aware of the dangers of phishing and some examples of the work conducted by other researchers in this area will be highlighted below.

Pattison *et al* [21] investigated the behaviour response of computer users when receiving either phishing e-mails or genuine e-mails. The study was conducted as a scenario-based role-play experiment where participants had to indicate what the appropriate response would be on certain e-mail messages. The study found that participants who were informed, prior to the experiment, that they are part of a phishing exercise performed better in handling phishing e-mail messages.

Simulated phishing attacks together with embedded training were used by Jansson and Von Solms [5] in an effort to cultivate users' resistance towards phishing attacks, while Kumaraguru *et al* [7] also conducted a study on anti-phishing training to proof that user training should be used in conjunction with technological solutions for security problems. Other studies include Dodge *et al* [9] who performed a practical phishing experiment involving students from the United States Military Academy, Jagatic *et al* [8] performed a study at the Indiana University, Steyn *et al* [22] conducted a practical experiment in South Africa and Hasle *et al* [23] a study in Norway.

It is interesting to note that all the practical phishing experiments referred to so far, were conducted using students as participants. Although these studies produced many advantages and insights, it is doubted whether the results can be generalised and extrapolated to industry enterprises.

Consistent with the research projects mentioned above, this study also performs a practical phishing experiment but uses an industry enterprise for research purposes instead of students in a university environment. In addition, the exercise is aimed at creating a climate for organisational learning. To ensure that the exercise is not a once-off event, the objective is to initiate a learning process and to show how security incidents such as phishing can and should be used for single and double-loop learning in an organisation.

The study was conducted at a large geographically dispersed utility. The organisation in question is a large multi-billion dollar entity with over 3500 IT users and they supply essential services to over 2 million customers. The organisation has an information security course that is mandatory for all employees and partners who have access to the IT infrastructure. The objective of the course is to make IT users aware of their responsibilities with regards to protecting the organisations' information and information systems from unauthorised access, loss or disclosure. Whilst the information security course is deemed mandatory, the records could not support this assertion as many staff was found not to have completed the course or no records could be found of their attendance.

3   Methodology

The successful implementation of an e-mail phishing exercise is dependent on how well certain issues, associated with the exercise, are considered. Jansson and Von Solms [5] categorised these issues into principles to be considered *before designing* the exercise, *before conducting* the exercise, *during* the exercise, and *after* the exercise while Dodge *et al* [9] simply refer to them as general and specific considerations. In this study considerations are also presented as general and specific considerations. The general considerations are concerned with those issues that may have an impact on the exercise as a whole while the specific considerations deal with aspects specific to the enterprise where the study was conducted.

General Considerations
The first and most important general consideration is the determination and definition of an objective. There should be a clearly defined goal and in this study the goal was

simply stated as the evaluation of security awareness associated with phishing and the creation of an opportunity for organisational learning to take place. The next consideration is critical for success i.e. to get ethical clearance and top management approval. This was achieved by conducting personal meetings with the CEO, the CFO and the IT manager where the purpose, actual steps and possible outcomes were explained. A formal project proposal detailing aspects such as the basic process, different phases, measures of success and possible risks, was also submitted for approval to management.

Other general considerations which were appropriately addressed included the timing of the exercise; maintaining the privacy of respondents; the selection of a random and representative sample of respondents; measurements to ensure that no information was disclosed prior to the exercise; and, a debriefing exercise following the test.

Specific Considerations

The central issue among the specific considerations was the construction of an appropriate e-mail message. The message had to be concise, credible and at the same time be enticing in order for participants to react.

To ensure that the phishing e-mail message complies with all the necessary requirements, it was decided to make use of aspects that may trigger certain emotions from participants. Jansson [6] presents a list of a large number of techniques that are based on negative, positive and neutral emotional exploits. For the construction of the e-mail message the following emotional exploits were used.

Legitimacy – when a user is made to believe that the source of the e-mail message is legitimate.

Authority – people tend to comply with instructions or requests issued by someone with authority.

Scarcity – when users believe that the time to react is limited.

Conformity – users who believe that other fellow-employees have already reacted to a request are inclined to also comply with the request.

Apart from these four techniques which were explicitly built into the e-mail message (see figure 2), three other important emotional exploits were also implicitly included. They were *urgency* (making users believe it is an emergency), *carelessness* (clicking on a link) and *diffusion of responsibility* (users believe that someone else is responsible for security). Users were asked to click on the link in the message which would then take them to another webpage where their usernames and passwords were requested. Figure 2 also indicates how the e-mail was constructed to provide clues to alert users that the message was likely not to be legitimate. The real name of the organisation has been changed in figure 2.

There were a number of other specific issues that also needed clarification before the actual exercise could take place i.e. it was important not to refer to any specific IT, security or internal audit staff as this may compromise the trust between users and

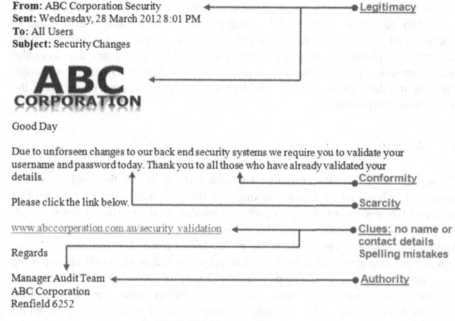

Fig. 2. Phishing e-mail message

staff. Steps also had to be taken to ensure that the enterprise's anti-phishing tools and spam filters do not identify the message as spam or a phishing scam, and Helpdesk had to be provided with a predetermined response should there be any queries from users. Provision was also made for respondents who reply directly to the phishing e-mail. Some of the technical considerations include the deletion of duplicate records (if a user responds more than once) and also a check to see whether the correct usernames were supplied (password were requested but not recorded).

The e-mail message (figure 2) was first sent to a small group of 10 employees. The objective was to test whether all technical aspects are functioning correctly and also to get feedback on possible improvements. After some minor changes were made, following the small pilot study, it was decided to go ahead and implement the phishing test.

The phishing e-mail message was sent to all employees at 8:00pm on a weekday night. The organisation is a 24-hour operation with activities taking place on a continuous basis. Statistics of user logs showed that there are on average about 1700 active IT users signed on during any night and to ensure that the night workers are included in the test, the 8:00pm sending time was chosen. This sending time would also guarantee that day workers should have the phishing e-mail in their inboxes first thing in the morning. The idea was to get users to respond early before they can discuss it with fellow employees.

A number of senior managers found the phishing e-mail very annoying and some of them sent out general e-mail messages to object to the phishing message (and the test). The security personnel were also involved and concern was expressed regarding the possibility of an external attack aimed at disrupting essential services. Due to this, it was decided at 8:30am the next morning to remove the phishing message and to officially end the test. The reasons for withdrawing the phishing e-mail relatively early the next morning were firstly, to prevent large-scale disruptions and secondly, because enough data has been recorded at that stage to draw meaningful conclusions. The data and the experience were sufficient and interesting results, presented in the next section, were obtained.

4   Results

The data recorded from the phishing awareness exercise include the employee name, department where the person is working and the username. Passwords were also requested but not recorded due to privacy considerations. As part of the exercise, passwords were validated but only the result was recorded in a simple yes/no format. Appropriate safeguards to ensure privacy were put in place. The recorded employee names were purely recorded for statistical purposes and nowhere during reporting were specific names linked to responses. The reason for recording usernames was to perform a validation test to ensure that users do enter valid usernames (and by implication valid passwords). All duplicate records (users who entered their details more than once) and records with invalid usernames were removed from the final data set.

The main result, before any further analyses were performed, was the number of negative responses received. A negative response is a response where a user provided his or her username and password. During the test 280 users responded to the phishing message of whom 231 (83%) entered their usernames and passwords on the webpage. Of the 231 users, 23 (10%) entered their valid details more than once. Although there were approximately 1700 active users logged on during the test, it would be incorrect to assume that all of those who did not respond acted in a positive way. Reasons for this may be the fact that many people do not respond immediately to e-mail messages, some users may have left their workstations logged on during the night while not there, some users may have been engaged in other tasks and simply did not check their mail inboxes, etc. A much more significant analysis was to link the 280 users who responded, to the information security course that all staff members are required to complete and which would have provided them with basic security information on how to react to possible phishing scams. Figures 3(a) and (b) show the results graphically. Figure 3(a) shows that an unexpected 69% of those users who entered their passwords did complete the security training in the past. Figure 3(b) shows the training details of those who responded without entering their usernames and passwords. These results indicate that there are at least two points of concern. Firstly, the high number of users who responded in a negative way despite their security training and secondly, the relatively high number of users that never completed the information security course.

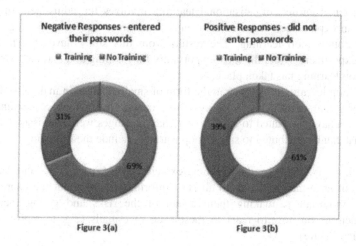

Figure 3(a)   Figure 3(b)

Fig. 3. Responses related to training completed

Figure 4 shows an analysis of responses (percentages) per experience category for those who entered their usernames and passwords. Experience in this case refers to the number of years a person is employed at the organisation. From figure 4 it can be seen that those employees with less experience at the organisation (and therefore less exposure to its security practices and policies) are more inclined to give away personal details. More than a third (35%) of those who entered their usernames and passwords have less than 5 years experience with more than half (52%) less than 10 years.

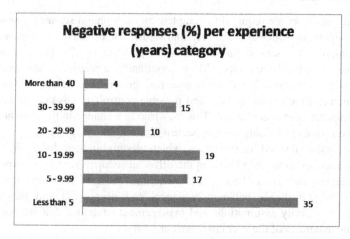

Fig. 4. Responses per experience category

The data that was captured during the exercise makes it possible to perform a number of analyses, e.g. responses per department, gender, age group etc. These types of analyses were not done in this study as the focus was more directed at possible organisational learning opportunities.

As explained earlier, organisational learning involves the adjustment of actions based on an experience. These adjustments, or learning, can then be categorised as single or double-loop learning. The results from this study have shown that the phishing experiment offers the ideal opportunity for learning and that both single and double-loop learning has taken place.

Single-loop learning took place in the form of small changes in making staff aware of the risks and consequences of phishing scams. Instructions concerning basic acceptable behaviour related to suspicious e-mail messages were also issued. Specific actions that can be attributed to single-loop learning include the following.

–   The first day, following the phishing exercise, the Manager Risk and Assurance sent out an e-mail message to all staff informing them about the exercise and, more importantly, making them aware of the risks and giving them basic instructions on how to react to these type of e-mails (e.g. to report it to the Service Centre).
–   The company's weekly in-house bulletin was used to reinforce the security awareness message and to instruct staff to complete the company's computer based information security course. This was done for two consecutive months following the phishing exercise.

The single-loop learning examples mentioned here did not change the status quo of any process but were quick and effective corrective measures to address a specific problem area. There were, however, other issues that needed a more comprehensive investigation that may lead to a change in policies and procedures. These double-loop learning issues include the following.

–   All staff members are required to complete an information security course which will equip them with basic security knowledge for different security situations including phishing scams. An analysis of the phishing results showed that not all staff has completed the course. More importantly, a relatively large number of those who have completed the course had given their passwords away. An assessment of the course content and possible controls to ensure that everybody completes the course is planned. This may lead to a change in the current security policy on issues pertaining to basic security training.
–   Another issue, planned for the future, which was highlighted during the phishing exercise relates to the gap between the different security views and expectations of managers and users. This gap is sometimes referred to as the information security digital divide between managers and users [24] and may lead to unrealistic security assumptions and management strategies that are not aligned with the dynamics of the user environment.

If one considers the results of the phishing exercise it seems permissible to draw the conclusion that the exercise has created opportunities for organisational learning. Basic problems were immediately corrected through an easy and uncomplicated single-loop learning approach while double-loop learning issues provided an opportunity for the organisation to adapt and adjust some of their information strategies.

5   Conclusions

Modern businesses are characterised by the increasing reliance on information assets. The protection of these assets depends to a large extend on the employees and users and it is not surprisingly that criminals tend to focus their attacks on humans. Phishing has become one of the most frequently used techniques to obtain personal or private information and to combat it, proper security awareness programs should be in place. To ensure that a security awareness activity does not become a once-off event, organisations may want to consider the use of various organisational learning models to enhance the awareness and educational value of such programs.

In this paper a successful practical phishing exercise was conducted at a large organisation. The aim was not only to record the number of users who are willing to give away personal information, but also to create an opportunity for organisational learning in order to improve the educational value of the phishing experiment. The results have shown that employees are prone to phishing attacks, but more importantly, the phishing exercise created an excellent opportunity for both single and double-loop learning activities. A single-loop learning approach was followed to immediately correct certain shortcomings without changing the status quo, while double-loop learning provided the opportunity to revisit and adapt some of the longer term information security strategies.

One security experiment linked successfully to organisational learning does not necessarily prove that all security exercises will lead to organisational learning. The exercise did, however, provide an insight into exciting possibilities to increase the value of security awareness exercises and that it may ultimately lead to the completion of the learning process described in section 2 of the paper.

References

1. Furnell, S., Clarke, N.: Power to the People? The Evolving Recognition of Human Aspects of Security. Computers and Security 31, 983–988 (2012)
2. Pfleeger, S.L., Caputo, D.D.: Leverage Behavioral Science to Mitigate Cyber Security Risk. Computers and Security 31, 597–611 (2012)
3. van Niekerk, J., von Solms, R.: Organisational Learning Models for Information Security (2004), http://icsa.cs.up.za/issa/2004/Proceedings/Full/043.pdf
4. Thomson, K., van Niekerk, J.: Combating Information Security Apathy by Encouraging Prosocial Organisational Behaviour. Information Management & Computer Security 20, 39–46 (2012)
5. Jansson, K., von Solms, R.: Phishing for Phishing Awareness. Behaviour & Information Technology (2011), doi:10.1080/0144929X.2011.632650
6. Jansson, K.: A Model for Cultivating Resistance to Social Engineering Attacks, Unpublished M-dissertation, Nelson Mandela Metropolitan University (2011)
7. Kumaraguru, P., Cranshaw, J., Acquisti, A., Cranor, L., Hong, J., Blair, M.A., Pham, T.: School of Phish: A Real-World Evaluation of Anti-Phishing Training. In: Proceedings of the 5th Symposium on Usable Privacy and Security (SOUPS), pp. 3:1–3:12 (2009)
8. Jagatic, T.N., Johnson, N.A., Jakobsson, M., Menezer, F.: Social Phishing. Communications of the ACM 50(10), 94–100 (2007)

9. Dodge, R.C., Carver, C., Ferguson, A.J.: Phishing for User Security Awareness. Computers and Security 26, 73–80 (2007)
10. Albrechtsen, E.: Barriers against Productive Organisational Learning from Information Security Incidents. Paper in the PhD course Organisational Development and ICT, Norwegian University of Science and Technology (2003)
11. Schermerhorn, J.R., Osborn, R.N., Uhl-Bien, M., Hunt, J.G.: Organisational Behavior, 12th edn. John Wiley & Sons, Inc., NJ (2012)
12. Lopez, S.P., Peon, J.M.M., Ordas, C.J.V.: Organisational Learning as a Determining Factor in Business Performance. The Learning Organisation 12(3), 227–245 (2005)
13. Kennedy, E.: A Critical Evaluation of the Organisational Learning that takes place in a Project Management Environment. Unpublished M-dissertation, North-West University (2008)
14. Argyris, C., Schon, D.: Organisational Learning II: Theory, Method and Practice. Prentice Hall (1996)
15. Buckler, B.: Practical Steps towards a Learning Organisation: Applying Academic Knowledge to Improvement and Innovation in Business Processes. The Learning Organisation 5(1), 15–23 (1998)
16. Ahmad, A., Hadgkiss, J., Ruighaver, A.B.: Incident Response Teams – Challenges in Supporting the Organisational Security Function. Computers and Security 31, 643–652 (2012)
17. Kane, G.C., Alavi, M.: Information Technology and Organisational Learning: Investigation of Exploration and Exploitation Processes. Organization Science 18(5), 796–812 (2007)
18. Chou, S.: Computer Systems to Facilitating Organizational Learning: IT and Organizational Context. Expert Systems with Applications (24), 273–280 (2003)
19. Oxford Dictionary (November 2012),
    http://oxforddictionaries.com/definition/english/phishing
20. Symantec Intelligence Report (June 2012),
    http://www.symantec.com/content/en/us/enterprise/
    other_resources/b_intelligence_report_06_2012.en-us.pdf
21. Pattinson, M., Jerram, C., Parsons, K., McCormac, A., Butavicius, M.: Why do some People Manage Phishing E-mails Better than Others? Information Management and Computer Security 20(1), 18–28 (2012)
22. Steyn, T., Kruger, H.A., Drevin, L.: Identity Theft – Empirical Evidence from a Phishing Exercise. In: Venter, H., Elofif, M., Labuschagne, L., Elofif, J., von Solms, R. (eds.) New Approaches for Security, Privacy and Trust in Complex Environments. IFIP, vol. 232, pp. 193–203. Springer, Boston (2007)
23. Hasle, H., Kristiansen, Y., Kintel, K., Snekkenes, E.: Measuring Resistance to Social Engineering. In: Deng, R.H., Bao, F., Pang, H., Zhou, J. (eds.) ISPEC 2005. LNCS, vol. 3439, pp. 132–143. Springer, Heidelberg (2005)
24. Albrechtsen, E., Hovden, J.: The Information Security Digital Divide between Information Security Managers and Users. Computers and Security (28), 476–490 (2009)

A Case for Societal Digital Security Culture

Lotfi Ben Othmane[1], Harold Weffers[1] Rohit Ranchal[2], Pelin Angin[2],
Bharat Bhargava[2], and Mohd Murtadha Mohamad[3]

[1] Laboratory for Quality Software, Department of Mathematics and Computer
Science, Eindhoven University of Technology, The Netherlands
{l.ben.othmane,h.t.g.weffers}@tue.nl
[2] CERIAS and Computer Sciences, Purdue University, USA
{rranchal,pangin,bb}@purdue.edu
[3] Faculty of Computing, Universiti Teknologi Malaysia, Malaysia
murtadha@utm.my

Abstract. Information and communication technology systems, such
as remote health care monitoring and smart mobility applications, have
become indispensable parts of our lives. Security vulnerabilities in these
systems could cause financial losses, privacy/safety compromises, and
operational interruptions. This paper demonstrates through examples,
that technical security solutions for these information systems, alone,
are not sufficient to protect individuals and their assets from attacks. It
proposes to complement (usable) technical solutions with Societal Digital
Security Culture (SDSC): collective knowledge, common practices, and
intuitive common behavior about digital security that the members of a
society share. The paper also suggests a set of approaches for improving
SDSC in a society and demonstrates using a case study how the suggested
approaches could be integrated to compose a plan for improving SDSC.

Keywords: Information Security, Security Culture, Security Usability.

1 Introduction

We commonly use pervasive computing systems, such as remote vehicle control systems [1], remote healthcare monitoring systems, and home automation
systems to improve our life quality; public information systems [2], such as online banking for personal business; and Internet telephony applications, such
as Skype for personal communication. However, these systems have security
threats–circumstances and events with the potential to harm an Information
System (IS) through unauthorized access, destruction, disclosure, modification
of data, and Denial of Service (DoS) [3].

Attackers exploit technical vulnerabilities and security policy violations to
trigger security threats and compromise the system's assets. Technical vulnerabilities are weaknesses and flaws in a system's design, implementation, or operation and management [4]. For example, sending data through networks without
assuring confidentiality and integrity [4] is a weakness of the system that manages them. Policy violations are faults in applying and enforcing security policies that provide attackers with confidential information or technical weaknesses

L.J. Janczewski, H.B. Wolfe, and S. Shenoi (Eds.): SEC 2013, IFIP AICT 405, pp. 391–404, 2013.
© IFIP International Federation for Information Processing 2013

Table 1. Impacts of security threats to systems

Impact	Example
Safety compromise	Attacker controlling the brakes of a vehicle [6] through remote access to the in-vehicle network of the vehicle using a mobile phone.
Financial loss	Attacker installing a key logger on the mobile device of a user to capture credentials for performing financial operations on his behalf [7].
Privacy violation	Use of information on an Online Social Network (OSN) for purposes they were not intended, as in the case of a teacher in training being denied her teaching degree due to her photos posted on an OSN [8].
Operational interruption	Attacker continuously sending messages to a vehicle to prevent it from sending e-call messages to a service center in case of an accident [9].

which allow them to compromise assets of the system. For example, an attacker could use social engineering [5] to get the secret password of an individual for online banking (e.g., when he/she gets drunk), which enables him/her to withdraw money from the victim's bank account. Table 1 provides an overview of the impacts of major security threats to information systems.

Figure 1 shows that the security threats for information systems we use fall into several categories: physical security violations, technical attacks, security policy violations, and errors caused by limited human knowledge. Technical security measures attempt to address these threats, but fall short in providing comprehensive security solutions in most cases.

This paper investigates two main questions: What are the limitations of technical security solutions used in pervasive systems, social networks, and public information systems? And, how can technical security solutions be supported to reduce the risks of security threats to these systems? We answer the first question through analyzing the efficacy of technical security mechanisms for two case studies: connected vehicle and online banking. The analysis shows that technical security solutions, alone, cannot protect individuals and their assets from attacks. Therefore, we propose to extend the technical solutions with Societal Digital Security Culture (SDSC), which answers the second question.

Digital Security Culture (DSC) in organizations is well investigated, e.g. [19], [20], and [21]. However, to the best of our knowledge, Colella and Colombini [22] are the only authors who–briefly–discussed security awareness to address threats related to pervasive computing. There is currently no work on SDSC. The main contributions of this paper are to: (1) demonstrate that technical security mechanisms, alone, cannot sufficiently protect individuals and their assets from attacks on systems they use, (2) propose to extend technical security mechanisms through SDSC, and (3) suggest approaches for improving SDSC.

The rest of the paper is organized as follows: Section 2 describes the limitations of efficacy of technical security solutions. Section 3 provides an overview of "usable security" and its limitations. Section 4 defines and describes SDSC. Section 5 suggests some approaches for improving SDSC, Section 6 presents an example for reducing the risk of security threats through improving SDSC, and Section 7 concludes the paper.

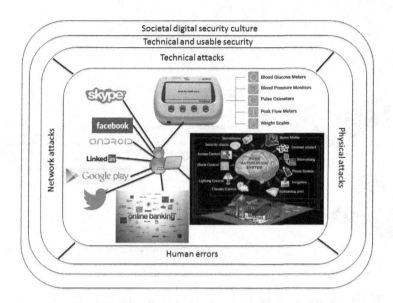

Fig. 1. Security environment for everyday information systems. (Image references clockwise from top right corner: [10], [11], [12], [13], [14], [15], [16], [17], [18].)

2   Limitations of Efficacy of Technical Security Solutions

2.1   Overview of the Limitations of Technical Solutions

Companies which develop systems and applications for public use implement technical security solutions, which cannot alone prevent and protect the user of the systems or applications from attacks (even if they were certified to assure the security of the user). The main limitations of the technical solutions are:

L1. *Policy violation.* Technical security solutions often rely on the user to comply with some security policies, e.g., not disclose a password. However, a user may violate the policy, e.g., provide his/her password to other individuals.

L2. *Weak mechanisms.* Companies often implement ineffective security solutions for protecting users' assets, so they preserve low product cost. For example, pacemakers and implantable cardiac defibrillators have weak security mechanisms although they are widely used [23].

L3. *New attack scenarios.* Companies implement security mechanisms for known attacks. However, attackers attack where they are least expected; they discover new vulnerabilities and exploit them.

2.2   Demonstration of the Limitations of Technical Security Mechanisms

This subsection presents two applications, describes their related digital attacks; and demonstrates the limitations of the technical security solutions for them.

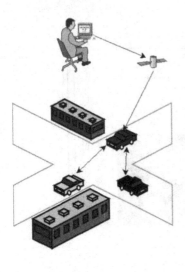

Date: Wed, 30 Jan 2013 11:18:37
From: Admin HDFC Bank <admin.securehdfcbanking@gmail.com>
Reply-To: secure.hdfcinformation@gmail.com
Subject: Survey Request

HDFC BANK

Dear Customer,

You have been selected for our reward survey offer. HDFC Bank values your feedback
and is doing a $50 Reward Survey. HDFC Bank will credit your account with $50 after
you complete this survey. It will not take more than 5 minutes. To get advantage of this
offer and start the survey, click on this link: www.getthisoffer.com/surveyhdfcbank. After
completing the survey, reply back with the information specified below within 30 days to
receive $50. We will send you a confirmation once you complete the survey and provide
your information.

Name:
Address:
Date of Birth:
SSN:
Bank Name:
Bank Account:

This message has been sent only to our special customers. Hurry this offer is open only
for next 5 days.

HDFC Bank Survey Department

Fig. 2. Remote access to a connected vehicle

Fig. 3. Phishing example

Case 1: Connected Vehicle. Every (motor) vehicle uses a set of sensors and
Electronic Control Units (ECUs) to collect data about the vehicle's behavior and
environment, and to control the functionalities of the vehicle. ECUs collaborate
by exchanging messages; they compose an in-vehicle network (a.k.a. on-Board
network). Motor vehicles, until recently, used to have a closed in-vehicle network, i.e. they did not have external connectivity. Messages exchanged between
the components of a vehicle were produced and consumed by the nodes of the in-
vehicle network. Today, several applications such as cooperative adaptive cruise
control, remote firmware update, e-call, and remote diagnostic of vehicles require communication with the in-vehicle network of the vehicle. A vehicle whose
ECUs communicate through an in-vehicle network, and which communicates
with neighboring vehicles and Road Side Units (RSUs), personal devices, and
Service Centers (SCs) is called a connected vehicle [1]. Figure 2 shows a scenario
for remote access to connected vehicles.

In the last decade, several threat analyses, security solutions, and security and
privacy architectures have been proposed for assuring secure communication in
in-vehicle networks, between vehicles, between vehicles and personal devices,
between vehicles and service centers, as well as detecting malicious data, protection against wormhole attacks, secure data aggregation for VANets, use of
devices that include a hardware security module, over-the-air firmware update,
protection against denial of service attacks, and access control to applications [1].

Car manufacturers implement security solutions to address the threats. However, there are reports that the security mechanisms they implement are sub-
verted. For instance, Checkoway et al. [24] performed a set of attacks on a vehicle
(a sedan) including the following:

A1. Exploit a weakness and a flaw in the authentication program of aqLink protocol implementation, namely, short (8-bits) random numbers and a buffer overflow vulnerability, to upload and run arbitrary code.
A2. Use trojan horse for Android-based smart phones to exploit a buffer overflow vulnerability in the car's hands-free application that uses the Bluetooth protocol. (The attack requires the smart phone to be paired with the car's Bluetooth device.)
A3. Call car and play a well-crafted "song" from an iPad, that exploits a logic flaw and a buffer overflow vulnerability in the authentication of aqLink protocol implementation to upload and run arbitrary code.

These attacks show the limitations of technical security solutions for connected vehicles. For instance, attack scenario A1 exploits an implementation weakness: random numbers are of 8-bits (limitation L2), which allows the attacker to upload an arbitrary program into the embedded system. The code may provide the attacker with the ability to inject messages into the in-vehicle network of the vehicle, such as increasing speed or disabling the brake. The other attack scenarios exploit source code vulnerabilities that the researchers found in the programs of the device: they are new attack scenarios (limitation L3).

Case 2: Online Banking. Hackers exploit online banking Web application vulnerabilities and user faults through means like social engineering. Social engineering, e.g. phishing attacks, exploit human cognitive biases–creating flaws in human logic using different ways to perceive reality–to trick humans into performing actions, such as disclosing sensitive information. Phishing attacks are conducted through (a) presenting illegitimate digital information that attempts to fraudulently acquire sensitive information, such as login credentials, personal information, or financial information, or (b) masquerading as a trustworthy entity–e.g. a well-known organization or an acquaintance.

The phishing information is usually distributed through emails that contain an attachment, or a web link. Figure 3 shows a phishing email masquerading as HDFC bank.[1] The attack scenarios posed by phishing email include:

B1. Fool online banking users to send the hacker their sensitive information, such as Personally Identifiable Information (PII) and financial information, which could be used for identity theft and financial fraud.
B2. Spoof the bank websites, deceive the users to provide their login credentials, and use the information to hack the users' bank accounts.
B3. Deceive users to install malicious software on their computers, which may give the hacker access to the users' computers and other computers accessible from the users' computers or capture their login credentials and personal data and send them to the hacker for malicious use.

Technical and usable security solutions are not sufficient to mitigate attacks B1, B2, and B3. For instance, attack scenario B1 succeeds for users who violate

---

[1] HDFC bank is a fictive name.

the policy (limitation L1): Banks do not request PII and financial information through emails, so users should not reply to emails requesting such information; attack scenario B2 exploits weak mechanisms (limitation L2) that do not detect Website spoofing; and attack scenario B3 often uses new techniques (limitation L3) to bypass anti-malware software.

3 Usable Security

Whitten and Tygar [25] have identified the weakest link property: attackers need to exploit only a single error, and human frailty provides this error: humans are, frequently, the "weakest link" in the security chain. Whitten and Tygar [25] pointed out that users do not apply security mechanisms, although they know them, simply because the mechanisms are not usable enough. A security software is *usable* [25] if the people who are expected to use it: (1) are reliably made aware of the security tasks they need to perform, (2) are able to figure out how to successfully perform those tasks, (3) don't make dangerous errors, and (4) are sufficiently comfortable with the interface to continue using it.

Security usability addresses the question: why users *can't* apply security mechanisms. The techniques for usable security aim to reduce the complexity of security mechanisms, improve the knowledge of users, and reduce the cost of applying them in terms of efforts and money. However, making security usable and changing users' knowledge doesn't enforce change in their behavior [26]. Sasse and Flechais find that security culture, based on a shared understanding of the importance of security, is the key to achieving desired behavior [26].

4 Overview of Societal Digital Security Culture

Members of the society need to gain knowledge and experience sufficient to **avoid** the consequences of the limitations of technical solutions. Security limitations have been addressed for the case of organizations using DSC, which extends (usable) technical security solutions [21]. The most common definition of DSC–that we adopt in this paper–is the collective knowledge, common practices, and intuitive common behavior about digital security (cf. [19]). This definition identifies knowledge and behavior (which includes practices) as the main levels of DSC.

Table 2 shows the differences between technical security solutions, usable security solutions, DSC and SDSC. It shows that technical security solutions, usable security solutions, and SDSC complement each other, and that SDSC extends DSC from organizations to the society.

SDSC is similar, in principal, to DSC in organizations; it helps individuals use pervasive computing systems, social networks, and public applications while protecting themselves and their assets from digital security threats. Since the limitations of the (usable) technical solutions affect the members of the society in general and an effort at the level of the society should be made to address them, we consider this challenge societal; that is, it does not only concern individuals

Table 2. Difference between the digital security approaches

	Technical security solutions	Usable security solutions	DSC	SDSC
Target entity	information systems	human-computer interactions	employees in organizations	members of the society
Protection target	information systems and their users	information systems and their users	information systems of organizations	users of the society
Beneficiary	individual	individual	organizations	society
Liability	information system operators	information system operators or distributors	organizations	members of the society, organizations, and law makers.
Preparation for unknown attacks	low	low	moderate	moderate
Technical knowledge requirement	high	low	low	low

who happen to be the victims. A second reason for considering the issue societal is the fact that people imitate each others' behaviors.

SDSC and DSC have several differences including the following.

- Organizations decide on the IS they use and can control the threats they are exposed to. In contrast, it is difficult for the society to limit the ISs used by its members–if not impossible.
- Organizations control the selection of their members–so it is possible to select only individuals who share certain values. In contrast, the society has limited control on the selection of the citizens.
- Organizations set the policies for using their ISs. In contrast, the security policies in the society are set in response to events related to using ISs.
- Organizations can set efficient measures for enforcing desired behaviors. In contrast, setting efficient measures for enforcing desired behaviors in the society requires important resources and long time.
- Organizations can easily set measures for detecting violations. In contrast, setting such measures in the society may cause privacy violation. (Recall that members of the society use ISs, in most cases, for private business.)

SDSC of a group has levels which range between weak and strong. Example for indicators of weak SDSC is the willingness of the members of the group to use the pervasive systems without checking associated security risks: potential threats with their occurrence and impacts [28]. Example for indicators of strong SDSC is the importance members of the group give to evaluating the risks associated with a system they intend to use.

Table 3. Password change habits in the society [27]

	weekly	monthly	twice/year	once/year	never	not sure
How often do you change passwords for your banking account(s)?	8%	16%	19%	18%	28%	12%
How often do you change passwords for your social media account(s)?	6%	11%	13%	19%	42%	10%

Table 4. Generic interest in security [27]

	yes	no	not sure
Does your company have policies/training/security requirements that you must follow when you use your personal device at work?	42%	44%	14%
Have you installed any security software or apps on your smartphone in order to make it more secure from viruses or malware?	31%	64%	5%

A survey conducted in USA in 2012 by the National Cyber Security Alliance (NCSA) and McAfee [27] reveals the weak SDSC in USA. For instance, Table 3 shows that 30% of the interviewees either never or do not recall they ever changed their online banking password (and more than 50% for the case of OSN) and Table 4 shows that about 70% of interviewees are either not sure or did not install a security software for their smart phones.

5   Approaches for Improving Societal Digital Security Culture

This section proposes three approaches for improving SDSC: instituting security policies, spread of knowledge, and behavioral improvement, which are complementary. The approaches are borrowed from DSC in organizations and adapted for society.[2] Table 5 lists the three approaches and the methods that implement these approaches. It specifies for each method whether it affects knowledge and attitude, behavior, or both.

5.1   Institute Digital Security Policies

A digital security policy specifies acceptable and unacceptable behavior in relation to security practices. A collection of security policies specifies, indirectly, the *target SDSC*: DSC that the society wants to "live in." The objective of a security policy is to influence and to direct the behavior of individuals on protecting their own digital assets and themselves (cf. [29]) from security threats to the systems they use and to discourage compromising the security of others.

---

[2] In this section we often use "confer" (cf.) because in the references the ideas apply to organizations; we adapt these ideas to individuals/members of society.

Table 5. Approaches for digital security culture enforcement

Approach	Knowledge and Attitude	Behavior
Institute security policies		
Develop security policies (P1.1)	x	
Spread the Knowledge		
Security awareness programs (P2.1)	x	
Leadership support (P2.2)	x	
Behavioral improvement		
Use of personal incentives (P3.1)		x
Use of games (P3.2)		x
Use of certification (P3.3)	x	x
Education of children (P3.4)	x	x

In order to be a deterrent for attackers and those justifying the abusive use of people's personal information with loopholes in the system, politicians, citizens, and security experts should collaborate to create SDSC in the form of laws. As evident from the aforementioned case study, instituting security policies will not be sufficient for a complete SDSC. The policies need to be (a) disseminated to individuals and (b) enforced through incentives and punishment by laws.

5.2 Spread the Knowledge about Security Threats

This subsection discusses security awareness programs and leadership support as methods that enable spread of knowledge about digital security threats.

Security Awareness Programs. They aim to improve the awareness of individuals about security risks [30]. They are used to change (and improve) the knowledge and attitude of individuals towards digital security threats. These programs may use (1) promotional methods, such as mugs and screen savers; (2) improving methods, such as rewarding mechanisms; (3) educational and interactive methods, such as demonstrations and training; and (4) informative methods, such as emails and newsletters [31]. Another means of raising security awareness is using OSNs to provide an effective way for information dissemination, especially for educating the public about policies and attacks.

Existing security awareness programs, although successful in changing the attitude toward security risks, are not effective in changing users' habits and intuitive behavior to respond as necessary to security threats [32]. Kruger and Kearney [32] report that trainees exhibit good level of awareness attitudes and knowledge, but exhibit poor security behavior. They report that awareness behavior is as low as 18% when it comes to adhering to the security policies. This shows the limitation of security awareness programs in effectively improving the intuitive behavior towards security risks, which further supports the use of the suggested approaches to improve SDSC.

Dodge et al. investigated the response of military cadets in USA to the phishing attack [20]. They sent phishing attacks to the students–without previous announcement of the exercise, evaluated the responses, and alerted students about the result of the test. The experiments showed that senior students had better security culture than junior students, which shows the difference between security culture and security awareness.

Leadership Support. Leaders support and commitment is crucial to changing SDSC (cf. [33], [29]). Leaders need to embody the security best practices; they should behave according to the policies, be engaged and live up to the security policies they set. The commitment and support of leaders to SDSC change helps disseminate the knowledge because their activities are visible to the society members, which encourage them to, also, practice the policy.

5.3   Improve Intuitive Behavior towards Security Threats

This subsection describes four methods for behavior improvement: use of incentives, use of games, use of certification, and use of courses.

Use of Personal Incentives. *Personal incentives* motivate individuals to change their behavior. They can be categorized in three classes:

- Material or morals rewards: Offering small rewards, e.g., money and praise by peers, to the users to keep them interested in the training program. Thus, over time, they undergo behavioral changes towards perceiving and reacting to the attack scenarios.
- Moral or material sanctions: The fear of embarrassment and punishment, e.g., penalty and blame, forces users to behave appropriately.
- Responsibilities and accountability for complying with policies [29]: Influence the users to be responsible in following the policies. For instance, non-disclosure agreements help preventing leakage of sensitive information.

The effectiveness of rewards and sanctions depends on the satisfaction of the receiving individual [34]. For example, (we expect) a small monetary reward may motivate a poor but not a rich individual.

Use of Games. Games are competitive interactions involving chance and imaginary setting and are bound by rules to achieve specified goals that depend on the player skills. By nature, games are competitive; users like to play the games and get better scores. Games could simulate attacks and protection mechanisms.

We propose to exploit the characteristics of games for creating competitiveness to improve SDSC of individuals. Games are already being used in security awareness programs to help employees gain skills to discover threats and develop reactions to them [35]. Users could play a game in which they are required to discover the threats and protect themselves. The games help users understand how to discover threats, know what protection mechanisms are and how they work and how to identify attacks and react to them. They transform the behavior of individuals from passive, i.e. knowing the impact of the threat, to proactive and engaging, i.e. acting spontaneously to limit the impact of the threat.

Use of Certification. Certification of knowledge is important for users handling sensitive information of other entities. It should be made mandatory and

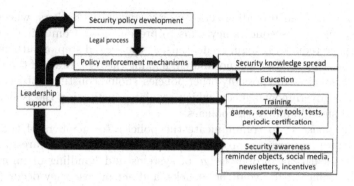

Fig. 4. The SDSC process

enforced by the legal and regulatory policies. Certification can be obtained after completing a certain level of education and training and demonstrating the knowledge through a test. Certifications should require periodic renewal to accommodate updated policies and new threats. For instance, a bank employee handling sensitive financial and user information should renew his/her certification periodically. The certification process enforces the change in user behavior towards securely handling information and prevents attacks.

Education of Children. It is very important to introduce children to SDSC when they start using computers and the Internet. Thus, schools need to adopt and offer mandatory classes to teach all children about the SDSC process and its importance. This will help the children easily develop the rightful behavior at an early age when they are just beginning to use digital information systems.

Figure 4 shows how the proposed approaches for improving SDSC should be integrated to achieve a high level of security for any information system. As seen in the figure, while there is a logical time ordering relation between most of the proposed methods, leadership support should come into play at every stage of the SDSC improvement process.

6   Example on Reducing Risks of Security Threats Using Societal Digital Security Culture

This section shows through an example how to improve the SDSC to address phishing attacks. We assume that the online banking system implements usable technical mechanisms and we develop a program that integrates coherently a set of approaches to improve the security culture of a society.

The first phase of the plan is to create two policies (P1.1): (1) no PII should be disclosed through email, and (2) two-step-authentication mechanisms should be required for accounts that use sensitive information (The second step could be providing a secret answer to a personal question in the case that the first step, the login, was performed at a host unregistered by the user). The first policy aims to prevent users from providing sensitive information to hackers, who pretend to be the bank. The second policy aims to prevent users from using a spoofed bank web page requesting login credentials, as the second step of authentication being unique to every user will not match, making the user aware of the phishing attack. The policies–and possibly other policies–should constitute objects of law, created by a government agency, which regulates instituting the policies. The government should enforce the policies.

The next phase is to communicate the policies to members of the society through security awareness programs (P2.1). Users become aware of policies and threats, learn the proper usage of systems and handling of information, develop the behavior to avoid the attacks, and act in case they occur (as they do for the case of a fire for example). The banks could motivate their users by e.g., offering loyalty rewards points (P3.1) for successful completion of training programs and for reporting phishing attacks. The incentives change the behavior of users towards the attack: they would learn to differentiate emails coming from a generic mail service (e.g., Gmail) and emails coming from a bank and recognize phishing email using their characteristics, such as generic greeting, fake sender address, false sense of urgency, and fake and deceptive web links.

Periodic knowledge check through renewable training and certification (P3.3) keeps the users updated about new policies and new threats.

7   Conclusion

The use of pervasive computing systems, social networks, and public information systems exposes individuals to the impacts of security threats to these systems. This paper demonstrates that technical security solutions cannot alone, effectively, protect individuals and their assets from attacks on the systems they use, and proposes to complement (usable) technical solutions with SDSC: collective knowledge, common practices, and intuitive common behavior about digital security that the members of a society share. It also suggests a set of approaches–borrowed from organizational DSC–for improving SDSC.

This work is a first step in investigating SDSC. Our future work will include the development of surveys for assessing the security culture, conduct case studies for improving SDSC (e.g., improve the security culture related to connected vehicles), evaluate the effectiveness of approaches for improving security cultures, investigate how to develop a coherent plan for improving the security culture in a society.

Acknowledgment. This work is supported partially by the Dutch national HTAS innovation program; HTAS being an acronym for High Tech Automotive Systems. Any opinions expressed in this paper are those of the authors and do not necessarily reflect those of Dutch national HTAS innovation program.

The authors thank Drs. Reinier Post and Joost Gabriels from LaQuSo, Eindhoven University of Technology for their valuable comments.

References

1. Ben Othmane, L., Weffers, H., Mohamad, M.M., Wolf, M.: A Survey of Security and Privacy in Connected Vehicles. In: Wireless Sensor Networks (WSN) For Vehicular and Space Applications: Architecture and Implementation. Springer, Norwell (accepted)
2. Sundgren, B.: What is a public information system. International Journal of Public Information Systems 1(1), 81–99 (2005)
3. Gilgor, V.: A note on the denial-of-service problem. In: Proceedings of the 1983 IEEE Symposium on Security and Privacy, SP 1983, pp. 5101–5111. IEEE Computer Society, Washington, DC (1983)
4. Kissel, R.: Glossary of key information security terms (February 2011), http://csrc.nist.gov/publications/nistir/ir7298-rev1/nistir-7298-revision1.pdf
5. Anderson, R.J.: Security Engineering: A Guide to Building Dependable Distributed Systems, 2nd edn. Wiley Publishing, Indianapolis (2008)
6. Bailey, D., Solnik, M.: iSEC partners presents: The hacked and the furious. (November 2012), http://www.youtube.com/watch?v=bNDvOOSGb6w
7. Grebennikov, N.: Keyloggers: How they work and how to detect them (part 1) (November 2012), http://www.securelist.com/en/analysis/204791931/Keyloggers_How_they_work_and_how_to_detect_them_Part_1
8. Rosen, J.: The web means the end of forgetting. The New York Times (2010) (published: July 21, 2010)
9. Society, E.I.: ecall: Time saved = lives saved (June 2011), http://ec.europa.eu/information_society/activities/esafety/ecall/index_en.htm
10. Bosch: Bosch health buddy (January 2013), http://www.bosch-telehealth.com/
11. SGRenovation (January 2013), http://sgrenovation.com/why-use-smart-home-appliances/
12. MyBankTracker (January 2013), http://www.mybanktracker.com/news/2010/05/27/
13. Twitter: Twitter logo (January 2013), https://www.twitter.com
14. Google: Playstore logo (January 2013), https://play.google.com/store?hl=en
15. LinkedIn: Linkedin logo (January 2013), http://www.linkedin.com/
16. Google: Android logo (January 2013), http://www.android.com/
17. Facebook: Facebook logo (January 2013), https://www.facebook.com
18. Skype: Skype logo (January 2013), http://beta.skype.com/en/
19. Williams, P.: What does security culture look like for small organizations? In: 7th Australian Information Security Management Conference, Perth, Australia (December 2009)
20. Dodge Jr., R.C., Carver, C., Ferguson, A.J.: Phishing for user security awareness. Computers & Security 26(1), 73–80 (2007)
21. Schlienger, T., Teufel, S.: Information security culture: The socio-cultural dimension in information security management. In: Proc. of the IFIP TC11 17th International Conference on Information Security: Visions and Perspectives, SEC 2002, pp. 191–202. Kluwer, B.V., Deventer (2002)
22. Colella, A., Colombini, C.: Security paradigm in ubiquitous computing. In: 2012 Sixth International Conference on Innovative Mobile and Internet Services in Ubiquitous Computing (IMIS), Palermo, Italy, pp. 634–638 (July 2012)

23. Halperin, D., Heydt-Benjamin, T.S., Ransford, B., Clark, S.S., Defend, B., Morgan, W., Fu, K., Kohno, T., Maisel, W.H.: Pacemakers and implantable cardiac defibrillators: Software radio attacks and zero-power defenses. In: Proceedings of the 2008 IEEE Symposium on Security and Privacy, SP 2008, pp. 129–142. IEEE Computer Society, Washington, DC (2008)

24. Checkoway, S., McCoy, D., Kantor, B., Anderson, D., Shacham, H., Savage, S., Koscher, K., Czeskis, A., Roesner, F., Kohno, T.: Comprehensive experimental analyses of automotive attack surfaces. In: Proceedings of the 20th USENIX Conference on Security, SEC 2011, p. 6. USENIX Association, Berkeley (2011)

25. Whitten, A., Tygar, J.D.: Why Johnny can't encrypt: a usability evaluation of pgp 5.0. In: Proceedings of the 8th conference on USENIX Security Symposium, SSYM 1999, Washington, D.C., vol. 8, p. 14 (August 1999)

26. Sasse, M.A., Flechais, I.: Usable Security: What is it? How do we get it? In: Security and Usability: Designing secure systems that people can use, pp. 13–30. O'Reilly Books (2005)

27. NCSA/McAfee: 2012 ncsa/mcafee online safety survey (October 2012), http://www.staysafeonline.org/download/datasets/3890/2012_ncsa_mcafee_online_safety_study.pdf

28. Shirey, R.: Internet Security Glossary, Version 2. RFC 4949 (Informational) (August 2007)

29. Lim, J.S., Ahmad, A., Chang, S., Maynard, S.B.: Embedding information security culture emerging concerns and challenges. In: Pacific Asia Conference on Information Systems, PACIS 2010, Taipei, Taiwan (July 2010)

30. European Network and Information Security Agency: A users' guide: How to raise information security awareness (June 2006), http://www.enisa.europa.eu/act/ar/deliverables/2006/ar-guide/en

31. Johnson, E.C.: Security awareness: switch to a better programme. Network Security 2006(2), 15–18 (2006)

32. Kruger, H., Kearney, W.: A prototype for assessing information security awareness. Computers & Security 25(4), 289–296 (2006)

33. Lapke, M., Dhillon, G.: Power relationships in information systems security policy formulation and implementation. In: Proc. 16th European Conference on Information Systems, ECIS 2008, Galway, Ireland, pp. 1358–1369 (June 2008)

34. Pahnila, S., Siponen, M., Mahmood, A.: Employees' behavior towards is security policy compliance. In: Proc. of the 40th Annual Hawaii International Conference on System Sciences, HICSS 2007, Washington, DC, USA, p. 156b (2007)

35. Cone, B.D., Irvine, C.E., Thompson, M.F., Nguyen, T.D.: A video game for cyber security training and awareness. Computers & Security 26(1), 63–72 (2007)

Secure Outsourcing: An Investigation of the Fit between Clients and Providers

Gurpreet Dhillon[1], Romilla Chowdhuri[1], and Filipe de Sá-Soares[2]

[1] Virginia Commonwealth University, Richmond, USA
{gdhillon,syedr2}@vcu.edu
[2] Universidade do Minho, Portugal
fss@dsi.uminho.pt

Abstract. In this paper we present an analysis of top security issues related to IT outsourcing. Identification of top issues is important since there is a limited understanding of security in outsourcing relationships. Such an analysis will help decision makers in appropriate strategic planning for secure outsourcing. Our analysis is conducted through a two-phase approach. First, a Delphi study is undertaken to identify the top issues. Second, an intensive study of phase one results is undertaken to better understand the reasons for the different perceptions.

Keywords: Secure outsourcing, congruence, client vendor fit, Delphi study.

1 Introduction

Information security is a significant sticking point in establishing a relationship between Information Technology (IT) outsourcing vendors and clients. While statistics related to outsourcing risks and failures are abound, there has been a limited emphasis on understanding information security related reasons for outsourcing problems. We believe that many of the problems stem from a lack of fit between what IT outsourcing vendors consider to be the key success factors and what outsourcing clients perceive to be critical for the success of the relationship. It is important to undertake such an investigation because of two primary reasons. First, majority of IT outsourcing projects fail because of a lack of appreciation as to what matters to the clients and the vendors [2], [14]. Second, several IT outsourcing projects fall victim to security breaches because of a range of issues – broken processes, failure to appreciate client requirements [10], among others. If strategic alignment between IT outsourcing vendors and clients is maintained, many of the security challenges could be overcome.

A first step in ensuring a strategic fit with respect to information security is to identify as to what is important for the vendors and the clients respectively. In this paper we undertake an extensive Delphi study to identify information security issues related to both the vendors and the clients. This is followed up by an intensive analysis of the issues through in depth interviews with several client and vendor firms.

L.J. Janczewski, H.B. Wolfe, and S. Shenoi (Eds.): SEC 2013, IFIP AICT 405, pp. 405–418, 2013.

2   Informing Literature

In recent years there have been several security breaches where privacy and confidentiality of data has been compromised largely because there was a lack of control over the remote sites. In 2011 an Irish hospital reported breach of patient information related to transcription services in the Philippines. Recently US Government Accounting office survey reported that at least 40 percent of federal contractors and state Medicare agencies experienced a privacy breach (see GAO-06-676)[1]. While it is mandatory for the contractor to report breaches, there is limited oversight. Given the challenges, many corporations have begun implementing a range of technical controls to ensure security of their own infrastructures rather than rely on the vendors.

In addressing the security challenges in outsourcing relationships or for that matter any kind of a risk, management of client-vendor relationship has been argued as important. Earlier studies on outsourcing have mainly discussed different phases of client-vendor relationships and the relevant issues in each of the phases [7]. For example, *Relationship Structuring* involves issues deemed important when the outsourcing contract is being prepared, *Relationship Building* involves issues that contribute to the strengthening of relationship between client and vendor, and *Relationship Management* involves issues that are relevant to drive the relationship in the right direction. Another study lists 25 independent variables that can impact the relationship between outsourcing client and vendor [18]. The most cited factors include effective knowledge sharing, cultural distance, trust, prior relationship status, and communication.

Studies related to secure outsourcing have been few and far between. In majority of the cases the emphasis has been on contractual aspects of the relationship between the client and the vendor. And many researchers have made calls for clarity in contracts as well as selective outsourcing [17]. Managing the IT function as a value center [36] has also been proposed as a way for ensuring success of outsourcing arrangements. There is no doubt that prior research has made significant contribution to the manner in which advantages can be achieved from outsourcing relationships, however there has been limited contribution with respect to management of security and privacy.

Internet Security has been considered as one of the technological risks [15], with data confidentiality, integrity and availability as the topmost concerns in an outsourcing arrangement [16]. While a few surveys report computer networks, regulations and personnel as the highest security threats to organizations [4], others recognize that not only technical, but also non-technical threats can be detrimental to an engagement [4], [8], and [28]. However, most of the work cited under the domain of IS outsourcing risks is generic and has a very limited focus on security [10], and [31]. Several researchers have provided frameworks to identify organizational assets at risk and to use financial metrics to determine priority of assets that need protection [3], and [27]. Research on security threats prevalent in an outsourcing or offshore environment and risk management models has also been undertaken [5]. The political, cultural and legal differences between supplier and provider environment are supposed to make the environment less favorable for operators. A multi-layer security model to mitigate

---

[1] http://www.gao.gov/assets/260/251282.pdf. Accessed January 29, 2013.

the security risks, both at technical and nontechnical level, in outsourcing domains is presented by Doomun [9], where eleven steps in an outsourcing arrangement are divided across three layers of security: identification, monitoring and improvement, and measurement.

Wei and Blake [37] provide a comprehensive list of information security risk factors and corresponding safeguards for IT offshore outsourcing. More recently, Nassimbeni et al [23] categorized the security risks into three phases: strategic planning, supplier selection and contracting, implementation and monitoring. In both the studies the issues have mainly been borrowed from existing literature. Some of the researchers have also classified the risks as external and internal threats to an organization and human and non-human risks. Non-technical concerns such as employees, regulations, and trust have emerged to be more severe than technological risks [21], [29], [34], and [35]. As such few studies are concerned with a specific type of security concern such as policies [11].

While the prevalent IT outsourcing research has certainly helped in better understanding the client-vendor relationships, an aspect that has largely remained unexplored is that of organizational *fit*. In the IT strategy domain organization fit has been explored in terms of alignment between IT strategy and business strategy [13]. In the strategy literature it has been studied in terms of the fit between an organization's structure and its strategy. Even though Livari [20] made a call for understanding organizational fit of information systems with the environment, little progress has been made to date.

With respect to IT outsourcing the notion of the fit between a client and vendor has also not been well studied. It is suggested that fit can be understood through the elements of congruence theory, which explains the interactions among organizational environment, values, structure, process and reaction-adjustment [24]. Based on congruence theory, an *outsourcing environment* thus can be defined as the existence of any condition such as culture, regulations, provider/supplier capabilities, security, and competence that can determine the success of an outsourcing arrangement. Organizational values determine the acceptable and unacceptable behavior. In this respect factors such as trust, transparency and ethics fall under the value system of an organization. Structure of an outsourcing arrangement defines the factors such as reporting hierarchy, ownership and processes for communication. Additionally reaction-adjustments are required, which entail the feedback and outcomes of an engagement and the related modifying strategy in response to the reactions of clients for a better strategic fit and alliance between outsourcing clients and vendors.

Clearly the existing literature on identification and mitigation of security risks is rich. The security risks at technical, human and regulatory levels are well identified; many of the studies highlight that non-technical risks are more severe than the technical ones. However, the literature is short of two perspectives: **First**, gap analysis of how outsourcing clients and outsourcing vendors perceive the security risks. **Second**, the existing literature does not discuss much about the congruence among different concepts in an outsourcing arrangement, particularly in the security domain. Hence to determine a fit between vendors and clients, we need to understand as to what security issues are important to each of them and then to establish a basis for their congruence.

3   Research Methodology

Given that the purpose of this study was to identify security concerns amongst out-sourcing clients and vendors, a two-phased approach was adopted. In the first instance a Delphi study was undertaken. This helped us in identifying the major security issues as perceived by the clients and the vendors. In the second phase an in depth analysis of clients and vendors was undertaken. This helped us in understanding the reasons for significant differences in their perceptions.

3.1   Phase 1 – A Delphi Study

To ensure a reliable and validated list of issues that are of concern to the organizations, both from client and vendor perspective, a process to inquire and seek the divergent opinions of different experts is provisioned. A ranking method based on Schmidt's Delphi methodology, designed to elicit the opinions of panel of experts through controlled inquiry and feedback, is employed [32]. Delphi study allowed factors to converge to the ones that really are important in secure outsourcing.

Panel Demographics
To account for varying experiences, and role of experts, both outsourcing vendors or providers and outsourcing clients or suppliers were chosen as the target panelists. A total of 11 panelists were drawn from the pool of 21 prospective participants. We identified senior IS executives from major corporations and asked them to identify the most useful and experienced people to participate in the survey. The participants were divided into two groups –*Outsourcing Providers (5)* and *Outsourcing Suppliers (6)*. The panelists had impressive and varied experiences in IT outsourcing and management. The number of panelists suffices the requirement of eliciting diverse opinions and prevents the panelists from being intimidated with the volume of feedback [32]. Moreover, the comparative size of the two panels is irrelevant since it doesn't have any impact on response analysis. For detecting statistically significant results, the group size is dependent on the group dynamics rather than the number of participants; therefore, 10 to 11 experts is a good sample size [26].

Data Collection
The data collection phase is informed by Schmidt's method, which divides the study into three major phases [32]. The first round - brainstorming or blank sheet round - was conducted to elicit as many issues as possible from each panelist. Each participant was asked to provide at least 6 issues along with a short description. The authors collated the issues by removing duplicates. The combined list was sent to panelists explaining why certain items were removed and further asked the panelists for their opinion on the integrity and uniformity of the list. In the second round we asked each panelist to pare down the list to most important issues. A total of 26 issues were identified which were sent to the panelists for further evaluation, addition, deletions and /or verification. This is to ensure that a common set of issues is provided for the panelists to rank in subsequent rounds. Ranking of the final 26 issues was done in

phase 3. During this phase each panelist was required to rank the issues in order of importance with 1 being the most important security issue and 26 being the least important security issue in outsourcing. The panelists were restricted to have the ties between two or more issues.

Multiple ranking rounds were conducted until a consensus was achieved. To avoid bias a randomly ordered set of issues was sent to each panelist in the first ranking round. For the subsequent rounds, the lists were ordered by average ranks. In this study we used Kendall's Coefficient of Concordance W to evaluate the level of agreement among respondents' opinions in a given round. According to Schmidt [32], 'W' can range between 0.1 (very weak agreement) and 0.9 (unusually strong agreement). Moreover, Spearman's Rank Correlation Coefficient rho is used to evaluate the level of stability of the panel's opinion between two successive rounds and between two different groups of respondents in a given round. The value of rho can range between -1 (perfect negative correlation) and 1 (perfect positive correlation) Subsequent ranking rounds are stopped either if Kendall's Coefficient of Concordance W indicated a strong consensus (>0.7) or if the level of consensus leveled off in two successive rounds.

At the end of every ranking round, five important pieces of feedback were sent to panelists: (1) mean rank for each issue; (2) level of agreement in terms of Kendall's W; (3) Spearman correlation rho; (4) P-value; (5) relevant comments by the panelists

Data Analysis
The analysis of the results was performed in two parts: First, an analysis of aggregated Delphi study treats all respondents as a global panel and thus presents the unified ranking results. Second, an analysis of partitioned Delphi study presents the ranking results based on respondents group, i.e. outsourcing providers and outsourcing clients.

3.2   Phase 2 - Probing for Congruence

The second round of data collection was based on two workshops with representatives from Fortune 500 companies. There were 11 individuals with an average of 8 years of work experience who participated in these workshops. The workshops were conducted from May 2012 to July 2012. In the first workshop, each participant was required to answer three questions for all 26 issues. Suitable probes were added following each question. This helped in developing a rich insight. The probes were:

1.   What do you think about the issue?
2.   Why do you think it is important for outsourcing provider?
3.   Why do you think it is important for outsourcing client?

The second workshop was concentrated to achieve congruence between outsourcing suppliers and outsourcing providers. Different ranks assigned by clients and vendors to particular issues were highlighted. The participants were asked to answer two questions so as to elicit their opinions on the gaps identified in the ranking sought by clients and providers for the issues.

1. Explain what do you think is the reason for assigning different ranks by outsourcing clients and outsourcing providers?
2. Explain what can be done to resolve the difference in order to seek a common ground of understanding between clients and providers?

4　Findings from the Delphi Study

For phase one, the results were analyzed from a global or aggregated view and partitioned or client vs. vendor view. The global panel reached a weak consensus by third ranking round (see table 1).

Table 1. Global Consensus

Round	W (Clients * Provider)	Rho
1	0.342(p<0.001)	
2	0.279(p<0.001)	0.568 (p<0.01)
3	0.102(p<0.727)	0.497 (p=0.01)

On the other hand, by the third ranking round, Clients had fair agreement whereas vendors had very weak agreement. Moreover, a weak positive correlation exists between round 2 and round 3 in global ranking as well as between clients and providers by round 3 (see table 2).

Table 2. Client and Vendor Consensus

Round	Clients' W	Providers' W	Rho
1	0.349(p=0.0121)	0.522(p<0.001)	0.374
2	0.486(p<0.001)	0.266(p=0.0297)	0.479
3	0.569(p=0.287)	0.100(p=0.94)	0.119

The weak consensus in global ranking clearly suggests that outsourcing clients and outsourcing vendors have conflict of interest. Moreover, the weak consensus within vendors indicates that not all vendors perceive the importance of security at same level. And finally the difference between ranks assigned to each issue by clients and vendors further highlights the conflict of interest between the two. Table 3 presents a comparison of the ranks from client and vendor perspectives and shows a significant divide between the two groups. The issues are sorted compositely; however, given the significant difference for most of the issues, the composite rank is irrelevant. For this paper we assume a difference of more than three, between the ranks sought by client and vendors, as significant. Thereby, a total of 16 issues out of 26 show significant difference between the rankings of two groups

Table 3. Comparison of Client and Vendor ranks (only significant issue are presented)

Rank of the issue	Issue Description	Client Rank	Vendor Rank
2	Comprehensiveness of information security outsourcing decision analysis	7	2
3	Information security competency of outsourcing vendor	8	1
5	Ability of outsourcing vendor to comply with client's security policies, standards and processes	2	10
7	Dissipation of outsourcing vendor's knowledge	10	3
8	Technical complexity of outsourcing client's information security operations	13	5
9	Trust that outsourcing vendor applies appropriate security controls	1	20
10	Diversity of jurisdictions and laws	4	17
12	Information security credibility of outsourcing vendor	15	9
13	Quality of outsourcing vendor's staff	18	6
14	Legal and judicial framework of outsourcing vendor's environment	9	16
15	Inability to redevelop competencies on information security	19	11
17	Audit of outsourcing vendor staffing process	20	12
18	Inability to change information security requirements	12	22
20	Transparency of outsourcing vendor billing	14	24
21	Audit of outsourced information security operations	25	14

5   Reviewing Congruence Amongst Issues

It is interesting to note that there is a significant difference in the client and vendor perspectives of the top secure outsourcing issues. In this section we explore these issues further to develop a better understanding. In terms of managing security of outsourcing it makes sense to develop a fit between what the clients and the vendors consider important.

Two issues that seem to be of significant concern for both the clients and the vendors is of *diversity of laws* and the *legal and judicial framework of the vendor's environment*. Both these concerns are indeed noteworthy. Our discussions with a CIO of a major bank in the US, which has outsourced significant amount of IT services to India, suggest jurisdictional issues to be a major concern. The CIO noted:

> I can say with absolute certainty that our outsourcing experience has been very positive. We found significantly high level of competence in our vendor. However there are constant challenges of dealing with the regulatory environment. Laws in the US are rather strict in terms of disclosure and we feel that to be an impediment to getting our work done.

The literature has reported similar concerns, albeit with respect to mainstream outsourcing issues rather than security. It has been argued that there are issues of conformance and contractual violations, which can have a detrimental impact on outsourcing relationships [28]. It is interesting to note though that both issues 10 and 14 rank higher amongst the clients than the vendors. It seems that regulatory compliance and prevalence of a judicial framework is more of a concern to the outsourcing clients than the vendors. Another IT manager in our study commented:

> Increased transparency regarding the laws governing the vendor may mitigate the risk for the client. However, the burden is on the vendor to reassure the client that the risk is minimal. Therefore the vendor should be supplying as much information to reassure the client that they are working under the same legal context and that their legal agreements are mutually beneficial.

In the literature several calls have been made that suggest clarity of legal and regulatory frameworks (e.g. [30]). Beyond clarity however there is a need to work on aligning the legal and regulatory frameworks at a national level. Country specific institutions shall play a critical role ensuring such alignment (e.g. NASSCOM in India). To better mitigate the risks and to ensure that the interest of both parties is secure, increased transparency in legal structure is required. The burden lies on the provider though. Therefore the vendor should be making available as much information to reassure the client that they are working under the same legal context and that their legal agreements are mutually beneficial. As a principle we therefore propose:

Principle 1 - Reducing the diversity of laws and ensuring congruence of legislative controls ensure security in outsourcing.

Another issue, *dissipation of outsourcing vendors knowledge,* emerged to be significant. While this issue seems more critical for the vendors, there are some significant implications for client firms as well. Vendors believe that because of the untoward need to comply with the whims and fancies for the clients, there is usually a dissipation of the knowledge over a period of time. One of the members of our intensive study was the country head for a large Indian outsourcing vendor. When asked to comment of this issue, he said:

> The outsourcing industry has a serious problem. While we have our own business processes, we usually have to recreate or reconfigure them based on our client needs and wants. We are usually rather happy to do so. However in the process we lose our tacit knowledge. From our perspective it is important to ensure protection of this knowledge. Many of our security and privacy concerns would be managed if we get a little better in knowledge management.

Perhaps Willcocks et al [39] are among the few researchers who have studied the importance of protection of intellectual property. Most of the emphasis has however been on protecting loss of intellectual property – largely of the client firm. Management of knowledge to protect tacit knowledge has also been studied in the literature (e.g. see [1], [25]), though rarely in connection with outsourcing.

It goes without saying that poor knowledge management structures will disappoint the prospects of procuring of new contracts. In comparison, the clients seem to either assume that the provider has a sustainable structure that prevents or minimizes the loss of intellectual capital and ensures confidentiality, or the client is ready to bear the risk for the perceived potential benefits. Clients expect skilled resources as a contractual requirement. As the risk for clients is minimal, they rank this in less importance in comparison to the vendor. Existing literature mentions that for the better management of expectations, both clients and suppliers need to understand the utility of knowledge management, implications of loss and structural requirement [39]. This is also reflected in the comments of one of security assurance manager:

> Suppliers need to minimize staff turnover and find ways to ensure staff retention and knowledge sharing. There are many methods to achieve this; such as better wages, benefits, flex time, encouragement, knowledge repositories, education opportunities, etc. They should pair veteran staff member with new staff members to improve their understanding of confidentiality, integrity and availability.

As a principle we therefore propose:

Principle 2 Tacit knowledge management and ensuring the integrity of vendor business processes, is a pre-requisite for good and secure outsourcing.

Our research also found *information security competency of outsourcing vendor* as a significant issue. Many scholars have commented on the importance of vendor competence [12], [19], [38]. It is argued that value based outsourcing outcome should be generated and transferred from the vendor to the client [19]. However, as is indicative from our study, clients and vendors differ in their opinions on what is most important when selecting and promoting outsourcing security services. While, vendors often believe that proving their competency through a large list of certifications, awards, and large clientele is important to have to prove their competency, the client's perspective is geared towards the application and utilization of supplier competency. One of the IT managers from a bank noted:

> The vendor is expected to be competent in their area of expertise, so the client needs to make clear to the vendor that a basic expectation should not be at the top of their list as there are more important factors that will be used to differentiate the vendors from one another.

As is rightly pointed out by the IT Manager, the issue with managing competence is not to present a baseline of what the vendor knows (i.e. the skill set), but a demonstration of the *know-that* (see [6]). Assessment of competence is outwardly driven and hence a presentation of some sort of maturity in security management is essential (e.g. ISO 21827). As a principle we propose:

Principle 3 - A competence in ensuring secure outsourcing is to develop an ability to define individual know-how and know-that.

Process is a formalized sequence of actions guided "informally" by the organization's structure and organization's value system. There is enough evidence in the literature about the impact of process standardization on outsourcing success [40]. However, the variations in the ranks of one of the issues identified - *ability of outsourcing vendor to comply with client's security policies, standards and processes* – is a cause of concern. The issue here is indicative of the need for facilitating communication and coordination required for the alignment of policies, standards and processes guiding information security in an outsourcing engagement. Clients certainly place high importance on its own policies and processes, giving this issue a higher rank. Meanwhile, providers view their policies, procedures, and standards as being best-in-class. Clearly the vendors seem to be ignorant of the fact that having a process framework that is not customizable to the individual requirements of different clients can be a potential hindrance. As one of the client notes:

> It is great that a company can claim they are competent in providing outsourced information security but it means nothing to the client unless the client perceives their specific policies as being effectively applied by the provider.

To eliminate the gap, processes and policies need to be comprehensive enough and the contracts need to emphasize the implications of non-compliance. For the sake of continued alliance, the responsibility lies more on vendor to ensure process compliance and governance. Another manager from a client organization commented:

> Clients are usually outsourcing to relieve their workload and performing a comprehensive analysis is viewed as adding to the existing workload they are trying to relieve. The more a potential supplier is willing to be an active partner and point out the pros and cons of their own proposals as well as the others, the smaller the gap will be.

As a principle, we propose:

Principle 4 - Establishing congruence between client and vendor security policies ensures protection of information resources and a good working arrangement between the client and the vendor.

If leveraging the core competency of suppliers is the main motive to outsource security operations, the lower ranking by clients for the issue - *audit of outsourced information security operations* - is justified. Clients expect competency of the outsourcing vendor to be in place. However, clients also seem to lack consensus on the need for continued monitoring and governance procedures. Auditing is one of the means for the client to verify whether the vendor is adhering to the security policies. Vendors by virtue of providing a higher rank in comparison to clients, appear to be aware of the importance of proving continued compliance with agreements. Providing audited or auditable information relating to the clients data and processes is a must for establishing trust. Much of the research in IS outsourcing has focused on different dimensions of governance procedures including contractual and non-contractual mechanisms of trust building [22]. Auditing and third party assurance, which leads to increased trust (see issues 4 and 9 in our study), typically do not seem to be touched upon.

A related issue (and also connected to principle 4 above) is that of a competence audit. Any audit of vendor operations must include several aspects including - overall competence in information security (issue 15 in our study) and quality of vendor staff (issue 13). Our research subjects reported several instances where there was a general loss of competence over a period of time. This usually occurs when either the vendor organization gets too entrenched with one client and hence overlooking the needs of the other or when internal processes are patched and reconfigured in a reactive manner to ensure compliance with the expectations of a given client (refer to issue 5 in our study). One Chief Information Security Officer from a healthcare organization commented:

> There seems to be this half-life of a security competence. I have seen that after a contract has been signed, there is a somewhat exponential decay in quality.

In the literature there is some mention of such decay in quality, although not directly in relation to outsourcing (e.g. see [33]). It is found that in many of the quality improvement initiatives can interact with prevailing systems and routines to undercut commitment to continuous improvement. While our research does not suggest this to be the case in terms of secure outsourcing, the difference in opinions between the clients and the vendors seem indicative. As a principle we therefore propose:

Principle 5 - An internal audit of both client and vendor operations is critical to understand current weaknesses and potential problems there might be with respect to information security structures, procedures and capabilities.

Based on our research, two major constructs seem to emerge – *strategic context* of secure outsourcing and *organizational capability* in outsourcing (Fig.1). The strategic context is defined by legal/regulatory congruence and security policy alignment. In our research organizational capability is a function of knowledge management, competence and audit. Combined together, our constructs define security congruence.

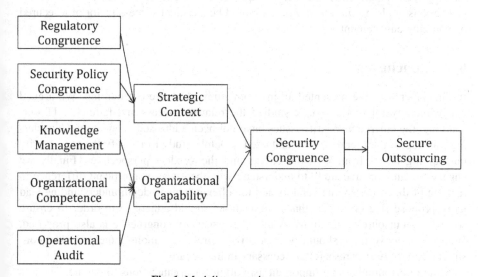

Fig. 1. Modeling security congruence

The level of congruence however can only be assessed through outcome measures (e.g. secure outsourcing). Such outcome measures could include reduced incidents of security breaches, high ranks from external vetting organizations etc.

A central theme in organization strategy literature is that of "fit". Findings from our research seem to be in resonance with that body of work. For instance, and as noted previously, Nightingale and Toulouse [24] comment on the mutual interaction amongst values, structure, process, reaction-adjustment and environment leads to the congruent organization.

In the context of security of information resources, the need to develop a fit between outsourcing partners seems to be appropriate. Significant variations in the rankings on part of vendors raise some doubts: if they value the sensitivity of client data; if they ensure adequate protection of the assets; if the vendor is aware of the vulnerabilities in their processes. All these issues would also raise concern about the attitude of the client, particularly in relation to shunning responsibilities. This can indeed be a classic example of strife between factions of affordability and availability.

In order to achieve the congruence between clients and vendors, the discussion so far leads to the emergence of one main theme - *managing expectations*. In the purview of congruence theory this requires elimination of gaps between the two parties and eventually align the two organizations (in our case, around strategy and capability as per Fig.1). Fig.1 provides a conceptual design of such an aligned organization. For better management of expectations, the supplier and vendor organizations need to communicate and coordinate their respective operations.

Both the organizations align to the required dimensions and in effect overtime the two organizations involved in an outsourcing contract appear to be one "virtual" organization, which has just one goal - delivering services in a secure manner (i.e. secure outsourcing). As long as a gap exists in processes, structure or values between the two organizations, the alignment is questionable. The time taken by the two organizations to align - *alignment latency* would be a critical success factor of a secured outsourcing engagement.

6   Conclusion

In this paper we have presented an in depth study of secure outsourcing. We argued that while several scholars have studied the relative success and failure of IT outsourcing, the emergent security issues have not been addressed adequately. Considering this gap in the literature we conducted a Delphi study to identify the top security outsourcing issues from both the clients and the vendors perspectives. Finally we engaged in an intensive study to understand why there was a significant difference in ranking of the issues by the vendors and the clients. This in depth understanding lead us to propose five principles that organizations should adhere to in order to ensure security of outsourcing relations. A model for security congruence is also proposed. While we believe there should be a positive correlation amongst the proposed constructs, clearly further research is necessary in this regard.

Secure outsourcing is an important aspiration for organizations to pursue. There is no doubt that many businesses thrive on getting part of their operations taken care of by a vendor. It not only makes business sense to do so, but it also allows enterprises to tap into the expertise that may reside elsewhere. Security then is simply a means to ensure smooth running of the business. And definition of the pertinent issues allows us to strategically plan secure outsourcing relationships.

References

[1] Arora, A.: Contracting for tacit knowledge: the provision of technical services in technology licensing contracts. Journal of Development Economics 50(2), 233–256 (1996)

[2] Barthelemy, J.: The hidden costs of IT outsourcing. MIT Sloan Management Review 42(3), 60–69 (2001)

[3] Bojanc, R., Jerman-Blažič, B.: An economic modelling approach to information security risk management. International Journal of Information Management 28(5), 413–422 (2008)

[4] Chang, A.J.T., Yeh, Q.J.: On security preparations against possible IS threats across industries. Information Management & Computer Security 14(4), 343–360 (2006)

[5] Colwill, C., Gray, A.: Creating an effective security risk model for outsourcing decisions. BT Technology Journal 25(1), 79–87 (2007)

[6] Dhillon, G.: Organizational competence in harnessing IT: a case study. Information & Management 45(5), 297–303 (2008)

[7] Dibbern, J., Goles, T., Hirschheim, R., Jayatilaka, B.: Information systems outsourcing: a survey and analysis of the literature. ACM SIGMIS Database 35(4), 6–102 (2004)

[8] Dlamini, M.T., Eloff, J.H., Eloff, M.M.: Information security: The moving target. Computers & Security 28(3), 189–198 (2009)

[9] Doomun, M.R.: Multi-level information system security in outsourcing domain. Business Process Management Journal 14(6), 849–857 (2008)

[10] Earl, M.J.: The risks of outsourcing IT. Sloan Management Review 37, 26–32 (1996)

[11] Fulford, H., Doherty, N.F.: The application of information security policies in large UK-based organizations: an exploratory investigation. Information Management & Computer Security 11(3), 106–114 (2003)

[12] Goles, T.: The Impact of Client-Vendor Relationship on Outsourcing Success. University of Houston, Houston (2001)

[13] Henderson, J.C., Venkatraman, N.: Strategic alignment: leveraging information technology for transforming organisations. IBM Systems Journal 32(1), 4–16 (1993)

[14] Kaiser, K.M., Hawk, S.: Evolution of offshore software development: From outsourcing to cosourcing. MIS Quarterly Executive 3(2), 69–81 (2004)

[15] Kern, T., Willcocks, L.P., Lacity, M.C.: Application service provision: Risk assessment and mitigation. MIS Quarterly Executive 1(2), 113–126 (2002)

[16] Khalfan, A.M.: Information security considerations in IS/IT outsourcing projects: a descriptive case study of two sectors. International Journal of Information Management 24(1), 29–42 (2004)

[17] Lacity, M.C., Willcocks, L.P.: An Empirical Investigation of Information Technology Sourcing Practices: Lessons from Experience. MIS Quarterly 22(3), 363–408 (1998)

[18] Lacity, M.C., Khan, S., Yan, A., Willcocks, L.P.: A review of the IT outsourcing empirical literature and future research directions. Journal of Information Technology 25(4), 395–433 (2010)

[19] Levina, N., Ross, J.W.: From the vendor's perspective: exploring the value proposition in information technology outsourcing. MIS Quarterly, 331–364 (2003)

[20] Livari, J.: The organizational fit of information systems. Information Systems Journal 2(1), 3–29 (1992)

[21] Loch, K.D., Carr, H.H., Warkentin, M.E.: Threats to information systems: today's reality, yesterday's understanding. MIS Quarterly, 173–186 (1992)

[22] Miranda, S.M., Kavan, C.B.: Moments of governance in IS outsourcing: conceptualizing effects of contracts on value capture and creation. Journal of Information Technology 20(3), 152–169 (2005)

[23] Nassimbeni, G., Sartor, M., Dus, D.: Security risks in service offshoring and outsourcing. Industrial Management & Data Systems 112(3), 4–4 (2012)

[24] Nightingale, D.V., Toulouse, J.M.: Toward a multilevel congruence theory of organization. Administrative Science Quarterly, 264–280 (1977)

[25] Norman, P.M.: Protecting knowledge in strategic alliances: Resource and relational characteristics. The Journal of High Technology Management Research 13(2), 177–202 (2002)

[26] Okoli, C., Pawlowski, S.D.: The Delphi method as a research tool: an example, design considerations and applications. Information & Management 42(1), 15–29 (2004)

[27] Osei-Bryson, K.-M., Ngwenyama, O.K.: Managing risks in information systems outsourcing: an approach to analyzing outsourcing risks and structuring incentive contracts. European Journal of Operational Research 174(1), 245–264 (2006)

[28] Pai, A.K., Basu, S.: Offshore technology outsourcing: overview of management and legal issues. Business Process Management Journal 13(1), 21–46 (2007)

[29] Posthumus, S., Von Solms, R.: A framework for the governance of information security. Computers & Security 23(8), 638–646 (2004)

[30] Raghu, T.: Cyber-security policies and legal frameworks governing Business Process and IT Outsourcing arrangements. Paper Presented at the Indo-US Conference on Cyber-Security, Cyber-Crime & Cyber Forensics (2009)

[31] Sakthivel, S.: Managing risk in offshore systems development. Communications of the ACM 50(4), 69–75 (2007)

[32] Schmidt, R.C.: Managing Delphi surveys using nonparametric statistical techniques. Decision Sciences 28(3), 763–774 (1997)

[33] Sterman, J.D., Repenning, N.P., Kofman, F.: Unanticipated side effects of successful quality programs: Exploring a paradox of organizational improvement. Management Science 43(4), 503–521 (1997)

[34] Tickle, I.: Data integrity assurance in a layered security strategy. Computer Fraud & Security 2002(10), 9–13 (2002)

[35] Tran, E., Atkinson, M.: Security of personal data across national borders. Information Management & Computer Security 10(5), 237–241 (2002)

[36] Venkatraman, N.: Beyond outsourcing: managing IT resources as a value center. Sloan Management Review 38(3), 51–64 (1997)

[37] Wei, Y., Blake, M.: Service-oriented computing and cloud computing: Challenges and opportunities. IEEE Internet Computing 14(6), 72–75 (2010)

[38] Willcocks, L., Lacity, M.C.: Relationships in IT Outsourcing: A Stakeholder Perspective. In: Zmud, R. (ed.) Framing the Domains of IT Management, pp. 355–384. Pinnaflex Inc., Ohio (2000)

[39] Willcocks, L., Hindle, J., Feeny, D., Lacity, M.: IT and business process outsourcing: The knowledge potential. Information Systems Management 21(3), 7–15 (2004)

[40] Wüllenweber, K., Beimborn, D., Weitzel, T., König, W.: The impact of process standardization on business process outsourcing success. Information Systems Frontiers 10(2), 211–224 (2008)

Performance Analysis of File Carving Tools

Thomas Laurenson

Department of Information Science, School of Business,
University of Otago. Dunedin, New Zealand
thomas@thomaslaurenson.com

Abstract. File carving is the process of recovering files based on the contents of a file in scenarios where file system metadata is unavailable. In this research a total of 6 file carving tools were tested and reviewed to evaluate the performance quality of each. Comparison of findings to a previous similar study was conducted and showed variable performance advances. A new file carving data set was also authored and testing determined that the wider variety of file types and structures proved challenging for most tools to efficiently recover a high percentage of files. Results also highlighted the ongoing issue with complete recovery and reassembly of fragmented files. Future research is required to provide digital forensic investigators & data recovery practitioners with efficient and accurate file carving tools to maximise file recovery and minimise invalid file output.

Keywords: File Carving, Data Recovery, Digital Forensics.

1 Introduction

File carving is a particularly powerful technique because computer files can be recovered from raw data regardless of the type of file system, and file retrieval is possible even if the file system metadata has been completely destroyed [1]. The process therefore provides additional data recovery methods to augment digital investigation where existing traditional data recovery techniques are not suitable or have been unsuccessful. Scenarios where file carving is exceptionally useful is when recovering data and files that have previously been deleted, extracting files from the unallocated space of a digital data storage device, and in cases when a storage device or a file system has been damaged or corrupted.

Previous research has advanced file carving techniques and algorithms resulting in newer state-of-the-art file recovery methods. Specifically, the Digital Forensic Research Workshop (DFRWS) conference promoted file carving techniques and tools by issuing a Forensic Challenge in 2006[1] and, again, in 2007[2]. The contests greatly extended file carving knowledge resulting in the discovery of new carving techniques and the release of associated tools.

---

[1] http://www.dfrws.org/2006/challenge/
[2] http://www.dfrws.org/2007/challenge/

L.J. Janczewski, H.B. Wolfe, and S. Shenoi (Eds.): SEC 2013, IFIP AICT 405, pp. 419–433, 2013.
© IFIP International Federation for Information Processing 2013

Additionally, academic research has also contributed towards the improvement of file carving techniques, such as increasing file carving speed using GPUs [2], advanced file structure carving for binary file types [3], and multimedia files [4]. Furthermore, methods have also been developed for scenarios including carving network packets; e.g. IP packets from forensic images [5] and carving file objects from memory dumps [6]. Advanced file carving techniques have also been investigated including *in-place* file carving to reduce storage space and processing time [7] and recovery and re-assembly of fragmented JPEG files [8].

1.1 Problem

Digital Forensics is a relatively new discipline which presents numerous challenges for researchers and practitioners alike. Unfortunately, current research intended for forensic applications often has little or no impact, because in many instances the researchers are poorly acquainted with the *real-world* digital forensic problems encountered and the practical constraints frequently placed on investigators [9]. The solution is to conduct research which is *investigator-centric* with the aim of providing findings of practical usefulness lessening the gap between academic research and requisite real-world investigation tools and techniques. Furthermore, the targets of investigations are increasing in size and complexity [10]. Practitioners need informed results to confidently identify the correct tool for a specific scenario in order to decrease the overall case processing time while also maintaining investigation integrity.

File carving can be a difficult and complex process which is further complicated by the variety of available tools. Many forensic investigators are unaware of the capabilities and/or the limitations of the various file carving tools. Despite targeted active research a number of problems still exist for the professional digital forensic investigator or data recovery practitioner: which file carving tools provide the best performance in regards to *1)* the percentage of files recovered; *2)* the correctness and reliability of tool output; and *3)* the processing speed of the tool.

This paper aims to provide digital forensic practitioners with practical information and recommendations to assist in reliable and thorough implementation of file carving techniques. An additional goal is to identify current weaknesses in file carving techniques and tools so that future research areas can be targeted for technology advancement.

1.2 Structure

Firstly, the basics of file carving is described in order to understand the subject matter. A tool testing methodology is then outlined including data sets, performance measurements and a thorough testing procedure. Carving tool results from the testing phase are reviewed and findings are discussed. Finally, conclusions are drawn and areas for future research are suggested.

2 File Carving

File carving seeks to recover files based on content, irrespective of supporting file system metadata being available. The following subsections include a detailed summary of the various file structures, established file carving techniques and the associated file carving tools used by investigators to recover files in digital investigations.

2.1 File Structure

The structure of data in computer based systems is controlled by the file system allowing users the facility of long-term storage and retrieval of data in a hierarchy of files and directories [11]. Fig. 1 displays the 3 major types of file structures encountered: contiguous, fragmented and partial files. Embedded files are also discussed in this section.

Contiguous Files: A file is said to be *contiguous* when the data held in the file is stored in blocks in a logical order of sequence on the storage medium. The file is therefore stored in a single fragment occupying sequential file system clusters. A contiguous file (*FileA*) is shown in Fig. 1, which occupies 3 consecutive blocks spanning from block 4 to 6.

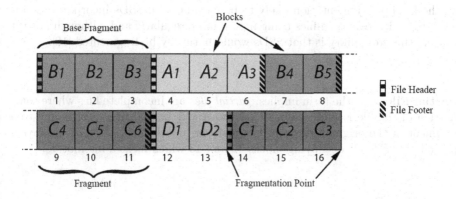

Fig. 1. A simplified diagram displaying various file structures where each square represents a single storage block. A contiguous (*File A*), linear fragmented (*File B*), non-linear fragmented (*File C*) and partial (*File D*) file structures are illustrated, where each block of a file is numbered consecutively (e.g. N_1, N_2 ... N_n). A base-fragment, file fragment and file fragmentation points are also displayed. (Source: Figure adapted from [8] and [12]).

Fragmented Files: A file is *fragmented* when one or more chunks of the file are not stored in a sequential order and, thus, are comprised of two or more fragments separated from each other by an unknown number of clusters [12]. As files are added, deleted or modified the structure of a file system becomes divided and files may not be stored on consecutive clusters. Fragmentation in hard disks is therefore a result of the file system's allocation strategy, usually to optimise techniques such as fast file access and increased storage efficiency [13].

Fragmented files have a variety of different forms. However, files with 2 fragments, known as *bifragmented*, have been recognised as being the most common [14]. Fragmented files can be found in a linear and non-linear structure[3] depending on where the separate fragments are stored on the file system. Fig. 1 displays a linear fragmented file (*File B*) stored on a total of 5 blocks, separated by 3 blocks which are occupied by *File A*. The base-fragment of *File B* occupies blocks 1 to 3. For comparison, a non-linear fragmented file (*File C*) is also shown, stored on a total of 6 blocks. The base-fragment of this file occupies blocks 14 to 16 while the second fragment occupies blocks 9 to 11.

The issue of file fragmentation and the potential occurrence in actual investigations is debated among digital forensic researchers and professionals. Analysis of 324 second-hand hard drives showed that a total of 6% of all files recovered were fragmented [14]. Additionally, of all the fragmented files approximately 47% were discovered to be bifragmented. Although 6% seems a relatively small amount in general, it is highly significant that file types of forensic interest (e.g. AVI, DOC, JPG and PST) had considerably higher fragmentations than file types of little interest (e.g. BMP, HLP, INF and INI).

The availability and uptake of Solid State Drives (SSD) also has an impact on the level of fragmentation likely to be encountered. SSDs incorporate wear-levelling which results in files being moved more regularly and, although not yet proven, the probability is that SSDs would naturally be fragmented [12].

Partial Files: As the term implies, *partial files* are incomplete files where some portion of the file is unavailable. The reason why partial files exist is due to a fragment of the original file being overwritten by other data. Fig. 1 displays a partial file (*File D*) occupying blocks 12 and 13 which lacks a file footer.

Embedded Files: When the contents of one file are added or stored in another file it is known as an *embedded file*. A common example is a JPEG image embedded within a Microsoft Word document or files embedded in an archive file; e.g. ZIP files. Embedded files can be contiguous, fragmented or partial depending on the scenario.

---

[3] Linear and non-linear fragmented files are also commonly referred to as sequential and non-sequential fragmentation files respectively.

2.2   File Carving Techniques

Previous research has identified various methods to perform file carving. An overview is provided outlining selected file carving techniques including header-based, file structure and block-based carving, as well as the role of file validation in the file carving process.

Header-Based Carving: Files have unique headers, also known as magic numbers or file signatures. These unique values can be used to help identify the beginning of a file and aid in carving files without the corresponding metadata. *Header-footer carving* is the most basic carving technique which searches data for patterns that mark a distinct header (start of file marker) and footer (end of file marker) [15]. The process is achieved by extracting all data contained within the headers and footers and copying that data into an external file.

An alternative header-based carving technique is *header-maximum size carving*. When a header is discovered (with no footer value available), the maximum carve size is used to calculate how far away from the header the end of the file might be [1]. As some file types can vary dramatically in size, this technique can have varying results and can also increase the size needed to store recovered files. However, it remains a viable approach because many file formats (e.g. JPEG, MP3) are not affected if additional data is appended to the end of a valid file [14]. Another header-based carving technique is *header-embedded length carving*. Some file formats have internal file information which specifies the length, or size, of the file and provides an identified point for the footer of the file [13].

File Structure Carving: Another file carving technique is based on the internal structure of a file, where specific knowledge of the contents can help reconstruct the original file. *File structure carving* is primarily aimed towards assembling fragmented files, where header-based carving fails to reconstruct multiple file fragments. An example is semantic carvers (also known as deep carvers) which use information about the internal file structure to control the carving process in some way [13].

Block-Based Carving: An advanced carving technique is *block-based carving* which calculates meta information of the content of a data block; for example, by implementing character counts or calculating statistical information [15]. The premise is that computer systems use fixed block sizes (sectors) for storing data (usually 512 bytes) and file carvers can examine every block for every file type definition [16].

File Validation: The method of *file validation* is an integral aspect of the file carving process. Validation provides the confirmation that the carved data actually results in a valid file output. Therefore, an automated format validator is a function that accepts a block of data and then determines whether it conforms to the defined structure of the file format before resulting in a validated file [17].

2.3 File Carving Tools

There is a wide selection of file carving tools available ranging from expensive proprietary forensic software suites (EnCase, FTK & WinHex) to open source software (Scalpel, Foremost & PhotoRec). A total of 6 file carving tools were selected for testing and are listed in Table 1. The basis for tool selection criteria included: wide file type support, advanced carving features and tool availability. Each tool listed has the associated license, tool version number and tool platform details. Additionally, the availability of tool configuration is also provided which illustrates the ability to modify the database of file signatures used by the tool.

Table 1. File Carving Tools Used During Testing

Name	License	Version	Platform	Configurable
EnCase	Proprietary	7.05	Windows	No
FTK	Proprietary	4.1	Windows	Yes
WinHex	Proprietary	16.8	Windows	Yes
PhotoRec	Open Source	6.13	Multi	No
Scalpel	Open Source	2.0	Multi	Yes
Foremost	Open Source	1.5.7	Linux	Yes

3 Tool Testing Methodology

In order to produce reliable and valid results a digital forensic tool testing methodology was used which implements function orientation testing to evaluate the ability of software tools to perform specific functions or tasks [18]. In this research the specific function to be tested is the ability of a file carving tool to recover assorted file types in various different scenarios. The following subsections outline the data sets, performance measurements and the testing procedure used during the experimental phase of this research.

3.1 Data Sets

Data sets in digital investigations and forensic research are usually comprised of a forensic image of a target device; for example, a bitwise copy of a computer's hard drive. However, in order to correctly evaluate file carving tools and produce reliable results, detailed knowledge of the data contained within the data set is essential. The use of documented data sets provide a baseline for scientific evaluation of tools and research reproducibility of useful findings to the academic community and practitioners alike [19].

Therefore, specific purpose based data sets for testing file carving tools were used. Each data set has extensive documentation including the following details: *1)* File name; *2)* File type; *3)* MD5 hash value; *4)* File location (offset);

and, if pertinent, *5)* File scenario. A total of 3 data sets were used to test tool performance:

1. Basic Data Carving Test #1 (11-carve-fat.dd)[4]
2. DFRWS2006 Forensics Challenge Data Set (dfrws-2006-challenge.img)[5]
3. Baseline Carving Data Set (bcds.raw)(see following section)

Baseline Carving Data Set: A new data set was created specifically for the second testing portion of this research. Justification for this is based on several limitations of data sets that are currently available. Firstly, the structure of files in the available data sets are not representative of, or in proportion with, data encountered in *real-world* investigations; for example, 11-carve-fat only contains contiguous files, while the DFRWS challenge data sets are predominantly fragmented (being designed to advance carving techniques, not test the performance capabilities of carving tools). Additionally, the variety of file types contained within the identified data sets are limited in scope.

The newly created data set was dubbed *Baseline Carving Data Set*[6]. The overall purpose is to represent a file structure that is indicative of what may be encountered in investigations in order to provide more viable carving performance results. It included numerous different user file types (a total of 25 different file types, and 67 files in total). Various file structures are also tested based on file sizes, fragmentation rates and gap sizes from an analysis of file systems from the wild [14]. The file types selected were classified into 4 distinct categories:

1. Documents: DOC, XLS, PPT, DOCX, XLSX, PPTX, PDF, TXT, HTML
2. Images: JPG, PNG, GIF
3. Multimedia: MP3, WAV, MPG, AVI, WMV, WMA, MOV, MP4, FLV
4. Archive: ZIP, 7ZIP, GZIP, RAR

The following file structures are to be tested: *1)* Contiguous files; *2)* Fragmented files; and *3)* Partial files. All documents and images used in the data set were sourced from the Digital Corpora, which provide an unrestricted file corpus[7] of 1 million *real* files sourced from web servers in the .gov domain and come with associated file metadata [19], while all multimedia and archive files were sourced from the public domain. This allows unrestricted distribution of the completed data set to other researchers or tool vendors.

---

[4] The Basic Data Carving Test #1 is authored by Nick Mikus and available from: http://dftt.sourceforge.net/test11/index.html
[5] The DFRWS2006 Forensics Challenge Data Set is authored by Brian Carrier, Eoghan Casy & Wietse Venema and avilable from: http://www.dfrws.org/2006/challenge/index.shtml
[6] The Baseline Carving Data Set is available from: https://github.com/thomaslaurenson/. All documentation including data set layout, hash sets, testing scenarios and file sources is also provided.
[7] Available from: http://domex.nps.edu/corp/files/govdocs1/

3.2   Performance Measurement

The performance of file carving tools can be measured based on the ability to recover correct files from a data set while avoiding the recovery of incorrect, corrupt or partial files. A widely known performance measurement used for Information Retrieval was applied to determine the performance of each tool. The measurements include versions of Recall, Precision and Fmeasure metrics which were modified specifically for tool testing performance[8]. The following 4 quality measurement metrics with associated symbols are defined below [20]:

$$carving\_Recall(_cR) = \frac{all - sfn - ufn}{all} \tag{1}$$

$$supported\_Recall(_sR) = \frac{sp - sfn}{sp} \tag{2}$$

$$carving\_Precision(_cP) = \frac{tp}{tp + ufp + \frac{1}{2}kfp} \tag{3}$$

$$carving\_Fmeasure(_cFm) = \frac{1}{\alpha\frac{1}{_cP} + (1 - \alpha)\frac{1}{_cR}} \tag{4}$$

- All (all) refers to the total number of files in a data set.
- Supported files (sp) define the total number of file types in a data set supported by the specific carving tool.
- True positive (tp) is a file that is correctly carved from the data set.
- False positive is any carved file which is not a true positive. Known false positive (kfp) are files identified by the tool output as incorrect or corrupt, while unknown false positives (ufp) are false positives not identified as incorrect by the tool.
- False negative is the fraction of a file that was not correctly carved. A supported false negative (sfn) is the fraction of a file not carved by a tool, while an unsupported false negative (ufn) is a file type not supported by a tool.
- Alpha (α) is the factor used to assign weight to the relative importance of recall compared to precision. For this research $\alpha = 0.5$, meaning recall and precision each make up 50% of the importance of the Fmeasure metric.

The speed of processing a data set, measured in Megabits per second (Mb/s), will also be recorded to determine the time taken to perform file carving on the various selected data sets[9]. Furthermore, each test will be run 5 times to calculate an average processing speed.

---

[8] See ref. [20] Chapter 4 for additional information and reasoning behind the modified metrics to suit file carving performance measurement.

[9] To ensure viable processing speed results, all testing was conducted on the same computer system with the following specifications: Intel Core i5-3570K CPU with 8GB RAM and running either Backtrack Linux 5R3 or Mircosoft Windows 7 depending on the supported platform of each file carving tool.

Score Interpretation: The tool quality is tested and scored with a value between 0 (low) and 1 (high). Each of the 4 performance metrics and possible reason(s) of the resultant score are reviewed below [20]:

1. **carving_Recall:** Tests the ability of a tool to extract a high number of correct files from the data set. Low scores are either caused by unsupported file types, file structures or tool failure.
2. **supported_Recall:** Similar to carving recall, but determines the ability of a tool to extract a high number of supported file types only. Low scores are indicative of tool failure to extract only supported file types.
3. **carving_Precision:** Measures the correctness of the tool, where low scores are usually indicative of a large number of false positive files carved.
4. **carving_Fmeasure:** The results of the recall and precision scores are combined to provide an overall score for a tool, thus enabling indicative comparisons to be made.

3.3 Testing Procedure

A rigorous testing procedure was implemented to ensure that correct data collection and analysis was achieved in order to provide accurate results. At the outset each file carving tool was sourced and the tool documentation reviewed extensively. The selected tools were then run against the 3 specified data sets and results compared to the appropriate data set documentation. The specific testing procedure used in this research is adapted from 2 previous similar studies [20,15] and is made up of the following phases:

1. **Determine true positives:** Calculate and compare MD5 hash values for all output from the file carving tool against the MD5 hash values from the data set documentation[10]. The remaining output files are then checked to determine if the carved file occupies the same block ranges as the file in the data set. If either of the 2 scenarios are true, files are marked as *tp* matches.
2. **Determine false negatives:** A combination of piecewise hashing [21] coupled with manual analysis was performed on tool output to determine any remaining false negatives and the fraction weight for files not already accounted for.
3. **Determine known false positives:** The log file created by each specific tool is then reviewed to identify any carved files which are marked as incorrect or corrupt. These files are marked as a *kfp* and counted accordingly.
4. **Determine unknown false positives:** The remaining output files are marked as *ufp* and counted accordingly.
5. **Calculate performance measurements:** The 4 performance metrics were then calculated using the defined formulae and the findings tabulated.

---

[10] The Hashdeep tool (http://md5deep.sourceforge.net/) was used to first create a list of the unique hash values of all files in the data set and then to compare the MD5 hash values to the list of known files. In digital forensic investigations this process is referred to as hash set analysis.

4   Carving Tool Review

Each selected file carving tool was run against the target data sets and the testing procedure implemented. Comparison of the results were made of the first two data sets against those of a previous similar study followed by testing results from the newly authored Baseline Carving Data Set.

4.1   Results and Comparison to Previous Research

The six file carving tools were each tested against the 11-carve-fat and the DFRWS2006 data sets. Tables 2 & 3 show the results as calculated from the defined performance measurements as well as the processing speed of the tool. The results were then compared to the previous findings collected by Kloet in 2007 [20]. An arrow is displayed to indicate either an increase or a decrease in the comparative performance score of each tool[11].

Table 2. File carving performance scores for 11-carve-fat.dd

Tool	Carving Recall	Supported Recall	Carving Precision	Carving Fmeasure	Processing Speed (MB/s)
EnCase	0.669	0.772	0.500	0.572	7.750
FTK	0.736 ⬆	0.736 ⬆	0.733 ⬇	0.735 ⬆	6.889 ⬆
WinHex	0.933	0.933	1.000	0.966	31.000
PhotoRec	0.933 ⬆	0.933 ⬆	1.000 ⬆	0.966 ⬆	20.667 ⬆
Scalpel	0.800 ⬇	0.800 ⬇	0.917 ⬆	0.854 ⬆	10.333 ⬆
Foremost	0.708 ⬇	0.708 ⬇	1.000 ⬆	0.829 ⬇	62.000 ⬆

A high overall performance was achieved by most tools on the 11-carve-fat data set, due to wide file type support and because only contiguous file structures make up the data set. WinHex and PhotoRec produced identical results and were noted for obtaining the highest performance scores, where only one false negative carving result was counted. Interestingly, all tools failed to carve a JPEG file with a corrupt header which demonstrates the importance of a complete and uncorrupted file header to allow correct file type identification from raw data.

In comparison to previous findings it was anticipated that there would be a widespread increase in tool performance. Both FTK and PhotoRec did have increased performance scores apart from the precision results from FTK which was caused by 9 false positive carved files. It was also discovered that decreases in performance were from tools with a highly editable configuration file (Scalpel & Foremost) and it is the author's opinion that a different method of tool configuration was possibly used in previous testing. This is justified by the lower

---

[11] For the 11-carve-fat.dd data set FTK, Scalpel, Foremost & PhotoRec have values to compare to previous results. For the dfrws-2006-challenge.raw data set comparative results are for FTK, Foremost & PhotoRec only.

recall but higher precision scores for Scalpel & Foremost. More file signatures could have been enabled during testing, but preliminary results indicated a very large number of false positives, thus, would have resulted in increased recall but decreased precision scores for each tool.

Each of the tools supported all 11 file types in this data set, apart from EnCase, therefore the carving recall and supported recall results are identical for each tool. Due to the very small size of the data set (62MB), the processing speed results are not conclusive findings of tool speed performance.

Table 3. File carving performance scores for dfrws-2006-challenge.img

Tool	Carving Recall	Supported Recall	Carving Precision	Carving Fmeasure	Processing Speed (MB/s)
EnCase	0.565	0.565	0.429	0.488	0.889
FTK	0.481 ⬇	0.513 ⬇	0.563 ⬆	0.519 ⬆	1.021 ⬆
WinHex	0.623	0.623	0.622	0.623	12.000
PhotoRec	0.813 ⬇	0.813 ⬇	0.963 ⬆	0.881 ⬆	0.980 ⬆
Scalpel	0.385	0.425	0.333	0.357	4.800
Foremost	0.546 ⬇	0.603 ⬇	0.341 ⬆	0.420 ⬆	9.600 ⬆

Although the DFRWS2006 data set contains only 6 different file types the image layout is significantly more complex than the 11-carve-fat data set. It includes 15 contiguous files and 17 fragmented files. Due to the difficulty of carving fragmented files, the scores for all tools were much lower. PhotoRec had the highest overall performance and extracted the most positive carving matches and lowest rate of false positive results. WinHex had the second highest overall Fmeasure score and the second lowest number of false positives.

Compared to previous findings all Fmeasure scores showed an increase indicating that the overall performance of file carving tools has improved for the scenarios in this data set. However, both carving recall scores were down albeit very close to previous findings. The decreases in performance may, again, be due to differences in tool configuration or operation varying between this research and the previous study. The exclusion of known bad file signatures recovering less true positive matches but also producing dramatically fewer false positive matches dictates higher precision but lower recall scores; e.g. by default Foremost has 3 file signatures for JPEG images one of which is known to produce high false positives but would have resulted in additional files recovered. Another potential reason for lower recall scores was that sector boundary scans (of 512 bytes) were specified during testing.

4.2 Baseline Carving Data Set Results

Slight changes were made to the testing procedure during testing the Baseline Carving Data Set as comparison of results to previous research was not necessary.

Firstly, carved results must validate in order to be counted as a true positive. A method known as *fast object validation* was implemented which attempts to open the file using it's native application without generating an error message, therefore, validating the carved file[14]. Secondly, the performance measurement scheme was updated to include the counting of true positives as a fraction, similar to the original method of counting supported false negatives as a fraction. The reasoning was that true positive matches are commonly carved as a fraction of a file, a notable example being a thumbnail image carved from a JPEG image which displays the original image but in a smaller file size quality. Additionally, with the updated procedure, true positives, supported false negatives and unsupported false negatives should always equal the total number of files in the data set. This can be summarised as: $tp + sfn + ufn = all$.

The results displayed in Table 4 show the performance results of each tool for each measurement metric along with the corresponding processing speed results. Additionally, optimised testing was performed for 2 of the tools identified as Scalpel Opt and Foremost Opt.

Table 4. File carving performance scores for bcds.raw

Tool	Carving Recall	Supported Recall	Carving Precision	Carving Fmeasure	Processing Speed (MB/s)
EnCase	0.390	0.413	0.093	0.150	0.029
FTK	0.445	0.508	0.098	0.160	0.714
WinHex	0.776	0.776	1.000	0.874	21.500
PhotoRec	0.825	0.825	0.938	0.878	3.822
Scalpel	0.428	0.453	0.004	0.007	0.068
Scalpel Opt	0.503	0.548	0.767	0.607	28.667
Foremost	0.421	0.452	0.004	0.008	0.065
Foremost Opt	0.539	0.587	0.694	0.607	24.571

Testing of the Baseline Carving Data Set revealed that the greater variety of file types and file structures proved difficult for most file carvers to efficiently extract a high percentage of files. Nevertheless, PhotoRec and WinHex were again the top performing file carving tools. PhotoRec had a slightly higher Fmeasure score due to obtaining a higher recall score. Both carvers also supported all 25 different file types, however, WinHex had a notably higher processing speed.

EnCase, FTK, Scalpel & Foremost all retained a high number of false positive files resulting in very low precision scores and in turn decreasing the overall Fmeasure result. The majority of the errors were caused by the MPEG file type, defined by short and very common header values which produced hundreds of false positive carved files. Both Scalpel & Foremost carved over 5,000 false positive MPEG files while FTK carved 300 false positive MPEG files. The low precision score by EnCase was due to carving numerous embedded files which were unable to be excluded using the embedded file hash set as most output files were corrupt. FTK, Scalpel & Foremost also carved out embedded files which were able to be excluded using the embedded file hash set.

The default file signature databases (conf files) used by Scalpel and Foremost proved to greatly decrease performance scores, especially precision and processing speed, mainly due to excessive numbers of false positive carved files. Therefore, both file signature databases were optimised in an attempt to achieve better performance results. This involved adding new file signatures for Office 2007, HTML, MP4 & FLV file types and updating existing file signatures for JPEG, PNG & Office 2003 file types. Additionally, maximum file sizes were updated and the MPEG file signature was removed from the databases. As the results indicate both Scalpel Opt & Foremost Opt had a dramatic increase in Fmeasure score from 0.007 to 0.607 and 0.008 to 0.607 respectively which demonstrates the importance of tool configuration and file signature databases used.

The use of a significantly larger data set (237MB) and complex file structure give a better understanding of the processing speed of the 6 tools. The results indicate that, as expected, processing speed decreases greatly as the number of false positives increase. This is specifically caused by the time required to write false positive file matches to permanent disk storage.

4.3   Discussion of Findings

The experiment results highlight numerous insights into the current performance of file carving tools in terms of capabilities and limitations. One of the most important factors is a detailed knowledge of tool configuration and the selection of file types, or signatures, chosen by the investigator for potential recovery; for example, MPEG and ZIP files proved difficult to carve without numerous false positives due to common header values. In this scenario manual analysis, or a specialised carver developed for a specific file format, may be implemented to enhance file recovery. However, with the increasing sizes of targets being investigated, such detailed analysis may be hindered by technical or time frame limitations.

Another important configuration option is the specification of sector size. Targeting the beginning of a sector offset for file headers greatly reduced false positive results for all tools where this option was available. However, enabling sector scanning also has the limitation of potentially missing files of interest and, as this research discovered, embedded files could not be recovered separately from the original container file.

The selection of the right tool for the job at hand is essential; for example, Scalpel uses header-based carving very efficiently with high computational performance on large data sets whereas PhotoRec uses predominantly structure-based carving with potentially lower computational performance. However, PhotoRec results illustrated that a higher percentage of correct files was usually carved while also minimising false positives. Knowledge of specific file types and associated file structure also contributes to more efficient tool usage and improved carving results.

In terms of file structure the results reinforce that contiguous files are much simpler to carve compared to fragmented files. Nevertheless, most tools were found capable of extracting the base fragment of a high percentage of fragmented files from each data set. Again, implementation of manual analysis may then provide complete file recovery. The inability to reconstruct file fragments, despite advanced academic research and proof of concept software development, is potentially troublesome to practitioners. However, it was identified that the type of data separating fragments is an important factor in how well a carver could extract the fragmented file; for example, an HTML file intertwined with a TXT file separating the two fragments was difficult to recover whereas a JPEG document separated by randomly generated data or another JPEG proved simpler to recover.

There are numerous factors influencing the processing speed of a file carving tool and it can be highly dependant on the avoidance of carving and writing false positive files. Additionally, the file carving technique used will also affect processing speed. In general, the more complex the extraction method, the slower the processing speed. Another factor is the scan type selected on tools; for example, PhotoRec has a *brute force mode* scan which greatly increases scan time while Foremost & Scalpel have a *quick mode* which decreases scan time by only searching the start of a block of the input file as specified by the investigator.

5   Conclusion

In conclusion, this research investigated the performance of 6 file carving tools by conducting testing on various data sets and analysing tool output. The fact remains that there is no single best file carver. However, informed selection of the correct tool for a specific task plus knowledge of tool configuration stand out as the most important aspects to increasing both the number of files recovered and the reliability of tool output. Additionally, the findings highlight the ongoing issue and limitations of reconstructing file fragments.

A selection of available tools has also been compiled from this research to promote and advance future research. A new file carving data set, post processing file validation scripts and tool configuration files have been authored and made available for use[12].

Future advancement of techniques and tools based on academic research could greatly improve the performance of file carving tools. Implementation of advanced data abstractions to store file carving metadata, continual advancement of file validation techniques and the automated post-processing of carving output can all help to increase file carving file performance. Additional research is also needed to reverse-engineer new file types to support the carving process. File carving, however, remains a valuable technique enabling the recovery of files and the retrieval of potential evidence for digital investigations.

---

[12] All files are available from: https://github.com/thomaslaurenson/

References

1. Richard III, G.G., Roussev, V.: Scalpel: A Frugal, High Performance File Carver. In: 2005 Digital Forensic Research Workshop, New Orleans, LA (2005)
2. Marziale, L., Richard III, G.G., Roussev, V.: Massive Threading: Using GPUs to increase the performance of digital forensics tools. Digital Investigation 4(suppl.), 73–81 (2007)
3. Hand, S., Lin, Z., Gu, G., Thuraisingham, B.: Bin-Carver: Automatic recovery of binary executable files. Digital Investigation 9(suppl.), 108–117 (2012)
4. Yoo, B., Park, J., Lim, S., Bang, J., Lee, S.: A Study on Multimedia File Carving Method: Multimedia Tools and Applications, 1–19 (2011)
5. Beverly, R., Garfinkel, S., Cardwell, G.: Forensic Carving of Network Packets and Associated Data Structures. Digital Investigation 8(suppl.), 78–89 (2011)
6. van Baar, R.B., Alink, W., van Ballegooij, A.R.: Forensic Memory Analysis: Files mapped in memory. Digital Investigation 5(suppl.), 52–57 (2008)
7. Richard III, G.G., Roussev, V., Marziale, L.: In-Place File Carving. In: Craiger, P., Shenoi, S. (eds.) Advances in Digital Forensics III. IFIP, vol. 242, pp. 217–230. Springer, Boston (2007)
8. Sencar, H.T., Memon, N.: Identification and Recovery of JPEG Files with Missing Fragments. Digital Investigation 6(suppl.), 88–98 (2009)
9. Walls, R.J., Levine, B.N., Liberatore, M., Shields, C.: Effective Digital Forensics Research is Investigator-Centric. In: 6th USENIX Conference on Hot Topics in Security, pp. 1–11. USENIX Association, San Francisco (2011)
10. Garfinkel, S.L.: Digital Forensics Research: The Next 10 Years. Digital Investigation 7(suppl.), 64–73 (2010)
11. Carrier, B.: File System Forensic Analysis. Addison-Wesley Professional (2005)
12. Pal, A., Memon, N.: The Evolution of File Carving. IEEE Signal Processing Magazine 26(2), 59–71 (2009)
13. Cohen, M.I.: Advanced Carving Techniques. Digital Investigation 4(3-4), 119–128 (2007)
14. Garfinkel, S.L.: Carving Contiguous and Fragmented Files with Fast Object Validation. Digital Investigation 4(suppl.), 2–12 (2007)
15. Tomar, D.S., Malviya, O., Verma, R.: Analysis Framework for Quality Measurement of Carving Techniques. In: 6th National Conference on Emerging Trends in Computing and Communication, Hamirpur, India, pp. 421–426 (2008)
16. Metz, J., Mora, R.J.: Analysis of 2006 DFRWS Forensic Carving Challenge (2006), http://www.dfrws.org/2006/challenge/submissions/mora/dfrws2006.pdf
17. Aronson, L., Van Den Bos, J.: Towards an Engineering Approach to File Carver Construction. In: 35th IEEE Annual Computer Software and Applications Conference Workshops, pp. 368–373. IEEE, Munich (2011)
18. Lyle, J., White, D., Ayers, R.: NIST Internal Report 7490: Digital Forensics at the National Institute of Standards and Technology. National Institute of Standards and Technology, Gaithersburg, Maryland (2008)
19. Garfinkel, S., Farrell, P., Roussev, V., Dinolt, G.: Bringing Science to Digital Forensics with Standardized Forensic Corpora. Digital Investigation 6, 2–11 (2009)
20. Kloet, S.J.J.: Master's Thesis: Measuring and Improving the Quality of File Carving Methods. Eindhoven University of Technology (2007)
21. Kornblum, J.: Identifying Almost Identical Files using Context Triggered Piecewise Hashing. Digital Investigation 3(suppl.), 91–97 (2006)

Author Index

Printed in the United States
By Bookmasters